Asia before Europe

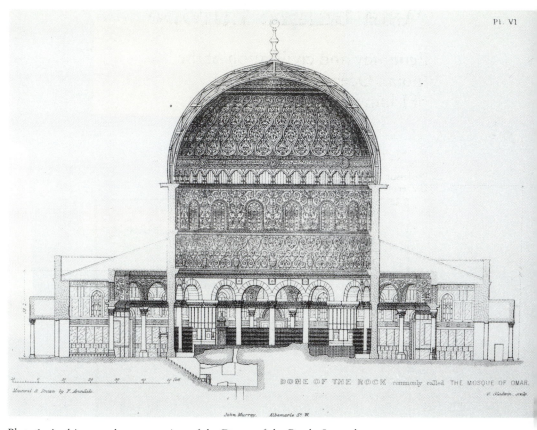

Plate 1 Architectural cross-section of the Dome of the Rock, Jerusalem.

Asia before Europe

Economy and civilisation of the
Indian Ocean from the rise
of Islam to 1750

K. N. CHAUDHURI

Professor of the Economic History of Asia,
University of London

CAMBRIDGE UNIVERSITY PRESS

Cambridge
New York   Port Chester
Melbourne   Sydney

Published by the Press Syndicate of the University of Cambridge
The Pitt Building, Trumpington Street, Cambridge. CB2 1RP
40 West 20th Street, New York, NY 10011, USA
10 Stamford Road, Oakleigh, Melbourne 3166, Australia

First published 1990

Printed in Great Britain by The Bath Press, Avon

British Library cataloguing in publication data

Chaudhuri, K. N. (Kirti N.), *1934–*
Asia before Europe: economy and civilisation of the
Indian Ocean from the rise of Islam to 1750.
1. Indian Ocean region, history
I. Title
909′.09824

Library of Congress cataloguing in publication data

Chaudhuri, K. N.
Asia before Europe: economy and civilisation of the Indian Ocean
from the rise of Islam to 1750. K. N. Chaudhuri.
p.   cm.
Includes bibliographical references.
ISBN 0-521-30400-8 ISBN 0-521-31681-2 pbk
1. Indian Ocean Region – Civilisation. 2. Indian Ocean Region –
Economic conditions. 3. Comparative civilisation. I. Title.
DS339.C48 1990
909′.09824–dc20   89–17284 CIP

ISBN 0 521 30400 8 hardback
ISBN 0 521 31681 2 paperback

WD

Contents

Part I

Fernand Braudel and 'Asia before Europe': a tribute, recollections, and a dialogue 3

Problems of comparative history 19
The choice of time period and spatial units, 19. Three sets of problems, 20. The structural approach, 'Incomplete Theorem', and the problem of categories, 21. The deconstruction of the concept of Asia, 22. The unity of space and time, 23.

The methodology and its application 24
Fernand Braudel, 24. Michel Foucault, 25. Georg Cantor and set theory, 27.

Space, time and structures in the Indian Ocean 28
Theoretical framework, 28. The comparative world views of Islam, India, South East Asia, and China, 30. The comparative civilisations of the Indian Ocean, 32. Economic structure and organisation, 37. The unity of historical time, 40.

The unity and disunity of the Indian Ocean 42
General principles, 42. Identities of discourse, 45. Rules of integration, 46. Levels of integration, 47. Contemporary awareness of comparative features, 47. The problem of limits, 48.

The identities of the four Indian Ocean civilisations 48
The topological structure of Islam, 48. Outer and inner limits of Islam, 50. Historical contradictions in Islam, 50. The universal and plural character of Sanskritic India, 53. The intellectual achievements of ancient Indian thought, 53. Albiruni's description of medieval India, 54. The structuring social codes in ancient India, 54. The sources of political power left

v

Part II

Plates

Figures

Maps

Diagram

Preface

In 1980 Dr Robin Derricourt invited me on behalf of the Syndics of the Cambridge University Press to write a two-volume history of the Indian Ocean based on my university courses. The first volume appeared in 1985 under the title *Trade and Civilisation in the Indian Ocean from the Rise of Islam to 1750*. The present work is a sequel to the earlier study. If the approach and the methodology of the first volume represented a shift from my *Trading World of Asia* (1978), *Asia before Europe* also differs from both the works. It incorporates the outline of a distinct theory for writing comparative history, which it is hoped, will be developed further for a more extensive future study of the premodern societies around the Indian Ocean. The question of the similarity and difference between my own theoretical approach and that of Fernand Braudel is discussed at some length in the Introduction, as also is the background to the formation of the theory.

It is my pleasant duty to acknowledge the help and assistance that I have received from many friends, colleagues, and institutions. The support given by the Editorial Office of the Cambridge University Press was invaluable in keeping the project alive through almost a decade of very hard work. The British Academy, the Leverhulme Foundation, and the Research Committee of my own institution, the School of Oriental and African Studies, University of London, have generously supported my field research in the Middle East, South Asia, South East Asia, and the Far East. I am grateful to my colleagues for bibliographical and linguistic help. I have learnt a great deal about premodern agrarian production from Madhavi Bajekal's detailed research on eastern Rajasthan in the early eighteenth century and I am also grateful to Dilbagh Singh for sharing with me his vast knowledge of the sources in the Rajasthan State Archives in Bikaner. I should like to thank G. D. Sharma for acting as a historical consultant during by field trips in south Gujarat in the winter of 1987–8. The invitation from Selma al-Radi and the University of Sana to give three seminars in the spring of 1987 enabled me to visit and see a part of the Middle East which always had close contact with the rest of the Indian Ocean.

Gopalan Balachandran who successfully completed his Ph.D. thesis while this book was being written, was a willing and sympathetic listener and his sharp mind could analyse a problem rapidly and elegantly. Conversations with Alexander Piatigorsky during the autumn of 1985, when I was constructing the theoretical framework, alerted me to several philosophical possibilities. *Trade and Civilisation in the Indian Ocean* contained a dedication to Fernand Braudel. This study acknowledges a similar sense of intellectual debt to Kenneth Ballhatchet, Professor of South Asian History at the University of London, until his retirement in 1988. During the thirty years or so that I have known him, his support and encouragement to research have always remained strong. Ken's wide knowledge of historical sources in many different archives in many different parts of the world, his intuitive grasp of complex theoretical problems, and deep understanding of social attitudes, have been a model and a source of inspiration to all those who have been fortunate to work with him. Finally, I should like to thank all my past undergraduates (there are too many of them to be named individually) who responded enthusiastically to the lectures and seminars on comparative history put before them during the last ten years.

K.N.C.

Acknowledgements

I should like to thank the following individuals and institutions for permission to use illustrative material: British Museum; Dr Chintamani Singh, Director, Jaigarh Fort, Jaipur; John Gollings, Staatsbibliothek Preussischer Kultur-besitz, Berlin, Orientabteilung; Topkapi Sarayi Museum; Victoria and Albert Museum; and Robert Young.

K.N.C.

Abbreviations

AH	The Hijra era (Muslim calendar, starting in AD 622)
BL	British Library
BM	British Museum
IOR	India Office Records, British Library
b. 720	Born in AD 720
d. 956	Died in AD 956
r. 756–68	Reigned from AD 756 to 768

Note to the reader

The basic plan of this study incorporates three features: the outline of a theory for writing comparative history, the identification of the stable and unchanging structures in the Indian Ocean societies, what Fernand Braudel called *la longue durée*, and the description of the historical processes involved. Part I generally deals with the theoretical issues, while part II contains case-studies and descriptive material. The arrangement of the book follows the logic of historical themes, economic and social, in the Indian Ocean regions. The book does not deal with the chronology of individual areas.

Non-theoretical readers are advised to skip chapter one and begin with pp. 48–66 of chapter two, pp. 79–88 of chapter three, pp. 97–110 of chapter four, pp. 127–48 of chapter five, and then go to part II, chapter six. Those who would like to read through the book sequentially but are not familiar with the theoretical terms are provided with a glossary which explains most of the concepts used in the book. The historical exposition is not conditional on a full comprehension of these terms, some of which necessarily refer to abstract and even difficult issues in philosophy and mathematics. But the theory provides historians with very powerful techniques of comparative analysis. Certain historical themes are discussed in more than one chapter and the basic propositions are recapitulated in order to add emphasis and familiarise the undergraduate students with the key conclusions. This is done quite deliberately in the manner of a composer repeating his fundamental musical themes in a structured composition. The index should be used for cross-reference to these common themes and also for explanations of non-English words.

PART I

Introduction

Fernand Braudel and 'Asia Before Europe': a tribute,
recollections, and a dialogue

Fernand Braudel made his last public appearance on 20 October 1985 at
Chateauvallon, a conference centre in the south of France. As usual *petit*
déjeuner that morning was served in the open air, on the terrace of Residence
Cap Brun overlooking the Bay of Toulon. The leaves of the carefully trimmed
plane trees bordering the terrace were beginning to change colour. The breakfast table was set with coffee, petit pain, and fresh croissants. The tall white-
painted windows of the slightly run-down villa opened on to the terrace, and
the gardens, planted with magnificent umbrella pines, sloped away towards
the cliffs which dropped down to the sea below. The whole scene was
inimitably French. After the summer crowds, a Mediterranean seaside resort
has a deserted air in the autumn, and the mood is well conveyed by the
common Franco-Spanish word 'triste', pensive. Braudel always came down
late for breakfast and was the last to appear, dressed immaculately in a grey
flannel suit with the famous rosette of the Académie Française in his button-
hole. The habitual warmth and friendliness with which he greeted everyone
and especially young people were another side of his personality that was in
some contrast to the formal and even formidable image projected on the
debating platform. There was a slight chill in the air that October morning.
Braudel sat down, his grey eyes resting on the distant sea, and turning to
Alberto Tenenti, a close friend and colleague, observed, his voice just a
whisper, 'Poco freddo, Alberto.' This was the last day of the 'Journées Fernand
Braudel', and later that morning Braudel would touch on the recollections of
a life-time.

The three-day symposium at Chateauvallon, organised by Marielle Paquet,
was a resounding success, a glittering affair, attended by many distinguished
international historians, members of the Press, and French public figures. It
also turned out to be a valedictory occasion, where Braudel's disciples, 'mes
élèves' as he affectionately called them, honoured the maître for the last time,
although they were not to know it then. There were three themes for discussion: the Mediterranean, capitalism, and France. Braudel's studies on the
first two themes of course provided the groundwork for the participants' con-

3

tributions; the first volume of his incomplete work on France would be published posthumously. On the last morning of the symposium, in the course of winding up the debate, Braudel spoke about himself and his work, besides commenting on other academic themes. Theodore Zeldin, he said, had accused him of being a strange and uncharacteristic Frenchman: a remark which irritated him a little, because it was both true and untrue. He continued:

I am afraid the sensationalism, which all of a sudden attached itself to me, is unfortunate from a historical point of view. I have had a very large number of students, and I have great regard for them, I have argued with them and they have argued with me in turn when necessary. They often say to me, you have had a particularly privileged life. And so I protest . . . that Jean-Paul Sartre had in a way a far more brilliant involvement in French and international public life than myself . . . It will perhaps amuse you to listen to me for an instance. I have had a difficult life. No, not difficult, very difficult. But I have never lost the joy of living. Equally well, I have never felt sorry for myself, because I hate vanity.

If these were surprising words for those who only knew Braudel as the greatest historian of this century, there was more to come. The comparison of his own with Sartre's celebrity status obviously had an inner meaning. The French university establishment, he said, had always blackballed him (he actually used the word 'blackboulé'). He had been elected to a chair at the Collège de France but had never had the right to confer degrees on his students.[1] To be a school-teacher was an ambition that would remain with him, he said, to the end of his life.[2] And he expressed great admiration for Jean-Paul Sartre. 'According to me, Sartre was often wrong, but I always admired his commitment. That is not so, in my case. It is a fault, I confess.'[3]

The light-hearted exchange between Theodore Zeldin and Braudel which followed these revelations put every one at ease. Pressed by Albert du Roy to agree whether or not he was an unusual Frenchman when judged by the foreign stereotype that the French were a nation of introverts who looked upon their culture as the only valid culture in the world, Braudel replied that the point should be put to Zeldin. After all, Zeldin had studied the French as one might study the guinea-pig. What then did he think of the French guinea-pig? Zeldin replied that he was delighted to have succeeded in urging so distinguished a 'guinea-pig' to speak about his life. As we drove back to Cap Brun after the session had ended, Professor Vitorino Magalhaes-Godinho, who was in high spirits, said to me, 'You must write down your first impressions of what was said at Chateauvallon'. The social highlight of the symposium was a banquet given by the Admiral of the French Mediterranean Fleet at his residence, a restored Napoleonic fort on the mountains above the town. It was attended by more than one hundred guests. The interior of the building was furnished in simple but exquisite taste, and the guests all sat down for the meal at tables laid for a dozen people. After dinner Madame Braudel said to me, 'Let me show you the view from the terrace. I was here yesterday, visiting the

Admiral and his wife, it is an astonishing sight from these heights.' Outside, the Mediterranean night was still warm: the elegant illuminated facade of the chateau, the galaxy of Toulon's lights across the Bay, the dinner and the fine wine, all fused into so many mosaic impressions of a magical evening.

Throughout the symposium, whether the discussions touched on the history of the Mediterranean or that of capitalism, Fernand Braudel restated and reformulated the two basic features of his methodology. An intuitive under-standing of social forms and structures must be related to a systematic theory of historical changes. He reminded the audience what Lucien Febvre had said: 'To pose a problem is the beginning and end of all history. Without problems, there is no history.'[4] During the session on capitalism Braudel swiftly dealt with the question of ideology. 'When you say that capitalism is a superstruc-ture,' Paul Fabra, the editor of *Le Monde* asked, 'are you using the word super-structure in a Marxist sense?' Braudel's response was that 'structure', which could be both superstructure and infrastructure, corresponded with the social, economic, and the cultural reality, as part of the 'longue durée' of which religion, for example, was a phenomenon. 'You are not using the word super-structure,' Immanuel Wallerstein added, 'in the Marxist sense. For Marx, infrastructure controlled the superstructure, while for you, in a sense, the superstructure is the dominant element.' Braudel concluded the exchange by saying that for him the phenomenon of structures was one which remained invariant over time. It had nothing to do with the structuralism of Lévi-Strauss or some of the French sociologists and philosophers.[5]

To be blackballed by an entire academic establishment, whether of the Right or Left, is no mean feat and one was beginning to understand the reasons. I was told by a close associate of Braudel that the Académie Française had offered him the membership before but that he had turned down the honour. Braudel not only remained neutral in his choice of intellectual methods, refusing to take sides in the ideological divisions of post-war France, but his ideas of reforming French higher education were another source of conflict with the establishment. The Director of the Ecole Normale Supérieure had said to him that if the students did not prepare for competitive examinations ('l'agrégation'), what would they do? Every one had told him that there were other alternatives. But he was not satisfied. The debate did not end in favour of Braudel and the reformers. Christian Fouchet had visited President Pompidou who had apparently told him, 'If you continue to talk about the "agrégation", I shall show you the door.' Fouchet had pondered on this and there had been no reform.

Braudel's *La Méditerranée* provides a methodological blue-print for his-torians looking for actual physical structures which lie invisible below the surface of social activities and which are subject to different rhythms of time. The work addressed itself with great insight and in considerable depth to the question of how unities of time and space are established at different levels of cognitive logic. His *Civilisation matérielle, économie et capitalisme*, on the other hand, goes beyond the problem of spatial unities and is concerned with the question of the direction of changes in world history from the fifteenth to the eighteenth century. While it is possible to criticise Braudel's works on matters of factual detail or interpretation, to do so is rather like standing in front of Michelangelo's statue of David in Piazza Signoria in Florence or looking up at his paintings in the Sistine Chapel in Rome and saying that the artist's grasp of the human anatomy was all wrong. Surely, it is better to think of Braudel's works as a statement of artistic creativity, in much the same way that Wittgenstein's *Tractatus Logico-Philosophicus* is a beautiful if austere example of intellectual reasoning. The fact that the world's greatest philosopher of the time had changed his mind about the validity of his own earlier work does nothing to deter other readers from reading the work. Similarly, Cantor's set theory is rightly regarded as one of the supreme theoretical discoveries of our age, even though many of his intuitively derived ideas could not be proved immediately and the 'continuum problem' still remains unsolvable. The relationship between formal proof of consistency and historical writings should be left undefined. History is not a series of photographic snapshots of 'reality' any more than scientific experiments are a *direct* explanation of how the physical world functions.

For the historians of the Indian Ocean, Braudel's studies of the Mediterranean and the emergence of capitalism in world history remain a necessary point of departure. His description of food, clothing, and housing as the ground-floor of material life, a part of the *longue durée*, obviously merits closer investigation in the context of societies other than those of Europe. He had included the Ottoman Empire, India, and China in the *Civilisation matérielle*, but he was necessarily constrained by considerations of the limits of his projected volumes. His view of long-distance trade and the activities of great merchants as the top floor of commercial capitalism was a reply to those historians who regard trade as a minor element in the quantitative sum-total of economic activities in premodern civilisations. Modern historiography, Braudel pointed out, is obsessed with the notion of numerical majority. 'The vital decisions in history were not taken in the past, any more than they are today, according to the reasonable rules of universal suffrage. There are plenty of reasons for arguing that the minority had a greater influence over the course of history than the majority.'[6] The historians' continuing preoccupation with the pepper trade as the motive force behind the Portuguese arrival in the Indian Ocean might be taken as an affirmation of the point. While defending his doctoral thesis at the Sorbonne, Magalhaes-Godinho had apparently conceded to Ernest Labrousse that the total Portuguese agricultural production exceeded the value of pepper and spice imports.[7] Yet, the Venetian and Portuguese role in the world distribution of pepper is still an active topic of historical debate. The late Professor Ashtor, who had written so much about the Levantine trade carried his obsession with the pepper trade to extreme lengths. When we were lunching together one day in Florence, every one was astonished to see him unscrew the top of the pepper-pot and empty half of its contents on his plate, saying that he had a personal obligation to promote the consumption of black pepper.

The preface to my *Trade and Civilisation in the Indian Ocean* acknowledged an intellectual debt to Braudel in the sense that not only do his works demonstrate to professional historians how to write history but the approach stimulates one to raise further questions and elaborate research on existing themes. He was pleased at the acknowledgement and sent me a card after reading the book, as he did also after he had read my *Trading World of Asia and the English East India Company* in page proofs. He was then working on the final version of the *Civilisation matérielle* and had asked to see the book before it was published. In 1975 Madame Braudel had told me at Prato that her husband was about to complete his trilogy. I asked Braudel if he would agree to read my typescript of the *Trading World of Asia*, the first version of which was then ready, and comment on it. Braudel readily agreed and wrote to me: 'Si la chose vous était possible, de m'envoyer votre ouvrage en consultation. J'en ai besoin, dans les quelques semaines qui viennent, pendant lesquelles j'achève la mise au point de mon livre, *Économie et capitalisme, 15ᵉ–18ᵉ siècle*.' I sent off to him three huge volumes of the original extended typescript and later the page-proofs, because he said he wanted to quote from the published version. The generous acknowledgement of the *Trading World of Asia* which appeared in the second volume of *Civilization and Capitalism* (p. 385) is explained by this exchange. The methodology of the latter work, if not that of the *Trade and Civilisation*, was very different from that of Braudel's and the difference would not have escaped him. His ideas and the capacity to highlight particular historical problems influenced other historians to continue and elaborate an ongoing intellectual debate. It may be instructive to study how Einstein's theory of relativity developed out of the contemporary theories on space and gravity or what Bertrand Russell had to say about the contributions of Frege and Peano to his own mathematical thinking.[8]

Asia Before Europe is a sequel to *Trade and Civilisation in the Indian Ocean*. It uses axioms of set theory and other theoretical concepts which at first sight may seem difficult or unnecessary to those who are accustomed to work mainly in terms of historical description. It does not need much reflection to realise that a treatment of the whole of the Indian Ocean for so long a time period would have been impossible at the level of mere description. But to identify the relevant themes and subject these to further analysis, even in terms of Braudel's intuitive posing of problems, I needed principles of selection. The decision to use the logic of mathematical set theory to trace out problems of historical unities and disunities came slowly. Although the research notes were ready and were accumulated over many years, it seemed premature to begin serious work before certain methodological questions had been settled. During the autumn of 1985, after returning from France, I began to work on the theoretical framework of the present study. This was a difficult period and the epistemological problems seemed particularly intractable. After a while, the outline of a possible theory began to emerge. In order to remind myself constantly what the main problems were, the propositions were written up on the blackboard in my office in algebraical notation. A series of dated notes point to the precise evolution of the methodology. Some of the complex issues took a long time before they were settled. For a time I could not see a way of resolving the problem of fixing the inner and outer limit of a set given by a linguistic expression and it was late one evening that the solution finally came quite suddenly. The technique of fixing these limits I regard as a key concept in the theory underlying this work and it is essentially derived from the notion that a set is capable of finite or infinite extension or division.

By Christmas of 1985 the basic ideas which are presented in chapter 1 and the glossary were fully worked out. It was only after the methodology had emerged that I began the laborious task of reading the technical philosophical works on the subject. It was reassuring to discover that the human mind is capable of reaching very similar theoretical conclusions quite independently and if other people had said the same things that I was trying to establish, it did not trouble me in the least. I was just glad to have worked it out for myself. Russell's article of 1915 on the theory of time, for example, I read only in January 1989 and found that the opening statement of the problem was almost identical with what I had written in my notebook in December 1985. But I did not and still do not make the distinction he did between the order of perceived time and real time. Wittgenstein wrote in the preface to his *Tractatus* that the book would be understood only by someone who had himself had the thoughts that are expressed in it, or at least similar thoughts. He added the modest qualification that he made no claim to novelty in detail and the reason why he had not given any sources was that 'it is a matter of indifference to me whether the thoughts that I have had have been anticipated by someone else'. But he acknowledged his debt to Frege's great works and to Russell.[9]

An examination of the linguistic logic of Wittgenstein, the semiology of Saussure, Jakobson, and Hjelmslev, Chomsky's difficult theories on generative grammars, the outline of Cantor's set theory, and Gödel's Incomplete Theorem, pointed towards the possibility of integrating certain common strands of analytical thought for the purpose of writing comparative structural history. Of course, the similarity between the structuralism of Lévi-Strauss and the logic of Boolean algebra was a striking reminder of how abstract reasoning could become a powerful instrument of applied research.[10] Bricolage, that happy phrase used by Lévi-Strauss, after all has many advantages. Michel Foucault approached the problem of establishing historical unity and disunity from a direction different from that of Braudel and Lévi-Strauss. While most historians and structuralists are preoccupied with rules, functions, and uniformities, expressed in terms of both time and space, Foucault examined rigorously and closely the entire foundation of human cognitive logic, a methodology which he called the archaeology of knowledge. His theory of 'Discourse' (a term used in a specific sense) tried to retrieve from beneath the smooth surface of temporal continuity, the discontinuities and ruptures which occur in the collective mental awareness of social structures. The intellectual appeal of Foucault's work lies in the fact that he was able to show that the objects of historical discourse are not independent of their context.

It was evident both before and after I had studied the theoretical literature that European thought and methods of logical reasoning had certain common features and a common path of development in spite of the proclaimed differences and oppositions between various protagonists. The critical period in the formation of this thought can be placed between 1870 and 1930. In the present work, Braudelian methodology is retained but it is also complemented by a more rigorous theory of the concept of unity and disunity, continuity and discontinuity, ruptures and thresholds. The interaction between the physical world and the mental has been made an explicit part of the theory and the integration represents the main difference between Braudel's approach and that adopted in this book. The attempt to combine the abstract reasoning of mathematical and linguistic logic with the discursive tradition of Continental philosophical and social thinkers may appear strange. It is justified not only on the ground of creating bricolage but by an appreciation that there is much common ground between the two, provided the technical differences are clearly kept in mind and the respective concepts are treated as instruments of historical explication. To outsiders, the difference between Braudel and the structuralists might appear as one of relative emphasis. The influence of intellectual thought created by Durkheim, Mauss, and Saussure must have been particularly strong among Braudel's generation, just as the authority and the innovative iconoclasm of Henri Poincaré, the French mathematician, at the turn of the century extended beyond France to raise issues of fundamental importance in science and mathematics. It is true that Braudel never referred to Foucault's assault on the unspoken and inviolable assumptions of classical history. This is something of a puzzle, considering the current upsurge of interest in Foucault's work. Foucault was neither a systematic thinker nor a careful historian. But the power of his prose and the novelty of his discursive, critical thought are undeniable. Braudel's own way of writing history was very much a break-away movement from the supremacy previously accorded to the unilinear narration of a certain class of events. His search for physical structures in the geography of the earth and of human societies might repudiate the idea of intentionality inherent in the principle of structures, a principle which acts as systems of classification. His vision of the historical unity of the Mediterranean as being the product of the *longue durée* was an artificial creation, in the sense that no one in the age of Philip II would have admitted that the Muslim Mediterranean was any longer a part of the Christian world and if they did, the level at which the comparison was drawn would have seemed self-evident. As Merleau-Ponty put it, 'Analytical thought interrupts the perceptual transition from one moment to another, and then seeks in the mind the guarantee of a unity which is already there when we perceive. Analytical thought also interrupts the unity of culture and then tries to reconstitute it from the outside.'[11]

However, it is difficult to remain ahead of Braudel even in the rarified world of set theory. One day, long after my own theoretical construction was completed, I casually opened volume 2 of Braudel's *Civilisation and Capitalism* and was surprised to see that the heading of chapter 5 was 'Society: A Set of Sets'. Braudel was commenting on the attempt of Georges Gurvitch, the philosopher, to define a generalised social structure, *La société globale*, as a transparent glass bubble inside which social action took place. For the historian of the concrete, however, society was not just one single container but several containers with different contents. 'It is with this in mind,' Braudel continued, 'and for want of a better term, that I have come to think of society as a "set of sets", the sum of all the things that historians encounter in the various branches of our research. I am borrowing from mathematics a concept so convenient that mathematicians themselves distrust it.'[12] Braudel did not apply the axioms of set theory rigorously to historical analysis and in my work the application for the time being has also been quite general. It is possible to take it much further. I am concerned at this stage not so much with the operative rules of Zermelo-Fraenkel axioms as with the *theory which has created the set theory*. The concepts of sets, the cardinality and the ordinal, topological space, logical space, logical necessity, limits, structural integration and differentiation, order and succession, and perpetual memory, are used to identify levels of analysis and objects of historical comparisons and to mark the interaction between physical structures and the mental world. What is mainly missing in the present work and has not been attempted is the presentation of a unified hypothesis of historical causality for the Indian Ocean civilisations.

Immanuel Wallerstein's work, in contrast, deals with the dynamic elements in world history from the sixteenth century to the present as an integrated process within the capitalist system of production and hence occupies a central stage in the debate among historians. This book merely offers a set of technical instruments for structural analysis and agrees with Braudel's view that to be successful the study of structures must assume the principle of temporal invariance. The description of the Indian Ocean civilisations is conducted mainly in terms of stable and unchanging structures and structural relations.

The experience of sifting through an enormous amount of raw data collected from a dozen different archives in different parts of the world, supplemented by another long and back-breaking 'prison-sentence' at library research, has taught me what the range of possibilities were in the past which society had to face and exploit. After spending a life-time behind the academic 'veil', I can almost hear the bells of an approaching caravan. The specialist historians of Asia, each examining his own narrow chronology and field, are often unable to see the structural totality of economic and social life and they are inclined to treat the experience of their own regions as unique or special. The decline of the Mughal empire is discussed as if imperial disintegration were a new phenomenon in history or confined only to the Indian subcontinent without any reference to similar happenings in Ming China, Safavid Iran, and the Ottoman empire. The historians of Asia, whether working on the Middle East, India, China, or Japan, seem to be much more interested in comparing the course of their history with that of Western Europe rather than with other regions of Asia. The colonial impact on Asia was not confined just to diverting the flow of trade in a longitudinal direction from the previous latitudinal flow; it reoriented Asian intellectual thought in a similar direction as well. This study attempts to show what the forces of expansion and contraction were in the history of the Indian Ocean; what were the limits of economic production and exchange; how social habits, consumption, and demand influenced the composition of goods and services; how people recognised themselves as being part of a community, society, religion, and civilisation. It raises the enigmatic problem of a 'perpetual memory' to explain the isomorphism of social structures over time (see below, pp. 375–7). The expression 'Indian Ocean' is redefined and extended, just as Braudel himself made a distinction between the 'true Mediterranean' and the 'greater Mediterranean'. The boundaries between each separate Asian civilisation are deliberately blurred, and if Orientalists find that the standard of scholarship is not rigorous enough to do justice to their own area and period of specialisation, I can only say that this is a work of synthesis which attempts to present a historical interpretation from the view-point of some one who has an insider's knowledge of some of the societies studied.

When Jacques Derrida reviewed Michel Foucault's *Histoire de la folie*, he offered an oblique apology: having had the good fortune to have studied under Foucault, the disciple's consciousness, he said, is an unhappy consciousness when he starts, 'not let us say to dispute, but to engage in dialogue with the master or, better to articulate the interminable and silent dialogue which made him into a disciple'.[13] There was no need for the apology. Derrida's criticisms have a very sharp cutting edge. If one were to ask Braudel in a similar silent dialogue why he did not take up the theoretical challenge of real structuralism which can be analysed, as for example, with the relation-arithmetic of Russell's *Principia Mathematica* (or a related system), how would he have replied? Let me try and answer for Braudel and then justify my own question. Braudel would surely have said that his structure was an analogue model or a system not unlike the mechanism of a watch. The task of the historian was to trace the time-duration over which the mechanism was capable of functioning, to examine its source of power, and to record the nature of the outputs or the positions of the hands on the dial. Having done that, he would also examine the way an entire structure changed over time. If an idea expressed itself through the concrete, an examination of its material expression takes care of the mental dimension. A structuralist like myself would look not only at the physical articulation between the different gear-wheels, pinions, and the main-spring of the watch but also at the generative principles which make it possible to make one wheel go round once an hour, another wheel 60 times, and the third 3,600 times. One would further wish to examine the impact of gravity, the principle of isochronism (the time taken by a pendulum or balance-wheel to complete an arc remains the same irrespective of its length) and the coefficient of metallic expansion under temperature variations, affecting the swings of that marvellous regulator of time, the balance-wheel, activated by the hair-spring and the escapement. There are two related concepts involved here: (1) the order of the wheels is *a series of a series of a series* and (2) if the third wheel z has the property c, the second wheel y will have property b, and the first wheel x property a, given the relationship w between them. The problem of gravity and isochronism due to the contra-directional metallic expansion of the balance-wheel and the hair-spring may be taken as one of destabilising influences on the structure. It is a structural contradiction which affects the accurate running of the watch.

In the context of social history, another simple example illustrates how structures function as principles of classification. Suppose in an Indian village there are a number of families and the rank-order of the married men is determined by their occupation and that of their wives by a ritual status before marriage which remains unchanged after marriage. If we take any two couples and if we know only the rank-orders of the husbands and wives, it will be impossible to match the respective husbands and wives. We need to look up the relationship in a second list and such a list is readily at hand in the family names. Furthermore, if there are marriage rules which allow only certain occupations to be matched with certain ritual rank, we would immediately know the possible occupations of the husbands from the ritual status of the wives and vice versa. In other words, the relationships, whether they are real or abstract, between different classes constitute a structure. Names classify members of a family and the marriage rules classify sets of family names. 'It has seemed to me,' Russell wrote, 'that those who are not familiar with mathematical logic find great difficulty in understanding what is meant by "structure", and, owing to this difficulty, are apt to go astray in attempting to understand the empirical world.'[14] It is doubtful whether Braudel would have agreed with this view so far as history was concerned. Intuitive reasoning and a careful observation of the *direction* of historical movements would have seemed to Braudel sufficient for writing structural history.

Braudel's work is a constant reminder that to write history with any kind of intuitive understanding, the historian must use his vision as much as his mind. Through words he creates a great gallery of mental pictures and perhaps it is because we share the same sensibilities towards visual images that certain similarities emerge in our respective studies. The theory of 'perpetual memory', for example, suggested itself when I was once looking at Salvador Dali's painting of 'soft watches' to which Dali gave the title 'Persistence of Memory'. Although it was painted in 1931, Dali was aware of the symbolism of genetic continuity and topological transformations present in the painting. Later, he claimed that the discovery of the deoxyribonucleic acid spiral (DNA), the fundamental molecular process of heredity, confirmed his surrealist thinking. When asked to explain the meaning of the painting, he had said enigmatically that the purpose of a watch, hard or soft, was to tell the exact time.[15] The shape of the watches may be melting but provided the dial and the hands are intact, time can still be read. This is essentially a topological concept, the structure remains isomorphic between different states of transformation. One may argue over the rationalisation of a surrealist painting but no one can deny its hallucinatory images. Gala's eyes had widened with shocked surprise when she saw the painting after Dali had just finished it. The soft watches in the painting certainly indicate time but a question persists: what is the image on that extended beach receding into the porcelain sea and the sky? Is it a fish, a sea-shell or a human embryo slumbering in unconscious sightless repose before assuming the full human form? Will it fall to the predators swimming in with the tide? Yet we know that, left undisturbed, the perpetual memory built into that as yet shapeless form (if it is that) will make it run its predetermined course, and even if it meets with tragedy, the possibility of the outcome will remain as a permanent memory.

Anyone who writes about the Indian Ocean from a European perspective, whether social or geographical, is acutely aware of the contrasting images between the two worlds and the difficult task of capturing those nuances in words. It may be instructive for the present-day observers to try to visualise how contemporary trans-continental travellers such as Ibn Jubayr or Ibn Battuta (the first was an Andalusian Arab and the second a Moroccan) reacted to the changing scene from the Mediterranean to the Red Sea and the Indian Ocean beyond. Braudel emphasised the sense of physical separation even between northern and southern Europe. In the preface to the first edition of his book, he wrote, 'I have loved the Mediterranean with passion, no doubt because I am a northerner like so many others in whose footsteps I have followed . . . The reader who approaches this book in the spirit I would wish will do well to bring with him his own memories, his own vision of the

Mediterranean to add colour to the text and to help me conjure up this vast presence, as I have done my best to do'.[16] Braudel was a North European but perfectly at home in the Mediterranean, a world of strong contrasts and brilliant images. Salvador Dali came from Figueras and spent most of his life in Catalonia. Port Lligat is a tiny fishing village under the towering mountain that divides France and Spain, where Dali made his first home. It is one of many similar places on that coast: a world of olive groves, pine forests, and deeply-indented bays. On a fine day the village, its houses, the beach, and the sea present a rainbow spectrum of intense colours. A narrow and difficult track turning off to the left just before Cadaques leads to Port Lligat. The village is much easier to reach from the sea than by land. Often my son and I have anchored our small boat in one of the 'calas' and watched the big fish swimming in the clear water below, their shape distorted by the refracted light. Huge pink sand-stone cliffs overhang these bays; geological pressure and the erosion from the sea have fragmented the rocks into fantastic shapes and jagged edges. The Mediterranean pine, a tenacious creature, seems to find a foothold in the rocky cracks almost down to the level of the sea. These small inlets always end in a pebble-strewn beach inaccessible from the landward side. The image of the pebbles on seashore exercised a powerful influence on Dali. In the Teatro Municipal at Figueras, which Dali turned into his studio and museum, he had painted a whole series of paintings on the second-floor walls. These suggest clearly that one is looking at the human form, reclining in different positions on the beach, with all the muscles of the body present: as one approaches closer the paintings resolve into pebbles. The paintings are made up of the images of pebbles.

It seems to me that some of the Surrealist thought depicted in Dali's paintings is also reflected in the historical contradictions seen in Islam or Sanskritic India. The personal impressions of the Mediterranean gathered over more than twenty years remain strong in my mind. Those of the Indian Ocean form another set of mosaic pictures no less suggestive. Early in the morning, the swallows, and house-martins set up a tremendous chorus in the interior court-yard of Archivo de Indias in Seville, a beautiful building designed by Juan de Herrera and completed in 1598. As the sun crosses the top of La Giralda, the birds suddenly fall silent. To walk back from the Archivo in the blinding heat of Seville's afternoon sun is as demanding of energy as walking through the suqs of Bait al-Fakih and Zabid in the Tihama. The sculptured tearful face of the Madonna, La Macarena, who is carried through the streets of Seville during Semana Santa, suggests the power of a religiosity which accompanied the Spaniard and the Portuguese everywhere in the New World and in the Indian Ocean. Looking at the strange garment of the participants carrying the *paso*, hooded figures in white cloaks and tall pointed hats, Lorca had written,

> Por la calleja vienen
> extraños unicornios.

Plate 2 Blockhouse on the Mocha seafront, the Yemen.

De qué campo,
de qué bosque mitológico?[17]

The nearby Sanlucar de Barrameda is not a derelict town as the ruined seafront of Mocha is today but the estuary of the Guadalquivir where the sluggish river joins the Atlantic, has the same melancholy abandoned air. It is difficult to imagine that this was once the landfall for the great galleons which set out for Spain from Vera Cruz and Havana. The ancient blockhouse on the beach at Mocha where the rowing boats from the English and Dutch East-Indiamen made their landings is still intact (see Plate 2). Under the round stone structure at the water's edge a group of wild cats were chasing each other in friendly play or staring at the distant Ethiopian coast in silent mysterious contemplation. In the seventeenth century, Mocha was one of the most prosperous port-cities in the Red Sea, with sumptuous houses and mosques. Today, only a few half-ruined mansions and Shaikh Sadhili's shrine stand in a landscape of gravel mounds that extend for several miles. To witness a similar scene of human withdrawal in the Mediterranean one would have to travel to the island of Krk in Yugoslavia. A few trailing vines remaining in stone-enclosed parcels of land are the only reminders that this was once a great wine-making region of the Adriatic. The population of the island has migrated en masse to the mainland and beyond. The carefully tended few acres of vineyards around the conglomerated cliff-town of Vrbnik showed, when I visited the place, that the perpetual memory linking the past and the present had not disintegrated altogether.

The silence and the isolation of the high mountains of Abruzzi in Italy match the wild ruggedness of Sierra de Francia and Las Hurdes, only 100 km or so from the baroque splendours of Spain's most ancient university town, Salamanca. No one who has travelled from one end of the Indian Ocean to the other in a single journey will ever forget the contrasting images, colours, and textures of natural objects. An onlooker standing on the Golden Horn and looking at the skyline of Istanbul will be immediately aware of two opposing influences at work. The slender, soaring minarets of the hill-top mosques proclaim the presence of Islam but the domes resembling gigantic seashells convey another message: the power of the great Christian basilica, Santa Sophia, to inscribe the spiritual strength of the Orthodox Church in symbolic architecture. This was a message which was carried across the Mediterranean to Ravenna and Venice. The Islamic failure to capture Constantinople (677) is permanently enshrined in the tomb of the Arab general who fell while attempting to storm the invincible defences of the city. The silence of the sand dunes on the edge of Rub al-Khali or in the Nafud is total. To come upon a desert oasis growing irrigated date-palms and banana-trees is disorienting, because the intense greenery is totally unexpected after the eyes have become accustomed to the prevailing landscape colours of buff, grey, or pink. The colour of the Nafud varies between mauve and buff, due to the presence of porphyri fragments in the sand. The Yemeni builders can rightly claim to be ranked among the world's greatest stone-masons. At the end of the fifteenth century, the last of the Tahirid sultans of the Yemen, al-Zafar Amir ibn Abdul Wahab (1489–1517), built a madrasa-mosque in Radda. It is a building unique for its eclectic style and power of design. The brilliant multi-coloured frescoes commissioned by the Sultan inside the mosque contain the distilled beauty of abstract geometric shapes and forms, no less imaginative than the mihrab of the Great Mosque in Cordoba. In the square below the al-Amariya mosque, a group of camels were quietly feeding during the mid-day break. The architectural splendours of Iran's desert cities, Isfahan, Yazd, and Kirman match those of the Yemeni towns in the interior mountains. These are places far from the sea and as one moves nearer to the coast and the world of seafarers, the objective symbols also seem to change their idiom. The vast date plantations of the island of Bahrayn, which sustained its economic prosperity for more than three millennia, kept the desert at bay. On the other side of the Arabian sea, in the wide creek at Daman, between the old and the new Portuguese fortresses which once commanded the sea approach, the scene was busy: lateen-rigged fishing vessels were loading up with blocks of ice before putting out to sea. The tangle of nylon fishing-nets and trawls on the quay and the shouts of the crew were exactly the same as in the Portuguese fishing-port of Sesimbra before the sardine boats sailed for their night fishing. The sailors of course were of dif-

Plate 3 Religious shrine adjacent to the convent of Nossa Senhora do Cabo, Cabo Espichel, Portugal.

ferent nationality. The high tide racing past the beach in the Java sea through the narrow opening between two islands produces a booming and incredibly melancholy sound. The volcanic landscape of Java and Bali often covered in mists seems gentle and threatening at the same time. It is difficult to forget the overpowering smell of thousands of fish strung out on lines and drying in the sun on a beach of silver sand near the Thai-Cambodian border.

Few seafarers in our period of study would have seen the world of ice and snow in the high Himalayas. One autumn morning, I rose early after having spent a bitterly cold night camping on a col at an altitude of some 6,000 metres, surrounded by magnificent peaks. A light fall of snow covered the ground but the sky was clear. Suddenly the snow-covered summits of the peaks lit up with bright rose-coloured light. The sun was rising from behind the Great Himalayan Range. As the morning grew warmer, a huge snow-field on the peak in front detached itself from the mountain and fell with a roar on the glacier below. High up in the sky a flock of geese was flying in formation, making its way to the winter feeding-grounds in the plains. If they had come from Siberia, they would have crossed the T'ien-shan mountains and the Takla Makan desert. In the mid-day heat, the deserted streets of Cambay would remind the visitor one moment that he was in Mughal India and another moment that he was possibly in Sintra or Evora in Portugal. The exquisite red sandstone mosque of Cambay inside the citadel facing the sea is the only surviving symbol of a past which at one time rivalled that of Venice. The huge maze of salt-streaked sandbanks and shoals out in the Gulf convey the same sense of awe as the Atlantic rollers breaking against the cliffs of Cabo Espichel, the lonely headland beyond the Lagoa de Albufeira to the south of Lisbon. On the cliff-top next to the strangely beautiful derelict convent of Nossa Senhora do Cabo, there is a small white-domed structure (see Plate 3): it has a startling resemblance to the numerous shrines dedicated to the memory of Islamic saints throughout the Middle East and India. On the edge of the Pacific, the Japanese countryside presents visual images one will not find anywhere else in Asia. The task of reconstructing the historical past of the Indian Ocean civilisations, the full interplay between society, science, technology, and daily life still remains ahead of us. This work is just the beginning of the journey.

1

The setting: unities of discourse

Problems of comparative history

The choice of time period and spatial units. This study is an exercise in the comparative history of the regions around the Indian Ocean from the rise of Islam to the mid eighteenth century. Its emphasis lies primarily on economic and social structures. Theoretically, all comparisons fall into three categories: those which are across thresholds of time, those which compare different units of space, and those which evaluate purely qualitative inequalities, as for example, the differences between physical sensations and abstract concepts, social structures, religious or moral systems. The purpose of comparisons may be general or specific. At this stage it is taken to be essentially the same as the historian's desire to reconstruct the past. The choice of our time period, its extended length, and the wide geographical space covered is neither arbitrary nor randomly selected. The title of the work and the theory of time and space outlined in chapters 3 and 4 point to a view of history which differs profoundly from the conventional approach. Few historians would dispute the fact that it is necessary to present the subject-matter of history mainly as a series of events or cognitive points arranged in the order of chronology. Thus history belongs to a 'well-ordered set'. It has a starting point expressed as a least number in a set of ordinal numbers (dates). The rule of induction then allows historical events to be presented in an ordered succession.[1]

The present work does not challenge the fundamental proposition of history that it is a sequential process ordered by time. But the assumption is modified by a theoretical investigation into the structure of time. The analysis shows that historical events, structures, or phenomena can be grouped into different classes of time which have different qualitative properties, different 'frequencies', and unequal 'power'. The definition of time accepted here is the same as that of Leibniz.[2] Fernand Braudel has outlined in his works some of these problems and the resulting perspectives which emerge from a more explicit awareness of the role of time. Braudel's ideas and the brief theoretical remarks of Lévi-Strauss on the distinction between history and anthropology and the problem of encoding historical events on a temporal scale are taken a step further in our study and applied in the light of a more rigorous reasoning.[3] It is also assumed further that the history of the societies examined here possesses an internal rationale which does not explicitly call for a comparison with European experience in order to make itself evident and understood. The *meaning* and the *evocation* of the Asian historical scene are taken to be *a priori*, even though there have been many common points at which Europe and Asia have met. Finally, the study also evaluates the spatial unity and disunity of the Indian Ocean regions in terms of both physical qualities and their mental perceptions. The historical interaction between units of space and society can be studied with the help of three suggested analytical instruments: the concepts of topology, order, and metamorphosis (see below, p. 113).

Three sets of problems. A comparative historian must initially address himself to several sets of problems and questions. First of all, there is the question of epistemology. How do people in different time periods and different places recognise themselves as being part of a common set whether that set is defined by ethnicity, language, religion, or geography? That they do so has never been in any doubt. But the principle through which notions of continuity and discontinuity, boundaries, and ruptures are established is highly complex and variable. It is essential to discover, as part of the second set of problems, rules of social practices which remain relatively stable if not actually invariant over a specific length of time. Economic or social structure is largely determined by these rules. Lastly, there is the question of presenting the substance of historical developments and suggesting possible explanations of their causation. However, a comparative study of premodern Asia in its social and economic dimensions poses many difficulties. It is not without reason that the history of the regions around and beyond the Indian Ocean is still awaiting its author. In contrast, students of premodern Europe have distinguished themselves in a proliferation of explanations that attempt to integrate the multiple strands of the economic past by means of a self-limiting range of causal theories. The rigours of linguistic demands alone on the Orientalist encourage intense regional specialisation which is reinforced by the task of unravelling the exceptional complexities of social structures found in many Eastern civilisations.

There are also important theoretical difficulties. Structural analysis is only one of several different conceptual techniques that can be adopted to mark, outline, and delimit the boundaries of the objective domains of comparative categories. Lacking a unified body of theories, the structuralist is forced to work with a heterogeneous and often ill-matched collection of theoretical propositions in the manner of a bricoleur creating bricolage and turning social or historical evidence almost into mytho-poetry.[4] In its classic form, history as a discipline also gives rise to a more fundamental problem. The historian, like the scientist, hopes to reproduce a segment of reality ('what really happened in the past') as a photographic image exact in all its details. Even when the details are lacking, it is impossible for him to admit that the deficiencies of the image could be due to anything other than technical faults. That there could be two or more valid yet contradictory explanations of an occurrence or phenomenon cannot be admitted, because the historian works with an absolute and idealised definition of 'truth'.

The structural approach, 'Incomplete Theorem', and the problem of categories. In 1931 the Viennese mathematician Kurt Gödel, who was only twenty-five at the time, published his famous paper 'On formally undecidable propositions of *Principia Mathematica and related systems*'.[5] Gödel's 'Incomplete Theorem' destroyed certain basic assumptions of formal methods of proof in mathematics and science and it modified the historian's implicit belief that the human mind is capable (through language) of providing a test of truth for every proposition derived from a given universe of observations. Gödel was able to work out a mathematical proof of the contradiction inherent in the class of paradoxes of which the ancient 'Liar's paradox' is one: Epimenides, the Cretan, said that all Cretans are liars. The mind and language can make a single statement appear simultaneously true and false. By using a unique mathematical technique, Gödel proved that even in elementary arithmetic there is a residual formula which is unprovable by the test of consistency. An extension of the reasoning which follows from Gödel's Incomplete Theorem is that the identity of historical structures cannot be taken as 'platonic': it is dependent on definitions, on the observer's time-frame, and location in space. The relevance of the Incomplete Theorem as a methodological device to this study lies in the fact that terms such as the Indian Ocean or food and clothing can be treated as if they were systems of classification rather than names and concepts rigidly attached to a particular set of meanings.

If the identification of a given historical structure presents difficulties, its description also creates similar problems. The fact that the boundaries of a 'structure' change discretely and continuously in any one of these three dimensions requires the construction of a dynamic theory which can handle synchronous movements in more than one plane. An alternative approach to that of static structuralism is to view historical processes as a series of 'transforms'.[6] A set of discrete objects, abstract relationships, even a family of movements, is carried over from one time period to another either in a replicated or a modified form. The density of the transformation function is less in the first case (exact replication or 'steady state'), greater in the second. A metallurgical process which involves the heating of iron ores in order to produce wrought iron is a historical transformation of maximum density (within the framework of metallurgy). The application of transformation functions to history weakens the notion of equilibrium which has played such an important role in human thought, a source of both strength and weakness.

What has been said so far leads to the conclusion that a comparative historian, wherever he decides to locate his field of study, should begin by defining the planes of his analysis by appealing consciously to the theory of knowledge. Primary knowledge gained through perception (historical evidence) is naturally rearranged in the course of historical description into concrete categories such as religion, political organisation, economic life, and social institutions, each of which contains its own rules of 'logical necessity'. Description and chronology (as defined by solar time) of course constitute the two strongest allies of the historian. Descriptive history creates its accessibility by spontaneously drawing on the powerful logic inherent in all natural languages. At the same time, it cannot avoid creating arbitrary constructions based on 'propositions', 'tautologies' and 'contradictions'. A proposition, according to Wittgenstein, has the form of its sense. A tautology is equivalent to an 'empty set' which leaves its 'logical space' empty, while a contradiction completely fills it up. Every word or a combination of words shuts out or excludes certain sense and thereby fixes the limits of its variability.[7] Accordingly, the idea that there exists a geographical continent called Asia inhabited by Asian people or a geographical set whose elements are composed of various spatial units defined by the term 'Indian Ocean' should be taken as a purely mental construct. These categories possess sense but they are not positively verifiable by experience. The historical unity and disunity of Asia, therefore, can be defined only by a series of mental processes. The logical frame constructed by the mind captures momentarily an image of the reality arranged in the triple order of tense: the past, present, and the future. In a generalised form, the sense of a proposition such as the 'Indian Ocean' resolves into the fundamental dialectics of space, time, and structures.

The deconstruction of the concept of Asia. An example of how the dialectics operate can be seen by going back once again to the concept of Asia as a continent. The term, it is recognised, is essentially Western. There is no equivalent word in any Asian language nor such a concept in the domain of geographical knowledge, though expressions such as the 'Sea of China' or the 'Sea of Hind' held certain analogous meaning in Arabic and some of the Indian languages. The geographical concept of Asia is derived through the following reasoning. Western civilisations and European people (identified by religion, colour, shared habits, and artistic expression) are to be found in a specific area of the northern hemisphere which is named 'Europe'. Eastern civilisations and their members are manifestly 'non-European'; neither are they to be found in Europe. Hence the geographical space associated with these latter civilisations can be given the identity of a separate continent. The 'mapping pattern' between the two categories, European people and Europe as a continent, is isomorphic. One set transfers its structural unity to the other in a one-to-one ratio. However, it is the principle of contradiction (non-European) that establishes the identity of Asia, even though its civilisations and people are markedly different from one another. Of course, besides being non-European, Asia is also non-African, non-American and so on. There is a sequence of exclusions of which non-European comes first.[8] For Europe, the notion of a continental unity is derived from that of the homogeneity of European people. But for Asian civilisations, their disunity or lack of apparent cohesion is not admitted as an argument against the use of the term Asia. On the contrary, the identity of people does not enter into the semantics at all. Geographical Asia is the inverse mirror image of geographical Europe. The logic appears as dialectical in historical application because of the contradiction contained in the implied original proposition. It is easily seen that the identity and the totality of the 'excluded set', Asia, will hold over time only as long as the identity of the 'set of sets', Europe, is intact. We might say that this is the hidden temporal structure of a concept that is objectified through reduction, a process in which tense is abolished.[9] The sense of the two expressions is understood by a large number of people without having to refer to the history of their meanings over time. Even when Europe or Asia is undergoing major structural changes neither of the two terms changes its meaning. Furthermore, specific sets such as Europe, Africa, or Asia contain the structuring principle of spatial categories called continents. The category remains empty and its derivation is completely arbitrary. It is impossible to distinguish a continent from an island, a peninsula, or a large land mass. The problem of discovering the actual dividing lines between Europe, Asia, and Africa or between the Indian Ocean and the Pacific consequently disappears at the level of physical space. The cartographic frontiers are either purely conventional or unimportant. They are certainly variable according to the chosen mental frame of reference. The implication of an empty set lies precisely in the fact that it can be given content in more than one grid of specification.

The unity of space and time. The deconstruction of the Western image of Asia as a distinct unit of space exposes several layers of logical reasoning which uphold the historical reconstruction of the past. The unity of the regions we have called the Indian Ocean and that of their economic and social life takes on analytical cohesion not from the observable unity of a spatial construct but from the dynamics of structural relations. The analysis is always conducted in the mental domain. As for the unity of the time period, no historian can deny the objective existence of historical 'facts' identified with an ordinal unit of solar time. Yet he is forced to admit that for him there is no other tense than the past and therefore, all that he has to work with is a mere record and a memory of the past. The historian is a spectator and not a participant, no matter how strong is the illusion of being a continuing witness to a continuous process. The objectivity of a historical fact, an event, or a particular period arises from an awareness of the ruptures in time (past, present, and future) which places it, at the time of its occurrence, in the present and assigns it an associative relation with absolute time.[10] All historical facts with or without a specific date possess a past and a future both of which are independent of observation.[11] If we take a date such as AD 622, the foundation of Islam as expressed through the association of the faithful ('umma'), we can see that everything prior to it constitutes its past and everything posterior, its future. It is the existence of this time-mark alone which makes the history of the region known as the 'Middle East' discontinuous and divides it into pre- and post-Islamic periods. The idea of continuity depends on the introduction of an arbitrary single point into a line or surface and the point belongs only to *one* of the two resulting sets. Historical action must necessarily take place in the physical domain but its manifestations are measured against temporal ruptures perceived in the mental domain as past, present, and future. The apparent contradictions and the complexity of movements which characterise the history not only of the Indian Ocean but also that of the West may owe their origin to the interaction between the physical and mental domains at the level of action.

The methodology and its application

Fernand Braudel. The question of whether our time-period, chosen regions, and historical themes possess any natural cohesion and unities can be answered at several levels of analysis. No one has done more than Fernand Braudel to explore the role of time, space, and structural relationships through a wealth of historical case-studies. Although Braudel was well aware of the abstract principles involved in constructing the theoretical arguments, he refrained from suggesting any rigorous exposition of his ideas. Moreover, he excluded from his studies mental perceptions, the impact of ideology, and the influence of religion. His intellectual interest remained focused primarily on the historical processes and the interplay between different physical systems. Climate, environment, and mechanisms of social control such as capitalism or the world economy constantly interact with one another to produce a whole stream of material consequences. In Braudel's scheme of historical reasoning, the explanation and description of the concrete expressions of the human mind would to some extent have taken account of the abstract dimension. In his essay 'History and Sociology' published in a volume edited by Georges Gurvitch, Braudel made his theoretical standpoint quite clear:

A historian faithful to the teachings of Lucien Febvre and Marcel Mauss will always wish to grasp the whole, the totality of social life. So he is led to bringing together different levels, time spans, different kinds of time, structures, conjunctures, events. These taken all together go to make up for him a fairly precarious global balance which can be maintained only through a constant series of adjustments, clashes, and slight alterations. In its totality, social reality in flux is ideally, at every instant, *synchronous* with its history, a constantly changing image, although it might repeat a thousand previous details of a thousand previous realities.[12]

The totality of a given historical situation and its changing boundaries remained the central themes for Braudel in his studies both of the Mediterranean and of the emergence of Western Europe as a world economy. Braudel saw the unity of the Mediterranean as being the product of the unities of material life and the physical environment. Against the slowly changing background, historical events, the fire-flies of time, played out their ephemeral course.[13] However, Braudel never thought it necessary to define what is meant by a 'totality' or describe the principles by which it is established. His description of Mediterranean history itself established the unity of the subject.

Michel Foucault. Braudel's reluctance to examine the role of ideas as structuring principles in social life may appear strange in view of his familiarity with German historical and philosophical thought. It is all the more striking when it is considered that during the years that Braudel was engaged in completing his massive historical work *Civilisation matérielle, économie et capitalisme*, Michel Foucault had already published his *Histoire de la folie à l'age classique*, *Les mots et les choses*, *L'Archéologie du savoir*, and other semi-historical studies. Foucault's abiding interest and achievement was to show how mental categories into which the totality of social phenomena are partitioned by contemporary observers change over time and how dangerous it is to assume that classificatory terms such as madness, capitalism, political economy, medical practice, or sexuality have universal meanings independent of the historical context. Even the unity of generic discourses (psychology, economics, grammar, or medicine) cannot be taken for granted. The ideas and methods of argumentation put forward by Foucault hold out a strong appeal to historians who are looking for structural relations in a social system resulting from the interaction between the mental and the physical domains.

In his theory of the formation of objects in discourse, Foucault specified three separate processes at work. First of all, there was a surface of emergence given by questions such as where, by whom, and by what norms are abstract or concrete categories recognised. If we take madness as a category, the context in which its symptoms are tested could be: family, the immediate social groups involved, the work situation, and the religious community. Foucault's second process is the delimitation of objects through different forms of authority. Law, social custom, medical science, or religion endow specific groups of people with the power to define objective categories. Thus it becomes possible in this process for medical practitioners to reclassify criminal behaviour as a subset of psycho-pathological disorder. Even the state might wish through its judicial apparatus to equate political dissent with insanity and confine those who express radical views to mental institutions. Finally, Foucault also specified grids of reference which are systems through which objective conditions and relations are established. These could be a theory of knowledge, scientific practices, a time sequence, all of which enable the phenomenon of insanity to be divided, structured, and compared.

Foucault recognised that abstract categories transformed through discourse as physical objects can exist, change, and make new appearances only if there is 'a group of relations established between authorities of emergence, delimitation, and specification'.[14] The primary relations between institutions, economic and social processes, behavioural patterns, systems of norms, techniques and types of classification, and modes of characterisation do not enable *existing* objects to be identified, nor are they derived from the objects themselves. The new themes of discourse result from a system of secondary or reflexive relations within the interstices of social categories. The historical linkages between the family as a social institution and judicial authorities can be studied in their own right as an example of primary relations between structures. The mental perceptions of these relations on the other hand might give rise to a system of discourse which in turn redefines entire categories of social conditions. New surfaces such as a changing notion of artistic expression, what is refined and vulgar, changing social identities expressed as changes in food habits, dress, and housing styles, a new concept of crime and punishment, could all appear as new categories in the mental domain which find equivalences in the physical domain.

Neither the materialism of Braudel nor the mental transients of Foucault called for an integration of the two respective methodologies. Within its own frame of reference, each is self-contained and perfectly comprehensible. Although Braudel chose to remain silent on Foucault's contribution to history, in the opening pages of *The Archaeology of Knowledge*, Foucault made an indirect reference to Braudel's theory of slow-moving changes as an antithesis to his own object of inquiry:

From the political mobility at the surface down to the slow movements of 'material civilization', ever more levels of analysis have been established: each has its own peculiar discontinuities and patterns; and as one descends to the deepest levels, the rhythms become broader. Beneath the rapidly changing history of governments, wars, and famines, there emerge other, apparently unmoving histories: the history of sea routes, the history of corn or of gold-mining, the history of drought and of irrigation, the history of crop rotation, the history of the balance achieved by the human species between hunger and abundance.[15]

The historian's classic preoccupation Foucault saw as an overwhelming compulsion to seek out continuities and unities so that 'discontinuity was the stigma of temporal dislocation that is the historian's task to remove from history'.[16] In the new kind of history which interested Foucault, the emphasis shifted to the task of tracing out ruptures, limits, thresholds, series, and transformations.

Georg Cantor and set theory. Braudel and Foucault both used the rhetoric of language to identify certain intuitive and selective operations of the human mind. It is possible to argue that they were the common products of a line of European thought which had its origin in the mathematical discoveries of the 1870s when Georg Cantor discovered the theory of sets and the infinite, leading to the unsolvable problem of the continuum and Gödel's Incomplete Theorem. Braudel's search for unities in the triple dimensions of space, time, and structures, his inclusion of the Sahara and Anatolia in the Mediterranean, his famous statement that the Christian and Muslim halves of the Mediterranean breathed and lived in the same common rhythms, Foucault's archaeological excavations on the fragile surface of perceived unities and his emphasis on ruptures, were already anticipated as a methodology by the axioms of set theory first propounded by Cantor and subsequently formalised by Zermelo and Fraenkel. By an 'aggregate' or set, Cantor had written, we are to understand any collection into a whole M of definite and separate objects m of our intuition or our thought.[17] The capacity of the mind to think of 'many' as 'one' and divide 'one' into 'many' Cantor took as the basis of his set theory. It draws on three key intuitive concepts: the awareness of a principle which separates one element of a set from another element (differentiation), a second principle which enables the elements to be classified into a single set (integration), and a principle of ordering or succession which derives one set from another according to anterior or posterior notions. By way of an example let us take the 'axiom of choice' which states that if there is a set of non-empty sets none of which have common members, then there exists a set with exactly one member drawn from each set.[18] This is a simple process of selection with which the historian is perfectly familiar. But the principle of its derivation involves enormous complexity, because it assumes that the criteria for making the representative selection from each set actually exist. For example, it is perfectly possible to select a member from Muslim, Hindu, Javanese, and Chinese societies respectively to make up a representative set of Indian Ocean civilisations. The principle which identifies an individual as a member of Islam, Sanskritic India or any other larger community (as we shall show) is different in each case.

The search for solutions to intractable and impossibly difficult questions raised by his own work proved too much for Cantor and he became insane. The continuum problem in particular has still not found a satisfactory answer. The logical paradoxes inherent in the set theory (for example, in the expression 'a set of *all* sets') created universal dismay and it was left to Bertrand Russell to analyse their true nature, leading to 'the amazing fact that our logical intuitions (i.e., intuitions concerning such notions as: truth, concept, being, class, etc.) are self-contradictory'.[19] Such was the impact of Cantor's discovery that as late as 1925 David Hilbert, the foremost mathematical theorist of his time, described it as one of the supreme achievements of purely intellectual human activity. No one, Hilbert claimed, shall drive us out of the paradise which Cantor has created for us.[20]

Set theory admittedly places at the disposal of the historian a powerful logical instrument for identifying unities and discontinuities. But the question remains whether or not the principle of identifying sets violates our intuitive notions of plausibility. If the Central Asian steppes and deserts are to be included in the regions of the Indian Ocean, a train of thought must be established which connects them together as being members of a common set. When the possibility is presented in this way, we can see that the term 'Indian Ocean' is nothing more than a *name* given to a set of principles which form not *one* but an *infinity* of sets, none of which is separable from its argument. The problem is exactly the same as the one raised by Cantor in his continuum question: 'how many points are there on a straight line in Euclidean space?', for which we substitute, 'how many interpretations are there of the Indian Ocean as a set of historical relationships?'.[21] There is obviously a *family* of hidden meanings with outer and inner limits. One possible interpretation is the following: the sea, fertile land, mountains, and the desert are the necessary elements of a space in which the interactions between seafarers, nomads, and the people of settled agriculture appear as a single indivisible historical process for more than a millennium. By this reasoning, there is a principle under which each element of the set 'Indian Ocean, Arabs, Indians, the Chinese and so on, is integrated into a common pattern of history. It may be asked, as a separate issue, why not use the more commonly accepted term Asia. It can indeed be so used, except for the fact that Asia has a specific meaning. As we have already shown, it is an empty set formed by its antithesis to Europe. The use of the term Asia forces the historian consciously or unconsciously to explain the history of Asia not in the light of its own rationale but by a reasoning which describes it as 'Europe and the people without history'. The words 'Asia' and 'Asian' are used in our study but always in the sense that they include singly or in a combination terms such as Arab, Indian, Malay, Thai, Chinese, or Japanese and do not refer to something that needs the prior concept of a Europe and people with history to make sense.

Space, time, and structures in the Indian Ocean

Theoretical framework. In a reflective essay, Roman Jakobson stated that the 'question of invariance in the midst of variation' has been the dominant topic and methodological device underlying his diversified yet homogeneous research work since 1911.[22] Jakobson's enunciation of the problem goes to the very heart of structural analysis: how to discover and recognise structural continuities and discontinuities (over time) when forms are variable. The canonical plan of Hindu temples or Islamic mosques must remain invariant but artistic and architectural forms are allowed free expression. The history of the people who lived in the lands adjacent to and beyond the Indian Ocean may be expressed through the history of food items, food production, settled agriculture, nomadism, and the inner social identities revealed through unchanging or slowly changing daily habits. These are set-theoretic concepts which enable us to compare the physical symbols and their mental representations responsible for ordering and structuring society in the Middle East, India, South East Asia, and China. The analysis will show that societies primarily dependent on bread or rice to sustain human life (as opposed to meat or dairy products) have their field of choices constrained by the priority given to cereal farming. The historical contours of wheat and rice cultivation not only follow certain attributes of the physical environment but are also influenced by relationships which exist within human society. The system of law, the concept of property, the wealth-generating quality of cleared land, the dependence of political agents on agricultural surplus to create state income, are all instances of structural relations which have closely interacted throughout history with the twin domesticated plants of civilisation, wheat and rice. The theory of Braudelian *longue durée* seems to operate in a decisive fashion on the temporal rhythms of our chosen categories: food and clothing habits in the Indian Ocean, the architecture of power, styles of housing, systems of agriculture, industrial production, and the patterns of urbanisation.

The methodology of this study and its theoretical premises do not deny the primacy of Braudel's three-fold physical dimensions in historical description and analysis. But the theory of our historical logic takes into account explicitly the mental transformations of space, time, and structures which act upon the physical symbols through action. For an illustration, take the Indian Ocean as a unit of space. The climatic and the environmental hazards of the sea obviously determined in an absolute sense the outcome of historical commercial voyages organised by merchants. It was the collective awareness of these dangers and the observed limits of their variability which marked out particular sea routes and landfalls as being permanently safe for navigation. Thus the Indian Ocean, so far as merchants were concerned, had three discernible qualities. Its distances were measurable by analogue methods (in leagues or miles) as well as journey-time (arithmetic ratios). The changes in the surface of the sea followed regular seasonal patterns. Finally, the sea expressed a relationship between itself and man not only in the opportunity it provided for transporting goods but also in the preference for a whole way of seafaring life.

We can see that each of these three attributes have projections onto other features of society. The distance is projected to the technique of ship-building and methods of navigation. The seasonal characteristics of the sea determines the sailing dates, the time cycle of caravans bringing goods to the ports of embarkation, and even the rhythm of industrial production. The structural relationship between the sea and merchants can be projected into attitudes which decide whether trade, merchants, the legal protection of commercial capital, and the operation of market forces, were worthy of further encouragement and extension. In the language of set theory, the structure of the sea is 'mapped' in this exercise on to the structure of society. When the mapping is in a one-to-one ratio it is isomorphic. For example, the life of a working sailor in the Indian Ocean and the structural features of the sea are isomorphic but the mapping pattern is different for merchants who use the sea only partially. Perhaps the isomorphism between the Indian Ocean and our subjects of study owed most to the climate, particularly the patterns of the monsoon winds which marked out zones of aridity and high plant growth. Societies which had access to ample water supplies were quite different from those which possessed only limited access, and it was the conjunction between the sea and the global climate which created the distinction.

Using the concepts discussed so far, we are able to specify for historical analysis an abstract structural 'space' with six dimensions: scientific space, real time, functions such as the causal relationship between rainfall and crop-raising, and the mental representations of each of these three physical planes. Any point in this structural space can be identified either by its co-ordinates to the six dimensions or relative to other points using the same dimensions. The relative positions of the points are defined as structural relations and the limits of their variability are given by the limits of the structural space. How are the limits determined? There is no difficulty with purely physical manifestations. When inadequate rainfall turns arid land into desert, farmers and nomads must move on or change their occupational life. There is little room for interpretation. However, in the mental domain a structural space is transformed into a logical space which is defined, following Wittgenstein, as the possibilities in the existence of states of affair.[23] The transformation of arid land into desert, in so far as it affects human survival, now reduces to the question, when is the process completed and how is it recognised to be so? In order to solve the problem a system of linguistic and physical tests is needed. As a mental concept the desert has an outer and inner limit in the logical space. The outer limit of the desert is fixed by its antithesis to land with water and all deserts can be classified into a set by this test. The inner limit of the concept is reached when the expression 'a grain of sand' is mentioned. Further linguistic and physical partitioning of a grain of sand leads us to chemistry, beyond the limits of the logical space and the principle which identifies the desert as a set. It is easy enough to see that the mere presence of sand whether in cultivable land or seashores does not lead to the concept of the desert which needs a dialectic image of space (i.e. completely antithetical images, desert and non-desert).

The comparative world views of Islam, India, South East Asia, and China. The outer limits of the Indian Ocean as a spatial set are given in the west by the Gulf of Suez and the marshlands of the Shatt al-Arab; in the east, the sea which lies beyond Japan forms an undefined barrier to navigation by sailing ships. When the identity of the great ocean and that of its sub-sets are projected on to the collective identities of the people who lived in the lands surrounding the sea, certain distinct sets of historical 'world' views emerge. As a set the Indian Ocean is not merely the two-dimensional unit of space depicted on most maps. It has a third dimension in the curvature of the earth. In order to see what the distribution of civilisational space looks like in three-dimensional form, the computer was instructed to draw four maps from the height of a space satellite with its eye centred on Mecca, Delhi, Jakarta, and Peking (see Maps 1–4). The exercise is highly revealing. The three-dimensional maps suggest that the mental projections of space are not entirely linear and additive. Beyond a certain point the representations of distances become logarithmic and exponential. What appear to be straight lines become at closer view curves and ratios. We shall see in chapter 5 that an anthropomorphic transformation of space among premodern people created limits beyond which societies ceased to be real and even human.

The cartographic world view of a Muslim as seen from Mecca, Cairo, or Constantinople radiated from the Red Sea and the eastern Mediterranean into adjacent areas as far as Spain in the west and the straits of Malacca and Sunda in the east. India is clearly as interesting an area for an expanding Islam as the Mediterranean (Map 1). High visibility of Central Asia rapidly distorts into a bare awareness of China. What is surprising and at the same time paradoxical in the cartographic image is the massive presence of Africa. The isolation of the rest of Africa stands in marked contrast to its eastern coast which is not only a part of the Indian Ocean in its physical dimensions but historically was incorporated into the world of Islam. The paradox of the situation lies in the fact that the interaction between the indigenous African cultures and that of Islam whether it was at the level of daily life or deeper mental constructs still remains only half understood in spite of its long history.

The world view of India (Map 2) echoes these nuances but presents fewer perplexities. The map shows the primacy of the Middle East, East Africa, and South East Asia and the halfway-house role of the subcontinent in the Indian Ocean. China and the Mediterranean are visible. Atlantic Europe and the Baltic are severely distorted. As the eye of the satellite moves eastward to Jakarta (Map 3) and Peking (Map 4), the respective images of the globe reverse themselves. The world of the Indonesian islands is highly oceanic: the southern Indian Ocean and the Pacific occupy large areas in the pictorial image. For China the landmass stretching from the trans-Himalayan and the Tien Shan regions to the southern tip of the Malay peninsula is the dominant perspective of space, though the South China Sea is also of obvious importance. The contemporaneous view of actual global space of course remained imperfect, and at the same time it is not entirely fanciful to suggest that there is a certain correspondence between the three-dimensional distortions we see

Eye   Long.   Lat.   Dist.
      40.0   22.0   10.0

Map 1 Three-dimensional view of the world centred on Mecca.

today with the aid of space satellites and the experience of distance filtered through travel by land and sea. The human eye reduces three-dimensional forms into two-dimensional images and the resulting distortions find an equivalence in the inability of people to conceive of remote places as being an entirely normal unit of space fit for human habitation. Space becomes mythological and is located either in a garden of Eden or in hell.

The comparative civilisations of the Indian Ocean. One of the main objectives of this study as an exercise in comparative economic and social history is to locate the outer and inner limits of the different civilisations which were recognised by their respective members in their own time-frame to be separate and distinct from one another. The limits and boundaries were established at

Eye Long. Lat. Dist.
     77.0   28.0 10.0

Map 2 Three-dimensional view of the world centred on Delhi.

several levels of perceptions and often the structural unities and disunities lay below the level of collective awareness. People who ate rice, fish, and the derivatives of the coconut, to take only one example, sharply distinguished themselves from those who lived on bread, meat, and dairy products. This was a separation largely mapped by climate and geography onto social habits and traditions. But the rice-eating communities were themselves divided by language, religion, culture, and ethnic identities. Farmers growing rice in tiny flooded fields, whether they lived in the Malabar coast of India, Ceylon, eastern Bengal, Java, Thailand, or China, would not have known that their houses shared a common style of construction. The technology of rice production on the other hand, particularly improvements in seeds and cropping cycles, had strong diffusive and imitative patterns. The participants were

Eye   Long.   Lat.   Dist.
        106.5   −7.0   10.0

Map 3 Three-dimensional view of the world centred on Jakarta.

strongly aware of the limits of possibilities in the methods of wet-rice cultivation and their comparative spatial dimensions. In this example, two
separate 'sets' identified by the terms 'food' and 'housing' are divided into
further sub-sets and elements each of which can belong to other independent
sets. Historical developments associated with food habits, food production
(techniques of rice growing), styles of housing, building materials, and construction methods, constitute further sub-sets or elements of the original sets.
The outer limits of the two sets 'food' and 'housing' are fixed in the first
instance by the linguistic sense of the words, and in the second by the
expression Indian Ocean. The inner limits are reached by a process of
linguistic differentiation verified by experience. Actual examples can be found
in the individual items of food and housing: bread, rice, meat, fish, protein,

Eye Long. Lat. Dist.
     116.0 39.5 10.0

Map 4 Three-dimensional view of the world centred on Peking.

carbohydrates, fat, stones, bricks, wood, and thatch. The process of differentiation is perhaps exhausted when any one of these terms, such as fish is further
categorised as food into raw fish (edible in certain societies), grilled fish, boiled
fish, baked fish, salted and smoked fish. Each of these categories occupies a
structural position on the logical space of our two sets and they are also related
in a symbolic or functional way to other sets (see chapter 5). The historical
trajectory of these sets follow different rhythms of time. Food habits and
preferred styles of housing may remain stable over long periods of time. They
may also change rapidly in response to fundamental technological transformations.

If Asia were the dialectic image of Europe, there is some justification for
thinking that a similar pattern of thought may also have existed among the

members of the four dominant civilisations of the Indian Ocean in our period. The sense of dissimilarity and distance which existed between the people of Islam, Sanskritic India, South East Asia, and the Far East was tempered by a conscious awareness of the attributes of societies other than one's own and the desire to import new forms of religion, social habits, technology, and artistic expression. A subject of the Celestial empire may have been a rare visitor to the Islamic world but cultural and political exchanges between China and Islam were not totally absent. The historical remains of ancient Java, Bali, Cambodia, Thailand, and Burma point to a conscious assimilation and trans-formation of cultural identities that originated in the Indian subcontinent. The historical destinies of Europe and Africa in contrast remained well beyond the limits of immediate perceptions. Even the assimilation of Greco-Roman cultural, scientific, and social traditions by the Muslims and Indians remained indirect and dialectical. The separation was highlighted and reinforced by the tradition of a perpetual war between Christendom and Islam. Few Asian societies realised the full historical implications of the arrival of the Portuguese, Dutch, and the English in the Indian Ocean and they remained non-participants to the great technological and social revolution which led to the rapid shrinking of the world in the nineteenth and twentieth centuries. The exclusion of East Africa from our civilisational identities needs a special word of explanation. In spite of its close connection with the Islamic world, the indigenous African communities appear to have been structured by a historical logic separate and independent from the rest of the Indian Ocean.

There were specific rules (not always fully visible) by which every member of the Indian Ocean societies could be classified into a common set and likewise, recognised as an individual (see chapter 2). An examination of these outer and inner limits in Islam, Sanskritic society, the communities of maritime and mainland South East Asia, and China, show that the tests were both simple and complex. The rules by which a Chinese Muslim recognised himself to be a subject of the Celestial emperor and at the same time to be bound by the Qur'anic laws were grounded on very different principles. The four great civilisations of the Indian Ocean can of course be identified with specific areas of space. While no contemporary thinker would have denied that he 'belonged' to one or other of these cultural sets, space itself assigned identities to people. The place of birth located a person absolutely in legal terms and relatively on the social map. In contrast, the nomadic peoples relied by definition on genealogy rather than a fixed locus in space to create a 'perpetual memory' of social replication. Sanskritic India used both genealogy and space as principles of primary identities. Pilgrims who had paid homage to the holy cities of Varanasi, Hardwar, or Mathura enjoyed spiritual and immediate social distinctions (as did also Muslim devotees visiting Mecca, Qum, and Mashhad) which only a spatial journey could convey. Above all, the strongest structuring principles of space in the Indian Ocean societies were to be found in its order, the typologies of fertile plains, the desert, mountains, and the sea (see chapter 5).

Economic structure and organisation. The theoretical framework adopted in our study enables us to view the articulation of the economy, society, and the state in the Indian Ocean as a totality. The idealised economic concepts such as market forces, subsistence production, capitalism and so on are treated as artificial constructs which are not directly visible as part of the social reality. Economic activities functioned within a larger structure and at each level of articulation a set of logical necessities governed the physical operation of a particular system. Interaction between these logical necessities and mental perceptions determined how economic production and distribution would move over time and whether new technological innovations could be assimilated into social practices. Settled agriculture needed logically not only land, labour, and capital but also a legal definition of property rights in cleared land and an agency of internal and external protection. The idea and practice of subsistence-oriented peasant agriculture were not fully compatible with the notions of a judicial and political authority which extended beyond the immediate locality of the farmers. The result was a structural contradiction and the possibility of endemic conflicts of interest between self-sufficient farmers, the political elites, the military, the inhabitants of towns, and the merchants (see chapter 3).

It is quite clear that the basic economic structures of Asian societies were worked out long before our period of study. The technology of agricultural and industrial production, the pattern of urbanisation, and the distribution of economic products through a mixed system of market forces and social entitlement had not only reached their mature forms at the time of the birth of Islam but over the next thousand years their historical trajectory display cyclical and counter-cyclical motions. Some areas suffered decline and relative institutional retrogression from time to time. One can cite the examples of Egypt and Iraq: their capital-intensive irrigated agriculture, articulated to a well-developed commercial and urban economy, suffered catastrophic disruptions in the thirteenth and fourteenth centuries, the causes of which are still not entirely clear. The political dislocation following the Mongol conquests and the demographic consequences of Black Death were linked to other long-term factors in bringing about the visible and recorded calamities which affected many parts of the Middle East in this period. The over-development of land through irrigation and the appearance of the plague and malaria in new and more virulent forms may have been responsible for a 'crisis' of the thirteenth century in the Indian Ocean. Under Ottoman rule the Middle East recaptured some of its former prosperity. The irrigated agriculture of Ceylon, the rice bowl of southern India, reverted to jungle. The experience of Cambodia was very similar. The landed economy of northern India and the riverine deltas of

China on the other hand continued to move forward in spite of temporary climatic and political setbacks.

The complex rhythms of time associated with the history of the Indian Ocean make it difficult to use the tripartite logic of European history as an analytical tool. There was no transition from a 'mode of classical production' into that of feudalism, nor a historical progression from the commercial capitalism of the sixteenth and seventeenth centuries to the industrial capitalism of the nineteenth. Examples of capitalistic production were to be found in most areas in a random distribution of temporal sequences. This is not to deny the considerable impact of a major world-wide economic phenomenon such as the discovery and the dispersion of American and Japanese silver from the sixteenth century onwards, which restructured the economic policies of centralised bureaucratic empires and strengthened the *de facto* position of merchants. The concentration of capital into the hands of the mercantile class in turn vitalised the role of bankers and merchants as intermediaries between farmers and the state. Market forces, however, existed alongside the logic of subsistence production.

Transcontinental oceanic and caravan trade remained the economic mechanism through which the economies of the Indian Ocean were linked to the rest of the world. The most tangible sign of the external economic dimensions was the movement of gold, silver, and copper which acted as currency. The distribution of precious metals within the Indian Ocean measured to some extent the degree of commercialisation achieved in agricultural and industrial production. Economic specialisation between regions was closely associated with the volume of trade and the sophistication of its institutional organisation. For the full development of capitalistic activities to which market operations gave rise, three further conditions needed to be fulfilled. Political stability not only ensured an orderly conduct of social life but also more specifically, whether the merchants' financial liabilities and assets could be converted into real wealth. The owners of capital did not enjoy in Asia the strict protection of the law but intransigent political rulers discovered to their cost that the supply of loans and credit to the state dried up if the bankers and merchants were persistently mistreated and expropriated for short-term gain. No Asian government would have denied that the maintenance of law and order within its jurisdiction was an essential obligation of political authority and that all subjects regardless of their occupation should be the beneficiaries of that duty. Yet the protection of merchants and trade routes involved something more than a technical expression of power. Merchants by definition operated across national political frontiers. The concept of a law of nation was required for the preservation of their personal safety and the value of their property. This necessary condition was satisfied for maritime trade by declaring the Indian Ocean a neutral zone and encouraging port towns to function as semi-independent commercial emporia. For caravan routes, the nomadic tribes assumed the role of protectors in return for financial indemnities.

The economic development of the Indian Ocean regions was the consequence of three structural features. A highly productive agriculture supported a complex system of political and social institutions. Industrial production for the export markets introduced some elements of capitalistic principles governing the relationships between the artisans and merchants. Economic exchange primarily took the form of local and long-distance trade and the market for agricultural and industrial goods operated on the allocation principle of relative prices indexed by money and currency. The distribution of natural endowments, of course, determined in the last instance whether a particular community or region was to enjoy relative affluence or remain trapped in a cycle of bare survival and destructive starvation. Nomadic societies were particularly vulnerable to climatic shifts. A central contradiction in all Asian economies was the co-existence of non-market and market relations. Farmers tilled their fields to raise crops which mainly went to feed their immediate families. Where the opportunity for marketing high-value food crops and agricultural raw materials for industrial manufacture existed, peasants allocated some of their land to cash crops.

The impetus for such diversification of agricultural production occurred long before our period of study. It is possible to show that the Arab military leaders in the newly-conquered land in Iraq adopted principles of taxation which were worked out by earlier political authorities in the context of the region's irrigated economy, a tradition which went back to the Babylonian times. The taxation problems faced by the centralised bureaucratic empires reflected the dual features of the rural economy. Where the state claimed a physical share of crops, the services of financial intermediaries were required in order to transform the revenue in kind into cash incomes. Money assessment on the other hand involved not only a detailed survey of land and the annual calculation of areas sown with cash crops but also the prediction of average prices and the cash revenue of farmers. That peasant producers should pay rents and taxes to the state and the dominant warrior classes controlling land was taken as axiomatic. What was less than clear was the degree of force which should be applied to determine the 'economic' relationship between the tax-payers, the rentiers, and the state agents. However, in spite of their depressed social status, the peasantry appeared not to have been reduced to slavery, though in India and China agronomic bonded labour was a common institution. Perhaps, the most enigmatic problem in the production relations was the process whereby industrial craftsmen worked for non-local export markets. There were artisans in the rural economy who produced only for tied clients and they were rewarded by a share of the local agricultural produce. It is difficult to envisage the chain of historical causation which transformed part-time craftsmen into skilled specialised industrial manufacturers dependent on the capitalistic apparatus for the distribution of their products and fixing the level of output. The logic of economic self-sufficiency remained firmly rooted on the structure of peasant production, on the technology of transport and the strength of local identities. It was however continually eroded, reshaped, and transformed by social and political forces which articulated the rural economy to towns and cities and the wider civilisational values.

The premodern towns and cities of the Indian Ocean represented the final point of convergence between settled people and the nomads, between the rulers and the ruled, between agriculture and industry, between foreign and domestic merchants, and the literate and illiterate. The primate capital city shared an urban image in common with the smallest town: they were 'signs', composed of a universal class of 'signifiers', as well as 'signifieds'.[24] Whether a particular urban location possessed in full or lacked the physical attributes of a 'true town' was immaterial to the concept which retained its elementary sense without the need for further explication. The signifiers included all the concrete images of the town and the city: the density of housing, its street plan, the presence of famous religious shrines, temples, and mosques, architecture of symbolical power, and above all, the social character of its inhabitants. The anthropomorphism of space – certain human qualities attributed to specific regions – was derived in the minds of our contemporary observers largely from stereotyped behaviour patterns found among urban populations. If this was one particular aspect of the significations associated with urbanisation, the other was the ability of central places to indicate a differentiated and hierarchically arranged economic order, a structure of political and military power, and the power of artistic traditions. The urban history of the Indian Ocean was its most permanent component of time. Even in cases where an ephemeral town rose to rapid fame and prominence only to be obliterated completely in the regional topography, the urge towards personal urbanisation by leaders of society remained constant and recurrent. The city was the repository of social habits associated with food, clothing, and housing: if these habits possessed the power to signify the inner identities of people, the forms of that power resided largely in the city.

The unity of historical time. The question whether the period from the rise of Islam to the mid eighteenth century had any inherent structuring principle in the history of the Indian Ocean regions is resolved only by bringing into play all the theoretical assumptions discussed so far. Mechanical time-marks such as the birth of Islam in 622, the foundation of the T'ang dynasty in 618, and the Revolution of Plassey in 1757 leading to the foundation of British political power in India, provide terminal dates easily recognised by historians accustomed to work with the idea of linear time. These three time-marks occupy points on the logical space of perceived time which are measured by co-ordinates to several different conceptual planes. Each is seemingly random and the precise moment of their occurrence is neither predetermined nor important. Each event has a 'power' of signification which goes far beyond Fernand Braudel's fire-flies of historical events. They illuminate stretches of time in the life-cycle of civilisations whose metrics include several centuries and even a millennium. The military re-unification of China by the Sui and T'ang rulers and the spread of Islam across the Mediterranean and the Indian Ocean symbolise expansionary forces in history. The Revolution of Plassey signified the final passing of the Mughal empire in India and the end of a political, technological, and cultural *ancien régime*. The political rupture was immediately visible to contemporaries, the concrete manifestations of the technological and civilisational breaks were just beginning to appear. Within our chosen time-frame, there were several specific historical movements which shared simultaneously the characteristics of long-term expansion, contraction, and the steady state. The expansion of the nomadic steppe people from Central Asia towards the Middle East, India, and China belonged to the *longue durée* as well as to the cyclical components of time. The recurrent rise and fall of political empires and dynasties in Asian history must be seen alongside the assimilative power of Islam, Hinduism, and Confucian ethics to restructure the volatile forces present in the state system into conditions of steady state. Their failure in the late eighteenth century to assimilate European militarism and separate civilisational identity also marked the end of a life-cycle.

2

Comparative civilisations of Asia: structural integration and differentiation

The unity and disunity of the Indian Ocean

General principles. Certain abstract principles determine the unity and disunity of different civilisations in premodern Asia. They act, without revealing themselves, as signifiers in the mental domain.[1] The coherence of chronological periods, the order of time rhythms, or the identity of geographical space and social structures are signified as so many imaginary constructs whose logical space is left empty, to be filled by individuals, historians, and whosoever chooses to think about such matters. The constructed images attempt to portray but cannot represent the historical reality. They are necessarily imprecise. Although few historians would admit the fact or even show any awareness of it, the principles through which they learn to recognise specific sets, categories, and classes of time, space, and structural relationships invoke methods of integration and differentiation. The life-span of a particular civilisation in Asia may be derived by a process of summation. The sum-total of the segments of its historical past and the continuity of its social traditions across those segments are integrated together to form a perceived unity: unity which thereafter appears as the self-evident internal quality of a pre-identified structure. The reasoning proceeds from a concept signified in the mental domain as a singular set to its morphism in the physical domain to another objective set, a process which involves the recognition of the plurality of the discrete elements of the latter set. The final stage of the integration or the secondary order of significance follows when the discrete objects identified in the physical domain are reduced to a singular idea in the mental.[2] Many historical examples illustrate the point. The agrarian life of civilised China would seem on one plane of analysis to stretch back in an unbroken sequence to the Bronze Age, an integral part of a single civilisation.[3] Dynastic changes, of course, punctuated China's political life. And yet, in all its long history, the accumulated regalia of a resplendent imperial heritage were carried across political revolutions through the invariant ideology of a divinely-ordained emperor assisted by a learned and meritocratic bureaucracy. The history of settled farming in other parts of Asia was no less ancient than that of China. But the civilisations which it helped to support have long since vanished. Archaeology alone reminds us how the political and economic superstructure of ancient Egypt, Babylonia, or the Indus valley rested on a flourishing agrarian base. The recognition of the temporal ruptures in turn introduces the principle of differentiation. From the life-span of a civilisation measured over a millennium, perhaps over several millennia, the historian progresses towards centuries, years, or even days and hours. All through the ages the Asian farmer who tilled the fields cleared by his forgotten forefathers regulated his occupational life in terms of the seasons of the calendar and the length of available daylight.[4] Every structure in the economic and social life of man possesses a proper cognitive logic and appropriate metrics of time and space. It can be easily demonstrated that the unity and disunity of geographical areas also obey the same principle of objective formation. It is entirely possible to add together all the rural hamlets of Asia to derive a logical space of arbitrary dimensions, defined by the single concept of food-crop production.

The proposition that the totality of the farming villages of Asia should constitute a unitary theme of historical reconstruction lacks an essential quality of space, the element of contiguity. Space cannot be recognised for what it is without the necessary condition of continuity. The contradiction serves to draw attention to an important point. It must be obvious that the principle of symbolic integration utilised by historians to establish a field of analysis is very different from the intrinsic unity possessed by a set of historical events.[5] It cannot be denied that historians work wholly in the domain of the mind, and therefore often transcend beyond the world of primary experience. Historical action on the other hand expresses its objective forms through an interaction between the mental and the physical domains. All action is initiated and regulated by an internal logic that matches its specific elements to the specific stages of the action. While capable of displaying the property of independence (axiomatic derivation) this logic is nevertheless extremely complex and not always consistent. Even so its outer and inner limits are identifiable, and the historian creates for himself a difficult decision in the choice he has whether to mirror the totality of the original logic of historical causality or to rearrange its constituent elements into some other constructs.

Another way of looking at the same problem but from a slightly different perspective is to ask how the independence of the historical logic is established in the first place. Since facts are the outcome of thought, and thought is prompted by facts, by perceptions of facts, or by other thoughts, there is obviously a complete structure of relationships between these entities incorporating order, sequence, and tense. When the mapping relations become time-invariant and facts are reduced to a singular abstract set in the collective mind, through the summation or elimination of individual mental frames, the historical identity of an entire civilisation reveals itself. It is inconceivable that human thought expressed through natural language should be without a logical structure, though that logic is not always apparent to external observers. The linkage between the intention of the thinker, his thought, and

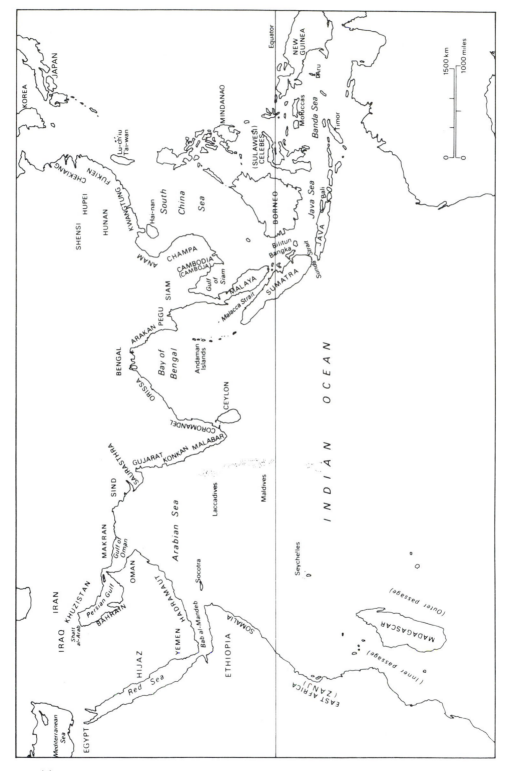

Map 5 The main historical regions of the Indian Ocean.

44

the subsequent experience reconstitutes itself as a concept in the mental domain. A representation or a sign bearing a resemblance to an object, it can be argued, does not signify it unless meaning exists in the form of intention in the cognitive field. Thus accidental sign-creation has no real meaning.[6] For a historian the point is of some interest. A prophet cannot carry conviction unless he creates the faith. A potter who accidentally discovers the technique of firing true porcelain is not able to recognise his creation as porcelain unless the concept exists in the first place. But he can learn to recognise that a new class of objects has been created by his own hands and mind. The people of the *ancien régime* identified their collective or individual place in the economic or social space by an intuitive or conditioned awareness of a larger construct formed by religion, language, political obligations and rights, artistic traditions, and the practices of every-day life. These visible and sometimes not-so-visible frontiers were drawn on the cultural cartography of Asia by four great civilisations in our period of study. From the high plains and the eroded valleys of the eastern Mediterranean to the pine-clad mountains of China and Japan, on the edge of the unnavigable Pacific, stood not only a dissimilar geography but also distinctive ways of life created by Arabs, Indians, the Cambodian-Javanese, and 'Maha-Chin', the name by which the rest of Asia knew the great Far Eastern civilisation.[7]

Identities of discourse. The determining principle of the structural unity of premodern Asia is capable of being expressed in the form of two separate arguments. On the one hand, there is the identity of each civilisation, complete in itself, dimensioned by its own history, and by an internal system of economic production, exchange, patterns of consumption, and the distributive role of the state. On the other hand, each of these latter elements can be taken as the unit of historical analysis, across the whole range of cultural frontiers, to provide the basis of a generalised discourse. The identity of the four Asian civilisations just outlined did not remain static in the millennium following the foundation of Islam or the T'ang unification of China. The constituent elements of all these civilisations underwent internal changes, i.e. the mapping relations defining the positions of the elements relative to one another in logical space shifted. Nevertheless, the awareness of a distinct cultural identity or that of the qualitative ruptures between categories of social sets was constantly reinforced through a dialectical process of comparison between one civilisation and another. Movements of ideas, of religion, of technology, or the exchange of economic and artistic objects through long-distance trade and even travel in the guise of pilgrimage and diplomatic missions helped in the formation of the differentiation so often expressed in the contemporary vocabulary of historical and reflective discourses.

There is no question that each separate civilisation of premodern Asia can be treated as the logical object of a historical study and of comparative analysis when other external social and economic structures are explicitly taken into account. In the past, Chinese, Islamic, and even Indian thinkers attempted to evaluate their historical conclusions and larger generalised reasoning in the light of a knowledge going beyond the immediate mental environment. Theoretical rigour gained from constant debate and interaction with other minds was a well-recognised quality. The basis of comparative analysis, however, suggested itself and was subsequently sustained through a set of propositions derived from a clearly demarcated and established area of thought. Mathematics, geography, religion, philosophy, moral issues, and forms of political behaviour represented ancient disciplines in more than one Asian civilisation. Theory and practice associated with them readily provided comparable normative rules for the whole society. Can the historian apply the same principle of integration to themes such as economic production and distribution, food habits and the mechanics of exchange? In what way, the sceptic might insist, do such themes appear as an analytic configuration in a logical space, in which the means of food production practised in the Nile delta could be described on the same reference grid as those of the Yangtze? The principle of integration in this case involves the discovery of new concepts in the order of knowledge. Within a given historical structure, identified let us say as food production, there are universal elements in a field of possibilities which reveal the inherent underlying logic present in the syntax of social relations. The differences on the other hand show at which point social practices branch off into unique paths of development.

Rules of integration. There is no theoretical difficulty in thinking that food production forms a conceptual category with other complete structures as its elements: settled farming, nomadism, hunting and fishing. Food production itself is a member of the set 'food', and each language of Asia would represent it by a different word, often derived by association from the name of a particular cereal. The set 'food' is recognised, selected, and responded to in the mental domain by all human societies irrespective of their practical preferences. But a particular society will select specific items as food from a set of possibilities located in the physical domain. The elements of the set 'food' will vary according to the individual or the class of individuals making the choice, according to the time of the year or day, and according to the spatial location of the selectors. The logic of comparative analysis relative to food habits or food production cannot be mistaken or confused, and having retrieved it from its objective and linguistic field, the specific forms of the structure identified by that logic can be viewed through a historical perspective. But that task, the structural analysis of the economic and social syntax, its changing form and configuration, is best attempted after a preliminary description and examination of the features that define the outer and inner limits of the four great civilisations in premodern Asia. Whether the historian's object of interest is monotheistic Islam, the Celestial empire, or the plurality of Sanskritic society, the identity of each civilisation included a dialectical element derived from the awareness of the external world. Economic and social practices were moulded as a result at several levels of logical integration.

Levels of integration. Perhaps the first and primary level of that logical integration (the process through which the different elements of social and economic relations and action are made part of a single structure) was the historical order itself: a particular and localised community's own structural trajectory over time. However, the appearance of towns and cities and the continuing strength of urbanisation throughout the period of antiquity in the history of Eurasia must point to an early separation between the structural logic of local communities and that of a society characterised by an urban-rural 'continuum'.

The second level was constituted by the rationale of this 'continuum' in all its aspects in the mental and physical domains, in economic activities, in the enforcement of the political will of the state system, in the expression of religious and spiritual leadership, in artistic creations, in the infinitely differentiated forms of cultural identities and preferences lying between a 'high' pole and a 'popular' pole. Urbanisation and a society that included a history of urban life within itself could not exist and continue to function without the concept of an operating system structured by the articulated logic of a multiple class of sets. The construction of a collection of houses, the provision of food, water, and fuel supplies, means of transport within and outside the urban locality, the reconciliation of conflicting social interests, all these necessary conditions of urban life demanded the integration of logical operations belonging to different structural systems. However the fusion between the urban-rural continuum and the political expression of the state does not require logically the conceptual identity of a distinctive civilisation or even precise geographical boundaries.

Yet, historically the idea of a 'civilisation' manifested in tangible and intangible language of signs, was a larger concept than a political empire or a 'world system' incorporating the urban-rural continuum. The temporal trajectory of a particular and individual social system obviously possessed the capacity to integrate external factors and move laterally over geographical and social space. This process may be described as the third level of integration, and it included the conscious borrowings and the syncretic tendencies between one civilisation and another in the long history of premodern Asia.[8]

Contemporary awareness of comparative features. From the middle of the seventh century, when Islam projected itself as a major force of expansion, to the beginning of the European colonial period in the late eighteenth century, the main Asian civilisations were identified and described in comparative terms by many contemporary observers. Hsuan-tsang was not the only distinguished Far Eastern pilgrim to visit Buddhist India. His description of the great monastery of Nalanda (633–7), in spite of many stylised comments, still conveys a vivid impression of how the 'Great Vehicle' of Buddhist thought was studied by monks, students, and laymen in a unique centre of learning in ancient India.[9] The description and analysis of the religions of Asia, its people, geography, towns and cities, economic products, and political life also occupied the attention of many Islamic writers and scholars: al-Jahiz, al-Muqaddasi, al-Masudi, Ibn Battuta, Ibn Khaldun, al-Qalqashandi, and even the 'serene majesty' of two Mughal emperors, Babar and Jahangir, both of whom attempted their hand at social analysis in their respective memoirs.[10] Below the level of the 'high' culture and the conscious knowledge of an exalted, authorised, and legitimate tradition of comparative discourse, there were multiple layers of a more popular awareness of the diversity of social life. Each year as the trading season opened, great merchants, small traders, pedlars, caravan masters, camel-drivers, sailors and officers of a multitude of ships, crossed the Indian Ocean and the great trans-Asian zone of caravan trading in the north. Large numbers of pilgrims swelled the size of this huge annual movement of people and commercial goods. In the course of their journey, the travellers not only traversed the different contours of physical geography in Asia; they must have observed clearly the cultural watersheds and the distinctive symbols of a collective mental world, which pointed towards the historical identity of each separate Asian civilisation.

The problem of limits. To repeat the historical problem set before us: it is to discover the principles which consciously or otherwise enabled different sets of people in premodern Asia to consider themselves as being an integral part of an entire structure. To state the problem in this way is to raise another fundamental question. What is the limit beyond which the concept of unity (of a particular entity) cannot be pushed and likewise what is the limit of the smallest fragment of the unit beyond which that element cannot be partitioned. What is the limit at which point terms such as 0.9, 0.99, 0.999 become 1 and in reverse order 0.1, 0.01, 0.001 become 0 itself? As we know, at the ends of both limits lies infinity. There is no bridge between the set of decimal fractions and the set of whole numbers. Like Wittgenstein, the philosopher and the theoretical mathematician who had set out to discover the limits of the human language, I aim to explore the limits of historical unity (integration) and disunity (differentiation) of Asian civilisations and to look for the principles which fix those limits.

The identities of the four Indian Ocean civilisations

The topological structure of Islam. The term 'civilisation' is of recent origin, perhaps no earlier than the mid eighteenth century.[11] However, the physical contours traced by the historical development of certain regions, their people and societies leave little doubt that the dialectics of cognitive logic appeared certainly before our period of study. In the West, the mental domain of Islam, unified by spiritual forces of astonishing intensity, radiated spatial horizons which had topological characteristics: an abstract area defined by limits which separated Muslims from non-Muslims. The expression Dar al-Islam or the House of Islam symbolised the abstract identity; its physical representation had another term. The geographical zone of Balad al-Islam expanded or contracted according to historical circumstances while retaining its fundamental structural features. The Muslim sense of identity, which took many tangible forms, reduced geographical definitions to a secondary set of considerations. Its latitudinal displacement, however, was of remarkable dimensions. From Hijaz to the high Atlas mountains in the Maghreb, Islam traced its area of influence along the Red Sea and the entire southern half of the Mediterranean. It crossed the Arabian Sea and the Bay of Bengal before coming to a rest in the islands of the Java Sea. In the north, Islam followed the ancient caravan routes across the European and Central Asian steppe-land and even traversed the Great Gobi to reach, but not penetrate much beyond, the Great Walls of the Celestial Empire. The spatial dimension of Islam did not always possess the quality of contiguity. The cathedral mosque, masjid-i-jami, represented the presence of the faithful in the mountains, in the plains, in the desert, and the tropical lands. Of course, Muslim philosophers, historians, and geographers were fully aware of the classificatory principles of space and global climate which they called 'iqlim'.[12] Furthermore, they could neither forget nor ignore the insidious political insubordination ('fitna') that would threaten and mock the imperial unity of the caliphate from the days of its Umayyad foundation. At the same time, everyone was aware that it was faith, and a unique faith at that, which bound Islamic people together. In language of extraordinary power, the Arab writer and thinker al-Jahiz (*c.* 776/7–868/9), argued the point with precise logic in a famous passage dealing with the Kharijites, the separatist followers of Ali. What was the principle, he asked, that united the members of the faith from all walks of life and from different corners of the earth:

when we see the people of Sijistan, of the Jazira, of Yemen, the Maghreb and ʿUman, the Azraqi, the Najdi, the Ibadi and the Sufri [four Kharijite sects], *maula* and Arab, Persian and nomad, slaves and women, weavers and peasants, despite their various origins and their different homelands all fighting on the same side, we understand that it is religion which creates this unity between them and reconciles their conflicts.[13]

The very same point could have been made for the Muslims as a whole.

The outer and inner limits of Islam. Islamic thought, always a leader in the rational theory of practice, left it largely to non-believers to misinterpret its spiritual fervour. St Thomas was not alone in believing that faith provided a better path to God than intellect.[14] If the Balad al-Islam is considered as a complete structure represented in both the mental and physical domains, it perhaps follows that its outer limits are fixed *a priori* by a morphism, an abstract mapping, between people, space and time. When the word faith is mentioned, using Arabic as the medium of expression, the linguistic symbol of the mapping relation is found and no further step in integration is possible. The temporal patterns of Islamic doctrines were by no means stationary. But its ideology ruled out any form of relativism and held fast to the notion of a divine, and thus constant truth. The method of differentiation yields groups of individuals and subjects in dialectical opposition: shiᶜa and sunni, pious and impious, just and tyrannical, rich and poor, 'umran badawa' (tribal-nomadic civilisation) and 'Umran hadara' (sedentary-urban civilisation).[15] The principle of undifferentiated status in piety, through its inverse image, uniquely identified the individual. The inner limits of structural Islam is surely reached in the mortality of the single believer, seeking in the shared equality of mankind, benediction and forgiveness in the grace and mercy of God.[16]

The historical contradictions in Islam. Muslim civilisation was nothing if not universalising. Its unifying principles sought out integral identities. The influence of Arabic as a language of communication, of religious and literary expression, and of administration remained central, even when Persian and Turkish emerged as significant linguistic rivals. To see this one has only to evaluate the Arabic content of these two languages. But Islam was not able and, more than likely, had no wish, to abolish contradictions. It absorbed nomads and farmers, believers and non-believers. It thereby unleashed, through the chosen instrument of that absorption, an inner political tension that was also economic and social. Military conquests insistently asked for a definition of the term citizenship. The Eastern Roman Empire had a perfect understanding of its meaning, one which was not readily comprehensible to the tribal followers of the Prophet in the early days of the Arab expansion. The powerful mind of Ibn Khaldun would correctly diagnose the problem in the fourteenth century, as he looked back over the historic past and the crumbling political world of contemporaneous Maghreb. Quoting the celebrated Sasanian King Khusraw I (AD 531–79), Ibn Khaldun argued that the power and authority of the state derived from finance and taxation which in turn rested on cultivation. The payment of taxes by definition implied submission to authority and a weakening of the fighting spirit of the independent tribes. No group was more humble and less able to defend itself than the peasantry. When Prophet Muhammad saw a plough-share in one of the houses in

Medina, he remarked that such a thing could never enter anyone's home unaccompanied by humbleness.[17] The policy of Umar, the great conquering caliph, in levying differential taxation on the non-believers of the conquered lands, especially the Kharaj, was justified on the ground of sound statesmanship.[18] The poll tax, *jizya*, however, was a distinct badge of collective humiliation. In AH 22 (AD 642–3), Shahrbaraz, the ruler of Derband in northern Iran, begged the victorious ʿAbd-ar-Rahman to spare his people the disgrace of *jizya*. Let political loyalty alone, he said, be our poll tax; the real *jizya* would turn us into your enemies.[19] Overwhelmed by the military disaster of the Arab conquest, the converted gentile Muslims could only reflect in despair that theirs was already a civilised world when the Arabs were still eating lizards in the desert.[20] The privileged distinction between Arabs and the converted (*maula*) could not be upheld indefinitely without reducing one of the fundamental claims of Islam to a hollow mockery.

Citizenship in Islam was replicated through faith, and the payment of taxation conferred no more than a limited subjecthood. Islam promised death to polytheists. The threat remained largely empty, as became evident when successive Islamic invaders from the end of the twelfth century moved into the vast geography of the Indian subcontinent. The freedom of life enjoyed by the proud and exclusive adherents of an alien faith, openly worshipping the remembrances of their divine Trinity, perpetually troubled the conscience of just Muslims. How could the Hindus, not only notorious polytheists but also open social enemies of Islam, be a party to the pact, 'ahl al-dhimma', which allowed freedom of religion to Jews and Christians on the payment of the *jizya*?[21] The poll tax was collected from the Hindus intermittently, but how was it to be justified? The problem remained theoretically unresolved: a fatal source – together with the intractable question of dynastic succession – of moral debilitation.[22] Religious orthodoxy and political expediency ultimately went their separate ways in the empire of Islam. After 971 when the Fatimid dynasty of Tunisia raised Fustat, Old Cairo, to the status of an alternative spiritual capital, the scandal of two rival caliphates could no longer be concealed and the world would soon come to view the Abbasid caliph, the imam of God, living in Baghdad as a parrot in a cage, reciting the words put in his mouth by his Turkish generals.[23] If human language cannot avoid creating paradoxes and contradictions, it is manifestly not possible to avoid these in social institutions which are structured on the human mind. Islam possessed neither political nor geographical unity. Its members, however, were clearly recognisable by a set of finite attributes. The language of the Prophet was also the language of the Qur'an. But no matter what was the linguistic expression of Islam, the script in which it found a visual symbol moved from right to left, lending itself to the rare art of the calligrapher's skill. Their place of worship always faced the direction of Mecca; the sacred *kaʿba* was a fixed object in a fixed point in space. Muslims wore distinctive clothing; the white laced muslin

Plate 4 Dome of the Rock, Jerusalem.

cap at once identified the religion of the wearer. Food prescribed or denied in the Qur'an found its appropriate mandatory role, though indulgence in prohibited alcohol could not altogether be suppressed. The Dome of the Rock and the jewelled mihrab in the great mosque of Cordoba continue to signify the unchanging image of created beauty.

The universal and plural character of Sanskritic India. The people of ancient India also fashioned a universal civilisation. However, the principles integrating their social order could not have been more different. Muslims and Christians, with revealed religion, found little difficulty in conceding the equality of human status but withheld freedom of conscience: truth was always addressed in the singular. Ancient Indians who accepted the vast authority of the immense corpus of Sanskritic sacerdotal texts handed down from the time of the four Vedas were not in the least concerned with the enforcement of beliefs or even sacred practices. But they discovered and applied with relentless energy an invariant principle in the mode of social transformation: the ways of 'varnasrama-dharma', a plural concept if ever there was one, encompassed the totality of life and pointed to the inviolable rules of human replication. Nothing illustrates the principle of differentiation in ancient India and its reverse, the dialectical unity, better than the fact that Indians learnt their singular 'Hindu' identity from Muslims. There is no single Sanskrit word that even attempts to describe the religion or the cardinal order of the people who lived in the land of the Aryas. The abstract idea of complementarity structured the elements of a society that had no wish to overlook descent but merely to raise it to a new level of meaning.

The intellectual achievements of ancient Indian thought. From the seventh century to the twelfth, and even beyond, Hindu civilisation remained the most formidable adversary of Islam in the western Indian Ocean and a far greater rival in the mental domain. No Arab or Persian thinker ever approached the intellectual depth or brilliance of a Sankara or Ramanujam.[24] Sankara (*c.* 788–820) died at the age of thirty-two, according to tradition. By then he had already composed a series of commentaries which elevated philosophical discourse to hitherto unseen heights of subtlety and power, based on a rigorous logic of dialectical unity. Shankara's views on the absolute non-differentiated idea of God, soul, and the universe, his discovery and advocacy of the empty set ('mayavada') containing within itself the single quality-less force, dominated for more than two centuries the studies of the Upanishadas, the main body of Hindu philosophical texts. It was challenged and, if not entirely replaced, at least complemented by the theistic and dualistic school founded by Ramanujam (*b. c.* 1017), a thinker of mental powers near equal to Shankara's. In addition, Ramanujam would appear to whole generations of devotional writers and leaders of religious thought as their ultimate spiritual fountain-head. The philosophical systems which emerged in India from the eighth century onwards, with the slow retreat of Buddhist influence, drew on the immense strength of Brahmanical learning. By the turn of the Christian era, Indian civilisation had already scored a series of triumphant near 'firsts' in human discoveries of the mind: scientific theories of linguistics, grammar, the mathematical concept of the empty set, zero, and negative numbers. These dazzling intellectual achievements accompanied a rapid material progress in technology, economic production, social organisation, and artistic expression which was there for the whole world to see. The inspiration for the dynamic movements came as much from the internal structure of Indian society as that of the neighbouring civilisations: Iranian, Greek, Central Asian, and Chinese. In the learned circles of ninth-century Baghdad, people belonging to the politically-distant Indian society could still be described as world leaders in astronomy, mathematics (especially numerals), and medicine; in the art of fashioning swords, in music, and poetry. 'They possess a script,' al-Jahiz wrote, 'capable of expressing the sounds of all languages, as well as many numerals. They have . . . many long treatises, and a deep understanding of philosophy and letters.'[25]

Albiruni's description of medieval India. By the time the Khurasanian mathematician and scholar Albiruni set out to learn the details of Indian scientific knowledge (*c.* 1020) and its social history, militant Islam had already embarked on a long and violent onslaught against the Hindu civilisation: the previous world view of India was no longer the same. The Hindu speculative mind appeared, on closer acquaintance, to have shut itself off from the external dimensions of knowledge and to have forgotten, in a spirit of overwhelming insularity and complacency, the injunction of the scholar Varahamihira that the Greeks, though impure in ritual order, should be honoured because they excelled in science more than any other people.[26] Albiruni was aware that his interest in Hindu civilisation and its scientific discoveries might appear repugnant to readers of his own faith. The systems of opposition he identified between Islam and Hinduism included the military confrontation and the resulting social antipathy that was already a historical reality. Albiruni was a true Muslim and a beneficiary of Mahmud of Ghazna, the desecrator of Somnath, the *sanctum sanctorum* of Indian temples. The Hindus, he observed with some discomfort, did not care much for theological disputations going beyond words. But when the ritual impurity of non-Hindus was the material point, it was another matter altogether: their fanaticism was directed against those who did not belong to the Hindu ritual order. Albiruni had consciously or otherwise come upon the basic principle of integration and differentiation in the structural life of Indian civilisation. Later on, he would specifically contrast the equality of Muslims as against the plurality of status embodied in the four estates of ancient Iran and India.

The structuring social codes in ancient India. When king Ardashir b. Babak restored the Persian empire, he also restored the Sasanian social estates composed by knights and princes; the monks, fire-priests, and lawyers; the physicians, astronomers, and men of science; finally, by husbandmen, and artisans.[27] Among Hindus, Albiruni observed, similar institutions were common. The quadratic term 'varna' clearly distinguished priests (Brahmans), warriors (*ksatriyas*), traders, farmers, and artisans (*vasyas*), and menials (*sudras*). While the 'varnasrama-dharma', the basic doctrine of temporal reproduction expressed (at a later historical period) the theoretical reference points on the economic and social grids of Indian civilisation, the operational spaces were signified at the level of everyday life by the practice of what Albiruni called 'jataka' or genealogy (which is known today as 'jati'). It is possible that the concept of a quadratic social order signified by the term 'varna' or colour represented the historical reality of a vanished remote past. Linguistic analysis has demonstrated that a similar term ('pistra') also existed for ancient Iran and the symbolism of colour originated with the colour of the clothing worn by the respective classes and associated with a cardinal point. The tripartite division of society into priests, warriors, and farmers was retained longer in Iran than in India where the 'varna' became a redundant theory.[28] However, it is true that both the doctrines, that of *varna* and *jati*, were distinguished by common elements in the mental domain. The principle of integration was represented at the level of cognitive logic by the system of ritual status, either of an individual or an entire community, superimposed on the system of economic or occupational functions, in the physical domain. Symbols of ritual hierarchy or ritual complementarity signified the differentiated identities. The outer limit of Hindu civilisation is reached in the concept of 'asrama', man's individual pledge to remain within the limits of society and acknowledge the rules of right conduct (*dharma*). Its inner limit was simply birth: Indian thought enshrined the unique view that no individual truly dies unless he ceases to be born. Individual conduct and birth were inseparable, in a cause-and-effect recursion. Whereas in Islam it is the idea of mortality, resurrection, and the Day of Judgement that identifies the individual within the collective destiny, ancient India found the limit of structural differentiation at the opposite end, birth. The Sanskrit composite expression 'varnasrama-dharma' included three fundamental propositions of Indian society. 'Varna' represented the structural code within which only the category of Brahman enjoyed an exclusively-defined status through his access to the performance of the Vedic rituals. 'Ashrama' with its notion of the distinct stages of life signified whether an individual identified at birth by the code of *varna* should choose to remain within the structural limits of human society or should become an ascetic or adopt any other non-scriptural and non-canonical identity. The term 'dharma' finally turned the other two propositions into an overarching idea of legality.[29]

Social forms specified by the order of *varna* and the stages of life were given content through prescriptions of right conduct. That the ancient Indian ideology of differentiated unity could not tolerate structural contradictions was obvious. Contradictions must be integrated, if necessary as exceptions that merely proved the rule. However, there were historical dilemmas that remained only partially resolved. The uneven pace of demographic movements combined with the exercise of free will made it difficult to prevent misalliances across the fundamental caste divisions; the same logic also applied to economic opportunities. Furthermore, if entire communities adopted the full range of Sanskritic ritual practices, not sanctioned by the immediate sacerdotal classification, what social or political force was to keep them permanently labelled as usurpers?[30] Both time and mobility worked against a static division of Indian society. Eventually, the system was forced to recognise the economic realities. It was permissible for Brahmans to engage in lower occupations if no employment was available in the traditional duties. Historically, a class of agricultural and farming Brahmans emerged unequal in caste rank to the priestly Brahmans. The occupational castes (*jatis*) at first sight would appear to have established an unbreakable link between religion and economic divisions of labour with ritual hierarchy as the principle of ordering. In reality, the *jati* system was fatally weakened by a lack of dynamic theory, which allowed structural contradictions to appear at the operational level. Its disciplinary character ensured the supply of skilled labour in essential economic functions and at the same time the hereditary principle took care of the transmission of the skills and knowledge. But difficulties arose when a particular occupational caste began to accumulate wealth or experienced a deterioration in its means of economic livelihood. The demand for social mobility in terms of higher ritual status and occupational changes came from both the rich and the under-privileged sub-castes. The members of a newly-rich sub-caste with lowly ritual status might unilaterally decide to adopt the religious practices of a higher group. Population pressure and the shrinkage of economic opportunities due to social or political catastrophes on the other hand might as easily lead to an invasion of economic occupations by other sub-castes. Historically well-recorded, both the processes caused many bloody social conflicts.[31]

The sources of political power left unidentified in India. Perhaps the real contradiction which the theorists of ancient India could not resolve was the source of political power. The king and the warrior class were separated in practice, and ritual status was not necessarily lost by the acceptance of non-Hindu political sovereignty as was proved during the period of Muslim rule in India. The concept of imperial unity and even the state system could not be uniquely identified. It was also obvious that social order and its theory constituted only one of the many different aspects of Indian civilisation. Its other expressions, in art, literature, music, food habits, and styles of clothing were as distinctive as equivalent forms in Islamic and Chinese civilisations: forms that were recognised without fail as having originated in the Indian subcontinent. No one with any claim to religious, philosophical, or literary distinction could

Plate 5 Hindu temple depicted as the universal chariot, Vijayanagara, *c.* fourteenth century.

forget the unchanging discipline of Sanskrit as a universal language. The epistemology survived in the mental domain even when practices varied in the physical plane. It is remarkable how strong and universal was the isomorphism between the concept of an integral Indian civilisation and its representations in the physical domain throughout the Indian geography. This fundamental spatial and conceptual unity of Indian history acquired a new character with the arrival and expansion of Islam in India. The Muslim state system, and sense of self-identity in general, could hardly remain unaware of the numerical strength of the Hindu society. Considerations of mere survival, if nothing else, demanded that a certain distance should be maintained between the formal expressions of the two competing civilisations.[32] At the level of everyday life, however, Islam and Indian systems freely borrowed from one another. Deviant forms of religious thought containing elements from both sides reinforced similar inter-cultural integration in architectural creations, in painting, and literature. The logic of economic production and political administration refused to admit a strict long-run separation between Muslim and Hindu talent.

The transmission of ancient Indian civilisation to South East Asia. There was an element of randomness or accident in the historical factors that influenced and directed the spatial expansion of the civilisation of ancient India. In the north-west, it encountered formidable rivals in the Iranian and Hellenistic empires before the rise of Islam. Although Central Asia accepted and retained Buddhism as a significant element of cultural life until its gradual replacement by Islam, it was in South East Asia that Indian civilisation was to find its most articulated expression. The nature of the transmission, its human agency and the forms of absorption, however, need to be carefully delineated and related to the wider historical movements in the area. It is necessary above all to banish the term 'Indian colonisation' from the vocabulary of social analysis. Migration of people for permanent settlement in regions outside their own environment was common enough in premodern Asia, as was also military invasions. For South East Asia the creation and the interweaving of India's civilisational superstructure, and later that of Islam, was a more complex process than the simple transfer of social and cultural forms by people who are already a part of these structures. Merchants and traders from the Indian sub-continent (and later from the Persian Gulf and the Red Sea) regularly sailed to the commercial ports of the Malayan archipelago and the Indochinese penin-sula. The vessels certainly carried Indian crew, whose number, as in the case of the ships of fifteenth-century Malacca, was to be counted in thousands. It is not improbable (although only indirect evidence supports the hypothesis) that stone-masons, painters, metal-smiths, wood-carvers, weavers, priests and learned men from pre-Islamic India might have also found employment in the generous patronage of the royal courts of Sumatra, Java, Funan and Cambodia. The question that still remains unanswered is that of the initial motivation and the impetus behind the transplantation of Sanskritic and Buddhist civilisation to South East Asia. At what stage did the purely Indian agency turn into an independent indigenous instrument of cultural con-tinuum? It is unhistorical and uncritical to assume that the mere presence of Indian communities on the Javanese or Cambodian soil was sufficient to pro-claim the authority of the Brahmanical or Buddhist way of life among people who were already endowed with organised social structures.[33] Merchants as a rule are disinterested in cultural transmissions; the transplantation of external cultural values and the appreciation of luxury objects obtained through long-distance trade is a diffused and adaptive social process.[34]

The structural identities of South East Asian civilisations. The general argu-ment that South East Asia should occupy a separate logical space for the purpose of comparative history on the same level as Islam, India, and China is open to debate. What is not questionable is the strong contemporaneous awareness of a series of separate identities to be perceived and seen in a world of islands and sea, in rivers and mountains, in the physiognomy of the people, in their dress, food, and houses, in the way of building religious shrines, in lands that grew sandalwood and aromatic spices.[35] A thousand visible symbols signified unambiguously the geographical and cultural ruptures between South East Asia, India, and China, not to speak of the Middle and Near East. But it is far more difficult to reconstruct the differences that existed in the mental domain below the surface of social realities. The technique of filtering the identity of a civilisation by fixing the outer and inner limits in the conceptual image of the social structure adopted for Islam and India, which is also relevant for China, breaks down in the case of South East Asia. There is no single dominating ideology here that creates through a dialectical process of acceptance and sanctions a single unified civilisation. The external elements of Indian, Chinese, or Muslim civilisations were absorbed progressively in different parts of Indonesia, in ancient Cambodia, and adjacent lands, by political kingdoms, societies, and communities (these terms are viewed as independent separate 'sets' which have common elements) that already possessed their own articulated internal identities. The principle of integration and differentiation in the structure of these civilisations as a result operated simultaneously at several levels and within a certain margin of tolerance.

Local geography and ethnic community provided first of all the ground-floor of the primary identity. The term *wong Jawa* (Javanese people) identified the inhabitants of an island in the archipelago that would establish a long historical claim to cultural and political leadership shared and contested with neighbouring Sumatra. But the people of Sumatra in so far as their island-based identity was concerned also belonged to the same Late Malayas who originally spread out over the islands of the Java Sea from the mainland. The principle of deriving such identities was common not only in Java and Sumatra but also throughout Asia. The Mons, Khmers, and the Thais who shared with other smaller tribal groups the land-area from Burma to the Indochinese peninsula, spoke different languages and preserved the cognitive techniques of cultural differentiation which coincided with territorial units (which were however variable). The performance of public and private rituals, the pattern of kinship, the division of the solar calendar into a hierarchy of sacred events, the mental submission to the idealised power of the departed ancestors – all these operating systems in the larger structure of society characterised as much the history of the Malayan archipelago and mainland South East Asia as that of India and China.[36] The dynamic process which introduced the element of plurality into the area as a whole was the partial transmission of the Sanskritic civilisation from India, followed by the two variants of Buddhism and the incomplete conversion to Islam after the thirteenth century. Islam was never able to cross the Gulf of Siam and its formal expressions even in Java and Sumatra included an inner view of man that was not entirely of orthodox

Plate 6 Buddhist temple and stupa (Pagnam pagoda), Bangkok river, Thailand.

idiom.[37] The propagation of Pali Buddhism through Sinhalese sources took place from about the twelfth century and it was mostly confined to Burma, Siam, Laos, and Cambodia, where it fused with active forms of existing royal and popular cultures to provide a general and more unified expression of religious identity. In Annam, Confucian China retained a cultural presence even when the imperial political links were broken off.

People of ancient Sumatra, Java, Champa, and Cambodia appear to have been highly selective in their approach and attitude towards the Sanskritic civilisation of the Indian subcontinent. It is clear that the totality of the Indian structures served to map out certain ordered ranks in religious life, state system, and artistic expression. The adaptation of the cult of Siva was a case in point. The abstract doctrines of Saivism, as they were formulated in ancient Javanese religious texts, were virtually indistinguishable from the concept of immanent theism in the classical Indian philosophical thought. Alongside, a more personal cult of Saivism, associated with particular temples and royal houses, expressed the morphism between the idea of divinity and the source of royal power. Perhaps the most striking asymmetry between Sanskritic civilisation in India and its adaptive elements in South East Asia can be traced to the different treatment of the social code embodied in *varna* or caste differentiation. The quadratic term was known and used in both maritime and mainland South East Asia. It is doubtful, however, whether the principle of birth was as invariant in the replication of social categories as in India. Brahmans, it has been argued, assisted in sanctifying the temporal authority of kings but could not establish an exclusive status in social or political hierarchy.[38] That they had a mediating role in the legitimacy of political authority seems historically well-documented. After the foundation of the kingdom of Ayuthya (1350), even the Thai royalty, already strongly Buddhist in beliefs and outlook, followed the practice of Brahmanic coronation and court rituals as a link between the idea of divinity and the theory of absolute kingship.[39] The rest of Thai society conformed in general to the Buddhist rules of conduct. But the structural relationships between the royal house, the members of the elite groups, and the common people were determined by a predominantly internal and indigenous historical logic, creating a direct mapping between the rulers and the ruled. The hypothesis of simultaneously operating dual principles structuring society and civilisations is inadmissible in a theory of finite axiomatic reasoning.[40] However, in historical situations a single structure with a continuum lying between an outer and inner limit often contained multiple relationships between identical elements defined by more than one principle, just as a single function could perform more than one role. The selective adaptation of the Indian structural codes in South East Asia supports the hypothesis of the duality, and it is also strengthened by the character of Islamic expansion in Sumatra and Java. Serious conversions began at the leading commercial emporia of maritime Indonesia from the end of the thirteenth century and very slowly spread to the inland communities during the next two centuries. By the beginning of the seventeenth century Islam had turned into a major ideological and social force in the archipelago, though Malayan-Javanese social forms retained many features of the earlier identities and could only be equated imprecisely with classical Islam of the Middle East.

The objective symbols of Chinese civilisation. It can be shown conclusively from Arabic historical sources dating from the ninth and tenth centuries that each year during the trading season the merchants of Basra and Siraf, the two most important ports in the Persian Gulf, sent out many ships to trade in India, the Indonesian archipelago, and China.[41] The crew of these vessels, their owners, and the *nakhodas* who sailed in them were unquestionably Muslims.[42] Yet, it needed more than three centuries for Islam to make substantial gains in maritime Indonesia and the process was set in motion only after Islam had reached coastal India in the late thirteenth century. The argument of a causal link between long-distance trade and the diffusion of religion and civilisation cannot hold in view of Islam's historical experience in the Malayan archipelago. It is true however that Muslim sailors, traders, and merchants who made landfall at one of the Sumatran or Javanese ports would have seen there geographical and cultural features that were not too dissimilar from Calicut and Quilon in the Malabar or the commercial towns of Bengal. As the Sirafi ships worked their way up the South China Sea towards the island of Honan, they crossed over an undefined contour of civilisations in the Indian Ocean. The first pointer towards the technological and cultural separation must have been the sight of an ocean-going Chinese junk flying fan-shaped sails made of bamboo mats. So striking and unfamiliar was the appearance of these vessels that the astonished reaction of the Moroccan traveller Ibn Battuta, who saw them in the Calicut harbour in 1342, can still be sensed in his description of Chinese junks.[43] When the Arab or Indian ships finally arrived at Chuan-chou or Zaiton, one of the greatest trading cities of the Indian Ocean during the southern Sung dynasty, the disembarking crew and the passengers would have been greeted with sights and sounds of an urban environment totally different from anything they knew at home. The world of Islam found itself very definitely out of depth in the Celestial Empire. Many habits of everyday life in a Chinese city, especially the sale and consumption of pork, deeply offended Muslim sensibilities. As Ibn Battuta recorded in his account, the Chinese civilisation contained many agreeable things, but the rejection of the true faith distressed the devout Maghrebi who mostly stayed at home in order to avoid catching glimpses of what he considered to be odious social habits.[44]

The principles identifying Chinese civilisation. It was precisely social practices, cultural tradition, and the shared experience of a long history that contributed in a large measure to the structural integration of Chinese civilisation. When Chao K'uang-yin ascended the Celestial throne in 960 and founded the Sung dynasty, the empire had already passed through its classical and medieval periods and was entering the modern phase. In the words of Chen Te-hsiu, a follower of the Neo-Confucian master Chu Hsi who died in 1200, officially condemned as a heretic and teacher of false doctrines, the 'Way' of Heaven shown by Confucian was lost and disrupted after the period of the Warring States and the Ch'in dynasty (190–316). Although the art of letters and good government flourished under the early Sung emperors, the true Way was rediscovered only later by four brilliant masters of whom Chu Hsi was the last. It was a measure of the spiritual and intellectual influence of the Neo-Confucian thinker that within thirty years or so of his death, Emperor Li-tsung (r. 1225–64) should have rehabilitated the memory of Chu Hsi by official kow tow at the temple of Confucius.[45] The suggestion of Chen Te-hsiu that the teachings of Confucius fell into oblivion for more than seven centuries can hardly be accepted at its face value. But the remarkable assumption in his thinking was the long memory of an unbroken historical tradition that included besides religious practices, the high status of scholarship and political statesmanship. It was all the more remarkable for the fact that the gilded life of pleasure led by the Southern Sung emperors in the luxurious capital of Hangchow was about to come to an end at the hands of Mongol 'Barbarians' (1279). The fall of the last of the Sungs did not de-Sinicise the Celestial Empire, just as the spread and acceptance of Buddhism in the earlier centuries and the mysterious rituals and doctrines of Tao cult failed to destroy the social differentiation codified by the followers of Confucian thought.

In the mid eighteenth century, the administration of the Ch'ing emperor Ch'ien-lung (1736–95) raised China to a new level of economic prosperity and cultural manifestations. By what linguistic symbols did his subjects, if asked to do so, derive their collective identities as members of a common Chinese civilisation? It is conceivable that two separate terms might have been used: *Hua* (standing for civilisation as an antonym to the idea of foreign or 'barbarian' world) and *Yan Huang tzu sun* (the descendants of the mythological Chinese founder-emperors Yan and Huang). Under Ch'ing rule, the enduring structural integrity of Chinese society and the state would not have been disputed by any members of the imperial government headed by a ruler whose immediate ancestors were non-Chinese northern-frontiers rulers. The early Ch'ing emperors had to address themselves primarily to political and practical tasks and they were more concerned with action than with abstract questions of principles.[46] All the same, even great K'ang-hsi (1662–1722), the founder of Manchu rule and an indefatigable soldier-statesman, let it be known in reply to the Catholic criticism of Chinese moral system that Confucius was venerated in China because of his doctrines of respect for virtue, his system of education, and his inculcation of love for superiors and their ancestors. The description *T'ien* or Heaven given to the ruler Shang-ti had no more significance than an honorific title.[47] The emperor was quite clear in his mind about the distinction between superstition and the rationality of religious devotion. The articulated relations between Confucian ethics and the state system in China was not something that a political leader in search of imperial legitimacy could easily ignore. K'ang-hsi himself had visited Confucius' home in 1684, made the ritual prostrations and offerings, and listened to the ritual music and lectures on the Great Learning.[48] The Sacred Edict (*Sheng-yu*) of the youthful emperor promulgated in 1670, when he was sixteen years old, contained a distillation of Confucian orthodox doctrines on social organisation. The classical text of the Edict was widely explicated in colloquial versions during the rest of his reign.[49]

If the expression 'Yan huang tzu sun' stood for the linguistic symbol that identified all individuals as members of a common set, it must follow that one of the principles of structural integration in Chinese civilisation was derived from the state system exemplified in the abstract concept of imperial office and its replication through successive rulers. The tripartite religious divisions of Chinese society fail to yield a unique identity either in the mental or the physical domain. The ideology and the ritual practices associated with

Confucian interpretation of the cult of Heaven were paralleled later by Buddhist and Taoist systems of belief and worship. The subscription and conformity to one set of religious expressions would not have created social contradictions if the members of the same community simultaneously professed adherence to the others.[50] The plurality of the cults of local deities, found throughout China, was a practical manifestation, lacking a central unifying theory of religion.[51] It can perhaps be interpreted as a sign that religious practices in China followed from the structure of society rather than structured it as an independent agent. The outer limit of Chinese civilisation may be found in the public and universal acknowledgement of the Mandate of Heaven held by the emperor, an admission that defined through its dialectical image the mapping relations between the ruler and the ruled. People who migrated overseas and lived under the jurisdiction of 'barbarian' princes did not entirely forfeit their Chinese identity. The Celestial Court and the imperial bureaucracy refused to admit any principle of integration other than the submission to the divinely-ordained authority of the ruler. The symbolic expressions of the exclusive mediating role between the Heaven and Earth were carefully formalised. Dressed in magnificent ritual clothes, the emperor performed the official rites and prostrated himself before the Altar of Heaven.[52] The cosmic dependence of the 'Son of Heaven' reversed itself when subjects were received in audience at the imperial palace, the Forbidden City in Peking during the period it served as the capital. It was they, the grand secretaries, the officials, commoners, and even foreign envoys, who were required to perform the kow tow on formal presentation to the emperor. In 1793, a British ambassador, Lord Macartney, was brusquely denied imperial audience because he declined to take part in a ceremony which he considered demeaning to the dignity of a sovereign representative.[53] Other cognitive symbols, besides the obeisance, distinguished the emperor from his people. In formal court, he alone faced south, while his ministers faced north. The colour red was exclusive to his calligraphy. The ideographs of his personal boyhood name were restricted all through the empire.[54] A strict tradition of royal protocol constantly identified the source and repository of political sovereignty.

The inner and outer limits of China. The historical unity of Chinese civilisation did not rest merely on the theory of absolute state power. The principle of integration consisted of a set of clearly-defined relationships between the central government, the civil administration, and the structure of society. It is true that ordinary people from different regions of China spoke mutually incomprehensible dialects. The language of government and administration on the other hand was one of classical uniformity, with a privileged access but a necessary one for the educated social minority. Chinese civilisation was almost unique in its treatment of education, religious learning, and high levels

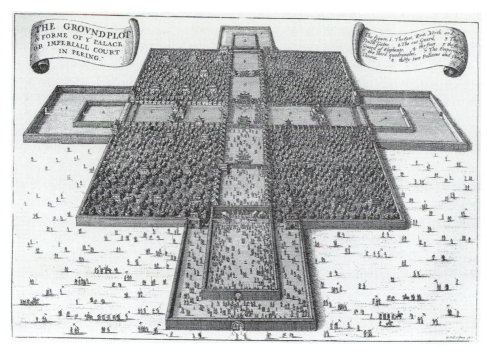

Plate 7 The garden and the Great Court of the Imperial Palace in Peking.

of scholarship as a combined instrument of the state system. Whether members of administration entered service through the state examinations or influential recommendations, the mastery of verbal and written communications was an essential condition of further promotions. The formal structure of educational degrees, set up by the state, itself introduced an abstract and invariant role in social mobility linked to academic merit. It was difficult enough for provincial candidates to gain the triennial national *chin-shi* examinations. Only a limited number of the ablest candidates entered the imperial Hanlin Academy, the prestigious school of Confucian scholarship.[55] The imperial bureaucracy in China was an open system in theory. Its restrictive character at the operational level arose from the necessity of paying for an expensive and competitive educational competence. Landed wealth opened the doors of scholarship and forged a firm link between the hierarchy of Chinese rural society, the state, and the unified imperial administration. The homogeneity of culture, which can be clearly specified on the elements of the social grid, and the general acceptance of the Confucian theory of inequality, maintained on the whole a general understanding between the people and the elite groups in China. The Imperial Board of Rites even attempted to bring some order or regularity into the multiplicity of local deities by keeping a register of officially recognised shrines and by conferring honorific titles on deities associated with the shrines.[56] The inner structural limit of Chinese civilisation reveals itself in the practice of ancestor worship and the death rites which identified uniquely the lineage family as the smallest divisible unit of society.[57] It is possible that in Chinese social thought there was no systematic principle corresponding to the individual's awareness of his conscious 'self'. Duties and rights assigned to an individual made sense only in the context of the family or the larger social environment.

Principles of integration and differentiation: a critique

Contemporary comparisons. In evaluating the historical relevance of the structuralism adopted so far, it is right to pose the question why should ordinary people in imperial China or ancient India, societies with immense geography and complex levels of differentiation, at all look for a linguistic symbol under which every one could be described as the subject of the Son of Heaven or the people of Vedic religion. Indeed, we have already seen that no such term existed for Sanskritic civilisation. If asked, the common man would in all probability have answered that he was a person of a named village, district, town, or a sub-caste and have shown little awareness of the outer structural limits of his particular civilisation. For a Muslim, a Thai or a Javanese, the social code was somewhat different, which highlights an important theoretical point to be examined shortly. It may readily be conceded that the concept of belonging to a common set or a totality (only indirectly indicated by a deeper structure) becomes weaker as the elements of the set are repeatedly differentiated. The question is in what circumstances would the Celestial Emperor or the chief priest of a great Indian temple fail to recognise who was a Chinese subject and who was a member of the Indian ritual hierarchy? There were clear rules in all Asian societies which allowed recognised authorities to delimit the formation of objects, and the rules were formulated both by internal rationality and external stimulus. The images of self-identities were often no more than mirror reflections of the perceptions of a world external to one's own. Whether the perceptions of other societies, their practices, and values, were favourable or unfavourable made little difference to the real purpose of the comparisons: to evaluate the self, individually or collectively, against *tensed* experience. In the seventh century, when Hsuan-tsang, the Buddhist pilgrim from China, wished to return home after his journey through India, the inmates of the great monastery of Nalanda begged him to remain, reminding him that China was a country of 'mlechas', unimportant barbarians who despised religion and the Faith. The gentle reply of the Chinese Buddhist monk was to outline to his listeners the just principles of government practised by the Celestial Emperor, the role of virtuous conduct in families, the fine artistic traditions reached in China: 'they have taken the Heavens as their model, and they know how to calculate the movements of the seven

Luminaries.'[58] The interchange, recorded by Hui Li, was clearly intended to point out the difference between knowledge and uninformed opinion.

In spite of its massive self-confidence, the Chinese civilisation retained a certain curiosity about the intellectual achievements of other Asian people. A story attributed to the Arab physician and alchemist al-Razi (850–925) recounts how a Chinese scholar came to his house and in five months learnt to speak and write Arabic. Before returning to China, the visiting scholar transcribed the entire sixteen books of Galen from dictation in remarkably accurate short-hand.[59] The ability to make enlightened analysis of comparative civilisations had reached a fine art in ninth-century Baghdad. Al-Jahiz saw divine intervention in the ability of particular nations to excel in areas of human attainments. Thus, the Greeks, spared from manual toils by their political masters, invented machines, tools, astrolabes, and musical instruments. They loved science but shrank from its application. The Chinese were specialists in metallurgy and metal-casting; in weaving and drawing; in everything concerned with practical skills in contrast to the Hellenic excellence in abstract thought. Indians, according to Jahiz, led the world in science, mathematics, and philosophy. As for the desert Arabs, they would not degrade themselves by paying taxes and making a living with a pair of scales. But when they turned their keen minds and clear brains to poetry, fine language, navigation, horse-breeding, and the mastery of weapons, they achieved perfection beyond the wildest dreams.[60] The text of al-Jahiz was not unique. A strong awareness of the comparative features of Asian civilisations often marked the thinking of Islamic writers. They could not have overlooked the fact that their own religion and society were of a diffusionist kind; Muslim thought reinforced itself by the conscious adaptation of the material achievements of non-Islamic people while rejecting at the same time a plurality of doctrines.

Sets and sub-sets as expressions of unities and disunities: the power of Cantorian analysis. A study of comparative civilisations in world history is not feasible unless the concept of a separation or rupture exists in the first place. The idea of structural integration and differentiation introduced earlier has been substituted in the course of the historical analysis by the more general term of a 'set' and its 'sub-sets'. The application of the two terms calls for the specification of a principle or property under which a set is identified. The technique of fixing the outer limit of a historical structure or a set, adopted so far, satisfies this condition. If it is accepted that the inner limit of a civilisation, the smallest divisible subset of the larger set, is the individual, then the historian must look for the principle which assigns a distinct role to the individual in any one of the subsets of the totality. Why is it necessary to derive such a rule? No problem arises if the individual is truly unique. He is different from every one else and he has no past and future. But an individual as a human being is a recurrent object and he can recognise himself through the conscious self. A rule is needed to separate the elements that are unique to everyone as an individual no matter how many times the concept of the individual is replicated. When the rule disappears, the individual also disappears.

The identity of a civilisation or a society can be derived by two separate theoretical principles: that of adding together the separate elements to form a common set or by dividing an integral structure into its natural elements. The civilisation of China, like that of India, was the sum total of parts rather than a totality reducible or capable of being reduced into further elements by differentiation, as was the case with Islam. Therefore, for Chinese or Indian societies the unity was much harder to define, as it was sensed more than perceived as a truth. The underlying principle of integration needs to be excavated from the depths of the mental domain or social practices. The application of the differentiating methods to historical China and India, in contrast, reveals at once the sets and sub-sets of structural relationships on the logical space. Members of Islamic, Thai, or any one of the different Indonesian societies in the archipelago, could be clearly enumerated by a single or a number of positive tests as belonging to a set. The Chinese and Indian social systems were not enumerable. It was always possible to generate a Chinese or Indian 'set' that was not a part of the larger set. The reason for this apparent paradox is to be found in the functional role of interpretation. The subjects of the Celestial Emperors were clearly Chinese. When they migrated overseas and lived under the political jurisdiction of a Thai monarch, their essential identity was not lost as long as the community retained its language and the obligation of ancestor worship. Varying definition made overseas Chinese, members of two different sets, neither of which could be reconciled under a single cardinal principle. The same logic of non-enumerability also applies to Indian social order. There was no formal justification as to why any ritual, functional, or historical divisions should exist between the four *varnas* or, to put the same point in another way, why Brahmans should need the services of any other castes. The quality of a Brahman could not itself be defined except by the prescription of birth and the willingness of society to admit a claim. Historically, there was not just a single 'set' of Brahmans but many 'sets' with differing interpretations attached to each one. The cardinal 'number' (defined here as a principle or quality) describing Chinese or Indian civilisations could be language, religion, social structure, social identities, political system, and law. A truth function relating to any one of these categories is sufficient to reveal the relevant identity. For Islam, however, religion took precedence over other attributes of civilisation and thereby made Muslims members of an enumerable set.

The application of the mathematical ideas of Cantor and Gödel to social history provides a formal proof of what can be already sensed or known intuitively through the use of descriptive language.[61] At first sight the application by itself does not suggest the answer to the question of why it is necessary to know whether a historical 'set' was enumerable or non-enumerable. Yet the implication of the analysis is far-reaching. A civilisation such as Islam enumerated by a unique cardinal 'number' was likely to prove highly resistant to the idea of fundamental social change or the absorption of external cultural symbols. While a non-enumerable society would readily add a new element to its total identity provided the rules of integration and the mapping-relations between the elements did not radically change. The problem in both the cases involves determining the exact nature of structural invariance under transformation. In the first case, the form and content of a category that acts as a cardinal number remain unchanged even when individuals and communities, who learn to recognise the category and act on its perception, are replicated over time. In the second case, the quality of invariance applies to the relationships between the categories rather than to their content. Rituals and social practices in China and India, for example, were codified over a long period of time and often in syncretic versions. However, it was impossible for a subject of the Celestial Emperor to repudiate the reciprocal relationship between himself and the repository of the 'Mandate of Heaven', just as in Sanskritic India the mapping-pattern between the category of Brahmanism and the rest of the society was independent of interpretative variations attached to the category. The partial order of the elements on the logical social space stays invariant under all types of transformations.

The obvious power of Cantorian theory is demonstrated in its ability to analyse sets consisting not only of forms and content but also ordered relations. Islamic societies, for example, do not constitute a 'continuum' over time, because the possibility of conversion places them in the same position as the set of rational numbers which do not have its own members as limiting values. On the other hand, any society such as the Indian or Chinese where the principle of birth is a primary identity constitutes a 'continuum' and is comparable to the set of real numbers. The analysis brings to the surface the deeper structures of human society and exposes to view complexities that cannot be grasped by intuitive reasoning alone. Earlier in our theoretical approach to the comparative civilisations of premodern Asia, a distinction was drawn between a proposition whose predicate was contained within itself and a proposition whose sense is validated by historical experience. For the historian wishing to draw on the enormous power of the Cantorian 'continuum' there are many practical dilemmas, not the least of which is the specification of the cognitive rules of a set, its sub-sets, and elements. To what extent, it may be asked, is an isolated rural community in Mughal India a part of the Indian civilisation? Does the fact that it is situated within India geographically constitute its sole claim to be called Indian? A similar question also arises with unauthorised and deviationist expressions within a given social structure. Changes in the cognitive rules constantly created new sets or additional sub-sets. The dynamics of structural changes and the character of invariance cannot be fully grasped unless the ordered relations between authorised and unauthorised social entities within the total structure are examined and the temporal trajectory of the ordered objects is traced. Unauthorised forms of social expression may constitute a parallel structure which is accommodated within the larger authorised one because it does not constitute a significant threat or its existence is made possible by an independent rationality. The authorities delimiting the conceptual forms may also remain ignorant that there is a parallel structure at all. A theory of structural changes formulated in terms of Cantorian ideas and methods must state clearly the entity that is being transformed. It could take the form of changes in the relationships or mapping patterns, complete transformations, changes in the values of elements, or variations in the possibilities of different states of affairs (movements on the logical space). A civilisation may or may not historically have a legitimate theory of structural change, though actual change could result from the conscious or unconscious social will. Does the perception of an external world cause images of identities to change over time and if so, does it bring about fundamental structural changes? The historical unity and disunity of the civilisations of Asia need to be evaluated against theoretical issues raised by such questions.

There still remains one final problem: the unities of material life. Below the level of mental unities created by culture, religion, social system, and all the nuances of human identities, lies another type of unity. It is the unity of objects and sights, constantly crossing and recrossing the civilisational and political frontiers. It is a morphism mapped and upheld by land, water, and the sky that looks down upon cultivated fields, orchards, houses, and cities built by man. The world of dry farming, of wheat fields, beehive villages, and the harsh landscape of rocks, barren hills, and mountains produces its own typology which is far distant from the world of rice terraces, of fish ponds, bamboo houses, coconut trees, and banana plantations. It is a kind of unity that has neither an outer nor an inner limit. Yet the mind can feel, if not articulate, the difference between the sight of the full moon rising behind palm trees in the huge arching sky of a tropical night and that of the moon which shows itself against the towering fir trees on the icy Himalayan heights. The desert after all does not, cannot begin until the rains cease to fall. The dry hot winds which blow across the Great Nafud and the North Indian plains would desolate human sensibilities that know only the moist and humid climate of Thailand, Java, and Bali. No camel nomad will ever see the green chess-boards of flooded rice fields surrounded by tropical forests. If he did, the greenery will disorient him and hurt his eyes. People accustomed to the bedouin tents, mud-and-brick houses, or the splendours of stone masonry seen against landscape-colours of yellow, buff, and grey will at first mentally reject wooden houses with sloping roofs framed by banana trees. The physical unities found in common ecological environments also creates social and cultural unities which are not immediately visible to the participants themselves at the level of cognitive awareness.

3

State, society, and economy: structural relationships and contradictions

The balance-sheet of great civilisations

The moral dilemma of absolute power. The great civilisations of the past had many spectacular items on the credit side of their collective account books. The ability to organise complex administration and enunciate just principles of government found a parallel expression in the creation of an economic structure that produced, as well as distributed, a wide range of material goods and services. Above all, a whole way of civilised life was refracted over centuries, in the vitality of a constant moral code made self-aware by a compassionate society. The different civilisations of premodern Asia in our period of study shared in this history of mankind's material and mental achievements. All the time, a debit column appeared in the ledger book. The visible successes, the obvious gains, and the advancements in knowledge were accompanied too often by failures that resulted in stark tragedy. This ineffaceable association between order and disorder, between good and evil, between suffering and contentment, seemed to permeate every aspect and level of society. The economic and political life of civilisations, not only in Asia but in all parts of the world, sustained themselves and absorbed 'order' from a force which clearly also contained an antithesis. Contemporaries, whether they were mere participants, observers, or thinkers, seldom lost sight of the contradiction present in human society: the inevitable result flowing from the action of men while they remained mortal *civitas peregrina* on Augustine's earthly city.[1] In the latter half of the fourteenth century, as Ibn Khaldun came to reflect on the seemingly inexplicable rise and fall of Islamic empires and states, the actual historical facts appeared to him as beyond questioning. The downfall of the later Umayyad caliphs he ascribed to disregard of the examples of their predecessors who had carefully deliberated on policy and religious truth. The later Umayyads, on the other hand, acted according to the nature of royal authority to suit their worldly purposes and intents. Popular censure of the Umayyad rule found one of its expressions in the willingness to believe in the propaganda made by the ᶜAbbasids, who would raise the flag to revolt against the Damascus caliphate in 749–50. The ᶜAbbasids, Ibn Khaldun thought, were second to none in their moral integrity and used royal authority to advance the different aspects and ways of the truth. Eventually, when power passed to their descendants, they became enmeshed in luxury and in worldly affairs of no value, turning their back on Islam: 'Therefore God permitted them to be ruined, and [He permitted] the Arabs to be completely deprived of their power, which He gave to others.'[2]

There were others, besides the political thinkers of Islam, who saw the reason for the historical decline of empires, societies, and even the entirety of economic life, in the deterioration of moral conduct and values. A belief in the withdrawal of divine support was the relentless corollary of this logic. For our next example we can move down two centuries and turn to a civilisation that possessed the most self-aware theories of its articulated political and social structures. In November 1565, Emperor Chia-ching of the Ming dynasty received an unusual memorial. In spite of his deep interest in the Taoist cult of longevity, Chia-ching would shortly come to the end of his long reign stretching over four decades (*r*. 1521–66). The memorial was written and submitted by Hai Jui, a junior mandarin, as the hierarchy of rank went in the imperial secretariat, who was serving at the time as a secretary in the Ministry of Revenue in Peking. It drew attention to the emperor's personal failures in preventing economic, administrative, and political troubles that surrounded the great Ming empire on all sides. For this was a time when Mongol military threat in the north found its unrelated counterpart in the south where famous cities and prosperous coastal areas were devastated by terrible samurai raids from Japan. Hai Jui cited ruinous taxation, the prevalent official corruption, palace extravagance, and unchecked rural banditry to conclude: 'It has already been some time since the people under Heaven started to regard Your Majesty as unworthy'.[3] The expressions used were harsh and the emperor appeared to have felt the weight of the criticisms brought against him. He hesitated for several months before ordering the arrest of the intransigent civil servant and kept the order for death-by-garrotting in suspension. Hai Jui was released from prison with the death of Chia-ching and the accession of the Lung-ch'ing emperor to the celestial throne. An awkward man with a sensational reputation, Hai Jui went on to hold distinguished office in the imperial bureaucracy and died twenty years later, when he was still the censor-in-chief of Nanking. The moral of the celebrated incident was clear enough to spectators. It needed reckless courage to play the dangerous game of giving disinterested advice to the holders of absolute political power. At the same time, men who were prepared to do so were not lacking. Almost a stereotyped figure, they appear regularly in Asian historiography.[4] In 1702, an English envoy reporting on the commercial affairs of the busy Mughal port of Surat recorded an 'incident' in the open *durbar* (court) during a public audience between the governor and the civic dignitaries. A Turkish merchant had stood up and made an astonishing charge against the Mughal authorities: the land, he said, might belong to the emperor (Aurangzeb) in theory and practice, but 'the Government [was] soe corrupted that the King's orders were not obeyed nor noe man could have rights.'[5]

The form and the tone of the criticisms signal in the clearest language the direction of certain historical attitudes and their dialectical nature. The source of the imperial or state power was not disputed, nor was the role expected from political authority. That the general economic and social life should have been conditioned by the fiscal policy of the government was in itself an admission of a strongly articulated relationship between the state and society. The audacity of a mere merchant, raising his voice in anger against the Great Mughal, one of the wealthiest and most powerful princes in Asia, must imply that the concept of economic justice and the continued functioning of economic activities as expressed through commercial relations were not strangers to the operation of the body politic. Yet the admitted splendours of royal courts, military displays, the piety of religious foundations, and the exalted examples of artistic creations, did not always imply the protection of the peasantry, artisans, and ordinary people from misery and exploitation. The present-day historian, surveying a period in which religion, myth-making, and magic were thought, mistakenly as it turns out, to have provided substitutes for the rationality of scientific thought, cannot avoid the obligation to explain why the failures were at least as numerous as the successes.[6] Is it possible to believe that the ancient thinkers may have been partially right, that both sides of the equation were an integral part of the same structure? This was a 'fact of life' that had troubled the vision of St John: the four horsemen of the Apocalypse seemed to ride on for ever, spreading conquest, wars, famines, and mortality over the land. The same problem in a more abstract shape would haunt the mind of Augustine, as he composed at the age of seventy-two the last book of *De civitate Dei* (AD 425). 'In its collective origin, from the evidence of life itself, a life so full of so many and such various evils that it can hardly be called living, we must conclude that the whole human race is being punished . . .' Farmers might hurry to put away their corn to save it from the ravages of pests and locusts, but 'I know of peasants, whose excellent harvest has been swept away, from out of their barns, by a sudden water-race'.[7]

The distance between the theory and practice of just government remained an unresolved source of torment to Islamic political thinkers, even though, faced by the real alternative of having to choose between anarchy and a tyrannical government, most of them came down on the side of the forces of law and order. But there were few illusions about the price that was to be paid. On being asked to point out a happy man, an ᶜAbbasid caliph in Baghdad is alleged to have replied, 'The best life has he who has an ample house, a beautiful wife, and sufficient means, who does not know us and whom we do not know'.[8] The stern *sufi* saint, Shaikh Nizam al-Din Auliya (*d.* 1325), the founder and the leader of the highly influential 'khanqah' (Islamic monastery)

Plate 8 The Great Turtle coming to rescue the shipwrecked people, frieze from Barabodur Temple, Java, Indonesia.

in Delhi, expressed a profound mistrust of political power in the reply he gave to a messenger of the sultan who had asked for an interview between the Shaikh and his master: 'my house contains two doors; if the Sultan entered it through one, I would leave by the other'.[9] Human failings were common enough. Even supplication for divine intervention in a society that believed in the regularity of its occurrence seemed not always to work. Huang Liu-hung, who wrote a much-read and much-admired administrative treatise at the time of emperor K'ang-hsi, recorded his own feeling of helplessness before mass suffering while serving as a district magistrate in an impoverished and exhausted province of northern China during 1670–2. True to his professional training, the Chinese mandarin composed an 'official' memorial to the local divinity.

We have had no rain since the sixth month. Now it is the eighth month and the grain crops have not yet been harvested. The seeds for next year's crops cannot be planted. Therefore, we cannot refrain from laying our prayers before the god. Although the people of T'an-ch'eng have repeatedly laid their woes before the god, they have no alternative. T'an-ch'eng has suffered the devastations of war and famine for a long time. We can afford no fancy offerings, only clean utensils with simple sacrificial objects to take the place of elaborate ceremonies with the music of stringed instruments. God, please grant our request.'[10]

Plate 9 Shipwreck: monster from the depths of the ocean threatening the sailors and passengers, frieze from Barabodur Temple, Java, Indonesia.

'Acts of God', social disasters, and public policy. The Celestial Empire was far from an impoverished nation, judged by contemporaneous standards, nor was it permanently in a state of warfare. The ravages and chronic devastations of civil wars spared the history of China to a much greater extent than was the case in Western Asia. The wealth and urban splendours of the Chinese empire which had astonished Marco Polo and Ibn Battuta in the thirteenth and fourteenth centuries would continue to impress Jesuit missionaries in the eighteenth. The crisis described by Huang Liu-hung was endemic in agrarian societies of premodern Asia. An unstable climate generated large annual fluctuations in food production and in the general level of income and consumption. A succession of bumper harvests would give way with catastrophic suddenness to scorched fields and pitifully meagre crops. Sometimes, the very measures designed to prevent natural calamities and to increase economic production through public investment in flood controls and irrigation works further debilitated a rural population already weakened by malnutrition. When Huang Liu-hung was in charge of the T'an-ch'eng district, construction works began on the huge and expensive Le-ma reservoir project. The local people were ordered to provide conscripted labour, though in the past the

district had been spared because its limited demographic resources were not unknown to officials. The magistrate reported to his prefectorial superior that he was daily faced by the sight of a procession of emaciated and hungry-looking people, followed by their dependents, begging and supplicating for exemption from the labour-service. To send them to the distant T'ao-su River project, in addition to the existing irrigation works on the lake, would be to condemn them to certain death.[11]

Huang's request was granted by his official superiors. Similar examples of a close link between the local administration and the economic policy of the central government could be multiplied for the same period from northern India. During the seventeenth and early eighteenth centuries, a great deal of agrarian development took place in the princely state of Jaipur, whose hereditary rulers were nominal administrative grandees in the service of the Mughal emperors. With the help of capital provided by local financiers many substantial farmers constructed irrigation works for growing commercial crops and the area was gradually brought into closer contact with the great urban markets further north. However, as time went on the number of farming families who were unable to service their debts during periods of distress rose disturbingly. The office of the central revenue chief in Jaipur expressed considerable disquiet at the level of land foreclosures and rural indebtedness, though perhaps more from fear of financial losses to the government than from consideration for the peasantry.[12] Agrarian prosperity manifested in good seasons could create its own structural contradiction through effects on grain prices. Between 1585 and 1590 throughout northern India the harvests were unusually large. While the increase in the absolute size of the crops retained for subsistence contributed to the welfare of the farmers, the urban population also benefited through lower prices of food grains. But the fall in the money income of the peasantry added severely to the rural tax burden. Referring to the last year of the agricultural abundance, the contemporary Mughal historian and statesman Abu'l Fazl commented, 'On account of the extent of cultivation, and the goodness of administration, prices fell very low, and many cultivators were unable to pay the government revenue. In the provinces of Allahabad, Agra, Oudh, Delhi, and sarkars of Saharanpur and Budaon, one eighth [of revenue] was remitted and in sarkars of Sirhind and Hisar one-tenth.'[13]

The courtier-politician in Abu'l Fazl perhaps saw a natural cause-and-effect relationship between the quality of administration in Mughal India and the economic plenty of the 1580s and 1590s. In reality, there was little awareness on his part of any possible structural contradiction between large harvests, the level of grain prices, and the obligation of the farming population to pay their taxes in money. That the pattern of articulation or the mapping relations between these three entities could be reduced to an abstract set of mathematical expressions (containing the economic logic) remained beyond the grasp of most premodern thinkers of Asia. In the existing order of knowledge, the baffling and the impossibly difficult problem of how to maintain the income of producers while safeguarding the living standards of consumers and the level of public revenue, found little explicit analysis. When an actual historical contradiction arose, the solution was necessarily at a practical level: if the peasantry are unable to pay, social stability called for an elementary administrative measure, the remission of revenue. What was an economic problem at a far deeper level of occurrence than the contemporaries could imagine, a problem that repeated itself inexorably with every temporal cycle of plenty and want, was transformed by them into the idiom of political action. This was a domain where familiar remedies were known to exist which, if not entirely guaranteed to bring success, at least provided the social engineers with a reasonable chance.

The structural contradiction embedded in the economics of premodern grain production stemmed, of course, from the difficulty in establishing an equilibrium price between supply and demand. The quantity of grain produced was not fixed by the price variable alone and the element of time delay between consumption and production introduced in any case a permanent disequilibrium in the pattern of prices. The impact of harvest failures and outright famines on the other hand could be reduced by the distribution of grain from state granaries, a practice which was normal in China. Although in the contemporary order of knowledge, economic reasoning remained rudimentary, there was some awareness among Chinese thinkers at least that thrift and frugality were virtues the aggregate effects of which were not always beneficial to the poor who had lost their livelihood through drought and flood. In such a year when peasants suffered from a loss of harvests, a Chinese text recommended, palaces, houses, towers, and pavilions should be built or repaired to create employment. Those who had 'no dogs in the front [yard] and no hogs in the back should be employed first'. Such construction works were not merely for the gratification of the sovereign but to help the economy of the state. The economic logic of public works on income-creation was clearly outlined in the remarkable policy adopted by the Sung statesman Fan Chung-yen (989–1052) when he was the governor of western Chekiang. In the aftermath of a devastating famine, he advised the leaders of Buddhist temples to undertake construction work because in a year of famine labour was very cheap. As a reply to official criticism of lavish public spending, Fan memorialised in detail the reason why he had ordered the banquets and construction works. It was to 'distribute surplus wealth and to benefit the poor. Traders and peddlers of food, and artisans and hired labourers, who relied on these public and private activities for their living, numbered several tens of thousands a day ... In that year in the two Chekiang areas only Hangchow was peaceful and the people did not wander to other places for refuge.'[14]

The principles of articulation. The articulated structure, of which the economy, state, and society are different elements, formed a totality which functioned as such over time and at a particular moment, whether or not the awareness of its existence existed in the order of knowledge. Movement in one element of the total set released energy spreading to its immediate neighbouring element in the chain of articulation and the transmission of the original movement through the whole system was regulated by the absorption of energy by each next-in-line element. While these movements are at the centre of historians' interest, their temporal profile depends on the specific character of the articulated structure. Let us imagine that each Asian civilisation is a continuum: it is spread over a range of possible states and interpretations (defined categories). The concept of kinship or family is a continuum both in its concrete and interpretative sense; so are the terms rulers and ruled, subsistence and exchange, urban and rural. How are these categories as 'sets' and their elements within the continuum interlinked? The historical examples cited so far suggest that a number of different principles can be identified as the operating rationale of the total set. The principle of kinship radiating through the extended family into a wider complex of social ties and political loyalty continually reinforced itself by the implicit or explicit use of force exercised through military power, although neither principle could rise above and free itself from the abstract and indivisible logical necessity underlying a particular system. Finally, there was the strange combination of a multitude of specific strategies maximising individual satisfaction and gain, constrained by religious and moral values. Our theory and analysis of the structure of articulation in the history of premodern Asia contain a key assumption: that the four principles just outlined operate simultaneously and constitute themselves into a single indivisible force in so far as actual practices are concerned. The idea that is being put forward in making the assumption is that of complementarity. The reality of the physical domain is different from the abstracted model seeking to explain it. One is complementary to the other and the latter is restricted by the problem of metrics and methods of validation. Historical action must necessarily manifest itself as a singular entity. The sum total of motivations that leads to its execution can be separated into different components like the sunlight separated into its constituent bands of colours. To those who are participants in the action, the logic remains integral, because in the end any one who initiates any action chooses a single option out of a binary alternative of 'yes' and 'no' (whether to act or not to act).

The sources of social conflicts. Structural contradictions which are systematic over any length of time may result from environmental factors outside human control; often they are thrown up by the incompatibility of logic inherent in two different systems articulated by an ensemble of our four principles. Variations in crop production due to climatic reasons would obviously set off a wave of reaction throughout the economy and the polity, becoming more intricate as the interactions multiplied over time. A remote farming community in historical Asia might organise its land utilisation and food supply on the basis of kinship and the pattern of dominance among the local families, although no one could overlook the fact that settled agriculture called for the performance of a succession of physical steps (which we have called the 'logical necessity' but which may also be taken as the 'forces of production' as interpreted by Marx). The political agent of the state in the locality, whether he was a district magistrate in China, a provincial governor of the Thai monarch, or a member of the cadre of military officers appointed by the Ottoman and Mughal imperial courts, could not allow the operating rationality of his administrative duties to be solely fixed by the structure of local kinship. If he was an outsider assigned temporarily to the area, it was only the discipline of his training and sense of moral responsibility that reconciled any possible contradiction between the objectives of the distant central government and the welfare of the inhabitants in the immediate rural neighbourhood. The logic of political power and military operations, linked to the logical necessity of maintaining public revenue, took precedent in the order of relations between the peasantry and the state agents. The practice of selling farming families, defaulting on tax payments, into temporary bondage was common enough, as was also the infliction of corporal punishment. Pushed to its limits, mass coercion depopulated entire agricultural districts and resulted in peasants absconding, destroying the state itself in the process. Whether or not the agents of the state possessed sufficient and effective political means and military force at all times and in every part of the centralised empire they served, to hold the people in complete coercion is still an open question. But the possibility of a contradiction in the articulation of the rulers and the ruled certainly existed.

The typologies of economic production: theories of subsistence and exchange as ideal types. The analysis of the articulated structure of Asian civilisations should perhaps begin by raising a basic question. What kind of economic structure did these societies possess in our period of study? It is not at all easy to answer the question and historians still profoundly differ in their interpretations of the surviving evidence. It can be put in relative perspective by asking a second, supplementary question. How did Asian people in different localities and in different time periods provide themselves with the necessities of life, replicate their families as social units, and organise political protection? It will be well initially to take into account two distinct lines of thought that have dominated for a century or more the formation of historical discourse. One is the idea of a subsistence agriculture or self-sufficient economy which is played off against the model of a market-oriented, exchange economy; the other is the notion of an evolutionary process from a simple 'primitive' social organisation into a more complex 'advanced' system. The argument is constructed in the following sequence. A particular unit of economic production such as a village, a group of villages, or a locality taken together produce all their basic necessities of life. The bulk of the crops grown is consumed within the peasant families and agriculture is practised jointly with weaving, pottery-making, and the manufacture of metal tools. The transition from a subsistence to an exchange economy is made when farmers begin to sell part of their agricultural production in the market either to pay for taxes or to buy goods that are not available locally. It is recognised in this reasoning that division of labour exists but perhaps within households and between different villages in the locality. It does not need much imagination to see that the concepts of a subsistence economy and the fully-developed market are two polar types that one would not find in a pristine form in any historical situations in Asia. Examples of uninterrupted evolution from a lower form to a higher one are even more diffi-cult to find, even if one could define the comparative categories. Historical developments in most parts of Asia seem to have been distributed in a more random temporal pattern. An area that was well-documented as being charac-terised by active inter-regional and long-distance trade, by the production of industrial goods for export, and agricultural specialisation underpinned by monetary exchange, would relapse into relative insularity due to political or climatic upheavals.

Some historical case-studies: the early Islamic Middle East and Sung China.
Such an area was Iraq after the Mongol conquest of the mid thirteenth century. The urban splendours of Baghdad under the ᶜAbbasids, its economic influence on the transcontinental trade of the Indian Ocean, and the fertility of the surrounding agricultural areas found many true as well as hyperbolic descrip-tions among Islamic historians from al-Tabari to al-Muqaddasi.[15] After the disaster of the Mongol conquest, the irrigational canals and the dykes fell into disrepair and the whole area gradually went over from the ideology of settled agriculture to the ways of a nomadic society. However, to Asian historians the polar concepts of subsistence and market economies, urban and rural, tribal societies and centralised political empires are perfectly clear. They have been an essential part of a long historiographical tradition. For example, in describ-ing the brilliant period of urbanisation and urban culture which accompanied the early Islamic expansion in the Middle East and the Mediterranean, von Grunebaum pointed out that the Arab empire, as well as its social life, was carried on the shoulders of the peasantry but dominated by townsmen in every sense. Mercenary soldiers, urban administrators, and princes helped to organise and exploit the countryside. Even when Turkish invaders of the Islamic East from the eleventh century onwards created a new class of military land-holders triumphing over the previous mercantile Arab and Arabising

aristocracy in civil government, towns remained at the centre of real political power. So pervasive was the influence of urban life that most Islamic historians paid little attention to the rural scene.[16] The cognitive techniques used by Grunebaum are almost identical to those of Yoshinobu Shiba in his study of the urbanisation and the development of markets in the lower Yangtze valley during the Sung period. On the basis of his own research and those of other specialists, he concludes that Sung China witnessed a significant impetus towards greater urbanisation based on the growth of agriculture in the huge delta-system of the Yangtze river. The improvement in food production and the cultivation of commercial crops was stimulated by the development of inter-regional trade and a restructuring of the administrative spatial units in terms of a new urban–rural relationship. It is significant that the Chinese historical sources also seem to point towards a greater exploitation of the rural areas from urban locations, and Yoshinobu Shiba concludes that a consequent impoverishment of the farming population may have restricted further urban progress. Although the mandarin class attempted to reduce the economic inequality between urban and rural areas, the efforts were not entirely successful.[17]

Historical attempts at monetisation: the policies of Wang An-shih, ʿAla al-Din Khalji, and Muhammad Tughluq. It is remarkable that two present-day historians as von Grunebaum and Shiba of such widely-separated regions as the Yangtze delta and the Middle East should nevertheless utilise near-identical theoretical tools to analyse the structure of economic articulation between town and country. Are we right in thinking from their historical case-studies that the nature of the relationship between the locality and the wider environment in historical Asia can be formulated in terms of a common model of development? The model yields two objective entities, countryside and towns, and three variable but interlinked flows of action – movements in agrarian production, inter-regional trade, and political control. The application of the model in historical analysis has made it increasingly difficult to sustain the nineteenth-century discourse on history that presents the economic life of Asia as the sum total of a large number of self-sufficient rural units inhabited by dispossessed, rights-less farmers who are under the direct control of the centralised bureaucratic states.[18] The economic and social stratification incorporated far more complex and varied forms and changed in various different directions.

The sophistication of policy and even the operations of the economy are revealed, to take another example from Sung China, by the famous reforms known as the 'New Programme' initiated by Wang An-shih, the celebrated prime minister (appointed 1069) of Sung Shen-tsung. The measures included land survey and land utilisation, irrigation and flood control works, the transport of government tribute to the capital, and the organisation of local militia. But the main thrust of the New Programme lay in commuting the land taxes in terms of copper money and financing agricultural development or the silk industry by setting-up a government-sponsored fund. The active marketing of rural products and the rationalisation of the system of tax receipts and disbursements were an essential condition for the success of the reforms. Wang An-shih was forced to resign after the empire suffered the calamity of a nationwide drought. A contemporary minister of finance, Shen Kua, reinforced Wang's argument for the monetisation of the economy in an observation to the Emperor which was nothing less than a theory of the velocity of monetary circulation.

The utility of money derives from circulation and loan-making. A village of ten households may have 100,000 coins. If the cash is stored in the household of one individual, even after a century, the sum remains 100,000. If the coins are circulated through business transactions so that every individual of the ten households can enjoy the utility of the 100,000 coins, then the utility will amount to that of 1,000,000 cash. If circulation continues without stop, the utility of the cash will be beyond enumeration.[19]

The New Programme attracted a powerful critic in the historian Ssu-ma Kuang (1018–86) who was also an influential court politician in opposition to the prime minister's faction. The critical document pointed out that human labour combined with the natural fertility of the soil produced such useful things as grain and silk, while money in the form of coins was an artificial index of value and an official monopoly. A wealthy merchant may possess stocks of money but farmers normally organise their activities in a different way. Even a rich farmer normally evaluates his welfare in terms of enlarging his land-holdings in order to harvest more crops, repairing or building houses, or owning his own oxen so that he has no need to borrow from others. As for a poor farmer, he has barely enough to eat and to wear. He may even be a share-cropper, toiling hard just to fend off starvation. Such people have little opportunity of seeing any copper coins, let alone of owning them. The enlightened governments in the past had taken into account the reality of agricultural production in the Celestial Empire and collected taxes in grain, silk, and labour services. It was not until the latter part of the T'ang dynasty that the revenue payments were enforced in cash. All that had now changed and 'individuals wherever they happen to be or whether they are rich or poor, are constantly pressured by government officials for money. After a bumper harvest when the price of grain is low, they have to sell their crops at one-third of their normal price in order to raise enough cash to pay the government.'[20] Although the dissenting view highlighted the virtues of commodity production for 'use value', the references to silk weaving and the prices of grain also reveal another aspect of the economy in which exchange transactions predominated.

The depth of urbanisation reached in Sung China or in the Middle East and India, from a much earlier period, could hardly have been sustained without a corresponding structure of distribution and the marketing of food supplies, raw materials, and industrial goods.

The observations of Ziya al-Din Barani (c. 1285–1357), the historian of the Delhi Sultanate, on this subject are highly suggestive. Barani noted that it was normal for grain prices in urban markets to fluctuate according to the expected distribution of rains or the movements of trading caravans. But ᶜAla al-Din Khalji, the ferocious warrior-sultan of Delhi (r. 1296–1316), imposed such draconian price regulations and penalties on grain merchants that the price of corn remained low in the capital even when the monsoon was uneven. The price control was introduced in order to reduce the burden of army pay on the government, which was faced with large military expenditures in order to fight the invading Mongol armies pouring into north India during this period. The items of daily life controlled by the regulations included cotton piece goods, sugar, vegetables, fruits, cooking fats, lamp oil, and manufactured goods. The pious Muslim historian, who would die in severe self-inflicted poverty, remained strongly critical of any public policy not in harmony with the religious traditions of Islam. He returned to the theme of economic affairs when describing the events under Sultan Muhammad Tughluq (r. 1324–51), whose brilliant but unstable personality disconcerted both friends and critics.[21] One of the innovative measures introduced by the sultan of Delhi was a token currency, nominated in copper, which had the same value as equivalent gold and silver coins. The Indian monetary experiment anticipated by some half a century a similar measure, the circulation of paper currency, instituted by the founder of the Ming dynasty in China, Emperor Hung-wu (temple name T'ai-tsu, r. 1368–98). The copper coinage of Muhammad Tughluq was legal tender for the government treasuries and the effect, according to Barani, was to turn the counting-house of every Hindu merchant into a mint. The general public, the aristocracy, the landowners, the village headmen, all grew rich and purchased horses, arms, and fine things of life. The resulting inflation had a serious effect on government revenue and Gresham's Law (bad money driving out good) rapidly came into operation. The central treasury eventually redeemed all the copper coinage at face value, suffering heavy losses.[22] The rapid depreciation of the early Ming paper currency also proved that there was as yet no real substitute for the usage of precious metals or commodity money such as standard baskets of rice or bolts of silk for measuring exchange values.[23]

The fiscal reforms of Wang An-shih analysed by the Sung historian Ssu-ma Kuang and the descriptions of Barani were separated by nearly three centuries. But the Chinese and the Indian sources alike seem to point towards certain common structural features that are not as a rule directly visible in the form of an aggregate or a totality.[24] The discussions suggest that in national economic life, the operation of the price mechanism, the use of money, and the influence of urban centres, had very distinctive roles. The market certainly existed. So also did food production for the direct consumption of the producers. In fact, there is no lack of historical sources from any period or area of our study to demonstrate the force of fiscal pressure on subsistence producers, pushing them in the direction of the market and the exchange economy, characterised and even dominated by inter-regional and long-distance trade. It is equally evident that peasants accustomed to grow food for their own use would find it difficult to pay taxes nominated in cash unless a part of the surplus produce could be sold. If any confusion or possible difference exists between the viewpoints of those historians who emphasise the self-sufficient, subsistent character of past Asian economies and others who assign a greater weight to the wider process of economic exchange, it is because the *levels* at which each subset or sub-structure was operating have not been examined in sufficient depth. It is particularly important to remember that the forms of the economic organisation of premodern Asia cannot be arranged as a complex of moments on an evolutionary time-chart without a beginning and an end. They are not yesterday's children who grow into tomorrow's adults. They may have their own temporal trajectory. But in their maturity, they represent totally different aggregate structures, ordered and articulated by their own logical necessity. The ceaseless quest of the modern historians looking for the 'origins' and roots of capitalism is not much better than the alchemist's search for the philosopher's stone that transforms base metal into gold. The temptation to write economic history from the vantage point of the present forces some historians of Asia to see the economic development of each area forever undergoing 'greater urbanisation' or 'increasing monetisation'. The subsistence agriculture of India or China, they would have us believe, was being commercialised as much at around AD 1000 as in 1800. In order to avoid such undifferentiated generalisations, it is imperative to locate the discontinuities and thresholds both in structures and historical time.

The structure of production

The economic rationale of settled farming, nomadism, and the mechanism of the exchange economy. Two invariant forms of articulation within the organisation of economic life clearly stand out in historical Asia. Whether the historian looks at the arid lands inhabited by great tribes of migratory nomads or the green field-systems of intense productivity created by the labours of people living in the deltas of the Nile, the Euphrates-Tigris, the Indus, the Ganges, the Mekong, and the Yangtze, food production was not only an economic activity but also a way of life. Farming or nomadism provided a direct linkage between social survival and the means of production. Against this fact stands out the other inescapable element of history. A great many people, members of the different civilisations of Asia, were *not* engaged in growing their own food or raising their own livestock. Farmers or nomadic communities who, it might appear at first sight, had no wish or incentive to feed any one else other than their own families and extended kinship groups, nonetheless provided food to classes without direct involvement in its production. How was the necessary connection between these two apparently contradictory situations established in the first place and by what means did the articulated structure perpetuate itself?

The question cannot be answered with direct historical evidence, as division of labour within the domestic and the impersonal, spatially-extended system of production had appeared very early in the history of Asia.[25] By AD 1000 many areas in the Near and Middle East had already passed through several complete civilisational life-cycles based on finely-differentiated economic specialisations and exchange. During the Sung period in China, if not much earlier, many separate categories of skilled agriculturists, growing rice, dry cereals, or producing silk-cocoons, were carefully distinguished from silk weavers, the makers of fine porcelain, bronze-casters, and lacquer-polishers by the technological demands of their professions as well as the economic forces of the market. Traders and merchants not only existed as separate social groups but also provided the necessary links between the farmers, industrial craftsmen, and the final consumers in rural and urban areas. Similar forms of labour division were also to be found in India, with the difference that under the influence of Sanskritic religious thinking these forms had become embedded into a system of hereditary sub-castes whose members were not easily permitted, or did not think it necessary, to change their pre-determined vocations. An identity between the idea of the 'inequality' of social stratifications and different types of economic functions appears to have been a deeply-rooted feature of Asian history. One of the strongest appeals of Islam and the reason for its universal adoption in many parts of our area lay precisely in the fact that Islam claimed to restore the lost equality of mankind. It is significant, however, that not even Islam was able to dissolve the economic distinctions between the leather-worker and the water-carrier (one manufacturing the water-flask and the other shouldering it for the use of others), between butchers and bakers, between the destitute and the over-rich. A recurring theme in the economic policy of pre-modern rulers is the notion of a just price for the daily necessities of life. A just price: but for whom? The self-sufficient peasantry by a double reasoning does not understand the justice of low prices for their products. All the same, abnormally high prices of food and the inflated profits realised by producers, merchants, shopkeepers, bankers, and money-changers attracted the attention of political authorities and jurists.[26] 'The king should settle before his own throne the prices of all things according to the principle of production-cost [*nirkh-i baraward*]', Barani wrote, so as to prevent profiteering by traders.[27] But beneath the multiplicity of the laws seeking to control the price of bread or rice, there lay submerged an entire structure of economic forces, social relationships, and individual motivations which made these attempts at regulations ineffective at best and very often totally futile. The division of labour and the simultaneous operation of the rationale of a market provided opportunities for making economic gains at the level of individual groups. There was no suitable instrument known to premodern rulers for curbing the operation of the market without also destroying the basis of their finances. The more complex the structure of the state and society, the greater was the dependence of the ruling elites on the uninterrupted functioning of the market.

Agricultural production and the market. The existence of economic specialisation going back by several millennia in Asian history is well-documented. It leaves unanswered the question raised earlier: why should peasants growing their own food and weaving the materials for their garments enter the market? An important factor, often repeated, was said to be the fiscal demands of the state. The proportion of rural production appropriated by the centralised military-bureaucratic empires of Asia remained substantial, from a fifth to a third of the total. The reasoning, though valid as a description, is not sufficient as an explanation. There were many regions and localities in Asia where the principle of a highly-organised state was either very weak or the government's capacity to tax the agricultural population directly remained limited; at the same time these areas were part of a flourishing economy. The available archaeological and historical evidence reveals, on a more careful collation, that the allegedly closed system of rural production was characterised by an active process of exchange from a very distant past. Asian food producers were no more self-sufficient in economic terms than urban-dwellers. Even the nomads, historically the most isolated communities, established reciprocal relations with specific groups of settled people, whether these were date-cultivators in a desert-oasis or grain farmers living at the margin of cultivation. The great chain of trading cities in Central Asia, in the Iranian central plateau, and North Africa, on the fringe of the Sahara, depended on the migratory warrior tribes to provide the visiting merchants with baggage animals and to secure by agreement the protection of their caravans. The nomadic exchange of livestock, horses, camels, and sheep, together with other items, dairy products, wool, hides, and carpets, for grain, sugar, coffee, tea, and fine textiles underlined a social and an economic necessity that was no less strong in the case of settled farmers.[28]

One of the tell-tale signs of the intrusion of the exchange and the market in the lives of such people was the large mix of crops, vegetables, and fruits cultivated in China, South East Asia, India, and the Middle East. The argument that the multiplicity of the produce owed its logic to the differential drought- or flood-resisting quality of the different varieties unravels only one of the many facets of the historical reality in the rural economy. The mixture included several high-valued cash crops: wheat, oil-seeds, cotton, hemp, indigo, and sugar-cane. These were all sold in the local or the distant markets. Areas with an ample supply of water able to grow rice could not compete with those of dry-farming in the number of crops grown. But was there just one single variety of rice cultivated by the Indian or Chinese peasantry? The Chinese work *Chi Min Yao Shu* dating from a time (*c.* AD 535) when rice was rarely cultivated to the north of the Huai, mentions twelve non-glutinous rices and eleven glutinous types. The *Shou Shih Tung Kao* (*c.* 1742) lists more than 3,000 varieties of rice. The grain markets of Hangchow and other towns and cities of China were not alone in selling a wide selection of rice.[29] There were shops in the bazaars of Delhi, the Mughal capital, where 'nothing is seen but pots of oil or butter, piles of baskets with rice, barley, chick-peas, wheat, and an endless variety of other grain and pulse, the ordinary aliment not only of the *Gentiles* [Hindus], who never eat meat, but of the lower class of *Mahometans*, and a considerable portion of the military.'[30]

The social gradations associated with the consumption of different types of rice did not go unnoticed. Shu Lin, a twelfth-century scholar, pointed out that the long-grained *keng* rice grown on fertile land was used to pay government taxes and was eaten only by upper-class people; whereas the small-grained Champa rice (*hsien*) gave high yields, commanded a low price and was eaten by people of modest and poor means.[31] Here is another description of the same social feature from the pen of Jean-Baptiste Tavernier (1665), a French dealer in precious stones and jewellery: the district of Navapura in Gujarat, four days' march from the port of Surat, through which the caravan road to northern India passed, not only specialised in the weaving of cotton cloth but also grew the famous thin-grained perfumed ('Basmati') rice of India. The composition of the local soil and the irrigation water raised from the local river contributed to its quality. This was a rice eaten by the Indian aristocracy and it made a valued present for the high-ranking people in Persia.[32] So sensational was the reputation of the Indian scented rice that Ghazan Khan, the Mongol ruler of Iran (*r.* 1295–1304), had attempted unsuccessfully to introduce its cultivation in the rice-growing areas of the Caspian Sea.[33] The necessity for insuring against the risks of crop-failure certainly led the farmers to sow a large variety of cereals. The range of food habits combined with technical factors such as crop rotation also accounted for the practice. The rapid adoption by the Asian peasantry from the sixteenth-century onwards of maize and tobacco, one a food item in farming households and the other a commercial crop sold in the market for cash, proves the degree to which farmers were accustomed to assimilate an advantageous innovation. As the depth of historical documentation increases in the seventeenth and eighteenth centuries, it is possible to demonstrate beyond any doubt that the cultivation of widely-traded crops such as black pepper, finer spices, indigo, tea, and coffee was controlled and regulated by careful economic considerations which underlie any competitive commodity market.[34]

Long-distance trade, closed economies, and urbanisation. The different levels of articulation in the economic life of Asian societies possessed varying structural features. Economic relationships within a village, or between the rural district and the urban centres were not necessarily of the same order and magnitude. Long-distance trade, connecting together international commercial turn-tables of the stature of a Canton, Malacca, or Alexandria, vitalised itself by a rationality that worked its way from the final consumers of the traded goods to their first producers. The ownership and utilisation of land in a village and the distribution of crops were determined in many areas by the pattern of kinship and the dispersion of power, all of which might operate without the direct intervention of a system of prices indexed by money and currency. In a closed local economy of this type, even the basic division of labour between the producers of food and makers of industrial artifacts leaves both the groups under-employed. The historical stereotype of the Asian rural craftsman practising his art alongside the tending of his agricultural holding is a common one, and its axiomatic corollary was the rewarding of service people, barbers, washermen, street cleaners, and night-watchmen, in kind. How far was this model of distribution and exchange indexed by social usage, the prevailing form of organisation in the rural society of premodern Asia? The question helps to highlight a puzzling contradiction. Even in those areas for which the sources indicate that the peasantry raised crops on the rationale of subsistence and co-existed with the part-time artisans in the village, producers were linked to the external locality by the extractive mechanism of an economic surplus, absorbed by the state and urban residents. In other words, part of the rural production left the circuit of 'use value' and entered the network of market relationships controlled by prices and money. But a more general pattern seems to have been a mixed system in which considerations of subsistence production were relaxed or constrained by differential opportunities for market transactions. Transport facilities, the availability of credit and capital, and profit incentives determined over what geographical area and period of time production would remain in touch with the market. There was one level, the top one in the economic articulation, that retained a fair degree of temporal stability. The great primate cities, characterised by political, religious, and commercial functions, supported their continued existence on the basis of a highly differentiated relationship with the countryside. Damascus, Baghdad, Cairo, Constantinople, Delhi, and Peking joined Mecca, Cambay, Malacca, and Canton in gathering their vital supplies and urban resources from areas going far beyond the immediate hinterland.

The structure of contradictions: the autonomy of social groups and the state. It may be asked, to what extent is the historical contradiction (between subsistence and exchange) explained by the autonomy of social categories? Were the peasants autonomous food producers or an exploited group forced to enter the market through the pressure exercised by the centralised states and by the dominant classes in the locality? Who provided political protection to the civil society? Did the peasants and rural artisans organise their own protection or was it in the hands of local power groups and the agents of the state? How far did the subjects look upon their rulers as wolves to be feared and slain? The great merchants often combining in their specialised profession the function of the banker and owners of loan capital acted in close partnership with the agents of the Asian states. But as social groups their autonomy from the rest of the society was remarkable. The daughters of a wealthy merchant were rarely offered in marriage to the sons of the aristocracy or high-ranking court officials. According to our theoretical syntax, every 'set' is autonomous in a sense, because the principle defining it is different in each case or it cannot appear as a set. What is important then is to examine the way the system of articulation (or the mapping relations) undermines the autonomy which can be both theoretical and empirical. It is important to repeat that neither the economic structure of premodern societies nor the practices are ever directly visible. It is the totality of a given historical situation that defines the theoretical or ideological categories under which practices can be distinguished as economic, social, or political. What appears as an exclusively religious ritual turns out to be an essential step in economic production and administrative duties if it helps to precipitate rains and thus avert the calamity of a famine. 'Untimely and inadequate rainfall or sunshine makes the growth of five grains impossible and causes pestilence among the people', was the observation of the mandarin Huang Liu-hung: 'It is the duty of the magistrate to pray for remedies . . . The magistrate should control his thoughts and fast and pray as a manifestation of his sincerity.'[35] The prescription came from the agent of a centralised bureaucratic state that claimed a fifth or more of the total agricultural production as its share of income, a practice that was common in India and the Middle East also. The pattern of articulation between the state and the economic producers in Asia certainly reduced the autonomy of individual producing-units and pushed them in the direction of the market and the surplus-creation. However, it is possible to put forward an opposite point of view, that it was the pre-existing structure of a differentiated exchange economy that created in the first place the conditions for the growth of the centralised empires.

Political thinkers and statesmen in Islamic states, India, Buddhist South East Asia, and China repeatedly noted the dangers of an alienation of identity and interest between the rulers and the ruled, between subjects and their legitimate representatives. The concern was expressed in more than one type of source. The Iranian model king Anushirawan is supposed to have said:

After this, I shall speak to the tyrannical only with the sword; I shall protect the ewe and the lamb from the wolf and restrain the hands of the tyrannical; I shall remove the corrupt from the face of earth and make the world populous by justice and security, because it is for this that I have been created.[36]

A Thai manuscript record of royal commands ascribed to King Mang Rai, the founder of the city of Chieng Mai in the north (1296), contains an article on the reclamation of waste land. A subject who converted such land into rice fields, gardens, or dwelling places enjoyed tax-exemption for three years. If any powerful local person relying on status tried to deprive the original owner of the land by offering money to the lord of the district, he was to be prevented from doing so and demoted in rank, so that idle men did not rule the land and cause the kingdom to decline.[37] The Ming official Lu K'un (1536–1618), writing in the tradition of Neo-Confucian scholars, disapproved of the growth of extravagant habits among the peasantry. He also thought that if the Celestial Emperor did not appoint officials, the worldly benefits would be appropriated by the strong, the lawless, and the greedy. The leaderless poor would gather together in rebellion, bringing disaster to the society.[38] Even the great al-Ghazali (1058–1111), who was perfectly aware that in his day the conjunction between the caliphate, the legitimation of the government, and military power was uncomfortably close, could not refrain from stating the obvious: the prosperity of the inhabited land and its depopulation depended on kings and the quality of their government.[39] The autonomy of the bureaucratic or military classes was universally feared as vitiating the existence of the state itself and encouraging rural unrest and banditry. The fears merely confirm the historical existence of all these practices that ran counter to the notion of good order, practices that were condemned but could not be eradicated. Rural traders, bankers, and merchants might compel their client farmers to grow crops for the market through the use of financial power. The government needed the service of such exploitative groups to turn commodities into disposable state income. The contradiction was irremovably built into the structure of the society and the state.

The role of force: an example from ancient Egypt. In the last analysis, force remained the strongest form of social and economic articulation. Here is a 'lament' for the earth's dispossessed, recorded by chance from the period of the New Kingdom in Pharaonic Egypt:

Remember you not the condition of the cultivator faced with the registering of the harvest-tax, when the snake has carried off half the corn and the hippopotamus has devoured the rest. The mice abound in the field. The locusts descend. The cattle devour. The sparrows bring disaster upon the cultivator. The remainder that is on the threshing-floor is at an end, it falls to the thieves . . . The yoke of oxen has died while threshing and ploughing. And now the scribe lands on the river-bank and is about to register the harvest-tax. The janitors carry staves and the Nubians rods of palm, and they say 'hand over the corn' though there is none. The cultivator is beaten all over, he is bound and thrown into the well, soused and dipped head downwards. His wife has been bound in his presence, his children are in fetters. His neighbours abandon them and they are fled. So their corn flies away . . . Mark it well.

The consequence of such brutalities were predictable enough as a different but similar ancient Egyptian papyrus document recorded:

Another communication for my Lord's good pleasure, to the effect that two of the field labourers of the *mine*-land of Pharaoh, which is under my Lord's authority have fled before the face of the stable-master Neferhotep, he having beaten them. And now, look, the fields of the *mine*-land of Pharaoh which are under my Lord's authority are abandoned and there is no one to till them. This letter is for my Lord's Information.[40]

4

The structure of time and history

The theory of time

Real and perceived time. The theory of time and its structure constitute two interlinked subjects of scientific investigation. The problems of comprehension and application raised by them differ in magnitude. The question of whether time is real or not — the possibility that it exists independently of human perception — assumes historical relevance as part of an enquiry concerning the interaction between the physical world and human agency. The mortality of all living creatures is a moment in time, unalterable in its reality whichever way time is viewed. The biological response to the finite outcome of the life-cycle and its evaluation through analytical intelligence produce consequences that are at the centre of the historian's craft. The mental evaluation is not confined to man alone; it includes the animal kingdom as well. Shortages of food and death resulting from the ensuing famine would cause many species of animals and birds to refrain from replicating their families. The interaction in this particular case is between 'real time' and 'perceived time'. The first is measured in units which can only be observed externally. Real time is neither fully comprehended nor explained. Perceived time is at the disposal of the observer. The world line or the axis of time as defined by a particular society or group of people fixes its rationale. Expressions such as 'time has gone fast or slowly' or 'a sense of history does not exist in the East' are evidence of either shifting or altogether independent world lines on the part of the same observer or different categories of observers.[1] In general, theories of time and space depend on the explicit recognition of time-like and space-like separations, ruptures on continuous surfaces: this is the real test, whether or not a society or a group of people possess any concept of time. The structure of time is more accessible and easier to describe than the theory of time. No physicist or philosopher would seriously dispute today that the definition of structural time given by Leibniz was the first step in its future extension: 'Time is the order of non-contemporaneous things. It is thus the universal order of change in which we ignore the specific kind of changes that have occurred.'[2]

Order and succession. The perception of 'before' and 'after' embodied in the notion of order and succession, as Claude Lévi-Strauss has reminded us, gives

92

history its entire distinction and originality as a branch of knowledge.[3] Without dates descriptive history cannot but lose all its power of interpretation and meaning. If this much is clear from an intuitive understanding of the problem of arranging a sequence of historical events or facts, it is also evident that the different components of 'history' are no more homogeneous than all the details of daily life that collectively constitute the totality of social activity. The defeat of the Sasanian 'King of Kings' Yazdigird in the neighbourhood of Nihavand in 642 is known in the history of Islam as the 'Victory of Victories', comparable to the Second Battle of Panipat (1192) which laid open the legendary wealth of India to Muslim occupation. The class of such events is not the same as the many thousands of battles and wars fought, won, and lost in the history of Asia. They cannot be treated as mere fire-flies of history, which momentarily illuminate a surface of darkness. These are events which express and generate historical forces with a life-span of many centuries, a temporal class of different order from the annual winter campaigns of professional armies. Both Lévi-Strauss and Fernand Braudel in their different ways have emphasised and outlined the technique of refracting the structure of time for historical and social analysis.[4]

Order and succession are accepted in our analysis as basic concepts essential to historical writing. Are they also necessary for arranging and organising social life? The question of whether past Asian civilisations and communities viewed their history in terms of the same temporal units as those of Europe can be decisively answered if we can show that the concept of time expressed as a series of non-simultaneous entities *was* or *was not* a necessary condition for producing food, sowing crops, weaving cloth, and organising complex operations in government and administration. The true answer is already found. Any society that is aware of the triple order of tense – past, present, and future – and embodies it in the structure of its language, is also aware of the physical presence of temporal order in the collective life. Even abstract ideas of destiny and fate, which reflect the awareness of absolute logical necessity in human life, operate through ordered tense. Order and succession are geometric concepts, verified by visual sense in the form of pictures and they are arithmetised through the three-dimensional space co-ordinates. Order can be defined as a principle through which a set of relative points in space is synthesised by the mind. Succession is a movement through a collection of such points sharing the attribute of inequalities, such as are found in a cumulative list of integers beginning with the cardinal number one. There can be no succession and therefore no measured time unless the method and the path for moving from one point to another exist. It can be shown that if a machine were to write out all the terms in a set of rational numbers between 0 and 1, there is no computational procedure that will enable the machine to reach the integer one and thus halt its operation. The world line or the axis of time for fractions is different from those of whole numbers. For historians and the theory of time structure in general, the significance of different sets of world lines can be stated quite briefly. Dates as measured by astronomical calendars enable history to anchor itself against real time. Ordinal numbers (first, second, third, and so on) equate historical time with real time. Regnal years, widely used by Islamic chroniclers in India, were an ordinal sequence of time whose metric was the lunar year of the Hijra (AD 622). The world line of the regnal years is the dynastic cycle, which could be both specific and general. The year 1368, for example, might express the finite beginning of the Ming empire in China, but the idea of successive dynasties ruling over a unified celestial kingdom was quite general and receded back into a non-enumerable past. The temporal world line of the Chinese or Indian agricultural year in contrast was topologically closed, it had neither a finite beginning nor an end, but is characterised by an ordinal sequence of agricultural tasks. The year 1368 held no meaning for the Asian farmer whose sole concern with time was to determine the right time for sowing rice or wheat.

Absolute and relative time. The nature of historical events or facts fixed the class of time, especially dates, and the metrics of real time defined in turn the notion of relative intervals or duration. Through their statistical formulae, the mathematicians of time have placed at the disposal of historians convenient and lucid tools for analysing the structure of the past. To what extent, it might be asked, were the abstract concepts, particularly the distinction between real time and perceived time, apparent to contemporary thinkers and authorities who codified and enforced the application of finite duration through the use of calendars and patterns of social behaviour? The awareness of the problem certainly existed in the mental domain, as we can see from a remarkable controversy between the tenth-century Ismaili philosopher Abu Hatim Razi and the famous physician al-Razi. Abu Hatim Razi set up the viewpoint of his opponent in the following summary:

Time is constituted by the motion of the spheres, the passage of days and nights, the number of years and months; are all these co-eternal with time, or are they produced in time? . . . Muhammad ibn Zakariya Razi . . . who will end by invoking Plato, begins by stating his own thesis in simple terms: 'For my part, I profess this: Time implies an absolute Time and a limited time. Absolute Time is eternal Duration; this is the time that is eternally in movement and never halts. Limited time is that which exists through the movements of the celestial spheres, the course of the sun and the heavenly bodies.'[5]

The distinction that was being drawn here between absolute time and astronomical time is of great interest to historians of scientific thought. For the passage reveals the elements of a cosmology that had a long history and was shared by many thinkers, in spite of individual points of disagreement. When the philosophical discourses are placed against the scientific measurements of

Plate 10 Sun dial from the al-Azahar mosque, Cairo, Egypt.

time, whether in the form of astronomical calculations or the movements of time-machines, clocks, watches, clepsydras, or sun-dials, the associative relations between social practices and a sense of history expressed through tensed order are seen to be no different in Asia than anywhere else in the world. The trumpets, drums, and cymbals in the royal palace in Delhi proclaimed in a thunder of musical sounds the hours of the day and night. On his first arrival in the city, Bernier found the performance quite overwhelming, but 'such is the power of habit that this same noise is now heard by me with pleasure, in the night particularly, when in bed and afar, on my terrace this music sounds in my ears as solemn, grand, and melodious.'[6] Even events seemingly without any systematic meaning, except the social consequences, were carefully recorded. In the year Hijra 1026 (AD 1617), the governor of Qandahar sent in reports of a strange plague of mice in the province, mice which completely destroyed all crops and even the fruit trees. After a time they disappeared as mysteriously as they had first appeared.[7] At about the same time, many towns and cities in the provinces of the Punjab, Delhi, and Agra experienced a new disease, with all the dreaded symptoms of bubonic plague. Demented rats, driven out of their senses by some malady of their own, rushed out into the streets and fell dead on doorsteps. If people fled the town at the very first sighting of dead rats and escaped into the jungle, they were spared the inevitable mortality that overtook other disease-stricken areas. The plague however stopped short just before reaching the former imperial capital of Fathpur Sikri. Physicians could make nothing of the epidemic, except to say that it might be related to the drought of the two previous years.[8]

The two random incidents recorded in the memoirs of Emperor Jahangir illuminate an important aspect of the 'causal' theory of time. Even a highly literate society with a complex structure of government was not able to make sense of contemporaneous events and occurrences without referring to the past. Neither the present nor the future could be reduced to the level of planned expectation, unless a sense of history and the knowledge derived from an analysis of specific historical case-studies existed in the universe of discourse. The possible conclusion to be drawn from the deduction is quite evident. The logic of tense, past, present, and future, together with any time marks serving the same purpose, is an inherent part of language and it is a topological structure. Whether it is expanded, shrunk or distorted in any direction makes no difference to the order; an event (point) or a series of events (line) will remain in ordered contact with the topological surface of perceived time. Although historical sense is a necessary condition of social existence and organisation, the art of historical writing itself makes no such assumption and is a matter of social preferences. A community may be aware of the functional role of history and yet not choose to write it down. The great prehistoric rock paintings did not come out of schools of fine arts nor were they preserved in public museums. Islamic writers however were convinced that temporal duration of the past was best preserved in written form. In 1143–4 Abul Qasim Muhammad b. Yusuf al-Madani al-Hanafi, who wrote on Hanafi law, stated the case for his *History of Balh*:

It revives the memory of the early and recent scholars of Balh . . . Remembering is [giving] new life, and restoring this [new life?] is like reviving all mankind . . . Of actual vision nothing remains but a memory in the mind. Therefore, hearing and seeing are equivalent, and the report [of a third person] is equivalent to actual vision, although in reality there is a great difference between them . . . The memory of pious men is a source of [divine] mercy, and an instructive memento for later generations. Without books, most historical information would be forgotten. After a short while, the memory of any human being, whatever his condition, would be lost.[9]

Metrics of time: the units. The relativity of time-classes can be seen quite clearly in the convention of astronomical measurements. History as a set of past events is measured in different units of time, centuries, years, months, weeks, days, and the sub-divisions of the daily cycle. It is not without historical significance that the actual metrics of time, both chronometry and chronology, widely varied between different civilisations of the past. Some societies chose rotations of the earth, others those of the moon; the beginning of a new year was quite arbitrary; weeks and hours were all defined in varying lengths.[10] The agricultural year, the Indian 'fasli', differed by convention from the calendar year.[11] The chronometric and chronological practices identified, for the members of a society or civilisation, those structures of time relevant to their physical and mental universe. The demarcation of the temporal units by religious or secular authorities and the appropriation of time by people in a position of social or political dominance created the ground-floor of historical action. Economic production, distribution, and consumption, because they were quantified against temporal units, regulated themselves through the rhythm of appropriated time. The length of the working day or the week, the number of public days of rest, and the length of religious festivities, were all fixed by mandates of power. Expressions such as idle, industrious, leisured, and even obedient had little meaning without a concept of authority that appropriated in the name of duty, the hours from the dawn to sunset in the lives of farmers and artisans.

Methods of periodisation

The frequency and class of time. For any historian, a theory of the structure of time must address itself to a central question. How are the chronological unities and disunities established in the first place for a chosen period? If there are recognised continuities in the pattern of time, the class of events need to be specified in terms of the frequency of occurrence within the unit of measurement. The daily events that took place in the history of the Ottoman, Mughal, and Ming empires were recorded with great care by many chroniclers. They were both random and systematic. The class of such events cannot be the same as the changes in the use of fire-arms, shipbuilding, and the diffusion of American silver which took place during the same period. The frequency of the former class was much higher than that of the latter. Furthermore, it is not only that the objective measurements in terms of duration vary between events belonging to different time classes but their mental images also convey meaning, sense, and intelligence which are not of the same depth. In the mental domain time is signified by the sequence and the number of relevant terms which cognitive logic identifies for the purpose of analysis. It is important to be aware that two separate propositions are involved here. In one case, the class of historical events is fixed by the relative frequency of occurrences within a fixed unit of time. Within one calendar year the agricultural tasks for a rural community could be counted in hundreds but the number of its religious festivals may not have been more than a dozen. In that of the second, the unit period itself is a variable. The distinction seldom appears to be explicit, because the chronometry itself takes care of it. There is no sense in counting the number of meals eaten over a whole year; the appropriate metrics is that of the twenty-four-hour day. Climatic and ecological variations on the other hand can only be measured over centuries, if not millennia.

The life cycles of Asian civilisations, three dates, AD 618, 622, 1757. Perhaps the most useful starting-point for the analysis and description of the temporal structure of Asian history is the concept of a civilisation's life-cycle which can be taken also as its world line or the time axis. The implied assumption that the period from the seventh to the eighteenth century constitutes a coherent chronological unit for Asia as a whole needs to be examined in detail and its rationale excavated from the intuitive domain. As we shall see, the assumption turns out to be a valid one, though only under the limiting concept of a life-cycle. Every community creates a continuum in terms of its past through social traditions, religious beliefs, and visual images seen in paintings, architecture, clothing, and even the local geography. The length of the continuum starting from the extreme point beyond which no memory and sense of collective identity is retained makes up the life-cycle. Two fortunate coincidences provide a time marker at the beginning of our historical cycle: the foundation of the T'ang dynasty in China (618) and Muhammad's journey to Medina (622) caused concentric ripples to appear on the surface of time which rapidly increased in spatial and structural dimensions. Somewhere along an invisible line in the Central Asian steppes and the South China Sea the topological expansion of Islam met that of China.[12] Is it too far-fetched to suggest that because the Celestial civilisation and the Balad al-Islam between them encompassed the whole of geographical Asia, the two above dates should be taken as the starting-point of our continuum?

The argument will not hold as a rigid exercise in symbolic logic. But it has certain historical validity. Let us take the year 1757, the date of the 'Revolution' of Plassey, as the formal, symbolic terminal point of our historical periodisation. At this time a Muslim living in the Middle East, India, or South East Asia, together with a subject of the Ch'ien-lung Emperor would have had no difficulty, given a certain level of education, in placing the dates 618 and 622 in a sequence of living traditions. Their way of life had changed in the intervening centuries but the changes were not new, unrecognisable, structural transformations. For the subcontinent of India and South East Asia the relevance of the time marks are derived through an indirect associative relation. In so far as there was a geographical and civilisational rupture between these areas and their neighbours in the east and the west, the dynastic cycles in China and the chronology of Islam introduced a time order between their autonomous internal developments and the relative rank of each in the logical space we know as the history of 'Asia'. The associative temporal scale enables us to make comparisons, even though neither ancient India nor South East Asia articulated their life-cycles in terms of our adopted terminology. Whatever the actual mode of expression, the principles which integrated people into a common 'set' in China, South East Asia, India, and the Middle East, did not fundamentally change during the millennium under study.

There were however important new intrusions which an Umayyad or Abbasid Muslim would have found decidedly strange, if not actually beyond the limits of comprehension. He would certainly have wondered at the presence of the Ottoman Turks, professing belief in the true faith, in the heartland of the Eastern Roman Empire and actually occupying Constantinople, a city that had proclaimed to the world not only the splendours of Byzantine life but also the earlier Arab military failures against itself. He would not have thought it possible that the Rumis and Franks, feared at the time for their naval mastery of the northern shores of the Mediterranean, could pose a similar danger to the Muslim right of free navigation in the Indian Ocean. Above all, he would have found it incredible that the same Europeans now held the key to collective wealth and material well-being through their knowledge of the sciences and practical arts far surpassing anything the most advanced civilisation of Asia could offer. It was perhaps not without reason that the knowledge of Western achievements, their true magnitude and significance for the future course of development, were slow to spread among men of power and learning in the east. Halet Efendi, the Turkish ambassador to France (1803–6), believed that the European economic competition could be effectively broken merely by setting up five factories for snuff, paper, crystal, cloth, and porcelain as well as schools for languages and geography.[13] If there was any doubt in the minds of the Directors of the English East India Company about the political implication of the Battle of Plassey and the year 1757, it was not shared by the Company's officials and military officers in Bengal, who were convinced that the political and military control of Bengal was at last about to fall into their own hands. As the Court of Directors would remind the Fort William Council in Calcutta, 'we conceive you would not presume to go on with your extensive scheme of fortifying Cossimbuzar, and we cannot avoid remarking that you seem so thoroughly possessed with military ideas as to forget your employers are merchants and trade their principal object.'[14] But even that dignified, commercially-minded body of men in London described the events of 1757 as 'the late very extraordinary Revolution' which, by opening the public treasury of the richest province of the Mughal empire to the Company's control, terminated the need to ship American treasure from Europe.[15]

The 'power' of historical dates in Asian history. The historical life-cycle which was about to come to an end from the second half of the eighteenth century affected as much the ways of the *ancien régime* in the Western world as in Asia. But the consequences were not symmetrical. The political weakness amounting in some cases to actual collapse was the forerunner in a larger theatre of decline on the part of the once-great Asian civilisations, the most telling expression of which was an inability to retain control over economic and social destinies. When after a disastrous war (1839–42) the Chinese government agreed to open its ports to British opium traders, it did not do so choosing between right and wrong: the choice was between survival and destruction. The year 1757 belongs to a particular class of dates, familiar to historians, sharing a common attribute. They are random or nearly-random in the first occurrence, but they have the capacity to mark and signal long-term movements lasting over a century, perhaps over many centuries. Examples of such dates taken from Asian history within our life-cycle can be easily identified and listed: 1739, the sack of Delhi by Nadir Shah; 1722, the fall of the Safavids in Iran; 1644, the overthrow of the Ming dynasty in China; 1526, the Battle of Panipat and the Mughal conquest of India; 1498, Vasco da Gama drops anchor in the harbour of Calicut; 1453, Constantinople taken by the Ottoman Turks; 1368, the accession of the first Ming emperor in China; 1347, the Black Death appears in Egypt; 1279, the Mongol conquest of China; 1258, Baghdad occupied by the Mongols; 1192, the Turkish victory over Hindu forces in the Punjab; 1071, Jerusalem falls to the Muslim Seljuk Turks; 969, the Fatimid conquest of Egypt; 960, the accession of the Sung dynasty in China; 749, the Abbasid revolution in Iraq; 641, Alexandria captured by the Arabs.

Four components of structural time. The list presented above is selective and leaves out many similar events. But it is able to drive home, by exclusion and inclusion, two important generalisations about the nature of the long-term in Asian history. The economic and social life contained few 'solar time' markers between stages of major thresholds. It is necessary to codify such changes either in terms of 'historical' time in the form of ordinal sequences or 'structural' time, divided into long stationary movements, Braudel's *longue durée*, trends, cycles, and the random. The second point concerns the causal nature of the long-term historical changes. The real force seems to have come from the establishment of great territorial empires, the movements of conquering people across the Asian geography, and the associative forms of religious and social systems. In either case, their frequency of time was low.

Historical examples

The history of the Black Death as an instance of the interaction between the random and the long term. The history of the Black Death in the Middle East can be taken as an illustration of how the time dimension operated. In the medical history of the time the previous incidence of the bubonic plague was imperfectly known and the visitation appeared to contemporaries as a totally unpredictable social disaster. Although the virulence of the epidemic lessened after a few years, the disease reappeared at irregular intervals of time and the original outbreak left behind a long legacy of psychological insecurity and a long-lasting impact on the overall levels of population, agricultural production, prices, incomes, and all those aspects of daily life which were quantified through production and consumption. In sonorous Arabic prose, the most distinguished historian of his time recorded the effects of the calamity, in which he lost his own parents:

in the middle of the eighth [fourteenth] century, civilization both in the East and the West was visited by a destructive plague which devastated nations and caused populations to vanish. It swallowed up many of the good things of civilization and wiped them out. It overtook the dynasties at the time of their senility, when they had reached the limit of their duration . . . Civilization decreased with decrease of mankind. Cities and buildings were laid waste, roads and way signs were obliterated, settlements and mansions became empty, dynasties and tribes grew weak. The entire inhabited world changes . . . It was as if the voice of existence in the world had called out for oblivion and restriction, and the world had responded to its call . . . When there is a general change of conditions, it is as if the entire creation had changed and the whole world been altered, as if it were a new and repeated creation, a world brought into existence anew. Therefore, there is need at this time that someone should systematically set down the situation of world among all regions and races . . . [16]

The plague was obviously a random occurrence in history and it was almost unique. The dates of its appearance and decline are of absolute importance in a chronological sense. On the other hand, the economic and social effects of the plague stretched out over two centuries or more. When historians attempt to describe the social consequences of the Black Death in Egypt, they cannot really ascribe precise dates because the turning-points in demographic movements and agricultural production cannot be identified exactly. Nor does it make much sense to select a cardinal unit of time such as a century to measure the effects. Instead, the power of historical explanations increases if the historians could say that 'it took ten generations before the economy of Egypt regained its former prosperity'.[17] The introduction of the term 'generations' changes the scale from solar time to social time. It will be seen that the latter is not expressed in terms of fixed units of duration and in this example, will vary with the average life expectancy of a single generation.

Military technology. The dynastic cycles and the periodic waves of conquests by spatially mobile groups of people could be causally related to distinct stages of technological developments related to social structures. It is possible to suggest that the military achievements or failures of successive Chinese empires were due to the mastery of new weapons, new techniques in warfare, a superior technology in iron and steel production, and the social will to apply these advances in knowledge and practices to military usage.[18] Taoist alchemists in China, according to recent historiography, had apparently invented gunpowder as a result of systematic research. From *c.* AD 1000 simple bombs and fire-projectiles were coming into use in China.[19] It was not until the invention of metal-barrel artillery between 1280 and 1320 that the explosive impact of the new chemical invention on warfare and social life found a proper channel of diffusion. Tavernier repeats a seventeenth-century historical tradition in India that gunpowder and guns were first invented by the people of Assam, which then passed on to Pegu and China; 'this is the reason why the discovery is generally ascribed to the Chinese'. The Mughal conqueror of Assam, Mir Jumla, brought back numerous captured iron guns, and the people there could manufacture Western-style gunpowder.[20]

It is not known how or where Tavernier learnt about the tradition. But the use of artillery in Western Asia can be definitely ascribed to the third decade of the fifteenth century. In 1422, Murad II battered the walls of Constantinople with cannon-balls.[21] The overthrow of the Mamluks in Egypt by the Ottoman Turks in 1517, may or may not have been due to the use of field guns by the Turkish forces (see Plate 11). There is no doubt that the Mamluks had given overwhelming importance to the mastery of heavy cavalry manoeuvres, nor that the Ottomans came to be regarded as the acknowledged masters in Asia of the art of gun-casting and the use of artillery.[22] A Yemeni historian Ibn al-Dayba has left a graphic account of the use of firearms by the invading Ottoman forces against the Tahirid sultans (1516):

The troops of the Ottoman sultan carried with them arquebuses which they fired. This is something strange. No one can fight one armed with it without being defeated. It is like a gun, but longer and thinner . . . The bullet sometimes strikes one person, passes right through him, and on to someone else. So both are killed.[23]

The description 'gunpowder empire' would fit not only the Ottomans but also the Mughals, though more in the context of siege warfare rather than the deployment of infantry armed with muskets. In 1665, Tavernier watched an artillery-train pass through a town in Central India. The guns were intended to reinforce Raja Jai Singh, then campaigning against the Marathas in the Deccan. Some of the cannon were forty-eight pounders, others thirty-six, and each gun-carriage was drawn by twenty-four pairs of oxen. An elephant followed the artillery train and whenever the oxen got into difficulty in a bad spot, pushed the gun with his trunk. The artillery-men numbered 2,000 and were all Muslims, with the exception of the gunners who were Europeans.[24]

Much earlier, the appearance of the foot-stirrup in the eighth century had a revolutionary impact on Western warfare, although its diffusion seems to have come from Asia. Gradually, the heavily-armed and armour-clad horsemen became a deadly tactical attack-force. As Jerusalem was lost to the Crusaders (1099), the Muslims no doubt drew their own conclusions on the Frankish style of warfare. The equestrian methods of the Latin knights were later consciously imitated by the Islamic rulers.[25] But the real Eastern counter-part to heavy-armoured cavalry was the mounted archer of the Central Asian steppes. In his description of the prowess of the Turkish horsemen, al-Jahiz admittedly engaged in a certain idealisation, perhaps to mitigate their otherwise evil reputation. It conveys a vivid contemporaneous impression of extraordinary fighting skills. The Turkoman cavalry could use a spear as well as any other heavy lancers, and if a thousand of their horsemen were hard-pressed they would fire all their arrows in a single volley and bring down a similar

Plate 11   Ottoman cannon cast for the Egyptian campaign of 1516–17.

number of enemy horsemen. Few body of men could stand up to such a test. Neither the Iranians nor the bedouins were famous for their mastery of mounted archery. But the Turk could hit a target from the saddle. His horse might be exhausted from being galloped hard and reined, wheeled to the right and left, but the rider went on shooting, firing ten arrows before the enemy could let fly one. Within the range of his bow, to try and run past a Turkish horseman was to court certain death, for he could shoot as accurately behind him as from the front (see Plate 12).[26] It is impossible to dismiss or overlook the close relationship between the means of warfare and the emergence of centralised imperial states in Asia with a life-span long enough to rank as a phenomenon of the *longue durée*. This conclusion, in fact, can be generalised. Technological innovations juxtaposed with the basic social urges created almost by chance, as it were, the ground-work of larger historical movements: examples of the random interacting with the long term.

Four expansionary forces in Asian history. Within the theoretical context of Braudelian *longue durée*, the chronological scheme just presented contains three structural elements. We can clearly identify an expansionary force which manifests itself all through history in one society or another and which has a distinct cyclical rhythm: a political, social, and economic high-pressure zone that steadily fills out over time. Then there was a process of assimilation and consolidation often leading to long periods of social stability, a structural 'steady state'. Finally, we can also see historical phases of general contraction and instability resulting from political and social conflicts with a corresponding closing of the mental doors and windows, a resigned acceptance of the politics of decline. Some historians would describe the period of expansion as the 'A phase' in a long cycle and the period of decline that of the 'B phase'. The combination of the total movements constituted *conjunctures*, or particular surfaces of time separated from their neighbours.[27] During the period from 630 to 1800, four significant expansionary movements profoundly influenced, directed, and shaped the course of Asian history. The first and foremost was the rise and spread of Islam, a truly long-term movement which remains beyond rational explanation. The second force was the unification of China and the expansion of Chinese civilisation in the Far East, Central Asia, and South East Asia. The third phenomenon was less positive in its immediate impact but very catalytic in its effects: this was the periodic migration of war-like nomads from Central Asian pastures in the direction of settled lands in the Middle East, China, and even India. Successive groups of invaders, Turks, Mongols, Mughals, and Manchus, able to utilise their vast herds of rugged steppe horses, overran the heartland of ancient Asian empires and established new and stronger forms of political and social structures in those areas. Finally, European maritime expansion beginning in the fifteenth century with the Iberian voyages of explorations and continuing through the discovery of America and the Cape passage to the Indian Ocean, completely transformed in time the balance of political power in the eastern hemisphere.

The foundation of the Dutch and English East India Companies in 1600–2 was part of a wider economic development which historians describe as the rise of commercial capitalism, leading eventually to the industrial capitalism of the nineteenth century. The technological revolution of this latter period created two unrelated forms of change. On the one hand, the ecological relationship between man, animals, and the physical environment faced potentially radical alteration. For animals life in general, the process of industrialisation, the capacity to produce more food and thereby support a far greater density of population, was both tragic and catastrophic. Furthermore, the advanced technology monopolised by the Western European nations gave rise to a form of political dominance which is known in the vocabulary of current historiography as economic imperialism. The course of Asian and African history entered after 1750 altogether a new period of violent transformations. Asian civilisations did not participate as direct agents in the new developments but they were large recipients of its operations. All four expansionary phases were articulated to those of long-term contraction, of which the decline in Egypt and Syria after 1400 was the most famous and controversial. But even in the Middle East the phenomenal expansion of the Mamluk

Plate 12　Central Asian nomadic horseman shooting backward arrow from the saddle, drawing by Mehmet Siya Galem, fifteenth century.

and Ottoman Turks was a qualitative displacement of the earlier Arab triumph by the Central Asian nomadic factor. Islamic historians were uncertain, at least in the context of the economic decline of Egypt following the Plague, how far Turkish administration was to be held responsible for the continuing depression. When the Mamluk Sultan Barsbai imposed an extra 'cavalry' tax on every household (1434), his clerks in the army bureau counted 'the villages in the whole of the cultivated land in Egypt' and discovered that there were 2,170 villages altogether. An earlier historian al-Musabbihi in his history had given the number of flourishing villages in the fourteenth century as 10,000. Ibn Taghri Birdi concluded this narration with a cryptic remark: 'Note the difference between the two periods, despite the security of the present time and the many conflicts of that time – but the reason is well known and silence is now more comely.'[28]

It will be seen that by giving emphasis to the four broader historical movements of expansion and their mutual interactions, a corresponding weight is placed on the influence of the core areas in which the movements originated: the Middle East, China, Central Asia, and Europe. The scheme seems to leave out the two most important civilisations of Asia in the Indian subcontinent and South East Asia. The historical role of these two zones can be categorised in the chronological structure as being the opposite of the expansionary forces. Sanskritic culture and ways of thought appear to have been turning inwards, towards a greater exploration of the inner meaning and the preservation of the fundamental social and moral values in the ritualistic hierarchy. When confronted with the political ideology of Islam after the establishment of the Delhi sultanate (1206), the Sanskritic militarism could only offer partial and incomplete resistance. Even in South East Asia, the earlier success of Hindu civilisation suffered eclipse at the hands of Buddhist preachers from Sri Lanka. The state systems which the historians are able to reconstruct in the Indian subcontinent, in Java, Sumatra, Burma, Thailand, and Indochina, expanded and declined according to an autonomous and semi-internal rationale whose rhythms cannot be related to the vast geographical topography of Islam, China, and maritime Europe.

The structure and examples of the long term and the stationary. The examples cited so far point towards two classes of historical time. A random event or a series of such events fuses with the latent long-term forces either in a particular society or a geographical unit and then spreads out. The turning-points in the conjuncture can be accurately dated. The second class is made up of movements over very long periods of time (in the technical language of mathematics, the average value expands or contracts over time) but the evolution is not capable of yielding precise dates. Religious devotion, technological changes in the methods of warfare, improvements in the strain of rice seeds, the greater use of astronomical calculations in oceanic navigation, and the accumulation of capital through an intensification of long-distance trade, all these are subjects that obey only imperfectly the cardinal identities of solar time. There was yet another class of the long term for which the ordinal sequences were important but not the average values. The stationary elements of time arranged themselves according to the logic of the situation, fluctuating around a static mean value. The most astonishing feature in the economic history of Asia was the equation between the monsoon winds and the limits of cereal cultivation. The height and the length of the Himalayan mountains played no small role in this process by blocking the path of the icy arctic winds blowing from the north. The distribution of rainfall in the monsoon belts of Asia varied according to a pre-determined and observable pattern within the annual cycle. The average precipitation did not, to the best of our knowledge, display long rising or declining trends during the period under study. In the mental domain, the meaning of terms such as Mahachin, al-Hind, or Ta-shi remained constant, though the actual nuances might vary.

It can be argued that by AD 1000 the social structure of Asian civilisations and the stages of technology associated with them had reached comparative stability. Through a process of diffusion or independent development, the relative levels were almost comparable. In methods of crop-growing, irrigation, the art of metallurgy, and industrial production only small differences existed between the Middle East, India, South East Asia, China, and Japan. The technological stability and the slow progress which did take place were accompanied by a 'steady state' in economic organisation and social institutions. Complicated forms of land-holding and tenurial arrangements co-existed with land markets, law courts, commercial contracts, money and currency, and fiscal systems. Practices changed within these categories which themselves, however, stayed largely invariant. When the great soldier-caliph al-Mu'awiya, after shifting the capital from Kufa to Damascus (661), issued gold and silver money without the emblem of the cross which marked Byzantine coins, it was rejected by the people.[29] The eternal image of value signified by the gold *solidus* of the late Roman empire and its Syriac variant, the *denarius aureus*, survived in the name given to the premier coin of Islam, the gold dinar.[30] The commercial world of Islam did not see proper Islamic coinage before the end of the century, when Caliph ᶜAbd al-Malik reformed the monetary practices. The stationary component of time is seen in many other examples, in the near-constant designs of industrial tools, the shape of artifacts (carts, pottery, patterns of rugs and textiles), food and clothing habits. The collective mental worlds changed least of all and then again almost imperceptibly.

The stationary components of time and the slow-moving changes, reflected in the concept of expanding or declining averages, are very difficult to explain in terms of a unified theory of historical causality.[31] Why should Islamic societies display expansionary time-trends during a period when Sanskritic civilisation was busy closing its mental windows, allowing social absorption of peripheral and marginal people only indirectly and through the back door? There is no fundamental climatic explanation for the stability of the advancing and retreating monsoon winds as annual events. On the other hand, the interaction between economic pressures, such as a chronic state of crisis in food supply or increasing demand for new types of clothing material (cotton), led to a systematic search for new technology and innovations. The best-documented examples are to be found in the Chinese historical sources. The introduction of the early-ripening Champa rice (*c.* 1012) during the Sung period and the spread of raw cotton a little later resulted from rational decisions and their expected benefits on the part of Chinese farmers and bureaucracy.[32] Cotton spinning and weaving did not occur as extensive rural industries in China until after the thirteenth century. In the profile of long time-scales these are infrequent and rare transient breaks which raise the graph of economic development to new and different levels.

Examples of the random. There were of course purely random events, the effects of which stable or retreating societies found difficult, if not impossible, to control. Social disasters following from harvest failures, epidemics, and warfare provoked resigned lamentations from contemporary historians. In al-Maqrizi's history of Egypt covering the period from 1172 to 1250, these irregular cyclical events, with a random expectation, are recorded with chilling precision. In 1172 the field mice increased in such numbers that they destroyed the date plantations and the standing crop of sugar cane. In the same year 'a severe misfortune afflicted all the people of Egypt. For the gold and silver coinage left the country as if never to return.' In 1184 the flood level of the Nile at the Nilometer rose nineteen arms less thirteen fingers and the excessive water caused much damage to the villages; also four ships with 1,300 pilgrims were lost in the Red Sea. In 1192 the Nile once again over-flooded, damaging crops. There was insufficient water in 1194 and the price of wheat rose to famine-levels. In 1201 the crops once again failed and the Nile all but dried up. The terrible and macabre consequences of the famine were only too evident and an estimated total of 220,000 people died within a very short time. In 1224 locusts descended on Iraq, the Jazirah, Diyar-Bakr, and Syria. In 1236 an epidemic struck Egypt and more than 12,000 people died in Cairo and Fustat alone. Suffering caused by military movements, particularly the raids and counter-raids between the Crusaders and the Muslims, was described by al-Maqrizi in greater and harrowing details.[33] The failure of the Nile to reach the right flood level in lower Egypt carried disastrous implications for a much wider region, as the areas around the source of the river probably experienced conditions of severe drought. Famine resulting from harvest variations was so endemic in Chinese life that Huang Liu-hung in his administrative treatise recommended that under such conditions if a few men, driven by hunger and desperation, robbed a family in an isolated village in an attempt to keep alive, they should not be viewed as having committed something really loathsome and atrocious. By a stroke of the pen, the magistrate could show grace to those who deserved pity.[34]

It is worth pointing out that the random character of the above events is only apparent in so far as their actual occurrence could not be accurately predicted in terms of calendrical measurements. When the time marks in the form of intervals (years, months, and so on) are removed, the links in the chain turn out to be completely deterministic. One famine follows another in an inexorable sequence, though separated by an irregular interval of time. The distribution of the chance occurrences embedded in the expression 'Acts of God' was just as systematic as any other planned social action within the control of man. What eluded human knowledge and understanding was the deterministic mechanism which generated the temporal pattern of the random elements in history. Rituals and astrology were both intended to reduce the errors of predicting the future in order to control the present. The Chinese historical work *Sui Shu* (History of the Sui Dynasty 581–617) suggested a specific analysis for social disasters: 'All epidemics, cattle plagues, harvest disasters arise from failure to be in accordance with the laws of Heaven . . . when there is disaster from heaven, there should be set out the Ming T'ang.'[35]

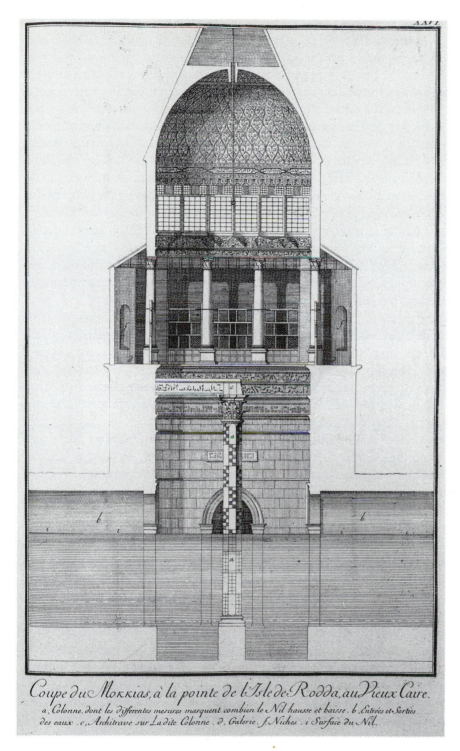

Coupe du Mokkias, à la pointe de l'Isle de Rodda, au Vieux Caire.
a, Colonne, dont les differentes mesures marquent combien le Nil hausse et baisse. b, Entrées et Sorties
des eaux. c, Architrave sur la dite Colonne. d, Galerie. f, Niches. i Surface du Nil.

Plate 13 Nilometer, measuring the level of the annual Nile flood.

Cyclical time. The assumption of deterministic processes was certainly true in the case of the cyclical variations. The conjunction of time associated with regular or irregular cycles, whether these are measured over centuries or much shorter segments of time, has exercised a peculiar fascination for historians of all ages. The debate has not yet ended. But in spite of disagreements certain facts are quite clear. The dynastic cycles in the history of Asia cannot be dismissed as merely spurious features of time. Periods of peace in civilian society alternated with those of disquiet and a general breakdown in order. The large-scale war cycles are the best recorded themes of premodern history. From the eastern Mediterranean to China, the political theory and practices underpinning the state systems were bonded together in a sequence of cyclical movements, punctuated by revolutions. The power and prestige of dynasties, Ibn Khaldun concluded from his reading of history and his knowledge of practical Islamic politics, seemed to obey a rule of four generations, though it may happen that a particular house is wiped out or collapses before this period or outlasts to the fifth and the sixth generations in a state of decay.[36]

As Marcel Granet has pointed out, the Chinese representation of time, coinciding as it did with the concept of 'liturgical' time, incorporated a cyclical structure of varying duration. The annual cycle of seasons had correspondingly larger projections in the history of the dynasties, the individual reigns, or their segments. The promulgation of the calendar, decreed as the inaugural act of a new reign was a decisive ceremony of imperial sovereignty.[37] The operation of the shorter cycles of liturgical time in Chinese social life can be seen in the timing of the annual performance of the ancestor cult within the lineage family, in the rituals of the imperial shrines, and various 'rites de passage' in an individual's life-cycle. After the spring had ended, the emperor could no longer use green robes. All banners and cult objects changed over to red, the symbol of fire, the element of the summer god Yen Ti.[38] Temporal cycles marked economic activities also. Some were irregular, others completely predictable. Favourable harvests seemed to stimulate consumer demand for luxury objects distributed through long-distance trade. There was a distinct cyclical pattern of ten to twenty years associated with commercial prosperity and depression in the Indian Ocean. The price movements through the year for food crops exhibited a deterministic, inverse relationship with the levels of grain stocks, falling sharply as the harvests were gathered and rising gradually thereafter. The same pattern was visible for commercial products sold in a competitive market during the period of active trading.[39]

Cyclical time in history has its own metrics, extending from a fraction of a second measuring heart-beats, to days, weeks, months, and the year. A cycle extending beyond fifty years, however, becomes difficult to recognise, as the size of the sample automatically decreases beyond this point. The dynastic or the war cycles, for example, still continue to elude real historical explanations.

The generating mechanism which systematically gave rise to these long movements remain obscure, and without the fundamental assumption of 'cause-
and-effect' relationships, some historians will find it difficult to accept the fact
that even the well-documented war cycles were not really random events. The
reason for this failure to explain may lie in the fact that each class of events is
studied as an individual phenomenon without taking into account the totality
of the situation. The problem is well described in the 'Reflection Principle' of
set theory, propounded by Zermelo that 'any specifically described model of
set theory can in some way be viewed as a set, that is, as an element of a higher
model of set theory'.[40] An analysis of the structure of time leads us to a strange
conclusion. Historical events are located not only in an order of succession,
measured by solar time, but they are also characterised by quality and power,
which have time and space dimensions. The annual Muslim pilgrimage to
Mecca belonged to a cyclical class of events. Its power to influence millions of
lives and human decisions was unquestionable and extended over very large
areas. That quality remained almost constant in our period of history.

5

The structure of space and society

Concepts of space and time

How the unity of space is established in the mental domain. Time and space are concepts of history which occupy separate but complementary fields of structural analysis. It can be shown that space is a more fundamental, rational, and *a priori* dimension for social action than time-order and succession. The primacy assigned to space in historical understanding takes precedence over actual dates and periods. It is possible, without referring to a specific order of time, to plot on a map of Asia the sites of all the important historical battle-fields, great urban centres, caravan routes, and the commercial emporia in the Indian Ocean. The exercise would reveal a series of pictorial images with a consistency of latent structural relationships, able to separate through an internal logic the ephemeral and the random from the permanent and the systematic. In a way, the internal logic is already identified when the selection is first made: out of a total set of finite events located in the time-dimension, the historian selects only those that are considered 'important', in other words, he endows them with certain quality and power before looking at the implicated structure enfolded in the dimensions of space. The plotting of historical events on a map explicates the unity and the totality of the subject of our thought, action, and life, which subsequent movements had dissolved.[1] This interaction between time and space proves a remarkable feature of 'perceived' time: its discrete and discontinuous nature as opposed to the apparent and perceived continuity of space. The sense of continuity in time is preserved only through the irrational and the abstract concept of the present, which links together the past and the future but which belongs to neither of the two segments.[2] The historical periodisation represents a transformation of time into space, in which discrete entities are arranged into a sequence seemingly without any intervals, and the period thus created appears as equivalent of the concept of 'now' with its own past and future.

In contrast, the unities of space are both real and imaginary. The mind constantly verifies through vision physical obstacles to motion and mobility and thereby marks out an imaginary area of space that is safe and habitable. Such a structure identified in the domain of the mind, through the images of physical space, is established by a dialectical process of recognising ruptures,

112

continuity, neighbourhood, proximity, and the idea of a limit. A spatial surface marked out in this way will withstand distortions without a loss of identity. The movement must not introduce a break or a hole in the surface, which restructures and modifies the fundamental notion of being inside and outside an unbroken unit of space. The geographical unity of the Indian sub-continent, for example, does not depend on its shape or the geomorphological character of its landmass as long as the surrounding sea and the great chain of mountains in the north remain as the limits of the concept. The early Indian Ocean sailors and merchants, whose annual oceanic voyages supplied existential proofs of several kinds, would have known for certain how to interpret the distant, grey silhouette of the Girnar mountain rising from the sea, a signal to the dangerous coastal waters of Gujarat's most prosperous ports.[3] The voyage was practically over and the landfall of India almost within their reach. The experience of the seafarers was matched by that of the Central Asian caravan traders, each year leading huge strings of precious equine cargo across the Himalayan passes.[4] They must have known the exact points when they were inside and outside the geographical and cultural frontiers of Sanskritic civilisation. That awareness would have been qualified by another set of mental registrations telling them that the spiritual limits of Islam traced out a different type of space with its own test of being an insider or outsider.

Three analytical concepts of space: topology, order, and metamorphosis. Once the singularity of a surface is established as a concept, further quantifiers are introduced in its analysis. A plain may stretch out to infinity through the illusion of an ever-receding horizon; it may contain arid lands and fertile corn-fields. It may be seen in Mesopotamia, Central Asia, India, and China. Like a town, a plain remains a plain, wherever it is found, never to be confused with mountains and valleys. The concept of a plain is independent of physical measurement and its limit is fixed by the notion of elevated contours. A secondary sequence of selection creates other forms of unities within the primary category. Geological movements might turn plains into broken ground. The small plains of the eastern Mediterranean in Syria and Palestine were not of the same order as those which continued for many hundreds of miles in northern India. A narrow plain flanked by the desert, created and maintained by a perennial river cannot be compared to one which terminates quite abruptly in snow-capped mountains. The principle of ranking, we must note, has changed here. Instead of looking for the continuity of surface, we are arranging unities by their dispersion. The order of inequalities whether expressed quantitatively or qualitatively fixes the patterns of dispersion. When a tenth-century Arab geographer put to himself a contentious question, how one and the same ocean, the Indian Ocean or the Sea of China, as the Muslims called it, could be divided into eight seas, his answer was simple: ask anyone who has to navigate and sail by sea; he would know the difference between the Persian Gulf and the Red Sea.[5] There is yet another type of spatial unity which depends neither on the notion of proximity-and-limit nor on that of order. This is a unity derived from action or the idea of 'becoming'. The fragment of a plain, valley, or a forest turned into agricultural land and containing a number of dwelling houses becomes a village. A new category denominated in terms of space is created through the combination of two separate rationales, the logic of an operation derived from the social domain and that of the potential quality of space itself.

The rule of formation in this case is complex but the result appears as an integral system. A premodern village generally satisfied some bounded conditions: it did not fall below or outgrow an expected or mean range of physical measurements (whether of population or land area), nor could it give up totally its annual cycle of agricultural activities. If there was a self-regulating mechanism which perpetuated the village as a spatial and social category over time, the rationale of that process also makes it possible to draw precise and specific historical comparisons between one village and another across the map of Asia. Once the category of the village is understood to possess a combination of certain necessary and sufficient qualities, all other villages can be derived from that starting position.[6] Every local community of Asia, all the major civilisations of the Indian Ocean, possessed mental linkages between social forms and the structure of space. The tripartite physical resolution of space, we can say, is a bounded surface, an ordered sequence, and the metamorphosis of given categories, all of which found a ramified echo in human imagination that was no less real than the reality itself.[7]

Social identities through space

The role of birth-place. The images of space inscribed for the people of the *ancien régime*, whether in Asia or Europe, their strongest and most tangible sense of collective identities. Filtered through experience and memories of experience situated in the past and the present, these perceptions provided at once the basis of concerted social action and an awareness of the limits enclosing the individual will and its larger aggregate projection. Place names created equivalences or morphisms between units of space and sets of people, and a simple mapping relation such as the principle of birth replicated the categories over time without loss of identities. The mandate exercised by the place of birth to locate an individual or a group of people on the grids of comparative civilisation was overwhelmingly strong, and yet there were complex alternatives as well. When Umar and his bedouin military followers established Muslim rule over the Aramaic-speaking people of Iraq, the Arabs discerned among their conquered subjects a superior attitude that was an infallible sign of orderly, ancient, and prosperous agricultural life, in which a man identified himself by his place of origin rather than tribal affiliation. The caliph, it was said, urged the Arabs to study their own lineage and avoid the example of the Nabateans of lower Mesopotamia; these were people who on being asked would reply that they came from such and such a village. Of course, the Anbats or the Iraqis were not granted a prophet as the Arabs were, but that did not alter the fact that a Nabati provided taxes for the benefit of Gentiles and Muslims alike.[8] There was a certain irony in the fact that by the time al-Muqaddasi came to write his great work on the world of Islam in the late tenth century, to be an Arab was to become synonymous with an Arabic-speaking, urbanised, trans-geographical culture, which looked upon the wandering desert-life with envious condescension.

The anthropomorphism of space in historical writings. The anthropomorphism of spatial configurations in al-Muqaddasi's thoughts however followed classic time-less forms. The association between the stereotypes of human nature and cartographic frontiers remained without explanation, but the imagery persisted. The province of Kirman in eastern Iran was singled out by him as a region which had the sweetest dates and the most cringing people. Infidels, sugar-candy, and musk distinguished Sind (an area of India where the Muslims would encounter their first political confrontation with Sanskritic civilisation). The region most favoured with blessings, pious men, ascetics and shrines, was that of Syria. The province where there were more devotees, scholars of the Qur'an, wealth, commerce, grain, and special products was Misr, the land held by its people as the gift of the Nile. The Maghreb had the unfortunate distinction of having the roughest, heaviest, and the most deceitful people but it was a province which also contained the largest number of towns and the most extensive areas.[9] To this a Maghrebi would probably have replied, in much the same way as Ibn Battuta did later, that the kinds of things which the Egyptians ate along with their bread would not even be looked at in the Maghreb. The Egyptians lived on a diet of lentils and chickpeas, cooked in enormous cauldrons on industrial scale. In north Africa, there was an abundance of meat, dairy products, and green vegetables.[10] The scheme of contrasted values and the opposition of qualities associated with particular types of geography exercised a strange fascination in the premodern worlds of the Mediterranean and the Indian Ocean. Critical men with enquiring minds would struggle all through the centuries with a central paradox. Theories of climate, environment, water supplies, and the recursive rhythms of aridity seemed to explain the juxtapositions of contradictions which escaped and baffled human reasoning and understanding.

Contradictions in spatial identities: the case of the desert. Perhaps the most inexplicable contradiction of all among Islamic theorists was the perpetual oscillation between the sedentarisation of the pastoral people and the qualified renomadisation of the settled societies. It was not easy to understand how a historical group of bedouins, the camel nomads of the true desert, who possessed the strongest sense of collective identities based on descent, would nevertheless one day forget their genealogies, mingle with Persians and non-Arab people, and be wiped out as tribes; all memories of 'asabiya', group feeling, lost in love of comforts and luxuries. Once settled, 'they take the greatest pride in the preparation of food and fine cuisine, in the use of varied splendid clothes of silk and brocade and other [fine materials], in the construction of even higher buildings and towers, in elaborate furnishings for the buildings, and the most intensive cultivation of crafts in actuality.'[11] The settlement of nomadic Arab tribes on the fringes of settled land began long before the birth of Islam. The Bakarite Arabs had given their name to the Syrian town of Diyar Bakr and its surrounding province. The members of the great confederacy of Tamim spread out along the shore of the Persian Gulf as far as Shatt al-Arab, while the Kalb had settled in the chain of oases in Wadi Sirhan and in the depression of al-Jawf. Internal conflicts and attacks from stronger external enemies made the semi-settled and the nomadic tribes alike seek spatial strongholds. A pre-Islamic poet spoke with pride of the Taghlib who alone had no shelter in their land and protected themselves solely by military valour. The Lukhaiz could flee from their land along the seashore to the inner uplands if a force from India threatened them. The Kalb retreated into the rocky heights of black basalt rocks where no mounted force could go. The Ghassan fought even the mighty legions and squadrons of Rome.[12]

But at the margin of civilisation, in the no-man's land between the oasis and the desert, corn and date growers would abandon their cultivation periodically and follow the example of the pastoral overlords in a nomadic way of life. The exact reason escapes the historian's scrutiny. The experience of Alois Musil at the beginning of the present century suggests that the rapacity of the government tax-collectors often caused the 'fellahin' (peasants) to flee from their irrigated settlements in the Euphrates and join the tribes engaged in raising sheep and goats in the desert.[13] Power struggles among the great Bedouin tribes of inner Arabia could result in attacks on the oasis-dwellers who were themselves allied to different opposing parties in the desert. The civil war was fought with savage determination: wells were blocked up or poisoned, mature palm groves cut down in an effort to ruin the foundation of the oasis economy.[14] In his history of Egypt, Maqrizi recorded the news from the Hijaz for the year 612 AH (AD 1216): Sharif Qatadah, the Amir of Mecca, attacked Medina, the Prophet's City, and cut down many palm trees. The Amir of Medina was in Syria with al-Malik al-Adil at the time. With an army furnished by al-Adil, the Amir set out to recover Medina but died on the way. His nephew Jumaz ibn-Qasim took command of the forces and captured Mecca. The fleeing Sharif was besieged in Yanbu[c].[15] Armed semi-tribal fellahin, fortified in high-walled garden houses were able to hold out and resist the bedouin attacks. The less strong generally had no alternative to submission

Plate 14 Irrigated oasis in the desert, Tihama, date-palms and banana-trees.

and ruination.[16] If the civil war continued in the desert, the inhabitants of a flourishing oasis settlement such as al-Jawf (Dumat al-Jandal) at the head of the Wadi Sirhan would be effectively cut off from the settled world by enemies prowling outside the fortifications. Their herds would soon die and the caravan trade come to a standstill. Only dates, grains, and vegetables raised in the oasis gardens sustained the beleaguered citizens.[17] The example of Mesopotamia itself after the Central Asian conquests of the thirteenth century was a perpetual reminder of how the irrigational investments of 2,000 years could be written off in a catastrophic long-cycle of decline. Above all, no one wholly succeeded in explaining why urbanised societies with all the advantages of their sophisticated, civilised life, would collapse politically before the onslaught of nomadic warriors. The prosperity of the irrigated agriculture of Iraq, especially in the Diyala plains, had begun to shrink in the late Abbasid period after the Revolt of the Zanj (868–83).[18] The withdrawal of sedentary life which almost reached the environs of Baghdad itself during the Ilkhanid period was as close to the essential as Turco-Semitic breakdown mirrored in the capture of the caliphate seat and the murder of the spiritual leader of Islam by the infidel Hulegu Beg in 1258.[19]

The role of travel and geographical descriptions in spatial identities. In a world starved of exact and reliable information, disbelief and incredulity at physical

Plate 15 Sand dunes, near the Empty Quarter, Rub al-Khali.

manifestations not seen, heard, or experienced could be partially overcome by first-hand geographical descriptions. Even the sober and practical Chinese who were apt to think that the Middle Kingdom occupied the centre of the earth adopted a prudent attitude when confronted with Master Ma Tsung-tao's (Ma Huan's) account of the Indian Ocean countries, which the Arabic-speaking linguist had visited (1413–33) in the course of the famous Ming maritime voyages organised by the Grand Eunuch Cheng Ho. The much-travelled author of *Ying-yai sheng-lan* himself admitted that in his youth when

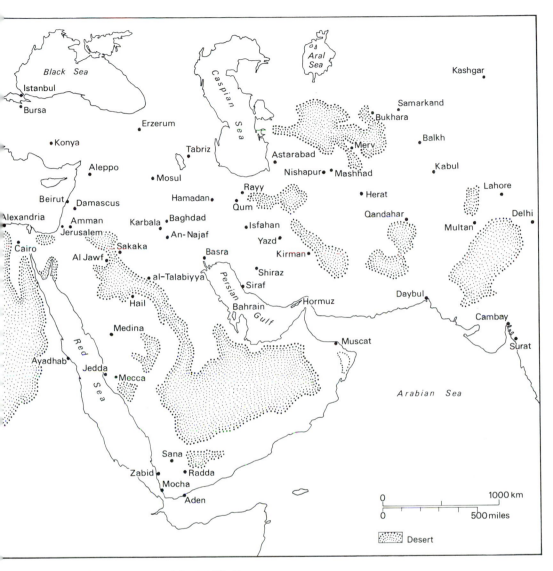

Map 6 Historical map of the Middle East.

he had looked at a book describing the seasons, climate, topography, and the people of distant oceans, he had asked himself in some surprise, 'How can there be such dissimilarities in the world?'[20] Lack of knowledge only partially explains the disbelief and the feeling of marvel. An acutely charged sensibility towards space exaggerated the scheme of physical differences, which seemed to lie in waiting just beyond the recognised limits of the familiar world. Distances appeared magnified, given the pace of human mobility as measured on a space-time scale. The memory of a long journey by land and sea reverberated

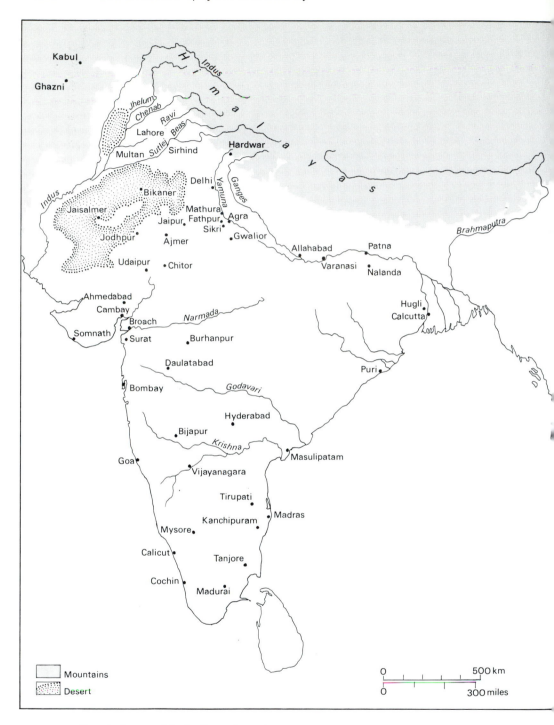

Map 7 Historical map of the Indian subcontinent.

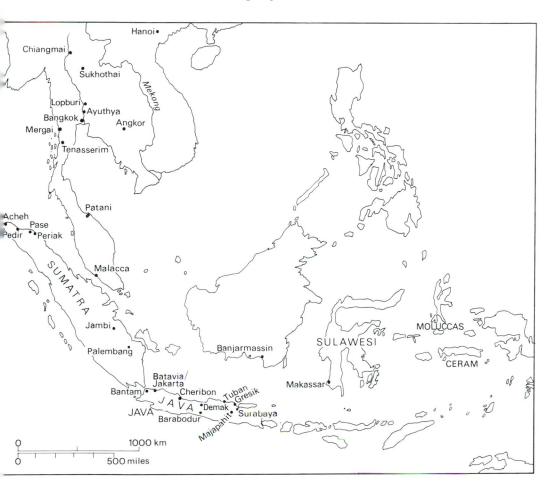

Map 8 Historical map of South East Asia.

against the outer shell of collective knowledge, eventually adding to its growth after the initial mental resistance to the assimilation of new information had been overcome.

The sea stories told by Buzurg Ibn Shahriyar in his *Incredible Book of the Indian Ocean* were set in the trans-oceanic world of Siraf in the tenth century, a period when Muslim ship-captains and merchants were already sailing on regular though hazardous voyages to India, South East Asia, and China. The mixture of fantasy, day-dreams, and sober narratives in the *Incredible Book* might have come from the remembrances of Ulysses himself. In the historical works of al-Masudi and al-Muqaddasi on the other hand, written at about the same time, the imaginative elements of space were severely kept out of sight, and the text al-Idrisi (*c.* AD 1099/1100–62) composed as a commentary on his planisphere known as the *Book of Roger* epitomised contemporaneous scientific geography. However, travellers' tales which claimed to describe the real world were another matter. Even Ibn Battuta was suspected of having invented his Indian experiences. In the times of the Merinid Sultan Abu Inan, Ibn Khaldun tells us, a shaykh from Tangier went on a long journey to the East, visiting Iraq, the Yemen, and India; he lived at the court of the sultan of Delhi who employed him as a Malikite judge. What he had to report on India was so fantastic that whispers went round doubting the shaykh's veracity. Ibn Khaldun's own scepticism was dismissed by the celebrated Wazir Faris b. Wadrar with the argument that knowledge confined and limited by man's immediate environment should not be a test of the truth. The minister humorously compared the young aspiring statesman, as Ibn Khaldun then was, with the son of another imprisoned wazir. The boy had grown up in prison in company with his father and asked him one day about the meat he was eating. On being told that is was mutton and on having a sheep described in detail, he replied, 'Father, you mean, it looks like a rat.'[21]

In the landscape of daydreams where the public opinion of the day located them, the trans-continental journey of a Hsuan-tsang or Marco Polo, the 'Rihla' of the Malikite jurist of Tangier, and the peregrinations of the Portuguese adventurer Fernao Mendes Pinto created two kinds of unities.[22] One was the unity of discourse, the other the unity of abstract topological space. Within a single discourse, the dispersion of objects, people, social systems, and individual responses to images of space were all brought together by an ongoing epistemology in the first place, which led to the appearance later of a new order in knowledge. The discourse suggested the unity of space in the manner of a line drawn on an empty background. The geographical contours of Ibn Battuta's 'Rihla' would trace an implicit unity of possibilities in the states of affairs, of which the ancient linkage between the Mediterranean lands and the Indian Ocean was not the least important. People in the Maghreb, in the Spice Islands of the Eastern Archipelago and the rice plains of Greater China, could discover for themselves in the discourse (assuming literacy) not only the existence of sea lanes and caravan routes that held together the commercial unity of the old world but also how exogenous societies organised and derived their civilisational identities under another sky. Of course, traders and merchants living inside their own communal shells like colonies of hermit crabs, had long profited from the trans-oceanic highways. But they refrained, as if by mutual agreement, from any explicit intellectual diffusion of the specialised knowledge available readily at their command.

The objects, which they knew other people fashioned in far-away places, were divine gifts fit to be carried by land and sea. It was not for merchants to explain, much less to speculate on, the abstract unity formed by silk, porcelain, and tea between a great Far Eastern civilisation, warmed by the tropical sun, and the inhabitants of a cold Western hemisphere. All three, as we know, were commodities, great products of civilisations, which could be placed very precisely in the historical interstices of space, time, and socio-economic trans-

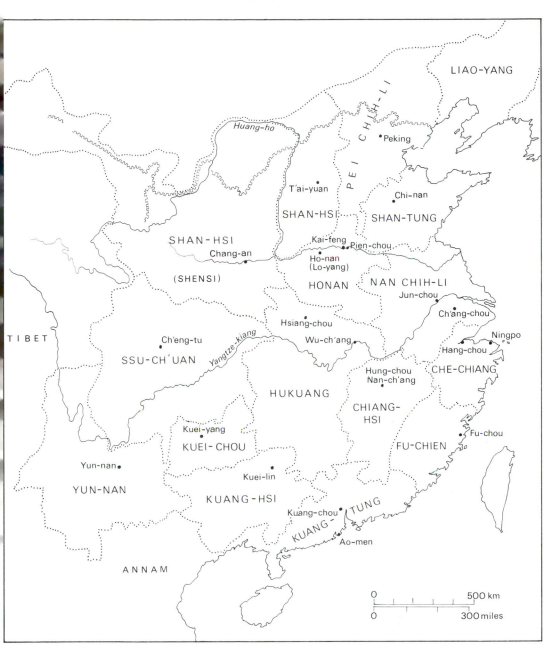

Map 9 Historical map of China.

formations. Human hands and mind changed beyond recognition the filament
spun by the silkworm, the leaves of the camellia, and the fossil-age white clay
kaolin, creating new forms, new substances with mysterious inner resonance.
Like tiny droplets of sounds echoing inside the sealed vase of unconscious time,

the sensibilities conveyed by these three most exotic objects of social usage and long-distance trade expanded in radial patterns of additive growth from a distant golden centre in the Celestial Empire. But the mental reverberations of the lost daydreams are no longer understood. The historian asks in vain: by what process of social adaptation, sensory adjustment, addictive habit, and aesthetic appreciation did the Eastern and Western man learn to drink a warming infusion served in a vessel which made a compulsive appeal to the visions of objective beauty? One end of the continuum was occupied by a strong infusion dispensed in rough earthenware cups to poorer people who could afford nothing better; at the other end lay the delicate perfumed beverage of rare cultivation and the entire ritualised ceremonies belonging to the select acolytes. Each group could be mapped by tea and porcelain on to a structure of space and time. Premodern merchants knew the contours of this abstract cartography because they were instrumental in drawing its first tracings. But the cracks made in the historical geology by the first appearance of the event and its subsequent discourse remained unexplored. Our sources are not of course altogether silent. The chinaware of Yueh and Yo were green and increased the natural colour of the tea, an eighth-century Chinese text on tea recorded in its commentary on porcelain kilns. Hsing ware being white gave the tea a red colour. The cups of Shouchou were yellow and turned tea into a purple hue, while in the brown ware of Hungchou tea looked black, an unsuitable colour.[23] The commentary merely relocated the undecidability of the first-order logic in the original discourse at a different level: why this particular sequence of preferred colours in tea rather than another? When the Sung tea-masters initiated the fashion of powdered tea, blue or dark brown bowls held a finer appeal; the light white porcelain of the Ming period complemented the method of making tea by infusion.[24]

Geographical descriptions of far-away lands and exotic people were both popular and necessary in the order of knowledge. Why then the innuendos, the accusing finger of disbelief pointing at the trans-continental traveller? The front page of Marco Polo's *Description of the World* addressed itself directly to an unspoken question: 'All the people who are pleased and wish to know the different generations of men and the diversities of the different regions and lands of the world, the diversities also of the kingdoms and provinces and regions of all parts of the east . . . take then this book and have it read.' But there were some things in the book which 'Master Marc Pol' did not see himself; he heard them from men fit to be cited and of truth. Things seen and those heard were clearly distinguished in the text.[25] Here was a possible answer. Even works of personal travel demanded in the name of geographical science that the totality of the Eurasian space and its topological boundaries should not be left without a description. The confusion resulting from this practice was unacceptable to those who had first-hand knowledge of Asia and other distant places. As Alexander Hamilton pointed out (1727) with acid frankness, referring to the popular description of the Indian Ocean by Reverend John Ovington (1696), 'I know his greatest Travels were on Maps, and the Knowledge he had of the Countries, any Way remote from the afore-mentioned Places, was the Accounts he gathered from common Report'.[26]

Iconographic themes and geographical theories of social identities. The con-temporaneous sense of unease which an analysis of the spatial and human geography aroused also stemmed from another dimension of the social psychology. The Islamic scholarly works passed on from one hand to another long-held textual views that climate influenced, if it did not entirely govern, societies and civilisations. In the latitudinal depiction of the earth, derived from Greek geography (especially the work of Ptolemy), seven imaginary zones appeared as divisions of the cultivated regions extending from the south to the north. The people of the middle zones were temperate in their physique, character, and in their ways of life. They had all the natural conditions necess-ary for a civilised life, such as economic production, houses, crafts, sciences, political leadership, and royal authority. They also possessed manifestations of prophecy, religious groups, dynasties, laws, and everything else that was temperate. Arabs, Greeks, Indians, and the Chinese were among the people of the middle zone for whom historical information was available. But human beings found beyond the southern edge of the civilised zones were closer to the dumb animals than to rational beings.[27] The iconographic themes equating social practices with climatic determinants existed simultaneously alongside a large body of practical information separating the myths from the reality and the stereotype from the particular. All the same, a subterranean feeling of psychological insecurity remained. What would happen to these theories and the moral basis of comparisons, external dominance, and even self-identities, if actual geographical observations gathered by respectable and authoritative men suggested, demonstrated, and even proved that the human form was no different, that societies were perfectly capable, and that civilisations could flourish and grow to maturity in a random latitudinal distribution of space?

The iconographic identities were necessary if only to preserve and re-create the abstract limits of space. It is noticeable that geographical works in China, the area most isolated from the rest of the Indian Ocean, tended to be more descriptive, neutral, and less theoretical or mythological than similar treatises in India and the Middle East. Drawings contained in the 'Illustrated Record of Strange Countries' (*c.* 1430), a work probably inspired by the early Ming Indian Ocean voyages, accurately depicted the African zebra and the Arab dress and features of the man leading the animal on a rope.[28] Ma Huan's own account of the Indian Ocean was severely factual by any standards. If the early Ming voyages organised by Cheng-ho (1403–33) partially reinforced Chinese curiosity about India and the Middle East, the arrival of the Far Eastern junks with the rich and precious products of China caused a sensation in the Islamic world. Ibn Taghri Birdi records the obvious interest of Barsbai, the Mamluk sultan of Egypt, when the Amir of Mecca and the Controller of Jedda reported in 1432 that a number of Chinese junks had come to the seaports of India and two of these were actually at anchor in Aden. Because of the prevailing political disturbances in the Yemen, the goods brought by the junks, porcelain, silk, musk, and so on were not landed there. The Chinese captains had requested permission to come up to Jedda. The request was granted and the sultan asked his officials to treat the visitors with honour.[29]

In the West, by the middle of the sixteenth century, an epistemological break was about to occur, after a period of actual contacts with Asia, Africa, and the New World, so that it was no longer necessary to rely on speculation of an inherited science to draw the physical boundaries of the earth. The insight gained from a closer knowledge of Asian societies and people partially dissolved the previous mental perceptions of socio-spatial topology, replacing them with new forms. An official of the English East India Company living in the great Mughal port of Surat in 1672 addressed a long letter to the Directors at home, in which he attempted to describe the way of life practised by the Indians and Europeans alike in the East. His aim was to remove the doubt expressed by 'my other good friends' in England that by observing the custom of the heathen Indians and listening to the subtle insinuations of the Jesuit priests he might have forgotten God and the principles in which he was brought up. The conclusion established the theoretical existence of two separate sets of interpretations on socio-spatial topology: the view point of an outsider from 'inside' and that of the outsider of the 'inside' from outside:

Whereas some think that the customs of the Indians are brutish and of such evil example to Christians that it is an occasion of their neglect of divine worship, I rather find the contrary, for the several sorts of the Indians are so strict to the Rules of their Religion in keeping their set times of prayer and fasting and other ceremonies that it is a provocation to the Christians to do the like in their way, so that there is an emulation between the Indians and us, who shall serve God most and best.[30]

Observations made in concrete reference frames and collected together within a new discourse of social-space by unprejudiced scrutiny were now to be substituted for the generalised knowledge of the past, creating a different kind of science. In 1677, John Fryer, a contemporary of our above author, travelled by sea from Surat to Bandar Abbas. The sense of euphoria that greeted a newly-arrived traveller in Persia expressed itself vividly in Fryer's disbelief how 300 leagues' space could make such a difference. He had left behind a sullen, melancholy, and sun-burnt nation and was now offered in exchange open, cheerful, and clear-complexioned mankind.[31] A century later, the emerging discourse had almost reached the margins of a new level of abstraction. Parallel to the objective information-gathering expeditions to the remote corners of the globe, alongside scientific map-making and voyages of new oceanic navigation, another corpus of theoretical literature would appear. Robert Orme, the historian of the British military transactions in India, once more returned to the ancient themes in his *Historical Fragments of the Mogul Empire* (1782). People born under a sun too fierce for physical exertion could be expected to earn their scanty livelihood in the easiest of labours. Spinning and weaving, light sedentary occupations by definition, were widely prevalent in India. The province of Bengal was the most fertile of any in the universe, more so than Egypt. But here people depended more on the elements than on themselves for subsistence.[32] Was the rice land of Bengal so carefully levelled, terraced, and surrounded by dykes also a gift of nature? There was no answer to the question in the rational discourse of the late eighteenth century, a discourse that would continue to unfold itself for another century and a half. That rationality, by placing European geography and Western civilisation at the centre of a scientific reasoning, could only make sense of the external units of space, the animal kingdom, exogenous forms of human society, and man's behaviour and conduct, through an evolutionary timechart, in which both the beast and the savage would learn to recognise themselves for what they really were and escape extinction, if not extermination.

The physical structures of space

The role of observation. The perceptions, we have studied so far, attempted to classify space by mapping its metrics, quality, and invariance on to society, groups of people, and their characteristics in one-to-one relations. There were unities and disunities in the structure of space seen against the totality of human response in the history of premodern Asia, which formed themselves at a more fundamental level. The biological clock or the pacemaker which lies buried in the unconscious depth of the human brain and the mind synchronises itself with space and real time through mechanical instruments. Astronomical movements were observed regularly from remote times in history, recorded and homogenised through mathematical calculations and, linked up with a perpetual memory, were able to replicate categories of objects and abstract concepts within the totality of social practices. The fixed images of space, expressed in varying durations of time, some permanent, others lasting only a moment, derived their historical power from an ever-present interaction between the sky, water, and land.

Nothing symbolised the awesome power of nature as much as the plasma of energy seen in a flash of lightning, which vanished from sight even before its thunder was heard. The tropical storms of the Indian Ocean represented extreme danger to ships caught far out at sea. In May 1652, a large, richly-laden ship belonging to the sultan of Golconda sailed from the Persian Gulf, on its way back to Masulipatam. Near the Maldive Islands, it ran into the onsetting monsoon and a severe storm. The ship was struck by lightning three times. The first lightning fell on the foremast, splitting it from top to bottom; then it ran along the deck, killing three sailors. The second strike killed two more men on the deck. The third strike occurred just as the cook came up to announce dinner to the officers. The lightning singed his hair and made a small burn in the stomach.[33] The cook was almost certainly wearing a copper amulet round the waist (as a protection against disease), which caught the electrical charge.

The climate and climatic changes. For the majority of the people living in the regions around the Indian Ocean the thunder storm was a divine gift. The appearance of the annual south-west monsoon winds, accompanied by heavy lightning and huge formations of cumulus clouds, carried an unambiguous message. The parched earth, baked by an overhead sun from April to June, was about to be revitalised by the rains. The haunting fear of starvation and death which faced men and animals alike throughout the lands bordering the great ocean could only lift through a miracle of nature revealing itself in an endless cycle of repetitive time. The wind directions, the rate of oceanic evaporation, variations in temperature, and the pressure gradients developing in the upper atmosphere determined the pattern of annual precipitation, which in turn fixed the limits of cultivation in Asia and the rhythm of economic life. As early as the first century AD a Greek geographical work on the Indian Ocean accurately described the reversing cycles of winds and the sailing routes of ships trading with India. Al-Idrisi had similar comments on the Sea of India and China: it was a sea greatly disturbed by strong winds and was subject to heavy rains. The seasonal winds blew in one direction for six months and in the opposite for another six.[34] The monsoon had enabled ships to navigate the maritime passage between Mesopotamia and India from the Sumerian and Babylonian times. However, the global climate of which the monsoon winds and the seasonal rains were a manifestation created much earlier conditions favourable for the growth of settled cereal-based farming over areas which appear to have been more extensive than in the period following the foundation of Islam.

Archaeological evidence unearthed at the urban sites of the Indus Valley civilisation points towards a greater rainfall, more vegetation, and the presence of animals which live in the tropical habitat: tigers, rhinoceroses, elephants, and water-buffalo. The area of Sind where the great city of Mohenjo-Daro once stood (*c.* 2500–1750 BC) is described as a treeless, arid, heat-furnace in all our historical sources, although the flood-plains of the river Indus were still able in the seventeenth century to produce an abundance of wheat, rice, and vegetables.[35] It is possible that progressive deforestation in the region gradually created the conditions of extreme aridity seen later and the true desert may have advanced in many parts of the western India as a result of ecological changes. There is reason to believe, from the distribution of fossilised pollens, tree rings, and the stratified remains of pine, elms, and oak trees in the Kashmir valley that the 0° centigrade January isotherm extended at a more northerly latitude in the third millennium BC representing a warmer and more moist climate in northern China, India, and the countries of the 'Fertile Crescent' in the Middle East. Snowfalls were rarely recorded in central China at that period. Rice could be sown a whole month earlier, and the bamboo grew more extensively to the north of the Yellow River than at a later period.[36]

Primeval flooding. The climatic evidence seems to suggest that the highest point of the inter-glacial warming phase in which we live today was reached some 5,000 years ago. The melting of the northern glaciers and the polar ice sheets, together with a period of 'over-developed' monsoon rains, could have produced extensive flooding, giving rise to the memory and the legends of a primeval flood in the Near East. The Islamic historian Baladhuri has graphic descriptions of cataclysmic flooding in lower Mesopotamia just before the Muslim conquest, inundations which changed the regional landscape and created the Great Swamp between the later towns of Kufa and Basra, extending more than two hundred miles in length and fifty miles in breadth. During the reign of the Sasanian King Kubadh I, at the end of the fourth century, the Tigris breached its banks and flooded the low-lying lands. The dykes had been left unattended for many years. The irrigation works were restored under Anushirawan and the land was returned to cultivation. But a few years after Muhammad's removal to Medina (*c.* 629), when Khusraw Parwiz was in power, the Euphrates and the Tigris once again rose to unprecedented levels and broke through the breaches. The blind terror which only a river in uncontrollable flood can arouse among settled people is still evident in the text. The king took personal charge of the flood control and spared neither treasure nor the lives of his men in the effort to hold back the rivers: 'Indeed, he crucified in one day forty dyke-men at a certain breach and yet was unable to master the flood.' The Great Swamp, 'al-Batiha', had come to stay for good, 'the breaches came in all the embankments, for none gave heed', the Iranian landowning noblemen, the 'Dihkans', were powerless to repair the dykes, so great was the damage; the swamps lengthened and widened in all directions year by year.[37]

The climatic mechanism of the monsoons. The alternating long cycles of desiccation and the abundance of rains operated over a time scale admittedly measured in several millennia. The same climatic instability generating the long cycles, through variations in the earth's orbit and the polar tilt, also influenced the shorter near-random weather fluctuations over much of the Indian Ocean and Central Asia. The quantity, distribution, and the incidence of rainfall had a vital bearing on the physical survival of entire communities and the economic prosperity of large empires. The two reversing systems of Asian monsoons, the south-west and the north-east winds which controlled the distribution of precipitation, acted as the single most important agent of an unintentional, unconscious unification for societies sharing little else in common. The local wind systems themselves were part of a single global climate: the circumpolar vortex, operating both in the northern and southern hemisphere, caused by the interaction between the earth's axial rotation and the differential thermal pressure gradients in the atmosphere. The meteorological observations made during the last century or so seem to show that the variations in the timing and the depth of the critical summer monsoons were a function of the westerly winds to the north of the Himalayan mountain barrier. The amount of winter snow and ice in turn affected the westerlies. The 'Southern Oscillation' leading to alternating low and high pressure over the Indonesian Archipelago and the Indian Ocean in some years and the Easter Islands and south east Pacific in others completed its whole cyclical movements in 2.5 years, though it could take as long as 5–7 years. Furthermore, when a trough developed in the circumpolar vortex at the longitudes of the Indian subcontinent in the northern hemisphere, the timing of the south west monsoon winds was accelerated.[38] It is possible that the historical changes in the fortunes of Asian agriculture, all the systematic determinants of food supply, could be partly accounted for by the latitudinal variations in the westerly winds regulating the levels of rainfall.

The conclusion is controversial and derived from observational correlations.[39] The theorem of falsifiability, however, can be easily applied to the major zones of agricultural production throughout the Indian Ocean for the entire period of our study. There is no doubt that climatic instability as manifested in disastrous flooding and prolonged droughts (over two to three years) exercised a relentless pressure against demographic movements and the stability of social investments in land. The space–settlement ratio, whether seen as the population density or the intensity of food production, was subject to a high degree of short-term fluctuations. Famines and the high rate of mortality resulting from unpredictable food shortages remained a never-to-be forgotten scourge for the peoples of Asia extending from the Arabian peninsula to China. All the same, the risks attached to settled agriculture were outweighed by the other incontrovertible fact of Asian history: the enormous and perpetual capacity of the land to grow plants for the subsistence of man and animals. The high civilisations of the Indian Ocean, all the material achievements and possibilities of human ingenuity, traced their final source to the dry- and wet-land farming symbolised as it were by two plants of life, wheat and rice.

Plains: the topological boundaries of space and settled agriculture

Two ecologies: crop growing and pastoralism. Social habits associated with the consumption of bread and rice followed closely the structure of the inhabited and cultivated space. The topological boundaries of settlements and their order on the other hand were created and sustained by the generic division of Asian agriculture into cold-weather dry crop-growing zones and those growing crops dependent on high ambient temperature, humidity, and water supply. There was yet a third variation on the ecological theme. Land unsuitable for the cultivation of major food crops had the capacity to grow grass and a number of hardy shrubs, on which domesticated herbivorous animals could feed. The typology of such pasture-grounds incorporated a whole spectrum of landscapes as variable as sand-deserts, mountain-slopes high above the snow-line, and the vast plains of Central Asia. All three classifications, based on historical motifs written by millet, wheat, rice, and scant-grass, can be seen and compared on a map of the Indian Ocean drawn by an index of plant productivity. The index takes into account four climatic elements which largely determine the natural growth of plants. It is not surprising that the equatorial band with its high incidence of rainfall and the largest constant heat-budget has the highest index rating. Intensive wet-crop agriculture was possible in the north-western tip of Madagascar, the Konkan-Malabar coast of India, and the Malayan-Indonesian Archipelago, although sizeable concentration of population in our period of study was only to be found in the Malabar, Java, Bali, and parts of Sumatra. The presence of dense tropical forests and undergrowth, as for example found in the Malayan peninsula, and the inherent fragility of the regional soil probably impeded land-clearance and the spread of intensive crop-production. It would seem that the best conditions for the development of settled agriculture and the formation of large territorial units into organised states were found, not in the zones of the highest plant productivity, but in those with a much lower index-value. Much of the Indian subcontinent, China, Japan, and parts of the eastern and southern Africa, fall into this category. The unities of human civilisations around and beyond the Indian Ocean made possible by common farming techniques, by the cultivation of common cereals and food plants, may or may not have been visible to the members of those communities in the distant past. To the present-day historians however, these transient unities present an uncomfortably high profile and throw out a dangerous challenge of explication. The structure of historical relationships, of social habits and traditions, the symbolism of food in religious thought, the distinctions between the sacred and the profane, economic production, and political control need to be placed, many would argue, in their respective dimensions of time and space by the twin theories of evolution and diffusion.

Land utilisation and water control. It was perhaps no accident that the ancient civilisations of the world should have arisen in the river valleys of the Nile, the Euphrates-Tigris in Mesopotamia, and the Indus in India, with similar but much later developments in the regions around the Yangtze delta and the Pearl River in China. The thriving agricultural population, the urban centres, and the high material standards of life, so amply recorded in the archaeological remains and historical accounts, can all be traced back to a combination of equitable climate, ample supply of water, and fertile land. The transformation of waste land into productive soil was not a spontaneous condition of nature. The rural geography of Egypt, Mesopotamia, Iran, India, South East Asia, and China was man-made. When the Zoroastrian God in the ancient Iranian text Vendidad was asked where was the earth most gladdened, he replied: wherever most grain was produced, and grass and fruit-bearing trees, wherever barren land was turned into watered fields and marshes drained dry. The earth mourned when it was sterile.[40] Besides the early nucleated areas in the river valleys, throughout the 'Fertile Crescent' in the Middle East, the northern regions of India and China, and the riparian plains of Java, Indochina, and Thailand, conditions were favourable for the emergence of an intensive agricultural technology centred on the cultivation of cereals. The dietary habits of the Indian Ocean people largely coincided with the two main geographical divisions. The lines of wheat cultivation which stretched from the west to the east in a huge arching band gradually reached their southern limits around the latitude 23.5° N., the extreme point of the sun's annual northward movement from the equator. To the south and the east of longitude 75° E. the wet-rice terraces dominated the rural landscape. The twin topologies created by wheat and rice also determined in subtle ways who was inside and outside a bread-eating society and a rice-consuming culture. The food habits were by no means exclusive, though the cognitive overtones were unmistakable. As Ma Huang's descriptions cross the straits of Malacca and Sunda and reach the Arabian Sea, the exotic products of the country are carefully noted together with the grains sold in the local markets. When the 'treasure-ships' from the Middle Kingdom arrived in the Yemeni ports people came to exchange their frankincense, aloes, myrrh, and benzoin for porcelain, silk, and hemp. This was a part of the Arabian peninsula where there was no lack of such things as husked and unhusked rice, wheat, pulse, glutinous millet, and all kinds of vegetables.[41] We know from other historical sources that rice reached the arid lands of the Middle East from Egypt, Iraq, and India. There were also people living in the Maldive-Laccadive Islands who were so isolated that they knew 'nothing about rice and grain' and lived on fish and shrimps.[42]

To identify a hidden unity of economic life and the alternatives facing societies in general across the entire civilisational water-sheds of the Indian

Ocean by the contours of wheat and rice is to pay a singular tribute to the notions of geographical determinism. However, the historical response to a specific problem, the utilisation of land for growing crops, can be seen in better perspective if we remember that for the greater majority of the agricultural population of Asia, water was without question a vital element of physical survival. It was available only seasonally and then only in limited quantities. Throughout the dry-farming zones, whether farmers practised the winter wheat, barley, and legume cultivation or the summer planting of millet, cotton, and sugar-cane, the average levels of precipitation remained uncertain and the incidence of rainfall even more so. If the land was to create wealth for every one in the social spectrum, peasants, artisans, merchants, and the ruling elites, the vital private and public duty which could neither be ignored nor forgotten was how to tame the powers of the great perennial rivers and reach the precious water below ground. Success in large-scale food production and the cultivation of industrial crops implied, besides the use of the plough harnessed to the traction power of the draught oxen, efficient storage, distribution, and management of water. The technology of extensive irrigational works was more complicated than that of water-raising equipment. But neither could be separated from the other. Canals, wells, and the controlled use of annually flooding rivers represented a long-drawn investment in land without which the civilisations of Asia would have shared their environment largely with animals in the manner of primeval Africa. A spectacular example of the combined technology of crop-growing and artificial irrigation is to be seen in the island of Bali in the Indonesian archipelago. Constructed on steep mountain sides the rice-terraces of Bali were among the most productive in the region and had been in operation well before AD 1000. Success in rice growing on these tiny plots of land depended on the excavation and maintenance of elaborate irrigation conduits and underground tunnels, often running over long distances.[43] The subterranean canals of Persia and the Yemen (known as 'qanats' and 'ghayls' respectively) called for engineering skills no less demanding than the Balinese. These irrigation works made it just possible to support crop production in an otherwise arid topography.[44]

In northern China careful management of the sowing cycle and flood control could secure a regular annual crop of wheat and sorghum. The technique was known to the Chinese agricultural experts and outlined by the famous Christian statesman of the Ming period, Hsu Kuang-ch'i (1562–1633) in his agronomic encyclopaedia.[45] Hydraulic knowledge obviously needed to be integrated with the right selection of crops. The use of the plough in the extensive agriculture of the Indian Ocean and the supply of oxen on the other hand established a secondary relationship between water supply and the technique of crop production because of the need for grazing and fodder. Well before our historical period, the settled communities of the Indian Ocean were locked into a grid-system with intersecting points made up by the optimum quantity of cultivable land, the animal-powered plough, irrigational works, the rate of demographic replication, and the entire external superstructure of exchange and consumption.[46]

The contemporary images of space: Ibn Jubayr and Tavernier. The topology of space defined by cereal farming extended from the flood plains of the Nile, across the Fertile Crescent to northern India, and thence to South East Asia and China. Many contemporary descriptions illuminate the moods and feelings of travellers journeying through unfamiliar landscapes enriched by man's effort to grow corn and rice. The images of space come through clearly in Ibn Jubayr's account of the pilgrimage to Mecca. On his way back to the Mediterranean through the Basra-Damascus route, the Andalusian minister and the caravan he was travelling with halted in May 1183 at a village called al-Qantara (The Bridge). It was surrounded by wide and fertile fields, which were irrigated by water drawn from the Euphrates through a canal. The beautiful village was shaded by the foliage of fruit trees. 'Over a branch of the Euphrates at this place, there is a large bridge, arched so that one must climb and descend it, that gives its name to the village . . . We found that in these regions the barley is reaped at this time, which is the middle of May.'[47] Jean Baptiste Tavernier, following the annual trade caravans from the great port of Surat to the imperial city Agra, talks about the countryside, as he found it in the middle of the seventeenth century. The distance between Burhanpur and the chintz-manufacturing town of Sironj was one hundred Indian leagues, which were reckoned to be longer than those used in the earlier stages of the route, for a cart took just over an hour to cover one league. In these 100 leagues the traveller passed through fertile fields of wheat and rice for whole days. The sight would remind him of the endless wheat fields of La Beauce in the Loire. Forests and waste scrub land were generally rare in this part of central India and the caravan route to Agra beyond Sironj traversed, according to Tavernier, similar cultivated tracts with closely-spaced villages.[48]

A contemporary comparison between Gujarat and Persia: John Fryer. An explicit comparative analysis of Asian geography was not common among our contemporary observers. John Fryer, the English physician at the East India Company's Factory in Surat, was an exception. In December 1679 Fryer was called out to attend a colleague taken ill at Broach, a town some fifty miles away to the north. A compulsive observer and writer, the curious doctor at once committed his impressions to paper. Fryer had just returned from a visit to Isfahan, the spectacular capital of Safavid Persia. It is clear that the impressions brought back by him formed into a contrasting mosaic of incredible richness and power, a backdrop to the long Indian experience. The journey to Broach gave him the opportunity to make a direct comparison between the topography of Gujarat and that of Iran. The empty, desolate land-

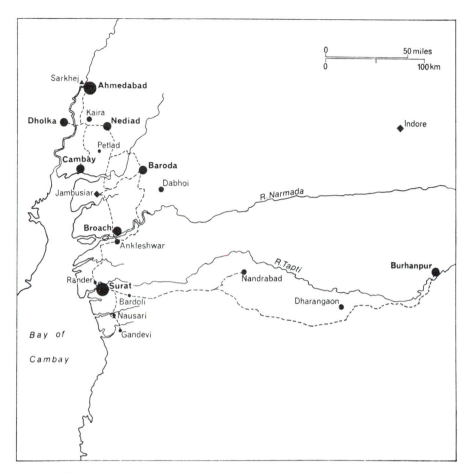

Map 10 Gujarat: textile towns *c.* 1700.

scape of rocks, sand, and salt deposits through which the road from the Gulf
port approached the oasis of Zayanda-Rud appeared as overwhelming as the
exquisite lapidarian sight of Isfahan itself. An eloquent tribute to the memory
of Shah Abbas, the creator and real architect of the refurbished capital, was
composed by Fryer.

The magnificently-arched buzzars, which form the noble square to the palaces; the
stately rows of sycamores, which the world cannot parallel, the glorious summer-
houses, and pleasant gardens, the stupendous bridges, sumptuous temples [mosques],
the religious convents, the colleges for the professors of astronomy, are so many lasting pyramides and monuments of his fame.[49]

The short journey from Surat to Broach could be made either by land or sea,
by taking a boat from Swally Marine to the river Narmada. Fryer set out on
horseback with a retinue of guards and a carriage in case riding proved

Plate 16 Step-well or 'baoli' near Broach, Gujarat, India (see p. 137).

Plate 17 The river-front in Broach, leading to the sea (see p. 138).

tiring.[50] The flat plains around Surat were among one of the most intensively cultivated and commercialised regions in Gujarat. Broach itself led the weaving and processing of cotton cloth, which was carried on in all the neighbouring villages and small towns. Fryer was at once struck by the visual difference between the thinly-populated Iranian plateau and the busy industrial and agricultural scene in southern Gujarat. On Persian roads there were neither carts, nor coaches and wains. Here in India the way was clogged and jammed with 'cafilas' of oxen and camels. Teams of bullocks in pairs of eight, twelve, and sixteen, were yoked to heavy waggons loaded with merchandise. In Persia, the caravans moved in all seasons of the year with escorts who would guide them through mountain passes infested with bandits. In India, the commercial traffic had strict seasonal routines because of the rains, and armed mounted guards accompanied the convoys. But here protection was needed against marauding soldiers from the regular army itself and the outlawed irregular cavalry squadrons. The most striking contrast between the two areas was the frequent sight of broad rivers and great tanks of water in India and their absence in Persia. Fryer saw huge underground storage tanks and wells accessed by long flights of stone stairways, off which opened cool large resting chambers. These wells were the famous 'baolis' of Gujarat with ornate galleries and vaulted skylights (see Plate 16), built as charitable deeds by princes and wealthy merchants.[51] Fryer noticed that water was raised from level to level by *norias*, earthenware pots attached to a geared wheel, or in huge leather buckets worked by oxen. The irrigated garden-land made 'one thing you are more sure here than there, and that is provisions of all sorts, in almost every village, which stand thick hereabouts'. The cavalcade had set out at dawn, and passing through flourishing fields of standing corn and tobacco plantations, halted in a grove of toddy-palms as the day grew hot. When the crows came to roost in the evening, wheeling about in great flocks, the party was on its way again. At midnight, they reached the little weaving town of Ankleswar, where they slept the night in the house belonging to the Company's Broker. At sunrise next day, the march was resumed. A cafila of five hundred oxen went past, laden with salt for the inland province. The country was all 'champaign' and delicate meadows. Beyond the plains and the broad, swift, deep river rose the whitewashed houses of Broach (see Plate 17). Large sea-going vessels were brought right up to the town by skilled pilots with cargo of corn and salt. The locally-grown wheat and cotton contributed in no small measure to the industrial and commercial prosperity of the area, so evident in this period of Mughal rule in Gujarat. Only the previous September, Fryer observed with professional humour, the annual Red Sea Fleet had returned from the hajj voyage laden with 'Religion and Pestilence', a Mughal version of Sebastian Brand's *Narrenschiff* (*Stultifera Navis*, 1497), an imagery that seemed to have persisted in European mental vision.[52] But more important than transporting 'Frenzied Fools', the Fleet also brought back five million rupees' worth of treasure in gold and silver. The river of precious metals flowing between the 'caja forte' of Casa de Contratacion in Sevilla and the Mughal minthouse in Surat continued to inject vast financial liquidity to the agrarian-based and at the same time highly commercialised economies of both India and China.

Nomads, arid lands, and the desert

The nomads in Asian history. The visions of plenty which the corn fields of northern India conveyed was perceived and reflected upon by a wandering warrior-prince 'on the run' from his enemies occupying Samarkand. Zahir al-Din Muhammad Babar, Padshah Ghazi, the charismatic founder of the Mughal empire in India, thought that the physical geography of Hindustan had few visual attractions to offer compared with his native homeland in the valley of Zarafshan. There was nothing in India equal to the sight of poplar and plane trees, or apples, pears, peaches, and apricots growing in walled gardens. It was, however, a large country, rich, populous and able to produce an abundance of crops without seemingly artificial irrigation. The years of exile spent in Kabul he would describe, on looking back after his victory over Ibrahim Lodi (1526), as a harsh school of poverty.[53] The taxes gathered from the land, the number of skilled artisans, and the size of the cultivated areas provided all the means for building a great Turkoman empire in India. The recovery of the Timurid inheritance in Samarkand and Bukhara was a mere dream. For more than a thousand years, to the steppe people of inner Asia and the pastoralists of trans-Oxiana, the rice and bread baskets of China and India held out an extravagant attraction which is difficult to comprehend and unravel. Neither the deserts, the fearsome Gobi, nor the Great Walls succeeded in containing the nomads beyond China's open frontiers in the north. India found only partial protection in the icy-heights of the Himalayas. The desert and the mountain without doubt symbolised in contemporaneous mind the spatial antithesis to sedentary life and even to civilisation itself. The Muslim urban sensibility of the fourteenth century would view the nomad and the desert through a very special reasoning. The Bedouin has no need to plan his vegetable garden, or take into account the direction from which the wind blows and construct water channels. In the desert the direction of the wind is not important, it comes from all sides. Only when people could not move as in a city that the wind turned bad. Towns built by Arabs with few exceptions quickly fall into ruin. The sites of al-Kufa and al-Basra in lower Iraq were chosen by the early Muslim conquerors with the sole thought of providing pastures for their camels and the proximity of the garrison-towns to the caravan routes. The 'Badawin' did not have to care about supplies of corn.[54] Al-Muqaddasi had already expressed his own opinion of the neighbourhood of Kufa: 'the heat is very great, and the air foul and oppressive. There is a perfect pest of mosquitoes and life is a misery. Their food is fish, their drink is hot water, and their nights a torture.'[55]

By this time advanced urban decay already marked many famous towns and cities of al-Iraq. The oasis agriculture of the central Euphrates-Tigris and the Diyala plains, the National Bank of Babylonia and the Islamic caliphate, were on their way back to the desert as the descendants of Chingiz Khan planned fresh onslaughts in Asia, this time in the direction of India. In 1321 Sultan Ghiyath al-Din Tughluq hurriedly built a great fortified town to the east of sprawling Delhi in case the Mongols once again broke through to the plains watered by the river Jamuna. A poor Turk by origin, the sultan had arrived in India as a groom in the service of a rich merchant and distinguished himself as a cavalry officer later. An inscription in the mosque at Multan described him as the victor of twenty-nine battles against the Tartar invaders.[56] The terror and loathing aroused by the nomadic style of mobile warfare among the settled and regular imperial soldiers bred its own counter-terror. Mongol prisoners of war died terrible and cruel deaths at the hands of their captors.[57] But even in captivity, as an Islamic portrait-painter saw with sensitive eyes, the valour of 'blood' remained defiant (see Plate 18). The army of Hindustan did succeed in containing the Mongol invasions, until Amir Timur and his steppe cavalry sacked Delhi in 1398, some would say with surprising ease. Soon the

Tughluq urban-fortress was abandoned and lay in utter ruin, as the political gravitation of the empire moved away from Old Delhi. By night travellers encamped on the main caravan road to Agra had their rest disturbed by lions roaring under the massive ramparts, thirty feet thick. By day, the occasional shepherd led his flock through the deserted streets in search of grass, watched by eagles and vultures soaring high above the roofless halls, fallen masonry, and blind arches pointing to the sky like finger-less hands. In popular memory, the curse of the Sufi saint reverberated in disembodied anger. When nomads came to graze their animals over the land where royal palaces and cities had once stood, civilisation found the final plenitude of death. Political injustice, violence, and religious impiety still occupied extreme positions. There was no appeal against punishment and retribution from the victim and the transgressor alike.

Central Asian pastures and the desert. All through our period, the mounted nomads had appeared among the settled people and cultivated fields from both the steppe and the desert. In the vast spaces of Inner Asia, the Turkoman or the Mongol rider learnt early his total dependence on the horse, which in turn needed pasture for grazing. Chingiz Khan, the destroyer of the finest Islamic cities of Oxiana, would recall (as recorded in the *Secret History of the Mongols*) his friendship with Bo'orcu, when as young boys they had both ridden out for three nights in pursuit of thieves who had stolen eight horses, the isabella geldings. The other boy put aside his leather milk-pail and the task of milking the mares, made Chingiz change his straw-yellow horse with hairless tail for a blue-white horse with a black stripe on its backbone and riding his own swift pale-yellow mount, he and Chingiz found the stolen animals and drove them back.[58] However, the pastures over which Chingiz Khan and his companion of youth rode lay far away, beyond the twin rivers, Syr Darya and Amu Darya, to the north of the Heavenly Mountains, the T'ien Shan, and the Zungarian Depression and they were too distant for most Asian societies to pay much attention. The desert was entirely different. It was almost at the very door step of the settled civilisation. The Great Gobi, the Takla Makan, the Thar desert of Sind, the Iranian salt desert, the Nafud and the Syrian desert, were like so many seas which finally merged with that great ocean of sand in the west, the Sahara. The horizon of settled farming was fixed by two separate types of limits, the real sea and the desert. The caravan cities which supported and fostered the transcontinental overland trade can be presented as the mirror-images of the Indian Ocean ports and harbours situated not on the sea-shores but around the edges of the deserts. In fact, the Arabic word 'sahil' meaning 'coast' was often applied to the Tunisian plains and to the country south-west of the Sahara.[59] The analogy helps to place in historical perspective another feature of the desert which it shared with the sea. Nomads make a living out of the desert in much the same way that in-shore and off-shore

Plate 18 Portrait of a Mongol prince as prisoner, Herat, late fifteenth century (see p. 139).

fishermen had learnt to live off the sea. Both obtained food from their natural habitat not only for themselves but also for others. The seafaring people of the Indian Ocean, especially the inward-looking communities of fishermen, constituted a very distinctive group, generally avoided by those who knew only the sown land. The people of the sea, however, did not view their environment as a place of exaggerated danger or of pastime.[60] The nomads living in and around the arid land and the true desert similarly adopted through long experience an outlook which completely integrated their ecology to the social life. To the Arabs, the desert appeared not, as it did to the hajj pilgrims, as a place whence a man was reborn on leaving it but as a plain covered with familiar centuries-old landmarks, countless grazing grounds, camping sites, water springs, and sites of battles won and lost.[61]

There were reasons for the ingrained fear which the settled people felt towards the desert. In the recorded history of mankind, over long periods of time, the desert has seldom retreated before favourable climatic conditions. The movement was mostly in the opposite direction. The desert has inexorably advanced at the expense of cultivation. The long-term degradation of the environment in semi-arid areas brought about by careless or ignorant agricultural practices was palpably visible. Once wars, epidemics, or even prolonged years of drought interrupted the regular rhythm of cultivation, the arable land quickly deteriorated; the fierce summer winds and torrential rains devastated the top soil. In the region of the 'Dead Cities' of Northern Syria, the lost earth is measured to a height of two metres or so. The very desolation of the desert pointed to another historical phenomenon. The periodic incursions of the warrior tribes mounted on camels and horses brought bloodshed, military conflicts, and enslavement for many peaceful and prosperous communities which had forgotten the rules of total war. The common belief that towns and civilisation did not need the nomads but that the bedouins needed them all the time underlined in reality a double dependence, not fully acknowledged by our historian.[62] It is true that the bedouins could not live without dates, bread, coffee, sugar, and clothing materials, just as the settled people needed the nomads for milk, wool, and hides. When the Ruwala tribe, belonging to the great ʿAnaza Confederacy, started on their annual northern migration towards the Syrian uplands, having spent the winter and spring in the oasis and pastures of northern Hijaz around the Nafud, food supplies often ran out and hungry camels stopped giving milk. A starving bedouin woman would say, despairingly, as the military leaders decided to avoid a dangerous oasis-town where flour and barley could have been procured, 'We are looking for bread, but the country where there is no bread is not sweet'.[63] Even the Amir's younger son Saud in the princely tents went without bread and cooked food for days on end. The bedouins were convinced, Alois Musil recorded, that the fellahin were obliged to supply them with grain. It was heard daily that if they did not do so of their free will, the 'badawin' should take from the fella whatever could be found. The rapacity towards the cultivator was in strange conrast to the hospitality of the tent to those who were without adequate sustenance. In the evening women short of food would cry before the mistress of a well-provided tent: 'Give me supper little sister. Give me supper.' When they received a ration of wheat, they carried it to the hungry children and the sick.[64]

The dependence of the settled societies on nomads was not quite of the same order of immediate urgency. It was all the same insistently pervasive, just below the visible surface of social structure. In the western Indian Ocean, the nomadic communities were the real and ultimate source of draught animals which provided traction power for the plough, an indispensable technological feature of settled agriculture. Economic calculations and the balance between grazing and arable land fixed the proportions of fodder and edible crops; the productive patterns had evolved in Asia in such a way as to maximise the returns from marginal areas unsuited to continuous human habitation. In this process the nomads fulfilled a crucial role in their ability to rear domesticated animals in the desert and on land suffering from extreme aridity. A similar argument also applied to the carriage of goods over long distances. It is inconceivable that the great urban centres and industrialised countryside in India or the Middle East could have provided many items of daily necessities, not to speak of the luxury articles of civilised life, without inter-regional and even transcontinental trade. Nomads in the last analysis were the indirect carriers and guardians of the caravan trade.

Spatial and historical images of the desert. However, it is far from easy to find a proper definition or a single description of the desert and its inhabitants. This is a fact that has bred a number of geographical paradoxes. Storms without rain, plants without leaves, springs without source, and rivers that lead nowhere, all these metaphors applied to the desert, even though they told only half-truths.[65] Not all deserts in our spatial study had the same historical features. The Gobi and the Takla Makan belonged to a class different from the Sind, Syrian, and the Arabian deserts. Camel caravans regularly crossed the vast empty wastes of the Great Gobi in journeys that stretched over many thousands of miles. The Takla Makan was impassable across its main breadth. Compared to the Central Asian deserts, the Sind and the Middle Eastern deserts were busy cross-roads of civilisation. Their proximity to the major centres of political power and economic activity provided tangible opportunities to the nomadic tribes for exchanging their animals, camels, horses, donkeys, and sheep for the products of settled society. Magnificent urban emporia sprang up in the Rajasthan desert, where the rich trans-continental caravan merchants built luxurious mansions and warehouses for their business. The periodic fairs in western Rajasthan, selling thoroughbred camels, horses, and even prized breeds of cattle were famous events in the annual calendar of commercial activity. The inhabitants of Deir as-Zor, a town on the upper reaches of the river Euphrates, carried on an active trade with the semi-fellahin and even the Bedouins. They bought wool, made it into carpets and blankets and sold the products to the nomads and the farmers. Rafts were also loaded up with the locally-grown wheat and barley together with the imported industrial goods of the Mediterranean. The traders went downstream once a year, offering their wares to the different settlements on the river.[66] In lower Iraq, the town of al-Najaf, which housed the golden-domed mausoleum of Ali and many religious houses and convents, lay at the end of the desert road from Medina passing through the awesome landscape of southern Nafud. The traveller marching with the Baghdad caravan entered the town through Bab al-Hadra and walking through the bazaars of green-grocers, cooks, butchers, tailors, and perfumers, he would come to the inner Bab al-Hadra and the public buildings beautifully decorated with the blue and green enamelled tiles of Qashan.[67] In the earlier stages of the journey, at Samira, Faid, and al-Thaʿlabiya, the Badawin gathered in large numbers, selling camels, sheep, ghi, and curdled milk to the pilgrims in exchange for coarse cotton cloth, which was imported in hugh quantities from India and sold at the hajj fair. In 1184 when Ibn Jubayr passed through al-Thaʿlabiya members of the caravan maddened by thirst fought so desperately for water that seven people were crushed to death in the stampede: 'May God pity and pardon them'.[68]

Pilgrims, oasis-dwellers and the Bedouins. When Ibn Battuta travelled on the Medina to al-Najaf route in November 1326 the Amir al-Hajj, 'Pahlawan' Muhammad al-Hawih, the noble 'strongman' of Mosul, commanding the caravan and its military guards, entered Faid in battle formation, as two brother-Amirs of the Arʿabs, Fayyad and Hiyar, were encamped there with their mounted bedouin warriors. However, on this occasion the Amirs offered their protection to the caravan, no doubt in return for a substantial officially arranged indemnity.[69] Nothing illustrated better the weight of the reciprocal relationship between the desert and the settled oasis cultivation of the Middle East than the regular exactions of these indemnities which the fellahin paid to the Arabs in wheat, barley, and dates. The bedouin political and military strength seemed to have been created and sustained by two striking paradoxes of the desert. It rained frequently during the winter and spring around the edges of the true desert and even in the Nafud the 'raza', a tree-like bush with long flexible boughs, grew on the crests of the sand dunes, 'giving [them] the appearance of a huge garden'.[70] The replenished water springs and the desert shrubs and grasses which the periodic rains brought forth enabled the migrating tribes to maintain the size of their herds. The collective animal wealth also acted as an instrument of war. Perhaps, the most terrible paradox of all seen in the desert-life of the bedouins was the 'ghazw' or the raids mounted by the bitterly divided tribes. In these deadly encounters, the aspiring tribal leaders and fighters learnt the skills of survival, showing off their ability to handle camels and shoot accurately. They also unknowingly proved a statistical law: the game of chance which ended in a zero gain. Camels taken in prize during a successful 'ghazw' sooner of later were made even by other surprise enemy raids. But the bloodshed and the constant actions kept up a relentless pressure on military leadership. For a party of Shammar camel riders in the Nafud to be surprised by a superior force of the Ruwalas, their traditional enemies, was to invite certain death, at times of general hostilities. Alois Musil was an eye-witness to one such encounter during the civil war of 1909. The victorious Ruwalas killed a number of Shammars in the first charge, and then allowed the rest of the victims to surrender, but took their mounts, provisions, and even water. When the Shammar asked to be shot on the spot rather than left to die of thirst in the waterless Nafud, the Ruwalas replied that they would not blacken their faces by killing unarmed men. From this engagement not a single Shammar returned to his clan. On hearing about the affair, the Amir of the Ruwala, An-Nuri Ibn Shalan, merely said that the sandy waste of the Nafud must have its sacrifice.[71]

The association between the desert and Islam certainly existed. It was neither direct nor simple. The religious orthodoxy of the ordinary Bedouin tribesmen could not be taken for granted as a constant through time.[72] The term 'Ar^cab' as applied to the nomadic clansmen who regularly migrated across the peninsula between the Red Sea, Iraq, and Syria, carried a message of fear for the settled farmers and oasis-cultivators. Even the tribes engaged in raising mainly donkeys and sheep were considered as being of separate genealogy and identity from the true Bedouins, who were their official protectors receiving financial indemnity in return.[73] The permanent irrigated farms near the Euphrates sometimes called 'al-Qasr' resembled a quadrangular fortress, their high walls pierced by loop-holes and strengthened by corner bastions.[74] Large oasis settlements such as Sakakah, al-Jawf, and even al-Qara would have many such fortified garden-dwellings containing several wells for irrigating the date-palms, figs, apricots, oranges, lemons, and grape-vines. The daily task of drawing water from the deep wells was excessively laborious and performed by both men and beasts pulling the leather-buckets. Periodically, an irrigated garden-settlement in the desert would be abandoned, even though permanent sources of water continued to be available. The ruins of al-Hadita visited by Musil contained a garden measuring 903 metres in length and 482 in breadth. It had been irrigated by an aqueduct built of black stones and reported to have come from al-Azraq.[75] The survey of the ruins interested Prince an-Nuri who thought that it might be possible to resettle the garden with cultivators brought from the Hawran. It is significant that the construction of a blockhouse was also mentioned during the conversation.

The inhabitants of an oasis such as Sakakah could not carry on their cultivation without an established political understanding with the stronger bedouin tribes. Many of the settlers would accompany the Ruwalas migrating towards Damascus in the spring and work on the Syrian farms in order to earn money. The cash income was spent on buying clothing, wheat, barley, and no doubt also coffee and sugar. The bedouins of the inner desert and the fringe areas guaranteed the protection of caravans and the personal safety of the merchants who traded both in transport animals and consumer goods. These services naturally were not free. In troubled times, if a party of neutral merchants, from the Iraqi or Syrian border towns, whose protectors and clients included groups at war, sold arms and munitions to the wrong side, their goods were subject to seizure by the opposite party. Such an operation was actually recorded and described in detail. A group of merchants from al-Mashad had supplied guns and cartridges to the enemies of the Ruwalas in the oasis of Sakakah. Should we not sell arms to the Krese, they pleaded, how would they treat us? The peace messages were ignored and armed fighters mounted on horses galloped off to intercept the camels as soon as the scouts detected the train. However, the Sleib, the raisers of sheep, responsible for the safe-conduct of the caravan, hid the camels in a depression taking care not to leave any tracks in the sand. The raiders returned empty-handed.[76] The most prestigious and perhaps financially lucrative was the protection of the three annual hajj caravans going to Mecca from Cairo, Damascus, and Baghdad. Al-Jaziri, a sixteenth-century religious official in Cairo, stated (*c.* 1565) that the Tarabin had the exclusive responsibility for the resting places and roads in east-central Sinai between Nakhl and al-Ga^c, while the tribes of the Wuhaydat and Rutaymat guarded the mountain pass above the gulf of Aqabah. The records of the St Catherine Monastery in the Sinai (of the Orthodox Church) also confirm that various bedouin tribes were in the pay of the establishment in semi-protective functions.[77] An English merchant writing a little later than al-Jaziri has left another detailed description of the entire sequence of the great Cairo pilgrim caravan setting out on its journey along the northern shore of the Red Sea. The Amir al-Hajj had a force of 400 soldiers, mounted on camels and horses, to guard the convoy, and six pieces of ordnance drawn by twelve camels to impress the Arabs and celebrate the safe entry to Mecca. The captain was guided by eight experienced Arab trackers who marched ahead. But beyond Nakhl he put his hand in his purse and distributed presents, garments, and turbans on bedouin leaders who bound themselves to protect the caravan and, according to the desert law, promised to make restitution if any one was robbed. The number of people who travelled in the Cairo, Damascus, and Baghdad caravans to Mecca could not have been under 200,000, according to this account.[78] To outsiders the inhabitants of the desert areas signalled danger. The insiders themselves lived in perpetual fear of the strong in their own ecology. What the Bedouins thought of the townsmen, however, was not always recorded.

Plate 19 Rural scene in Bengal.

Sea

The Indian Ocean trade as an agent of spatial unity. The cultivated fields, the desert, and the mountains, each perceived category established real historical unities through our tripartite theoretical elements of space, topology, order, and the human transformation of the geography. The Indian Ocean itself created a different kind of unity through long-distance trade and the great urban emporia. The free port and the trading city of caravan routes represented the essence of many different civilisations, a distillation of a multitude of geographical images. The mountainous coasts of southern China would have been the dominant views associated with Canton, Amoy, and other ports of Kwangtung and Fukien. Both the coast-line and the urban spatial projections in China were of an entirely separate order from that of the Indian subcontinent. The voyage to the commercial emporium of Hugli, 150 miles upstream, would have begun among vast sandbanks and half submerged forests of mangrove trees, where the turbulent estuarial waters of the river Ganges met the huge tidal waves of the Bay of Bengal. The journey would terminate among the flat, soft landscape of rice fields surrounded by tall coconut trees. The skylines of Canton and Hugli were pierced by buildings of totally dissimilar architectural forms and idioms. The soaring roof of the Chinese pavilion-styled houses symbolised the Celestial Empire as much as the Indo-Islamic architecture of power with its arched gateways, domes, cupolas, minarets, and latticed balconies. In Canton and Hugli many splendid examples of public buildings were to be seen and both cities lived mainly from the profits of maritime trade. The collective symbols of regional architectural expressions were the superstructure of the state and the society. The humble dwellings of the poor, using mud walls, bamboo matting, and thatch roofs, brought the countryside deep inside the urban environment. The basic shape and the building material of farm houses differed little between south China and Bengal. The visual contrasts and the awareness of their inner meaning strengthened the identity of each civilisation which considered itself as being separate from the others in the Indian Ocean, and at the same time added to the sense of belonging to a common league. Above all, trade which flowed through the caravan towns, major seaports, and primate cities fashioned an immense chain of economic and cultural interdependence that was as integral and indivisible as the monsoon rains fusing together the common elements of rice and wheat farming.

PART II

6

Social identities I: food and drink

General theory

Food, clothing, and housing as social signifiers. Food and drink together with clothing and housing constitute the ground-floor of material life, a level of history that changes only slowly over time. This famous conclusion of Fernand Braudel, which lies at the very heart of his theory of the *longue durée*, is so compulsively obvious, so immediately accessible that it runs the risk of being taken for granted by historians.[1] The age-old adage that people do not live by bread alone merely reconfirms, through the perverse logic of a contradiction, the physiology of starvation, the delights and excesses of a 'high table', and the infinite gradations of narcotic stimuli found in alcoholic and infused beverages that relieve both hunger and the monotony of daily life. Asian armies did not march on empty stomachs. Offerings of food pleased the divine pantheon, or so it was believed. The ritualised replication of meals offered to the dead, enjoyed during their mortal lives, underlined further the distinction between the sacred and the profane in food preparations and serving. A Han noblewoman, who died (168+ BC) shortly after eating a large quantity of musk melons, was buried with forty-eight bamboo cases and fifty-one ceramic vessels containing food in formal ceremonial presentation.[2] Even in monotheistic Islam the distribution of food to the devout and the indigent outside the mosque and the shrine remained a fundamental part of religious duty. The spirit of piety in such offerings is idealised in a most evocative manner by the early seventeenth-century Mughal painter Mir Hashim. One of his miniatures depicts a blind pilgrim obtaining food at the famous 'dargah' of the Khwaja Sahib Muin al-Din Chisti at Ajmer. The artist catches with great sensitivity the social nuances of the occasion in the careful and even elaborate arrangement of the bread, rice, confectionery, and the fruits in lacquered trays and enamelled dishes; in the expression and the clothing of the religious disciples serving the food; in the serene presence of the resting dog, symbolising the tolerance of the humble and the intolerable (see Plate 20).[3]

The way people ate, dressed, and housed themselves revealed at once their personal identities and social affiliations. The historic image of Asia as a separate and distinct continent, it was stated earlier, was a composite one rooted in the different cultural traditions of the Middle East, India, South East

151

Asia, and China. How did people recognise one another as members of other civilisations? The symbolic space of unfamiliar material life must have had social pointers. When an Arab or a Persian ship, let us say one of those described by the Sirafi shipmaster Buzurg ibn Shahriyar (*c*. 900–53), left the Gulf and sailed for a voyage to India, Java, and China, its first port of call would have been Quilon or Calicut on the Malabar coast.[4] At the level of everyday life, the Islamic crew and the merchants who sailed in the ship would have had to ask themselves three questions as they went ashore. What kind of food are we going to eat during our stay at the Malabar port? And then, what kind of ceremonial clothes shall we wear when paying a formal visit to the shahbandar or the king? Finally, where were the visitors usually housed as they conducted their temporary business in town? Contemporary historical sources which describe the Indian Ocean civilisations in comparative terms leave little doubt that food habits, articles of clothing, and housing were considered as the three fundamental material expressions of other more profound senses of collective social identities derived from religion and moral systems. The symbolism of clothing even in the form of a remembered personal response could signal memories of cataclysmic past events. Thus the famous Umayyad general al-Hajjaj, the victor over the anti-caliphs of Mecca (AD 692) and the 'hardest arrow' in the armoury of caliph ʿAbd al-Malik, inaugurated his iron rule over Iraq (694) by entering the mosque at Kufa, where he ascended the steps of the *minbar* (pulpit) and removing the red silk headcloth that covered his face, proclaimed, 'I am the son of majesty, the one who mounts the high places, when I take off my turban, you know who I am.'[5] The slaughter of the faithful by al-Hajjaj even within the precincts of Ka'ba could not have been forgotten. In the ripe corn fields of Iraq, the terrible general would gather another harvest of rebellious heads.

Food habits and social identities. Collective food habits had more than a functional meaning. Brillat-Savarin's aphorism 'Tell me what you eat, and I will tell you what you are', was as valid for Asian history as in European.[6] An early Chinese text from the Han period expressed the belief that the social habituation to the imperial cuisine could have the effect of changing the political allegiance of the powerful but barbarous tribes on the northern frontiers. If the Hsiung-nu (possibly Hunas of European and Indian memory) could be persuaded to develop a craving for Chinese cooked rice, keng stew, roasted meats, and wine, it would become, the writer hoped, a source of their ethnic weakness.[7] The fourth Mughal emperor Jahangir (see Plate 21), a connoisseur of fine paintings, a crack shot, an Epicurean, and an observer of social customs, expressed his amazed reaction when some Burmese or Mongkhmer visitors arrived at the imperial capital in 1613. 'I made some inquiries as to their customs and religion', he wrote in his *Memoir*, 'they eat everything there is either on land or in the sea, and nothing is forbidden by their religion. They eat

Plate 20 Blind pilgrim obtaining food at the dargah of Muin al-Din Chisti,
Ajmer, India, attributed to Mir Hashim, seventeenth century (see p. 151).

with everyone. They take into their possession [marry] their sisters by another mother . . . They have no proper religion. They are far from the Musulman faith and separated from that of the Hindus.'[8] The transgression of cultural watersheds always attracted notice. Bishop Heber's visit to the Nawab of Oudh in Lucknow during his journey through northern India (1824–5), was marked by an invitation to a public breakfast at the palace, served in European-style on a long table laid with fine English and French china. The king began by putting hot rolls on the plates of the distinguished guests:

Coffee, tea, butter, eggs, and fish were then carried round by the servants . . . The king had some mess of his own in a beautiful covered French cup, but the other Mussul-mans ate as the Europeans did. There was a pillaw, which the king recommended to me . . . this was really an excellent thing, with neither ghee nor garlic, and with no fault except, perhaps, that it was too dry, and too exclusively fowl, rice, and spices.[9]

Heber noted that the late Nawab Sadat Ali Khan spoke English without any accent and had frequently worn English uniform, though his son received a mainly Islamic education.[10]

The bishop's concealed sense of wonder at the sight of a European meal served in an Indian palace can be matched by the astonished reaction of an Iranian diplomat when he was a guest together with his ambassador of the English governor of Madras. The mission was on its way to Siam in 1685 and had broken the voyage in India. During the first formal reception given by the Fort St George to honour the guests, wine and hors-d'oeuvres were served on arrival. After the toast was drunk and gun salutes fired, Ibn Muhammad Ibrahim observed, dinner was served on a long table covered with a white cloth and laid with silver plates, silver knives, spoons, and forks, and napkins. The English governor himself carved the joint and served his honoured guests personally. The second reception coincided with the celebrations of James II's accession. The news had just arrived in Madras. On this occasion, the authorities in Madras thought it proper to include Persian cuisine in the official menu and the loan of the Ambassador's chefs was requested as none of the caterers in the service of Fort St George had a knowledge of the food and dishes which would please the diplomatic guests. The English themselves were interested in trying 'our kind of food'. The reception was held in a marquee and the floor was spread with carpets. When the Iranians arrived and were about to remove their shoes, they saw that not only did the English hosts walk about on the rugs with their shoes on but even had the dogs running about the place. If the canine presence was a little unwelcome, the decided highlight of the evening, and a delightful surprise, was the public appearance of the English ladies at the banquet and their free participation at the dancing. As for the food, one of the outstanding delicacies served was a white rooster made in sugar confection: 'When it was brought out before us, we were obliged to examine it twice to be sure that it was in fact made of candy.'[11]

Plate 21 Mughal Emperor Jahangir, early seventeenth century.

When people belonging to one cultural tradition as defined by food, dress, and housing met members of another culture in the course of trade, diplomatic missions, or religious pilgrimage, they had the obvious option of changing their identities for a brief period of time. Did they take that option? The analysis of this question brings to the surface the depth of tradition in comparative Asian societies and the element of change that was permissible or possible. In so far as food habits were observable historically, the French Huguenot jeweller Sir John Chardin, who lived in Persia and India for many years (1664–77), summed up the differentiating principle admirably: 'In the Indies, as up to China and Ispahan, whether in the Islands, or the Terra-Firma, the Religions divide People in their Food, as well in their Beliefs and Worships'.[12] It is apparent that our anonymous Muslim merchants in Calicut or Canton faced immediate food barriers which they could not easily cross. In India, the permitted indigenous food exchanges between social groups rigidly excluded non-Sanskritic people. In China, Muslims themselves would have refrained from eating with the Chinese because of ritual prohibitions. It was forbidden as a matter of general principle for Muslims to eat with 'kafirs' (infidels), though which people exactly fitted the description was difficult to decide. Meat obtained from an idolater, a Mazdean, a pagan, or an apostate could not be eaten by an adherent of orthodox Islam. Such travellers in China carried their own bread in order to avoid having to eat food prepared by infidels.[13] There was another dimension to food conventions. In Asia, as elsewhere in the world, in addition to being a part of religious and social systems the dietary traditions were closely related to the physical sense of taste and smell and therefore were habit-forming. They had tangible as well as symbolic meaning. The human nose and the tongue taken together constitute an amazingly sensitive chemical laboratory, instantly able to detect members of homologous alcohols, aldehydes or acids, and complex mixtures of compounds present in food.[14]

The symbolism of clothing and housing. The conventions on clothing, however, were in a different category of cognitive logic. The connection between the sensory process of assimilating information and the symbolic meaning of dress was much stronger than in the case of food habits. If an individual changed his clothing, he automatically changed his social identity and became another person. It is not only that an Arab would become unrecognisable as an Arab, if he changed his dress, but if he put on the habit of an imam and covered his head with the black turban of tightly-rolled muslin, he was no longer a layman but a religious leader of Islam. The sacred thread of the Brahman in India was inviolable. The rejection of the sacred thread also meant the repudiation of his religion and a disavowal of his membership of the Indian society. Change of clothing implied in our scheme of historical differentiation permutations at two levels: between one society and another and between different levels of the same society. This duality of course holds for food habits as well. In every Asian society in our period of study, there was a qualitative and quantitative contrast between food eaten by the wealthy and the food eaten by the poor. The gastronomic conventions were divided moreover into a high cuisine and low, and for non-Islamic religions there was a third element in the special food preparations offered to gods and spirits. On ceremonial and festive occasions both the rich and the poor cooked meals prescribed by tradition, which differed from everyday food. The dimensions of space, time, and structures strictly ordered the elements of the two 'sets', food and clothing. But for the history of Asian housing, the overall picture is not quite so schematic. Although all the main influences of social stratifications and categorisation were present in the styles and forms of housing, the margin of choice was limited by technical considerations. Travelling merchants, for example, would not have had any option other than of staying in local dwellings such as were available. The fact that a Chinese or Arab merchant in Calicut housed himself in a bamboo-and-palm-leaf house during the trading season would not necessarily have changed his social identity. He would certainly note the difference between his accustomed style of housing and the foreign offerings, rationalising the temporary situation as best he could.

Contemporary comparisons of food and housing: al-Muqaddasi, Bernier, Della Valle, and Hamilton. The historical material illuminating these analytical points is exceedingly rich. Al-Muqaddasi, the Syrian scholar, geographer, and traveller, draws a stylised picture of the contrasting features of life in Damascus in the tenth century. The climate was pleasant, though somewhat dry. But the citizens were turbulent, fruits insipid, meat was tough, houses were small, and the streets gloomy. Bread was also bad there and it was difficult to find employment.[15] Here is François Bernier from Louis XIV's France, contrasting (1663–4) Europe and Asia on the roads, his heart and prejudice forever pulling in opposite directions. Bernier thought that if Europe had the same system of government as Asia:

The excellent accommodation for travellers would disappear; the good inns, for example, between Paris and Lyons, would dwindle into ten or twelve wretched caravansaries, and travellers be reduced to the necessity of moving like the Gypsies with everything about them. The Eastern Karavans-Serrah resemble large barns, raised and paved all round, in the same manner as our Pont-neuf. Hundreds of human beings are seen in them, mingled with their horses, mules, and camels. In summer these buildings are hot and suffocating, and in winter nothing but the breath of so many animals prevents the inmates from dying of cold.

The shops in Delhi could never equal the brilliant appearance of those in Paris, in Rue St Denis for example, nor would any true gourmet, a lover of good food, quit Paris for the sake of visiting the Mughal capital.[16] Unlike Bernier,

Plate 22 Caravanserai, Iran.

Pietro Della Valle, the aristocratic Roman traveller in the Middle East and India, refrained from the subject of comparative sociology while describing the 'caravanserai' of Ahmedabad. On arrival at this great political capital and industrial city (1624), Della Valle and his party went straight to the house of the English merchants, where they dined while other lodgings were being prepared for them. Afterwards, the party went to one of the houses in the street called the Tailors' Caravanserai:

> For you must know that the Caravanserai, or Inns, in Ahmedabad, and other Great Cities of India, are not, as in Persia and Turkey, one single habitation, made in the form of a great Cloyster, with abundance of Lodgings round about, separate one from another, for quartering of strangers; but they are whole great streets of the City destined for strangers to dwell in, and whosoever is minded to hire a house; and because these streets are locked up in the night time for security of the persons and goods which are there, therefore they call them Caravanserai.[17]

Some idea of the comparative perspective on Asian food and housing can be gained from the entertaining descriptions left by Alexander Hamilton. In 1703, the Scottish ship captain and private trader went to trade at the Malabar port of Badagara. The local Raja was strengthening his navy at the time in the European style and came aboard Hamilton's ship, fitted out as a warship, to look at the naval architecture. Hamilton offered him coffee, tea, wine, and brandy which were politely refused, as these were polluted by being served by Europeans. 'Next day I waited on him ashore, and he carried me to his Palace, which was very meanly built of reeds, and covered with cocoa-nut leaves, but very neat and clean . . . and there he treated me with Rice, Fowl, and fresh Fish drest after their Way.' A few years later when Hamilton called again at the port, he was warmly welcomed by the ruler and 'lodged in a Stone House, the common place for Ambassadors to lodge in . . . The Bedding was only some Mats spread on a Couch; but it is the common Bedding of the Country, and his

Highness has no better. Before I was conducted to my Lodgings, there was a Present of Rice, Butter, Hens, Fruits and Roots put into a Pantry for me, and my Retinue.'[18] Hamilton's account of the social scene in eighteenth-century Malabar informs on several aspects of our analysis. It can be seen that the dietary laws are very strict for the Raja and his people but not at all important in a religio-ritual sense for Hamilton. He can temporarily eat Malabari food without being accused of having gone 'native'. On the other hand, Hamilton's European notion of a royal palace was much more rigid than that of the Raja's as were his ideas of the standards of furnishing. The emphasis on the contrast between a wooden or bamboo structure meant for local usage and the stone building that houses visiting dignitaries reveals the asymmetry between the functional and the symbolic. Hamilton was unable to appreciate that in a humid tropical climate a finely-woven mat bed was much more comfortable than one spread with mattresses and cotton sheets. Almost two centuries later, a British civil servant in Burma commented on similar mat beds used there, 'no one has anything more elaborate, and indeed nothing better could be wished for. A cooler bed could not easily be found.'[19] We can say that during this period in Malabar, the functional meaning of housing and furniture was still intact and determined perhaps by the local climate and the availability of the necessary building materials. The traditions have not been modified by a high culture which states that what is fit and proper for a king is different from the needs of the subjects and common people. From the early sixteenth century, as European observers began to write about the Asian social habits and customs, they were astonished to discover that what was purely functional in Europe had strong symbolic meaning in Asia which appeared totally irrational. At the same time, they were unable to shed their own symbolic ideas about these material expressions of everyday life.

The structural elements of food, clothing, and housing. Two important historical determinants of food, dress, and housing have now been identified: social identity and functional usage. Another pair of fundamental associations can also be established at the level of the concrete. The first of these is the system of economic production. Local climate, geography, technological methods, and institutional organisation determined the composition of everyday life and the range of articles that could be produced at least cost. The second association is the binary distinction between the masculine and the feminine. The sexual differentiation permeated all aspects of Asian life but were not strictly speaking always symmetrical. For instance, men and women generally ate the same kind of food but they did not eat together in every society. Within households women mostly prepared the meals and processed food items. The high cuisine was always in the domain of men. In the professional kitchens where food was prepared for sale in the restaurants or in the markets and in royal palaces, it was men who acted as cooks. In the case of housing, where the better-off people could afford to build large houses, the quarters for men were separated from those assigned to women and children. The formal conventions about the time and the occasion for men to visit the women's quarters remained highly structured. In dress of course the separation between men and women was total and achieved through marginal symbolic transmutations in shape, colour, texture, and patterns of material, jewellery, and toilette.

The tripartite combinations and oppositions in food: a critique of Lévi-Strauss. The different dimensions and categorisation of food, clothing, and housing can be highlighted and analysed by using the logic set out in the accompanying diagrams. The central triangle marks out the logical space for all three, arranged in the triple dimensions of nutritional-functional usage, social-religious symbolism, and economic-technical production, with each axis scaled between the ordinal values of 0 to 100 to convey the idea of a 'continuum'. The graphing technique makes it possible to locate the historical identity of an item of food, such as rice, bread, meat, or wine, on each axis of the triangle according to its relative strength for a group of people, for a period of time, and for a unit of space. Staple items such as bread or rice will lie close to each apex of the central triangle, because these contribute the highest input of nutritional/functional value to diet, because their symbolical significance in social life, religion, and myths is strong, and because economic production is overwhelmingly oriented towards the supply of bread or rice to the respective civilisations that consume them. Our diagrams furthermore seem to indicate a generative scheme that gives rise to 'sets' in triple units of oppositions, with elements drawn from a larger set. Some of the elements are partially interdependent; others stand alone. Thus roasting or grilling (the act of exposing raw food to direct heat radiation) will generate roast meat, grilled fish, parched millet and rice, roasted nuts, and even bread. Each of these elements in turn becomes the generative principle or the cardinal number of other tripartite sets. It should perhaps be noted that the distinction between 'food' and 'non-food' or the presence and absence of binary oppositions in food preparations, identified by Lévi-Strauss (endogenous/exogenous, staple/garnish, bland/savoury) is unnecessary for an empirical description of comparative cuisine and diet.[20] The first (food) is a tautology that leaves the logical space empty, while the second (non-food) is a contradiction that completely fills it up. It is impossible to make any theoretical sense of the fact that sharks' fins (endogenous) and rare birds' nests (exogenous) should be prized items of *haute cuisine* in China and nowhere else in Asia. The terms 'endogenous' and 'exogenous' are defined in this context spatially, because sharks are caught in the home waters, while the birds' nests are imported from South East Asia. It might be noted that both the items of Chinese cuisine are exogenous in the sense that they are not items of an ordinary meal but are delicacies. In other

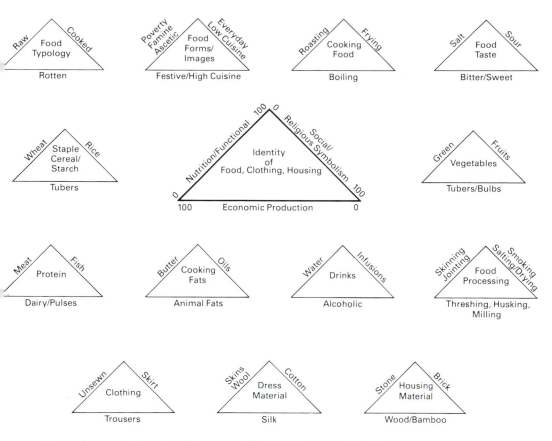

Triangular oppositions/combinations of food, clothing, and housing.

words, the definition can include the qualitative structure of a meal. There is also a temporal dimension. An Iranian breakfast composed of thin hard bread, white cheese, and fruit preserves will be considered non-food for the evening meal by the very same people. The trajectory of the food sets over time, social groups, and space is constantly generating positive and negative values, according to the scheme of whether a particular combination is present (+) or absent (−). The trajectory is so unstable that its explanatory power remains low.

Food and cuisine

Processing and preservation. A description of the Asian food habits should properly begin with the different categories of its processing. Settled agriculture specialising mainly in the production of cereals and different kinds of beans and pulses naturally gave rise to threshing, husking, and milling. The mortar and pestle, flat grinding stone used with a heavy stone or wooden roller, and the more elaborate rotary grinding stones cranked by hand had the advantage of decentralising the production of flour, whether made from wheat, millet, or rice. These mills had become universal in farming-households throughout Asia and were widely used in India, where it was important to authenticate the source of a basic food item. In China and the Middle East large-scale professional mills driven by water-power also operated alongside the domestic machines. In Egypt, an entire town derived its name and economic livelihood from flour mills: Mashtulu-t-Tawahin or Mashtul of the Mills supplied the camel caravans and the corn ships which provisioned Jedda and Mecca. The daily ebbing tides racing through the canals at Basra worked the mills built at the headworks. In the mid sixteenth century, Muhammad Ibn Nasir al-Din, the Amir of the Biqa and Karak Nuh in Syria, established a 'waqf' which contained, besides other property, two mills with their mill-stones mounted on the rivers Ghazir and Birdawn respectively.[21] If the rotary mills were worked by animals, camels, donkeys, or oxen, for grinding corn and pressing oil (see Plate 23), a compassionate attitude at least characterised the civic authorities. The animals must be permitted to rest by day and night and not allowed to be worked for more than a certain measure of time at a stretch. The other two categories of food processing, the slaughtering and butchering of meat and the drying, salting and preservation of fish, vegetables, and half-cooked cereals needed little mechanical aids but were performed by specialised and skilled personnel. In China, a whole industry of salting and pickling various kinds of food existed in each district and the mandarins knew exactly how many sheds manufactured the pickles and how many jars were actually made.[22] Shops in the 'street of blown sugar' ('batasagali') in Mughal Delhi, Shajahanabad, sold nothing but the confectioners' marvellous creations in spun and blown sugar, crystallised fruits, and an infinite variety of pickles.

Food preparation: the distinctions between the raw, the cooked, and the preserved. The technique of food processing synchronised closely with the symbolical grid of food preparations. All Asian civilisations maintained the triple distinctions between the raw, cooked, and the preserved.[23] In the Middle East and India many vegetables were eaten raw but meat, fish, and eggs appeared as food only in cooked or preserved forms. But it was permissible to serve milk in fresh, cooked, and decomposed variations. The fermented element in the food triangle of the Far East and in some of the mainland countries of South East Asia can be found in fish and shell-fish, soya-beans, and eggs. Fish and oyster sauce brewed with the same technical elaboration as the fermented soya-beans in China and Japan provided a subtle and graduated scale of tastes in both everyday and high cuisine. However, the Burmese 'raw-eaten fish paste' (*ngapi seinsa*), was so strong and pungent that only long

Plate 23 Oil-press being worked by camel, the Yemen.

habituation could make it acceptable as an essential accompaniment to rice.[24] Fermented soya-flour in the form of bean-curds almost equalled meat as a source of protein.[25] Preserved eggs, another prized delicacy of Chinese cuisine, called for a considerable mental adjustment before unaccustomed palates could regard them as food. A chemical mixture composed of salt and ash was applied to the shells, which turned the eggs through osmosis into blue-coloured jelly. The result appeared on the table as one of the ingredients of a cold hors d'oeuvre no less subtle than marinated duck, strips of jelly fish, and the preserved 'translucent peony' fish in sauce.[26] In traditional Japan, the preparation and the presentation of raw fish, in exquisite combinations of colour and shapes, reached almost the level of a fine art. The highly flavoured sauces (containing a large proportion of pounded ginger) that accompanied these fish dishes created in turn a perfect blending of tastes.

The structure of collective food habits identified by Lévi-Strauss in the semantics of the raw, cooked, and the decomposed has two separate areas of application. The primary consideration on food for all societies in any given period and environment is that of storage and nutrition. Through evolutionary experimentation, man must have discovered in Asia, as in other parts of the world, the necessary elements of a balanced diet and the degree of processing required before organic matter could be turned into safe edible food. Elaborate medical and therapeutic treatises existed in the Middle East, India, and China which outlined the relative properties of different kinds of food.[27] Although ice was available as a luxury depending on the local geography, the storage of fresh and cooked food raised severe problems. During his diplomatic mission to China, Lord Macartney and his entourage discovered on one occasion that the fresh food supplied to the party had deteriorated; the Chinese officials responsible for the supply had the buttons of their coats torn off on the orders of higher authorities as a ceremonial punishment.[28] The only safe way to keep cooked rice overnight in warm temperatures was by soaking it in water, which would often produce a slight degree of fermentation. In southern India, steamed dumplings ('idli') made from ground rice underwent such a process of natural fermentation. Similarly, kneaded flour dough left to ferment through the action of yeasts could be mixed with fresh dough to produce the risen leavened bread. The daily purchase of fresh food and the habit of not leaving any cooked food after the last meal of the day was so common in Western Asia that Chardin observed with just a hint of surprise that 'the Persians provide nothing before hand . . . but they buy every Day what they have occasion for . . . They never likewise dress Meat a Day before hand, nor keep any thing from one Day to another.' The left-overs in a rich household were immediately given to the poor.[29] Even Islamic travelling dervishes, who strictly divided their collected alms of food in equal proportions among themselves, kept nothing for the following day and redistributed the cooked food to others who needed it.[30]

Whatever may have been the social symbolism attached to the culinary triangle investigated by Lévi-Strauss, historical experience must have indicated to people that certain kinds of food had different taste appeals when eaten raw, cooked, or in fermented forms. Indeed, the concrete traditions of high and low cuisine probably derived from such experimentations and from the willingness of a society to tolerate the habits of eating non-standardised food on the part of a minority of its members. The ground-floor of food-habits in historical Asia is entirely visible. The essential cereals supplied the bulk of the nutritional needs of the greater majority of people, supplemented by small quantities of meat and fish. Vegetables and fruits were important as were also cooking oils and fats, salt, and various kinds of relishes that made bread and rice palatable. The list of such garnishes and condiments was not short: olives, onions, radishes, garlic, fresh ginger, green pepper, green chillies, pickles, fish pastes, salted plums, and soya sauce. The impeccable Chinese social logic separated a meal into two generic categories: the first part consisted of 'fan' or grains and starchy food; the second was 'ts'ai' or vegetables and meat which garnished the cereals.[31] The contrast between a protein-eating Europe and a mainly vegetarian Asia provoked amused reaction. Chardin thought that the Asiatics were nothing near so great eaters as the Europeans: 'we are Wolves and Voracious Beasts, when compared with them'. The austere nature of local agriculture in Iran or the Middle East explained as much the popular food-habits as the cultural traditions of sober eating and the avoidance of gluttony. However, an over-blown eater, 'mujallih', was disliked in Arab society.[32]

The food of the poor: the porridge and the stew. The diet of those people at the bottom of the social pyramid, as we know only too well from numerous sources, reflected the constant struggle to produce and retain sufficient food to replicate the family.[33] Throughout the areas of dry farming, the poverty line and sobriety in eating could be seen in the daily diet of some kind of porridge made from boiled millets, barley, and rice, often mixed with peas and pulses. In India, the dish was known as nutritious 'khichri'. Its distribution from 'soup-kitchens' in times of famine was the first act of both public and private charity. Emperor Jahangir recorded in his memoir that he tasted khichri for the first time during his visit to Gujarat in 1618. It was made from millet and split peas which were abundant in the area, and the dish suited him well. The emperor ordered that on days of abstinence when he refrained from eating meat, khichri should be prepared for him.[34] In the seventeenth century, the standard field-ration of the Mughal cavalry appears to have been khichri. Not many troopers were able to eat meat, according to Bernier, but they were 'satisfied with their kichery, a mess of rice and other vegetables, over which, when cooked, they pour boiled butter'.[35] The technique of food preparation which is seen in the boiling together of different kinds of whole grains, vegetables, and meat also reflects a mixed system of food production. In Han China, the dish known as 'keng' was a thick broth made from meat and grain. The Middle East had several near-relatives of the Indian porridge, though they were enriched with the addition of meat and lumps of fat. The early Islamic sources describing the life of semi-sedentary people living between the margins of cultivation and pastoralism mention 'tharid', a stew made from crumbled bread, meat, and vegetables, and 'hays', the ingredients of which were dates, milk, and butter; both were favourite food of the Prophet.[36]

Another staple dish, 'harisa', eaten by the poor and the better-off people has survived the passage of time from the Abbasid period to the present day. An elaborate *pot-au-feu* 'harisa' needed many hours of cooking on a slow fire, stretching out well into the night. Of all the foods a man could taste, al-Mas⁽udi related in a story, harisa was the best and favoured by the starving, the humble, and the powerful.[37] A recipe written in the classic style of gastronomy by a connoisseur of Baghdad (AD 1226) tells us exactly how to cook the harisa. Take six 'ratls' (Iraqi lb) of fat meat cut into strips and simmer slowly until the meat is tender. Remove all the bones and add four ratls of cleaned and washed wheat to the stock. Simmer further through the first quarter of the night. Before allowing the dish to cool, add a diced chicken with seasonings of cinnamon and salt. In the morning, pour hot melted fat cut from the tail of the fat-tailed lamb and serve with sprinkled ground cumin seed, cinnamon, and lemon-juice. The Indian recipe given by Abu'l Fazl in the sixteenth century agreed almost in every detail with the list of ingredients mentioned in the Baghdad cook-book except for the addition of the finer spices and saffron. The recipes suggest that harisa was probably best made on an industrial scale by the professional cook-houses in the suqs of Baghdad, Fustat, and Aden. The 'hisba' or the public regulations for 'Muhtasib', the official in charge of the law in medieval and late Islam, stipulated that the makers of harisa, the 'hurrasin', must add a minimum quantity of meat to the meal and that strict vigilance should be exercised to prevent the adulteration of the fat used and the contamination of the vessel in which the dish was prepared. The sellers of harisa in Baghdad had places above their shops furnished with tables and mats for the customers, though the better-off people with higher social claims might express disdain at the idea of eating at an establishment run by a harisa-cook. The eleventh century commercial documents known as the 'Cairo Geniza records' mention an incident involving some Jewish merchants at Aden who lost status by eating in the houses of Samaritans, Karaites, and hurrasin.[38]

Food prepared and sold in the bazaar. The loss of face involved in eating an identical food preparation in the market-place, as opposed to its consumption at home, points to a dichotomy that was noticed by Bernier and Chardin also. In the bazaars of imperial Delhi, meat was sold everywhere either roasted or cooked in a sauce, but Bernier thought that the meat could have come from camels, horses, or oxen which had died of disease. Neither bread nor meat cooked in the cook-shops could be wholly trusted. During the time Bernier was in the employment of a Mughal courtier in Delhi, he obtained food from the purveyor of the emperor's kitchen. Of course one of the express duties of the Muhtasib in fourteenth-century Misr was to supervise the cook-shops in town and ensure that the cooked meat of different animals, goats, sheep, oxen, and camels, were kept separate, 'so that no invalid may eat of them and suffer harm. Meat boiled in impure water will become entirely impure.'[39] The concept of public health certainly existed in the urban administration of pre-modern Asia, though the enforcement of the regulations presented difficulties. In contemporaneous Isfahan, Chardin noticed that the richer households prepared elaborate food in their own kitchens; but the ordinary people cooked nothing at home. After the day's work everyone gathered at the cook-houses to buy pulau rice and other things for supper. The huge kettles and saucepans, thirty inches or so in diameter, could be seen boiling on the stoves in these professional kitchens and there was a raised area at the back spread with carpets and separated from the front by a curtain, where the diners could sit down and eat their meal. In Cairo professional cooks, the 'tabakhs', kept similar food shops selling kebabs, boiled beans, and bread. However, it was only the poorer people who ate in the bazaar; the better off preferred to send their servants to buy cooked food from the tabakhs.[40] One area of cuisine where the domestic

Plate 24 The preparation of a Central Asian nomadic banquet, fifteenth century.

cook always compared badly with the professionals was in the domain of the pastry cook. The art of making confectionery, the wafer-thin pastries, and the savoury appetizers was best learnt from acknowledged masters in the bazaar by serving as apprentices. The concentration of skills needed and the advantages of large-scale production made it all but impossible for individual households to compete with the commercial confectioners. But in general, the tradition of public and professional cuisine perhaps reached its highest forms in China and the habit of eating and dining in restaurants and tea-houses had become common at least from the Sung period. Food stalls and food vendors also supplied the needs of the poorer people.[41]

Poverty food and festive food. The historical evidence on urban life and the vigorous, continuing culinary traditions indicate that the generic distinction between the high cuisine and the low can only be identified imperfectly with social hierarchy. Food eaten by the rich and food eaten by the poor did not symmetrically divide itself into two separate groups. The typology of 'abstinence' or 'poverty' food, festive food, and offerings distributed in the name of God constantly moved in and out of particular social categorisation (defined by income, status, or birth). It shifted over time and space as well. An enormous variety of food preparations and range of tastes characterised even folk cooking; nor was it universally true that Asian farmers or the urban working populations were uniformly deprived and under-nourished. In areas of high agricultural productivity, in India, South East Asia, or China, the farming population could choose their items of diet from a wide selection of food produced by themselves. The range of ingredients was reflected in a multitude of recipes actually used to cook vegetables, fish, meat, dairy products, and coconut derivatives: a rainbow spectrum of tastes drawn from very simple techniques to the highly elaborate. An active international maritime trade in food stuffs supplemented local production and added to the variety of cooking styles. Ibn Jubayr, the Andalusian secretary to the court of Granada who performed the hajj in 1183, has left an account of the supplies available in Mecca during the pilgrim traffic. 'Concerning the foods, fruits, and other good things,' he writes,

we had thought that Spain was especially favoured above all other regions. So it was, until we came to this blessed land, and found it overflowing with good things, and fruits such as figs, grapes, pomegranates, quince, peaches, lemons, walnuts, palmfruits, water-melons, cucumbers, and all the vegetables like egg-plant [aubergine], pumpkin, carrot, cauliflower . . . All these various kinds of vegetable and fruit had an excellence of taste greater than those of other lands, and our surprise at that lasts long.[42]

Emperor Jahangir's Epicurean mind constantly sought out the exotic fruits available in India and imported from abroad: pineapples from the Philippines and Goa, fruits with an extraordinary intensity of fragrance and flavour, pomegranates from Mocha, the unrivalled saffron grown in the valley of Kashmir. The pineapple was obviously a royal favourite, for many thousands were produced each year in the Gul-afshan garden at Agra.[43]

The idea of festive food or sacred food on the whole did not distinguish between a high cuisine and low. If there was any difference, it was to be found in the quality of the ingredients used and the number of dishes offered. A Javanese charter inscribed on two copper plates (AD 901) and issued by the 'rakryan' i Watu Tihang for the foundation of a religious domain in Central Java mentions a ceremonial meal attended by men and women; among the dishes enumerated there are names that can still be recognised today.[44] Consecrated food offered at the great Jagannath temple in Orissa, a shrine visited by many pilgrims from other parts of India, was wholly ascetical in its simple combination of rice, pulses, and ghi. Indeed, to offer food to a Brahman on anything other than a banana leaf or leaves of other trees sewn together was to invite summary refusal.[45] Ancient India undoubtedly had the most developed forms of sacred cooking incorporating a huge corpus of regional variations. Symbolic transformations strongly marked the ingredients used, the style of cooking, and even the cooking stove. In south India one of the festivals in the agricultural calendar is still celebrated by the religious offering of 'ponkal' rice, cooked in plain and sweet glutinous forms, which differed from the style of everyday rice preparations.[46] While festive food by definition included rich or elaborate cuisine, the opposite end was occupied by the continuum of poverty food or famine food. To a rich household, in times of scarcity items of peasant diet would appear as the fare of poverty. The farming family considered itself fortunate in finding anything edible at all when their harvests failed. The Chinese mandarin Huang Liu-huang would voice the eternal problem of feeding the crop-less, starving people: 'Fat years come to the land after lean years ... Since lean years are inevitable, preparations should be made to neutralize their harmful effects.' The institution of distributing rice gruel from free kitchens in towns and cities provided only a partial answer to the task of rural relief. Huang estimated that in the situation of a total famine, the average daily food needed by a family with three adults and two children would amount to 1.6 pints of rice (about 0.96 kg or a mere 3,408 calories). What items of food were considered as indispensable necessities of life in normal times of course depended on the variable notions of living standards and the productive resources available. During the period of the Southern Sung, the Chinese author Wu Tzu-mu reported that 'the things people cannot do without every day are firewood, rice, oil, salt, soybean sauce, vinegar, and tea.' Those who were a little better off could not do without 'hsia-fan' (food accompanying rice) and soup in addition to the above. When an agricultural community was stricken by absolute famine, there was of course little alternative choice in food. If the starving peasantry were unable to migrate, they were reduced to foraging for wild plants and trees. The Chinese herbal expert Chou Ting-wang who lived in Honan and Yunnan (*c.* 1382–1425) compiled a treatise on famine food, listing 414 plants altogether. Of these, 245 were herbs, 80 trees, 20 cereals, fruits 23, and 46 vegetables.[47]

Diet and nutrition. The tradition of an abstentious diet retained a strong appeal among the religious adherents of Islam and Hindu India. The Sufi saint Shaikh Nizam al-Din would not eat more than a mouthful of his morning meal during one Ramadan because of the thought that so many poverty-stricken people were sleeping in the corners of the mosques and shops in Delhi without having eaten at all.[48] Stories recorded by al-Muhassin in the tenth-century Baghdad shed interesting light on the food habits of the poor. The munificent and wealthy vizier Hamid b. ʿAbbas had forty tables set out daily in his mansion and entertained every one with meat and white bread, grandees and the poor, attendants and slaves. His servants however sent their mid-day

ration of bread and meat to their families at home and ate dry beans themselves, not wishing to indulge themselves at the expense of their wives and children. When the master of the house learnt what was going on, he ordered a
double-ration to be issued to the servants and still the practice continued.
Finally, it was discovered that the menials used the second meal to accumulate
credit with the butchers for a special feast. Date-cakes and beef, generally
regarded as inferior food, were considered by the upper-class of Baghdad as
perfectly fit for religious mendicants seeking alms.[49] The question of minimum
nutrition and living standards measured in terms of food consumptions is
impossibly difficult to answer for any period of our study. Premodern
economies, especially agricultural production, contained an enormous
amplitude of fluctuations from year to year and the variations in income distribution were equally marked. It is not possible to believe that the working
population in general and in times of good harvests would have been deprived
of the essential intakes of calories needed to generate muscular energy.[50] By
what process of scientific reasoning, based on experience and deductive
expectation, man learnt to live on a diet of millet, rice, and legumes escapes us.

The nutritional quality of the diet however is not in doubt.[51] The essential
supply of proteins, vitamins, and carbohydrates was maintained through an
optimising combination of available food items that included fish, peas and
beans, cereals, dairy products, vegetables and fruits. The propagation and
spread of high-yielding fruit trees throughout Asia in different time periods
were sure signs of the peasant response to subsistence needs and market
opportunities for generating money incomes. The diffusion of the sour orange
in the Islamic world probably occurred from India; al-Mas'udi attempts to
trace its passage from India, through Oman to Basra, and thence to Syria,
Palestine, and Egypt.[52] A pre-T'ang Chinese farming treatise (Northern Wei
c. AD 535) was quite specific about the role played by fruit trees. During the
years of trouble when the Central States fell into disorder, the starving people
found the cultivation of apricots 'a heaven-sent gift'; as the trees on the mountain slopes glistened in golden profusion, people ate their fill of the fruit. If a
single species, the apricot, could help the poor and save the starving, the source
went on, then all the five fruits and the different vegetables together must
mitigate the effects of hunger and add variety to cereal foods.[53] The Ming
statesman and scientist Hsu Kuang-chi (1562–1633) recommended that new
plants such as maize, sweet potatoes, and tapioca should be grown on
marginal land unsuitable for the main cereals in order to provide 'famine' food
though the Chinese would not have considered eating these in prosperous
times.[54] The food of the rich and the well-off in the Middle East and India
included mutton, chickens, geese, fish, rice, rare fruits, and an astonishing
variety of professionally-prepared confectionery. A character in a
seventeenth-century Egyptian text exclaims, 'Why do I see you forgetting

yellow rice seasoned with honey and turning away from peppered rice, almond cakes, fattened geese, and roasted chickens?'[55]

The role of rice and bread in Asian history. Rice and bread were staples for both the rich and the poor. The daily consumption of rice in Persia and India and the different ways of cooking it struck Sir John Chardin so forcefully that he has left a long explanation of its gastronomic and nutritional merits. He was the only contemporary European to observe the unique rustic method of cooking rice in a piece of hollow bamboo, which produced a delicious glutinous dish.[56] It was flavoured with either coconut-milk or pieces of chicken and pork. Chardin also mentioned the scented rice with red streaks on the grain which contained the perfume. It is evident that rice grown on different soils had its own characteristics. Abu'l Fazl's description of the Mughal kitchen in Akbar's court refers to the imperial Inspector of Stores obtaining 'Sukhdas' rice from Bharaij, 'Dewsirah' rice from Gwalior, and 'Jinjin' rice from Rajori and Nimlah. His recipe for a rice dish cooked in the royal kitchen in the Kabul style specifies rice, meat, ghi, gram, onions, salt, fresh ginger, cinnamon, pepper corns, cumin seeds, cardamoms, cloves, almonds, and raisins.[57] There is no difficulty in recognising the kind of rice that was served on the dining carpet of the greatest monarch of the Mughal dynasty; the dish is still cooked today virtually unchanged. Straight boiling however remained the most common and preferred way of cooking rice, the retention of the starchy water being determined by regional conventions. We can see such a method in an early Javanese relief depicting a woman steaming rice in a conical basket with a lid resting on a pot containing water.[58] While rice would have been eaten plain-boiled in most of India, South East Asia, China, and Japan, its elaborate treatment in Islamic countries underlined a cultural duality. Rice was a staple as well as a gastronomic variation on bread. There was even a special variety of bread made from rice, the 'khubz al-aruzz', which appears to have been a poverty-food in the marshland of lower Iraq. The Arab philologist and poet Jahza (*d.* 936) exclaimed in one of his verses that he would be content with bread made from rice flour, a few pickled vegetables, and a morsel of salted fish, washed down by a skin of date-syrup wine which had been matured in an earthenware jar. Ibn Battuta shared a meal of 'khubz al-aruzz', fish, milk, and dates with the inmates of a religious shrine near Wasit.[59]

It was not uncommon for rice-eating societies to serve rice both in plain and ornamented forms. But they would not willingly have eaten baked bread of the Islamic and Indian types. In China alone, wheat flour was welcomed as noodles and steamed buns. The contours of bread-eating zones in Asian cartography were as visible as the frontiers of wheat and millet cultivations. Al-Muqaddasi bought the very best and whitest bread in Fustat during his stay in Egypt and noted that the bakers did not make anything other than white bread.[60] The technique of baking bread reflected a skill handed down from the Pharaonic times. Oval and round loaves, some of them still in their wrappings of papyrus, from Deir el Medineh (New Kingdom) bear a strong resemblance to the type of bread made in present-day Egypt. One variety of the Pharaonic loaves found in archaeological sites had a hole at the centre, suggesting that the bread may have been eaten stuffed with eggs and vegetables, as it is still done in rural areas.[61] From Fustat to Damascus and indeed all the way to Delhi, the art of the baker included varieties of bread that ruled out direct comparisons almost by definition. The differentiated traditions of bread-making in the ancient world has no better description than that of Pliny:

In some places, bread is called after the dishes eaten with it, such as oyster bread; in others, from its special delicacy, as cake-bread; in others from the short time spent in making it, as hasty bread; and also from the method of baking, as oven bread or tin loaf or baking-pan bread; while not long ago there was even bread imported from Parthia called water bread because by means of water it is drawn out into a thin spongy consistency full of holes; others called it just Parthian bread. The highest merit depends on the goodness of the wheat and the fineness of the bolter. Some use eggs or milk in kneading the dough, while even butter has been used by races enjoying peace, when attention can be devoted to the varieties of pastry-making.

The Roman naturalist who was also a farmer observed that the common wheat flour made the best bread and the most famous pastry. In India, people made bread from cultivated and wild barley, although rice was their favourite grain.[62] Compare Pliny's comment with the section on bread in Abu'l Fazl's encyclopaedia of Mughal administration:

Bread is made in the pantry. There is a *large* kind, baked in an oven, made of ten seers [6.3 kg] flour, five seers milk, one and a half seers ghi; quarter seer salt. They make also smaller ones. The *thin* kind is baked on an iron plate . . . There are various ways of making it: one kind is called *chapati*.

Bread made in the imperial kitchen used refined flour (1:0.5 reduction) with a small addition of wholemeal flour and bran.[63] The Indian preference for chapati bread represented a cultural tradition which insisted that bread must be eaten fresh and hot. It was also the result of each family making sure that the bread was unadulterated and cooked under hygenic condition.

All bread-eating societies treated the cooked product with due symbolic respect. The Arabic term 'aish' applied to bread also signified life and subsistence, and it was used for rice as well in the Persian Gulf. The common bread of Islam, 'al-khubz al-huwwara' (white bread) or 'al-khubz al-khushkar' (whole meal bread), was a round loaf, about an inch thick made from wheat flour mixed with a starter dough which provided the yeast. The baking was carried out in a round oven, shaped like a large water-jar, and lined with fire-proof clay; the loaves being stuck on the side walls of the oven. The explosive rising of the bread during baking suggests that the leavening was due to the steam generated inside the loaves rather than the fermenting action of the yeast. In Egypt, besides the Balady (country) bread of the Nile Delta, there was also a sun-baked bread made in the Upper Valley, which received its final baking in the oven. If a list of Islamic bread were to be compiled, it will not be short. Furthermore, Arab authors on cooking were aware of the difference between their bread and that of the Franks and Armenians.[64] The 'Aish shamy' or Syrian bread was complemented by the very special 'khubz markouk', a paper-thin bread which the baker shaped by rapid and repeated upward throwing. It was either plain baked on a concave iron pan or fried in butter in a flat pan. A highly popular and spectacular example of the pastry-cook's art, the fried multi-leaved wafer pastry made its way to India, the Indonesian islands and even as far as Thailand, where it is still sold today under the name of 'martaba roti' and eaten sprinkled with sugar, an exotic and amusing creation of the Indian cook-shops.

Chardin's account of bread-making in Persia refers to three types: flat bread baked in a pit oven (probably 'nan' made in a 'tannur'), parchment-thin bread which he calls 'Lavach' (Lavas) cooked on a round tinned copper plate, and long flint-loaves ('Senguck' or Sangak) made in ovens lined with flint-stones.[65] Poppy and sesame seeds, plain and roasted, flavoured the loaves. Oven-baked bread enjoyed economies of scale in production and remained in the hands of professional bakers, though richer households with a large retinue of servants could mill their own flour and bake bread. The poorer people either bought bread in the market or took kneaded dough to the bakers' ovens. To buy bread from the owners of the 'furn', the communal ovens, was not altogether socially acceptable. The baker's assistant generally went round the well-to-do households collecting kneaded dough and brought back the baked bread on a tray (see Plate 25). The fee for the service was a small proportion of the dough. For the desert Arabs, baking bread was a mark of distinction and wealth. In many bedouin tents, bread was made only once or twice a year and its rarity indicated by the saying, 'This is the tent of bread; here bread is baked. So and so is very rich and bountiful, he has bread, he is the master of bread.' The nomadic Arabs refused to admit that ground wheat was genuine food and their staple diet remained boiled crushed grain.[66]

Styles of cuisine. The actual style of cooking, whether the historian looks at the high cuisine or the low, of course varied according to certain regional patterns. In terms of techniques, three separate culinary traditions can be discerned. The first typology included dishes cooked on the principle of roasting, grilling, and baking with the addition of simple herbs and spices. Then there were the fried dishes which also incorporated a variable scale of seasonings. The third category consisted of what later came to be labelled as 'curries', a technique of cooking which called for first, frying the ingredients in highly aromatic spices and then simmering them slowly in water, milk curd, or coconut milk. The actual recipes used showed a sharp regional contrast between the western and the eastern Indian Ocean. From Syria to Siam and Cambodia, the Middle Eastern and the Indian styles prevailed with varying degrees of local influence and independent traditions. A transcontinental traveller such as the Moroccan scholar Ibn Battuta would have encountered in his journeys from the West to the East an entire gastronomic continuum composed of many separate combinations of herbs, spices, and basic culinary ingredients: basil, rosemary, thyme, fenugreek, saffron, olive oil, lamb-fat, and milk curd, changing into coriander, cumin, cinnamon, cloves, nutmeg, cardamom, coconut milk, coconut oil, sesame- and mustard oil, and lard. The full spectrum of tastes created by different combinations of cooking fats, basic seasonings, yoghurt, coconut milk, fish pastes, soya sauce, garlic, and ginger cannot be realised in depth unless the dishes are eaten simultaneously.

The theory and practice of a high cuisine were an integral part of every Asian civilisation. Sanskritic India occupied a special rank in the total matrix of practical and symbolic meaning. In common with many other forms of social usage, Indian food habits were also deeply influenced by ritualistic theories. It was not only that vegetarians shared a common background with Buddhists, Jains, and Vedic adherents, but the idea of moral purity strongly permeated food habits. Certain foods were ritually pure, others were neutral, while the third category included those beyond the limits of the permissible. Secret feasts where prohibited food and drink featured as special highlights expressed a strong social necessity for deviationist group behaviour, and such meals were common both among the Muslim and Sanskritic communities.[67] The most striking features of the high cuisine in India were the generic divisions between Brahmanic tradition and the Islamic. Rice cooked in ghi and served with an endless variety of vegetables and pulses commanded ritual purity and if the dishes were dispensed by Brahmans, they could be eaten by all. As a result, the profession of the cook was an honourable one for the Brahman, however demeaning it might be in terms of financial status. Indian high cuisine of course strictly outlawed the consumption of beef, which was disliked even by the Islamic societies.[68] The universal habit of eating mutton or goat may have come to India with the arrival of Islam.

Indian aristocrats and the upper classes developed a dual personality from at least the Mughal period, when the norms of refined life crystallised into a recognisable pattern. There was a ritualistic Brahmanic tradition that emphasised the idea of simplicity and poverty-food, complemented by an Islamic royal convention of elaborate cuisine. The two were not necessarily exclusive. When Ibn Battuta arrived at the frontier town of Multan in the Punjab, he found Indian meals sufficiently distinctive to write a detailed account of the various courses served and their order. The first course consisted of roast mutton served with thick chapatis, parathas, and a sweet cake made from

Plate 25 Servant collecting bread from a bakery in an Islamic town, seventeenth century, detail from plate 63.

flour, sugar, and butter. This was followed by curried dishes served in large porcelain bowls. These dishes were cooked in ghi with green ginger and onions and were accompanied by chicken-rice and 'samusas' (triangular pastries filled with meat, almonds, walnuts, pistachios, onions, and spices). The dessert included small Indian confectionery and sweet condensed milk. The meal finally ended with betel and araca nuts. The feast was not very dissimilar from one which would be served today in the same region of the subcontinent. An eighteenth-century Bengali literary work that has some historical themes in it contains a unique description of an elaborate Indian banquet. The first course, composed of twenty-three different vegetables and pulses, is followed by fish, meat, sour dishes, and sweets. The meat course included not only kebabs and 'biriyani' but also three distinct surprises, Turkish 'dolma', vegetables with meat stuffing, Arab 'sikbaj', a highly complex spiced dish of meat and vegetables, and stuffed goat's head.[69]

In the Far East, the professional Chinese cooks created a tradition of high cuisine totally different from the Indo-Islamic, and societies under Chinese influence decisively rejected milk and dairy products. The Iranian diplomat Ibn Muhammad Ibrahim noted that it was impossible to obtain ghi in Siam for the use of his mission. For the resident foreigners, Muslims and Indians, ghi was imported from the Indian subcontinent. When the Thai king ordered the peasants to milk the buffalo cows and make butter for the distinguished visitors, the herdsmen protested in anger saying that never in history had they witnessed such a tyranny which sought to deprive the young calves of their mothers' milk. In fact, the Iranian envoy did not enjoy Thai cuisine and declared that the Siamese were ignorant of right table manners and did not know how to prepare normal, proper food. That this was more a case of unfamiliarity and the inability to appreciate exotic food is shown by his own description of a Thai banquet in which more than fifty exquisite dishes were served in fine porcelain saucers covered with silver lids.[70] The common people in Thailand admittedly lived on a diet of plain boiled rice eaten with fried green vegetables and fish. But festive food in South East Asia included all the elements of high cuisine. The preparation of gourmet dishes, whether grilled, roasted, or boiled, invariably began with a long assembly of the ingredients marinated or fried in spices or aromatic herbs. The spices were roasted first and then carefully ground. Professional food-vendors specialised in grilling whole chicken and pork over open fires. Fish wrapped in banana leaves and broiled over charcoal fire acquired a delicacy of flavour perfectly set off by the scented white rice and fresh vegetables served in a light pickle sauce. Throughout the Indonesian archipelago, the variety of local dishes rivalled the cuisine of the Indian subcontinent. But the saffron rice of the Middle East complemented in the Malayan archipelago the purely indigenous offerings, perhaps under the influence of Islamic traditions. The similarity in the style of cooking between South East Asia and India was so striking historically that it is legitimate to ask whether this was not a case of direct imitation by one civilisation from the other. When it is considered that many of the finer spices used in Indian cuisine originated in South East Asia and that coconut milk was an essential ingredient of some of the dishes, it is not improbable that the style of cooking may have been imported to Ceylon, South India and Bengal from the Indonesian archipelago.

On finer points of technical skills and the knowledge of ingredients and flavours, a Chinese cuisinier would have found few rivals in Asia, though the

Plate 26 Food preparation and banquet, wall-painting, Bali, Indonesia.

traditions of Thai cooking could make a fair bid for the second place. The grandeur of a formal Chinese banquet was just as overwhelming for foreign visitors, as its gastronomic nuances were exotic. Lord Macartney recorded in 1793 his impression of a reception given by the Emperor in the garden palace at Jehol:

We then descended from the steps of the throne, and sat down upon cushions at one of the tables on the Emperor's left hand . . . The tables were then uncovered and exhibited a sumptuous banquet. The Emperor sent us several dishes from his own table, together with some liquors, which the Chinese call wine, not, however, expressed from the grape . . . The order and regularity in serving and removing the dinner was wonderfully exact . . . The commanding feature of the ceremony was that calm dignity, that sober pomp of Asiatic greatness, which European refinements have not yet attained.[71]

Western visitors to the Celestial court were generally rare and the few envoys who did succeed in gaining access to the imperial presence were not always as favourably impressed as Lord Macartney. A century earlier, the Dutchman Pieter van Hoorn (1667) and the Jesuit Father Francisco Pimentel (1667–70) both commented on the semi-barbarous eating-habits of the Manchu dignitaries at the court banquets. Food was served on dirty silver dishes and huge joints of meat, including whole sheep's head with the horns still in place, appeared during a meal attended by Father Pimentel.[72] But these were banquets enjoyed by Tartar frontiers-men with Central Asian food-habits. The highest art of the cuisinier in China was no different from that of his counterparts in the rest of the world. A Ch'ing literary work which included a biography of the author's cook stated the problem admirably. Good cooking did not depend on the relative values of the ingredients. If the cook had the necessary skills, a piece of celery or salted cabbage could be made into a marvellous delicacy.[73] But that could have been said also by Dunand fils,

Napoleon's chef, who created the incomparable 'Chicken sauté Marengo' out of scrap food to celebrate a famous victory.[74]

Beverage in Asia. What kind of drinks accompanied food in historic Asia? The question has been left till now, not because the general diet excluded liquids, but because the tradition of serving food with drink followed a different logic from that of Europe. There was little appreciation that alcoholic beverages, as for example fine wines, might enhance the quality of a meal and provide as subtle an *ensemble* of tastes as particular dishes of well-cooked food. The supply of clean, safe and cool water taxed the ingenuity of hydraulic engineers as much as that of an individual host entertaining his friends to a celebratory dinner. Al-Muqaddasi noted down carefully the taste of water in the various wells and canals as he travelled from one city to another in the empire of Islam. A special accolade was reserved for the river Tigris which appeared feminine in the quality of its water, sweet and beneficial to scholars.[75] The earthenware industry throughout the Middle East and India prided itself on manufacturing water-jars which could cool the water through the natural capillary action. Drinks accompanying food in Western Asia were intended mainly to quench thirst: plain water, weak tea or fruit juice, that of lemons, oranges, and pomegranates, mixed with water and powdered sugar, took precedence over stronger beverages. Fermented milk curd diluted with water was a more substantial thirst-quencher. In climates marked by bitterly cold winters and summers of torrid heat, the provision of ice and refrigerated water was almost a necessity during the warm months. The ice-sellers of Isfahan gathered in open spaces around the outer suburbs. Huge blocks of ice, five or six feet thick, were made in winter with potable water and stored in ice-chambers dug deep into the ground. Similar ice pits were to be seen in China also.[76] Commercial ice travelled surprisingly long distances. When Akbar's court was in residence at Lahore, ice supplies were brought down from the distant mountains by pack horses, boat, and human porterage; the trade yielded great profits to the suppliers. A cheaper way of refrigerating water was the Indian method of rotating a metal water vessel in a solution of refined saltpetre.[77]

The religious prohibition of alcoholic beverages in Islam and in Sanskritic India commanded little popular influence, though it might have discouraged the practice of serving such drinks with a meal. The Abbasid caliph Mansur (*r.* Ad 754–75) denied the request of his Christian physician to drink wine at the royal table. One of his extravagant descendants, Mutawakkil (*r.* 847–61), drank so heavily in the evening that his servants had to prop him up against cushions. The Caliph was helpless when his trusted Turkish bodyguard Baghir betrayed his master and brutally murdered him, using the famous Indian 'jauhar' sword of which he was the official custodian.[78] Wine was served on formal occasions at the Iranian court during the Safavid period. When Shah Abbas III entertained (1673) foreign ambassadors, among whom were those

Plate 27 Cold-drink seller, early seventeenth century.

from France and Muscovy, to a round of public ceremonies and parades, fifty gold flagons of wine accompanied the magnificent banquet. Iranian wine made from fermented grape 'must' enjoyed a certain reputation for quality. Armenians, Georgians, and even Europeans found wine-making a profitable occupation in Persia and the wines of Shiraz, matured in glazed earthenware amphoras, fetched the best prices and compared well with the European wines.[79] Shirazi wine was popular among aristocratic Indians accustomed to alcoholic drinks, as were also wines imported from Europe after the sixteenth century. A Rajput prince notorious for his violence treated Tavernier with exceptional kindness because he had received gifts of European brandy and Spanish wines from the French travelling jeweller.[80] The tradition of serving wines made from rice or wheat as an indispensable part of a meal was, of course, universal in China and Japan. In the rest of Asia, strong spirits distilled from sugar, starch, or the juice of palm trees served the purpose of inebriation for the rich and the poor alike. Excessive and regular drinking of the fiery double-distilled Indian arak was to invite certain and irreversible damage to health. For the civilised, refined, and the sober, from the eastern Mediterranean to the Pacific, coffee and tea had no real rivals.

The power of food to signify. Our peregrination across the food map of Asia has been structured on certain theoretical ideas. A brief summary of the main analytical points will help to place the historical and the substantist exposition in perspective. Food as a 'category', whether it is identified by an abstract term or the name of a cereal preparation such as bread and rice, exists only in the mental domain according to our reference frame. In its generalised form the category does not need a space dimension and is constant through time. Food is recognised as a category by all human minds. Therefore, the non-singular mental categories called foods are made singular by *identity*.[81] The logical space constituted by food is occupied by ordered elements drawn from concrete objects in the physical domain. Selected food is a variable category in space and time according to *who* selects, *where* the selector is situated in space and time, and *where* selected food is found. Food is eaten or responded to as a variable category in space and time, according to who is eating (children/adults, men/women, rich/poor), according to the geographical location of the person eating (home, market-place, restaurants, friend's house, or on journeys), and according to the time of the day, month, annual seasons, and even centuries (incorporating technological and social frequencies of time). Did food habits change in any fundamental way in Asian civilisations during our period of study? The answer would depend on how the qualifier 'fundamental' is defined. The historians of the Middle East are unanimous in their views that wheat bread was the food of the common people, as opposed to bread made from barley or millet. The opposition between an urban-inspired bread-eating culture and that of porridge or stew made from whole grains, meat, dates, and milk can be fastened upon Ibn Khaldun's famous dichotomy of urban and nomadic ways of life. Each respective food tradition in that case would gain or lose strength according to the variable opposition between these two basic historical forces in the Middle East. The frequency of change identified here is not a monotonic function of time but is cyclical. The habit of coffee-drinking (not widely known before the sixteenth century), the permanent appearance of maize in Asian diet, and the increasing importance of rice in Chinese food with the southward shift in agriculture, can all be taken as elements indicating once-for-all changes.

7

Social identities II: clothing, the architecture of symbolic power, and housing

Clothing and social habits

The power of clothing to signify social categories. The patterns embodied in the historical structure of food and cuisine in Asia are clearly visible for our period of study. At the same time, it is evident that the morphism between food habits and social categories could never reach a one-to-one transformation. The reason is obvious. Personal taste diluted collective mandates. The technology of food production moreover was not stable even in the short-term, and because of the number of food items concerned, the possible permutations at each level of the food chain linking together the social categories were very large. The association between clothing and these categories on the other hand was not only in near-unit ratio but strongly reinforced by unconscious habits. The symbolism of dress manifested itself in the capacity to signify different categories of people, to distinguish between men, women, and children, between the powerful, rich, and the poor; the same power of symbolism is revealed in its ability to mark out particular social occasions, to act as objects of value, and indicate status which only a legitimate authority could confer on the receptors. Articles of clothing were distributed to servants as part of their regular wages and given to the needy on feast days. The presentation of a robe of honour, 'khilʿa', by the sultan possessed only one meaning and interpretation. It was the acknowledged mark of high distinction in Islamic statecraft.[1] The symbolic reversion of rank was obtained through the exclusive royal appropriation of certain kinds of garments; only the chosen few have the right to wear such clothing. In the twelfth year of his reign, the Mughal emperor Jahangir revived this custom which had been adopted by his father, the great Jalal al-Din Muhammad Akbar. The first item reserved for the imperial wardrobe was a sleeve-less 'nadiri' coat in the Kurdish style which was worn over the 'qaba', the principal Islamic outer costume. The royal qaba itself could be distinguished by its folded collar and the embroidered ends of the sleeves; other appropriated types of garments included a 'tush' shawl, a qaba made from Gujarati satin, and a silk sash interwoven with gold and silver threads.[2]

The structure of clothing habits is the nearest the historian can get to the structure of language which has dominated for so long certain techniques in social analysis. To say this is not to deny the importance of the functional

182

aspect of clothing in our earlier theoretical triangle. Form, however, generally took precedence over substance when a choice had to be made over the question of dress. Such an argument, which is also a historical explanation can be explicated by examining the generic dress styles in geographical Asia and relating them to the materials used in making the garments. The tradition of using unsewn materials as clothing probably derived from a remote past, which mainly survived in India during our period. The Islamic custom of wrapping up in white seamless cloth, 'ihram', before approaching the sacred enclave of Mecca is no doubt of ritualistic authority that perhaps reflected also an earlier tradition of clothing. In 1183 Ibn Jubayr and his fellow pilgrims put on the 'ihram' at al-Qurayn, a place about two days' march from Mecca. But within the holy mosque, while the visiting public covered themselves in the seamless cloth, the preacher ('khatib') wore the ceremonial dress of Islam, a black robe worked with gold, a black turban similarly ornamented, and a 'taylasam' or shoulder scarf of fine linen.[3] Tunics and skirts, worn in the Middle East, South East Asia, and parts of Central Asia, incorporated a certain amount of sewing and constituted an intermediate level. The necessity for combat clothing may have provided their logic and such garments intended for field duties were reinforced by padded quilts, leather, metal studs, or even chain mail. Finally, there were the fully sewn garments in the form of shirts, shaped jackets, and trousers often worn in conjunction with knee-high boots, a combination that unmistakably pointed towards an equestrian way of life.

These three generic divisions prevailed with varying degrees of uniformity in different geographical areas and they can be given fairly precise associations with our earlier quadratic identities of Asian civilisations. The Brahmanic sacerdotal tradition of wearing only unsewn material while performing the essential rituals radiated over other social categories in the Indian subcontinent and refused to make any distinctions of age, sex, or rank. The clothing habits retained remarkable constancy over time. The Islamic world, on the other hand, moved back and forth between the semi-sewn and the fully sewn, depending on the presence and strength of Central Asian, Turkish or Mongol influence. The Far Eastern clothing styles as a rule fall into the general category of the fully sewn, though ceremonial uniforms often retained the shape of tunics. The mosaics making up the geographical or civilisational patterns in Asian clothing history were cast and recast in contra-points of time by multi-layered mandates stemming from the mental domain. The saffron robe of the Indian ascetic included the garments of the Buddhist monks. A sudden flash of the ochre colour in a Thai village or in a Chinese and Japanese town is enough to remind the onlooker that the priests who proclaimed their identity through the yellow garments of the 'samha' represented a distant transplanted religion. The congregations attending the Buddhist temples in Thailand, Cambodia, Vietnam, or China, however, belonged to an entirely dissimilar cultural habitat. While clothing forms were dominated by a deeper and concealed structure of social identities, made explicit only in the transgression of the assumed rules, substance was much more dictated by the functional role of clothing.

The typology of clothing and social occasions. At one end of the substantive continuum stood the twin needs of cover and protection from the natural elements, while the other end was occupied by fashion, display, ritual associations, and gift exchanges. Neither of these two logical necessities could be satisfied without taking into account the nature of available material, colour, design, and patterns. In the northern highlands and plains of Asia, characterised by low winter temperatures, the use of woollen materials remained widespread, supplemented by fur skins and padded quilts. The woollen textiles varied from coarsely-spun and woven blankets to the superfine Kashmir shawls made from the under-hair of the magnificent white pure-bred goats of the high Himalayas.[4] The Astrakhan fur caps and coats made in Iran signified a similar symbolic position of high status. But there is no question that for the rich and poor alike from Egypt all the way to China and Japan, the most favoured dress materials were cotton textiles and close substitutes such as hemp and linen. Here again the range and variations in fineness, weight, and textures were enormous. The social usage reflected inner sensibilities visible only to the participants. Of course, the premier symbolic position in materials was held by silk, a product which man could improve upon but could not really manufacture. Silk garments signified power and wealth. To them belonged the quality of ritual purity. The aesthetic desire for beauty and colour was fulfilled by no other object at the level of daily life to the same degree as by materials made from silk. A gigantic mantle of silk covered even the ka'ba inside the mosque at Mecca. All the brocade factories of the Middle East measured their skill by weaving a piece fit for the holiest relic of Islam. The Tustar brocade of Khuzistan was famous and exported all over the world. The mantle for Mecca was woven there each year until the sultan fell into poverty and was unable to continue the practice.[5]

Clothes worn by the Muslims revealed their religion and identity in the same manner as those used by the Indians, the Javanese, Thais, or the Chinese and the Japanese. Under Islamic law, there were certain regulations which even attempted to separate the dress of the Christians and Jews, the 'dhimmis', from that of the true believers.[6] The repudiation of the orthodox and 'correct' dress by the spiritual head of Islam had serious implications. In 817 Caliph al-Ma'mun ordered the personal retainers, soldiers, and commanders to discard the black robe of his forefathers and wear green-sleeved coats ('qabas') and tall pointed caps. These innovations were, however, rejected by the people and provoked near mutiny among the troops.[7] The feeling of visual or cultural shock produced by the sight of unfamiliar formal dress can be sensed from the way the Islamic, South East Asian and the Far Eastern painters depicted the costumes of European dignitaries arriving at their royal court: even in serious works of art, there was just a hint of caricature, of jarring grotesque impressions, while the clothing worn by the indigenous people in the same paintings is drawn in fluent idiom. Eyes accustomed to see turbans or embroidered cloth caps as normal head-gears viewed European tall hats as objects of ridicule and mirth; from the sixteenth century to the eighteenth, Europeans in India were popularly known as 'hatmen'.[8] By the late eighteenth century, Indian artists had become thoroughly accustomed to the sight of European dress and the style of interior decorations and found many European patrons for their skills. Even for this period a scene depicting both Eastern and Western themes in material life could produce conflicting impressions which the artist himself must have sensed.

Within Asia, the desirability of proper dress habits led to considerable self-reflections when people crossed over the cultural watersheds. Al-Muqaddasi with his western Mediterranean outlook on clothing, noted that in the Yemen, people who wore trousers were laughed at. The usual dress consisted of a single garment 'izar' which was wrapped round the body.[9] The materials for the izar were woven in an infinite variety of checks and stripes in all the textile towns and villages of Gujarat and Sind down to the eighteenth century. During his visit to the Maldive Islands, Ibn Battuta found the habits of cleanliness among the islanders impeccable. But he was much disturbed by the sight of women and girls dressed only in sarongs or the straight skirts which covered only the lower part of the body. Islamic custom of course severely frowned upon any kind of physical exposure on the part of both men and women. Ibn Battuta refused to act as a qadi unless the women, involved in legal disputes, came to his presence properly covered. The Moroccan scholar admitted in the end that his exhortations had little success: 'I had some slave-girls who wore garments like those worn in Delhi and who covered their heads, but it was more of a disfigurement than an ornament in their case, since they were not accustomed to it.' He would return to the same theme when describing the Malabar coast of India. Women there wore only loose unsewn garments, one end of which they gathered round their waist and draped the rest over their shoulders. In spite of the obvious exposure which this style of clothing allowed, the beauty and the virtue of the women apparently remained unimpaired.[10]

The tradition of wearing only a minimum amount of clothing distinguished semi-tropical India and the whole of South East Asia. The convention included every level of society. Ceremonial dress in these areas formed at the same time a separate parallel stream which had all the ingredients of high fashion. An ancient Indian text of Jain origin in fact clearly differentiates categories of clothing by functions and occasions. In the first level were clothes of daily use; in the second, clean and washed garments ready to be used after a bath. Festive clothing formed another category, while at the very top level were costumes fit to be worn only while visiting the royal court.[11] The basic distinctions between unsewn and sewn garments were not rigidly upheld for either the Indian or South East Asian societies. The Indian clothing traditions historically remained centred on the habit of wrapping a long piece of material around the waist and it was combined with a long shirt for men and a short blouse for women. The variations in colour and the style of constructions in the upper garments underlined the difference in gender. The colour white was almost obligatory for men, a thin gold or coloured border to the material being the sole ornamentation allowed, if at all. The feminine 'sari' in its most expensive variant received all the imaginative lavishness and baroque motifs in design and colour the textile artist could devise. Della Valle pointed out that the upper-class Muslim ladies in India used silk materials of all kinds of patterns and colours. But the Hindu women in contrast usually 'use no other colour but red, or certain linen stamped with works of sundry colours, (which they call Cit) but all upon red ... whence their attire seems only red at a distance.'[12] In mainland and maritime South East Asia, the basic cover was provided by a rectangular piece of material, which was worn either knotted around the waist or sewn into a tubular skirt. Shoulder cloth, blouse, and half jackets, combined with belts and sashes, completed the totality of the costumes according to gender, rank, and occasion. In southern and northern Thailand, in the inner and outer islands of the Indonesian archipelago, in the tribal hills of Indo-Burmese frontier, fine and coarse textiles, made into traditional garments, acted as splendid symbols of social usage. The symbolism of dress and textiles was all pervasive. An Indian bride would wear at her wedding a red sari of silk or cotton. The performance of the marriage rites would have been preceded and followed by an exchange of ceremonial textiles. The parents of an Indonesian bride bestowed on her at the wedding a ritual garment which she would use to strengthen her life-force when it was weakened through child-birth or illness.[13]

The functional and symbolic role of clothing: fashion in Asian history. The garments of everyday wear and of special occasions in Islamic and Far Eastern countries retained their basic constructional features in common. The symbols of wealth or fine taste in clothing were signified by costly materials, by high standards of workmanship, and a multiplication of dress items. Three basic pieces linked together the entire structure of Islamic and Chinese clothing; the body shirt, the drawer or trousers, and an outer garment that was sometimes a tunic, an apron, or a coat. These were supported by peripheral items such as scarfs, sashes, belts, turbans and caps, slippers, shoes, boots, and personal jewellery. While in contemporaneous Europe, the binary distinction between the masculine and feminine attire was created by radically different styles, in Asia it was mostly achieved by varying the combination of the basic pieces and through design, patterns, and colours. The argument and the historical explanation that social identities and clothing habits represent mirror images (unit transformations) leads to the deductive expectation that if the explanations changed in any fundamental way, the objects of explanation would also shift. We know that neither in Europe nor in Asia, social identities changed fundamentally in our period. Yet, in European societies fashion was a major component of taste and the apparent lack of fashion-induced changes in the Middle East, India, or China caused many contemporary Western thinkers to make offensive remarks about Asian social and political systems. Take Jean Baptiste Say, for example, who wrote (1829): 'I confess that the unchanging fashions of the Turks and other Eastern peoples do not attract me. It seems that their fashions tend to preserve their stupid despotism'.[14] Sir John Chardin, an undisguised admirer of Persian and oriental culture, had made the same substantive point a century and a half earlier. The clothes of the Eastern people were in no wise subject to 'Mode'; 'they are always made after the same Fashion, and if the wisdom of one Nation appears in a constant Custom for their dress, as has been said, the Persians ought to be mightily commended for their Prudence, for they never alter in their Dress.'[15] Chardin claimed to have seen in the royal treasury at Isfahan, clothes worn by Timur which did not differ from contemporary style. Only when great political events swept across the social scene, such as the cataclysmic Central Asian invasions of Eurasia, did the Indian or the Chinese dress habits show signs of inner tensions.[16]

This conclusion of Fernand Braudel, however, is open to revision. The term 'fashion' in our theoretical analysis is as much an empty set or a set of sets (power set) with a continuum, as the larger set 'clothing' of which it is an element. Neither the couturier who practises the art nor the social theorist such as Say has an absolute patent to proclaim to the world how marginal variations to the basic constructions of dress should be interpreted under the guise of fashion. It is impossible for the foreigner and the uninitiated to detect changes in fashion when these take the form of slight alterations to styles and patterns in material, because the construction of dress generally changes very slowly over time. Would a Chardin or a Say be able to read the symbolic meaning of a three-, four-, or five-clawed dragon image woven on the ceremonial robes of imperial China? Would they know the difference between a 'hsuan-tuan-fu', the emperor's own robe in black with blue borders, a 'pao-ho-fu' in plain blue with cloud-figured blue borders, or the 'chung-ching-fu', presented to the mandarins as robes of honour, which had animals or birds instead of dragons to indicate rank? Why did the Ming emperors after Yung-lo gradually bring back the 'mang-i', the dragon robes, after the reaction against the Yuan or Mongol practices had softened over time?[17] In 1518 the Cheng-te Emperor of the Ming distributed robes with the three-clawed dragon to those of the third, while the second rank received the emblem of the flying-fish. Twenty years later, his successor, the Chia-ching Emperor whom we have met before, was angered by the sight of his President of the Board of War (Chang Tsan) appearing in Court in a robe with the emblem of the four-clawed 'mang'. Chang Tsan was of the second rank. How could he, the Emperor asked, take it upon himself to wear a mang? The Prime Minister replied that what Tsan was wearing was really a 'flying-fish', a new design which had been made to look like a mang. Why does it have two horns, the Emperor persisted, when that was strictly forbidden?[18] The 'chi-fu' decoration symbolised a schematic diagram of the entire universe and if the embroidered satin was of greenish-gold, it indicated that the robe was worn by an eunuch serving in the imperial palace.[19] Fashion in dress was as much a part of Asian culture as European, though its forms were not immediately intelligible or accessible to outsiders. An Islamic visitor to Paris, Shaikh Rifaᶜa (1826) showed great insight in his analysis of French fashions. In matters of dress, he pointed out, the French are constantly looking for new things and no fashion or adornment has remained with them for long. This does not mean that they change their dress completely and replace a hat with a turban. The hat continues to be used but its shape and colours are different.[20]

Expressions of individual tastes and preferences in Asian dress were immediately recognisable to participants in the number of pleats which the valets of an Indo-Islamic nobleman put in his master's superfine cotton girdle or turban; in the patterns of embroidery around the shirt-opening and round the collar; in the width of the sleeves in a Chinese dragon robe and the length of the dragon's tail. Aristocratic Indians who used the 'dhoti' together with the 'kamiz' or the shirt looked to their cloth merchants and tailors to furnish fashionable borders. The favoured garment of the Abbasid Caliph al-Mutawakkil (AD 847–61), made from a material of mixed silk, was imitated first by his household staff and then by the people. The popularity of the material drove up the price which in turn increased its production.[21] By the time the Mughal emperor Jahangir inherited the imperial wardrobe, the Indo-Islamic dress was already quite distinctive. The fashionable high-heeled shoes were replaced by equally fashionable soft slippers and the Safavid turban of multi-coloured striped stuffs had become popular.[22] Akbar himself intro-duced many new trends which were adopted by the fashionable courtiers. The traditional coat, the 'jamah', he renamed 'sarbgati', and the 'izar' was called 'yarpirahan'. His wardrobe contained 1,000 complete suits, of which 120 were kept in constant readiness. Each suit occupied a precise recorded place in a complete hierarchy of season, colour, value, and weight. The rank of pre-ferred colours was astonishingly long: ruby, golden orange, brass, crimson, grass-green, the colour of cotton-flower, sandalwood, almond-coloured, purple, grape-coloured, mauve . . .[23]

The universal human craving for symbolic distinction found an eloquent description in the pen of Ibn Khaldun:

It is part of royal and governmental pomp and dynastic custom to have the names of rulers and their peculiar marks embroidered on the silk, brocade, or pure silk gar-

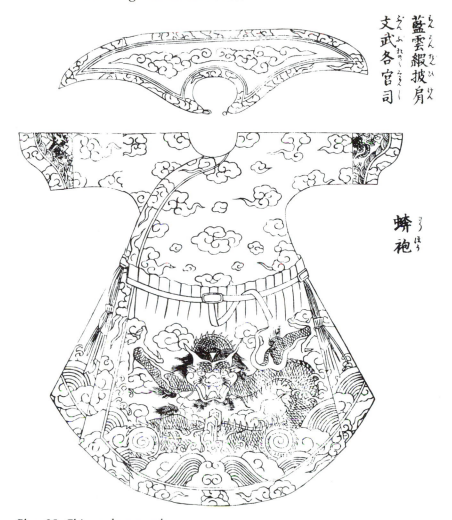

Plate 28 Chinese dragon-robe.

ments . . . The writing is brought out weaving a gold thread or some other coloured thread of a colour different from that fabric itself into it . . . Royal garments are embroidered with such a *tiraz*, in order to increase the prestige of the ruler or the person of lower rank who wears such a garment, or in order to increase the prestige of those whom the ruler distinguishes by bestowing upon them his own garment when he wants to honour them or appoint them to one of the offices of the dynasty.[24]

Even the puritanical Almohad dynasty which had at first shunned the tiraz, restored it later. The art historians Kuhnel and Goetz had delivered their own verdict on the question of fashion in Asian dress as early as 1926. The unchangeable character of oriental costume, so often repeated by foreigners, could not be sustained as a proposition even for the Indian traditions which were alleged to have been more conservative than elsewhere in Asia.[25] Pietro

Della Valle's interest in oriental social life, riddled as it was with European prejudice, caused him to take some account of the variations in costume. In India, both Muslims and Hindus, he observed, dressed only in white cotton which differed in quality and fineness according to the rank of the people and their spending habits. While the long upper robe and the associated tight trousers were cut in standard shapes, it was considered fashionable to pleat the material around the legs in fine folds. Furthermore, 'they who go most gallant, use to wear their Turbant only striped with silk or several colours upon white, and sometimes with Gold, and likewise their girdles wrought in Silk and Gold, instead of plain white.' Della Valle was so taken with the Indian outfit, for its cleanliness, comfort, and the show it made on horseback when worn with a sword, buckler, and shoulder belts, that he had a complete suit made for him to take back to Italy.[26]

The clothing of a politician and a royal connoisseur: Asaf Khan and Ibrahim Adil Shah. Asian sensibilities towards personal image, which lies at the root of the distinctions in dress, can be gauged from two seventeenth-century Indo-Islamic portraits. The subject of one is Emperor Shah Jahan's powerful prime minister and father-in-law Asaf Khan (1634). That of the second is Sultan Ibrahim Adil Shah of Bijapur (1580–1627). Asaf Khan is painted dressed in a simple qaba of flowered muslin. His trousers however are fashionably pleated. The richly-worked multi-coloured sash and the turban reflect the jewelled image of a great Mughal 'Amir' even though simplicity was the theme of the nobleman's clothing. The real personal badge of high office in the portrait was the huge damascened shield hung from a leather shoulder strap. The formidable Mughal mounted lancers shown faintly in the background and a small group of chained prisoners perhaps convey just a hint of the kind of political might that was at the disposal of Asaf Khan (see Plate 29). Wealth and power surrounded Sultan Ibrahim as well. He was also a poet, a connoisseur of art, an accomplished musician, and a student of philosophy. The portrait of Ibrahim depicts a man dressed in finery that was full of individual touches: the flowing qaba of transparent muslin blowing in the wind, the brocaded gold shoulder scarf and the matching sash and head band. Between the fingers of one hand rests a pair of Indian castanets, symbolising the princely musician. The other hand is holding a blue handkerchief (see Plate 30). There can be no possible confusion between the statesman with his hands held out in pious Islamic benediction and the courtly aesthete.

Architecture and housing

The house as a projection of the human body and social structure. The history of housing shared a feature in common with clothes. A house is an extention of the human form, a three-dimensional projection which transposes the mental perceptions of the scientific engineering represented by the human body. A double reasoning underlies the construction of houses. The primary need to provide shelter is taken for granted by everyone except the homeless. But a house is also something more than a mere utilitarian object with an economic value. Characterised by a complex internal logic at once functional and abstract, it ranges over a far wider mental and social universe than is the case with clothing. A house reflects and represents the structure of society at two separate levels of operation: that of the family and the collective will of which the individual family is an element. The arrangement of space within a house takes into account not only the physical needs of man, the provision of sleeping quarters, kitchen, and bathroom, but it addresses itself to the whole question of the relationship of individuals within the family unit. It can be seen by axiomatic reasoning that even a purely engineering detail such as the ground-plan of a house cannot be independent of the wider social conventions. In so far as a house is an integral part of a neighbourhood, it is of course directly influenced by the society's attitude towards individual rights and obligations, by the role of collective mandate, and the means available to society to enforce its will. The building and planning laws were born with the first house built by man. A medieval Islamic work on architecture and building regulations written by the Tunisian master-mason Ibn al-Rami (*d.* 1334) illuminated the point with a striking example. The case appears as a ruling ascribed to Caliph Umar al-Khattab (*r.* 634–44):

Umar passed by Abu Sufian while he was building his house in Madina, and he noticed that the foundation of the exterior wall protruded into the street. Umar said, 'Abu Sufian, you have exceeded your rights and protruded into the rights of others, so remove your wall.' Abu Sufian obeyed Umar and began to remove the foundation stones until completed, then asked Caliph Umar where he wanted him to place the wall. Umar replied, 'I want what is right'.[27]

The symbolic role of architecture. The construction industry in premodern Asia absorbed one of the largest proportions of the total available economic resources. For the farming population, house-building or repairs was one of the essential tasks in the annual work-cycle; or alternatively, depending on the depth of the exchange-economy, a source of employment during the slack agricultural season. At the upper level of the social stratification, large and sumptuous houses symbolised not only the personal wealth of their owners but also their status and taste. Building constructions, of which domestic housing is a part, possessed other attributes of human sensibilities. Marie-Antonin Carême (1784–1833), one of the greatest exponents of the *grande cuisine* of his age, claimed that architecture was the junior branch of the art of confectionery and he supported the claim with wonderfully ornate engravings of *patisserie* and creations in icing-sugar.[28] An artist-cuisinier who lived and worked in some of the greatest European royal houses and one who could

Plate 29 Asaf Khan, early seventeenth century (see p. 190).

Plate 30 Ibrahim Adil Shah II of Bijapur, *c.* 1615 (see p. 190).

Plate 31 Domestic dining scene, Iran, early seventeenth century.

name the First Consul (Napoleon), Prince Regent (George IV), Czar Alexander, and Prince Talleyrand among his patrons, Carême no doubt had ample opportunity to reflect upon the restless urge for creativity that often distinguish those who are endowed with political power and enjoy exalted social position. For such minds, the ability to organise splendid banquets was matched by the symbolic image of power inherent in public architecture which revealed the nature and source of royal majesty.[29] It was surely not entirely by accident that the Prince Regent, Carême's generous employer in England, should have been also the author of that bizarre architectural extravaganza, the Brighton Pavilion, which symbolised the exotic Orient and the princely yearning to escape from the scarcely-endurable rigidity of a formal and 'correct' public life. Whether the historian looks at the arid scenery of the Islamic Middle East, the vast geographical diversity of India and China, or the mist-covered volcanic landscape of Java, religious shrines of monumental proportions, palaces, citadels, fortifications, and even caravanserais and rest-houses for travellers, proclaimed the glorified image of the royal builders and their aristocratic followers. The Umayyad caliph ʿAbd al-Malik replaced the simple Bedouin mosque in Jerusalem with the Dome of the Rock (690–2) conceived and designed in the style of Islamic mosques. He had done the same with the mosques in Mecca, Medina, and Damascus. The architects and craftsmen who constructed these landmarks in the collective identity of Islam were sent, according to Ibn Khaldun, by the Byzantine emperor.[30]

The role of public buildings in Islam. Monuments built by the early Islamic rulers expressed in concrete visual forms the spiritual force of the new religion. The buildings and the decorative motifs also revealed the artistic ideas and thoughts of its adherents in a language of signs which were both assimilative and new. The motivations which inspired them were analysed and recorded by later historians, as we can see, to take only one example, from the work of the Damascene scholar al-Muqaddasi.[31] The Great Mosque in Damascus (709–15), he wrote, was the fairest jewel which belonged to the Muslims now. The most wonderful sight to be seen in the mosque was the setting of the various coloured marbles, perfectly matched with one another. It was said that the caliph al-Walid, the son of ʿAbd al-Malik, had employed on its construction skilled workmen from Persia, India, Western Africa, and Greece; he spent the revenues of Syria for seven years. The Byzantine emperor had given him additional materials and mosaics. In conversation with his uncle one day, al-Muqaddasi happened to remark that al-Walid had wasted the resources of Islam in building the Great Mosque, resources that would have been better spent on making roads, water cisterns, or on the restoration of the fortresses. He was gently corrected with the reply that the caliph had seen in Syria 'a country that had long been occupied by the Christians, and he noted therein the beautiful churches still belonging to them, so enchantingly fair, and so renowned for their splendour: even as are the Qumamah (the church of the Holy Sepulchre) and the churches of Lydda and Edessa. So he built for the Muslims a mosque, by which he diverted them from these, for he made it one of the wonders of the world.'[32] The outskirts of Damascus were landscaped by successive civilisations for a long time. Ibn Jubayr saw the large village of al-Nayrab (1184) close to the town on his way back from the hajj. The village houses were completely concealed by gardens and trees; only the tops of its buildings were to be seen from a distance. It had a cathedral mosque of unsurpassed elegance, the roof of which was set wholly with mosaics of many coloured marbles which an onlooker would have taken for a carpet of silk brocade. There was a fountain of exquisite beauty in the village and a place of ablution with ten doors, and water running in and around it.[33]

Abu'l Fazl clearly perceived the association between imperial power and architecture. The Mughal statesman missed few nuances of contemporaneous social and political practices. House-building, he said, was a necessary activity for governments. Houses were required for the army and they were a source of splendour for the administration. It was for this reason that Padshah Akbar had raised mighty citadels which protected the timid, overawed the rebellious, and delighted the obedient. Fine palaces provided accommodation for the ladies of the harem. Caravanserais, wells, and tanks likewise comforted the poor strangers.[34] The imperial historian was primarily a practical administrator and a statistician. He went on to write down the wages of building workers and the prices of all kinds of materials, red sandstone, three kinds of bricks – fully-burnt, half-burnt, and unburnt – wood, sweet limestone, lime, mortar, iron clamps, iron door-knockers, nails, rivets and heads, tiles, bamboo, thatch, glass window panes, and silver clay for whitewash. A skilled plasterer and carpenter earned the highest wage-rates, followed by stone-masons, brick-layers, and thatchers. The details listed by Abu'l Fazl are not of antiquarian interest alone. They shed illumination on a subject that is least documented in premodern Asian history. The Great Mughals in India were among the greatest builders of Islam, but their personal interest in the constructional techniques and planning was not unique. Ghazan Khan, the Mongol ruler who converted to Islam, drew up the ground-plans of his mausoleum near Tabriz (1299); according to the historical chronicle, the engineers consulted the monarch personally before locating the windows in the crypt.[35] The Islamic tradition of public building had a reverse side; it was noticed by the Dutch merchant Francisco Pelsaert. Once the builder-patron was dead, his successors showed little interest in maintaining or repairing the edifice. The roads leading to the towns and cities of Hindustan were strewn with fallen ruins of gardens, tombs, and palaces.[36] It was no doubt to prevent such consequences that private mansions, educational institutions, and mosques were turned into religious endowments, 'waqfs', which ensured that the financial resources for repairs as well as the charitable purpose were available and continued in a legally recognised form. In 1038 the Great Synagogue of Ramle granted a twenty-year lease for a ruined property belonging to itself to Sedaqa b. Yefet al-Shiraji (the sesame-oil maker) for the annual rent of half a dinar, which was to be invested in its repairs. The lessee expressly declared his intention to carry out the restorations. The court records of Ottoman Cairo also contain many references to contracts and judgements relating to building repairs under waqf control. The supervisor of the Madrasat al-Malik al-Nasir Farag Ibn Barquq concluded a contract with two master-builders to rebuild in 1581 the well and the water-wheel of the institution for a sum of fifty-five dinars. The contract was agreed in the presence of nine other fellow builders who declared that they could not undertake the work at a lesser estimate.[37]

Architecture in South East Asia and China. Similar arrangements also existed for Hindu buildings in India and Buddhist temples in South East Asia and the Far East.[38] A great temple-complex in India was almost 'a state within a state' once it was built and consecrated. Barabodur (*c.* 775–800), the largest Buddhist 'stupa' in the world, points to the religious and artistic aspirations of a Javanese monarch who undoubtedly possessed huge and stable economic resources in the wet-rice agriculture of his island-empire to have undertaken building-works on such a visionary scale. Seen against a background of intensely green tropical landscape of rugged volcanic mountains, the massive stone-built structure rises up in a series of platforms, culminating in a bell-shaped *stupa* at the top. The scenes of daily life, by land and sea, depicted in the hundreds of friezes that decorate the walls of the platforms, are as evocative of the civilisational vitality of Barabodur's creators, as any written records could have been had they survived. There were other examples of the architecture of symbolic power in South East Asia. Angkor Wat (*c.* 1131) in Cambodia expresses a spiritual affinity with the Hindu shrines of Bali, that merely points to the origin of an 'idea' and a sacred 'ideology' in the distant Indian sub-continent, transformed by other receptive minds. The splendours of Ayuthya, the capital of Siam for 400 years, were witnessed by Tavernier and Alexander Hamilton a century or so before the city was completely destroyed by fire during the Burmese war (1767). Covered with gold-leaves the temple spires of Ayuthya in a 'sunshine . . . reflect the rays so strongly that, at two or three miles distance, they disturb the eye, when looked upon . . . I [Hamilton] was in one temple pretty large, built exactly four square, and each square contained just an hundred images . . . The priests told us, that some were of pure gold, others of *Tecul* silver, which has no alloy in it'.[39] Both Tavernier and Hamilton actually saw the great image of the Buddha sixty feet high, Buddha who sat without a roof over his head for nearly two centuries after the sacking. The gold leaf rubbed around the base by generations of pilgrims as votive offering had accumulated into a thick layer. Ayuthya, one of the greatest capital cities of Asia, burnt for three days, vitrifying the crumbling bricks. The molten gold went to Burma to enrich Shwe Dagon and other Buddhist shrines. The beauty and the devotional intensity of Siamese religious architecture found such profuse expression throughout the land that Tavernier wondered 'at the industry of this nation'.[40]

The unity and disunity of the concrete visual images were underlined nowhere as strongly as in the case of houses and public monuments constructed from different building materials. Towns and cities composed of stone and brick-built houses presented a view very different from those in which wooden or bamboo-and-thatch structures predominated. The English private trader Thomas Bowrey (1669–88 in Asia) would voice this contrast in his statement that even rich and populous Acheh, the capital of the powerful maritime kingdom of Sumatra, fell far short of the appearance of the cities in Arabia, Persia, and India.[41] The great urban centres of China and Japan shared with eastern India and South East Asia similarities of architectural construction, though the actual idiom was different in each case. Western opinion on the artistic merit of Chinese housing differed. Matteo Ricci, the remarkable Jesuit priest who lived and worked (1583–1610) in Ming China, thought that Chinese architecture was inferior to that of Europe in every way with respect to the style and the durability of the buildings. When the Chinese set about building, they seemed to measure things by the span of human life, building for themselves rather than for future generations. Europeans on the other hand appeared to strive for the eternal in their attitude to civilisation. It was impossible for the people of China, who were otherwise in no way inferior to the rest of the world, to appreciate the magnificence of Western architecture and building forms.[42] Ricci was aware how passionately interested Emperor Wan-li was in building the magnificent royal tomb to the northwest of Peking, surrounded by bare mountains. Ricci and his fellow Jesuits presented the emperor with a picture of the San Marco piazza in Venice and an album of prints depicting the church at El Escorial in Spain. Emperor Wan-li laughed openly when the Jesuits told him that in Europe princes sometimes lived on the upper floors of their palaces, so absurd did the idea appear to him. Ricci reflected, 'thus are all the people kept content to remain in the modes in which they were brought up.'[43]

The difference between vertical and horizontal projections in building construction was noticed by more than one contemporary observer. De Magalhaens explicitly mentioned that whereas in Europe buildings were multi-storied, in China buildings extended horizontally. Bernier had said much the same thing for Delhi, pointing out that 'Paris consists of three or four cities piled upon one another, all of them containing numerous apartments.'[44] No disagreement exists among historians and contemporary observers that the architecture of symbolic power in China expressed the same inner urges as it did in other parts of Asia. The image of imperial majesty and artistic perfection were signified by the 'Purple Forbidden City' in Peking, forming a combination that was overwhelming to the beholder. Jan Nieuhof, the ambassador of the Dutch East India Company to the celestial court, described the Forbidden City in 1669:

This Imperial Court, which is exactly square, contains three miles in circumference, within the second wall of the city on the north side, being fortified also with strong stone battlements fifteen foot high; in this wall are four gates . . . we passed when we went to appear before the Emperor's Throne, through this gate, and from thence into a base court, which had a well-paved crossway of 400 paces, with a water-trench cut through the middle . . . All the Edifices, which are so many, are most richly adorned with gilt galleries, balconies, and carved imagery, to the admiration of all that ever saw them . . . Most of the timber which appears on the outside of the house, is either gilt or coloured over with a certain gum, called by the Chinese *cie* . . . wherewith they colour or paint their household-stuff, ships, and houses that they make them shine and glitter like Looking Glasses.[45]

Almost a century later Lord Macartney would make a sensitive analysis of the Chinese architectural traditions, observing that, although they differed markedly from European rules, nevertheless they were completely consistent in creating an integral system which combined perfectly water, landscaped garden, and roofed structures.[46]

The generative scheme of domestic housing: function and design. In common with food and clothing, domestic houses in Asia also resolved into a generative scheme that included double and triple sets of opposition. Urban and rural housing at times coincided with the typologies of the rich and the poor. Stone, brick, and timber on the other hand underlined a triangular pattern of opposition that was not always mutually exclusive, even though the regional distribution of houses distinguished by building materials was very striking. The choice of right materials was partly a question of costs and individual taste; partly, of climatic and ecological determinants. The ground-plan and the elevation of the housing-types are clearly recognisable. From the eastern Mediterranean to the northern and western plains of India, stone and brick works predominated, with a limited use of timber in the main constructional structure.[47] Hard-wood poles often provided supporting framework filled in by coursed clay or unburnt bricks. In general, the use of wood in the western Indian Ocean remained confined to doors, windows, and interior fittings. The basic plan of domestic housing, which was more than just a one-room shelter or a nomadic tent, revolved around a central theme, the interior courtyard. The two Arabic terms for a dwelling, 'bait' and 'dar', point towards a binary opposition (to take an etymological view rather than cultural or geographical): the first signified a covered shelter or a room, the single module of human habitation, while the second bore the meaning of a space surrounded by walls, buildings, or nomadic encampments.

In a classic description Georges Marçais makes the distinction clear and puts forward an European interpretation of the dar:

From the earliest times there has been in Muslim dwellings a tendency to arrange around a central space: the park, where the shepherd's flock will be sheltered from the blows of enemies; the courtyard, where the non-nomadic family will live cut off from inquisitive strangers . . . This arrangement, of a central open space, surrounded by habitable rooms, certainly does not belong exclusively to the Arab world. This disposition is also characteristic of the primitive Roman house, with its *atrium*, and the Hellenic house with its peristyle; it must have been adopted very early by the Mediter-

Plate 32   Orchard in the Yemen, trees being grown against walls (see p. 200).

ranean countries. But this type of domestic architecture seems to offer an ideal frame-work for Muslim life.[48]

The difference between the two concepts was important to the typology of Asian housing. Rural houses controlled their spacing by adopting the modular approach, even though an extended farm-house might be planned on the principle of an interior courtyard surrounded by high walls, against which fruit trees or vegetable plants were grown (see Plate 32). Urban housing in the Middle East and India on the other hand took the courtyard as the first principle of architectural planning. The desire for domestic privacy was not the only reason for locating the open courtyard within the outer walls. The interior of houses needed to be protected from the heat, noise, and dust from unpaved streets. The arrangement of the rooms and the service facilities followed on from this primary logic. The exceptions to this rule, if it could be described as such, were the square multi-storied tower houses of the Yemen, Hadramawt, and Hijaz, which had their free space distributed mainly around the buildings rather than inside them. These tall constructions often over-looked market-gardens, the produce from which was sold to the house-owners (see Plate 33).[49] But even in the Yemen a second type of garden-house was to be found in the suburbs which had interior courtyards landscaped with fountains, water pools, trees, and shrubs.

Carsten Niebuhr who visited Sanͨa in 1762 describes both the high-rise

Plate 33 Tower-house in San'a, the Yemen, vegetable-gardens in the square (see p. 200).

buildings and the courtyard house. The first, he noted, were constructed on principles different from Europe. Cut stones and burnt bricks were used. But the windows were only shuttered, without any glass-panes, though coloured Venetian glass was to be found in some houses. Niebuhr also saw the chief minister's country-house. Although not large, it was entirely open, on one side:

A number of fruit-trees grew in the garden. In the midst of it was a *jet d'eau*, similar to that which we had seen in the Imam's hall of audience. The water was put in motion, by being raised in a reservoir, by an ass and a man who led him. The *jet d'eau* was no ornament; but it cooled the air; a thing very agreeable in hot countries. We saw others of the same sort, in the garden of all the principal inhabitants of Sana.[50]

The single-roomed modular construction was more prevalent in rural areas and in the coastal towns such as Lohaya. A species of grass roofed over the mud-walled structures which were surrounded by a strong wooden fence.[51]

The design of a tenement house and large residence in Cairo. That the multi-storied tenement buildings and the extended family residences were common in other parts of the Middle East also, we know from a legal settlement of property in the famous Cairo geniza sources (*c.* 1190). The proprietorship of the two houses seemed to have been transferred as part of a marriage portion. The mother and the unmarried sister of the settler already had a five-eighth share in the tenement house, in the Mamsusa quarter of the city. It had a ground-floor and nine upper apartments and was owned jointly with the family of the physician al-Wajih and the Muslim Ministry of Pious Foundations. The second property (being transferred), bordering the well-known Hudayji lane, was altogether a larger complex, comprising several houses, a ruin, a cattle pen, and a well with a waterwheel (see Plate 34, for a similar type of house). For the larger house in the complex an arched doorway led into two halls through a double corridor paved with marble. The main reception hall here had a wind-tower, ventilating the room, and this too was lined with marble. A gilded cornice encircled the hall and the ceiling was painted with decorations in oil after the Syrian fashion. A marble fountain stood in the inner courtyard, flanked by two loggias, a kitchen, and a bathroom with marble floors and a gypsum-lined cupola. The upper floor contained the living-rooms and additional washrooms.[52] The *geniza* legal deed went into a characteristic level of details no doubt prescribed by the need to establish exact identity of the property and prevent encroachments and unauthorised modifications.

The functional logic of houses and building materials. The document reveals at the same time the standards of an opulent private house in a great Islamic capital city. The descriptions left by Chevalier Chardin and François Bernier of the aristocratic houses in Isfahan and Delhi show a fundamental unity of

Plate 34 Interior courtyard of a mansion in Cairo (see p. 202).

domestic architectural forms that had some kind of common origin or functional logic. The need to provide security and privacy, together with the problems of ventilation and physical comforts, led to the invention of the inner courtyard and the latticed windows, on which earthen water-coolers were often placed.[53] The projecting windows built on the upper levels of a house were known as 'mashrabiyya' in Egypt (see Plate 35) and 'bait al-sharbah' in the Yemen, a place for drinking, so to say; in India, the term 'jharoka' or view described such a balcony. The finely decorated window and the balcony found all the way from Egypt to India signified an important architectural theme. The magnificent cantilevered timbered windows of old houses in Jedda, rising up in a series of bays, reveal the finer aesthetic points involved in the presentation of a particular type of building facade.[54] Not all houses in the Indo-Islamic world presented a blank exterior. A good house in Delhi, according to Bernier's summary of contemporary ideas, should be in a flower-garden, with courtyards, fountains, water-pools, and large elevated 'diwans' or public apartments designed to catch the breeze. Chardin says much the same for Persian houses: 'the noblest are commonly raised between two and four foot above the surface of the ground, with four fronts, that face the four cardinal winds.'[55] The tower-houses of the Yemen also had diwans, placed on the second floor, though the sumptuous private sitting-rooms, the 'mafraj', were generally situated just below the roof-top.[56] The problem of ventilating inner and underground chambers without external windows presented a considerable challenge to the architects of the Middle East and India, who showed considerable engineering skill in constructing flues and chimneys. The magnificent ornate wind-towers of Yazd, still to be seen in their original form, are a direct descendant of an ancient art (see Plate 36). Thick walls and cross-ventilation achieved through windows placed on opposite walls partially protected the buildings from the effects of high summer temperature. There was also a conscious attempt to introduce an artificial cooling-system into the architecture. Ath-Tha'alibi, the tenth-century scholar of Nishapur, records in his book of curious and entertaining information that the Persian emperors used to have the roof of a summer-house plastered over with clay each day during the hot season. Lattice screens made from willow were placed outside the walls and large pieces of ice placed in the interstices. Al-Mansur adopted a similar technique for 'air-conditioning' his summer-houses. Wet canvas screens were substituted for ice and later the use of woven reed mats moistened with water became a regular method of cooling.[57]

The design of a substantial Indo-Islamic house provides some indication of the social usage of space, which is not always well documented in the historical sources. Women and children were not rigidly confined to particular parts of the house, though there were strict conventions about their appearance in the public rooms. The basic distinctions followed from the separation between sitting, dining, and sleeping quarters, while the functional rooms, the kitchen

Plate 35 The projecting wooden lattice in the window of a Cairo mansion (see p. 204).

Plate 36 Wind-tower in Yazd, Iran, ventilating several floors below ground (see p. 204).

and the bath, together with storage areas were arranged according to climatic conditions and the force of tradition. The standards of interior furnishings and decorations likewise reflected different shades of social tastes but did not on the whole vary on matters of form. The raised mattress covered by freshly-laundered sheets and fine carpets was the basic module of furnishing, supplemented by low chairs, tables, cupboards fitted to the walls, and ornamental plaster and inset-works in coloured stones. The premium attached to high-quality plaster-decorations perhaps explains why a skilled plasterer earned the highest rates of wages. Years of training followed before the aspiring craftsman could call himself a 'master' or 'ustad' in the profession.

Plate 37 Clay domes in a covered market, Kirman, Iran, sun-dried bricks.

The building materials were just as differentiated as the workmen who used them. The character of the stones determined how they were to be cut and shaped; the use of granite, basalt, or sandstones for different types of walls and structures were as well-understood as the use of hard kiln bricks and soft sun-baked ones. In the best type of masonry, the cut stones were so closely joined and fitted that it was impossible to insert even a needle into the joining. Plaster made from burnt alabaster, and mixed with lime and pounded sea-shells (in parts of India) could be polished to a surface finer than the best-grained marble.[58] In northern India, milk, resin-gum, and sugar were added to unslaked lime to prepare the plaster-mixture and after it had dried, the surface was polished with an agate-stone until it shone like a looking-class.[59] Even the humble clay strengthened by straw-cuttings yielded results in the hands of a master-builder, surprising to strangers (see Plate 37). 'It is universally common to spherical, arched, or plain buildings, to lay vast loads of mud at top,' wrote John Fryer in his account of Persia (1677), 'and what is more wonderful, only with mud and clay, they will rear most spacious arches, without other matter of assistance.'[60] The choice of building materials on the part of the builders and the patrons who commissioned the houses must have been determined by technical considerations as well as those of costs. The interior walls of houses in Sanᶜa for example were lined with unfinished stones or built with rubble. Our sources lack precise accounts of building expenses; Abu'l Fazl was the only contemporary author to give exact figures for different kinds of building materials needed for construction works. A seventeenth-century French account refers to the high building costs in Surat. Bricks and lime were expensive and timber had to be transported from northern Gujarat by sea. Even an ordinary house could not be built under 500–600 'livres for bricks and twice as much for lime.'[61]

Commercial buildings, rich, and poor housing. Commercial buildings, parts of which were also utilised for residential purposes, and the dwellings for the poorer people in towns and country constitute two additional typologies, different from aristocratic and well-to-do houses. In the seventeenth-century Mughal Delhi, even the better housing belonging to merchants and petty officials was not entirely built of stone or bricks, but space, shade, and good ventilation marked most of the structures which were whitewashed and roofed over with thatch and cane.[62] Intermixed with the richer houses, there was an immense number of small ones, built of mud and straw (see Plate 38). These were the homes of the common troopers, of the vast multitude of servants, and working people attached to the court and the imperial army. The wide usage of thatch and bamboo matting posed a serious fire hazard. Bernier mentioned three fires during a single year, which destroyed 60,000 dwellings in Delhi. It was because of these 'wretched mud and thatch houses' that Bernier took the imperial capital to resemble a collection of villages or as a military encampment with a few added civic amenities.[63] Furniture was scanty or lacking in the humble homes. Cooking stoves, earthenware water jars and a few utensils for cooking and eating supplemented the family beds covered with a sheet or two.[64] The swing-cot for the baby and smaller children added a tender note to an otherwise austere and hard life-style (see Plate 39).

Buildings where the merchants, traders, and artisans met to conduct business fall into two recognisable groups in the western Indian Ocean. The arcaded shops lining the main city streets opened onto warehouses at the back, where stocks were kept overnight. In Mughal Delhi, the upper parts of the warehouses were built over to provide accommodation for the owners of the shops: they looked handsome enough from the street, as Bernier observed, and appeared tolerably spacious within; they were airy at a distance from the dust and communicated with the terrace-roofs over the shops, on which the inhabitants slept at night.[65] The rich merchants, however, lived elsewhere and retired to their fine houses after the day's business. The covered bazaars of Safavid Isfahan impressed John Fryer not only by the elegance of their construction but also by the range of goods offered for sale.[66] The second type of commercial buildings was given the popular description of caravanserais but the actual linguistic terms varied from area to area. The Fatimid quarter of al-Qahira in Old Cairo contained about 200 'wakelas' or large commercial complexes (also known as funduqs and khans), housing merchants who

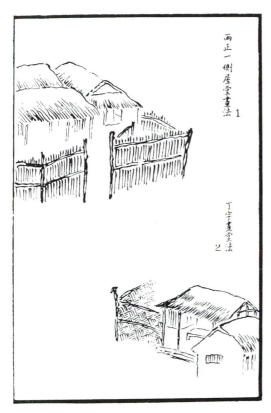

Plate 38 Peasant huts in bamboo mat and thatch
(see p. 208).

gathered at this most famous turn-table of the transcontinental trade of the Indian Ocean, the Mediterranean, and the Atlantic. In Bulaq, the port-area of Cairo built in the fourteenth century, there was a proliferation of wakelas which served the needs of merchants trading with Syria and the Red Sea.[67] The caravanserias of the Yemen, the 'samsarahs' of Bait al-Fakih and Sa^ena, functioned both as inns and centres of business. Constructed in burnt bricks or stones, they were often set up as pious institutions by wealthy citizens, and those situated on the road between Mharras and San^ea, while providing the travellers with accommodation, according to Niebuhr, served 'no other sort of food than coffee, rice, bread, and butter'.[68] In 1666 the French traveller Jean de Thevenot saw the beautiful caravanserai of Ahmedabad near the public green. The facade of the building was decorated with delicate latticed bal-conies supported on pillars. An archway with octagonal vaulting led into the handsome inner courtyard, two stories high; the stonework inside was plastered with the famous 'liquid marble'.[69]

Domestic housing in South East Asia and China. The visual and functional contrasts between urban and rural housing, or between the rich and poor housing, were greater perhaps in eastern Asia than in the west. A Middle Eastern or north Indian village composed of clay-walled or rough stone-built houses presented a view qualitatively different from the sight of large urban or garden houses built by the wealthy. It did not however express a fundamentally dissimilar identity. In eastern and southern India, where the dominant idiom of popular housing came from the use of bamboo, thatch, and occasionally, also timber, there was an upper level of house-building that followed the Middle Eastern pattern under the dominant influence of Islam. The architectural dichotomy lessened as Islam moved eastward towards the Indonesian archipelago. The mosque or the ruler's palace, the 'kraton', represented a new variation on the familiar constructional themes in overall planning, shape of the constructions, and building materials, without introducing radically new sensibilities. But the question remains: are the simple bamboo or wooden huts supported on timber piles, which provided housing to the bulk of the population to the east of the Bay of Bengal, of the same civilisational identity as the architecture of power and material splendours? The answer must be left open for the time being. Jan Nieuhof was emphatic in describing the ordinary houses in China as being 'mean built' without much comforts. They had only one door and a single room, roofed over with pan tiles, and the walls were whitewashed. People living in these houses drove very 'mean Trades'. But the shops of the rich merchants and the houses of the chief citizens were filled with all kinds of rich objects, cotton textiles, silk, porcelain, and jewellery.[70] The engraving of the working houses and shops in a Chinese street which accompanied Nieuhof's comment reveals an architectural form that was not different in terms of expression from the architecture of symbolic power in China. They were however different from the peasant huts of eastern Bengal with their soft, rounded, thatched roofs.

The symbiosis between the landscape and tropical housing. There can be nothing but unanimity on one historical point. In a landscape where flooded rice-fields were the dominant visual image of collective well-being, the scattered homesteads, surrounded by the banana plantations, clumps of cane and bamboo, and the coconut trees, shared a physical unity, born out of a functional usage and the limits of artistic ideas. Individual huts arranged within a fenced area were occupied by different members of the extended family and at the same time provided demarcated space for social occasions such as dining, reception, and family worship. Stilts, scaffolded platforms, or a banked plinth protected the houses from the annual flooding during the wet season.[71] If the household possessed a fish-pond, the excavated earth supplied the material for the raised area. The distinctive feature of the bamboo-and-

Plate 39 Domestic scene in Agra, the house of Nafahat al-Ums, poet and dervish, 1603 (see p. 208).

timber houses of Bengal and South East Asia lay in the shape of their roof and the methods of construction. In Javanese rural society, the status of a house was signified by the type of its roof which in turn identified the status of the owners. A simple sloping roof, with single or angled lines of elevation, carried the association of an ordinary farming house. The more elaborate roofing structures, the 'limasan' or 'joglo', rising up in tiered pyramids, suggested higher social rank.[72] Even the rounded humble thatch of the farmer's hut in Bengal, which recalled the haystack or the paddy-stores, held a certain visual fascination for eyes unaccustomed to such impressions. The splendour of Shah Jahan's Red Fort in Delhi (1638–48), built by architects Ustad Ahmad and Hamid, rested on the Mughal adaptation of the classic Iranian-Islamic architectural lines. But the shape of the emperor's pavilion in the hall of the public audience, 'Diwan-i-Khas', imitated in marble the peasant-dwellings of Bengal, perhaps reminding the 'Peacock-Throne' which province in the empire deserved to be called its rice-bowl.

The inversion of the usual symbolic meaning in this case, the transposition of the farmer's hut into a royal seat, suggests that architectural ideas cross and re-cross cultural watersheds in a more complex way than either food habits or clothing. The interaction between the senior architect-designer, his builders, the available technology and materials, and finally, the patron who commissions the work produced forms that were at once subtle and original. The overall idiom could not of course completely disregard the limits of social acceptability. But the ornamentation of a Thai or Chinese timbered-framed house must have taken into account the personal taste of the owners. The use of perishable building materials (bamboo, various kinds of vegetable fibres, and wood), did not mean that these houses lacked craftsmanship or artistic creativity. A rich house constructed with bamboo screen-walls and cane furnishings exhibited exquisite workmanship. A Thai house built in teak wood was a massive structure, with carved eaves brackets and finely-woven cane screens; the parquet floors were polished with transparent lacquer which brought out the grain of the timber to perfection. Plaster-work and gilding which ornamented public buildings, the Buddhist monasteries, temples, and royal palaces, varied the style of presentation, as did also the orange-gold tiles, covering the soaring roof (see Plate 40). On the whole, according to the French diplomat Simon de La Loubere who visited Siam in 1687, Thai public constructions lacked the profusion of columns, architraves, and friezes which characterised European planning. The real dignity of royal houses and temples did not consist among the Siamese in the 'ornaments of architecture'. It was found in a complex variation of the horizontal elevations. The public rooms and the apartments of the king and the queen were placed at different levels and connected with steps. At the very top, one high-ridged roof followed another in descending lines. 'At the Palace of the City of *Siam*,' wrote La

Plate 40 The ornamental roof of the Emerald Temple, Bangkok (see p. 212).

Loubere, 'I have seen seven roofs proceeding one from under another before the Building: I know not whether there were not others behind.'[73]

The constructional principles of Chinese architecture. The perceptive French envoy also thought that the principle behind Chinese architecture was the same as he had seen in Thailand. The ascending or descending succession of horizontal lines seem to point towards the idea of the inequality of objects. A modern historian of Chinese technology suggests that qualities of hierarchy, liturgy, axis, and symmetry distinguished Confucian architectonics.[74] There is little difficulty in recognising the basic form of the timbered structure in Asian society. It could be described as a raised pavilion with a frame construction. A series of columns and load-bearing pillars supported the roof, and that was all. Where needed, the walls acted merely as screens. Marble slabs, intricately perforated into latticed panels, appeared alongside bamboo or cane basket-work and wooden frames with panes filled by white oiled-paper. Even massive stone or brick walls in many Chinese constructions were not probably proper load-bearing structures (see Plate 41). The typology of the open pavilion did not remain confined just to eastern Asia. The famous Hall of Forty Pillars in Isfahan was a spectacular example of the architect's skill in combining the ver-tical column projections with the Islamic traditional style of solid construction

Plate 41 Main Hall of a Group of Temples, Shan Hsi Province (see p. 213).

(see Plate 42). The delicate marbled mausoleum of Itimad al-Daula in Agra (1621–28) may appear at first sight far removed from T'ai-ho Tien, the Hall of Supreme Harmony in the Forbidden City. The similarity of horizontal lines broken by vertical columns, arches, minarets, the cupola, and the curved roofs is all too evident. The open pavilion with timber frame and the sloping roof, either thatched or tiled, dominated building designs all the way from Java to China and Japan. In parts of South East Asia and China, there was in addition a strange religious structure, the 'meru' or pagoda, a tower-like construction composed of articulated stories.

Although Chinese architectural idiom was very different from those of the Middle East and India, the domestic housing shared a design feature in common with those areas. The central courtyard was as much a part of the Chinese scene as it was in western Asia. However, the principle of arranging living quarters in the form of partitioned cloisters, several stories high, was replaced by designing a number of self-contained pavilions within the rectangular courtyard enclosed by blank walls. These rooms were occupied by different members of the extended family. The courtyard or the enclosed area of land gave the Chinese architect the opportunity to combine landscaped garden and houses as a single entity, and the concave roof could be used with great effect to complement the shape of trees and shrubs planted in the garden.[75] A timber

Plate 42 The Hall of Forty Pillars, Isfahan, Iran (see p. 213–14).

structure cannot, of course, compare with stone and brick in durability, and the periodical rebuilding of Chinese houses has removed from the historian's eyes the chance to study the details of architectural evolution in China. Paintings dating from the Sung period show urban streets lined with buildings which are two- or three-stories high. The dominant single-storied structure built on a raised platform with a verandah protected by long eaves appeared to have evolved later on. On the other hand, the general functional and social features in architecture were enunciated very early. Mo Ti (*c.* 480–390 BC), for example, stated that the guiding principle in house-building should be the need to construct high in order to avoid damp and moisture. Thick walls kept out the wind and the cold. The roof must be strong enough to withstand snow, frosts, rain, and dew. High partitions within the palaces maintained social proprieties between men and women. It was unnecessary to expend labour and money on building features that could only indicate luxury and complications.[76]

Money and much artistic effort were nevertheless lavished on houses, as Juan Gonzales de Mendoza, the Spanish priest, noted in his account of China (1585). The houses were as grand as those in Rome and the interiors were

Plate 43 Dining scene in Sung China (see p. 216).

painted in brilliant colours and burnished-gold. All the fine houses had orna-mental pools and gardens. Chinese urban landscape could easily hold its own with that of Brussels, Venice, Seville, and Mexico City.[77] Interior scenes of social life painted by Ku Hung-chung (910–980) reveal a time-less dimension of material perfection: lacquered tables set with tea-pots, jugs, and bowls, low chairs, a long, screened platform used as an extended easy chair; the lady play-ing the lute is entirely at ease before her distinguished audience (see Plate 43). The grandeur of life-style was not without its cost. When Emperor Wan-li's projected mausoleum was completed after much labour and financial expen-diture, his officials represented to him how the weather had turned fine that day and the building workers expressed great joy on the occasion. But the emperor must also have known that old men and children had been drafted to work at the site, frail creatures who shed tears as they laboured in the bitter cold of a Peking winter.[78]

The isomorphism between housing and social structure. The architecture of symbolic power and private housing (taken together) signified historical identities in ways that differed from food and clothing. At the same time, all three signifiers preserved certain powers in common. The four civilisational identities, so strongly articulated by religion and social systems, were not isomorphic to the structure of food, clothing, and housing. Architectural forms and expressions indicated the presence of Islam within a continuum through visual images which could not be mistaken. Islamic clothing to some extent shared the same attribute, as did also Chinese and Sanskritic garments. But food habits were influenced as much by environmental factors as social and cultural. The unities of ideas, building materials, and functional usage in public and private architecture in the geographical area to the east of the Bay of Bengal can be arranged as a common 'set' with a continuum of its own. The brick or stone structures in Thailand, La Loubere thought, were so foreign to the natural constructional idiom of the country that these buildings, where found, pointed to the presence of foreigners and innovations introduced by them.[79] It is obvious that the technology of the building industry travelled over great distances irrespective of the civilisational frontiers. Its assimilation into local artistic or constructional forms indicated a different level of cognitive identity. The limits of social acceptability would determine how far new and visually attractive techniques, let us say, plastering, gilding, lacquer-work, stone-inlay, or the art of building true arches and domes, should be incorporated into the traditional methods of construction. Such changes went on all the time, in subtle ways marking the pace of wider social transformations. The Buddhist *stupa* in South East Asia, the Chinese pagoda, and the marble pavilions of the Mughal emperors in India, were joint heirs of a great transregional migration of inner identities which were supplemented by a new arrival in the eighteenth century, European building designs. Their adoption by Asian craftsmen however remained limited until much later.

The linguistic term for architecture and housing would yield in any language of Asia a common set defined by function and social meaning. The set can be further partitioned into two sub-sets formed by the symbolism of ceremonial power and private domestic usage. Unlike the elements of the sets 'food' and 'clothing', those of housing have no power to indicate either a temporal occasion or a precise spatial location. But the set can differentiate rank separating people by wealth and social position. The time dimension in the set is effective only at the level of the internal design of a house, which assigns particular roles to rooms and demarcated space. The usage in turn expresses itself through a daily time-sequence. The siting of the religious shrines in Sanskritic, Buddhist, and Chinese households reflected the importance of both internal planning and temporal routine. Because of their permanent and inflexible physical forms, buildings are not able to act as sensitive mirrors of transient mental reflections. But even here there is some room for movement. The garden house and the town house distinguished by a particular attitude and usage of space represented also the different rhythms of daily life and different aesthetic needs. Travellers approaching a large capital city and an industrial centre, such as Ahmedabad, would have been struck, as Jean de Thevenot was, by a sight reflecting many separate collective moods, exquisite gardens and houses enclosed by high walls and fruit trees, inter-mingled with rural housing, forming so many villages, as it were, in the outer suburbs.[80]

8

The land and its products: the structure of rural production

The rationale and typology of settled agriculture

Farming as a way of life. Settled farming in premodern Asia shares a common attribute with natural language. It is at once simple and complex. The nature of agrarian production, its purpose and objectives, can be grasped more or less intuitively, just as the meaning of words and linguistic expressions are understood without further explication. A historical description of the structure of rural life would appear at first sight both easily accessible and analytically incapable of over-elaboration. If the bulk of the Asian population lived on a diet of cereals and vegetable products, the regular supply of food was secured through one of the striking technological discoveries of the prehistoric age, the intensive use of land for crop-growing, market-gardening, and the development of domestic or commercial orchards.[1] Farming was more than a system of food production. It formed itself into a way of life as well. People in almost every stratum of society appeared in one way or another linked to the rural mechanism of wealth-creation. All the way from the eastern Mediterranean to the edge of the Pacific, rich and powerful centralised empires lived on the economic surplus created by a huge mass of toiling peasantry. For the majority of the Asian population there was no alternative to the logic of a reciprocal relationship between physical survival and the hard task of working the land.

However, beneath this unbroken surface of immediate comprehension lie submerged, like giant reefs of coral encrustation built up over several millennia, a whole complex of tangled organic relationships and even scientific facts. The historical interactions took place at the level of everyday life and the random movements of longer time-cycles, between the knowledge and practice of soil chemistry and plant-breeding, the utilisation of human and animal energy, the mastery of hydraulics and civil engineering, the innovation of mechanical aids, and accurate climatic observations. The technology of crop production did not stand alone. By a process of fusion with the social structure and dominant forms of political control, it reacted, changed, and responded not only to its own internal and external dynamics (the appearance of a new plant or the collapse of the soil productivity) but to pressures generated by the whole society. It is evident, Abu'l Fazl remarked in his chapter on the 'Means of Subsistence' in the *Ain-i-Akbari*, that in all cultivated tracts

218

people who own and hold title in land are numerous. But man's base nature and the passage of time obscures all true facts. It is only the just ruler, his administrators and judges who can restore the pristine quality of a lost liveli-hood.[2] The complex interplay between land, society, and its food have remained largely undocumented. It is almost a certainty that the historian will never be able to recover and only hint at the detailed rationale which con-trolled and governed food production based on crop-growing and land-management.

The basic patterns of Asian settled farming were worked out over many millennia and belonged temporally to the Braudelian *longue durée*. As Hans Helbaek has reminded us:

What was achieved during the first millennia of agriculture is still of paramount importance to modern society and will for ever so remain. Unconscious of his impudence, man forced plants to grow beyond the areas where by nature they were at home and, in doing so, was instrumental in reshaping their genetic constitution, thus enabling them to follow him in his expansive migrations practically all over the world.[3]

Fundamental changes in the social relationships and the technique of farming, when these did take place, were limited to a number of permutations between nomadism, swidden culture, and sedentarisation, utilising the full range of crop production and land-holding. In general during our period of study, three different types of rural production can be identified. First of all, there was a sizeable nomadic economy based on stock rearing and the herding of camels, sheep, horses, and cattle. Secondly, the farming equivalent of pastoral nomadism was the swidden or the shifting cultivation of the slash-and-burn type. Finally, by far the most important category of food production incor-porated arable farming practised on the basis of permanent land-holdings. The technology of arable production remained tied to a number of basic physical and social factors: implements such as the plough and the hoe, animal and occasionally water power, labour supplied by the peasant household, and permanent capital investments exemplified by cleared and terraced fields, wells, reservoirs, canals, and underground conduits. A smaller but not unimportant variation on this larger rural theme was to be seen in the commercially-operated plantations growing various kinds of palms (dates, coconuts, and betel-nuts), fruit trees, and even valuable timber such as teak. The cultivation of tea in China, coffee and 'qat' in the Yemen, and the tapping of incense from gum-bearing trees fitted almost into the same pattern of production.[4]

Shifting cultivation. It is a historical fact that the size of population that a diet of meat and milk can support in relation to a given area of land is much smaller than one dependent on vegetable food. As has been seen already, the diet of sedentary people in the Middle East, India, and the Far East consisted mainly of cereals, leguminous and root plants, vegetables, fruits, and occasionally, meat and fish. This single fact is perhaps sufficient to account for the wide prevalence of arable farming throughout the Indian Ocean. However, just as the existence of open grass land and the seasonal growth of vegetation in the desert areas created the conditions for nomadism based on a meat-and-milk diet supplemented by grains obtained from settled farmers, so the presence of tropical jungle in parts of India and South East Asia was responsible for the shifting cultivation of dry and semi-wet crops. Rural people practising this type of mobile tillage had certainly developed a social structure comparable to that of the settled villages, though in the remote areas aboriginal communities combined it with the habits of hunting and gathering of food. The system of shifting cultivation was essentially a common response of man to a particular environment. The thick jungle and its rapid re-establishment after an initial clearing provided the means for preserving the fertility of fragile tropical soil, and it was a practice aimed at rotating the fields rather than crops. The usual method of shifting cultivation in the forested areas of Asia was to clear a plot of land by cutting down trees and burning the wood. The ash acted as a fertiliser to the ground which was dug with either a sharpened stick or a hoe. Dry rice, millet, and maize (after its introduction in the sixteenth century) were the most common crops grown in the clearings, and these were left fallow after two or three seasons. It has been estimated that the period of rest required by the soil in the tropical regions of Indonesia was about nine years and after the average yield is taken into account, a family of five would have needed about twenty-five acres of suitable land to support itself. Under the system of shifting tillage, the density of population must have remained very low. A situation of chronic under-population and an abundance of forested land justified the survival of swidden culture through the centuries.[5]

The diffusion theory of crops. This particular approach depends on a distinctive epistemology: the hierarchical partitions of the totality for the purpose of scientific explanation. Applied to the historical topology of cultivars, the diffusionist would argue, drawing on his knowledge of biological evolution and the monumental work of the master-geneticist Vavilov, that domesticated wheat travelled eastward in the direction of northern India from a West Asian hearthland as a cold-weather crop.[6] Sorghum and millet (primarily monsoon-fed summer-crops) came to the Near East and India from Africa. The diffusion of banana and sugar-cane was a westward movement with its origin in South East Asia; from the same region wet-rice cultivation spread in every direction.[7] A whole range of crops originally cultivated in India as part of the earlier harvest cycle within a double summer and winter cropping system are mentioned in the early Islamic texts from the eighth century onwards. Pliny himself has a surprising reference to the bullrush millet of India and its westward diffusion: 'A millet has been introduced into Italy from India, within the last ten years that is of a black colour, with a large grain and a stalk like that of a reed. It grows to seven feet high, with very large hairs.'[8] The precise dating of the information would have appeared inherently improbable but for the fact that Pliny was a landowner and an agronomic expert with an accurate knowledge of practical farming techniques. The new food plants grown in the Near East, North Africa, and Islamic Spain within our period of study included hard wheat, rice, cotton, sugar-cane, sorghum, watermelons, oranges, and aubergines.[9] In this scheme of the historical topography of crops, there appears a complete two-way traffic system, following the existing routes of communication, trade, and cultural exchange going towards all four cardinal points of the compass. The trans-Atlantic (and even trans-Pacific) movements of the New World crops, maize, tobacco, and potato, during the sixteenth century and the rapid assimilation of the first two in Asian agriculture lend apparent strength to the diffusionist's armoury of arguments.

The origin of the domesticated plants is a problem mostly for the archaeologist rather than the historian. The question whether the basic cereals, wheat, barley, sorghum, millet, and rice, spread from a single point of domestication or whether they were independently developed as cultivars is different from the actual historical process that might have caused either of the two possibilities to occur. The history of the diffusion of the New World crops and the spread of coffee and tea from east to west not only reveals the complexity of the factors involved but also the severe limitations on our knowledge. Maize and tobacco were readily accepted by the Asian farmers; the first as a food crop and the second, as a source of cash income. Neither of the two plants were known to the Old World farmers, nor their agronomic behaviour in a transplanted environment. The rapid rate of diffusion must imply that both maize and tobacco found an immediate opening in the economic and social surface of existing farming practices, something that eluded potato for at least two centuries. But nothing is known of the actual historical rationale of the farming communities which made the process possible in the first place and a reality subsequently. Apart from the question of assimilating a root crop in the social matrix of diet and cultural habits, potato is difficult to harvest and needed substantial labour just when it was likely to be scarce. The cultivation of potato in the Middle East and India seldom went beyond horticulture and garden production. Coffee and tea were diffused by the Dutch and the English East India Companies in the eighteenth and nineteenth centuries as part of a self-conscious urge to enlarge the sources of supply. Tea was an ancient plant; the cultivation of coffee in the northern Yemen is documented only from the beginning of the sixteenth century. The habit of coffee-drinking however was associated with the fifteenth-century saint Ali b. ʿUmar al-Shadhili (1424–51).[10] The mosque dedicated to him still stands intact among the ruins of Mocha. The plantation method of cultivating coffee and tea, in Java, in the

Caribbean, Latin America, and India fitted into an emerging world-wide capitalist system of agricultural production, which was structurally different from the original historical situation in the Yemen and China. The same process could also claim responsibility for the economic death of Mocha, one of the most prosperous commercial cities in the seaborne trade of Asia.

The public awareness of agricultural technology. It is clear that the transmission of agronomic skills and the management of land by the rural communities had become well-founded long before our period of study. There are many historical examples which reveal the care and attention given by the Asian rulers and their political advisers to the technical management of agricultural practices. A Rasulid monarch of the Yemen, al-Malik al-Afdal al-ʿAbbas b. ʿAli, personally composed a treatise on cereal cultivation for the guidance of farmers (*c.* 1371), which showed an astonishing mastery of practical details and the knowledge of sources. A passage in the *Bughyat al-fellahin* reads (referring to the work of Democritus)

The cultivator must not sow on a day when the north wind is blowing because it spoils the ground, nor does the seed flourish and establish firm roots . . . Wheat and barley seeds must not be washed, for, if washed, its grains turn out thin and do not fill out much. When the cultivator sows at the waxing of the moon and the ascension of the preponderant Zodiacal signs, which cause generation, that seed will thrive and produce abundantly.[11]

Contemporary agronomic experts whether in the western or eastern Indian Ocean had little difficulty in understanding the importance of crop rotation and water control. The scientific work of Hsu Kuang-ch'i, as we have already seen, emphasised the point in some detail.[12] The worst category of land in northern China apparently was one subject to random and sudden flooding. The local people usually grew sorghum on such land and they could secure on average only a single crop every other year. As a result, rural communities in such areas suffered from chronic grinding poverty. But they were instructed by the Ming experts in better crop-growing techniques, which involved the selective planting of wheat at a time when flooding was not expected. As a rule, the inundations came in late summer or early autumn, a season when the wheat crops could have been already harvested. On land where it was possible to build drainage canals, the autumn floods receded quickly and allowed the soil to dry out. The autumn planting of wheat became feasible here. In localities where there was no means for drainage, the land did not dry out till winter, but even there spring wheat could be raised effectively. The introduction of wheat in areas of intermittent sorghum cultivation practically assured nine harvests out of every ten years.[13]

The profusion in the different varieties of crops, vegetables, and fruits cultivated by the Asian farmers reflected the influence of certain geographical

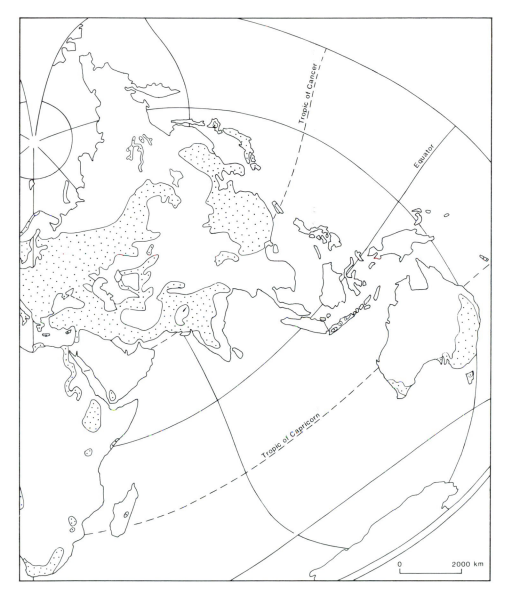

Map 11 Distribution of wheat cultivation.

and climatic determinants. It was also an index of social preferences and
economic considerations. Among ten to fifteen major cereals grown, wheat
and rice held the premier positions, symbolising two basic systems of crop production in Asian history: the methods of dry and wet farming. This was the
point of intersection where the climatic powers of the Indian Ocean, the
Mediterranean, and the Himalayas merged with the technology of agriculture,
man's constant effort to breed new strains of seeds within the same species of

plants and match them with soil conditions and the use of fertiliser. But in the last analysis it was the amount and incidence of rainfall, a function of the monsoon winds, the depth of water-tables, the flow of rivers, and the relative humidity in the atmosphere which marked out the zones of dry farming and wet. However, the map drawn by wheat was only one side of the picture in the historical evolution of dry farming. At its most intensive and productive form, the system incorporated a double cycle of summer planting (the 'kharif' crop), followed by a winter one ('rabi'). Because of its versatile capacity for producing a wide range of prepared food-items, cous-cous, pasta, best white bread, and refined flour for the fine-art of the skilled patissier, wheat captured high grounds in the collective imagination of every Asian society living on the uncertain yields of dry farming. Islamic sources took pride in the fact that even the ordinary people in urban areas ate bread baked from wheat-flour rather than from coarser grain.[14] The claim was not true for the Indian subcontinent and may not have been the case even for the Middle East. Wheat was a luxury crop saleable for cash and had distinctive characteristics in the texture and taste of its flour. In the *Bughyat al-fellahin*, the variety known as Wasni was considered to be one of the best. Its grains were red, heavy, thick, and with a tail. It was mainly sown in the temperate mountainous areas of the Yemen during the monsoon rains (July), in al-Qasaibah and parts of the Taiᶜzz district, and harvested in about three months. ᶜArabi wheat was white and fine-grained; the flour for making the open Egyptian bread came from the ᶜaqar variety.[15]

The technology of dry crops: wheat, barley, and millet. If the Middle Eastern and Indian peasants reserved their best land during the winter harvest cycle for wheat, the first position in the subsistence cereal-matrix was occupied by barley. Wheat was highly demanding in terms of soil nutrients and needed careful application of water during early growth. It could not be grown on the same plot of land for more than two years in succession without seriously impairing its productive capacity. Wheat land needed to be left fallow or rotated with other crops able to restore the soil. In Egypt and India, where the length of the growing season and artificial irrigation permitted two harvests to be raised annually, wheat land was alternated with green crops such as beans, peas, lentils, mustard and other oil seeds. In Mesopotamia, after the harvesting of the winter crops the fields were largely left fallow.[16] The Chinese work *Chih Min Yao Shu* recommended that wheat should be preceded by millet and followed by coriander and dye plants.

The system of rotation in dry winter cropping followed a highly complex pattern and incorporated also a great deal of inter-planting.[17] Mughal revenue practices in northern India distinguished four different types of land-usage. 'Polaj' land was annually cultivated for each crop in succession and never allowed to lie fallow. 'Parauti' land was left uncultivated for a brief period in

Plate 44 Agricultural scene in Egypt, women fetching water.

order to restore its fertility. Land fallowed for three to four years was known as 'chachar'. Finally, there was 'Banjar' land left untilled for more than five years. Rabi crops grown on polaj land included wheat, vetches, lentils, barley, linseed, safflower, millet (*panicum miliaceum*), mustard, peas, fenugreek, and 'kur' rice.[18] Land classification in Egypt, based on crop rotation and fallow patterns, was even more elaborate than in India. Ibn Mammati's list of thirteen different kinds of land was copied and summarised by Qalqashandi and Maqrizi respectively. In the crop cycle the most productive phase occurred between the planting of clover ('qurt'), legumes ('qattani'), and various gourds ('maqati') followed by wheat and flax.[19] Barley was a hardier crop compared with wheat and better able to withstand adverse factors such as drought and rising sub-soil salinity. In Mesopotamia, wheat cultivation retreated before barley as land was progressively subjected to salinity through excessive canal irrigation.[20] The combination of the two main cereal crops during the winter harvest with a large number of legumes reflected an important technical aspect of dry farming, the fact that legumes can fix nitrogen, supply their own need of the nutrient, and even leave a residue for subsequent crops.[21] Crop rotation preserved or enhanced the physical productivity of agricultural land. There was another technique practised by farmers which reduced the risk of crop failure within the same harvest cycle. A field would be planted with different types of crops in alternating bands with different rates of growth and resist-ance to drought, pests, and weeds. The method of inter-cropping and the sowing of mixed seeds derived its logic from scientific factors as well as the

avoidance of risk on the part of the Asian peasant-household. Its wide prevalence was a reflection of the extent to which agronomic specialisation fused
with economic and social considerations. Low-value crops inter-planted with
the valuable, marketable ones provided at once the opportunity for subsistence food and cash incomes.

The role of subsistence and cash crops. While wheat and barley economised on
the use of labour, both were plagued by the problem of low relative yield. For-
tunately for the Asian peasant societies, the arrival of the monsoon rains during mid-summer also created the conditions for raising a number of important
subsistence crops. Various kinds of millet, maize, and rice were sown in
summer and harvested just after the rains ceased in September. In areas
marked by absent winter rains and artificial irrigation, these were crops which
the cultivating communities had to live on for the rest of the year. In so far as
they needed a cash income, sugar-cane, cotton, and indigo, all grown during
the period of the monsoon rains, were extensively marketed as semi-processed
industrial raw materials over wide areas. Cane-pressing and the manufacture
of raw and refined sugar together with the oil-mills featured extensively
among rural and semi-rural industries closely linked to the crop patterns.
During his journey through Upper Egypt Ibn Battuta counted eleven sugar
factories in the small town of Manlawi, built two miles from the Nile. Poor
people would come to the boiling sheds with freshly-baked bread, throw it
into the vat in which the cane syrup was being cooked and go off with a cheap
ready-made confectionary.[22] The historical sources hint but do not fully
describe the complexity of the interaction between mainly ecological factors
and the economic environment which characterised settled agriculture. A clear
manifestation was the enormous range of some thirty to forty varieties of
winter and summer crops, regularly grown in northern India and recorded
with such painstaking care in the Mughal land and fiscal records.[23] It is
difficult to imagine that the proliferation of the crop-types was solely determined by the desire on the part of the peasants to avoid the risks of environmental hazards. In fact, it can be argued that a farmer who tries to grow a large
number of crops is certain to encounter bad weather for some of his crops all
the time. Most individual farmers probably concentrated on an optimum mix
of not more than half a dozen crops, and the rationale of the choice would have
been fixed by the subsistence needs of peasant households, the opportunity for
marketing the crops, the fiscal policy of the state, and the availability of water,
fertiliser, and labour.

These conclusions are not entirely conjectural, undocumented by historical
evidence. It is obviously true that the farming communities were not literate
and able to leave behind accounts and documents as did the merchants. The
routines of rural production and the prosperity of material life only attracted
the attention of the historian and the chroniclers by the violence of their

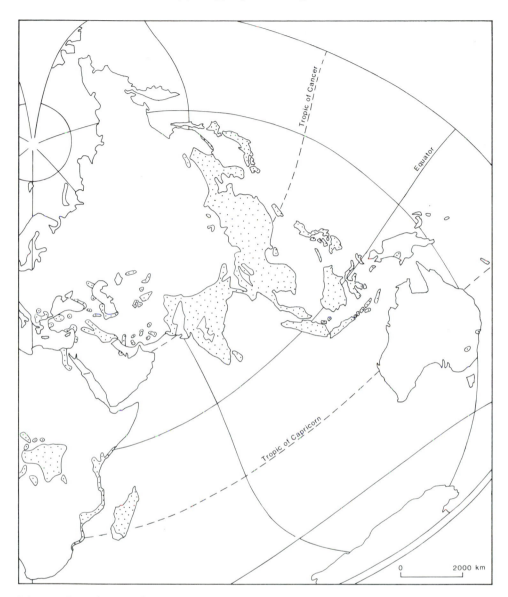

Map 12 Distribution of rice.

sudden, unexpected disruption and even total demise. An Indian historical text (1357) records one such event during the troublesome reign of Muhammad Tughluq:

At this time the country of the Doab was brought to ruin by the heavy taxation and the numerous cesses. The Hindus burnt their corn stacks and turned their cattle out to roam at large. Under the orders of the Sultan, the collectors and magistrates laid waste the country, and they killed some landholders and village chiefs and blinded others.

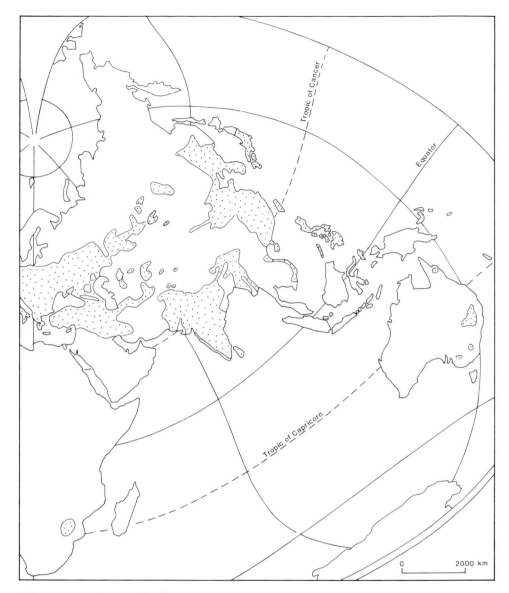

Map 13 Distribution of millet.

Such of these unhappy inhabitants as escaped formed themselves into bands and took refuge in the jungles. So the country was ruined. The Sultan then proceeded on a hunting excursion to Baran, where under his directions, the whole of that country was plundered and laid waste . . . [24]

The historian was not an impartial witness of the sultan's impious deeds. Even so, it is clear that the organised departments of the state displayed an interest in matters of agriculture which carried a burdensome message for the rural

Map 14 Distribution of sorghum.

population. Administrative reorganisation following political conquests especially led to the revision of the structure of agricultural taxation. This in turn called for the discussion and codification of the new measures.

The differential tax assessment of high-value crops: the example of early Islamic Mesopotamia. In the aftermath of the Islamic conquest of Mesopotamia, for example, a crucial point of political decision arose over the

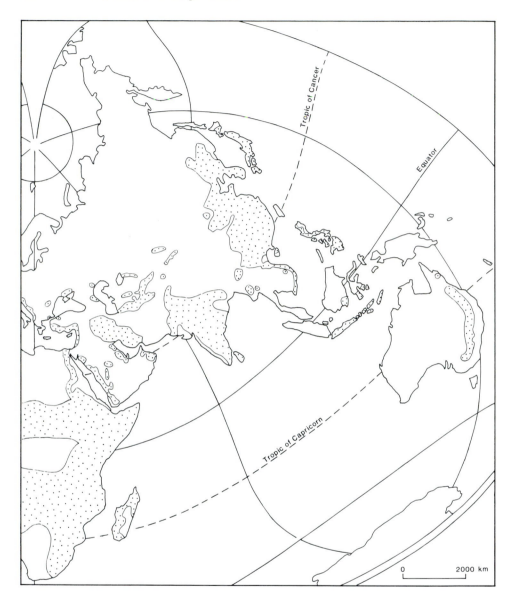

Map 15 Distribution of maize.

status of the Nabatean peasants tilling their legendary fields in al-Sawad, the complex of highly-developed irrigated 'oasis-land' between the Euphrates and the Tigris.[25] To Arab tribal conquerors hungry for prize, the question was a simple one: divide al-Sawad among the Muslims, leaving a fifth to the caliphate. No lesser authority than the Qur'an could be invoked to justify the division. The statesman in Caliph Umar ibn al-Khattab refused the importunities, on the ground that such a policy would leave nothing for the generations of Muslims yet to come. His proconsul ʿUthman ibn-Hunaif, sent to assess the harvests of al-Sawad, put seals round the necks of 550,000 Nabateans, declared them 'protected people' and proceeded to measure the land.[26] Standardised assessment rates based on Sasanian conventions eventually emerged.[27] In villages irrigated by the Euphrates, wheat land, if closely sown, incurred for every 'jarib' the rate of one and a half dirham, if thinly sown, two-thirds of a dirham, and for average production, one dirham; barley paid only half of the wheat average. Garden land which included palm trees, vines, vegetables, sesame, and cotton, was assessed by differential rates. Date plantations in regular commercial production paid ten dirhams for each jarib; vineyards planted for more than three years yielded a similar amount. Nothing was taken from plots growing vegetables, cucumbers, and cotton. Date palms growing outside the village boundaries were also exempt and their fruits belonged to the public.[28] The original survey of ʿUthman ibn-Hunaif had included a rate of six dirhams on a jarib of sugar-cane, four dirhams on wheat, and two on barley. The cautious and considered treatment given by the early caliphate rulers to an area which had the reputation of a model agriculture was to create the later tradition that the land of al-Sawad could not be bought or sold because it was a pious foundation held in trust for all Muslims.[29]

The schedule of rural taxation, imprecise and variable as it appears in the traditions recorded by al-Baladhuri, nevertheless unearths the archaeology of a lost inner reality which few thought of preserving at the time. The sown land of lower Mesopotamia was structured by a tripartite logic also reflected in the fiscal scheme. A clear dividing line runs between crops grown for feeding the local population and those raised for cash sale in the market. The first category deserved a lower rate of assessment not only because of a low nominal value expressed in its price but also because the essential cereals were inseparable from the welfare economy of the village. To deprive the peasant society of its threshold needs of barley, sorghum, millet, and rice was to invite an inevitable flight from land and a restructuring of the landscape of food production. Captive peasants unable to flee in large numbers responded to the crisis levels of appropriations by dying through malnutrition. At the second level of rural logic, the insurance of survival underwritten by the subsistence crops was articulated with a system of carefully-thought options which included the cultivation of high-valued cereals and industrial plants. Finally, the irrigation works of Iraq (and other similar regions of Asia) created the corn fields, the garden-land, the vineyards, and the date-palm orchards, representing capital expenditures and investments in agriculture undertaken by successive generations of Nabatean farmers. The state and society were willing up to a point to transcend the immediate future and adopt a longer time horizon. Such an outcome could not be thought of without an unambiguous concept of rights, usage, and property in land.[30] What at first sight seems little more than a few simple examples of Bedouin statecraft and financial wisdom assumes a different meaning when the archaeological excavations are taken a stage below the visible surface of history. Evidence from a later period confirms the degree of productive differentiation in agricultural land. The entire economic logic of dry farming in northern India can be studied in depth and in detail from the sixteenth-century Mughal administrative encyclopaedia composed by Abu'l Fazl. The fiscal and statistical templates, drawn up by the Chief Diwan's office in Delhi, the central finance department, defy imagination as they were completed and returned by thousands of district officials. The huge range of crops, the cadastral survey of individual fields, the collection of prices current in different markets, the tabulation of water resources, the differential fertility of soil, and the records of land rights, all these operating parts of the agricultural machinery were encoded and documented in disaggregated units of space. The Mamluk and Ottoman practices were not very different from those of the Mughal empire. Many tell-tale signs point towards a universal Babylonian-Sasanian and Indo-Islamic model of rural life, remarkable for its syncretic convergence on a set of limiting values.[31]

Clay tablets from the Sumerian period (*c.* 2000 BC) not only record the technique of cadastral mapping as a means of fixing property boundaries but also the diagrammatic depiction of canals, cultivated fields, and the site of villages.[32] Mesopotamian farmers already possessed the essential requisites for growing crops, the wild variants of which were not common to the local topography, 4,000 years ago. This was an area of strong contrasts: empty desert on one side flanked by the intensive cultivation of corn fields, palm groves, and one of the greatest systems of artificial irrigation known to the ancient world. The highland of upper Iraq, the Jazira, and the alluvial plains of the Euphrates-Tigris were primarily regions of dry farming, although around the Great Swamp and the Shatt al-Arab rice fields were common enough during the Islamic period. The historical experience of Mesopotamia lends conviction to an important point. Without the management of existing water resources and those created by human efforts, matched by a number of water-lifting devices, the productive cultivation of cereals, whether dry or wet, would have been impossible.[33] The size of the economic surplus could not have supported the flourishing and highly developed urban life. Even in northern India, where the regularity of the monsoon winds and the average levels of precipitation gave the rain-fed crops certain priority, absence of irrigation works signified either single harvests or the perpetual fear of a total famine. The task of constructing wells and tanks appears repeatedly in Indian history as one of the pious and royal duties undertaken for the benefit of the whole community. The monumental flood control works and the huge canal projects of China of course symbolised at once the power and the grandeur of the Celestial Empire and its unquestioned technological superiority in Asian agriculture.

Water supply and the technology of rice cultivation. Indeed, irrigation and the proper management of water resources constituted the two indispensable conditions for the successful development and extension of the method of wet-rice farming. This was as true of areas with an ample annual level of rainfall as those with a lesser amount of precipitation. The minimum water requirement for wet-rice cultivation extends from 1,240 mm to 2,200 mm according to the varieties grown.[34] The problem of an uncertain or inadequate incidence of rainfall was overcome historically by harnessing the supply of water carried by the perennial rivers, streams, and mountain-lakes. Shortage of water however was not the only consideration in growing rice as a major food-crop. Archaeological evidence going back by several millennia and supplemented by later written texts shows that the emergence of rice in its domesticated form incorporated three evolutionary elements. The time-sequence is not clear, but we can discern, first of all in order of relative ecological complexity, the development of upland rice varieties sown in prepared fields and watered by natural rainfall. By far the most prevalent, productive, and labour-intensive form was the lowland rice grown in flooded fields surrounded by low dykes. The central unit in this particular system of production remained the small terrace. Its economic viability derived from an unambiguous scientific relationship between the controlled usage of water and the growth habits of the rice plant. This was the point of intersection where the third element in the historical evolution of rice acquired its importance. The rice-farmers of the Indian Ocean could draw on a vast selection of different seed-types. Through a process of deliberate adaptation or accidental selection, the domesticated rice separated into late-ripening and early-ripening varieties, into glutinous and non-glutinous types, round-grained and long-grained, brown, red, and white, fragrant and non-scented, sensitive and non-sensitive to photoperiod. A British statistician counted in 1875 ninety different kinds of the 'aman' or winter rice grown in the Bengal district of Bakarganj. The autumn rice ('aus') could be differentiated into twenty-one varieties.[35] A spectacular example of primitive natural selection, re-adapted to human needs, was the floating rice of eastern Bengal (also sown in South East Asia); the plant grew in proportion to the water depth and typically the length varied from 1 m to over 6 m, the head always remaining above water.[36] In areas susceptible to sudden flooding, it ensured an automatic survival of the crop.

The construction of the terrace, levelling its gradient to allow a certain flow of water, and the whole work-cycle from the period of initial ploughing and puddling of the field to its controlled flooding and final drainage, were of course highly demanding of labour. The amount of work needed in creating the field and its surrounding dykes meant that the size was kept to a minimum. The typical rice-terrace was a tiny plot of land, which drew its nutritional

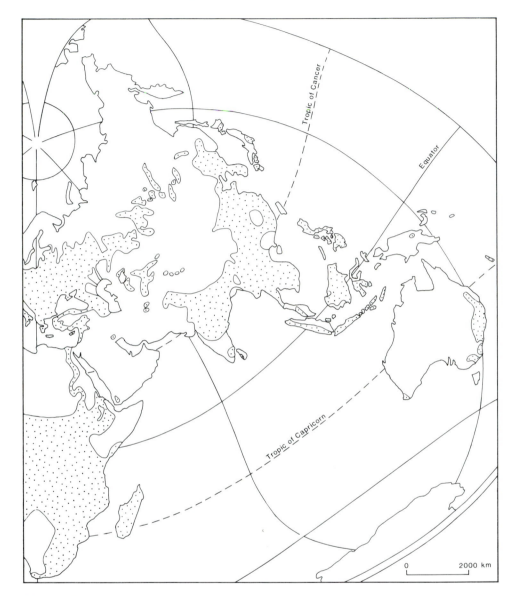

Map 16 Distribution of sugarcane.

qualities less from the soil than from aquatic flora and the solvents found in the water. After the field had been flooded with rain or irrigation water, it was ploughed several times until the soil was completely puddled. The seedlings were generally sown in raised nursery-beds and were transplanted by hand into the flooded terraces. From this point onwards, the management of the terrace became a fine operation: the level of water at each growing stage had to be kept constant and the temperature controlled by allowing the water to

挿苗

Plate 45　Planting rice in China.

flow through. By the time the crop ripened, the fields were completely dry.[37] A description of the ecology of the rice-field demonstrates the reason why the wet-rice cultivation was beyond the competence of individual families. It called for concerted social efforts on the part of the entire village community. In this respect, the contrast between wheat or dry-farming and rice cultivation could not have been more striking. The lower labour input of wheat was more than off-set by its lesser calorific value in relation to yield. The ratio between seed to harvest could be as high as 1:100 in the case of rice. Carsten Niebuhr observed in the course of his scientific work in the Middle East that the wheat ratios were thirty to seventy-fold in Egypt, twenty-fold in Iraq, and fifty-fold in the Yemen.[38] The rice-field is thus a factory, in the words of Fernand Braudel.[39] But like all factories, it needed a regular supply of man-power. The higher yield of rice enabled a greater concentration of population,

the labour of which was in turn absorbed by the routines of wet-rice cultivation. Which came first: the denser population or the higher yield?

The history of wet-farming in our period of study does not allow a clear
answer to be given to the question. But there is no doubt that the presence of
wet-rice fields in any area of the Indian Ocean was indicative generally of a
high productivity of labour, of the mastery of a complicated agronomic technique, and a strong socio-religious symbolism attached to rice as the premier
seed-plant of Asian civilisations. Although rice was originally domesticated as
a dry grass and used as such by the swidden farmers, in the greater part of
India, South East Asia, and the Far East, the transplanted method of growth
in standing water gave uniformly better results. In northern India, where the
monsoon rains were adequate, rice was grown as a kharif or autumn crop to
be followed by the dry winter crops. It was part of either a single crop or a
mixed-double cropping system. Heavier and more prolonged periods of rainfall in Bengal and on the western coast of India, from Konkan to the Malabar,
permitted the rice-farmers to practise a three-crop but mono-culture cereal-
planting during the annual cycle. The agricultural productivity of these areas
was such that they were treated as the rice granary of not only India but also
of the trading emporia of the Middle East and South East Asia. The economic
impoverishment which had overtaken Bengal during our century would have
been unbelievable in the seventeenth and eighteenth centuries when all the
contemporary historians united in extolling Bengal's overflowing agricultural
wealth founded on its export of rice and fine cotton cloth. By the time Bernier
visited Bengal and came to describe its economy, he had forgotten his earlier
strictures on oriental despotism:

Egypt had been represented in every age as the finest and most fruitful country in the
world . . . but the knowledge I have acquired of Bengale, during two visits paid to that
kingdom, inclines me to believe that the pre-eminence ascribed to Egypt is rather due
to Bengale. The latter country produces rice in such abundance that it supplies not
only the neighbouring but remote states. It is carried up the Ganges as far as Patna, and
exported by sea to Masulipatam and many other ports on the coast of Koromandel.
It is also sent to foreign kingdoms, principally to the island of Ceylon and the
Maldives.[40]

This was a period when Bengal exported rice to Sumatra and may have also
sent it to Malacca a century earlier when that port was at the height of its trade
in the Indian Ocean. Another great source of rice for the commercial emporia
came from the Javanese 'sawah' system of wet-rice cultivation. The Javanese
sawah and the Balinese mountain terraces were even more complex and man-
made than the paddy fields of southern India, Indochina, Thailand, and
China. For in addition to the usual method of terracing, collective social
organisations were needed here in order to build flood-control works in a
landscape deeply scored by volcanic activities. In the equatorial regions of the
Indonesian archipelago, the annual rains were variable. Hydraulic works,

水碓

Plate 46 Agricultural machinery in China, the turbine being
driven by water.

whether simple or elaborate, were essential for the sawah cultivation. The
Balinese underground irrigation tunnels and surface conduits tapped water
from volcanic lakes on the higher slopes of the mountains. Rice fields located
further down the valleys received their water supply later than the upper fields
and were vulnerable to any interruptions in the flow. Warfare and disputes
between different communities and their respective chiefs could lead to a
deliberate release of flood-water that would drown the standing crop of rice.[41]
A high premium was attached to social consensus and its legal definition in
such a system of economic production which started off with an initial expenditure of collective labour and capital and could function efficiently only as
long as the allocation of water and the maintenance of the irrigation-works
remained effective.

The discovery of early-ripening rice and its historical implication. Enough archaeological and historical evidence has now accumulated to show that mainland South East Asia, the region extending from present day northern Thailand to the Gulf of Tonking, had contributed significantly to the technique of wet-rice cultivation as well as to the simpler upland methods. The historian is seldom able to assign a period or a date to even simpler forms of technological improvements in agriculture and trace its motivation. The introduction of the early-ripening rice from the ancient kingdom of Champa to China around 1012 is an exception. The actual historical traditions differ: one version assigns its spread to the policy of the Sung emperor Chen-tsung who sent 30,000 bushels of Champa seed to the Lower Yangtze and Huai provinces for distribution to the farmers. Within a century or so the new rice had widely replaced the older slower-growing varieties in south China. In the twelfth century Shu Lin could write that the early-ripening Champa rice, which he called the lesser cereal because of its smaller grain, could be grown on any land, fertile and infertile.[42] The early lead taken by the Chinese rice-farmers in the northern provinces and the close historical links between Indochina and Yunnan make it implausible that the appearance of the early-ripening rice in China was accidental or due to ignorance. The agricultural resources of North China and the population balance had become unfavourable by the Sung period. The opening up of new riceland in the Yangtze delta was associated with a southward migration of Chinese people. The opportunity for double-cropping rice by shortening the period of growth could not have been lost on farmers anxious to increase the supply of a relatively coarse subsistence cereal and combine it with finer varieties of grains. The contemporary *Sung History* summed up the possibility for the economic development of southern China in the following words: 'After the Sung dynasty crossed the Yangtze valley to settle in the south, the productivity of irrigated land was found to be richer than in the central domain'.[43] There were, however, technical factors associated with water supply which also determined the short-term decision of the farmers to sow late or early-ripening rice. Robert Knox, who spent nearly twenty years of involuntary exile in the kingdom of Kandy in Ceylon (1659–79), gave a perceptive and accurate description of the method of rice farming on the island. Some varieties of rice, he observed, matured in seven months, while others needed from three to six months. The quick growing rice tasted better than all the others, though it had the lowest yield. Why then did the farmers not sow only the slow maturing variety with the better yield? The answer, according to him, lay in the farmers' assessment of the amount of water available through the growing season. If the water level in the tanks and canals happened to be relatively low when the rains came and it was feared that the terraces might be short of running water during the critical period of growth, the early-ripening rice was planted by the farmers.[44]

Hydrology in the history of settled farming

The irrigation systems of the Indian Ocean. A historical comparison between dry and wet farming reveals certain distinctive social, economic, and political associations differentiating them as separate systems. Food habits, the work-cycle, the sanctions and the coercive techniques in social control, the nature of agriculture's linkage with the state: all these are topics which could be taken as obvious examples for further analysis. But the contrasting patterns of dispersion are also matched by uniformities. The role played by irrigation in dry and wet farming was the most important element bridging both the systems. Hydraulic engineering associated with settled farming reached its highest art in many different and unconnected areas of the Indian Ocean and the Mediterranean. Not all of them were endowed with the most favourable conditions for cereal cultivation, nor were they able to maintain the irrigation works uninterruptedly. The famous historical examples can be cited readily: the basin-irrigation of the Nile during the period of its annual rise in depth; the permanent canal system drawn from the Euphrates-Tigris and harnessed to the water-wheels, the 'naᶜura'; the underground channels (the 'qanats') of Yazd and Kirman in the arid Iranian plateau; the integrated network of dams, reservoirs, and canals in ancient south India, Ceylon, and Cambodia; the irrigation conduits of the steep Balinese rice terraces; the four-hundred-mile long embankments containing the turbulent waters of the Yellow River, the Huang Ho, in northern China. Each of these examples represented an entire structure composed of ecological factors, social usage, and technological considerations. It is clear that the selective application of water to wheat, barley, and millet during the growing period could be accomplished only with the aid of artificial irrigation since the winter rainfall in most areas of dry farming was too uncertain. Permanent wells lined with bricks or cut stones provided a classic answer to the problem of water supply. The lifting device was a set of simple pulleys attached to a horizontal cross-beam. These held the ropes in position as the leather bucket filled with water was drawn to the surface by draught animals walking down a ramp, and emptied into a small tank connected to the irrigation channels. Fields adjacent to perennial streams and rivers could be watered also by using the cantilevered beam attached to a counter-weight at one end and a bucket at the other. It was known as a 'shaduf' in Egypt and 'dalia' in Iraq.[45] But the most striking and widely utilised water-lifting machinery of the premodern world were the geared wheels powered either by animals or the water race.[46] The technique of gearing, using two cogged wheels, enabled a horizontal circular motion to be transformed into a vertical rotary one (see Plate 47). Found throughout India, the Middle East and even Spain, the large 'naᶜura' (water-driven) or the 'saqiya' (worked by animals) evoked comments from many Islamic geographers and travellers (see Plate 48). Here is Yaqut describing the great wheels of Hama

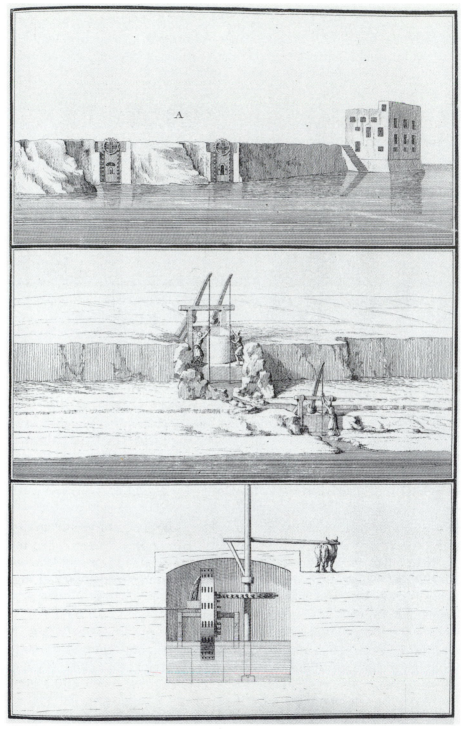

Plate 47 Different types of water-raising machinery in Egypt and gearing method (see p. 239).

Plate 48 Water-raising machinery in Egypt powered by oxen.

(one of which measured 20 metres in diameter) in Syria: 'On the [river] Orontes there are several waterwheels, which raise the water so that the garden can be irrigated and pour water out in the cistern of the mosque . . . Hama is a town with a stone wall, beside which there is a big stone building. The river flows and waters the gardens and drives their waterwheels.'[47] The detailed description of the mechanism of the Persian wheel by Babar, the first Mughal conqueror of northern India, is a pointer to the sense of wonder which the ancient agricultural systems of the Indo-Islamic plains inspired among the mainly nomadic Central Asian intruders into these areas.[48]

The qanats, underground channels, and canals. The mechanical aids in distributing water from pre-existing sources were, of course, useless when the supply itself failed. But many arid regions with an inadequate incidence of rainfall and surface streams could utilise either subterranean aquifer or springs located in the mountains which received winter rains or snow. A large proportion of dry crops raised in Iran, Afghanistan, and Oman was watered by underground channels often running more than twenty miles in length. A regular line of stately plane trees seen near an Iranian village invariably indicates that the underground conduit has come to the surface and is flowing as an open stream. The trees were planted to protect the banks and reduce evaporation through their shade. The technique of construction had developed very early and followed methods similar to those of mining. A whole network of canals and underground tunnels branching off from the

Greater Zab River irrigated the luxuriant gardens and plantations around Nimrud during the height of the Assyrian empire.[49] Archaeological excavation at Negub has revealed the engineering features of a water-tunnel system which was probably built by Esarhaddon (681–669 BC). The underground galleries were excavated through a number of vertical shafts. The gradient of the tunnel from the entrance was up hill in order to slow down the flow of water and there were sluice gates as well for regulating the volume.[50] Although the Negub tunnel was served by a river and was not connected to an underground water-table as in the case of the Iranian qanats, the use of shafts for the initial construction and the subsequent maintenance of the horizontal sections establishes a common technology between the two systems and points to its origin in quarry and mining activities.

It seems plausible to suggest that the qanat-builders may have learnt the essential engineering principles from the problem faced by ancient miners, that of removing excess water and the danger of flooding in mine-shafts and underground galleries.[51] Practical treatises on civil engineering have rarely survived in the historiography of Asian technology. An exception is *Anbat al-miya al-khafiyya* (*c*. AD 1000) of Muhammad Ibn al-Hasan al-Hasib, an Iranian who claimed to have written many large and small works on mathematics and engineering while he was resident in Iraq.[52] The author describes the method of locating an aquifer in the mountains and higher ground by means of a source well and the subsequent construction of vertical air-shafts and the horizontal tunnels lined with clay pipes. The mathematical problem of finding the ground-level and fixing the correct gradient was discussed in detail as were various precision instruments used for the purpose. The main levelling instrument was a tube made of glass, hard wood, or bamboo of exact straightness, top and bottom being perfectly parallel. It had three evenly spaced holes drilled in a straight line. The inclination of the land was easily found by filling the tube with water and ascertaining whether it remained inside the tube or came out through one of the end holes. The technical skill of the professional qanat-builders ('mukannis') in finding the correct gradient equalled that of the hydraulic engineers in ancient rice-growing regions.[53] Old qanats remained operational for many centuries, even in cases where the location of the source-well was forgotten. Polybius pointed this out in his *History*, referring to the campaign of Antiochus the Great against the Parthians (212–205 BC):

They say that at the time when the Persians were the rulers of Asia, they gave to those who conveyed a supply of water to places previously unirrigated, the right of cultivating the land for five generations, and consequently as the Taurus has many large streams descending from it, people incurred great expense and trouble in making underground channels reaching a long distance, so that at the present day those who make use of the water do not know whence the channels derive their supply.[54]

The scientific and economic calculations involved in constructing both qanats and surface canals were well understood by Islamic engineers and were actually written down for the benefit of theorists and students.[55]

The qanat system of irrigation was vital for the survival of many agro-urban centres in Iran and Afghanistan. The classical historians even claimed that in India there were officials who inspected the closed canals and organised the distribution of water so that every one had a fair share of it.[56] The statement is not supported by archaeological evidence from northern India. On the other hand, it is true that water rights carried important legal protection both in the Middle East and India. The ownership of a qanat or a well could be held by private individuals, communal authorities, and religious foundations. Such rights were often saleable.[57] The distribution of water from a common source to different agricultural users posed a different problem. It needed a corresponding social grid reflecting the general consensus and the sense of fair play.[58] A direct relationship is easily traced between the monetary value of land, its physical productivity, and hydrographic considerations. Land brought into cultivation from waste and existing arable irrigated by newly-constructed wells or canals under private enterprise enjoyed a lower rate of taxation for a limited number of years. In the early Islamic period, when al-Mahdi excavated the canal Nahr as-Sila near Wasit, share-croppers brought in for developing the land were allowed to pay two-fifths of the produce for a period of fifty years after which they were to pay one-half. However, the state income was treated as being part of a *waqf* and assigned to the citizens of Mecca and Medina.[59] The sense of pious duties associated with land development remained strong. The petition of Ahmed Bey and Grand Vizier Sokollu Mehmed Pasha (*office* 1568–79) to the Ottoman court seeking permission to construct irrigation canals for rice cultivation near the village of Yenice was accompanied by the promise to burn three candles at the shrine of Ak-Sams al-Din and to construct a caravanserai and five fountains in the town of Goynuk.[60] One of the greatest Grand Viziers in Ottoman history, Mehmed Pasha's pious duties though personal in this case were at the same time public in character. This soldier and statesman also had plans for constructing a canal between the Volga and the Don and in the isthmus of Suez.[61]

The irrigation works in India and South East Asia. In most cases, a reverse logic applied when the state itself initiated the irrigation schemes. The reign of Firuz Shah Tughluq, the mild and just ruler of Delhi (*r.* 1351–88), was seen by contemporary historians as a welcome contrast to the period of famine, depopulation, and political catastrophes witnessed under his predecessor Muhammad Tughluq, whose fiscal policy, as we have already seen, laid waste many flourishing rural districts. In 1356 Firuz Shah founded a new town Hisar Firuzah, about forty miles to the west of Delhi, and constructed two canals to supply the town with water and irrigate the surrounding countryside. The headwork was situated on the river Jamuna and the Sutlej. The fresh supply of water not only irrigated the gardens and fruit orchards but also enabled the farmers to grow an additional harvest. Previously only the kharif crops planted during the monsoon rains were successful, as winter wheat could not be grown for lack of water. In addition to Hisar and a new capital near old Delhi, Firuz Tughluq also built Fathabad which was again served by a network of canals. The increasing productivity of land visibly added to the prosperity of the local population and created a dilemma for a just ruler. The sultan convened an assembly of distinguished jurists and asked the question, 'If a man with great labour and expenditure of money conducts water into certain districts, so that the inhabitants thereof realize a large profit ought he or not to receive any return for his trouble and outlay?' The opinion of the learned counsels was unanimous: the king was entitled to the traditional right of 'sharb', a water-tax of ten per cent. The enlightened policy of constructing new and large-scale irrigation canals provided two sources of extra revenue for the sultanate, the tax on water itself and the normal dues on the additional harvest and fresh land brought under cultivation.[62]

The irrigation works of Firuz Shah were constructed on the principle of contour canals which originated in the upper stretches of a river and gradually descended into another river valley round high contours to effect a junction with other river- or canal-systems. The Jamuna and the Sutlej to the north of Delhi besides having very wide flood plains also flow at such a rate that even a strong swimmer is unable to make way against the current. The engineering problems in building the headwork from these rivers were considerable. The Tughluq canals apparently fell into ruins soon after and the supply of water from them dwindled. The Jamuna canal was re-excavated twice; first, during Akbar's reign by Shahab al-Din Ahmad Khan who wished to redevelop the agricultural land in his 'jagir' and later under Shah Jahan.[63] The utilisation of tanks and wells by north Indian farmers in areas of dry-farming in preference to extensive canal irrigation perhaps points to a decentralised social structure that was relatively mobile spatially, and it may also reflect conditions of chronic under-population. The historical relationship between water-resources, economic returns on crop-growing, available labour supply, and the exact impetus towards an intensified usage of land, is still an obscure and speculative subject. On the Indian subcontinent large-scale hydraulic projects, comparable to those of the Middle East, South East Asia, and China, were more common in the south than in the north.

The kingdom of Golconda, Tavernier observed, contained numerous large reservoirs fed by rivers and streams:

They are generally situated in somewhat elevated positions, where it is only necessary to make a dam on the side of the plain in order to retain the water. These dams are sometimes half a league long, and after the season of the rains is past they open the sluices from time to time in order to let the water run into the fields, where it is received in divers small canals to irrigate the lands of private individuals.[64]

This was an accurate description from an eye-witness of the technique of canalising a main stream, which had reached its highest development on the Kavery river in Tanjore and in the Sinhalese dry zones. The Grand Anikat of the Kavery-Coleroon built at about the second century AD and periodically reconstructed, was an enormous stone structure measuring 304 m in length, 16–18 m in width, and 4.5–5 m in height. It remained in operation almost continuously, while many of the large reservoirs and feeder canals in other parts of south India fell into disuse.[65] This was a historical feature also shared with Ceylon. After the thirteenth century, the magnificent system of tanks, 'anikats', and feeder-canals were quite suddenly abandoned. The flourishing rice-terraces, irrigated by the hydraulic works, were no longer cultivated. Signs of catastrophic and inexorable demographic decline appeared over the whole region. Several competing theories attempt to explain the remarkable historical decline. First, it will be useful to set out a few brief comparative examples against which these theories can be evaluated.

There is little doubt that during the active period of their life-span, the irrigation systems must have produced a large surplus of rice and other food crops and hence supported a fairly dense level of population. A detailed study on the history of rice-growing in northern Thailand has attempted to make some quantitative estimates of the effects of canal irrigation. The Muang Khaeng trunk canal on the left bank of the river Ping, excavated according to tradition by a retainer of king Mang Rai in 1281, extended for about thirty-four kilometres and provided water for a theoretical ceiling of 10,000 hectares of new rice land. If the yield is taken at 2–2.4 tons per hectare, the total output would have provided enough rice for 89,000–110,000 people (at an average per head consumption of 225 kg).[66] The conclusion is unmistakable. The potential level of absolute surplus yielded by the technique of wet-rice cultivation was far greater than the premodern population densities in rural areas and their possible food consumption. The irrigated system of wet-farming acted as the power-house throughout the Indian Ocean for state formation, the growth of urban markets, and all the supporting services which reached such profusion in India, Java, Thailand, Cambodia, and China. Almost within the range of historical memory, the late sixteenth-century Tokugawa Japan provides the most striking evidence for the wider economic and social impact of the introduction of wet-rice terraces. The rapid expansion in population and agricultural output represented, it has been argued, a radical transformation within the Japanese society of labour relations and consumption patterns in the households. These developments were accompanied by a growing power of the centralised state in Japan.[67] The process of development of course had its limits created by a semi-static technology and by demographic expansion. By the early eighteenth century many coastal provinces in south China, previously highly productive, were experiencing rising pressures on food supplies. The causes of the subsistence crisis and the prevailing poverty among farmers were analysed in a local gazetteer which stated:

When there are too many people there is not enough land to contain them, there is not enough grain to feed them, and there are not enough wealthy people to take care of them . . . Water rushes down violently from the mountains and the mountains become bare, earth is dug out from rocks and the rocks are split; there is not an inch of cultivable land left.[68]

The ruin of the irrigational works in Ceylon: a historical puzzle. The Sinhalese irrigation schemes, the weirs, the embankments, and the feeder canals supplying the reservoirs were constructed on a scale that would have needed a substantial labour force for the initial building-works and for the subsequent maintenance.[69] A topographical survey dating from 1897 discovered two huge 'anikats' (weirs) in the ruined uninhabited country to the north-east through which flowed the twin rivers of Yan-oya and Ma-oya. The weirs were still perfectly preserved and built of wedged stones placed alternately parallel to and at right angles to the stream-flow. The measurements of some of the slabs and one of the anikats were impressive by any standards: cut stones 353 cm by 18 cm. The second anikat measured 28 m in length, 12 m in breadth, and 3 m in height above the river-bed. The two long-abandoned ancient reservoirs of Padawiya and Wahalkada served by the irrigation systems clearly testified to a vanished agrarian prosperity derived from rice fields almost stretching down to the coast.[70] Where was the surplus rice, if any, consumed in Ceylon? Was it exported from the island to other areas of the Indian Ocean, some of which were deficit in food by the very nature of their geography? Was pre-thirteenth century Ceylon a rice basket in the same way that Szechwan and the lower Yangtze were at various times in the history of China? Was the agrarian system of Tanjore linked in any way to that of Ceylon? These questions, unanswerable with the present available historical evidence, help to highlight an important general point. The peaks and troughs in the history of rural development followed different and non-linear time-sequences in the various Indian Ocean regions. The rationale which underpinned one particular system in its entirety remains tantalising, beyond the historian's documented knowledge. We know that long-distance oceanic and caravan trade expanded, sustained, and quickened the urban economy. Without the economic surplus drawn from land neither cities nor the political order could have survived for any length of time. Wars, famines, and epidemics periodically interrupted, and in some cases, altogether destroyed the basis of orderly life. If the wet-rice cultivation was capable of and perhaps even intended to produce a surplus of food beyond the immediate needs of the rural population, what was the historical context of the hydraulic engineering in Ceylon and its sudden, catastrophic demise after about AD 1236?[71]

First of all, let us note that the Sinhalese collapse was not unique. The period from the 1220s to the 1350s was one of deep crisis for many societies in Asia.

The catalogue of disasters, migrations, conquests, defeat, and depopulations is full and endlessly researched by historians, though not necessarily on a comparative basis or as a topic deserving to be studied on its own. A historical process which began as a southern migration of the Turkish-speaking people (several centuries earlier) ended almost apocalyptically for the Muslims with the Mongols occupying the heartland of Islam. The Celestial Empire likewise had succumbed by the end of the thirteenth century. Large parts of Sanskritic India bore the full weight of the pressure generated in the north, as militant Islam tried desperately to roll back the Central Asian non-Muslim advance and seek new land and sources of wealth. By 1310 the mounted Turkish warriors had reached the Indian Ocean and entrenched themselves in Gujarat and southern India. The transcontinental war-cycle of this period should be viewed against the ruin of the Mesopotamian irrigated agriculture and the decline of the Cambodian civilisation yet to come. The appearance of the Black Death in Egypt and the Mediterranean must have seemed to contemporaries as the impending sign of an end to all the achievements of the ancient civilisations. Were these events all coincidence?

The effects of malaria. Fernand Braudel ascribed (on the basis of the detailed research of Pierre Gourou in French Indochina) the destruction of the Cambodian rural population during the period of Angkor Wat to an ecological change. The dangerous species of mosquito, the anopheles which harbours the malarial parasite, finds it difficult to breed in the stagnant, muddy water of the rice fields. The larvae's progress is hindered by the albugo of the aquatic plants and by the insects and fish present in such waters. The two most lethal varieties, the *Anopheles minimus* and the *Anopheles maculatus*, select as their breeding ground clear, sunlit pools where the water is calm but renewed by running streams. The mountainous regions in Cambodia became at some point in history the favoured habitat of the malaria mosquito, whereas the plains remained free from this terrible disease.[72] 'In the fifteenth-century Angkor Wat was a thriving capital with rice-fields irrigated by muddy water. Siamese attacks were not themselves responsible for its destruction: but they threw daily life and agriculture into confusion. The water of the canals cleared and malaria triumphed, and with it, the invading forest.'[73] Is it possible to believe that a similar tragedy had occurred in southern India and the dry zone of Ceylon at an earlier period or that malaria first appeared in upper Iraq and then spread eastward over time?

Robert Knox, whom we have already met, spoke of 'ague and fevers' generally suffered by the Sinhalese people, and using the same terms he described the unmistakable symptoms of malaria which attacked him and his father, Captain Knox, during their first year of shipwreck on the island. The father died from the disease. The son, then aged nineteen, survived but the fever returned every three days and the whole malaria cycle lasted for sixteen months.[74] The precise date of the advent of malaria in Ceylon and in the dry zone cannot be determined. People living in the dry zone appear to have been permanently weakened by its ravages, incapable of the physical exertion needed for repairing and dredging the irrigation channels. The question still remains: did malaria appear before or after the hydraulic works and the rice-terraces were abandoned? There is a final speculative point which no one has raised so far. The water supply itself may have failed all through the monsoon belt as a result of recurrent droughts or climatic oscillations leading to a steady erosion of cultivation. The effects on the demographic viability of wet-rice farming would have been just as severe as large-scale warfare and virulent epidemics. Robert Knox had something to say about the drought too in the dry zone:

The North End of this Island is much subject to dry weather. I have known it for five or six years together so dry (having no Rains, and there is no other means of water but that, being but three springs of running water, that I know, or ever heard of) that they could not plow or sow, and scarcely could dig wells deep enough to get water to drink.[75]

The voice of existence, Ibn Khaldun had said recalling the effects of the Black Death, called out for oblivion and decline: the world had responded to its call. That was a reason by itself why the history of these events should be carefully recorded.[76] Islam was a religion of the 'Book' and the present-day historian is fortunate that it could not live without written history. No one wrote down the origins of the agrarian disasters which took place in Ceylon and Cambodia. Indeed, it is possible that the decline was so unpredictable, slow, or unimaginable that none could believe in a point of no return. That near-total demographic catastrophes resulting from floods, earthquakes, or volcanic eruptions took place in every region of the Indian Ocean is not in question. The miraculous element of history was the capacity of the Asian rural population to recover from the effects of the recurrent crisis.

Hydrology in China. The Sinhalese wet-rice production, small as it might seem, bordered on the substantial when judged by the population densities of the time. Its destruction in the dry zone should be seen against the continuation of the intensive systems of production in other areas. No such doubt about the viability or the continuity attaches to the scale of the agrarian production in China, which more than any where else in Asia, profited from and needed large-scale flood control measures and irrigation works. The taming of the Yellow River and the productive use of its silt-laden water through canals and embankments go back to the Han times. Over the centuries the action of the annual flooding and the containing dykes have raised the level of the river almost to that of the surrounding plains. Chinese hydraulic engineers and government policy-makers were divided between those who believed in allowing the Yellow River plenty of room to expand its channel and those who thought that it should be constricted to force the water to dig a deeper bed. While the two schools differed in their views over a period of two millennia, the construction of retention basins at various points of the main stream in recent times seems to vindicate the expansionists.[77] At the end of the seventeenth century, a Frenchman paid a tribute both to the Chinese efforts to master the river and its continuing restlessness: 'This river [Hoambo, Yellow River] hath in former times caused great desolation in China, and they are still forced to this very day to keep up the water in certain places by long and strong Banks, which notwithstanding does not exempt the Cities thereabouts from Apprehensions of Inundation.'[78]

A passage in the history of the Yuan dynasty also emphasised the collective responsibility for digging wells, canals, and reservoirs which were essential for avoiding droughts. If the peasantry were unable themselves to undertake the necessary works, it was the duty of the district magistrates to initiate and supervise these measures.[79] Living in a society with a deep respect for literacy and the power of the written words, Chinese historians, administrators, and the men of practical arts united in setting down the actual facts and their own recommendations of how agriculture and the management of water-resources should be conducted. In the *Nung Shu* (Treatise on Agriculture, 1313–14), Weng Cheng described the prevailing system of intensive wet-rice cultivation in which the farmers themselves constructed surface tanks and reservoirs to store the water and built dykes and sluices to control its flow to the terraces. The transplantation of the seedlings from the nursery beds to the flooded main fields was followed by all the subsequent stages of controlled water usage. Weng Cheng slipped in a sentence which may be of significance: 'All farmers now use this method.'[80] It is obvious that an important historical development (with an uncertain chronology) was going on in the different parts of the Indian Ocean. This was the transition from a purely rain-fed system of rice-growing to one making a greater utilisation of the existing or seasonal water resources through either simple decentralised irrigation-works or more elaborate state-sponsored schemes. The construction of reed, bamboo, and brushwood weirs across rivers and streams by the peasant communities themselves was as wide-spread from Mesopotamia to China as the digging of ponds and small canals. In wet-rice agriculture, the provision of irrigation water complementing the monsoon rains added a second or even a third harvest to the annual cycle of production. Whether farming communities would take advantage of the possibility depended on several factors: the density of population, the pressure on food supply, the strength of the exchange economy, and the extent of the labour-expenditure needed. The motivation of the government in promoting more complex and extensive hydraulic projects incorporated besides all these considerations, the desire to increase its revenue from agriculture and make its collection easier. The construction of the ambitious

Grand Canal connecting the lower Yangtze with the Huai and the Yellow River systems and its later extension to Peking under the Yuan dynasty may have been prompted in the first place by the easier transport of tribute rice to the imperial capitals. The various sections of the Grand Canal were built at different times but combined together by the Sui Dynasty (AD 581–618): its total length measured 1,100 miles and around the mountains of the Shantung province the canal reached a height of 42 m above sea level.[81] The imposition of corvée through which the large reservoirs, canals, and dykes were built in China reduced their immediate economic attractions for the farming population. The direct and indirect effects of canal-building on rural welfare were summarised by Ssu-ma Ch'ien in the Book on Rivers and Canals. The waterways were all used for the navigation of boats and if the water level was sufficient, irrigation was also allowed. A huge network of ditches and channels connected the canals to the rice-terraces.[82]

The historical significance of dry and wet farming. The role played by canals as waterways in China can be taken as a convenient starting-point of a discussion on the relative position of wheat and rice as the two food-plants of civilisation. If the historian is able to see and make a valid distinction between the dry and wet farming as social systems, its primary level must necessarily rest on technical features. Wheat and low value dry crops can be collected in kind as agricultural taxes. But it is difficult to store such grains for any length of time without the risk of spoilage and insect attack. Their transport by camels and oxen was certainly feasible but costly as compared with water-carriage. It was possible to store rice for many years, and indeed its taste improved a year or so after it was harvested. Even peasant households in Thailand and other rice-surplus areas preferred to put aside their newly-husked rice until the starch stabilised. The long tradition of tribute collection in rice was surely not accidental in the history of South East Asia, imperial China, and Japan. Rice was an article of wages and acted as currency. Standard baskets of rice became a universal measure of value and money of account. The relationship between state finance, the structure of administration, and the rice economy could take on a more direct form than for governments in areas of dry farming. The state in wheat growing regions of Asia often needed the intervention of metallic money and social intermediaries in order to extract and circulate income generated by crop production. The point should not be pressed unduly but perhaps the opportunity for centralisation and its continuity was better provided in rice economy than wheat. The time and effort expended by rice farmers on their land made it difficult to recruit them as soldiers and they themselves were not prone to military careers. The professional soldiers and the military chiefs held the terrible weapon of mass starvation in the easy destruction of the infrastructure of rice land. It is a historical fact that village communities in areas of dry farming could spare men who readily enlisted in the army and the villages were often self-policed and self-defended. The two-way social traffic between the nomadic pastoralists and the settled farmers, as we have already seen, encouraged mutual militarism and the growth of fortified agricultural settlements.[83] Throughout the wheat growing regions of the Middle East and India, successive centralised and bureaucratic empires would struggle with a perennial problem: how to prevent their military administrators from becoming hereditary landed chiefs with local roots and local armed supporters.

The structure of rural society: the levels of stratification

The Malthusian population theory and 'Oriental Despotism'. It is not difficult to accept the proposition that the history of settled farming in Asia during our period of study raises many unresolved problems. At the centre of the historiographic debate is the paradox posed by the Malthusian theory of population growth and its economic counterpart, the principle of diminishing return in agricultural development. The two separate concepts are linked together by a more generalised and descriptive historical theory known as 'Oriental Despotism' which re-emerged in the writings of Marx as the 'Asiatic Mode of Production'.[84] In 1798 Malthus published his famous essay on the principle of population. It claimed to have discovered a simple law regarding the relationship between population and economic development. Population, Malthus claimed, grew exponentially while the means of subsistence expanded only in terms of a fixed multiplier. Therefore the weight of demographic number constantly exceeded the available food supply. Famine, disease, and warfare, or the consequences of 'Oriental Despotism' constrained the inexorable mathematical logic of unqualified demographic replication.[85] Malthus had formulated his original reasoning with careful thought and later introduced the notion of positive as well as negative checks. In the hands of historians, the complexity of his arguments is often forgotten. The doctrine of diminishing return in agricultural production was as appealing as the classical theorem of population growth, in which any increase in the number of people was primarily seen as an increase in consumers. The theory stated that if the total supply of land is fixed, there is a point beyond which no further increase in crop output is possible through intensive methods of cultivation. Any addition of labour or capital merely leads to an unfavourable ratio of yield. The result is a fall in the availability of food per head of population.[86] The historical validity and the application of these propositions, are, as we shall see, seriously limited.

The theory of 'Oriental Despotism' has been almost as influential as the Malthusian theory in explaining an ancient historical puzzle relating to Asian settled farming. European travellers in Asia from Marco Polo onwards were powerfully impressed by the visible wealth and grandeur of Asian royal courts, by the active economic life of Asian cities, the large volume of long-distance trade organised by an enterprising merchant-class, and above all, the productivity of a multi-seasonal agriculture. As Western first-hand knowledge of Asian societies increased after the sixteenth century, the observers also noted that in spite of the flourishing cultivation of land, the condition of the peasantry was far from prosperous. The apparent contradiction between a wealth-creating agriculture and the poverty reflected in the miserable life-style of rural Asia found an explanation in the mind of contemporaneous Europe in the notion of 'Oriental Despotism'. The wealth of the political elites, merchants, and traders, it was believed, really derived from a steady and disproportionate expropriation of the agricultural surplus created by the peasantry. Bernier stated (1664) the case, as always, with exuberant rhetoric. The tyranny of the Timurids in India, their governors and revenue collectors, was so excessive

as to deprive the peasant and artisan of the necessaries of life, and leave them to die of misery and exhaustion – a tyranny owing to which those wretched people either have no children at all, or have them only to endure the agonies of starvation, and to die at a tender age . . . As the ground is seldom tilled otherwise than by compulsion, and no person is found willing and able to repair the ditches and canals for the conveyance of water, it happens that the whole country is badly cultivated, and a great part rendered unproductive from the want of irrigation . . . The peasant cannot avoid asking himself this question: 'Why should I toil for a tyrant who may come tomorrow and lay his rapacious hands upon all I possess and value . . . '.[87]

Bernier thought that in Iraq, Ottoman Turkey, and Egypt, agriculture was equally ruined by the exactions of Islamic governments. Regions once well-cultivated and productive had now returned to the desert and the marsh, pestiferous and unfit for human habitation. In this reasoning, the quality of political administration and the welfare of rural society appeared to many contemporary thinkers, European as well as Asian, as two inseparable links in a cause-and-effect recursive chain. The principle seemed to transcend nationalities or ethnic identities, although an obvious contrast was often drawn between the European scene and that of Asia. Edmund Burke's historical description of southern India (1785) surpassed Bernier's prose in eloquence but it reversed the view point:

The Carnatic is refreshed by few or no living brooks or running streams, and it has rain only at a season; but its product of rice exacts the use of water subject to perpetual command. This is the national bank of the Carnatic, on which it must have a perpetual credit, or it perishes irretrievably. For that reason, in the happier times of India, a number almost incredible of reservoirs have been made in chosen places throughout the whole country . . . there cannot be in Carnatic and Tanjore fewer than ten thousand of these reservoirs of the larger and middling dimensions . . . These are the monuments of real kings, who were the fathers of their people; testators to a posterity which they embraced as their own . . . to perpetuate themselves through generations of generations, the guardians, the protectors, the nourishers of mankind.[88]

It is striking that both the passages should have drawn attention to the dialectics embedded in the structure of Asian rural production. One of the constant themes in the agrarian history of the Middle East and India was the attempt made by the political authorities to keep the peasantry on their land. It was achieved by a combination of coercive methods and the offer of direct economic incentives. The financial interest of the state required the system of taxation to maximise revenue. But if the cultivators were left without sufficient food and capital resources to replicate their families and replace the draught animals, ploughs, and seed-corn, it was axiomatic that steady demographic decline would become an eventuality, activated by the Malthusian checks. The uncertain rainfall and the variations in the water supply called for large capital expenditure on irrigational works. State intervention was essential both in order to draw out the investment funds and protect valuable rights in irrigated land. Where the state agency did not undertake the irrigational works directly through corvée or advance loans to the farmers, finance for rural development was often provided by the local bankers, landed magnates, and revenue officials who were all drawn from the same social background.[89] An undifferentiated theory of 'Oriental Despotism' completely disregards the finer details of inter-locked and contradictory interests involved in crop production and the different methods adopted for resolving actual or potential conflicts. Even in areas of high relative population concentration, the demographic resources often remained below the level needed to maintain optimum agricultural production, a situation which produced a perfect paradox, the simultaneous existence of rural poverty and surplus land. The Malthusian checks seldom brought about an equilibrium between population size and economic resources. Generally, famines and epidemics devastated communities below the level of efficiency. It can be argued that all the evidence of history indicates that social conflict and tension in rural areas arose as much from chronic under-population as from too many workers competing for scarce land.[90] Furthermore, there is no indication that past societies, when faced with the long-term dilemma of static food production and rising population, failed to draw an obvious conclusion: the possibility of technological progress. To suppose otherwise is to assume that the application of irrigation to crop-production, the improvement in seeds, the use of fertilisers, and the development of agricultural implements, including the harnessing of the plough to draught animals, even the emergence of settled farming itself, took place in a historical vacuum, without motivation. All these technological discoveries could have taken place in conditions of crisis as well as of rising productivity and growth.

The relationship between the state and the rural society: role of money. The state systems of the Indian Ocean were commanded by princely warriors and financed by merchants. In the last analysis, the economic resources extracted by both the groups came from the labours of the farmer and the artisan. That the control over land and its products was vital to the whole process of the social appropriation of power was never in any doubt. Legal theorists tended to support and uphold the absolute power and authority enjoyed by the political ruler or the emperor, within the operation of the economy and society, as against the feudal and administrative claims to independent rights. The absolutists were constrained or diluted in practice by the inability of the state exchequer to pay the salaries of the administrators directly in cash. Problems of time and distance were both responsible for the logistical difficulties in organising the payments mechanism. The structure of rural production evolved over time in such a way as to interact with the economic interests of the state and the landed intermediaries on whose support the centralised empires ultimately depended for their existence and survival. Because a pre-industrial economy was only imperfectly monetised and remained dependent on metallic currencies composed of gold, silver, copper, and in some areas cowrie shell money, shortage of money and the means of payment was endemic. The paradox of the situation lay in the fact that many areas of the Indian Ocean possessed at the same time an advanced exchange economy. They did not live in a state of primitive isolation. The concept of economic values, whether of services or of goods, was grounded on a clear notion of their scarcity or plentifulness. Gold and silver served universally as common units of monetary values, and the economic ideas were as widely prevalent as they were influential in guiding government policy. But the historical reality all the same posed intractable problems in reconciling the logic of subsistence food production with the demands of the exchange economy. It was not only the physical shortages of money that created the obstacles. The extraction of a surplus from the peasant communities and its redistribution over the rest of the economy posed difficult social and economic problems.

The problem of paying for civil and military administration. In Europe, after the disintegration of the traditional feudal relations, the connection between the finances of the sovereign and the agrarian classes went through a prolonged period of fragmentation and ultimately became separated. In Asia, on the other hand, the connection remained strong throughout and took a path very different from that of the West. The question to which the head of a centralised Asian bureaucratic empire had to address himself was embedded in a central contradiction: if the civil and military officers in charge of administering the rural areas could not all be paid by the exchequer and had to be rewarded through the assignment of revenue collection from rural producers, what was to prevent them from becoming permanent landed magnates? Alternatively, in areas still politically dominated by the traditional landed chiefs who were only imperfectly shorn of their military power, how could the central government turn this class of people into loyal supporters and tax-gatherers? The solution adopted of course lay in shifting the administrators periodically from their provincial bases. The assignment of revenue-yielding units of land seldom exceeded a period of three years. The institution of 'iqta' developed by the Abbasid caliphate, the Ottoman 'timar', and the Mughal 'jagirdari' systems supported both civil and military establishments through a tripartite relation between the state, administrators, and the farmers.[91] Whether the 'men of pen', who translated the wishes of the emperor, or the 'men of sword', implementing those commands, would remain content to divide their mutual spheres of influence in equal measure depended on the ideological and practical strength of the central government. In times of political weakness or changing ideology, the men of sword often seized undeclared political independence in the distant parts of the empire. Furthermore, the agrarian history of China in particular was marked by repeated peasant uprisings against rent-collectors and the local gentry. Rural banditry was a desperate if powerful weapon in the hands of the dispossessed. During the closing years of the Ming rule, many rural areas in China suffered severely from harsh collection of rents and taxes, leading to widespread peasant disturbances.[92] But the examples of sporadic violence in the countryside can be considered unusual in the sense that these events point towards a breakdown of the normal patterns of social and political behaviour. Asian farming people seldom had the time or the inclination to take arms on their own behalf, while the landed gentry always included a warrior element. They were able to recruit through their financial power armed retainers to intimidate either the peasantry or fellow-landed magnates. Detailed agrarian studies on the Ottoman dominions, Iran, India, China, and Japan prove conclusively that the common factor in the rural relationships of all these areas was an underlying threat of armed force which became explicit in the event of peasant uprisings or resistance. In quieter times, the general acceptance of a hierarchy of power which controlled and directed the use of economic resources in the countryside rested on the implicit acceptance of this ultimate sanction.

The political systems of Asia in our period of study could not dispense with the intermediate role of the rural landholders and the latter's bureaucratic counter-parts. The elaborate structure of agricultural taxation, its theory and practice, created by the central administrators contained an element of indeterminacy through its inability to predict the degree of co-operation which the stratified rural society was prepared to give to the state. The informal alliance of interest between the Asian rulers and the local landed gentry may have reduced the full interplay of market forces in fixing the economic usage of land by restricting proprietary rights, creating a web of privileged tenures, and even discouraging the growth of productivity. Agricultural production however was finely adjusted to the reality of social structure. The long-run changes in the distribution of agrarian income were determined by the relative capacity of land to yield crops, the ratio between cultivable land and rural population, and 'class' structure. It is possible that demographic trends in the last analysis controlled the relationship between the landed magnates and the peasantry, the people who actually tilled the land and made economic decisions. For many centuries agricultural land in southern China was considered highly productive and it was intensively cultivated and improved. But by the sixteenth and seventeenth centuries the process of expansion had run into serious difficulties and environmental degradation was beginning to impinge on rural well-being. The relative overcrowding in the Chinese countryside and the consequent land hunger created painful economic pressures on the poorer peasants, even leading to the practice of infanticide.[93] In Mughal India, slow population growth was responsible for weighing the balance between demographic factors and the availability of cultivable land in favour of the peasantry. Local landed classes were always careful not to drive away their privileged tenants and share-croppers by rack renting. The scarce factor of production in the drier and arid areas of northern India was capital. The development of irrigation and water resources depended critically on the supply of loans from private and government sources. The distribution of finance and the method of repaying the loans in turn determined how far farmers should benefit from the addition of an extra harvest in winter to their existing rain-fed autumn crops. If the prosperity of the cultivating classes in Mughal India appeared uneven and at times even precarious, there were two main reasons for it. The level of state demand whether expressed directly or through revenue farmers remained relatively high. But the burden of agricultural taxation was not shared equally. The dominant power structure within Indian rural society, itself hierarchically arranged, created privileged and non-privileged status. The Brahman, Rajput, and the administrative groups with proprietary interest in land paid a lesser share of the surplus to the state than those with a lower ritual and social rank. In the Middle Eastern rural society similar examples of stratified landholding and differential tax payments are well-documented.[94]

The social structure of the 'village'. Variations in agricultural yields and demographic trends raised or lowered tensions within a functioning system of rural class structure. In general, these semi-autonomous changes were not able to dissolve from within the established social bonds. There seems to have been some kind of replicating mechanism, a 'perpetual memory', which went on reproducing the agrarian relations over long periods of time. Fundamental structural changes occurred either in a slow process of mutation or as a result of cataclysmic disasters. The village of course constituted the basic unit of social and economic reproduction. It was also the primary module in the entire scheme of social stratification prevailing over the wider rural scene. The social and economic dimensions of the Asian village were to be found in its twin physical features: it was a collection of family households and a geographical locus with dwelling houses and cultivated land. The system of landownership within the village in most parts of the Indian Ocean did not coincide strictly with the technical requirements of land usage. For example, in India the total land area could be owned by a large number of proprietors each of whom possessed only a minute share. It did not necessarily follow that the actual size of the fields was subdivided to the same extent. There was a minimum size beyond which the units of agricultural land were not permitted to vary and these boundaries were fixed by local soil conditions, micro-climate, the irrigation facility and the range of crops planted. For the inhabitants of the village the most important and difficult problem lay in finding a method of reconciling the rights of ownership and the social aspects of landholding with the operating rules given by agronomic factors.

Indo-Islamic land usage. A common Indo-Islamic pattern seems to have been prevalent throughout our period of study stretching all the way from the Middle East to India. The allocation of the economic resources of the village can be differentiated into three theoretical and practical types. The first method was to hold all land in joint ownership and divide the crops after the harvest among the members, each share being determined by the pattern of kinship and the value of services rendered by weavers, potters, blacksmiths, carpenters, barbers, and washermen if any of these craft and service communities were present in the village. The allocation of agricultural labour and tasks followed a traditional pattern based on the structure of power within the extended family. The practice of sharing out the harvested crops bypassed the use of money and the indexing of value by prices. The exchange mechanism was an analogue system, and it can be concluded that where such localised economies existed, economic value was determined by commodity money rather than a metallic currency. In the second typology, the ownership of land still remained common but each individual field was marked out by its location, fertility, and access to water. The fields were cultivated by different families each year and the rotation method ensured that the distribution of wealth did not become extreme. Finally, there were villages in which all land was permanently divided among the community according to the principle of ancestral inheritance or by sale and purchase. Here the inequality of wealth was likely to be a significant feature of the agrarian economy and the system needed a parallel market structure based on money and prices to operate efficiently. In the fully partitioned villages, the distribution of income from land moved away from the principle of social entitlement to the concept of monetary values and incomes.

The three types of land usage were so widespread in the Levant, Iraq, Iran, and India that the combination could be taken as the dominant form of agrarian relations in Western Asia.[95] Although in the Middle East and India concentration of landed property and agricultural holdings was a common historical feature, the dominant groups could not completely disregard the rights of intermediate proprietors or cultivators according to customary laws. It was only the exercise of violent means and uncontrolled force which radically reshuffled the existing structure of rural relationships. The legal restrictions on land rights by sale or inheritance may explain the endemic violence which characterised the Islamic and Indian countryside. The easiest path to land acquisition by the local political chiefs was to use military force to drive off rival claimants from the adjacent villages. The social stratification of the countryside in the western Indian Ocean followed a tripartite division. The majority of the rural population consisted of peasants who actually ploughed and sowed the land. Above them there was another category composed of intermediate proprietors receiving rent or a share of crops from the peasants. At the very top, great landed magnates exercised semi-political rights and played an important role in linking their locality to the structure of imperial power at the centre. The relationship between each category of rural society was carefully defined and strictly enforced. The rights of individual peasant families recognised as hereditary cultivators could not be taken away by superior groups. But they were expected to surrender a high proportion of crops to the landlords, the exact share being determined by the types of land and crops grown. Landless families or those with insufficient hereditary land worked as annual share-croppers for landowners who had surplus land or had lost their permanent tenants. The position of chiefs in the rural hierarchy varied between a high official of the state empowered to collect taxes and a genuine landed magnate with proprietary rights over their estates. The relative weight of these two definitions depended on the power and will of the central government to impose an independent political administration in the distant provinces. In the Ottoman and Mughal polity, the concept of a non-hereditary military class supported out of agrarian resources was at its strongest and the indigenous military landed chiefs were quickly reduced to the status of princely administrators.

The control of the agrarian economy in the western Indian Ocean was a complex social process. In spite of the existence of bonded labour in agricultural production, the bulk of the peasantry managed to resist political and economic pressure to bind them permanently to large units of land as serfs. The price paid by them was admittedly high and even in cases where the appropriation of the economic surplus exceeded no more than a third of the total crop yield, the margin between bare survival and relative prosperity remained problematic for the farming communities. If the superior landed classes were not able to coerce the farmer into serfdom or slavery through force, what was the nature of the sanction that allowed them to extract an economic surplus and social compliance at all from the cultivators? There is little doubt that the military power of the conquering people in various parts of the Middle East and India gave rise to a distinct class of rural elite groups, though landed estates could grow in size through the normal process of sale and purchase. The political traditions of the centralised empire, handed down from the Egyptian and Babylonian times, prevented the peasantry from being reduced to the status of slaves. Throughout the western Indian Ocean, the tillers of land remained free citizens within a stratified social and political system, in striking contrast to the practices of the Greco-Roman civilisations. The slow demographic expansion and the low absolute population density obviously forced the owners of land to compete for farming labour. The size of the economic surplus yielded by land, sometimes double- or treble-cropped, on the other hand was relatively high in relation to the internal consumption needs of the rural population. The peasantry found it possible to part with a high proportion of their crops without suffering an immediate demographic loss. The policy of the centralised empires restricted the power of the landed elite through the recruitment and the maintenance of a professional armed force and at the same time political and legal support was lent to them to create and extract an agricultural surplus. But the attitude of the elite groups towards farmers and the practice of agriculture in both Islamic lands and Sanskritic India remained one of profound contempt. Such an environment severely restricted the room for social mobility.

Land usage in South East Asia and China. The historical reconstruction of the structure of rural society in mainland and maritime South East Asia suffers severely from inadequate sources, in marked contrast to India and the Middle East. Although the state and society has successively incorporated Sanskritic, Chinese, and Islamic concepts, terminology, and operating rules into indigenous usage, the assimilative process was never complete or exact. The use of Sanskrit, Pali, or Arabic terms may have been little more than a historic renaming and reclassifying of existing structures and social forms which displayed important differences with South Asian and Islamic practices. Of course certain basic common denominators remained. The available information indicates that the pattern of land utilisation and the technology of agricultural production in South East Asia were derived as much as elsewhere in the Indian Ocean from an observed relationship between climate, crops, collective human efforts and needs. On the other hand, the relationship between the state and rural communities whether they were organised in the form of nuclear settlements or scattered farming households expressed wide regional variations. In centralised states, as for example in the Thai and Khmer theory of kingship, where the idea of absolute political power was strong, the status of the cultivators reflected a high degree of dependency if not

actual bondage. That the villages continued to operate an internal organisational rationality based on the twin principles of kinship and functional
relationship is not in doubt. What is not clear is the historical articulation
between the ruling elites outside the locality and the farming community. The
appropriation of the economic surplus in South East Asia by the state and its
representatives basically fall into two categories. Farmers who had received
their land allocation from village headmen or district chiefs, appointed by the
ruling court, paid a part of the rice crop as rents or taxes. They were also liable
for corvée or labour services on the land held by the elite groups and on public
works schemes whether these were the construction of irrigation works,
canals, or public buildings. The prevalence of intensive rice farming, the relative density of population, and the opportunity for marketing the rice determined which of the two methods should be given priority.[96]

In China and Japan agriculture and the prosperity of the peasantry were
considered as the roots of the social fabric. This is not to say that there was no
hierarchical status in Chinese and Japanese societies. On the contrary, one of
the basic conclusions of Confucian ethics was to view all things, including
people, as unequal by nature. In Chinese moral and social thinking the status
differences were clearly institutionalised and each category was given an
official ranking. Chinese passion for a systematic treatment of people performing different economic functions could be seen in the creation of special
service groups such as soldiers, military agricultural colonisers in frontier
areas, artisans, and salt boilers. Although the early T'ang emperors had
attempted to redistribute land according to family size and the notion of a
minimum holding, the rural districts for a long time continued to be dominated by the great lineage families and their large estates. Serf-like peasants
worked and lived on these estates.[97] But alongside the large landowners, there
were also free small-scale farmers who practised commercial cultivation either
on the basis of private ownership of land or fixed tenancy contracts. After the
establishment of the Ming dynasty the institutional framework of Chinese
agriculture gradually moved towards a greater reliance on the market
mechanism. Even though each extended family tried to preserve its holdings of
land as an economic unit, the principle of private ownership and land utilisation introduced an element of flexibility in agricultural decision-making.
Farmers could decide as household units what crops to grow according to the
prevailing market prices. The trade in rice and other crops throughout the
major regions of China not only made it possible to develop urban industries,
it also brought the rural specialisation much closer to the national market.

The discovery of a large number of tenancy agreements from the early
eighteenth century has led to a fairly detailed reconstruction of the pattern of
landholding in the early Ch'ing period.[98] In 1714 a tenant who was described
in the contract as being landless agreed to lease a parcel of land belonging to
Fo-chou City. The field required 0.55 tan (2.75 kg) of seeds and the tenant was

to pay annually 11 tan (55 kg) of unhusked rice as rent. The heavy burden of rent in this case was compounded by the fact that it remained fixed irrespective of seasonal variations in harvest yields. The proprietorship of the land, of course, remained with the original owners. In fact, under the Ming dynasty sub-infeudation had become a feature of land utilisation. The person recorded in the government registers as being liable to pay the tax assessment was treated as the first owners. Below this level there was another class of proprietors who had purchased long tenancy rights to the land. An active market in leasehold land seemed to have developed in southern China and it is possible that the labour-intensive rice cultivation in the delta areas gave rise to a more permanent and alienable right to land. The favourable picture of Chinese agriculture given in some historical sources is of course contradicted by other writers who emphasised the harsh demands on the peasantry which led to widespread depopulation and regional migrations. The rural devastations which took place during the fall of the Ming dynasty were made good only slowly but by the early eighteenth century agricultural population had recovered and was even impinging on the available good land.

Land as economic and social capital. Land usage and social stratification in premodern Asia falls into two dominant typologies. On the one hand, the traditional distinctions between peasants, proprietors, and overlords are found in most areas. But the economic relationships binding one group to the other are not uniform. Where national markets were absent or imperfectly organised, a system of physical exchange prevailed such as the rotation of land or the division of crops. The development of the market on the other hand encouraged the growth of private ownership of land and the sale of crops for cash sums. In each case, there are associated systems of customary or codified laws to define the rights and obligations of the rural population. The position of the overlords in relation to the state and the local village continued to be ambiguous in the Indo-Islamic empires. The central government discouraged concentration of power in their hands, even though it was not able to dispense altogether with their local functions. In Chinese statecraft there were no such uncertainties. Large landowners needed to become civil servants through the due process of selection before they could exercise legitimate power. The appearance of warlords during the periods of political disturbances in China was common enough. The phenomenon never succeeded in challenging the basic centralising principle of Chinese political order.

The historical structure of Asian rural societies was shaped and sustained by the 'logical necessities' of settled agriculture. In order to bring waste land into productive use, it was necessary to invest a substantial amount of labour which in turn could only be obtained if there was a surplus fund of food, clothing, and shelter. Even peasant farming needed the fulfilment of three conditions: the undisputed possession of land, the security of the standing crops, and an economic mechanism through which the surplus yielded by the land could be distributed to services other than agriculture itself. It is axiomatic that no individual or community would go to the length of clearing the land, constructing irrigational works or undertaking costly improvements unless they were reasonably certain of enjoying the rewards of their labour. It was for this reason that the ancient Indian legal treatise, the Manusmriti declared unequivocally that whoever brought waste land into cultivation were also its legal owners. But the operating principles of ownership of land did not reside just in an original title. It was related to the wider social relationships among the agrarian communities. The taxes paid by the peasantry to the state agents or to the dominant local groups represented theoretically an economic transaction in which farmers exchanged a proportion of their crops in return for protection.[99] It is debatable whether in the history of the Indian Ocean the peasantry took this view of their obligation to the political overlords. Quite often the only protection they secured was partial exemption from the latter's own violence.[100] The redistributive functions of the state in the pre-industrial economies ultimately hinged on the productive capacity of land. The twin agrarian institutions of land tenure and land taxation made it possible for the state and the agrarian society to co-exist as an articulated entity.

9

Animals and their masters: nomads and nomadism

General problems

The definition: who is a nomad? Nomadism is a convenient theoretical term. It is also a continuum. A wide variety of people with different types of social organisation, degrees of mobility, and livelihoods can be classified by the term. It is significant that in most Asian societies, precise linguistic terms exist which describe the 'nomads' either by their wandering life, tribal and clan affiliations or economic occupations. The Turkish word 'köc' as it occurs in the Iranian texts was a generalised term carrying the entire shades of meaning from spatial movements, to migration routes, and mobile people.[1] The term 'yüruk', used in the Ottoman regulations ('kanums') to describe the Anatolian nomads, derives from the verb 'yürumek' meaning to walk or wander. It reflected the obvious ideological perception by a highly structured state of the difference between those subjects who were 'reaya' ('ra°iyat'), peasants, and those who were yüruks or nomads.[2] The local communities however would have identified the Turkish sheep-tending nomads by tribal names.[3] The complex variations of the category and the differing forms of nomadic relationships with the settled society make it difficult to look upon the term nomadism as anything other than a literary expression. However, for the purpose of a historical evaluation of the phenomenon, economic dependence on domesticated animals associated with a migratory way of life may be taken as one of its possible working definitions.[4] But it is well known that not all pastoralists were nomads nor all nomads keepers of animals. Shepherds and cattle-tenders practising transhumance could belong to the same community of settled farmers living in ancient villages: professional groups of people entrusted with the sheep, goats, and cattle owned by the villagers, who migrate during the dry season when there is no local grazing either to the forested areas or to the high mountain slopes well-provided with rich and nourishing grass. The social base of such animal-tenders remains firmly located in the fixed rural settings. On the other hand, in many parts of Asia there were completely nomadic communities such as iron-smiths who travelled from place to place with their entire families and possessions, carrying the foundry equipments and the raw metals in ornate metal carts drawn by oxen or camels.

The famous grain and salt traders of India, the 'Banjaras', were definitely

263

nomadic. Whether they were also pastoralists in the strict sense of the term is doubtful. Many contemporary observers spoke with a sense of wonder about the huge caravan of oxen owned by the Banjaras and employed in the carrying-trade. In 1622 when Emperor Jahangir was preparing an army for the relief of Qandahar, which was being besieged at the time by the forces of Shah Abbas, it was decided to use the Banjaras for provisioning the army and the artillery-trains during their difficult march from Multan to Qandahar. The emperor added by way of an elucidation that the grain-sellers who in the language of India were called Banjaras were a tribe: 'Some of them have 1,000 bullocks and some more or less. They take grain from different districts into the towns and sell it. They go along with the armies, and with such an army there would be 100,000 bullocks or more.'[5] Important as the Banjaras were to the army commissariat, their contribution to the commercial traffic was even greater. When the North Indian merchant houses wished to get their goods quickly to the great Mughal port-city Surat, well in time for the monsoon winds, wagons were discarded in favour of the Banjaras' bullock-trains. For small groups of private travellers, the nomadic caravans were a source of considerable delays. Jean-Baptiste Tavernier described the situation in detail:

As all the territories of the Great Mogul are well cultivated, the fields are enclosed by good ditches, and each has its tank or reservoir for irrigation. This makes it so inconvenient for travellers, because, when they meet caravans of this description in narrow roads, they are sometimes obliged to wait two or three days till all have passed. Those who drive these oxen follow no other trade all their lives; they never dwell in houses, and they take with them their women and children.[6]

Each group had a chief who acted as the political negotiator. The role was vital when two caravans travelling in opposite directions met head-on and each refused to give way to the other, often resulting in bloody clashes. According to Tavernier, two leading Banjara Chiefs were recently (1665) summoned to the imperial court and Aurangzeb persuaded them to come to a mutual agreement avoiding future conflicts. Each received a present of 100,000 rupees and a string of pearls.

Young animals born to the Banjara herds were looked after as caringly as children and a successful birth was greeted with much rejoicing. But the cattle owned by the Indian grain-carriers obviously had an economic function and value which were different from those owned by the true nomadic cattle-breeders in the subcontinent. The patterns of Banjara movement arose from the rationale of long-distance caravan trade and the dispersion of surplus-producing grain-districts. The community was the creation of the outside world and its economic needs. The true pastoral nomads were not unaware of the symbiotic relationship between themselves and the sedentary peasant farmers. Their animals however could not be fed from the profits of a carrying-trade. The search for suitable seasonal grazing and water as well as the size of the flocks and herds determined to an overwhelming extent how their masters would organise the rhythms of work and social life.

The historical role of nomads and their way of life have attracted a great deal of scholarly attention. From the Greco-Roman times to the present, historians have tried to account for the origin of nomadic pastoralism, its purpose, consequence, and even its true meaning. Whereas settled agriculture is mostly treated as being given and swidden culture dismissed as a primitive forerunner of intensive farming-techniques, nomadic communities practising pastoralism seemed to defy all through the ages rational analysis and remain at the same time one of the strongest forces of historical development. One of the reasons why pastoral nomadism presents such a wide variation of forms and different history is because of its relative freedom from structural constraints. Settled agriculture, as we have seen, must satisfy a large number of logical necessities ranging from land-clearance to the legal definition of property. Pastoral nomadism in contrast has just two structural decision-variables: whether the number of animals owned by the family unit is enough to live on their economic products and whether there is enough seasonal pasture for the animals themselves. As the nomads utilised mostly marginal land, they competed for optimal conditions: the grass and plants on which the camels, sheep, or cattle subsisted were completely exhausted in season as was also the supply of water. In such a situation, the pastoral nomads could articulate a whole range of social and political relations within the nomadic society as well as between themselves and the sedentary population. Whether the two-way traffic between the nomads and the settled land was fraught with tension, whether it was friendly or antagonistic, whether one side exercised political domination over the other, and whether it was conducted on terms of equal economic exchange, depended on historical circumstances. The relationships were neither static nor did they follow any definite rule of social behaviour.

The historical role of nomadic pastoralists

Nomads, states, and society. There are several reasons why nomadism as a historical phenomenon has aroused such strong interest and even a scholarly debate. It may be useful to make an initial distinction between 'encapsulated' and 'free' nomads: the first category included those who were already living within the bounds of sedentary society and established state systems, while the second group comprised nomads in relatively empty lands with weak state formation. The Central Asian deserts and mountains, the Eurasian steppes, the arid regions of the Arabian peninsula, and the Sahara provided the main camping grounds and seasonal pasturage for the free nomads. The encapsulated nomadic pastoralists were to be found in Anatolia, the Syrian upland, Iraq, Iran, Afghanistan, the high Himalayas, and in many parts of the northern and western Indian plains. The constant migrations of nomads from one pasture ground to another generally means crossing the 'political' frontiers of different social groups, nations, and states which raised awkward questions of both jurisdiction and loyalty to the legitimate authorities. In 1499, the Turkish Pasha of Morea wanted to prohibit the Albanian and Greek subjects of the little town of Coron, under Venetian control, from grazing their sheep in the territory of the Grand Signore. The Rettori of Coron pointed out with calculated logic, 'Our flocks may go to your land in summer, but your flocks come to ours in winter.'[7] It was a fact that many nomadic communities had their own independent political organisation and it was not easy to integrate them into the existing structure of state systems. Furthermore, not only were the encapsulated nomads, living in uneasy and negotiated relationship with the sedentary society of the established empires, regarded as a potential Trojan Horse, capable of undermining the stability of the state, but in the case of Central Asian tribal groups equipped with huge herds of war-horses, the external military threat posed by nomadic armies was very real. The settled societies of the Islamic Middle East, India, and China, sharing common political frontiers with the warlike tribal neighbours, went in constant fear of the military consequences of their periodic dispersion from the customary homelands.

The assimilation of the nomadic pastoralists into the social structure of settled agriculturalists is usually described as the process of sedentarisation. It was accompanied by a reverse movement: the intermittent relapse into nomadic ways of life on the part of people who were accustomed to produce part of their food supplies from crop-raising. In the main, the historical changes relating to encapsulated nomadism came from two separate directions. In a situation where the presence of nomads was considered to be a threat to the state or society, constant pressure was kept up by the political authorities to force or induce them to settle down permanently or to expel them beyond the state jurisdiction. The rural society seemed to have also an in-built mechanism for the absorption of the pastoral nomads and recreate them by turns. The wealthy owner of a large flock and herd of animals was likely to settle down and buy landed property, just as the impoverished nomadic members who had lost their flocks and herds through misfortune or acts of war had no alternative to becoming agricultural labourers.[8] Peasant farmers who practised small-scale subsistence crop-raising together with transhumant animal-tending in areas of marginal rainfall were also vulnerable to prolonged periods of drought. For a season or so they could just survive living on the acorns of the mountain-oak. If the drought continued, as it frequently did, the stark possibility of starvation would have driven them to become completely nomadic. As a form of economic activity, nomadism functioned as an indispensable part of the Asian food-production and its evolution was closely related to the history of urbanisation and long-distance caravan trade. Contemporary Asian historians and political authorities dealing with the daily impact of pastoral nomadism were very sensitive to its political and social implications, though they did not entirely disregard its economic role. European observers on the other hand were immediately aware of the contrast between their own agriculture and that of Asia as manifested through pastoralism. In Europe, stock-raising had become completely assimilated into settled farming, which was made possible by a combination of climatic factors and historical developments. The stable rainfall yielded a steady supply of grass and hay during the summer and early autumn, some of which could be saved as fodder for the winter. Although livestock suffered from chronic malnutrition during the winter months before the invention of cold-weather green crops, there was no real economic incentive or even the political possibility for the sheep and cattle farmers to migrate over long distances. The institution of the 'mesta' in Spain, allowing the Castilian merino sheep-owners to move their flocks over arable land, was a form of transhumance with serious implications for the prosperity of corn-growers.[9] Animal husbandry in the arid regions of the Indian Ocean on the other hand was never properly absorbed into the pattern of settled agriculture and remained largely mobile.

The western Indian Ocean civilisations were characterised by strong centralised empires and monarchies, and yet they appeared on the surface only too willing to tolerate the uncertain political presence of pastoral nomads. Why was this so? European scholars, in contrast to the attitudes of past Asian historians, have attempted to answer the question mainly in terms of the economic value and motivation of nomadism to Asian societies.[10] But when nomadism is examined as a historical process, it is clear that the social and political accommodation of the pastoralists within the structure of the centralised states was due not merely to a recognition of their economic importance but also because of a fundamental operating distinction made between the state and nations. The centralised states and empires of the Indian Ocean were invariably multinational and composed of plural societies. It was impossible for the successive rulers of northern China, India, and Iran to make a rigid separation between many different ethnic and linguistic categories of subjects, and the concept of citizenship as a strictly-interpreted legal definition remained decidedly vague. Furthermore, the heads of states in many instances were themselves of distant nomadic origin. The memory and the social traditions of the steppe and the desert were kept alive by a constant stream of aristocratic migrants seeking employment as military officers and administrators from the centralised states which derived their huge tax-revenue from the labour of peasant agriculturalists. Without a defined relationship with the rest of the Asian society, nomads ceased to be nomads. Ghazan Khan (1271–1304), the first Mongol head of state to convert to Islam, a great administrator and statesman, put the dilemma facing the nomadic warriors with considerable force:

I am not on the side of the Tazik [Iranian] raᶜiyat. If there is a purpose in pillaging them all, there is no one with more power to do this than I. Let us rob them together. But if you wish to be certain of collecting grain ['taghar'] and food ['ash'] for your tables in the future, I must be harsh with you. You must be taught reason. If you insult the raᶜiyat, take their oxen and seed, and trample their crops into the ground, what will you do in the future? . . . The obedient raᶜiyat must be distinguished from the raᶜiyat who are our enemies. How should we not protect the obedient, allowing them to suffer distress and torment at our hand.[11]

While it was difficult to control or suppress the military contingents of the powerful Mongol leaders, the semi-encapsulated nomads were easier to deal with. The Iranian minister of Ghazan, the famous historian Rashid al-Din (1247–1318) sent an officer to Khuzistan, an area through which the Zagros pastoralists migrated between summer and winter pastures, to try and prevent the various tribes from grazing their animals on village land and causing damage to the crops. The pastoralists were ordered to remove their flocks to Qara Tappa and the Ala-maran river. The officer had the power to arrest those who returned to the prohibited area, confiscate their property, and send them to the court under guard.[12] Later on when the Ottoman Turks had progressed from being Anatolian nomadic chiefs to the status of a Great Power presiding over a regular imperial administration from the former capital of the Eastern Roman Empire, regulations were framed which attempted to define the distinction between the peasants and the nomadic pastoralists. The yüruks did not cultivate the land, nor raise vineyards, it was noted. They tended sheep and the sheep tax was paid to the village officers ('sipahis'). They had no fixed home, no special relations with the governors, and were ruled by their own chiefs. A proven yüruk wrong-doer was punishable by his own law-enforcing agents.[13] If the Ottoman sheep-tax was indeed regressive and against the economic interest or even the survival of the yüruks as nomads, it failed in its intended design. For the Anatolian nomadic sheep-farmers have continued to exist to the present day. It was impossible to raise a large number of sheep as part of the regular arable farming cycle in the absence of permanent pastures, and as long as the sheep and its wool remained respectively the favourite item of food and the basic raw material for clothing, the pastoralists also received a political guarantee of survival. Economic necessity combined with cultural plurality to create a continuing historical tradition which assimilated the nomads with the sedentary society without complete structural absorption. Even when the Mughal princes in India only read about their Mongol past in historical texts, they still built marble pavilions which had to be overhung with heavy fabrics, creating the illusion of ceremonial tents. But Emperor Shah Jahan's new capital in Delhi contained entire quarters which were called after the names of their nomadic visitors, the Kizilbash, Uzbegs, and Mughals. The Central Asian horse-traders not only supplied the imperial army with valuable mounts but were important dealers in Indian export products.[14]

The historical role of nomads. The encapsulated nomads and the transhumant pastoralists were an indispensable part of the Indian Ocean economy, howsoever it is viewed. But it was not the breeders of sheep, goats, donkeys, and cattle who captured the attention of political leaders and thinkers. What really threatened the survival of ancient empires and sedentary peace was the periodical incursions of nomadic armies from the steppe and the desert, followed by their human dependents and animal supporters. The nomadic expansion towards the settled land in China, India, and the Middle East goes back to the age of antiquity, far earlier than our period of study. It continued as a political process to the sixteenth and seventeenth centuries, when the Mughals and the Manchus respectively conquered northern India (1526) and China (1644). To describe these two groups as nomadic may be strictly unhistorical, but they were certainly descended from people who had once been true pastoral nomads of inner Asia.

There is no question that the political thinking of successive imperial dynasties in China was profoundly influenced by the experience of having to defend repeatedly a geographically open northern frontier. It has been also suggested that the Great Wall of China built in different sections and at different times marked the limits of Chinese expansion towards the steppe: 'this frontier was the voluntarily demarcated limits of the convenient expansion of the Chinese Empire . . . it was not necessitated by the aggression of the nomads against China. That aggression came later, as a consequence of the demarcation of the frontier by the Chinese, and was due largely to the inequality of the terms of trade.'[15] Whether the Great Wall marked the voluntary outer limit of an expanding China is debatable. What is not in doubt is the fluctuating control of the border zones exercised by 'Han' China in differing periods of its history. Nothing illustrates this pulsating relationship better than the archaeological sites discovered deep into the northern deserts far beyond the margin of true cultivation. In the first century BC Chinese forces were still holding a long line of walls and fortified posts near the Tarim basin of the Takla Makan desert. The fragment of a regimental record found in a ruined outpost dated *c.* 65–67 BC reports the sighting of a barbarian horseman riding towards the watch-station with drawn bow. The rider withdrew on a discharge from the cross-bows. The appearance of the scout alerted the garrison to the possibility of a more serious attack. The chariots and the horsemen were directed to remain in readiness and look out for fire signals from other watchtowers.[16] The inventories show that the cross-bows issued to the company were fearsome weapons needing an effective bending strength of three to six 'shih' (216–432 kg).[17] The barbarian nomadic tribes which Han China attempted to subdue through the planting of military agricultural colonies on the desert-fringe may have been the ancestors of the later Hun warriors who would one day water their horses on the Danube and the Po.

The Islamic and the Middle Eastern perception of the nomadic danger or the contrast between the nomadic society and the sedentary was less tangible than that of the Chinese empire. It was nevertheless sharply expressed. Here is Ibn Khaldun expatiating on the evils of nomadic 'Arab' expansion:

It is noteworthy how civilization always collapsed in places the Arabs took over and conquered, and how such settlements were depopulated and the [very] earth there turned into something that was no [longer] earth. The Yemen where [the Arabs] live is in ruins, except for a few cities. Persian civilization in the Arab Iraq is likewise completely ruined. The same applies to contemporary Syria. When the Banu Hilal and the Banu Sulaym pushed through [from the homeland] to Ifriqiyah and the Maghrib in [the beginning of] the fifth [eleventh] century and struggled there for three hundred years, they attached themselves to [the country] and the flat territory in [the Maghrib] was completely ruined.[18]

Ibn Khaldun's factual details were not entirely accurate but his words expressed a widely-held sentiment that the 'badawin' were in a state of perpetual tension with the sown land, their political advance carrying a message of destruction for the civilised values of urban life. This over-statement was corrected elsewhere in the *Muqaddimah*. Ibn Khaldun showed that there was indeed a long history of sedentarisation on the part of the bedouin going back to the period of the early Islamic conquests.[19] His analysis brings to the surface some of the contradictions inherent in the nomadic political conquests which took place throughout Asia from the seventh century to the seventeenth. In the initial stage of the conquest, the tribal leaders and the elected head of state retained their nomadic identity and close relations with the mounted animal-tending warriors. It was a form of political domination in which the financial tribute paid by the subdued sedentary populations was treated as a real and potential source of income for the nomadic overlords. The civil administration remained under the control of previous leaders and continued to function in cases where life was not too severely disrupted by the political conquests and the massacres of the local people. In the second stage, the ruling nomadic elites became integrated with the old aristocracy and adopted the values of a sedentary-urbanised society. The political structure of new 'nomadic' state reverted back to the formalism of the traditional centralised bureaucratic empires with their marked separation between the men of the pen and the men of the sword.[20] The nomadic elements in the new state were no longer seen as the valued supporters of their former leaders. The pastoralists became people who at best were no more than a useful appendage of the crop-growing economy and at worst only fit to be moved on as they attempted to migrate through the village land from the summer pastures to the winter.

The nomadic conquests: the debate over bedouin and Turkish expansions. The above model just outlined is derived from the historical process of nomadic assimilation at the political level. But it does not resolve two fundamental questions. All through our period, various groups of pastoral nomads speaking different languages and dialects have formed and re-formed as tribes and political confederacies, ranging in size from a few hundred tents to tens of thousands. Why did they do so and what was the economic and social mechanism which maintained the ecological balance between the size of nomadic-pastoral population and physical resources? When the free nomads decided to leave their remote pasture grounds in the desert and the steppe, embarking on permanent militaristic migration, was it because of demographic pressure among themselves, climatic disaster, or some other unknown social factor? The problem has given rise to a number of famous debates. The advance of the desert and the spread of extreme aridity over once-cultivated land, it was held, may have contributed to the nomadisation or the bedouinisation of sedentary communities which knew both crop-farming and urbanisation. The theory of a climatic desiccation of the Arabian peninsula was suggested by Leone Caetani as a factor in the bedouinisation of the Arabic-speaking people which eventually led to the great dispersion under Islam.[21] The theory of the desertification of Arabia was vigorously refuted by Alois Musil with historical argumentation and geographical counter-examples based on his formidable first-hand knowledge of the Middle Eastern topography.

Musil argued that Caetani gave no explanation how the desert Arabs, unconscious sacrifices to the cosmic decline of Arabia and a prey of famines for thousands of years, could have continued to preserve their strength and vigour. How could the starving Arabs, he asked, so easily conquer societies which did not suffer from a shortage of food and material wealth?[22] Musil suggested that the agricultural settlements around Mareb on the edge of Rub al-Khali created by the great dam were abandoned not because of a climatic change but because floods had destroyed the dam. No starving people, he concluded, could ever have laid the foundations of a new civilization.[23] Musil's own theory of the Arab nomadic expansion was very similar to Ibn Khaldun's political analysis. When the strong frontier states failed to keep law and order, the bedouin would raid and drive out the transhumant nomads raising sheep and goat on the desert fringe. These people in turn raided the villages and towns. Eventually, the true pastoral nomads themselves struck at the core areas of the great empires and states. The Persian and Byzantine regimes in the Fertile Crescent and Egypt were already in decline and needed very little force to overturn them. The alternating cycles of strong and weak political states created a similar pattern of retreating and advancing desert. The Arabian peninsula lacked water; it did not lack plant life which grew luxuriantly after each shower of rain. The abandoned wells, the wadi irrigation works, and the once-cultivated land which had turned into semi-desert could be easily restored if the right developmental policies were re-adopted.

The history of the political and social opposition between the nomads and the settlers has continued to attract scholarly interest, and the controversy shows little sign of reaching a consensus. Werner Caskel suggested in an essay published in 1954 that the bedouinisation of pre-Islamic Arabia was the result of the collapse of the border states following the Roman withdrawal. The impoverishment of the ancient world, the decline of caravan trade, and the ruin of the cultivated settlements caused the population of the frontier towns to move away. Some settled in more favourable regions, the rest took to a nomadic way of life.[24] The suggestion of an increase in bedouin number and activity was questioned by Walter Dostal. However, he accepted the evidence on the historical collapse of the frontier states. The changing political and economic conditions resulting from the collapse were exploited by the full bedouin rather than recruits, new to nomadic pastoralism. According to Dostal, the real reason why the bedouin became militarily powerful between the decline of classical Arabia and the rise of Islam was the use of a new camel saddle, the saddle-bow (for a modern version, see Plate 53), possibly borrowed from the Parthians. The device enabled the camel rider to sit more securely and develop the military potential of the dromedary.[25] The difficulty of interpreting the fragmentary historical evidence is shown by the fact that Talal Asad could argue with equal conviction that far from dominating the settled society, it was the frontier states which exercised political power over the bedouin.[26]

There is no question that as long as the established states of the Indian Ocean remained stable and powerful, the pastoral nomadic warriors of the desert and the steppe could make little inroad against their regular armies. How is it possible then to explain the repeated success of nomadic forces in overwhelming sedentary communities from the time of the Indo-Scythians to the great Turkish migrations of the eleventh century? The Turco-Mongol expansion, of course, continued for the next four centuries in different parts of the Indian Ocean and the whole phenomenon seems to have been accompanied by a parallel dispersion of Arabic-speaking nomadic pastoralists in Iraq, Syria, Egypt, and North Africa. First of all, a residual doubt remains how far the military leadership of the new conquerors could actually be described as nomadic. Secondly, whether nomadic expansion should justifiably be regarded as a special phenomenon, different from other types of political or imperial expansion, is uncertain. Military conquests by one sedentary state over other sedentary states were common enough in Asian history. No special theory is needed to explain these events. On balance, the historical verdict on the early Islamic conquests seems to be an ambiguous one. Soldiers recruited from the settled elements in the Hijaz and adjacent areas were at least as numerous as the true bedouin. The cavalry and the camel-riders were also supported by infantry.[27] The rapid development of a powerful Islamic state replacing the Irano-Byzantine power-blocs carried few overtones of its nomadic origin. It was only when the Abbasid caliphate began to disintegrate as a political and civilisational force in the tenth and eleventh centuries that the

Muslim world experienced in real earnest the foundation of new dynasties which were either bedouin or Turkish.[28] The explanation for these new appearances may lie more with the economic and social changes within the old Islamic order than with the rationale of nomadic hostility towards the sedentary state and society. The gradual decline of the irrigated agriculture of Iraq, the urban decay, and the poverty witnessed by al-Muqaddasi during his travels in the tenth century are reminders that the lands of the eastern caliphate were no longer economically flourishing.

The arrival of the Seljuk Turks in Iran during the eleventh century and their subsequent political victories in Syria and Palestine were preceded by a long process of Turkish settlement in the Muslim world, induced by the active official policy of recruitment into the Abbasid military administration. If the Abbasids ultimately lost their power to the Turkish warlords, the successive caliphs could in a sense blame themselves for having initiated the policy of arming the Turkish slave soldiers as a counter-weight to the Khurasanians, Arabs, and the Khawarajis.[29] The Seljuks were a wing of the Turkish Ghuzz tribal confederacy practising typical Central Asian and steppe pastoralism based on raising sheep, horses, and the two-humped Bactrian camels. By contemporary standard the Seljuk cavalry was not large. When Alp Arslan (*r.* 1065–73), the celebrated soldier-sultan, defeated and captured the Byzantine emperor at Manzikert in 1071, his forces were reported to have numbered 15,000 horse and 5,000 infantry.[30] The migration and settlement of Turkish nomadic pastoralists in Iran, Diayarbakr, Jazira, and Anatolia was a gradual movement involving small groups. But the process was to continue for the next five centuries both at the economic and political levels and give rise to a sharp distinction between the peasants and the encapsulated nomads migrating over long distances between summer and winter pastures with their entire households and families.

The disintegration of the Abbasid caliphate and the competition between Egypt and Iraq for the political and spiritual leadership of Islam provided the backdrop to the Turkish westward expansion. The theory of a power-failure within Islamic society, however, points to only one side of the equation: the actual conditions in the steppes which gave rise to endemic conflicts among the powerful nomadic tribes, spilling over in the direction of Sung China and the Muslim west, still remain unknown. A climatic hypothesis similar to the desiccation of central Arabia was put forward by the geographer Ellsworth Huntington as an explanation of the Turco-Mongol migrations and in the face of persistent criticism, subsequently modified. But he continued to believe that the progressive loss of pasture-resources in the Eurasian steppes during the twelfth century was an important factor reinforcing the direction of political events.[31] There is no doubt that the various Turkish confederacies not only fought among themselves but were also under intense pressure from other, more powerful tribes further east. The Turkish migrations to the south and the west represented a response without an alternative. The permanent Islamic conquests in northern India under Qutb al-Din Aibaq (1192–1210), the slave-commander of the Ghorids in Afghanistan, could be seen more as a Turkish military triumph rather than as a religious victory of Muslims over unbelievers. The Turkoman style of mobile warfare and the mounted archery were highly effective against the rigid battle-order of the Rajput military chiefs using infantry, slow-moving lines of elephants, and some cavalry.[32] It did not save the Turks from a nomadic enemy using the same tactics as themselves on a far grander scale. The military unification of the fragmented Mongol tribes by Chingiz Khan may have appeared to outsiders at first as no more than an event in the local politics of inner Asia. Within a decade of the foundation of the Delhi Sultanate (1206), the civilised world of China, India, and the Middle East, was to experience a type of onslaught it had never seen before.[33] The army which accompanied Chingiz Khan during his campaign against the Khwarazm-Shah of Samarkand (1219) has been estimated as between 150,000 to 200,000 men.[34] The destruction of some of the greatest cities of Islam, Merv, Balkh, Herat, and Nishapur was followed by the terrible devastation of Iran. Islamic chroniclers record independently horrifying figures of people massacred by the Mongols. Najm al-Din Razi estimated that 700,000 people were killed or captured in and around his home town Ray, while Juvaini gives the casualties at Merv as 1,300,000.[35] After the conquest of Samarkand and Bukhara, according to Juvaini, the Mongols pacified and reconstructed the devastated countryside around these towns. But in Iran and Iraq at the time he was writing, 658 AH/AD 1259–60, every village and town appeared to be suffering, having been sacked many times, so that 'even though there be generation and increase until the Resurrection the population will not attain to a tenth part of what it was before'.[36]

To Razi, the Mongol eruption was nothing short of an act of punishment from God, a view also shared by Ibn al-Athir whose apocalyptic words describe it as a disaster such as had never happened before and which struck all the world, though the Muslims above all:

If anyone were to say that at no time since the creation of man by the great God had the world experienced anything like it, he would only be telling the truth. In fact nothing comparable is reported in the past chronicles . . . it may well be that the world from now until its end . . . will not experience the like of it again, apart perhaps from Gog and Magog.[37]

The Mongol expansion was certainly nomadic but it was different from the previous Turkish migrations, not only because the tribesmen were still pagans; the process of empire-building went on for more than a century and included an area extending from China to eastern Europe.

Amir Khusru, a Muslim writer living in India, describes (1289) in language mixed with fear, fascination and loathing, the Mongol forces invading India:

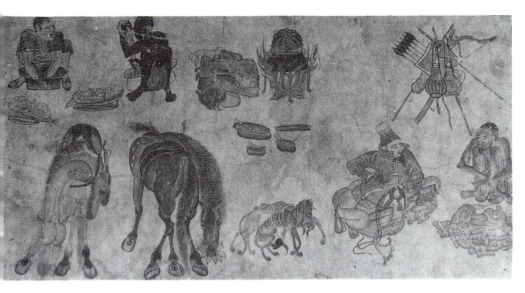

Plate 49 Central Asian nomadic camp, fifteenth century.

There were more than a thousand Tatar infidels and warriors of other tribes, riding on camels, great commanders in battle, all with steel-like bodies clothed in cotton; with faces like fire, with caps of sheep-skin, with their heads shorn. Their eyes were so narrow and piercing that they might have bored a hole in a brazen vessel. Their stink was more horrible than their colour. Their faces were set on their bodies as if they had no neck. Their cheeks resembled soft leathern bottles, full of wrinkles and knots. Their noses extended from cheek to cheek, and their mouths from cheek-bone to cheek-bone. Their moustaches were of extravagant length. They had scanty beards about their chins . . . The king marvelled at their beastly countenances, and said that God had created them out of hell-fire.[38]

Mongol prisoners of war generally suffered mistreatment from their Muslim captors. But the regular state armies often recruited them into their ranks. The Turkish sultans of Delhi were constantly reminded by their warrior followers that the Turks lived by plunder. In his history of the Delhi sultanate, Barani makes Balban recite the recent history of the Mongols in reply to questions from friends why he never stirred from the capital Delhi in spite of having a well-equipped army at his disposal. The Mughals, the Sultan said, had established themselves at Ghazni; Hulegu, the grandson of Chingiz Khan, had subdued Iraq and taken Baghdad. These accursed wretched had heard of the wealth and prosperity of Hindustan and were intent on conquering and plundering it. Lahore had fallen to them and not a day passed when there was not some scare of their attacks on India. The Sultan considered himself the defender of Islam in a hostile land. He would be only too pleased to raid the territories of Hindu landed magnates and princes. If the victims were non-

Muslim the ghazi ideology obviously legitimised for the Turks the illegality of the ghazw. But the relentless Mongol pressure on the Islamic world continued, causing the militant Turks to move southward. By 1310 the Turkish heavy cavalry had reached the Indian Ocean in Gujarat and southern India.

The bedouin were accustomed to talk of their raiding expeditions as equivalent to the agricultural occupation of the fellahin.[39] Juvaini likewise described the Mongol army as one constituted after the peasants. In time of action, the Mongols fought like disciplined wild animals and in days of peace, they were like sheep, yielding milk, wool, and many other useful things.[40] The pastoral economy of the Eurasian steppes may have been adequate historically to support the weight of human and animal populations. But the hostile migration of the mounted nomads accompanied by huge flocks of sheep and herds of horses into settled land signalled disaster for the farmers and their crops. The provision of fodder and corn for the army horses must have presented the Mongol chiefs with serious problems. When Chingiz Khan arrived in Bukhara and the assembled citizens opened the gates of the city to his forces, the first words addressed by him to the civic deputation of learned imams and notables were 'The countryside is empty of fodder. Fill our horses' bellies.'[41]

The early Islamic conquests were not, as we have already seen, strictly nomadic, though the desert Arabs supported the religious leaders of Medina and were in turn carefully fostered by them. On the other hand, the pastoral nomadic origins of the Turks and Mongols were very much in evidence. The true explanation for their dispersal from the desert and the mountains of Central Asia and the Eurasian steppes continues to elude the historian. Climatic changes, burden of overpopulation, the fragile nomadic ecology, and political development, are all likely candidates for a general theory of nomadic migrations in the direction of the civilised world of the Indian Ocean.[42] In order to view these different factors in proper perspective, it is well to recall that pastoral nomadism as an economic system always included a symbiotic relationship with the settled society practising crop-farming. Neither the plough nor the irrigation works, the two essential technological conditions of Indian Ocean agriculture, could effectively function without the traction power of domesticated animals. The nomadic or professional animal-breeders supplied a large proportion of draught animals used by farmers in the Middle East and India. The sedentary society needed the pastoral nomads as much as the latter needed the economic products of civilised life. The rationale of this two-way traffic brought the farmers and the nomads constantly together. Even the remote pastoral tribes of Central Asia and the outer steppes were not likely to be unaware of the existence of long-distance caravan trade and the civilisational contributions of China, India, and Iran. The cultivated land of Asia could not provide permanent pasture to the nomadic flocks and herds. Nomadic conquests implied for the victors almost by definition the abandonment of the pastoral economy and the ideology of the old way of life. Sedentarisation was an inevitable consequence of the political process set in motion by the military expansion of the free nomads. So why did they leave their idyllic pasture-home in the Eurasian steppes? The historical paradox remains as yet unanswered.

Animal-tending

From the late tenth century to the early fifteenth, the sedentary experience of the nomadic pastoralists remained adverse, even when the general picture was confusing and diffused. A long list of distinguished writers can be cited to show how the first-hand experience of Turco-Mongol politics deeply coloured contemporary thought: Nizam al-Mulk, the political thinker and the Iranian minister of the Seljuks, Al-Ghazali, the great theologian haunted by the fear of civil war and religious dissension, Juvaini, the biographer of Chingiz Khan, Rashid al-Din, the historian and the minister of Ghazan Khan, Amir Khusru, the Indian historian and poet, Ibn Khaldun, and even the Mughal prince Babar who had a great deal to say about Central Asian politics which lost him the Timurid patrimony in Samarkand. This preoccupation with the state and society has obscured the humbler role of the nomadic pastoralists as breeders and keepers of domesticated animals, essential to themselves and to the sedentary communities. There are few historical sources which describe in detail the structure of nomadic tribes and clans, the migration patterns, and methods of raising animals. Contemporary field studies undertaken by anthropologists shed some light on the social habits of the pastoral nomads but raise the question whether present-day conditions can be extrapolated backwards into history.

The horse in Asian history. In the past, it is only when travellers, merchants, soldiers, and diplomatic envoys came into contact with the pastoralists that an occasional glimpse of their main activity can be discerned. Of all the domesticated animals raised by the nomads, the most prestigious was the horse. The speed, strength, endurance, and the noble character of the pure-bred horse gave rise to a cultural tradition throughout the Indian Ocean which exceeded even the religious symbolism of the bull. The horse was seldom used in Asia as a draught animal harnessed to the cart or the plough, which was mostly drawn by the camel, oxen, and the buffalo. Mules and donkeys were preferred to horses as load-carriers over short distances, the longer hauls being reserved for cattle and camels. The primary function of the horse derived from its role in warfare and as a personal mount. The possession of a fine pure-bred horse signified both status and wealth, and most Asian states had ample proof of the need to reinforce their infantry with cavalry. Even the bedouin camel-riders were vulnerable in battle to horsemen and sought to supplement their regular long-distance camel mounts with horses. The extent to which the breeding of fine and specialised horses had become the preserve of nomadic pastoralists in Central Asia, Iran, and the Arabian peninsula can be seen from the fact that the two leading trading nations of Asia, India and China, preferred to import their war horses rather than breed them at home. Parts of northern India and China were not altogether unsuitable for horse-breeding and indeed a pure-bred Marwar, Kach, or the Punjab horse fetched high prices. But as compared to a Badakshan pony or the Arab blood-stock, the indigenous Indian horse remained a second-best choice. There was another aspect to the trade in imported horses. Even the best Arabian or the Iranian horse was likely to degenerate in a humid climate and the Middle Eastern experts often accused the Indian trainers of mishandling the horses in their care. But Abul Fazl's elaborate tabulation of the feeding schedules of horses in the imperial stable make it quite evident that the Mughal officers in charge of the best stock understood thoroughly how to care for the expensive and rare breeds.[43] The constant need to renew the original stock, Abdulla Wassaf wrote in his history (1300–28), worked to the best financial interests of Muslim merchants, for it was 'a providential ordinance of God that the western should continue in want of eastern products, and the eastern world of western products'.[44]

The bulk of the horses raised in the three main breeding areas of Asia can be associated with three ecotypes. Firstly, there was the 'equus przewalskii', the red-brown ancestor of the Central Asian steppe ponies whose distribution included Mongolia, Korea, and Japan. The leading northern breeds however were derived from 'equus tarpanus', the dun-coloured horse of the Russian steppes, which were still wild and found as far west as Poland in the late eighteenth century.[45] All the nomadic invaders, from the time of the Scythians and the Huns, to the Turco-Mongols, rode on the descendants of the Russian tarpan. Finally, the equestrian specialists have identified the third ecotype, the 'equus agilis' of the high, dry plains of Arabia and north Africa, popularly known in the West as the hot-blooded fiery horses of the South.[46]

The two great transcontinental travellers of our period, Marco Polo and Ibn Battuta, were both interested in horses and have left full accounts of the areas where they were raised. The Eurasian steppes and the valleys of the Central Asian mountains provided ideal breeding conditions for horses, with plenty of pasture and right ambient temperature. According to Marco Polo the horses of Badakshan, to the north of Afghanistan, could run over stony ground without any iron on their feet. These animals were so courageous and so well-trained that their owners galloped them over mountain slopes where no one else would have dared to do so.[47] Ferghana and Ili valley were homes of famous breeds which regularly found their way to the animal-fairs of India and the oasis-towns of Chinese Turkestan. Horses exported to India also came from regions much further west. When Ibn Battuta reached Azov, at the end of the sea named after it, beyond the Black Sea, he found the whole region

Plate 50 Emperor Babar's run-away thoroughbred horse.

inhabited by nomadic Turkish pastoralists who bred huge herds of horses for sale in India. These were non-pedigree animals and Ibn Battuta used the Arabic term 'kadish' to describe them, as opposed to horses of pure blood which were known as 'kochlani' or 'asil'. So numerous were these Turkish herds that the price of a good horse was almost negligible by Near Eastern standards and the animals were counted in units of a thousand heads. The pastoralists used a thin pole with a piece of felt attached to it as a counter for every thousand horses belonging to an owner, and it was not unusual to see Turkish women riding in waggons with ten such flag poles attached to the roof. The horses from the Black Sea steppe were driven all the way to India in droves of 6,000 animals, each trader bringing up to 200 horses each. When they reached Sind, the regular feed changed from barley to dry forage. By this time, after their long march through the desert and the mountains the horses were in poor condition; many animals either died or were stolen. Indian owners bought horses selectively and did not look for speed or running qualities in the Central Asian imported breeds. As the regular mounted troops were clad in coats of mail, strength and length of pace were more important than speed, and in addition to the rider, the horse had to carry armour for itself in combat. The real racing horse destined for the stables of the Indian princes came from the trading ports of the Yemen, Oman, and Fars and fetched 4,000 silver dinars each as against 500 for the Azov breed.[48]

The Turkoman breeders of Central Asia believed that their horse was a cross between the native ecotype and the Arab blood stock. Timur's military expeditions to the Middle East had yielded many thousands of prized Arabian mares which were dispersed among the nomadic pastoralists of Trans-Oxiana. General Ferrier, a French officer who served with the Iranian army, had closely studied the nomadic way of raising horses, as he was intrigued by the capacity of the Turkomans to make forays into Iranian territory riding on animals which seemed to possess legendary stamina. The winter snow and the spring rains in the steppes produced grasses which were highly palatable to the horses. The rich feed allowed the animals to obtain a high blood temperature and a wonderful elasticity of nerve and muscles. From August to winter, the horses lived on dry food and the daily feed consisted of seven pounds of barley, mixed with dry chopped straw, lucerne, and clover-hay. So skilled were the Central Asian trainers in feeding and exercising their horses that General Ferrier attested from his own experience the authenticity of a record held by a horse belonging to the Commander of the Iranian artillery. The animal had gone from Teheran to Tabriz and back again, a distance of 420 miles each way, in twelve days with twenty-four hours' rest after each journey.[49]

The Turkoman raiders prepared their horses carefully before setting off to plunder caravans. During the first month of the training, they were kept on a reduced diet of six pounds of hay and three pounds of barley. When the horses had lost their 'grass belly', they were galloped at full speed for half an hour

Plate 51 Arab horse and Mamluk rider clad in chain-mail and wearing helmet.

each day. They were not fed until some time after they had come in and were given very little water to drink. If a horse showed signs of being thirsty, he was kept fasting a little longer. After the second month's training, the horse was ready for its final diet of concentrates which included four and a quarter pounds of barley-flour, two pounds of maize-flour, and two pounds of sheep's tail fat chopped very find and all well mixed together in balls. The horses ate this food eagerly and it put them in tip-top condition, capable of sustaining the longest forced marches.[50]

The right kind of horse-feed appears to have exercised contemporary opinion a great deal. The Middle Eastern and European view was that the Indian trainers either overfed their fine imported breeds or failed to keep them in the right condition. Powerful animals who would race without the whip in their own natural habit, lost the competitive spirit in India. However, Marco Polo's statement that the Gulf horses were given cooked meat to eat in India or that there were no grooms to look after them there was a fine piece of travellers' fantasy.[51] Islamic India was crowded with Arab, Iranian, and Central Asian horse-dealers and cavalry officers who certainly knew how to look after horses. These people remained in the permanent employment of Indian princes anxious to preserve the value of their investment in blood stock. Emperor Akbar had set apart a special place for the stabling of imported horses in his capital so that careless and greedy horse-dealers were prevented from mistreating the animals. Upright and humane dealers were free to quarter them wherever they wished. Horses in the imperial stable had a complete schedule of feeds scientifically arrived at. The pedigree horses generally received a daily allowance of 4.7 kg of fodder, boiled peas or grain. In addition, they were also given 1.25 kg of flour. Horses worth 30 gold muhurs (300 grammes of pure gold) received half a kilogram of sugar; those worth 21–30 gold muhurs received a quarter kilogram. Horses of lesser value got no sugar at all. The amount of sugar and ghi added to the daily or weekly diet varied according to the season of the year. In the imperial stables, there were horses costing as much as 70 gold muhurs (700 grammes of pure gold).[52]

The Central Asian pastoralists had an obvious advantage over the horse-breeders of Iran and the Arabian peninsula. It was easier to export horses to India and China by land than by sea. But the reputation and the high prices commanded by the Arab and Iranian pure-bred horses more than made up for the inconvenience involved in transporting them in ships. In contemporaneous literature, the original Iranian blood-stock was referred to with the highest respect, and as Marco Polo found, Hormuz and the adjacent ports sent a large number of fine war-horses to India by sea.[53] This was a period when the horse trade appears to have been particularly prosperous. The Turkish military success in northern India and the continuing pressure on the southern Hindu states may have stimulated an urge to upgrade the cavalry. Abdulla Wassaf has left some details of the trade in Arabian and Gulf horses on the west coast of

Plate 52 Pedigree horses being fed in Chinese stables.

India. Abdar Rahman, a Muslim, was appointed as a minister by Sundar Pandaya, one of the Hindu princes of Malabar. Muslim influence may have been deliberately sought in order to facilitate commercial contacts with the Middle East. For example, according to Wassaf, an agreement was made between the merchants and Malik al-Islam Jamal al-Din that 1,400 horses from the latter's own stud should be exported each year from the island of Kish to Malabar. The breed was so celebrated for the purity of its blood that 'in comparison with them the most celebrated horses of antiquity, such as the Rukhs of Rustam should be as worthless as the horse of the chess-board'. Altogether more than 10,000 horses were sent to the Malabar ports and Cambay from Bahrain and other places of shipment in the Gulf at a total cost of 2.2 million dinars and the trade was officially financed out of the revenues of the Hindu religious endowments and by a tax on the 'Devadasis' (courtesans) attached to the temples.[54]

The reputation of the bedouin horse-breeders (as compared to the Iranians) for keeping up the purity of blood bordered on fanaticism. The code of personal honour associated with horsemanship made it impossible for the bedouin owners to misrepresent the pedigree of their horses. Indeed, to buy and sell fine horses carried a pejorative meaning for the desert tribes: it was an activity reserved for the 'jambazes' or the horse dealers who were apt to be regarded as liars.[55] Good horses were not generally for sale in the horse-fairs and transactions involving the best animals remained personal, qualified by guarantees of good treatment given by the buyers. The members of a bedouin tribe who had lost pedigree horses in a raid were bound in honour to treat the enemy scouts as inviolable when they came to demand the breeding details of the captured animals. The next throw of the ghazw dice might not only recover the stolen horses but also yield a bonus from the opposition.[56] The bedouin traced the pedigree of their horses through the mare. The stallion was chosen with infinite care for breeding purposes but it was valued to a lesser extent than in Europe. Extravagant care and affection in comparison were lavished on the mare. A mare which was in foal with a 'kadish' or non-pedigree stallion forfeited for ever the right to the blood line.[57] The pure strain of Arab horses generically known as 'Kuhaylan' was a rare and minor element in the herds of mainly kadish horses belonging to the bedouin and the horse-breeders of Mesopotamia. These may be just as noble as the true-bred horses and have better points than the aristocrat.[58] The pure strain of Arab horses was divided by tradition into five sub-categories collectively known as the al-Khamsa. These were the Kuhaylan, Saqlawi, Ubayn, Hamdani, and Hadban.[59]

The type of pasture available in the Arabian peninsula was not really suitable for large-scale horse breeding. Whereas the camel could thrive on prickly, saline vegetation, the horse needed rich and sweet grass, supplemented by corn. The highlands of central Nejd had the reputation of being the best breeding ground for fine horses, a claim which was disputed by Lady Anne Blunt.[60] There was no water in Nejd above ground level, she argued, nor any pasture fit for horses except during the winter months. For part of the year the mares kept by the bedouin there were fed on dates and camels' milk. The Nejd horses were of pure blood because of the isolation of the region but the lack of proper food stunted the breed. Horses raised in the Hamad were taller and faster than the average Nejdi. The country best suited for breeding horses, Lady Blunt thought, was the great pastoral district bordering the Euphrates. Although critical of the Arab owners' strict adherence to inbreeding and line-breeding in horses, Lady Blunt was enthusiastic about the character, strength, and the racing qualities of the Arab 'asil'. Other European experts had already confirmed the gentleness of the Arab horse and its extraordinary courage. The Arab would stand his ground before lions and tigers which made him the favourite of Indian princes for big-game hunting. An Arab stallion generally refrained from kicking or biting and even a foal would approach a stranger without fear. The little creature was often separated from its mother and was treated by the bedouin almost as a member of the human family. As for the galloping power of the Arab, Lady Blunt believed, it had little chance over a three-mile course against an English thoroughbred but over and beyond that distance no European horse could keep pace with it. Her own purebred mare Hagar once broke into a gallop on a desert expedition, refused to slow down, and ran for twelve miles or so at full speed. 'There is no doubt', Lady Blunt concluded, 'that the pure bred Arabian possesses extraordinary powers of endurance. On a journey he may be ridden day after day, and fed only upon grass. Yet he does not lose heart or condition, and is always ready to gallop at the end of the longest march, a thing we have never ventured to propose to our horses on any previous journey.'[61]

Raising camels and sheep. Central Asian and the steppe nomads could survive and even live well on the economic products of their herds. Mares' milk, horse-flesh, hides and skins, horse-hair, were all useful as direct means of sustaining nomadic life in the vast pastures of Inner Asia. The possibility of trading the surplus stock of horses for grain, tea, sugar, and silk from China and cotton textiles from India added an indirect economic dimension to nomadic pastoralism based on the horse. The bedouin of the Arabian desert were in a different situation. Their pastoral economy derived its rationale not from horse-breeding but from tending camels. Most nomadic communities, however, combined multiple animal-tending, and even the Central Asian nomads raised a substantial number of sheep and the two-humped Bactrian camels for their own use and for trading with the sedentary societies. The feeding and drinking habits of the small stock, sheep and goats, were so different from those of the larger animals, camel, horse, and cattle, that nomads who practised mixed herding faced considerable logistical problems in finding the right type of pasture and enough water for all their animals. The prestige and rank associated with each type of animal-tending were also different. There is a true story current in one of the tribal areas of Oman that two brothers, each looking after camels and sheep respectively, met at the well and neither would give way to the other for the honour of watering their animals first. The quarrel reached murderous proportions and was only settled by a happy accident.[62]

The adaptation of the nomadic domestic animals to their ecology was a continuing process both by selective evolution and human intervention. The type of plant-life which the desert, mountains, and the scrub provided of course determined in the first instance the composition of the nomadic herds and flocks. The camel is a natural browser as opposed to the sheep which is a grazer. The goat is both a grazer and a browser. With the exception of the camel, all other nomadic animals need daily watering and the young offsprings may have to be watered twice a day. If the daily grazing area is extensive (15–20 km), shepherds and cattle-tenders must divide their tasks so as to round up the animals before dark and bring them back to the source of water for the evening drink and milking. In the high Himalayas, the sheep and goats graze in summer at an average altitude of 5,000 metres or more. The shepherds who look after these animals lead exceptionally lonely lives even by the nomadic standard.

The physiological adjustment of the camel to the ecology of the arid regions made it the ideal drought animal in the Middle East, north Africa, Central Asia, and western India. The evolutionary separation between the dromedary and Bactrian camel underlined also two distinct zones of their usage and breeding. The single-humped dromedary was an animal of the hot, dry semi-desert and its distribution extended from the Sahara, through the Arabian peninsula to the Thar desert of India. The Bactrian camel was confined to the cold northern regions of Central Asia and Iran. Its thick woolly coat and the ability to traverse steep mountain-passes made it ideal for long caravan journeys across the Gobi and the Central Asian mountains in low winter temperatures. Before setting out on a difficult march across the northern deserts, Chinese caravan masters carefully calculated whether the business of the Gobi was sufficiently profitable to justify sacrificing valuable pack-camels, in case some of the animals died from thirst and exhaustion. If a caravan was delayed on the way, it would encounter snow on the mountain passes before reaching Kashgar, Samarkand, and Bukhara. Moving a major caravan composed of more than a thousand heavily-laden camels through snow-filled defiles needed all the skills of the camel-masters. The two-humped camels were apparently to be found at one time not only in the area of its later distribution but also in parts of Iraq, Mesopotamia, Anatolia, and India.[63] Its gradual retreat and eventual disappearance from the plains remains without a historical explanation. Cross-breeding between the Bactrian camel and the dromedary of course continued and produced an animal which was better suited to its tasks than any of the parent-stock, though for obvious reasons the practice of cross-breeding remained localised to the marginal area between Central Asia and the Iranian highland. But as late as the sixteenth century, the two-humped camels were still found in the imperial stables of Mughal India and were known by the generic name of 'bughur'. Cross-breeding between the bughur and the Indian variety ('lok') took place even in India.[64]

The camel was extensively bred in all the arid zones of the Indian Ocean. Much of this type of breeding, carried out by settled farmers, produced good baggage animals without particular attention to selective qualities. Raising thoroughbred dromedaries however was an exclusive occupation of the nomadic and semi-nomadic people practising either transhumance or lengthy annual migrations. Abu'l Fazl boasted that thanks to the interest taken by Emperor Akbar in improving camel stock, the Indian country-bred animals surpassed even the breeds of Iran and Turan. But he added, the best camels were raised in northern Gujarat (Kach), while the racers came from Ajmer. In

Plate 53   Resting camel with bow saddle, Zabid, the Yemen (see p. 272).

addition, a large number of camels were bred in Sind, Jodhpur, Nagor, Bikaner, and Jaisalmer.[65] Arab attitudes towards the camel and its usefulness found a perfect expression in a 'Hadith' which said that 'Camels are a source of power to their owner, sheep a blessing, and good is attached to the forelock of horses until the Resurrection'.[66] The Prophetic tradition had no need to elaborate further but the sedentary mind needs to be reminded that there were several complex layers of meaning and nuances attached to the ownership of camels by the desert Arabs. The size of the herds possessed by the tribal owners was a general signifier to the collective power of the clan. The camel was a bride's dowry; ransom and blood-money were paid in camels. According to another tradition, it was unwise to speak ill of the camel if only because it was a means of avoiding bloodshed. In a society which regarded the plundering raids, the ghazw, as a legitimate form of sport and acquisition of wealth, the camels were a prime target. The aristocratic military tribes among the bedouin obtained their best breeding stock through the ghazw and particular groups of camels taken in a raid could be traced back through successive owners to the original breeders of the Empty Quarter (Rub al-Khali) and Oman. Alois Musil recorded the following ethnographic note in his diary for 15 February 1915:

The camels searched for pasture, and each selected her favourite plants. Although our camels were all obtained from the Ruwala, not a single one had been reared by them. They had all been captured. The black she-camel Malha on which I rode to al-Ela had been brought by a son of Chief Fahad Ibn Tnejjan as spoil from a raid on the southern tribes. He had sold her in Brejda, where she was purchased by an Akejli, who was robbed of her by the Shararat. They sent her to an-Nuri [the Amir of the Ruwala] in lieu of contributions. My second riding camel, ash coloured Sa'ela, had been reared by the Shararat, from whom Ibn Rba'i of the Tuman had taken her as spoil. In a time of abundance [Rabi], Ibn Rba'i mounted on her back and proceeded on a raid against the Ruwala, but when he got as far as al-'Ajli, to the southwest of Laha, he was waylaid by a troop led by Trad, son of Sattam, and lost both the camel and his arms. Thus it happens that many a camel is known to tribes camping even as much as fifteen hundred kilometres apart.[67]

Arabic terminology divided people into settlers (hadara, those who lived in permanent houses) and nomads ('Arab, who dwelt in movable tents). Among the 'Arabs, there were further groupings. The raisers of sheep and goat had two things common in black: their tents made from black felt and the wool of their flocks. These nomadic pastoralists did not go into the interior of the desert and remained close to the fringe areas where sufficient pasture and water were available for the daily needs of the small stock. The shepherds were regarded as distant relatives of the fellahin.[68] The term bedouin was more precise than 'Arab, and these were the true camel-breeders of the Arabian peninsula. The Shararat and al-Murrah of Rub al-Khali not only produced famous breeds known for their speed, strength, milk-yield but also utilised the ecology of the desert to the best advantage of both the animals and their masters. For al-Murrah, the Empty Quarter, which was dreaded by even ordinary bedouin, provided everything one could wish for, the best camels, plenty of best camels' milk, good hunting, clean sand, fresh air, and all one's own brothers.[69] It is axiomatic that to survive in an environment avoided by everyone else, the camel breeders must have had a perpetual memory of the location of the seasonal pasture and permanent wells in the desert.

The Arabic word for the territory associated with the annual migration or the transhumance of a particular tribal group was 'dira', a term also used for the navigation route of a ship. The analogy between the sea and the desert expressed itself through a number of common symbols of which the image of the port, ship, and the camel was the strongest.[70] As breeders of the best riding camels, the Shararat organised their seasonal migrations between the inner desert and the cultivated fringe with utmost precision. If the rains were abundant during December, the nomads and their beasts could look forward to a 'rabi' season, a time of plenty, when the Nejd was miraculously covered with luxuriant grass, and rain pools provided ample water for the herds. The different clans moved backward and forward along the migration route according to pre-arranged plans best suited to each group. The failure of rains either over

Plate 54 A drove of camels with bedouin camel-herd.

a single season or a number of consecutive seasons, not an infrequent event, signalled the much-feared 'ajjam al-hawa' or the time of want. Only seeds of the grass and the roots of the perennial remained in the dry, hard ground and many camels perished from starvation and thirst.[71] The 'dirat-al Murrah' was a vast area stretching from southern Iraq and Kuwait in the north to the Rub al-Khali in the south. Al-Murrah exercised traditional and exclusive rights to the wells located beyond the oasis of al-Hasa up to the centre of Rub al-Khali.[72]

The wide range of terminology used by the bedouin in connection with camel-tending is an indication of how far social survival was associated with this particular form of pastoralism. There were separate words and expressions for a captured camel, a lost camel, one which was between the age of six and twenty-six, a load-carrying camel which belonged to a herd numbering not more than ten heads, a riding camel, and so on. The training and care of camels was a serious matter. A good camel will stand motionless until asked to move and remain silent while being saddled and unsaddled. This was an important point when their masters were camping at night in dangerous territory. The bedouin camels were easily frightened by the shade and rustling of palm groves in the oasis and by the high walls of the 'qasr'; without proper training they could become unmanageable. When camels were taken on forced marches lasting days and nights in a country where there was neither good pasture nor enough water, they were entitled to a mandatory three months' rest.[73] A starving camel would use up all the fat stored in the hump, its loins would sink, and the exhausted animal would insist on kneeling down if urged to move. A thirsting camel likewise would murmur pitiably, its eye overflow with tears, and every little while it would attempt to urinate. An onlooker would inquire of the herdsman on seeing such animals, 'How long have the camels thirsted?' To which the answer might be, 'they have thirsted four, five, seven, eight, and even fifteen days'.[74] While the patience, good nature, and the legendary stamina of the camel were universally admired by the bedouin, there were also bad points associated with particular animals. The habit of running away the moment the rider dismounts, running from plant to plant sniffing but not eating any, and above all kneeling down suddenly when on the march and throwing off the rider, were all bad points to watch for. A camel, capable of causing the death of the rider, through an incurable fault itself deserved the 'sentence of death' according to bedouin custom. In general, the bedouin looked after their camel herds with professional care and knowledge and would not willingly lend their she-camels to the settled people, fearing that the animals would not be properly cared for.

The quality which gave the camel an absolute advantage over all other domesticated animals in an arid environment was its ability to live on marginal plant-life, thorn bushes, prickly grass, and the scant foliage of thorn-trees. If rich and nourishing grass was available for grazing after ample rains and the ambient temperature was not too high, the herds could go without free drinking for several weeks. In summer when they fed on salty and bitter vegetation, it was necessary to water them almost everyday. Modern scientific experiments show that the body temperature of the camel rises by an average of 6.2° centigrade in eleven hours when deprived of water, whereas it varies by only two degrees C when allowed to drink freely. Similar observations for wild herbivorous desert animals such as the oryx and gazelle yield a rising temperature curve of 6.8° C which does not vary with watering conditions. These experiments prove that the camel is well-adjusted to water-loss but not to the same extent as the wild animals. It will not survive prolonged exposure to extreme stress, though it can withstand for some time a fluid loss of 24 per cent of its body weight without a fatal rise in body-temperature. In a single session, the camel is capable of ingesting water up to 30 per cent of its total weight. Human beings in contrast will not recover from a 12 per cent dehydration without assistance.[75] Musil estimated that camels which had fed on the salty 'hamz' plants exclusively will hold out no longer than four or five days without water. Those feeding on dry plants and grasses such as the 'tenn', 'hemri', 'nasi', and 'sobot' can endure one to two weeks at the maximum. During the rabi season the camels will not drink for a month or so.[76] Watering thirsty camels after a long day's march in the desert involved considerable hardship and self-discipline on the part of their masters. Often wells which had caved in had to be dug out afresh and pulling the heavy water-skin was excessively laborious. It was not easy to restrain twenty or thirty camels who had scented water and prevent them from stampeding the men working the water-hoist, knock over the folding trough, or even fall into the well.

Compared to the horse, camel, and the cattle, the sheep were truly blessed with a serene temperament which earned them quiet affection in every nomadic society. Any one who has seen for the first time a flock of fat-tailed 'dumba' sheep or the pure-bred long-haired goats belonging to the nomadic

'Gaddis', is not likely to forget the sight easily. The large cushion of fat carried by the sheep in the place of a normal tail is a survival insurance under semi-desert condition, though the variety was found all over north-western India and the Middle East. The fat from the dumba sheep's tail was a source of culinary distinction in communities which relished mutton. The dumba is a common sight but the Gaddi goats are rarely seen by the people of the plains, as they never descend below a certain altitude and are generally grazed on the Himalayan slopes just below the snow-line. A full-grown Gaddi goat will easily measure four feet in height and its fine white hair is a much sought-after ingredient for spinning and weaving superfine woollen textiles.

From Anatolia, through Kurdistan, the Iranian central plateau, the Zagros mountains, Afghanistan, Baluchistan, the Himalayas, and Rajasthan, the sheep provided the main sustenance to the nomadic pastoralists. The type of sheep kept by the nomads had adapted closely to their particular environment and was likely to die if moved suddenly to a different habitat. Indeed, looking after sheep was a hazardous business and entire flocks of several thousand animals could be wiped out by epidemic diseases and natural calamities. Unseasonal hot winds in the plains or heavy and prolonged showers of rain in the mountains often led to the mass destruction of sheep left out in the open without shelter. Apart from its role as a source of milk, wool, and occasionally meat, the humble sheep also had another utility in the Himalayas. In summer they crossed the glacier-passes from the plateau on the other side of the range, carrying salt packed in leather pouches slung over the back and descended to the cultivated valleys below. On the return journey, they helped to take back rice, flour, sugar, and other household items. Shepherds practising ordinary transhumance of course returned to the valleys in the autumn and the safe arrival of the flocks was greeted with much rejoicing if the village population were also the owners of the sheep. Animals belonging to the larger and independent nomadic groups however needed pre-arranged political accommodation with the villages before they could settle down in their winter pasture.

Nomadic cattle-breeding: some examples from India. The symbolic and practical significance of cattle in Asian societies was a remarkable feature of their history and yet little information is presently available on cattle-breeding. Together with the buffalo, the cattle were a necessary condition of settled agriculture in India, South East Asia, and China. Whether the animals pulled the heavier ploughs of northern India or the light variety used in the rice-paddy, without their traction-power the ratio between cultivated land, the quantity of cereals produced, and the density of population could not have been sustained. In India, well-irrigation was almost totally dependent on the cattle for pulling the water-bucket, and the success of nomadic breeders was judged not so much by the milk-yield of the cattle as their muscular power and the capacity to work long hours. As the Indian people lived on a diet composed largely of cereals, legumes, and vegetables, dairy products of course provided a welcome addition of proteins, though as we have already seen, in China milk products were not valued. But even in India the market for fresh milk remained limited and it was difficult to transport ghi and cheese because of the awkward bulk of the containers. A large number of cattle and buffalo were bred by specialist groups in South East Asia and China. However, it was the interest taken by British veterinary scientists in nineteenth-century India which has generated a substantial literature on the subject of tropical cattle-breeding. The Indian subcontinent was the home of the world's finest breeds of tropical cattle. It is possible that the quality of the Indian cattle has declined during the last century or so with the shrinkage of natural pasture and the extension of arable cultivation into forested areas.

Most nineteenth-century observers were agreed that the cattle bred by peasants as part of the village economy failed to meet the standard of nomadic cattle and degenerated in size as well as in milk-yield. Francis Buchanan who took a special interest in different types of cattle during his ethnographic tours of eastern and southern India at the end of the eighteenth century had a poor opinion of the village-bred cattle. In the high south Indian plateau, above the steep hills, he identified two main breeds. One was a small, gentle animal, red-brown or black in colour; the other was a larger and very fierce breed, the cows being pure white and the bulls either black or a mixture of black-and-white. The short thick build of the first variety made the oxen suitable for working the small rice-plots. But the villagers allowed the animals to degenerate quickly, as no one took much care to separate the young bulls from the heifers. Wealthy farmers who were anxious to improve their stock, sent some cows to be kept in the folds of the larger breed and obtained the use of good bulls. Animals bred in this way lost their parents' degeneracy in three generations.[77]

The observations made by a British veterinary officer in India still provide one of the classic accounts of nomadic life and its impact on cattle. 'Cattle breeding in India,' he wrote,

in the past has been very largely, and in many areas almost exclusively carried on by professional breeders, who raised their cattle on large waste areas . . . These breeders have usually been nomadic tribes who raised their cattle by migrating from place to place according to the abundance of food and water. The year, for these breeding tribes, usually commences with the Diwali festival, which occurs in the latter part of October or early November. At this time, each breeder and his family left the place where they had been settled during the monsoon, with his herd of cows headed by a selected bull, in search of good grazing and water. The herd was taken into all parts of the country, through thick jungle and sandy waste, and, as cattle were of little value, the sick, weak, and lame animals were left behind and either died or were devoured. The whole method led unconsciously to the survival of the fittest, and disease was stamped out . . . Owing to lack of roads and communications between different parts of the country, so that each breed covered a well defined area, the breeds were kept pure, at least in their country of origin.[78]

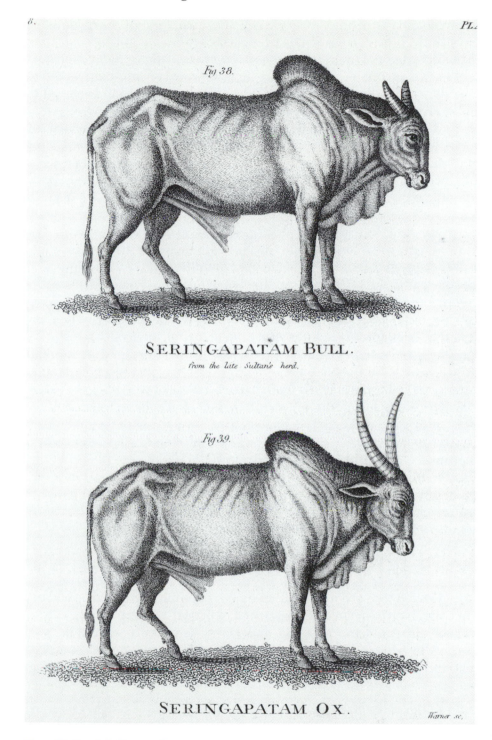

Plate 55 South Indian cattle.

The larger and better breed identified by Buchanan in Mysore originated as nomadic cattle. It was raised mainly by the tribes of Gollas and their sub-tribe the Hallikars who had migrated to the south from northern India in ancient times in several successive waves with a superior breed of cattle and settled in the Chitaldurg and Tumkur districts. During the sixteenth and seventeenth century under the patronage first of the Vijayanagara viceroys and then that of the Wadayar dynasty, the Hallikar cattle strain was officially selected for state breeding and came to be known as the Amrit Mahal breed. Under the celebrated ruler Chikka Devaraja Wadayar (*r.* 1672–1704), the state breeding stations became a regular part of the administration. But even the Amrit Mahal cattle were raised on the nomadic principle of free-range grazing which caused a considerable variation in their condition according to the availability of pasture.[79] During the dry season, according to Buchanan, the Mysore nomadic cattle looked painfully thin with their ribs showing through. With the advent of the rains and winter, the condition of the cattle improved and they began to put on weight rapidly. Being kept in a semi-wild state, the nomadic cattle had adapted well to their natural environment which offered rich grazing only seasonally and in the valleys. The total area over which the tribal or the state cattle grazed was immense, involving long journeys. During the time the cattle were on the move, the cattle-tenders penned them at night in folds surrounded by a high fence so as to keep away the tigers. Even so at time, the tigers broke through the thorn barrier, killing or wounding the cattle. The village cattle, Buchanan noted, often got stolen by thieves. But the Hallikar cattle were so fierce to strangers that not only were they safe from theft but the untrained bulls and even the cows needed more than three months to break in.[80]

In northern India, the finest breeds of cattle were raised in the area around Delhi, in the Punjab, Sind, Rajasthan, and Gujarat. A curious paradox emerged in north Indian cattle breeding: the drier the climate, the better the quality of nomadic cattle. The lush meadows of Bengal admittedly supported a huge number of cattle but this was not a region known for the excellence of its cattle stock. The Bengal cattle produced an ample supply of milk, giving rise to a prosperous dairy industry. This was achieved by maximising the number of cattle grazed over a given area rather than by optimising the milk-yield per head of cows. North Indian cattle, imported to Bengal, needed extreme care as they could not stand the humidity and heavy showers of rain. The twin paradox of the desert, the simultaneous presence of aridity and luxuriant seasonal grazing was highlighted by Major Erskine in his report on Jodhpur in Rajasthan:

The main wealth of the desert lands consists of the vast herds of camels, cattle, and sheep which roam over its sandy wastes and thrive admirably in the dry climate ... Horned cattle are reared in such numbers that they supply the neighbouring States and Provinces; they are almost wild and in excellent condition, but when taken out of the country, languish and get thin unless supplied with grain and condiments to make up for the loss of rich grasses on which they had been accustomed to feed.

The huge bulls bred in the Nagor district were particularly suitable for heavy-duty transport and for working the wells. At the two annual cattle-fairs of Marwar, the Parbatsar and the Tilwara fairs, more than 10,000 people came to buy cattle and donkeys.[81]

Historically, the much-prized Hariana breed came from the Delhi territory. These were large-limbed placid cattle with fine white or ash-white skin, the classic humped zebu type. Further west, the Bar and the Kacchi cattle were raised in the semi-desert tracts to the north of the river Ravi, and in the northern Punjab, three characteristic breeds had developed known as the Dhanni, Potwar, and Talaganj cattle. These were all powerful animals, able to work well at the irrigation-works and with the heavy plough. They were drought-resistant and thrived on dry fodder. The Muslim tribes who bred the cattle were regarded as professional graziers and their status varied from large landed magnates whose herds numbered by the hundreds to small owners of two or three head of cattle.[82] The big cattle-owning landed magnates (zamindars) looked on their herds as symbols of wealth which upheld the social status and the economic needs of the family directly and were less inclined to exploit the cattle commercially. Dairy production in particular always remained secondary and the Punjab breeds were never intended to give large quantities of milk. Whereas the bull calves were allowed as much milk as they needed, the females were neglected. However, there were also some special northern breeds which held record milk-yields; these were Hansi Hissar and the Sahiwal in the Punjab and the Red Sindhi and the Tharparkar in Sind.

The Hariana cattle-breeders generally practised transhumance rather than long nomadic migrations and during the dry season their cattle were fed on a diet of millet or sorghum fodder supplemented by gram, wheat, and oil-pressings. In the Bar region of the Punjab, the nomadic pastoralists were entirely dependent on natural grazing and when the scanty rains failed, they were forced to migrate as far north as beyond Gurdaspur to the Himalayan foothills and towards Bhawalpur on the lower Indus in the south.[83] One of the most sought-after and interesting breeds of cattle came from the area around the town of Bhag in western Sind on the Baluchistan border. The terrain was a hard alluvial plain with an annual rainfall of 50–125 mm. The summer temperature regularly reached 45–50° C and in winter fell to almost freezing. In this desolate country, the cattle found enough grass to eat after the scanty rains and for the rest of the year they were stall-fed on fodder and concentrates. The main problem in the dry season was the water supply. The perennial wells generally provided enough water for both crop-raising and for the cattle when the rains were normal, though scanty. If they dried up, temporary water-holes were dug in the dry river-beds and the cattle-tenders moved to these places with their herds. The cattle also needed to be shaded from the sun during the hottest part of the day. They were sent out to graze early in the morning and returned before midday to be penned in straw-shelters.[84] In the south-west, the nomadic cattle-breeders of Gujarat, the Rabaris and Bharwads, produced two famous pure-breeds, the Kankrej and Wadhial.[85] The nineteenth-century experts who examined the different forms of cattle-raising in the subcontinent were unanimous in their conclusion that the professional breeders thoroughly understood the genetic principles involved in line-breeding and were experts in selecting the right feed for their animals. The quality of the Indian cattle in our period of study seems to have been strongly related to the economic objectives which the rural society wished to optimise. Dairy production was decentralised and considered a next-best option to breeding bulls for transport and agricultural work. The pastoral nomads and semi-nomadic professional cattle-tenders separated stock-raising from arable farming. Cattle in premodern India did not really compete with crops for scarce land.

10

The human hand and its products: the structure of industrial production

The rationale of pre-machine industries

The competitive position of Asian industries. By the beginning of the sixteenth century, with the arrival of the Portuguese in the Indian Ocean, European historians, thinkers, and men of affairs became aware of what they had vaguely suspected and perhaps also known before. India, China, and many other nations of Asia were capable of manufacturing industrial goods at a level of costs and a profusion of varieties which even the highly developed economic regions in the Mediterranean, southern Germany, and Flanders were unable to match. As the volume of Europe's maritime trade with the Indian Ocean increased in the following centuries under the impetus of the English and Dutch East India Companies, the flood of Indian and Chinese textiles pouring into the consuming markets of the 'industrialised' West assumed proportions that seriously affected the livelihood and the competitive position of domestic textile workers. The rapidly increasing demand was of course brought about by a remarkable transformation of tastes and habits among people of all income-groups and social status. The European adoption of Asian textiles as an indispensable item of daily life made a profound imprint on the industrial scene of India and China. The phenomenon also stimulated technological developments in the West leading to the mechanisation of the entire cotton industry.[1] However, the memory and the tradition of a superior Asian technology and the quality of the products, built up over a period of nearly two centuries, was so strong that even in the third quarter of the eighteenth century, when the Indian textile industry was about to face a crippling challenge from the discovery of machine spinning and weaving in Britain, many contemporary observers continued to believe that the superfine cotton fabrics of Bengal could never be imitated by anyone else in the world.[2]

It was taken for granted that the manual dexterity possessed by the Indian weavers and spinners gave them a comparative advantage which was further strengthened by an austere if not poverty-stricken life-style. Daniel Defoe, the champion of a populist cause, had commented earlier that if people knew how the Indian weavers actually lived it would cause nothing but horror in Europe.[3] Another contemporary English economist, writing on a more neutral note, stressed that the wage cost of industrial production in Asia was so low that twice as much labour would be needed in England to produce the same amounts of goods. The cost of transporting a bale of raw cotton, he pointed out, from Asia to Europe was not much higher than that of shipping a bale of finished cloth. Yet no European textile manufacturer could even contemplate importing the essential raw material to produce goods of comparable quality and price in Europe.[4] Robert Orme, the historian of the foundation of British imperial power in India, finally summed up the myth and reality of Indian industrial production in his reflective work entitled *Historical Fragments of the Mogul Empire* (1783):

The women likewise spin the thread designed for the cloths, and then deliver it to the men, who have fingers to model it as exquisitely as these have prepared it. For it is a fact, that the tools which they use are as simple and plain as they can be imagined to be. The rigid, clumsy fingers of an European would scarcely be able to make a piece of canvass, with instruments which are all that an Indian employs in making a piece of cambric. It is farther remarkable, that every distinct kind of cloth is the produce of a particular district, in which the fabric has been transmitted, perhaps for centuries, from father to son, a custom which must have conduced to the perfection of the manufacture. I should perhaps, with my reader, have thought this detail of so simple a subject unnecessary, had I not considered, that the progress of the linen manufacture includes no less than a description of the lives of the half the inhabitants of Indostan.[5]

The role of industrial production in society and economy. Orme's justification of his subject by appealing to the weight of number contained an obvious exaggeration. The rhetorical trick nevertheless served to emphasise that textiles together with ceramics and metal objects fashioned from bronze, iron, and copper laid the foundation of civilised life in Asia no less than in other parts of the world. Industrial production is an eternal and ever-present activity in human society like its twin-brother, local and long-distance trade. A necessary assumption made in our study of Asian economic structures so far is that the evolution of settled agriculture and even nomadism implies an early and fundamental division of labour which is expressed in a separation of functions between food-producers, artisans, and the service people. The actual details of the methods of production and the nature of specialisation varied and were certainly conditioned by the overall features of the regional economy. Peasant communities in most parts of Asia were capable of weaving cotton cloth and other textiles within single households and there were skilled industrial workers, carpenters, blacksmiths, and potters who practised part-time crop-raising alongside their respective hereditary crafts. While division of labour within the family and agricultural land-utilisation by artisans was most prevalent in China and Japan, these features of craft production were also present in other parts of Asia. Village records from eastern Rajasthan in India, recently studied by historians, reveal that in many districts a special form of land tenure existed which was related to the industrial castes.[6] Yet, these areas of India had become commercialised by the first half of the eighteenth century and did not depend entirely on subsistence production of food or industrial goods.

Incomplete specialisation and the rural economy. However, it is easy to see why complete economic specialisation in rural societies is difficult to achieve. Industrial production even on the basis of pre-machine technology required certain economies of scale. A full-time worker or craftsman cannot earn a living from his manual skill alone if the size of the market is strictly limited. A village market, as Adam Smith pointed out with an amusing example, is highly limited. A single metal smith was capable of making upwards of 300,000 nails in a year, but in remote rural areas not even the output of a single day could be disposed of over a period of twelve months.[7] The division of labour was also emphasised indirectly by a Syrian jurist (Saharsi) in a definition of the Islamic concept of a township ('al-misr al-jami'): 'Some of our teachers . . . said [it is a place] in which every artisan can make his living from [the practising of] his craft throughout the year without needing to change into another craft.'[8] If the size of the market and cost of transport were important determinants of industrial production, the existence of surplus cultivable land provided the artisans with a natural insurance against any sudden or unexpected variations in demand. By being a subsistence farmer or the owner of share-cropped land, tilled by landless labourers, the rural craftsman made sure that his family would not be deprived of a minimum supply of food. There are numerous references in our sources which show that in all parts of India and China at a time of commercial depressions, the unemployed industrial worker turned to agricultural work such as helping with the harvesting in order to earn a wage.[9] Even in Hindu India where the caste system organised the bulk of the population on lines of horizontal divisions and retarded upward social mobility, the low ritual status of the artisans (relative to the twice-born castes) made it unimportant whether he was a weaver or a cultivator of land.[10]

Social attitudes and the status of the artisans. The picture drawn in this general analysis is that of a local rural economy which has reached in some way a long-run equilibrium between land usage, food production, and industrial manufacture and it is assumed further that the model is applicable to Asia as a whole, whether the historian is looking at the Middle East, India, South East Asia or China. In the short-run, the stability of the system was constantly disturbed by historical developments. Warfare, famines, and other natural calamities affected the balance between industrial prosperity and sudden destruction of the means of production and distribution. In the last analysis, at the level of the more permanent Braudelian *long durée*, social attitudes towards those who worked with their hands determined together with economic considerations, how far they were to be rewarded in material terms. If land was not a scarce commodity, it was easier to share it with non-agricultural groups. In a community suffering from land hunger, it was not unusual for the industrial worker to be driven off the land altogether in the direction of towns or reduced to very low occupational status.[11] In many Islamic countries, there was a long history of industrial craftsmen suffering the effects of a bitter antagonism between themselves and the ruling elites.[12] It is possible that the non-Arab origins of most of the urban workers made it difficult to assimilate them fully into a social structure based on the notion of complete political equality, even though the acceptance of Islam by these artisans made them equal in the eyes of the law with all members of the faithful. Whatever the reason, many historians would agree with the view of the Dutch seventeenth-century merchant Francisco Pelsaert that the Asian workers suffered from two terrible evils – low wages and political oppression. Individual artisans noted for the quality and beauty of their work might be rewarded by symbolic gifts and high prices. At the same time, powerful rulers and military invaders did not hesitate to enslave whole communities of craftsmen to suit their exceptional needs. According to tradition, in the aftermath of Chingiz Khan's conquests the silk and cotton weavers of Samarkand were pressed into the service of his military followers.[13] Timur's harsh treatment of architectural workers, his destruction of public buildings in conquered land, and the banishment of Indian stonemasons to Samarkand, were the most infamous examples among many similar episodes. The settlement of Chinese craftsmen in Trans-Oxiana was part of a great re-distribution of industrial skills brought about by the eruption of the Mongols across the map of Euro-Asia.

How far the popular and the generally-accepted image of the poverty-stricken and politically-oppressed artisan was grounded on real facts is a question which still remains open. At the turn of the eighteenth century, Francis Buchanan who made an exhaustive ethnographic study of southern and eastern India, gave a revealing description of the silk weavers of Bangalore:

It is not unusual for weavers of any kind in this country, except those of the *Whalliaru* cast, to employ any part of their time in agriculture; but many persons of casts that ought to be weavers, are in fact farmers. The *Cuttery* are more affluent than the *Pettegars*, and these again are more wealthy than any other kind of weavers.[14]

Apparently constant economic and social pressures combined with random disasters kept Asian industrial developments all through history in perpetual motion. Above all, there was a universal tendency for the craftsmen at a time of crisis to degenerate into simple urban or rural labourers and even to sell themselves into bondage.[15] If the crisis was caused by warfare many enlisted themselves as soldiers. Fighting was an honourable profession and the warlike community of Kaikkolar in south India which adopted textile weaving as a major vocation retained its warrior image all through our period. That the artisans themselves were aware in spite of the external pressures of their particular status and distinctive role in society can be measured from the fact that in Islamic societies and in Sanskritic India there were corporate associations ('sinf' in Islam and 'sreni' in India) which looked after the interests of the members, whether these were pious duties, the regulation of the professions, or the task of protecting the craftsmen from political oppression.[16] Neither the artisans' associations nor the financial power of the merchants who were indirectly involved in industrial production, however, succeeded in creating a general climate of supportive social opinion towards them. The law of contract and private debt worked inexorably against those who were unfortunate enough to default on their contractual deliveries of goods.

The analytical distinction between local and export production. The impact of external events differed qualitatively according to a basic binary characteristic of craft production. A clear analytical distinction can be made between industries that are strictly localised and those which serve a wider market and varied population. The distance scale of local production, even when it was not confined to the immediate locality of a particular village, seldom exceeded one day's travel on foot or by slow-moving carts. Production for the inter-regional or transcontinental trade on the other hand involved much longer journeys and called for an elaborate commercial organisation. Fine cotton textiles woven in major weaving towns of India or Chinese porcelain and silk fabrics produced in specific regions of specialisation travelled several thousand miles to be consumed in the aristocratic households of the Indian Ocean and the Mediterranean. The distance-time established the vital and necessary link between commercial capitalism and industrial production and it was only this kind of industrialisation which properly measured the depth of economic specialisation within the given constraints of subsistence food production and high transport costs. The accumulation of non-agricultural wealth, the rate of monetisation throughout the economy, and the production of commercial crops, cotton, mulberry, linen, and indigo, were determined to a large extent by the pace of industrial activity extending beyond the immediate locality. In our period of study, many parts of Asia had developed industries with all the attributes of an export-oriented demand, and it was not until the latter half of the eighteenth century that Europe was able to challenge Asia's traditional supremacy in industrial technology, cost efficiency, and the range of manufactures. A simple question still remained unresolved: what was the economic process which made it possible for India and China, to take the example of Asia's two great trading nations, to achieve this status in their industrial performance? The key to finding an answer lies in tracing the linkage between commercial capitalism and industrial production, between socially-determined needs and technology, and the response of craftsmen to new economic opportunities.

Industrial production, consumer demand, and commercial capitalism. The three great crafts of Asian civilisations were of course textiles, cotton and silk, metal goods including jewellery, ceramics and glassware. There were in addition a whole range of subsidiary craft manufactures which shared all the attributes of industrial technology and organisation: paper, gunpowder, fireworks, bricks, musical instruments, furniture, cosmetics, perfumery, all these items were an inseparable part of daily life in most parts of Asia. It is apparent that objects such as clothing fabrics, articles made from raw metals, and pottery have a common utilitarian origin as well as aesthetic and symbolic appeal and they are capable of being produced at the levels of both local consumption and the export trade. The distinction between the purely functional and high-value, luxury production is significant for the artisans in providing them with a choice whether to manufacture for the local or the external market. The historical dimension of the problem can be emphasised by asking, why should the weavers of cotton and silk and potters making simple earthenware move over from a system of non-specialised production to one requiring a high degree of specialisation, concentration of skills, and a larger margin of working capital? Many contemporary Western observers in Mughal India denied altogether that indigenous craftsmen were even capable of understanding such finer points. Here is an unflattering description of the 'mindless' south Indian cotton painters given by Daniel Havart, an agent of the Dutch East India Company:

Chintzes are painted here according to musters which are given to the painters which they then imitate completely and extremely well, for their national character is so stupid that they cannot imagine anything by themselves, but can only imitate something so that it has a complete likeness . . . This painting of chintzes goes on very slowly, like snails which creep on and appear not to advance. Yes, he who would wish to depict Patience would need no other object than such a painter of Palicol.[17]

Pelsaert, another Dutchman, had similar comments to make about the artisans of the imperial capital Agra: they could imitate everything they saw neatly but design nothing by themselves.[18] The Dutch observations were correct as a statement of facts but oblivious of a fundamental feature of traditional craft production. Artisans who fashioned the objects were not free agents who could draw on their individual imagination to produce works of art. They were rigidly bound by social conventions which specified, accepted or modified industrial designs and artistic expressions. The actual motifs themselves often had symbolic, hidden meanings attached to them, understood and recognised by the members of the community. In the manufacture of simple earthenware pottery, certain recurring themes have persisted for more than 3,000 years in the Middle East and India.[19] The design of bullock carts in Sind has not changed since the age of the Harappan civilisation, and it remains something of a mystery why in the case of such a functional object the village craftsmen should continue to make an identical model from one generation to another. For textile goods and other articles of everyday use, industrial workers producing for the export trade always responded to the tastes and preferences of the consuming markets. There were certain kinds of printed cotton fabrics manufactured in western India and exported to the Persian Gulf which would fail to find buyers unless they were glazed as smooth as paper.[20] The commercial risk in producing these special fabrics with a localised demand in overseas markets was underwritten by the merchants and not by the artisans. European officials employed by the English and Dutch East India Companies in procuring Asian textiles knew these facts well as did also their corporate masters in London and Amsterdam. By 1732 the wheel had begun to turn in the opposite direction and, tired of sending out Western designs to be copied by Indian textile designers, the Court of Directors wrote:

We send you some patterns, which may govern you so far as to see thereby that we want some new Works . . . endeavour to send us every year New Patterns, as well of the Flowers as Stripes, at least five or six in a bale, and let the Indians Work their own Fancys, which is always preferable before any Patterns we can send from Europe.[21]

The articulation between commercial capital and craft production carried an obvious danger for producers. Dominance of artisans by merchants was a reality whenever the force of competition on the buying side weakened. The historical sources also demonstrate that Asian merchants, whether they were operating in India, the Middle East, or China, intervened directly in industrial production as a result of particular commercial needs. The logic and rationale of marketing the products gave rise to institutional relations between the distributors and producers. These needs can be identified as relative costs of industrial products, their designs and specifications, delivery time, transport facilities, provision of working-capital, and underwriting the commercial risks. While the available material illuminate the operation of all these factors, it is much more difficult to find a reason for the motivation of industrial workers to move from a system of local production to one supplying the inter-regional markets. As soon as the question is raised, it can be seen that in the context of European industrial history, the problem is generally resolved by referring to the destruction of the feudal mode of production and the disappearance of the manorial economy. In Asia, however, there was no such periodisation nor a similar set of economic and social relations. Very far back in history, the great civilisations of the Indian Ocean had derived some of their identities and attributes from a highly developed system of industrial production and all through the ages they had actively participated in long-distance trade.

The theory of capitalistic domination and the historical evolution of industrial production. It was suggested earlier that the artisans producing cloth, pottery, metal objects, and works of carpentry for local communities were in some kind of economic and social equilibrium through their dual status of part-time artisans and part-time agriculturalists. If this image of a static continuing structure is correct, there is no reason why artisans should allow merchants to establish a relation of dominance over them and externalise their economic relations by producing goods for the export market. Even in cases where local craftsmen are required to pay taxes to government agents in terms of cash payments as opposed to levies in kind, market relations cannot be established unless industrial workers find it profitable to do so or unless they are coerced by the political power of the state. In fact, the image of a stationary subsistence-oriented production system in Asian history is an abstract dialectical concept and it is possible to suggest a number of historical factors which influenced the development of exchange relations between trade and industry. Internal pressures in rural societies in the form of demographic expansion, the consequent scarcity of cultivable land, and the general instability of crop production have already been mentioned as some of the contributory causes encouraging the artisans to migrate to towns. The migration of silk weavers from western India to Kanchipuram in the south was one of many such examples. Industrial craftsmen should be distinguished further between the partially-skilled and highly-skilled groups. A partially skilled artisan could work as a substitute metal smith or carpenter but it was inconceivable that a goldsmith making delicate filigree work should also serve as a lacquer-finisher working in wood. Premodern division of labour was not entirely a matter of relative costs and prices. Its rationale stemmed as well from social preferences and individual gifts with which people are born. A trained silk weaver, ivory carver, or porcelain maker is rewarded by society for the quality and beauty of the objects he produces. He may not only prefer and enjoy practising his art but be quite unfit to undertake hard agricultural work.

The products of these craft-skills were universally desired by most societies irrespective of their scale of internal values. The social or group preferences for luxury objects produced by a non-local industrial source strongly underlined the character of premodern trade. Japanese aristocratic consumption of Chinese silk before the age of Tokugawa isolation (*c.* 1650–1868) kept alive the Sino-Japanese trade even in times of chronic political tension. The demand provided the Portuguese in the mid sixteenth century (when the Ming embargo against Japan was in full force) with the opportunity for creating one of the most profitable channels of their trade in the Far East. Islamic rulers including the Mughal princes paid high prices for Chinese celadonware. These heavy sea-green dishes were appreciated not only because of their beauty and lustre but also because of a belief in their prophylactic quality. Art, religion,

Plate 56 Indian miniature ivory-carvings from Delhi, seventeenth century.

and magical transformations overlaid a perpetual patina of sensibilities on all forms of craft production. However, the inner appeal of luxury objects is not the only reason for industrial specialisation and the involvement of artisans in market relations. An active and varied trade developed in all parts of Asia in coarse cloth, earthenware pottery, iron implements, and brass utensils. Ordinary people as well as the well-off bought these simple goods of everyday use. At the great annual cloth market held in Jedda and Mecca during the period of the Hajj, the bulk of the textiles sold consisted of the cheaper products of Egypt and western India. The enormous social demand provided employment to a large number of cotton and linen weavers in the urban and rural areas of the Nile valley, Gujarat, and the Deccan. These particular categories of cloth exported to the Hijaz were also sold in large quantities in the internal markets close to their centres of production. Textile workers thus had a choice of two separate markets for their products. The examples of the Red Sea can be supported by other similar instances. Throughout the Indonesian archipelago, the checked, striped, and printed cotton of the Coro-mandel coast found a ready market. In China, with the rise of a prosperous cotton-weaving industry from the thirteenth century onwards, exchange relations were established both in town and country. Cotton cloth even became part of government-finance through the payment of salaries in kind, the provision of army clothing, and official export to the northern frontier areas for the procurement of horses and livestock from the nomads.[22] The image of a self-contained, self-sufficient village community living in perfect and ideal equilibrium was an attractive one to the nineteenth-century European observers in Asia. As Marx stated in a famous passage, 'The broad basis of the mode of production here [India and China] is formed by the unity of small-scale agriculture and home industry, to which in India we should add the form of village communities built upon the common ownership of land, which, incidentally, was the original form in China as well.'[23] This was an inverse mirror-reflection to an emerging machine-age industrial society, an imaginary antithesis created by historians and European colonial administrators as an antidote to their own disturbing experience of structural changes taking place at home.

Dynamics of specialisation. Artifacts and objects going back to the Pharaonic-Assyrian period in western Asia and to Han China in the east indicate that a skilled industrial craftsman in the past was more than likely to have been part of a fully differentiated form of labour and a unit of production. His value to the social community originated in being able to produce goods which non-skilled people could not produce. He needed long and meticulous training as well as inborn gifts. The family or the caste of the potential craftsman provided the means of transmitting the hereditary skills. If an industrial production unit composed of such men was forced to become part-time producers of industrial goods and rely on agricultural work to supplement their livelihood, this could have happened as a result of adverse historical forces of accidental nature, wars, political disturbances, and famines, which destroyed the basis of inter-regional and long-distance trade. Asian history is full of examples revealing the constant movements and migrations of craftsmen from one locality to another in search of better opportunities. The movements were not always in one direction alone, from the countryside to towns. During the period of Maratha expansion in eighteenth-century India, whole families of weavers fled from urban centres threatened by military sieges to settle in rural areas or in towns which previously had no weaving industry of their own. The phenomenon of migrating craftsmen was not confined to the Indian subcontinent alone. When the early Ch'ing government closed Amoy as a port open to foreign shipping, silk weavers and porcelain-makers who had previously settled there attracted by the custom of visiting ships, dispersed and many of them settled in Canton. Migration and movement provided a common remedy against natural disasters, political oppression, and shrinking economic opportunities.

The textile industries

Variations in design and regional locations. Product variations and a fine differentiation in technology gave to the traditional industries of Asia their most striking characteristics. The shape of porcelain vessels and earthenware pottery, their colour, design, and utilities incorporated as wide a range as in the case of cotton and silk textiles. Household utensils made from brass, copper, or precious metals were more functional, but even here the opportunity for individual designing was not neglected. Product variations were strongly associated with the locations of manufacture. The textile industry was perhaps the most dispersed one in Asia among those craft manufactures oriented towards the export market. It is clear that the pattern of dispersion was not a random one; it had identifiable regional configurations. In the Middle East from ancient times Egypt had specialised in the production of linen fabrics and the main centres of trade in the eleventh century were Damietta and Fustat. A remarkable picture of the export of linen goods from Egypt emerges from the documents of Jewish traders found in the Cairo geniza. The overseas markets included north Africa, Spain, Sicily, Constantinople, and other parts of the Islamic world.[24] Silk weaving had also developed in Damascus, Baghdad, and Basra. The brocaded work in silk and gold thread probably originated in Syria and Iraq and spread to other centres of textile weaving in the Middle East and India. Religious laws denied the wearing of silk and gold to Islamic men as also the use of silk carpets, the burning of incense in censers of gold and silver and drinking from vessels made in these precious metals.[25] The prohibitions were seldom honoured by the wealthy and the powerful. The importance of the textile industry in the urban economy of Iraq continued, as one Arab chronicler recorded in a graphic passage (AD 999):

Abu Nasr Sabur had endeavoured to impose a tithe on all silken and cotton goods manufactured in Baghdad. This caused a riot on the part of the people of the ᶜAttabi quarter, and of the Damascus Gate, who proceeded to the public mosque on Friday the tenth, stopped the sermon and prayer, clamoured and appealed, and went into the streets in this style . . . It was arranged that the tithe should be taken from the price of the silken goods only, and to that effect a proclamation was made on Sunday.[26]

Cotton and silk woven in all the major urban areas of the Middle East were supplemented by a woollen industry based on the manufacture of carpets and coarse materials. From the sixteenth century Iran and Ottoman Turkey emerged as producers of highly-prized woollen or wool-and-silk rugs and carpets, which were produced not as part of a nomadic economy but as an urban industry, located especially in Bursa, Tabriz, and Isfahan. A similar pattern of regional concentration of the textile industries was to be found in the Indian subcontinent which remained one of the greatest exporters of cotton goods to the world market. The four significant industrial regions of India specialising in the manufacture of cotton fabrics were the Punjab, Gujarat, the Coromandel coast, and Bengal. Important textile-weaving centres had developed in northern India in response to export demand. Weavers here had two main outlets for their products, besides the purely domestic markets. The caravan trade with Afghanistan, eastern Persia, and Central Asia complemented the river traffic to the ports of Sind, Daybul and later Tatta. The maritime trade to the Persian Gulf was as important to the cotton industries of the Punjab as it was to those of western India. There is little doubt that the coarse white, striped and checked cotton woven in innumerable villages and small towns of Gujarat clothed a large proportion of the population in the Middle East. Ahmedabad, the regional capital, was a famous producer of heavy silk cloth with magnificent decorative patterns. Gujarat had no indigenous sericulture: the basic raw material, silk filament, was imported from northern Bengal, Ajerbayjan in the Caspian, and China. High quality cottons woven throughout southern India and Bengal found a large market not only within India but also in the Middle East, South East Asia, the Far East, and after the sixteenth century in Europe. There were specific towns and rural districts where the basic white cloth was bleached, finished, and printed with patterns. Masulipatam, Sironj, Broach, and Ahmedabad, all these famous textile towns of India were as much concerned with the basic weaving of white cloth as finishing it in a final form ready for overseas shipment.

Textiles in China. In China, the traditional textile industry serving mass demand was hemp weaving, and it was only in the late Sung and Yuan period that the cultivation of shrub cotton became an important part of the agricultural economy, leading to the establishment of an associative cotton weaving industry. In contrast to the Indian experience, Chinese cotton never found its way into the world market. The premier historical exports from China remained silk and porcelain. Sericulture enjoyed a status in the political economy of the Celestial Empire which could have come only from the large and socially diffused demand for silk garments among all sections of the population. The ritual and ceremonial usage of silk in China was as distinctive as it was in other parts of Asia. But ordinary people demanded and purchased silk goods on a scale which made it almost an article of daily necessity. Robert Fortune, the nineteenth-century English traveller in China, described the people of Hangchow as being over-indulgent in their display of fine and costly clothing: 'all except the lowest labourers and coolies strutted about in dresses composed of silk, satin, and crepe . . . '. Fortune's Chinese servants, who came from the northern provinces were critical of the local habits. 'There were many rich men in their [own] country,' they said, 'but they all dressed plainly and modestly, while the natives of Hangchow, both rich and poor, were never contented unless gaily dressed in silks and satins . . . one can never tell a rich man in Hangchow, for it is just possible that all he possesses in the world is on his back'.[27] In common with many other aspects of Chinese civilisation, sericulture and silk weaving had spread from the north to the north-east and eventually to the south. Szechwan, specialising in the production of brocade, was complemented in time with the great silk producing centres in the lower Yangtze regions, Chekiang and Kiangsu with the industry concentrated in Hangchow, Hu-chou, Soochow, and Nanking. The southernmost coastal province of Kwangtung and the great port-city Canton also produced silk. The promotion of the premier Chinese textile industry through the administrative and imperial encouragement of mulberry cultivation reflected a close bond between the Confucian values of agricultural development and craft production as the two essential pillars of society.[28]

Theories of industrial locations. What explanation can the historian offer for the regional location of the textile industries in different parts of Asia? Orme had observed and reflected on the diffusion of the craft throughout eighteenth-century India and had a simple answer. There were few villages in Coromandel and Bengal which did not have at least a few families of weavers. People adopted the industry because of their weak physical constitution and the debilitating nature of the tropical climate. Weaving was a sedentary occupation requiring little active energy. It may seem strange that Orme and other European social observers in India who had a great deal to say about the caste structure of Indian society should nevertheless have overlooked the fact that the cotton textile industry in common with all other economic occupations was organised in India on the basis of caste groups the members of which had practically no say in the choice of their hereditary profession. The real explanation for the development of certain areas as export producers must be sought at a different level. Industrial location even in the age of non-mechanised production is strongly influenced by the relative costs of labour, wage goods, and capital which are distributed unevenly over space. Absolute advantages such as a favourable climate and the availability of water transport are strengthened by the easy supply of raw materials, access to markets, population density, and the quality of local political administration. An examination of the dispersion pattern of Asian textile weaving at once shows that there were two types of regional specialisation. Certain well-known types of cloth were woven only in particular cities and towns. The concentration of silk weaving in Soochow was closely related to the production and supply of raw silk in the surrounding districts. Dacca, the provincial capital of Bengal until the early eighteenth century, produced very fine transparent cotton muslin called 'ab-i-rawan' (flowing water), which were embroidered or even flowered on the loom. There were other towns in northern India which exported similar muslin to the Middle East and Central Asia. The two desert-cities of Yazd and Kirman in the Iranian plateau had sizeable weaving industries with well-known varieties of textiles. An English traveller who visited Kirman has left a detailed description of its textile trade.

Printed cloths and handkerchiefs are manufactured here also in great abundance, and carpets are wrought which are thought to be equal to any produced in the whole empire. These are chiefly the work of females of distinction, since to spin, to sew, and to embroider are the chief accomplishments of their education. These carpets are mostly made by the needle, with coloured worsteds on a woven substance . . . Others again of an inferior quality are altogether woven in colours and sold at a cheaper rate, these being the work of men. There are no large manufactories of either, however, as both are wrought in private dwellings and, when finished brought into the bazaar for sale.[29]

The location of these textile centres was probably independent of the consideration of transport costs, as the products were mostly high-valued goods consumed in richer households and the cost of carriage was not likely to be a large proportion of their final cost. The geographical pattern in the manufacture of these urban fabrics must be explained by the combination of favourable natural endowments and the cumulative effect created by a hereditary concentration of craft skills. In the case of Dacca or Soochow, an important encouragement to specialisation was their proximity to the supply of suitable raw materials. The quality of Dacca muslin especially in our period resulted in great measure from the quality of the cotton grown in the area. Similar arguments were also suggested in the seventeenth century for certain Indian towns being able to produce brighter and faster colours in chintz printing; the water supply in these places carried important mineral constituents which determined the technical balance of the natural dyes used. However, the theory of a possible connection between industrial location and the sources of raw materials is weakened by the existence of silk weaving in Ahmedabad or Varanasi which imported all their yarn from distant places. It is obvious that the specialised urban manufacturing centres in Asia expanded their production on the principle of a central place. An initial spatial advantage had brought together a whole range of associated and complementary skills. A labour force composed of fine spinners, weavers, embroiderers, and finishers had grown up around the city over many generations and the concentration of these skills in turn attracted the great merchants who distributed and marketed the products. What is significant in the context of urban textile industry is that, though the production is identified by a locus in space, the consuming markets are completely scattered and held no particular economic meaning for the primary producers. The urban centres and final consumers were brought together through the mechanism of commercial distribution.

The rationale of the rural location of the textile industries. Whatever may have been the historical reason that led to the rise of urban-based textile industries and their well-advertised products, there was no compelling social or economic reason why weavers and other craftsmen should be exclusively located in towns rather than in the countryside. In fact, textile production was particularly suited for rural areas. There were entire regions in the Middle East, India, and China which produced textiles intended for export both

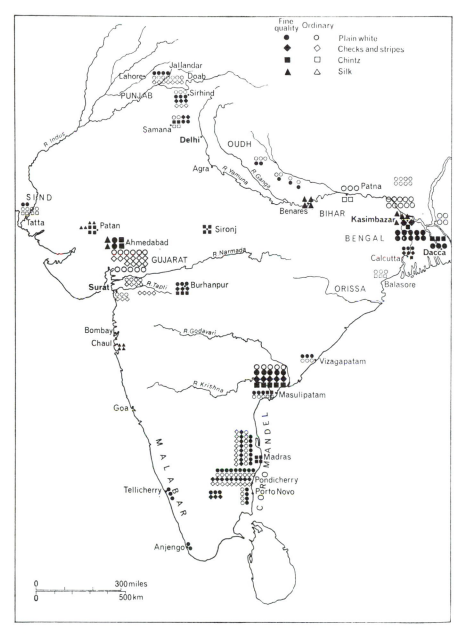

Map 17 India: main textile weaving areas 1600–1750.

within and outside the national frontiers. The main economic determinant of these regions was the contour of market areas. At an abstract level the theoretical problem was to define the boundaries of an economic region from the view point of producers as well as consumers. If the location of the textile workers is fixed, the consumers have a choice of alternative sources from which they can draw their supplies. On the other hand, distinct regional markets such as the Persian Gulf, the Red Sea, or the Spice Islands in South East Asia provide the producers with an opportunity to develop particular areas of export demand. In either case, the effect of market orientation was to create identifiable units of industrial zones. The most important influence in shaping the structure of exchange was that of transport costs. In northern and western India, the textile industry was largely located in towns. The wheeled vehicles used as industrial transport could travel easily over the flat plains and roads were easy to construct. In Bengal and south India the textile industry was scattered throughout the rural areas and it was highly decentralised. Here again the possible reasons for this characteristic were not identical. Bengal was a low-lying province with a magnificent system of rivers and canals which provided a cheap means of transport between the weaving villages and the urban markets where the products were sold for export. In the south, the landscape was constantly broken up by deep and rapid rivers, by mountains and ravines, making it very difficult to build suitable roads. The pack oxen were the main carriers of industrial goods and bulk articles in these regions. The role of nomadic carriers as cattle-breeders in national life and the pattern of agricultural specialisation added another dimension to the question of relative transport costs. It was by no means proven that pack oxen were less economic than the use of carts or wagons and they were certainly more mobile.

Costs of transport: an example from 1733. India's historical experience suggests that the location of the textile industry was sensitive to economic considerations. The records of the European trading companies in Asia contain numerous references to the detailed calculations of costs in alternative areas of production. In 1733, the English East India Company carried out a lengthy exercise in industrial costing. The surviving accounts show all the items of transport charges and road tolls for every type of textiles exported by the Company from about twenty different areas of southern India. It was found that there was only a difference of six per cent in buying the cloth from villages far distant from Madras as from towns nearer to the port.[30] The Company's commercial council in Madras thought that there was some risk in concentrating all its textiles purchases solely in one or two urban areas, as the growth of the industry and the increase in demand was likely to drive up quickly the price of food and raw materials. The basic costs of production even in this early period responded to variations in the prices of wage goods, yarn, and raw cotton. The analysis of the structure of textile industries suggests that production for the purely local markets needed few considerations other than the supply of suitable raw materials and a simple system of distribution. The bulk of the rural production of textiles probably never travelled beyond the locality. Weaving for an inter-regional or international market in contrast was a different matter altogether. Merchants who primarily exported overseas had to find sources of supplies which minimised transport costs between the production areas and the ports of shipment. Textile workers on the other hand tended to settle in places where they were sure of obtaining food and the necessary materials for their trade, and a certain measure of benign administration. It is evident that in regions where the export trade was most active, there was also a large trade in yarn and dyeing substances. No region could prosper industrially unless the political elites succeeded in maintaining law and order and repelling possible military incursions. Premodern industries were particularly vulnerable to economic devastations caused by wars and troops movements. The periodical rise and fall of different industrial regions in Asia were mainly due to this single element of disruption.

Technology in the textile industries. The technological conditions underlining the textile industries, whether cotton, silk, or linen, are subsumed by the three general problems inherent in historical developments. The level of technical inventions and scientific knowledge available to industrial producers at any given time determine the basic structure which is influenced in turn by economic calculations relative to the choice of alternative techniques in production. The rate of innovation and the willingness of society to tolerate institutional changes brought about by a new technology finally affect the pace of industrial growth. The introduction of the single- or multi-spindle spinning wheel which supplemented hand spinning with the spindle and distaff and the gradual development of the treadle-looms and the drawlooms reflected the most significant technological development in textile production. Once this particular set of innovations had been assimilated, these industries remained in a steady state until the mid nineteenth century when Western machine technology was imported and put into operation. Before this period, when an expansion in output was required either because of an increase in export demand or internal consumption, it was always achieved by expanding the size of the labour force rather than the development of capital intensive equipment. The phenomenon of an expanding and flexible labour force able to switch occupations between agriculture and industry was to be found both in China and India.

In the context of Chinese historical experience, Mark Elvin has sought an explanation in the economic model of a 'high-level equilibrium trap'.[31] As long as Chinese and Indian agriculture was able to cross each threshold of given technological constraints and continue to expand food production, the Malthusian demographic expansion also continued, providing the essential labour force for industry as well as agriculture. The adoption of machinery as a labour-saving strategy was retarded historically by this particular characteristic of Asia's two industrially most advanced nations. The absence of international competition also perpetuated to some extent the basic features of the Chinese and Indian textile production. While the use of the spinning wheel and

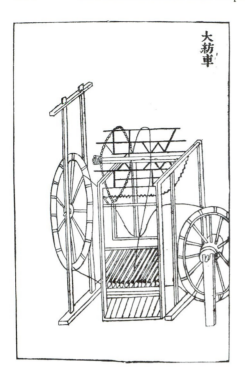

Plate 57 Spinning machinery and five-spindled spinning wheel in China (see p. 000).

the drawloom undoubtedly increased productivity, for certain particularly fine categories of textiles, simpler looms and hand-twisted yarn were preferred. Such threads were more uniform and harder in strength and the individually-operated looms gave greater control to the weaver. The capital cost of the traditional loom or the spinning wheel was negligible in total costs of production, and it is clear that the technological superiority of Asian fabrics rested largely on human skills transmitted on the basis of hereditary knowledge. If there was a precocious sign of machine-spinning, it was to be found in China. An agricultural handbook published in 1313 provides the first and authentic reference to an instrument described as the big spinning wheel which was mounted with thirty-two spindles. It could be cranked by hand or powered by animals and water-wheels. The instrument was capable of spinning one hundred catties (59 kg) of yarn in twenty-four hours. The Chinese work mentioned that it was applied generally to the spinning of ramie, although the silk industry was beginning to adopt a smaller version of it also.[32] The mechanical device appears not to have been applied to cotton spinning in China and there is no reference to any such instruments in Indian sources. Chinese cotton spinning remained confined to three or four spindle wheels. Five spindles were known to exist but were a rarity (see Plate 57). A late-eighteenth-century authority on cotton textiles (Chu Hua) raised a technical

Plate 58 Indian treadle-loom.

point in the use of five spindle wheels: 'I have seen the 4-spindle spinning wheel with which the spinners has to use five fingers to hold the four rovings. In employing a 5-spindle wheel, how can one hold five rovings?'[33]

The simple treadle looms (see Plate 58) which raised and lowered a given set of warps for the shuttle to be passed through was suitable for weaving either plain cloth or patterned fabrics which did not require more than two overhead harnesses controlling the pattern. For weaving highly complex 'picture' patterns on silk, the Chinese technicians had invented the drawloom which needed more than one person to operate. The chief weaver was assisted by drawboys who operated the complicated harnesses (see Plate 59). Sung Ying-hsing, the Ming author and an expert on Chinese technology (1637), included in his works fine drawing of the drawloom and described its function in producing the complicated patterns:

The artisan who makes the figure design for weaving is the most ingenious person. The pattern and colour of a fabric design are first painted by an artist on a piece of paper. The artisan takes the painted design and translates it, precisely, in terms of the silk threads used, down to the last thousandth of an inch, and makes a pattern for weaving. This pattern is hung up in the 'figure tower' of the drawloom; [it guides the drawboy] to lift the correct 'rigid rods' of the heddles. Even if the weaver does not know what the figure and colour on the fabric will turn out to be, he has only to follow the figure design and interlace the weft and warp threads according to specifications . . . when the shuttle passes, the desired figure appears on the fabric.[34]

Although China was evidently ahead of India in the use and application of mechanical instruments and machinery to textile production, the classic description of the Dacca cotton industry by John Taylor in the second half of the eighteenth century shows how far quality and the excellence of the fabrics depended on manual control:

Thread for coarse assortments is spun by a Wheel, for fine by a Spindle. Thread is made at all the aurangs [weaving centres], but the greatest quantity, and with few exceptions the best, is spun at Junglebarry Bazetpore; the fabrics from the greatest skill with which the thread is prepared, possess a peculiar softness . . . The heat of the climate will not admit of Thread of that quality being spun but at particular hours, usually from half an hour after day light, till nine or ten in the morning and from three or four in the afternoon till half an hour before sun set. Of spinners of this sort of Thread there are in all not above thirty.

Taylor wrote down in minute detail the preparation and the processing of the thread before the cloth was actually woven and concluded his report with the remark, 'The preparation of the tanna or warp thread of a full piece of plain or striped cloth of the Dacca aurang employs two men, according to the quality of the thread, from ten to thirty days. The [weaving] of such cloth employs two persons, one to weave, the other to prepare thread and attend the loom.' The superfine fabrics needed as many as sixty days per piece.[35]

The Asian weaver traditionally produced four generic types of fine cloth: plain fabrics, those painted or printed with patterns, cloth made from a mixture of cotton and silk thread, and pure silk pieces. The first category had an intermediate type which, as we have just seen, was patterned on the loom. Apart from the manual dexterity of the weaver and his ability to handle the

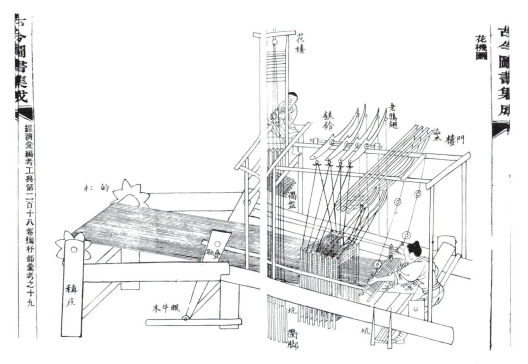

Plate 59 Chinese draw-loom with two weavers and the full harness (see p. 316).

tools of the trade which called for a long period of training, the most important factor in the manufacture of these cotton and silk goods was the preparation of the yarn. The reeling, spooling, spinning of the silk from cocoons to the final stage of the weft and tram threads was an excessively laborious and skilled process.[36] While workers in Italy and France in our period of study learnt quite easily the technique of sericulture and spinning silk thread and were able to weave highly sophisticated silk cloth, the knowledge of cotton yarn production remained virtually a closed secret. The chemical treatment of the raw thread before it was ready for weaving belonged to a whole series of chemical processes. The bleaching and dyeing the grey cloth was part of the same technology which had reached the limits of its advancement by the eighteenth century. The most splendid example of the Asian dyeing techniques could be seen in the elaborately painted Indian chintzes which involved no less than ten or twelve separate dye transfer processes being applied to the cloth. The brilliance and fastness of colours achieved through the use of vegetable and organic dyes in combination with chemical washing were characteristic qualities of Indian cotton cloth. The actual process of dyeing was taken down in detail by many contemporary Western textile experts and there is no doubt that the textile-finishers had a strong grasp of the empirical properties of the chemicals used.[37] In the second half of the seventeenth century the East India

Company sent out some English dyers and silk throwers to Bengal in order to instruct Indian workers in the art of producing glossy black colours, the indigenous forms of which were held to be inferior to the European finish. What success they had is not known, but by the end of the century the experimental technological transfer appears to have come to an end.[38] Evidence from the records of the European trading companies in the seventeenth and eighteenth centuries suggests that international competition in the manufacture of silk or cotton was so weak that India and China enjoyed a virtual monopoly in the export markets. Such conditions *ceteris paribus* were not conducive to a technological transformation.

The organisation of the textiles industries. Earlier, an analytical distinction was made between industrial production at the local level and one which required access to larger markets separated by great distances. Of course, the two categories of production were not completely exclusive and the mobility of the weavers and other artisans combined with the decentralised production processes constantly kept them in contact with the commercial world. But the organisation of village industries in Asia was closely connected with the social structure of agriculture. In the absence of substantial local markets and a monetised economy, craftsmen served a group of rural families and received their reward in kind. All economic decisions concerning the price of the goods, the amount of output, and marketing were a function of localised social conventions which determined the scale of economic values. The best example of such industrial stratification comes from India. The hierarchy of the caste system assigned different levels of rewards to different workers, though the forces of supply and demand also constrained and influenced the ritualistic considerations. Weavers enjoyed a higher social status than leather-workers and traditionally received a higher rate of remuneration. The social relationships were highly exploitative but at the same time allowed a basic subsistence to all. India was certainly an extreme historical case. But the custom of paying local craftsmen in kind was prevalent throughout Asia. A greater degree of sophistication is evident in the organisation of the second type of industrial production which depended on the market mechanism to control and regulate its temporal rhythms and decision-making. It was not only that the weaver, the metal smith, or the potter was paid a cash price for his product; the finishing, distribution, and the creation of new consumer demand called for a whole range of commercial services. Whether it was in the Middle East, India, or China, a clear vertical link appeared between marketing and industrial production. The Asian craftsmen appeared to have adopted two distinct approaches to the problem of productive decision-making. The question of what kind of goods should be produced is always related in manufacturing to that of the size of the production. Some artisans solved the problem by manufacturing traditional and well-known goods for sale in the open market.

Others needed the commercial services of brokers and merchants to establish the necessary linkages between production and the final consuming markets.

There are many historical examples from the seventeenth and eighteenth centuries which illustrate in a profusion of details how the textile industry was organised in India and China.[39] Cotton weavers in Indian rural areas would bring their middle-quality white cloth unbleached to the nearest market-town, where it was bought by traders. Normal forces of supply and demand fixed the price paid to the weavers, though a discount was also often applied to the agreed rates in order to compensate for variation in quality. The traders undertook to have the cloth bleached by professional washers and the finished pieces were then exported to the great cities in northern India.[40] Similar conditions also obtained in the cotton weaving areas of China. In the prefectural capital of Soochow a large quantity of green and blue cloth was bought for sale and it was glazed by finishers employed by the merchants. Although in these instances the weavers sold directly to the merchants or their agents, the transactions took place at the level of wholesale and not retail trading. The reason for this particular form of market structure is not difficult to find. The demand for textiles derived mainly from the garment trade is a continuous function of time, although religious and social festivals often created a distinctly seasonal pattern. Textile weavers actually engaged in the production seldom accumulated enough capital to hold substantial stocks of finished articles. That function was performed for them by the wholesale merchants and the overseas shippers. The economic role of the middlemen and the distributors in premodern industrial production was to build up a sufficient stock of goods from a large circle of producers and to supply the consumers all through the year from such inventories.[41] The surviving historical material, whether relating to the process of manufacture or the system of distribution, shows quite clearly that most of the Asian craft industries had become highly differentiated. The technology of production involved many intermediate stages, and the separation of functions was social as well as technical. In the textile industry before a single piece of chintz or muslin reached the hands of the public, it needed the services of farmers growing raw cotton, harvesters, those who ginned the cotton fibre, carders, spinners, weavers, bleachers, printers, painters, glazers, and repairers. If a thread in the superfine cotton muslin was found to have broken after its chemical treatment, it had to be replaced by hand using a needle for the entire piece of some fifteen yards in length by a class of workers who specialised in this type of repair work. Robert Orme, the author of a distinctive theory of Oriental despotism, pointed out that whereas the free commandeering of the artisans' services was common enough in Islamic societies in India and the Middle East, the political elite found it difficult to arrest the textile workers because no single social group was involved in the manufacture of cloth. The Mughal imperial agents purchasing Dacca muslin may have paid less than the full market price to the weavers, just as generous patrons anxious to secure the best quality work were often willing to exceed the market price. It may be argued that one of the reasons for the apparent prosperity and the continued expansion of the cotton and silk industries in the Indian Ocean regions probably lay in the relative absence of direct political interference with the artisan communities engaged in their respective tasks of specialisation.

The independent artisan who manufactured at his own risk but sold to the wholesale dealer constituted one typology in the organisation of production. The second type consisted of those who were far more specialised than the first group and these artisans generally worked for particular merchants and brokers who supplied them with working capital. The products were manufactured for a strictly limited export marked and consumer taste played a large part in determining the quality, design, and the costs. If the external demand failed, these objects could not be marketed in the local areas of production. The functional distinction between the two systems did not of course imply that in practice they were mutually exclusive. During the slack months, when the Red Sea or the China fleets had left port, the same weaver or potter who worked to order on behalf of the exporters for the rest of the year, might decide to work at his own risk either in the same profession or in some subsidiary occupation. The organisational link between the industrial producers and the wholesale merchants in this arrangement was a financial contract which stipulated that a substantial proportion of the final costs should be paid in advance against stipulated timed delivery. The wide prevalence of the system throughout the Indian Ocean has prompted many historians to describe it as equivalent to the European 'putting-out' method. The analogy is not quite correct for all parts of Asia. In Europe the true putting-out system involved an advance of raw materials to the craftsmen by merchants who commanded a substantial supply of capital and it represented a direct intervention in industrial production by the owners of commercial capital. Although large clothiers or silk weavers in Europe could become contractors to merchants utilising the putting-out method, it was the distributors who were responsible in the final instance with the adjustment of the production decisions. In China, the putting-out method was most visible in the silk industry which needed costly raw materials. In a typical Chinese silk weaving workshop, the workers might be members of a household who accepted the necessary yarn from wealthy commercial firms or they might weave either as piece-rate workers or with their own materials.[42] By the eighteenth century, commercial forces in the Chinese silk industry had reduced many highly skilled urban weavers almost to the status of daily wage workers completely dependent on the export demand. A local gazetteer of Soochow described the uncertain lot of these wretched people:

The inhabitants of the eastern section of the prefectural city [Soochow] are all textile workers . . . Each weaver has a special skill, and each has a regular employer, who pays him a daily wage. Should anything happen [to the regular weaver] the employer will get a worker who is without regular employment to take his place; this is known as 'calling a substitute'. The weavers without regular employers go to the city's bridges each day at dawn to await the calls. Satin weavers stand on Flower Bridge, damask weavers on Kuang-hua Temple Bridge, and spinners who make silk yarn at Lin-hsi Ward. They gather by the score and by the hundred, scanning around expectantly with outstretched necks, resembling groups of famine refugees. They will stay until after the breakfast hour. If work should be curtailed at the silk textile workshops, these people would be without a living.[43]

In contrast to the Chinese experience, Indian textile industry almost always demanded an advance of capital rather than raw materials. Historians familiar with the European model of the putting-out system have generally interpreted the Indian or the Middle Eastern advance contractual arrangements as a universal sign of the poverty of artisans who were held to be incapable of raising sufficient working capital to buy food and their own supply of raw materials. The role of the first group of artisans, those manufacturing at their own risk and selling directly to the merchants, is forgotten in this context and their ability to engage in independent production is left unexplained. There is no doubt that many weavers needed money to buy yarn and to support themselves while the cloth was being woven. But even more important was the indispensable role of the advance contract system in securing cloth in large enough quantities and with product control. It was a commercial contract which imposed definite legal obligations on either side. The merchant was reasonably certain of receiving a sufficient amount of cloth as the shipping season approached, and the artisan on his part had a customer for his goods. It will be remembered that the most difficult problem for any industrial producer is to match his output to the level of demand and to obtain information about the product itself. The craftsman who remains in full-time production has little time or opportunity to find out for himself how the market is moving over time in distant areas. He has to rely on the trader to supply him with the necessary information. It is possible that the origin of the advance contract system in industrial production of the Middle East and India can be traced to the Islamic juridical practices. According to the legal treatise *Hidaya* which incorporated the Hanifite school of law, the delivery of goods ordered from a manufacturer at some future date becomes binding only if the customer advances a part payment of the final price and specifies the dates. Once the artisan has accepted the advance, the transaction became a sale and it could not be interpreted as a mere promise to deliver.[44] Of course, in the Middle East as well as in India in non-commercial situations instances of a direct relationship between the industrial workers and their final customers could be cited. Ibn al-Ukhuwwa in the chapter on weavers in his guide for the Muhtasib laid down that the weaver must receive thread by weight and return the woven cloth of the same weight to avoid any doubt that the thread had been fraudulently changed. A workman hired for the purpose of weaving a specified piece of material would forfeit his wages if he made the cloth different from the sample.[45]

The structure of production and organisation adopted in the textile industries could be expected to be replicated in other areas of craft manufacture. Little information is available on the internal workings of the metal or porcelain industries. The presence of imperial directors at the kilns of the great pottery town Ching-te-chen would seem to suggest that there was a strong link between the final markets and the individual producers. European commercial documents dating from the early eighteenth century suggest that in Canton leading merchants contracted with the porcelain factories well in advance of the arrival of European ships to supply them with the right kind of export china. Many fine and expensive sets of porcelain bought by the English and Dutch East India Companies with special design and decorations were ordered several years in advance. It is very probable that the organisation of the potteries would have included a large element of vertical connection between the producers and distributors. The widespread use of advance contracting, however, calls for an economic explanation. The uncertainties of long-distance trade obviously needed an institutional safeguard against losses due to the non-clearance of the market. By working to orders the premodern artisan transferred some of the risks to the traders.

A vivid picture of how the system worked in actual practice can be gathered from a collection of English documents of the 1670s, which originated in the textile town of Broach in Gujarat. The East India Company was rapidly expanding its import of Indian cotton textile in this period and had sent its agents to purchase directly in the weaving districts of Western India. Centred around Broach there were a number of busy small towns and large villages which wove cotton cloth mainly for the Middle Eastern markets. The European companies were anxious to break into this particular network of textile production. From the month of September onwards the brokers employed by the merchants in the great Mughal port of Surat came down to the area and gave out financial advances to the weavers. There was strong competition for the services of the best workmen and the European buyers whose demand was comparatively large were obliged to follow the traditional method and pay the going market rates both for advances and the final price. This was a period when the export trade in Indian cotton was particularly strong in the Red Sea and the Persian Gulf and the producers were very sensitive to the market price. English merchants found that if they did not accept the cloth brought to the warehouse and pay the price demanded, the weavers took it to the Dutch or Indian export merchants. The advance previously given out was forfeited.[46] The question of standardisation and product control led to a running struggle between the wholesaler and the craftsmen in other parts of India. In 1675 the East India Company's merchants in Madras reported to the Council that the weavers had found themselves in great financial difficulties because the price of raw cotton, yarn, and food grains had risen substantially since the advance contracts were made. They were now using inferior thread to reduce costs, and if the Company insisted on receiving the same quality of goods as specified in the samples, the weavers would be unable to keep up the supply and the entire deposit already paid would be lost.[47] The problem was created by a basic logical contradiction between the needs of long-distance trade and the methods of artisan production. No wholesale dealer can function properly unless there is a certain measure of standardisation of products. The weavers accepted the mandate for product control from merchants and the final consumers. At the same time, it was impossible for the handicrafts industry to produce two identical pieces of cloth and at times of crisis brought about by harvest failures or political calamities, weavers found it difficult to maintain strict standards. Variation in quality was inevitable and no satisfactory solution was ever found to the endemic problem of matching trade samples.

The metallurgical industries

The importance of metals. Neither textile-weaving nor glass and ceramic industries, indispensable as these were to Asian civilisations, involved much use of metals. But there is no doubt that political and economic life over much of the Indian Ocean was closely associated with the metallurgical industries in one form or another. The use of metals in any society and in any historical period generally measured its relative technological and economic development. There were other social nuances to the significance of metals. The symbolism of iron as an element in the cycle of cosmic creation was particularly strong in the minds of Chinese scientists and philosophers. When one sees the melting of the metal in the great blast furnace, Chan Jo-Shui said (*d. c.* 1560), one understood the beginning and end of Heaven and Earth. The fusion inside the furnace was like the beginning of the formless embryo and the solidification the attainment of form. The beginning and the end succeeded one another in a finite cycle but the metal itself never really changed.[48] A list of historical objects fashioned from metals would be a long one. Agricultural tools and implements, metal fastenings, doors and locks in buildings, cooking utensils, heavy and fine armaments, religious artifacts, coins, and jewellery, all these generic categories occupied precise positions in the relative scale of development, refinement, and functional role in society through the Asian metallurgist's skill in handling copper, bronze, iron, gold, and silver. In his discussion of chemistry in the *Muqaddimah*, Ibn Khaldun raised a fundamental scientific question: 'The philosophers base their discussion of alchemy on the condition of the seven malleable minerals: gold, silver, lead, tin, copper, iron, and *kharsini*. The question is whether [seven metals] are different in their [specific] differences, each constituting a distinct species, or whether they differ in certain properties and constitute different kinds of one and the same species.'[49] He must have been aware that at the level of the symbolic (social)

Plate 60 Casting large bronze objects in China in prepared moulds (see p. 325).

and practical (scientific) usage, the refining and alloying techniques mastered by the early metal smiths, made each one distinct and combinational. Pure gold was the noblest metal occupying the premier rank in the hierarchy of ritual and aesthetic meaning. 'God sent iron down to earth,' it was recorded in the Qur'an, 'wherein is mighty power and many uses for mankind.'[50] Bronze remained the preferred alloy for representing the divine image in hypersensitive Sanskritic temple worship. The metallurgy of bronze and its variations were at once difficult and complex. But the technology of bronze casting not only continued to be handed down from generation to generation for several millennia; by the Sung period in China the ancient religious objects, the 'ting', had become collectors' pieces to be studied by emperors and scholars. In the Han period they had proclaimed the power of objects to mediate between the immortals and the mortals.[51]

Plate 61 Multiple bronze furnaces used for casting very large bells, showing the channels for the molten metal leading to the mould.

The spatial distribution of metal industries. The location of the metal industries specialising in the manufacture of high-value products was almost entirely in urban centres, though the raw metal itself was smelted close to the sources of ore and fuel. The small-scale of production, relative to the post-Industrial Revolution period, made it unnecessary to locate the secondary manufacturing in areas of coal mining. Apart from the urban workers, travelling metal smiths in Asia quite often carried their entire foundry and forging equipment in carts and river boats with a supply of raw metals ready to fashion whatever article was in demand. The ornate iron carts of the nomadic blacksmiths are still a familiar sight in the north Indian rural scene. Specialised metal goods produced in localised foundries and workshops also travelled over long distances. Indian swords, armour, guns, and ornamental metalware were exported to the Middle East just as many similar objects were imported into the subcontinent from Syria, Egypt, and Iran. The Cairo *geniza* sources dating from the twelfth century show that brass foundries in western India were manufacturing artifacts for the Middle Eastern markets and the raw metals used by the Indian metal smiths were often brought to them by traders from Aden. Broken copper and brass vessels were sent to India to be reworked there into new products and the practice seems to suggest that the local supply of the essential metals was either insufficient or irregular.[52] While tools, implements, nails, and bolts were mostly made by forging and hammering, large objects such as guns, bells, and the finer religious regalia were cast directly from the furnace. In every Middle Eastern or Indian manufacturing town, special streets or areas were set aside in the souks, qaysariyas, and bazaars where the metal smiths carried on their trade amidst the deafening sounds of hammering. Thin sheets of copper or brass were moulded into the required shapes of household utensils and their surface decorated with fine repoussé work. The noise from these workshops, if nothing else, would guide the unfamiliar visitors without fail to their location in the maze of narrow streets and alleys. Travelling platers in urban and rural areas went from house to house tinning the inner surface of copper vessels used for cooking. Chardin wrote with just a touch of wonder: 'The tinners of kettles and pans ... who use so many things in *Europe* about their work, go to people's houses in *Persia*, and work there for the very same charge. The master with his little apprentice, brings his whole shop with him, consisting in a sack of coal, a pair of bellows, a little solder, some *sal amoniack*, some bits of pewter in his pocket.'[53]

The technology of bronze casting. The tin was imported mainly from the islands of South East Asia, while China and Japan were large exporters of copper. The Chinese imperial government, however, periodically imposed restrictions on the outflow of copper from the Celestial Empire in order to protect its low-value transaction-oriented currency. Most of the ateliers making jewellery and the metal shops producing articles of everyday use needed little specialised equipment and techniques. Casting large bells and guns called for far greater organisation, team-work, and the preparation of plants. Sung Ying-hsing in his detailed technical treatise has left an exact description of the methods followed by Chinese bronze and iron workers making bells, cooking pots, and statues. Some of the imperial bells were of huge size and weight. The North-Star Pavilion in the Imperial Palace in Peking used one which weighed 20,000 catties (11,936 kg). In order to cast a bell of this size, 47,000 catties of copper were needed together with 4,000 catties of tin, 50 ounces of gold, and 120 ounces of silver. The moulds were prepared first by building up the clay core which was then covered with a coating of tallow and wax several inches thick. When the wax had dried a further coating of fine clay and charcoal was applied. The finished mould finally received heat-treatment to remove the wax. Sung reckoned that 10 catties of copper were needed to fill the cavity previously occupied by one catty of tallow and wax. The copper alloy was melted when the cavity of the mould was thoroughly dry.

But as it is not possible to cast such 10,000 catty quantities of molten copper by hand, [melting] furnaces are built all around [the moulding pit] and earthen trenches are made which decline towards the pit and connect the furnaces with the copper-holes on the bell mould. The trenches are surrounded with red-hot charcoal. When the metal

Plate 62 Heavy cannon cast in the Jaigarh cannon-foundry, Amber, Jaipur, seventeenth century.

is melted in the furnaces, the plugs are removed (the trenches are first closed by earthen plugs), and the molten metal flows like water down the trenches and eventually gets into the mould. [see Plate 61][54]

Heavy armament: the Jaipur gun-foundry. The basic technology of similar metal casting was well-known in India also. It is remarkable that Sung's account of the Chinese techniques are strongly corroborated by the surviving archaeological evidence from the great seventeenth century gun foundry and arsenal located in a fortress near Amber, belonging to the Rajas of Jaipur. The stronghold served as the treasure-house of the Jaipur State, and the arsenal and its working equipment remained sealed long after the workshops had ceased to operate. As a result these are still in a remarkable state of preservation. The main difference between the method of large metal casting described by Sung and the method followed in the Jaipur arsenal was that the Indian furnace where the bronze alloy or iron was melted was a single brick-built structure equipped with bellows to provide the air blasts (see Plate 63) and with an over-head ventilation system. In front of the furnace, there is a deep pit in which the gun moulds were placed just below the spout through which the molten metal flowed out. The moulds (see Plate 64) would have been pre-heated before casting began and traces of fire are still visible on the clay walls of the pit. The surviving gun moulds demonstrate that the large-bored guns, up to 2 metres

Plate 63   The bellows-opening of the blast-furnace in Jaigarh cannon-foundry, Amber, Jaipur, seventeenth century.

long, were cast in the form of a solid barrel and afterwards bored out in a gigantic lathe. The specially-hardened steel bits of different calibre were mounted on long steel rods which were held rigid while the crank of the lathe turned the gun barrel.

The technique of casting large cannon from bronze or iron was evidently quickly mastered by the Asian metallurgists, once the use of artillery had become well established. Ottoman Turkey led the heavy armament industry in Asia but the government arsenals in Mughal India (of which the Jaipur foundry was a part) rapidly caught up with the early start made by the Western manufacturers. According to Abu'l Fazl the interest taken by Emperor Akbar in gun-making was a major factor in the development of advanced technology. Barrels of muskets were made by twisting steel plates in the form of a roll and hammering the heated tube. Cylindrical pieces of iron were also bored out with 'an iron pin'. The complete barrel in the case of a long gun consisted of three or four such bored pieces welded together.[55] The method of boring guns appears to have been followed throughout the Indian Ocean. The nineteenth-century naturalist, Alfred Russel Wallace, discovered that in the island of Lombok to the east of Bali, the gun-smiths were still turning out beautiful

Plate 64 Integral moulds for casting large guns in Jaigarh cannon-foundry, Amber, Jaipur, seventeenth century.

pieces following the old technique. 'Two guns were exhibited,' he wrote,

one six the other seven feet long, and of a proportionately large bore ... I was anxious to know how they bored these long barrels, which seemed perfectly true and are said to shoot admirably; and, on asking the Gusti, received the enigmatical answer: 'We use a basket full of stones' ... I asked if I could see how they did it ... He soon returned with the most extraordinary boring-machine, the mode of using which the Gusti then explained to me. It was simply a strong bamboo basket, through the bottom of which was stuck upright a pole about three feet long, kept in its place by a few sticks tied across the top with rattans. The bottom of the pole has an iron ring, and a hole in which four-cornered borers of hardened iron can be fitted. The barrel to be bored is buried upright in the ground, the borer is inserted into it, the top of the stock or vertical shaft is held by a cross-piece of bamboo with a hole in it, and the basket is filled with stones to get the required weight. Two boys turn the bamboo round. The barrels are made in pieces of about eighteen inches long, which are first bored small, and then welded together upon a straight iron rod. The whole barrel is then worked with borers of gradually increasing size, and in three days the boring is finished ... when examining one of the handsome, well-finished, and serviceable guns, it was very hard to realize the fact, that they had been made from first to last with tools hardly sufficient for an English blacksmith to make a horse-shoe.[56]

The technology of iron and steel production. The fact that the Asian metal smith was capable of casting large objects in iron as well as in bronze was due to the fact that the essential technique of iron-working was mastered well before the Christian era. The famous iron-pillar in Delhi which has resisted rust and corrosion for more than two thousand years exemplified a long tradition of iron smelting and producing steel directly in the furnace. The high-carbon 'Indian' steel from which the celebrated Damascene swords were made had in fact a much wider provenance than the subcontinent itself and steel of similar metallurgical qualities was to be found throughout the Islamic world. The main feature of the Damascene blade was the 'jauhar' or the water of the etched metal, an irregular pattern visible on the surface of the swords. The Damascus blade, as C. S. Smith has pointed out, was made from a steel with a 1.5–2 per cent carbon content and the pattern appeared from the crystalline structure of the metal after it was elongated by moderate forging. A pre-Islamic writer Aus b. Hajar has left a lyrical description of the blade, a corrugated surface of glistening water resembling a pond over which the wind was blowing.[57] Manufactured all the way from Damascus, Isfahan, and southern India, the Damascus swords were obviously articles of exceptionally high value and at the very top of the metal smith's art. Iranian merchants travelled to the Deccan (Hyderabad) to purchase steel made at the great medieval iron-furnace of Konasamundram and Dimdurti. So legendary was the reputation of the Indian Damascene swords that the Abbasid Caliph Mutawakkil, who was a connoisseur and a collector of fine objects, offered an unlimited sum for a fabulous weapon which had found its way to Basra. The sword was found, purchased for the Caliph, and entrusted to a specially-appointed aide, Baghir, the Turk. It became the Caliph's murder weapon when Baghir joined a conspiracy against his master. Steel weapons were also exported to the Middle East from the iron-works in the Malayan peninsula and the swords were tempered in the Yemen.[58]

Metallurgists in India, China, and the Middle East had discovered from long practical experience that the quality and the utility of iron depended on the chemical transformations of the metal during the process of heat-treatment. The first stage in the production of Asian iron in the charcoal-fired furnaces was the smelting of cast-iron from the raw ores or metal-bearing sand. In China, as the supply of wood in the vicinity of the northern iron-works was depleted, other methods of smelting were developed using coal.[59] During the second stage, cast iron was transformed into wrought iron, by re-heating and stirring the molten metal in a reverberatory (puddling) furnace or by repeated forging and hammering of the original blooms. Finally, steel was produced either by combining cast and wrought iron or as in the case of India by smelting small quantities of wrought iron in crucibles with an admixture of wood and green leaves.

Although before the Western discovery of the large-scale iron plants of the nineteenth century, China was the only country in the world known to have used the blast furnace to produce molten cast iron, it would seem from Albiruni's description that the method was followed in the Islamic world also.[60] The Chinese furnaces producing both cast and wrought iron were described in detail by Sung Ying-hsing. The furnace walls were constructed from a salt and mud mixture. Any crack in the surface of the refractory clay within the furnace would condemn the process of smelting to certain failure. The push-and-pull bellows were operated by a team of six men and a complete cycle of casting lasted for a period of twenty-four hours, after which the molten metal would flow out from an opening at the side of the furnace. If it was intended to produce wrought iron immediately after the first smelting, the mixture was allowed to run off into square holes where it was vigorously stirred with willow sticks to create the necessary oxidising conditions. The malleable pure iron slabs were subsequently hammered into round pieces before being sent to the market.[61] Indian furnaces were similar to the Chinese ones in construction. But the ore was fused at a lower temperature producing bloom iron.[62] It was necessary to re-heat the blooms in a secondary furnace and forge them in order to produce proper wrought iron which could be used by the blacksmiths. The key to successful iron production in China and India lay in the development of the air blast supplied by the push-and-pull bellows. Buchanan's drawings and description of the south Indian furnaces make it quite clear that the action of the Indian bellows was basically similar to that of the Chinese ones. However, some of the Chinese furnaces were equipped with water-driven bellows and the piston operating them worked through a crank-shaft converting the rotary movement of the water wheel into longitudinal motion.[63]

If the essential technology of producing malleable iron and pure steel was known in both India and China, the question remains as to why Indian metallurgists did not utilise high temperature fusion to make cast iron. The clue to a possible answer lies in the nature of objects manufactured from metals in the two respective civilisations. In India metal-casting was confined to smaller objects than in China and the preferred technique appears to have been welding, hammering, and the use of cold chisel. On the other hand, the technology of bronze casting directly from the smelting furnace into the object-moulds may have given the Chinese metallurgists an insight into and the necessary experience of working high temperature furnaces. The technology had clearly appeared very early in the history of China, though cast iron, as we have seen, needed to be converted into wrought iron by a secondary process as much in China as in India. At what period Indian smiths mastered the art of casting iron objects is not known for certain. Alexander Hamilton mentioned at the turn of the seventeenth century that large anchors for ships were cast in moulds at the Orissa foundries, though the quality was not as good as in Europe.[64] Little information is available in the sources on the organisation of the metal industries and the system of commercial distribution. According to Buchanan a typical smelting-house would employ four bellows men, three men to prepare the charcoal, and three women and one man to collect and wash the iron-bearing sand. The furnace worked for four months in the year, as the sand mining was seasonal. Some of the workmen cultivated their land during the off-season or supplied charcoal to the towns. The remuneration of the workers including the profit of the master-craftsman owning the furnace and the equipment took the form of a distribution of either the iron ingots or finished objects such as plough shares.[65]

Glass and ceramics

Glass-making. The attainment of high temperature and its control were critical not only for the metallurgical industries in Asia but also for the manufacture of fine glassware and porcelain. The Islamic world had inherited a long tradition of glass-making from the period of antiquity and carried it to a new level of development. Damascus and other Syrian towns took the lead in the production of export ware but glass was also made in Egypt, Iraq, and Iran. The translucence of the Syrian glass and its extreme delicacy gave rise to proverbial comparisons which used expressions such as 'more delicate than Syrian glass' or 'clearer than Syrian glass'.[66] Muslim glass-makers utilised the blow-pipe, rods, pliers, and shears to work the molten glass into finely shaped objects, and a cutting wheel mounted with abrasives or steel wire was used to engrave decorative patterns on the glass surface.[67] Social conventions and aesthetic sensibilities created a distinctive assembly of glassware forms and shape in the Muslim West which was shared with Europe when Italian glass-making became a market-leader. But in the Indian subcontinent ritualistic authority and the laws of religious pollution ruled out the usage of fragile but high-valued glass and porcelain as objects for serving food and drink. The manufacture of beads and bangles remained the basic outlet for glass-making in India. Raw glass of different colours was purchased from the furnaces by travelling artisans who fashioned it into bangles in various urban bazaars.[68] Indian ornamental beads enjoyed a high reputation in the export markets and have been found in places as far away as West Africa. Islamic and Indian glass was essentially of soda-silicate type and the technique of manufacture involved a two-stage process. A mixture of silicate sand and quartz or flint was first heated and melted in crucibles in the furnace and allowed to cool. The resulting 'frit' was subsequently crushed and mixed with silica and re-melted to produce pure glass. The fire was kept going in the furnace for up to eight days, though the temperature remained lower than that producing frit.[69] The technology of fine glass production had evidently reached a high point among the Islamic craftsmen and there is evidence that there was a westward move-

ment of the workers in the aftermath of the political devastations in Syria
brought about by the Mongol invasions of the thirteenth century.

Ceramics. Objects made out of glass held a strong aesthetic and luxury appeal
in most premodern Asian societies. Pottery on the other hand traced its origin
to the strictly functional and only after a long period of time stretching out
over many thousands of years did the art of the potter reach the status of
refined objects. Without pottery there would have been no settled agriculture
and no crop production. This generalisation however is axiomatic and non-
historical. It is likely that the art of making storage jars and cooking pots in
unbaked and baked clay progressed alongside the larger historical development in sowing crops and developing land for intensive food production. It is
not possible to determine to what extent the manufacture of pottery based on
the technique of firing earthenware became in our period of study a separate
industrial activity extending beyond its immediate locality. The decentralised
nature of pottery-making and its wide dispersion in urban and rural locations
would suggest that coarse earthenware products were traded over relatively
short distances. An additional constraint on the wider exchange of pottery was
the fact that communities developed as in the case of textiles individual forms,
design, and shapes to suit their particular functional and symbolical usage. In
Sanskritic India dietary laws made people unwilling to use clay vessels as anything other than disposable articles. As a result pottery in South Asia did not
progress beyond the art of the village workman. The traditional Indian potter,
whether making purely functional objects or the images of deities for religious
occasions, did not lack artistic skills. The profusion of pottery types found
throughout the subcontinent prove that the usage was finely differentiated by
social norms. It was unthinkable that particular types of vessel used respectively for storing oils, ghi, molasses, grain, or water should be interchanged.
Similar conventions also prevailed in the Islamic world, South East Asia, and
the Far East.

Among all the craft products nothing illustrates better than ceramics the
separation between the functional, aesthetic, and the luxurious. Fine stone-
ware, decorated glazed pottery, and the true porcelain, whether made in the
Middle East or China, found markets far distant from their place of origin.
Even when the objects did not travel far and were manufactured to a standard
less than the luxury level, the aesthetic expressions displayed by the ceramic
artist placed their products in a world entirely different from that of earthenware. The point is well illustrated by the fragment of a bowl excavated at the
Ghubayra site (late 13th century) in the Kirman province of Iran. The inside
of the bowl is painted in black under blue glaze and the effect is obviously
intended to represent the sea. The outline of a large shark swimming through
shallow water is captured to perfection on the concave surface of the bowl (see
Plate 65). The piece was apparently of middle quality. The flow of artistic and

Plate 65 Islamic pottery from the Ghubayra site in Iran, showing the perspective drawing of a shark swimming in clear sea, black painting under blue-glaze, concave surface.

technological ideas between China and the Middle East effected through Central Asia in our period vitalised the ceramic industries of both the regions.[70] Muslim potters had a good knowledge of the technique of polychrome glazing and their mastery of tile-making in blue or green colours kept the Islamic ceramic industry at the forefront of development in mass production. The blue-and-white painting under a transparent glaze so commonly seen on Chinese export porcelain after the Mongol period may have owed its inspiration to the pull of Islamic demand. The ability of Asian countries to produce true high quality porcelain was constrained by technical knowledge and experience, and it was also influenced by the dominant position occupied by China, the world's leading porcelain manufacturer before the eighteenth

Plate 66   Caravan train transporting porcelain, fifteenth century.

century. Fine porcelain was made in Siamese kilns and commanded the attention of contemporary collectors. The scale of the Chinese porcelain industry
exceeded anything other regions could master. Archaeological findings
throughout Central Asia, the Middle East, East Africa, India, and South
East Asia show conclusively that Chinese export porcelain dominated the
Asian markets. The domestic demand within China likewise created a vast
outlet for ceramic products which differed in points of detail from the specialised items made for the overseas consumers. In common with silk and brocade,
the imperial demand for porcelain was a major element in sustaining the
industry at a high level of activity.

By the T'ang period the Chinese ceramic artists had mastered the technique
of firing clay vessels with coloured or transparent glazes. The purity of form
and design reached in this age remained a model for the future generations of
potters. Under the patronage of Sung ceramic collectors the porcelain industry
of China attained full maturity and a freedom of expression in artistic forms
that was both classic and innovative.[71] With the expansion of China's sea-
borne trade from the eleventh century, the diffusion and acceptance of Chinese
ceramics in Asian societies matched the earlier and better documented demand
for prized silk pieces. The export trade continued vigorously under the Ming
and Ch'ing dynasties and by the time Sung Ying-hsing came to write his
technological treatise, the two pottery towns, Ching-te-chen in the Kiangsi
province and Te-hua in Fukien, occupied the premier positions in manufacture
and export. The china-clay used in the kilns of Ching-te-chen was brought
from the neighbouring quarries in Wu-yuan and Ch'i-men. The clay was
moulded into square blocks and transported in small boats. Sung's account of

the preparation of the clay, glazes, and the firing sequence in the kilns is extremely detailed and he clearly identified the deep blue glaze used in Ming chinaware as a Muslim innovation originating in Persia.[72]

Miscellaneous industries. Textiles, metalware, porcelain, and glass distinguished in many striking ways the attributes of great Asian civilisations. Many other forms of industrial and semi-industrial production fused with agriculture, trade, and the services to constitute an entire structure of essential economic activities. Sugar-pressing, refining, and the manufacture of confectionary from white sugar progressed from the processing of an agricultural product to the use of large industrial plants.[73] The manufacture of edible oils was less complicated but it was an indispensable part of the urban and rural life. The distillation of alcohol and delicate perfumes from flower petals called for a considerable capital outlay on stills and the raw materials and it was technologically demanding. Leather tanning and saddlery, shoemaking, bookbinding, enamelling, mirror-making, coral- and jade-carving, all these permanent features of civilised life in the Indian Ocean sustained themselves on a hereditary transmission of crafts skills which finely differentiated objects of daily use from those valued by collectors and connoisseurs. In his chapter headed 'Of Mechanicks and Trades', Sir John Chardin was guilty of contradicting himself when he castigated the Persians and other Asians for their apparent laziness, lack of innovation, and insensitivity to European aesthetics:

The *Eastern* people are naturally soft and lazy, they work for, and desire only necessary things. All those beautiful pieces of painting, carving, turning, and so many others, whose beauty consists in an exact and plain imitation of nature, are not valued among those *Asiaticks*: they think, that because those pieces are of no use for the occasions of the body, they do not therefore deserve our notice: In a word, they make no account of the making of good pieces; they take notice only of the matter, which is the reason that their arts are so little improved; for as to the rest, they are men of good parts, have a penetrating wit, are patient and sincere, and would make very skilful workmen, were they paid liberally.[74]

Chardin's own descriptions of the Persian brocade-weavers, enamellers, goldsmiths, plasterers, and gunsmiths prove that his real meaning was quite different from the stereotype intended to satisfy the theorists of oriental despotism. He must have been aware that without generous patronage, the exquisite skills of the hereditary craftsmen could scarcely have been preserved from the Babylonian times to his century. The carpets and fine brocades were admittedly woven by people working long hours in unhealthy conditions, very often by young female children. The objects themselves however display a vigour of mind and spirit which is in strange contradiction to the alleged exploitative status of the workmen.

Plate 67 Chinese blue-and-white dish, from Hsuan-te period, 1426–35.

Plate 68 Overglaze enamelled tea pot, Ch'ien-lung period, 1736–95.

11

The historical dimensions of towns and cities

Semiotic topology and urban history

The formation and structure of the urban sign. The symbols which signify the urban and the rural are an integral part of the collective memories and consciousness of mankind.[1] The historical separation between the two categories was of course a finite process in time but it is no longer capable of exact measurement. The mental images derived from the objective reality of the town and the countryside tend to possess strong dialectic overtones. One set of signs and significations would exclude the other and at the same time, establish its own limits of comprehension with reference to the excluded set. The urban history of towns and cities is more than a history of concrete objects. It is constantly transformed into an entire system of signification. The image of the city extends beyond the city itself to its articulation, in precise and distinctive ways, to the abstract concept of the state, government, society, and economic activities. The subterranean structure of thought and language relating to urban life is so strong that few historians ever think it necessary to examine explicitly the theoretical foundations on which they have built their description and analysis of towns and cities as recognisable entities in history. From Max Weber onwards the role of urbanism as social constructs, whether in the historical context or in contemporaneous life, has been almost exclusively the preserve of social thinkers.[2] A notable exception is of course the work of Fernand Braudel. The history of the Mediterranean, as he has demonstrated so powerfully, revolved around the history of towns:

The prevailing human order in the Mediterranean has been one dictated primarily by towns and communications, subordinating everything else to their needs. Agriculture, even on a very modest scale, is dictated by and directed towards the town; all the more so when it is on a large scale. It is because of the towns that man's life has taken on a faster rhythm than it would under natural conditions.[3]

Although the emphasis here is placed on the physical linkages between towns and the order of social activity, in a later work Braudel would elaborate on the mental domain of the urban world. The problem at the centre of his perception of historical urbanism is embodied in the statement that a town is a town wherever it is. The reflection was prompted by the long European search for

338

Plate 69 An Islamic town-scene, seventeenth century.

the ideal urban type in which the original and creative power of Western towns, Braudel felt, occupied too much limelight.[4]

The historian of the Indian Ocean finds little to disagree with in this particular view of urbanism as a universal and abstract historical category. A simple proof can be offered in its support. In all the major languages of Asia the equivalent word for a town is understood by the speakers without the help of a lexicon. The sign ignores the specific form of urban characteristics for a generalised one, in which defensive walls, the density of housing, the splendour of public buildings, concentration of people, and the presence of markets can all be combined or interchanged as signifiers to a universal set of signification. The articulation of the signifiers to the signified is always a selective process: the totality of the physical urban characteristics represents a logical space from which only certain features are selected in order to symbolise the idea of the urban.[5] Thus, the unit of space signified as urban is both a construction and a variable.[6] Nevertheless, a town is never confused with a village, a hamlet, army camp, or with any other objective category of space. The word establishes many different levels of signification, with a remarkable disjunction appearing between the objects and their symbolic inscription in the domain of the mind. Actual physical differences between the urban and the rural cannot be perceived, nor evaluated without a 'pure sign' of the town establishing itself rigidly as a category through a process of exclusion. The signification of the urban thus acts as a signifier to a wider range of historical contexts and associated signifiers.

When all the detailed, empirical studies on separate themes of Asian history are taken into account, when we have finished examining the multi-dimensional features of settled agriculture, nomadism, the role of long-distance trade, and industrial production, the historical conclusions seem to converge. The point of that convergence is the function of urban centres in the wider development of society and even of civilisation. Towns and cities have existed in Asia longer than recorded history. The archaeological remains of the ancient Indus valley and those of Mesopotamia enable us to infer some striking points about the process of urbanisation in human history. The large size of the houses and public buildings, the elaborate town planning, and the careful provision of the essential services such as water supply, drainage, and access suggest that man was capable of conceiving urban life as an entity constant through time and not subject to later improvements. Like the knowledge of fire or the technique of metallurgy, the urban environment and its full attributes must have emerged after a very short period of evolution. Just as iron production required the provision of fuel and ores, the construction of a furnace, and the means for creating high temperatures as a single integrated process, so the urban phenomenon was a structured unity. Its component parts were no more divisible than the human body and its limbs. The evidence of the Harappan or Mesopotamian cities leads to another important deduction. Substantial urban sites called for an entire system of economic, social, and political institutions that stretched out beyond the limits of the city itself and included wider areas of geographical space. Therefore, the urban-rural polarity, as old as settled agriculture and state systems, has a continuous history as an abstract idea in recognising the quality of what is rural and what is urban.

Urban typology in Indian Ocean history. To Asian historians, the ideological and the conceptual opposition between urban and rural, subsistence and market economies, between tribal life and centralised political empires, are perfectly clear and they have been part of a long historiographic tradition. An ancient Sanskrit text on architecture and town-planning went to the extreme length of giving the exact specifications of different types of towns and villages. The *Manasara* (*c.* 5th–6th century AD) identified no less than eight kinds of urban conglomerations with varying levels and attributes of political sovereignty.[7] In the receding world of fourteenth-century Islam, Ibn Khaldun would make an explicit connection between the rationale of urban settlements and political power. 'Sedentary culture in cities comes from dynasties', because it was a condition that was the result of custom and went 'beyond the necessary conditions of civilization'.[8] Sedentary culture as a historical and social phenomenon was always evaluated in Ibn Khaldun's mind as an opposition to the nomadic, bedouin way of life. In this reasoning, the relative prosperity and the political strength of nations fixed the urban limits of the economic divisions of labour and social differentiations. A simple conjunction existed between the power of the state and the economic fortunes of cities. Industrial crafts multiply, thrive and prosper in cities, 'because cities have a highly developed civilization and their inhabitants are very prosperous, and the dynasty is at the root of it, because the dynasty collects the property of the subjects and spends it on its inner circle and on the men connected with it who are more influential by reason of their position than by reason of their property'. Cities close to the centres of political power, Ibn Khaldun thought, would naturally grow wealthy, living off the public treasury in much the same way that the water of a river made everything green around it. Urban settlements at the periphery of the empire seemed in contrast to be predominantly nomadic in character, their markets lacking the variety and richness of markets in the primate cities.

The opposition between the sedentary (*umran hadara*) and the nomadic (*umran badawa*), as presented in the *Muqaddimah*, can be taken as the mirror image of our view of the urban–rural dichotomy. It is evident that Ibn Khaldun's city derived its dynamics from certain particular elements of Islamic history and the ecology of the arid zones. The historical theory and the observations embodied in the presentation are all the same capable of wider and more generalised transformations. Ibn Khaldun significantly refrained from suggesting any specific origin of cities in the life of Islam. The present-day historian likewise looks in vain for a unique set of conditions that explain the rise of urban settlements in the remote prehistoric past. It is apparent from an examination of the historical evolution and the function of towns and cities in the Middle East, India, South East Asia, and China that each particular region which seems to form a unity of some kind created its own conditions of urbanisation. In their attempt to isolate urbanism as a unique social entity, the historians have been asking themselves the wrong question. The rationale for the emergence of towns and cities, the historic process which created the rupture between the urban and the rural, lies beyond our exact comprehension. It is, however, possible to look for the consequences of urbanisation on premodern systems of economic production, social structure, and political control. Can one really escape the conclusion that the human preference for living in nuclear families is echoed in their preference for living in urban locations? The historical phenomenon of urbanisation must be taken as a given and become the nodal point for further subsequent analysis.

The necessary conditions of urbanisation in Asia: the principles of urbanisation. The depth of urbanisation in the regional history of premodern Asia depended to a great extent on three interrelated conditions. If the locality was part of a centralised political empire, it was almost axiomatic that the imperial capital would serve as a model for locating power and delegated sovereignty in an urban environment. Active long-distance trade and a dominant role played by merchants and bankers in turning rural production into disposable state finance also strengthened the position of central places in the spatial hierarchy of social consumption and economic production. A strong association between religion, cultural life, and towns produced very similar results. These three conditions for urban development were present in varying degree and intensity in the lands bordering the Indian Ocean and in the vast open spaces of Inner Asia. It is true that towns were the products of communication, just as they influenced it in turn. But their capacity to respond to changing conditions, their rise, growth, and decline, the hierarchy of function and physical size, were related to the conjunction between religion, political power, and economic considerations.

The social dimensions of urban settlements in Asia were linked to those of space through the need for centrality.[9] It is obvious that there are substantial savings in transaction costs if central places serve as redistributive points in a multilateral exchange system.[10] This particular theory of the central place demands an additional condition, the necessity for political order which provides security, the storage facilities, and the contractual conventions for transactions involving a time-delay. The services in turn are supported by taxation and the growth of political power on the part of central authority which may well create the kind of market-less trading cited by Karl Polanyi in his study of ancient Mesopotamia.[11] The location of such central authority in urban settlements is connected with an apparent paradox emphasised by most urban historians of premodern Asia. The towns needed to draw their food supplies and industrial raw materials from the countryside but gave very little in return. The traffic seems to have been decidedly one-way. A possible explanation of the imbalance can be found in the fact that the process of exchange was not always symmetrical as between the same categories of objects. Commodities could be exchanged for money as a store of wealth, for services, and most important of all, for political considerations. The buying of protection from violence was as much an act of exchange as any other 'market' transactions. Our historical evidence fails to support the view that the major civilisations of the Indian Ocean were the sum-total of inward-looking agrarian communities without the need for trade and urban centres. Contemporaneous descriptions of space and travel accounts highlight the role of towns and cities as much as the productive capacity of rural areas. The linkages between the towns and the countryside were expressed through a mechanism of exchange, the exact form and pattern of which varied over time and in different regions. Fernand Braudel has isolated the historical variations in his three-fold typology of towns: open towns, undifferentiated from their hinterland and which even merge into it, towns closed in on themselves in every sense, their walls marking the boundaries of a particular way of life more than just a unit of space, and finally, those that are held in subjection by the whole range of known controls by the prince or state.[12] Braudel is here looking at the evolution of the urban phenomenon through the eyes of the townsman. When the viewpoint is reversed, he is able to see that all world economies recognise a centre, some focal point that acts as a stimulus to other regions and is essential to the existence of the economic unit as a whole. In the Mediterranean that centre in the fifteenth and sixteenth centuries was a narrow urban quadrilateral composed of Venice, Milan, Florence, and Genoa.[13]

The urban history of the Indian Ocean towns in our period of study yields many similar structures with clearly demarcated spatial boundaries which vary in size and complexity. Long-distance trade in the whole of the Indian Ocean and the Mediterranean, it is possible to argue, was held together by the urban pull of Canton, Malacca, Calicut, Cambay, Hormuz, Aden, Alexandria, Aleppo, Venice, and Genoa and it added in turn to the urban growth. The ceaseless circulation of goods and men on the latitudinal axis of the world is difficult to think of without the history of these trading cities.[14] Braudel's concept of the urban typology can be extended further to include a functional hierarchy of towns measured against the dimensions of both space and time.[15] The influence of a primate city such as Constantinople, Damascus, Baghdad, Delhi, or Peking, occupying a rank at the top of the spatial hierarchy, extended to the whole area of the empires over which they presided and it remained stable over a reasonably long period of time. The next in order of space is the regional city, followed by the provincial and district towns serving localised areas. The method of scaling (by taking a single function at a time) results in variable hierarchies. For example, a great capital city (Cairo, Isfahan, or Agra) would unquestionably be placed in the primate category when ranked by its political influence, but its economic or cultural roles may have a different spatial classification. Furthermore, the city is both a producer and a consumer.[16] The population size of an imperial capital and its correspondingly large consumption needs again locates it as a central place with the highest spatial rank. Needless to say the trajectory of time would switch between the different functional role of the city, placing it now at the top of one classification and that of another later.

Religion and the pattern of urbanisation

Islam and urbanisation. The argument adopted so far leads to the conclusion that any complex civilisation has an in-built political, economic, and social structure that makes it gravitate towards the formation of multi-functional urban localities. Certain historical facts clearly stand out. Like the Mediterranean, the Middle East derived its historical vitality from the presence of towns and cities. Wherever Islam made its presence felt as an indivisible combination of power, communication, and exchange, urbanisation flourished and expanded. As a religion born in Medina and growing up in Mecca, the urban origin and the urban leadership of Islam would remain a constant among the members of the 'umma' all through the centuries. When Basra was founded as a winter quarter for the army (*c.* 14, AH 16–17), the mosque appeared within the 'Dar al-Imara' (the quarter for the chief). At first it was nothing more than a simple structure built of sun-dried bricks ('labin') and thatch. The modular plan of Kufa was very similar, and at al-Fustat, the site of an older town, the new camp contained a mosque in the garden where ᶜAmr Ibn al-ᶜAs had planted his famous victorious standard. The tradition was carried to al-Mada'ain (Ctesiphon), Damascus, and Jerusalem in greater splendour. The Church of St John in Damascus, according to later Muslim historians, housed both Christians and Muslims in two separate partitions, giving rise to the belief that the capital of the Byzantine empire in Syria came into Arab possession by conquest and capitulation.[17]

The form and the architectural details of the mosque in Mecca, the external curtain-walls, the cloister ('riwak'), the open courtyard ('sahn'), the pillared hall facing the kibla ('liwan'), the mihrab and the minbar, the soaring corner spires, and the dazzling white of the whitewash, signified through tangible visual symbols an original association between the twin-cities of Hijaz and their innumerable transplanted off-shoots in the Yemen, Iraq, Syria, Egypt, the Maghreb, Andalusia, and India.[18] The strength of that idea can still be sensed today in Zabid, a walled oasis-city surrounded by the burning desert of

Plate 70   The Great Mosque in Zabid, the Yemen (see below).

the Tihama, as the Great Mosque (see Plate 70) dramatically comes into view
through the tangled alleyways of the busy souk. Zabid was one of the earliest
centres of Islamic theology and learning, almost contemporaneous with
Mecca and Medina in its adoption of Islam (AD 631). The morphism between
religion, society, town planning, and architecture remained strong throughout
the towns and cities of the Tihama, the narrow coastal plain which stretches
from Aden to the Sinai, and in the highlands of the Hijaz and the Yemen.

No one could deny that if there were such a thing as an Islamic city, its
signifier should be Mecca, followed by Medina. Here is al-Muqaddasi describing the spiritual fountain-heads of the Balad al-Islam:

Makkah, the metropolis of this province, is laid out around the Ka'bah in a narrow
valley enclosed by the surrounding hills. I saw three other towns similarly situated,
'Amman in Syria, Istakhr in Faris and Qayatu-l-Hamra in Khurasan. The houses of
Makkah are built of black, smooth stones and also of white stones; but the upper parts
are of brick. Many of them have large projecting windows of teak-wood and are
several stories high, whitewashed and clean . . . In breadth the town is as wide as the
valley. The masjid which is somewhat oblong in form, is situated two-thirds down the
city, towards the Masfalah quarter . . . Round the court three porticoes have been
erected on pillars of white marble which al-Mahdi brought from al-Iskandariyyah to
Jedda by way of the sea. The mosque in its present form was founded by him. The
porticoes have their walls decorated on the outside in mosaic, artisans from Syria and

Egypt being specially imported for the work. The names of these still appear on their work.[19]

The Andalusian pilgrim Ibn Jubayr actually transcribed the inscription on the wall of the west cloister: 'The servant of God Muhammad al-Mahdi, Prince of the Faithful, may God have him in His care, ordered the enlargement of the Sacred Mosque for the pilgrims to God's House and for those upon the ʿumrah, in the year 167 [AD 783].'[20] Yathrib (Medina) was the City of the Prophet, about half the size of Mecca, and surrounded by gardens and palm-groves. Although the town had a bright and cheerful aspect, its houses were built of sun-dried bricks and mud walls. The original mosque had been replaced by al-Walid and built on the plan of the Great Mosque of Damascus.[21] Al-Muqaddasi visited Zabid also. It was a splendid, well-built town; known commonly as the Baghdad of the Yemen. The citizens included men of letters, merchants, and political leaders, and it was a rich town. The mosque was at some distance from the market, clean and well paved. 'In short, Zabid was a noble town, unequalled all over al-Yaman', even though its streets were narrow, prices high, and fruits scarce.[22]

The plurality of the urban images: Jain, Islamic, and Portuguese influences in Cambay. It was to be expected that at the centre of Islam the isomorphism between the mosque and the city should be almost canonical. A Moroccan sultan, it was said, reproached his subjects when he saw a street without a mosque.[23] The endless descriptions by Muslim writers and European travellers of the religious shrines in Cairo, Damascus, and Baghdad were an expression of another, more fundamental projection of the collective mind on to the urban planning. The mapping relations held when Muslims crossed the Mediterranean and the Indian Ocean but the physical representations of the form changed. The mosque was still needed to proclaim the Islamic identity of a town and Islam is still an urbanising force in the lands of its recent settlement. But the architectural idiom could not always be kept in orthodox mode. By the time Islam reaches the Indonesian archipelago and the fringes of China, the architectural details of the mosques underwent a near-complete transformation and the structures are recognisable only by their conformity to the original plan.

In distant Cambay, one of the greatest commercial emporia of the Indian Ocean, as the Muslim ships arriving from the Red Sea, navigated their passage through a maze of vast salt-streaked sandbanks and submerged shoals, the first view of the town offered to sailors, merchants, and passengers would have been a symbol of political power, the massive ramparts of the fortress, commanding the landing points at the end of that dangerous gulf. Once inside the walls, passing through the vaulted sea-gate, the visitors would have been greeted by the sight of Cambay's beautiful cathedral mosque built in pink sandstone. The ornate carvings on the pillars and even whole structures could be identified as having been Sanskritic before an Indian temple was turned into a symbol of Islam. The canonical perfection of the plan and the design was such that there would have been no question whether the *masjid-i-jami* belonged to the faithful or the infidels. The city of Cambay however was predominantly of Jain faith and its adherents on their part would have seen and recognised in the mosque how the community's own religious and artistic sensibilities suffered a sea-change through the realities of Islamic conquest. When the Turkish warrior-sultans of Delhi conquered Gujarat and Cambay (1304–5), they had no wish to destroy the predominantly Hindu way of life prevalent in the region.[24] Cambay's beautiful brick-and-wood houses with fine projecting windows (see Plate 71) continued to shelter both the Hindus and Muslims alike, with only the architecture of power added to symbolise the Islamic conquest. The urban distinction of Cambay was not derived through religious associations during the period of its active life. That function was performed for itself by a splendid and ramified commercial structure which included the Middle East, east Africa, and the Indonesian archipelago. In the sixteenth century, the strong Portuguese presence in Cambay gave to the city an additional cultural identity. The 'armada de remas' organised by the viceroy of Goa each year escorted three separate convoys of local ships to Cambay in order to protect them from the Muslim privateers of the Malabar.[25] The Portuguese residents of Cambay had grown wealthy from their trade and empire in the Indian Ocean and there were many visible signs of their wealth and presence. The massive gates enclosing the Portuguese mansions pointed to the identity of the owners by the unmistakable Iberian emblems of the lions rampant and the triple crossed lances behind coats of arms (see Plate 72). 'In the quarter close to the sea,' wrote Tavernier in the 1660s, 'many fine houses, which they built and richly furnished after the manner of Portugal may still be seen; but at present they are uninhabited, and decay from day to day.'[26]

Was Cambay an Indian, Islamic, or Portuguese city? The question helps to demonstrate the multi-formed significations of urban images. It was all three simultaneously as an abstraction but one or the other according to the viewpoint of its inhabitants who were the principal actors in the city's functional life. No such doubt would have been voiced about the identity of Mecca, Meshed, Qum, or even Ajmer, a Rajput town which housed a famous shrine of Sufism in India. All these towns derived their signification from Islam. But they also shared one other quality with Cambay: each one was a metropolis in its own right, a primate city with the highest hierarchical rank in the order of space. The generative principle for Cambay was trade; it was religion for the others.

Towns in Sanskritic India. The famous Sanskritic temple towns of India, Varanasi, Mathura, Hardwar, Puri, Kanchipuram, Tirupati, and Madura,

Plate 71 Ancient wooden houses in the Indian-quarter of Cambay (see p. 347).

also possessed the quality of primate central places. Not all centres of Hindu pilgrimage were substantial urban complexes even when their sacred rank was high. The temple-site of Tirupati, one of the most sacred in southern India, was almost a town.[27] Albiruni was a contemporary of Mahmud of Ghazni who was to pillage and sack repeatedly the wealthiest temples in northern and western India (AD 1000–27), and he pointed out the mysterious quality of divinity which the Hindus assigned to the landscape of water ('tirtha'). Where flowing streams and rivers were lacking, enormous sacred reservoirs constructed with solid blocks of stones attracted throngs of pilgrims.[28] It was easy for fanatical Muslim rulers in search of financial prize to attack these places and despoil the visitors. The penultimate Afghan ruler of Delhi Sikander Shah Lodi (1489–1517) wanted to massacre the Hindu pilgrims at Thaneswar. When one of the leading Muslim jurists advised him against committing such an atrocity, the sultan replied in anger, 'If you had permitted me to do this, many thousands of Musulmans would have been placed in easy circumstances by it.'[29]

Plate 72 Gateway to a sixteenth-century Portuguese mansion in Cambay with lions rampant and triple crossed lances behind coats of arms (see p. 347).

In Albiruni's account both Varanasi and Mathura appear as places endowed with high sacerdotal qualities: to die in the city of Varanasi was to receive absolution from all sins and escape from the ever-repeating cycles of birth and death. Mathura, the city of the Krishna cult, was crowded with Brahmans, a sure sign of its role as a centre of learning. The urban splendours and the accessibility of the twin pilgrim-cities of northern Sanskritic India exposed them to repeated Muslim attacks and devastations. In 1194 the Turkish slave-commander Qutb al-Din destroyed nearly one thousand temples in Varanasi and ordered mosques to be built on their foundations.[30] The city and the image of its eternal sanctity possessed obvious powers of regeneration. While most Hindu urban centres in the north suffered near-complete metamorphosis from the thirteenth century onwards, Varanasi retained its original function and civic life. When Tavernier visited the place in the seventeenth century he found it a large and well-built town. The majority of the houses were made from bricks and cut stones and the structures were taller than in most other towns of India. The narrow width of the streets however created considerable inconvenience. Varanasi at this time had many fine caravanserais and the river-front once again presented a magnificent vista of temples and stone steps coming down to the water. But the premier and celebrated Visvesvara temple, built in the figure of a cross with towering cupolas, was soon to suffer destruction (1669) from the iconoclastic Mughal emperor Aurangzeb. Tavernier's description of the old temple just before its disappearance is a unique historical record. It is also a testimony to an institution which refused to die. Varanasi was a celebrated centre of Sanskritic learning in common with most pilgrim-towns of India. Mirza Raja Jai Singh, one of the most powerful Rajput princes in Aurangzeb's court, had founded a college next to the great temple for the education of the youths of distinguished families. 'On entering the court of this college,' Tavernier recorded, 'being curious to see it, and throwing my eyes upwards, I perceived a double gallery which ran all round it, and in the lower the two Princes [sons of Raja Jai Singh] were seated, accompanied by many young nobles and numerous Brahmans, who were making different figures, like those of mathematics, on the ground with chalk.' On seeing an European, the princes sent for Tavernier and asked him many things about Europe and especially about France. One of the Brahmans had two globes, which the Dutch had presented to the college, and Tavernier pointed out the position of France upon them. As a dealer in *objets d'art*, the French jeweller had time to note that the galleries of the largest caravanserai in Varanasi were used as markets where artisans themselves came to retail the fabulous, costly silk and brocaded fabrics woven in the suburbs: 'In this manner foreigners obtain them at first hand'.[31] Varanasi derived its primate role from religion. At the same time its large traffic in basic subsistence goods, pilgrims, and powerful patrons, gave to the city an import-

Plate 73 Palace on the Ganges in Patna, Bihar, India.

ant secondary function as a place of industrial production, banking, and finance.

The religious shrine and the school as urban symbols: the Middle East, South East Asia and the Far East. If the construction of the mosque was a duty and an attribute of royal power associated with Muslim urbanisation, so was the 'madrasa' or the college. Those founded in Syria and Egypt were especially splendid. Maqrizi in his description of medieval Cairo takes an imaginary walk from Bab Zuwayla to the Bab al-Futuh. Along the Bayn al-Qasrayn on the right there was the madrasa al-Salihiya where the teachers of the Hanifite and Hanbalite jurisprudence gathered. In fact, this area of Cairo contained seven major collegiate institutions.[32] The temple and the school were as much a part of urban signifiers in Muslim Middle East and Hindu India as they were in Java, Bali, Burma, Thailand, Cambodia, China, and Japan. The two greatest temple-complexes of Asia, Barabodur and Angkor Wat, must have had primate role in space similar to urban central places, although the extent of urbanism associated with the shrines cannot be known for certain. The profusion of temples (and institutions of Buddhist learning attached to them) in Ayuthya and Bangkok, successively capital-cities of Thailand, signified a distinctive theory and practice of both political sovereignty and social structure.[33] Kyoto and Nara in ancient Japan were temple-towns apart from being repositories of political power.[34] With the growth of Edo as the real capital of Tokugawa Japan in the seventeenth century, the titular presence of the emperor in Kyoto and its incomparable hill-top shrines, beautifully landscaped and surrounded by pine and cherry trees, heightened the cultural role of the imperial city at the expense of the political. The formal symbolical element in urban construction was present in most central places in the Eastern Indian Ocean. But the relationship between religion, society, and the city was not strictly isomorphic. The architects who built Chang-an, the capital of the Sui and T'ang dynasties in China, appeared to have discarded classical Chinese cosmological principles in urban construction and followed a practical plan.[35] Buddhist, Confucian, and other sectarian temples were nevertheless present in all towns and cities of imperial China. The small island of Bali contained so many temples of ancient Sanskritic origin that the morphism between its rice-growing wealth and social well-being was clearly articulated through religious architecture.

A comparative analysis of the primate cities and the principles which generated the spatial hierarchy reveals a substantial difference between the Western and the Eastern Indian Ocean. There is no question that temples, shrines, schools of religious instruction, and charitable houses run by priests and monks were an important attribute of cities wherever they were located in Asia. But the primate pilgrim-city which derived its first identity mainly from religious principles became fewer in an eastward direction and they disappear altogether in China. The Celestial Empire did not lack cities of premier rank and the influence of some extended even beyond China's political frontiers. People who visited them in the course of diplomacy, trade, or travel discovered that the grandeur of Chinese capital cities reflected the grandeur of Chinese culture and imperial traditions more than the projections of a universal religion. The contrast between the Indo-Islamic cities and those of South East Asia and China was grounded on real facts. Yet, the precise location of a city on the spatial grid of its influence are determined by complex and subtle historical interactions between different levels of social activity.

The permanent images of urban space. When the political and spiritual leaders of Islam decided to move the centre of power successively to Kufa, Damascus, and Baghdad, they ensured that the continuing process of Arab emigration out of the peninsula would reduce Mecca and Medina to places with a special urban status. The very word 'Haram' signifying the sacred territory of Mecca placed it directly on a relative scale of distances for all members of the faithful who wished to perform the hajj. Mecca remained all through the centuries a primate city with virtually unlimited spatial domain. For Muslims the 'Haram' as a point in social and physical space was both real and theoretical. Devout pilgrims from Granada, Tangier, Samarkand, and Malacca must undertake long and hazardous journeys by land and sea to reach Mecca; for a large number of Muslims the idea of the hajj would remain only a pious wish. The spatial role of Mecca held a different meaning for non-Muslims. They could see and appreciate its primate role as a theoretical construct. For the Hindu merchants of Surat, wishing to export cotton cloth to the hajj fair, the place had another meaning and another role. They would compete with the Indian Muslim pilgrims for shipping space but would not have been allowed to approach the 'Haram'. For traders and merchants, whether Muslim or non-Muslim, the perception of Mecca's role as a world-wide holy city was linked with its economic function as an important outlet for textiles and other goods. The relevant area of space in this case was fixed by the distance between Jedda and the textile-weaving centres in Egypt, Syria, Iraq, and India. Mecca had no direct primate political role in terms of space. Yet to be the custodian and guardian of the 'Haram' remained an idealised aspiration of most great political powers in the world of Islam.

It can be concluded from the historical examples discussed so far that the urban signification derived from religion operated at two levels of space: one was internal to the city, the other external. Where the religious signification created the dominant identity of a town, the mode of articulation to the larger social structure was 'extra muros' so to say: on the cognitive map the locality occupied a special position in relation to other towns and cities and other mental constructs. The nuances of a pilgrim-town visited by the adherents of its religion from a distance of perhaps many thousands of miles ignored the physical arrangement of space within the town in favour of the external projections. 'Many times we died and lived again – praise be to God,' exclaimed one distinguished 'hajji' as the party of which he was a member crossed over to Jedda from Aydhab, on the Sudanese shore of the Red Sea. The 'jilaba', the local variety of sewn ship ferrying the pilgrims, had met with gale-force wind in its perilous navigation through the coral reefs and the passengers listened with fear at the crash of the ship's hull grinding against under-water obstacles. Aydhab at this time (AD 1183) had no external walls and most of its houses were mere thatched huts, though some of the newly-built houses were made of plaster. It was in the desert with no vegetation and nothing to eat except what was imported from a distance. Yet, the port was crowded with ships from India and the Yemen and the local people made a large living by sailing the jilabas for the use of the hajj-pilgrims.[36] Compared to the opulent splendours of Mecca, even Jedda seemed much decayed (to the point of being just a village), though traces of its old walls and former habitations were still visible.[37] In Ibn Jubayr's account, as in many similar contemporary descriptions, an entire syntax of significations is revealed by the articulation between land and sea, between people and the means of transport, and between the final object of the journey and the places encountered on the way.

The political and economic dimensions of the urban hierarchy

Control over urban space as an attribute of power. Where urban centres enjoyed a distinctive place on the hierarchy of space through political or economic functions, the religious architecture of the city emphasised its intramural dimensions. The number and magnificence of sacred buildings in a political capital signified power together with other signifiers such as citadels, palaces, royal tombs, and caravanserais which in turn reflected its primate role. One of the most revealing expressions of the practical and symbolical power associated with urban architecture could be seen in a Mughal newsletter dated January 1670: 'in the month of Ramadan, the religious-minded emperor [Aurangzeb] ordered the demolition of the Hindu temple at Mathura known as the Dehra of Keshav Rai. His officers accomplished it in a short time. A grand mosque was built on its site at a vast expenditure.' The temple had been built by Raja Bir Singh Dev Bundela at a cost of thirty-three lakhs (3.3 million) rupees.[38] The urban central place and the hierarchy of towns were of course described, commented upon, and even analysed by many contemporary historians and thinkers. The present-day theorist in search of definitions and the typology of towns would find himself anticipated by a thousand years in a surprisingly comprehensive discussion on the subject written by al-Muqaddasi as a preface to his long list of towns and cities in the Balad al-Islam.

The geographical rank was arranged by al-Muqaddasi according to the analogy of political administration. Capitals are treated in his description as kings, provincial capitals as chamberlains, ordinary towns as cavalrymen, and villages as foot-soliders. He was aware that the word 'metropolis' had different meanings. The jurists defined it as a town with a large population, which has courts of justice and a resident governor and which meets the public charges from its own revenue; examples of such towns were ʿAththar, Nabulus, and Zuzan. The lexicographers explain it as a place which stands as a partition between two regions, such were al-Basra, ar-Raqqa, and Arrajan. The common people applied the term to any large and important town such as ar-Raiy, al-Mausil, and ar-Ramla. But our author would use the word metropolis to designate a city where the supreme ruler of a country resided, where the state departments had their quarters, in which the provincial governors received their investiture, and to which the towns of the province were referred. Damascus, Qayrawan, and Shiraz were such places. Some of the metropolises and district capitals had dependencies so large as to contain a number of towns. For example, there was Tukharistan in Balkh, the Bata'ih of Wasit in Iraq, and the Zab of Ifriqiyya. The list of primate political cities compiled by al-Muqaddasi included Samarkand, Iranshahr, Shahrastan, Ardabil, Hamadan, al-Ahwaz, Shiraz, as-Sirajan, al-Mansura, Zabid, Makka, Baghdad, al-Mausil, Dimashq [Damascus], al-Fustat, al-Qayrawan, and Qurtuba.[39] In our own time, Max Weber differentiated the 'city' in the economic and political sense from its social dimensions as seen in a 'commune'. Apart from its non-agricultural and commercial functions, the city as a commune must have, Weber thought, five physical and institutional features: fortifications, markets, courts of law, an associative structure, and finally, partial autonomy. The historical evidence however showed that the definition was only partially applicable even to the European cities of the Middle Ages and it excluded altogether those in the Middle East, India, China, and Japan.[40]

Primate cities in the Indian Ocean. Al-Muqaddasi's operational treatment of the Islamic primate cities as the repositories of political power and centres of administration was closely modelled on his first-hand experience of travelling through vast and diverse geographical regions united by a shared-theory of government and political administration. But in India, South East Asia, and the Far East, areas outside the direct influence of Islamic institutions, the association between the primate role of cities and the exercise of imperial power was even stronger. The Indian Ocean did not lack urban central places with primarily commercial or industrial functions. On the other hand, it was rare and even difficult for these cities to rival the visual appearance of Venice, Seville, and Amsterdam, places which lived mainly from the profits of long-distance trade and at the same time signified a larger, political role. There were of course exceptions. Marco Polo's famous account of Hangchow during the Mongol rule of China clearly indicate that the former capital of the Southern Sung was a thriving consuming, trading, and producing city with a still-large political presence.

Along the principal street of which we have spoken, which runs from one end of the city to the other, there are on one side and on the other houses, very large palaces with their gardens, and near by them houses of artisans who work in their shops, and at all hours are met people who are going up and down on their business, so that to see so great a crowd anyone would believe that it would not be possible that victuals are found enough to be able to feed it; and yet on every market day all the said squares are covered and filled with people and merchants who bring them both on carts and on boats and all is disposed of . . . this city had twelve different manner of trades, one of each craft . . . And each of these twelve has . . . 12,000 houses for each trade . . . And in each house . . . there were at least ten men to exercise those arts, and some fifteen, and some twenty, and thirty, and some forty.[41]

The economic and administrative importance of Hangchow made the Mongol rulers garrison the city with a force of 30,000 soldiers, which could be called out if any of the neighbouring districts or towns rose in rebellion. The sea-borne trade of Hangchow converged from all directions of the Indian Ocean and its merchants and traders built themselves sumptuous and richly-decorated houses, taking 'so great a delight in ornaments, paintings, and buildings, that the sums they spend on them are a stupendous thing'.

Were the epithets lavished by Marco Polo on the former Sung capital, the case of a Venetian finding things which he wanted to believe and see in another land? There are obvious exaggerations in his account. But European travellers in a Chinese or Indian town were more apt to criticise and notice the deviations from their own visual and social images brought from Europe than to super-impose these onto an Asian scene. On the other side of the Indian Ocean, the towns and cities of Gujarat received careful attention from Western travellers, just arrived from the Middle East or Europe. When Pietro della Valle went to Cambay (1623) he noticed that the houses were roofed over with tiles and the rain-water running off the roof was collected in cisterns. But he also observed that in Europe these buildings would be considered ordinary houses: here they were counted good and perhaps the best in the whole province. Earlier he had commented that the textile-weaving town of Broach, perched on top of its steep hill, was no bigger than Sienna in Tuscany and yet its population was three times larger. The cotton weavers of Broach supplied cloth to places as far away as Aleppo and Italy and the town yielded a large revenue in customs dues to the government.[42] Ahmedabad, founded in 1411 by Sultan Ahmed Shah of Gujarat on an older site, was to play a multi-functional role in its future history.[43] As the capital of maritime Gujarat, one of the most prosperous and agriculturally productive provinces in western India, it could boast of fine buildings and wide streets, and the city was a great industrial centre as well. Ahmedabad's dual status and its civic attractions gained from the conjunction between the political and economic factors, which was noticed by many con-temporary observers.[44]

On Monday, 25th of the first lunar month in AH 1027 (1618), the Mughal emperor Jahangir mounted his favourite elephant Surat-gaj in eager antici-pation of his first-ever visit to Ahmedabad. Crowds of people, men and women, had assembled near the walls, the gates, and the bazaars to greet the emperor. The first glimpse of the city however proved a little disappointing and not 'so worthy of praise as I had heard'. It was true that the main street leading through the bazaar was wide and spacious. But the shops were not proportional to the layout of the street. The buildings were all of wood and the pillars of the shops slender and mean. The prevailing dust annoyed the

Plate 74 Panorama of a Chinese town.

emperor sufficiently for him to say that the 'City of Ahmed' should be renamed the 'City of Dust'.[45] However, the *masjid-i-jami* commemorating the founder was a noble and large structure. Almost half a century later another stranger, this time from Europe, arrived in Surat and travelled to Ahmedabad (1666). In a description longer and more detailed than that of Jahangir's, Jean de Thevenot emphasised, how the city functioned both as a fortified political capital and a busy, well-planned place of business and industrial production.[46] In fact, the French traveller was unusually perceptive and his account of the Indian cities is an important source of information for the urban historians of

Mughal India. The road approaching Ahmedabad passed through a lovely plain watered by the river Sabarmati. This was the place where the wealthy citizens had built many beautiful summer-houses with large enclosed gardens; the still water of the huge masonry-lined lake Hauz-i-Qutb mirrored an exquisite pavilion-garden in its middle. The scattered outer suburbs led through a postern into the true suburb with continuous housing, and the town itself was strongly defended by stone and brick walls 'which at certain distance are flanked with great round towers and battlements all over. It is one of the places of Guzerat that is most carefully kept in order, both as to its walls and garrison, because it lies most conveniently for resisting the incursions of some neighbouring Rajas.' One of the signs of the commercial traffic coming to Ahmedabad was the fact that there were no less than twelve gates. A large square, the *maidan-i-shah* dominated the city-centre. It was 400 paces in breadth and seven hundred in length and planted with trees on all sides. Six or seven large cannon mounted on carriages were lined up on one side of the maidan. There were so many gardens and trees in Ahmedabad that from a high place the whole place looked like a forest of trees, the houses being concealed by them. Thevenot's description ended by listing the commodities manufactured and traded in the city; indigo, dried and preserved ginger, sugar, cumin, incense resins, tamarind, opium, and saltpetre. Among Ahmedabad's large variety of textiles the most notable were the satins, velvets, taffetas, and brocaded tapestries.[47]

Long-distance trade and urbanisation: economic factors. To go from the thirteenth-century Hangchow to the seventeenth-century Ahmedabad is to move a long way both in time and space. But the contemporary descriptions underline certain invariant principles in the urban category. Whether in China, India, or the Middle East, an important central place performed practical and symbolic roles for princes, soldiers, merchants, and artisans. The economic function of a capital city would grow in proportion to its primate status. A city of trade and industrial crafts inevitably attracted the attention of imperial powers in search of financial revenue. Thevenot concluded his chapter on Delhi with a revealing observation:

The ordinary Houses are but of Earth and Canes; and the other streets are so narrow, that they are altogether incommodious. But that inconvenience seems to contribute somewhat to the reputation of that Capital City of the Empire of the Mogull, for seeing that there is an extraordinary crowd in the Streets while the Court is there, the Indians are persuaded that it is the most populous City in the World; and nevertheless I have been told, that it appears to be a Desert when the King is absent. This will not seem strange if we consider, that the Court of the Great Mogul is very numerous, because the great Men of the Empire are almost all there . . . and then the great number of Merchants and other Trading People, who are obliged to stick to them, because in that Country there is no Trade nor Money to be got but at Court.[48]

Thevenot's Delhi was a new city founded by Shah Jahan and it had all the characteristics of an administrative enclave. In Surat, the treasure-house of the Mughal empire, the merchants had no need for aristocratic patronage in order to make a living. They managed a transcontinental trade on their own and the profits accumulated so relentlessly that reinvestment remained a perpetual problem. The millionaire bankers of Surat financed trade to Delhi, Agra, Bijapur, Golconda, Mocha, Hormuz, and Bandar Abbas. They lent money to the leading multinational corporations of the day, the Dutch and English East India Companies. So large was the financial presence of Surat in the Mughal empire that its governorship and political custody remained a matter of vital concern to the Durbar in Delhi. Yet, the city grew to its primate commercial status within a half a century or so as a successor to Cambay in the 1570s. John Henry Grose who saw Surat in the middle of the eighteenth century reflected that it was one of the best examples known in history of the power of trade to bring wealth, prosperity, and industrial skills to a particular geographical point in space within a short period of time.[49]

The association between political power, long-distance trade, and a high level of economic activities in cities of substantial status appears to have been almost taken for granted by many Islamic historians, even when the place in question owed its origin and development to the politics of power. The site of Baghdad, the Madinat as-Salam, was so closely associated with the artery of transcontinental trade passing along the Iraq-Syrian axis, that many contemporary writers recorded a tradition which ascribed its choice to a conscious decision taken by the caliph al-Mansur.[50] Al-Muqaddasi, for example, makes the wise inhabitants of the area say to the caliph:

We judge it advisable for you to settle in the midst of four districts, on the east Buq and Kalwadha, and on the west Qatrabbul and Baduraya. In this way, you shall always be surrounded by Palm trees and be near water, so that if one district suffers from drought, or fails to yield its harvests in due time, there will be relief in another. While being on the banks of as-Sarat, provisions will reach you in the boats which ply on the Euphrates. The caravans from Egypt and Syria will come by way of the desert, and all kinds of goods will reach you from China on the sea, and from the country of the Greeks and from al-Mausil by the Tigris. Thus surrounded by rivers, the enemy cannot approach you except in a ship or over a bridge, by way of the Tigris or the Euphrates.

Al-Mansur thus came to build the four main quarters of Baghdad, the Madinat al-Salam, Baduraya, ar-Rusafa, and Nahr al-Mu^calla.[51] The rapid expansion of the Abbasid capital, its suburbs and markets, since the completion of the Round City in 766 was no doubt a genuine urban process resulting from the growth of population and economic needs. For nearly 500 years, Baghdad would remain in the minds of all devout Muslims as a city which epitomised the political power of Islam, even when it was 'an effaced ruin', the statue of

Plate 75   An Anatolian mountain town.

a ghost, as Ibn Jubayr put it, without beauty and attractions to detain a stranger who was anxious to leave.[52]

The temporal dimensions of urban history

The perennial city and the ephemeral city: a twin typology. The palace or the citadel city built by ambitious rulers seldom succeeded as a metropolis unless it was able to acquire an independent economic base. The history of Samarra, founded during the reign of caliph al-Muʿtasim (836), illustrates the point. At the height of its life under al-Mutawakkil (847–61), the architectural and the artistic reputation of Samarra as a capital city of Islam was unrivalled. After Samarra ceased to be the official seat of the caliphate (889), its civic history fell into obscurity. By the tenth century, when al-Muqaddasi saw the site, the town was in total ruins. A traveller would walk two or three miles without coming upon any inhabited place.[53] In Mughal India, emperor Akbar chose the site of his magnificent new capital at Sikri to honour the local saint Shaikh Salim who had predicted the birth of his first male child (1570). The name 'Fathpur' signified the commemoration of the emperor's victories in Gujarat. The palace-complex and its surviving buildings still bear testimony to the cosmic vision of the society he ruled over. But the place was abandoned as an imperial city after only sixteen years.[54]

The temporal measure of urbanisation in our period of study is reflected in the difference between 'perennial' towns and those which were no more than the 'fire-flies' of history.[55] Urban sites in the Middle East and India going back to the period of antiquity or those of the early dynasties in the case of China provided a continuity of social life remarkable for its adherence to the civic forms. The 'ephemeral' towns also enjoyed intense activities and brilliant reputations during their brief existence, lasting in many cases for no more than half a century or so. Once such a town was abandoned, whether as a result of political or natural catastrophes, there was no further revival of its site. The perennial towns of course had their own history of expansion and recession. The slow decline of Baghdad or the successive foundation of new townships around an ancient site in Delhi did not indicate a total eclipse of the urban functions. The historical fortunes of Nanking in China changed many times but even when the Ming emperor Yung-lo transferred the capital to Peking in 1400, the city recovered from its initial demographic decline and retained its primate identity as a centre of scholarship, industrial production, and trade.[56] Of the six new Arab garrison-towns ('amsar') founded by Umar, three (Basra, Kufa, and Fustat) became perennial towns; Medina was already well established, while Jabiya and Jawwatha were soon abandoned.[57] The deliberate destruction of Fustat by fire in 1168 was prompted by the fear that the besieging Frankish army might capture it and pose a greater danger to neighbouring Cairo. Parts of the old town however were rebuilt when Saladin restored order in Egypt and contained the power of the Latin states in Palestine. Foreign travellers continued to visit Fustat to see the ancient relics and architectural remains.[58] Political events, unstable and unpredictable by the very nature of their occurrence, were a significant determinant in the growth or decline of towns. Referring to the famous Sikh destruction of Sirhind in the Punjab in 1708, the Mughal historian Khafi Khan lamented, 'Sirhind was an opulent town, with wealthy merchants, bankers, and tradesmen, monied men, and gentlemen of every class; and there were especially learned and religious men in great numbers residing there. No one found the opportunity of saving his life, or wealth, or family.'[59] For more than a century Sirhind had been a flourishing town in northern India, producing high-quality cotton textiles and containing 300 mosques and many Islamic shrines ('dargahs') and caravanserais.

The perennial cities of the Indian Ocean were the outcome of a number of complex historical forces acting together. Favourable geographical location,

Plate 76 The gateway to Lefke.

transport facilities, concentration of population, and the symbolic value of an exalted reputation, all played their part to ensure that an urban centre would retain a place on the hierarchical grid of central places. But all along, there were also famous and great historical cities in Asia which rose and fell with unexplained frequency. The ephemeral city, thrown up by the play of historical events, might possess many of the attributes of a perennial city and yet suffer destruction and total demise as if it had never existed. The history of Samarra and Fathpur Sikri was brief. That of Vijayanagara, the City of Victory, lasted more than two centuries, though it ended with just as spectacular suddenness. The capital was founded about 1335 by two Hindu princes in the Deccan, who succeeded in holding back the tidal wave of Turkish advance towards the south at a time when the Delhi Sultanate was beginning to lose the initial momentum gained from an invincible conquering reputation. The successor-rulers of Vijayanagara created one of the strongest military states in the region, and even in the early seventeenth century, as William Methwold, an official of the English East India Company recorded, the fortunes of the

Plate 77 The ruined fortifications of Vijayanagara.

'Lion Kings' (Narasingha) remained a topic of political news. The empire had already disintegrated and was well beyond any recovery.[60] In 1442, the Iranian envoy Abdur Razzak arrived at the imperial capital on a diplomatic mission. His astonished reaction at the sight it presented to the first-time visitor can be clearly sensed in the text.[61] Seven concentric rings of fortifications running along hills surrounded the inner city and the plains beyond the outermost walls were protected against massed cavalry or infantry charge by a passage about fifty yards in width in which stone shafts of the height of a man were driven firmly into the ground at close intervals. Between the first and the third walls, there were cultivated fields, gardens, and some houses. Beyond that point the true suburbs began with shops and markets, which continued into the inner city. The bazaars were flanked by arcades and magnificent galleries, and the jewellers sold their precious wares openly in the market. Streams flowing in stone-lined channels surrounded the king's palace, on one side of which stood the chancery ('diwan khana'), looking like a Persian 'chihal-sutun' or a hall of forty pillars. For the purpose of direct comparisons

Abdur Razzak took Herat, at that time the most celebrated Islamic capital city and pointed out that the inner city of Vijayanagara was about ten times the size of the chief market in Herat.[62] In 1566 after the battle of Talikota, Vijayanagara at last fell to a confederacy of Muslim powers in the Deccan. The city was pillaged and destroyed by fire. The capital of the shrunken Hindu state shifted to the far south and the ruins of the old town were soon claimed by the jungle from which it had risen in the first place.

Political power and urban geography: Mughal India. Nothing highlights more the historical role of the perennial city as the political map of the western Indian Ocean. Constantinople, Damascus, Baghdad, and Fustat were signifiers to a permanent signification of power. A score or more of lesser towns could easily be attached to the four primate cities. No Islamic ruler with aspiration to the caliphate could ignore the function of these places in the theory and practice of imperial legitimacy. It was not without reason that successive invaders from the Seljuk Turks to Amir Timur and Ottomans would attempt to capture at least one of these three key cities in the Islamic Middle East. A similar pattern is visible in the historical geography of the Mughal empire. Imperial control in Mughal India depended vitally on the control of six primate cities: Lahore, Delhi, Agra, Patna, Burhanpur, and Ahmedabad. If the north-western frontier is included in the empire, Kabul and Qandahar could also be added to the list. The control of these eight primate cities signified the possession of the peacock throne, the true sign of the Padshah of Hindustan. A single dissension or loss was a public proclamation of the weakening power of the reigning emperor. When a royal prince raised the flag of rebellion the capture of one of these cities was an inevitable part of the military campaign. The governor of Patna, Burhanpur, or Ahmedabad was often a close relative of the emperor. At the height of the Mughal imperial power, the main function of the eight primate cities was political. Their strategic or military significance was decidedly secondary. But there was an additional string of garrison towns, such as Gwalior, Allahabad, Chunar, Aurangabad, and Junnar, which provided the military sinews of the empire. The pattern of political conflicts in the subcontinent indicates clearly the key role played by towns and cities. The early life of Babar was a fierce and continual struggle for the mastery of Samarkand and Tashkent. As long as he remained a wandering warrior encamped in the high valleys of the Hindu Kush mountains, the political basis of his power also remained strictly limited. It was the possession of Kabul which eventually provided the real foundation of his later success in the plains of India. The military campaigns of Akbar followed a similar sequence. Of the thirty or so rebellions committed by insubordinate Amirs during the half-century of his reign, twenty-eight took place in towns, and the list included Agra, Lahore, Kabul, Allahabad, Jaunpur, Patna, and Ajmer.[63] When Akbar slaughtered the entire garrison and the civil popu-

Plate 78 Panorama of Damascus.

lation of Chitor (1567) in the aftermath of a strong resistance, he was sending a clear message to the Rajput princes of his determination to overcome the dangerous resistance at the flank of the empire. Chitor was perhaps the greatest fortress-town in northern India at the time. Its fall held the same meaning as the conquest of the impregnable Golconda fortress did in 1687: the elimination of the fortress towns as military machines was a signpost to the futility of resisting the territorial expansion of the Mughals.

As seats of imperial power, the capital cities of the western Indian Ocean together with lesser satellite towns functioned as central places exchanging political information and providing access to political influence. To secure advancement in career the ambitious 'umara' must secure admission to the imperial presence. For the Persian and Turkish nobility seeking patronage and lucrative employment, the Mughal capital cities proved unfailingly attractive for more than two centuries. The constant migration of the administrative and military personnel from the periphery of the empire to the primate cities and from the latter to the lesser towns in search of higher financial rewards was both a demographic and a social phenomenon, which had important political consequences for the survival of the Mughal imperial institutions. The foreign administrators and high-ranking officers receiving land assignments as their official salaries were less likely to put down local roots than the indigenous personnel and at the same time the role of the central financial department in Delhi as the final arbiter of the assignment-system kept the entire class tied down to the centre of power.

Urban centres and the politics of decline. The urban orientation of Islamic states was not without its source of weakness. The loss of a symbolic town or a city came as a grievous political and economic blow. Ibn Taghri Birdi relates in his 'History of Egypt' how on 1 June 1434 al-Malik al-Ashraf Barsbai, the Mamluk sultan, received terrible news from Baghdad. Isbahan ibn Qara Yusuf, the leader of the barbarian Turkomans, 'heretical infidels', had taken Baghdad and driven out all its inhabitants from the rich to the poor after despoiling them of their property. People had scattered with their wives and children in all quarters of the earth. Only three ovens were left in Baghdad for baking bread. The city resembled a deserted ruin, a refuge only of the owls. Mosul, the premier city of Jazira, also shared a similar fate.[64] Writing in a similar tone of resigned melancholy, Francisco Pelsaert would claim in the 1620s that Jahangir whose name implied that he grasped the whole world, was no more than the king of the plains or the open roads. For rebellious chiefs, thieves and robbers did not hesitate to pillage up to the very gate of Ahmedabad, Burhanpur, Agra, Delhi, and Lahore.[65] Compare the Dutchman's statement with the preamble to Jahangir's accession farman in which the emperor ordered his provincial or district officials to construct rest-houses, mosques, and water-tanks as the basic infrastructure of urbanisation in order to encourage people to come and settle in these places, because thefts and violent crimes occurred in isolated places or in highways.[66] The foundation of new townships was typically seen as an answer to lawlessness. By 1725, in the general collapse of Mughal provincial administration, even officials were turning into plunderers and openly moving into commercial towns in search of prize money. A letter from Daniel Innes, the English East India Company's agent in Cambay, describes in stark language the consequences of one such arrival:

A new Deputy Governor some days since arrived here. He was sent on his promising in twenty days to send to Ahmedabad 18,000 rupees, on which the merchants hid themselves and retired to neighbouring villages. Soon after his arrival, he beat a drum about the city warning the inhabitants to open their doors, or [he] would force them to it by plundering the city. Yet for six days after his arrival not a man was to be seen in the streets. He has since caught a few Banias whom he keeps prisoners to get hold

Plate 79 Fortifications of Broach, Gujarat.

of the heads of them; so that at present there is no manner of business going on, but we have several rumours that Hamid Khan intends to depart.[67]

   The historical connection which existed between long-distance trade and the process of urbanisation was a simultaneous phenomenon, a source of both strength and weakness to the towns and cities of the Indian Ocean. Wholesale merchants and bankers engaged in the transcontinental trade found all the necessary supporting services in places such as Alexandria, Cairo, Cambay, Surat, Malacca, and Canton.[68] Industrial producers also gained from the access to the larger demand through urban markets. These advantages were off-set by the periodical breakdown in law and order and instability of government. When the centralised bureaucratic empires lost control over their administrative subordinates or failed to check external invasions, the urban centres paid a heavy price for the failure.

The social dimensions of urbanisation

The homogeneity of urban life. The separation between the urban and the rural is most evident in Asian history at the level of political and economic structures. The rupture is less visible, less distinctive when social forms are taken into account. The urban poor faced the same problems as their rural counterpart in the daily struggle for physical survival. The artisans in towns paid taxes to the agents of the same state which collected its share of crops from the peasantry and the landed classes. The Brahmanic priests who performed the religious worship in urban temples were in no way distinguishable from their fellow-caste members in the Indian villages. The urban elite all through the Indian Ocean could claim that they were better educated and better informed than the upper members of the rural society. They did not enjoy rights and privileges which would separate the townsmen from other citizens living beyond the city walls. The presence of garden-land, orchards, and even fields within the towns or just outside the boundaries implied that a proportion of the urban-dwellers retained its links with the farming community. In most north Indian towns people depended on milk and dairy products to provide a substantial part of the diet. Cattle stalls were run within the towns by professional milk-suppliers and were also attached to the richer private households. In the early hours of the morning large herds of slow-moving cattle filed through the narrow congested streets to graze on pastures in the flood-plains of the larger rivers. The countryside was never far from the periphery of the city, and the premodern people may have had a different measure of urbanisation than their later descendants.

The hazards of urban life: fire, flooding, and pollution. For many social observers of the time, the disadvantages of urban life probably outweighed its many benefits. The physical hazards associated with towns were also present in the countryside, but in a confined location the effects were both more concentrated and immediately visible. Fire, flooding, pollution, epidemics, famines, and endemic social tension were feared and tolerated with a resigned expectation. The historical sources point to the universal prevalence of these natural and man-made catastrophes for urban-dwellers in every region of the Indian Ocean. But the examples taken from two well-documented primate cities of the Middle East, Baghdad and Cairo, are particularly graphic and even horrifying at times. The use of timber and thatch as building materials in the souks and the careless handling of combustibles led to frequent occurrences of large fires in Baghdad. The Great Fire of 1057 affected the Food Market, Ram Street, the flea-market, Barley Gate, the Perfume Market, Bride's Market, Timber Market, and the Carpenters' Market. A contemporaneous report quoted the historian Ibn al-Sabi's verdict that this fire did more damage than any previous ones. Vast spaces on the west bank of the river

Plate 80 Religious structure in Mahan awaiting repairs, sun-dried bricks.

lay in ruins and people were seen walking about with burnt and tattered clothing.[69] Sixteen years later torrential rains and the swollen water of the Tigris flooded Baghdad on both sides of the river. The water entered the caliph's palace and he had to be carried by his bodyguards to a place of safety. People fled from their homes in great panic and many public buildings including mosques fell down.

The worst effects of such flooding generally came in their aftermath when the contaminated drinking water produced cholera and other epidemic diseases. Environmental pollution was a serious health hazard even in times considered normal. The Egyptian physician Ali ibn Ridwan (998–1067/8) narrates with almost scientific detachment the level of pollution in Egypt and the degradation of the environment. The urban layout of Fustat fully justified, in his view, the warning of the Greek physician Rufus of Ephesus: if you enter a city and see that it has narrow alleys and tall buildings, flee from it because the city is contaminated.[70] In Fustat people were accustomed to throw out all the household rubbish and dead domestic animals into the streets where the decaying matter fouled the air. The Nile was also used for the general dumping of waste and the same river supplied drinking water. When the level of the Nile was low in the dry season, the sewers emptying into it polluted the water completely. The streets of Cairo were broader and less dirty than those of Fustat and people there drank mostly well water. But even in Cairo the level of water in the wells was shallow and it was invariably contaminated by the under-ground seepage from sewers. The Arab physician considered that the removal of rubbish from the streets and its dumping outside the town were essential for preserving civic health.

With the customary confidence derived from mapping two separate obser-vations, Ibn Ridwan concluded that the valley of the Nile generated tempera-ments devoid of courage and generosity, so that lions do not live in that country. If brought to Egypt, they become meek and refuse to breed. However, our author knew that the Egyptian people were far from sterile and he admitted that during his long period of residence in Egypt he could remember five incidents of pestilence out of twenty years: only one was really disastrous, the rest were the usual illnesses.[71] Egyptian cities were not the only places where insanitary habits and difficulties in waste disposal continued to baffle city administration, as we can see from a letter written by the authorities responsible for street-cleaning in Madras (1727). The inhabitants of Black Town had complained to the Council that in spite of the taxes paid by them, the streets were in a 'most abominable and filthy condition'. This, the 'Scavengers' thought, was wholly due to the insufferable habit of using the streets as toilets, throwing out ashes and household rubbish, and keeping hogs, buffaloes, and horses. Furthermore, pedestrians and children frequently fell into the open sink-holes which received the waste water from each house.[72]

Urban population, food and fuel supplies. The natural immunity to diseases acquired through continual exposure to the health hazards prevented the urban population from being entirely decimated but the susceptibility to illnesses remained.[73] The high infant mortality, the inevitable consequence of bad living conditions, probably kept urban demography relatively stable. It is something of a mystery why the level of population in many towns and cities of the Indian Ocean should display relatively stable features. Limits on employment opportunities were one explanation, difficulties in providing adequate housing, water, transport, and food another. A city without fuel was little better than one without food. In the aftermath of the terrible famine of 1201 in Egypt, when the price of wheat, barley, and beans reached unheard-of levels, the working ovens in Cairo and Misr (Fustat) were fuelled with wood taken from deserted houses.[74] The scarcity of food had either driven away or killed the firewood carriers. Even in normal years firewood was scarce and expensive, and poor people in Indian towns burnt dried cowdung mixed with straw. The smoke from these fires, Pelsaert complained, hung all over town making eyes run and choking the throat.[75] The tenements of Cairo ('rab') and the mud-and-thatch huts of Indian towns housed people with different food habits. In Cairo people without proper kitchens or cooking facilities in multi-occupied buildings purchased cooked food in the market; in India even the most humble household would attempt to prepare its own food.[76] In either case, the high price of grain and other foodstuff caused by harvest failures and wars brought desperate hardship to the urban poor. When the municipal authorities in Madras made a survey in 1727 of the tax-assessable households in the Black Town and the outer suburbs, the surveyors were shocked to discover the depth of poverty among the 14,000 households in the Muteah Pettah: 'widows and children who threw themselves at our feet as we passed along' begging for exemption from the house-tax.[77] These were crisis years in southern India which was devastated by famines and food scarcities.[78] The bad years witnessed the usual procession of emaciated people from rural areas pouring into towns and selling their children in an attempt to save them from starvation. A few years later the wretched cloth-bleachers of Madras would petition the English Council for an increase of their wages on the ground that they were so weakened by malnutrition, three men were needed to do the work of two.[79]

Factors of urban growth. The demographic stability of Asian towns is explained not only by the constraints on their physical size but also by their origin and function. Some cities of course grew rapidly and the reason for their sudden expansion was quite apparent. The spectacular growth of Surat could be attributed to a shift of trade away from Cambay, cut off from the open sea by the gradual silting up of its harbour. But it was difficult to make an estimation of Surat's population because of the number of temporary visitors. During the busy trading season from January to March, as the ships were preparing to sail for the Red Sea and the Persian Gulf, the town was so full of people that lodgings were hard to find and the three outer suburbs were all overflowing.[80] Agra, Lahore, and the new town of Shahjahanabad in Delhi experienced sudden construction booms when successive Mughal emperors chose these cities as their principal place of residence. In the words of Francisco Pelsaert, Agra was not much better than a village in the district of Bayana until Akbar made it his capital. Gardens were laid out, trees planted, and the luxuriance of the groves around Agra made it look like a royal park rather than a city. Every one rushed to acquire or purchase a piece of land that suited him best. As a result Agra had no remarkable market-places or bazaars as were to be found in Lahore, Burhanpur, Ahmedabad, and other Indian cities. The whole place was closely built over and densely populated, the Hindus mingling with the Muslims, the rich with the poor.[81]

Sources of social tensions. Although the residential quarters in many Near Eastern cities, were marked by segregated religious communities, Muslims, Christians, and Jews, the lack of urban distinction between the Hindus and Muslims in India was noticed by Pietro della Valle also. The Hindus were obviously more numerous than the Muslims but 'they live all mixt together,

and peaceably, because the *Gran Moghul* . . . altogether he be a Mahometan
. . . makes no difference in his Dominions between the one sort and the other;
and both in his Court, and Armies, and even amongst men of the highest
degree, they are of equal account, and consideration.'[82] In spite of della Valle's
reference to the apparent social harmony between the two communities in
India, there is ample evidence that the close urban proximity of the religious
groups could have explosive consequences. In 1713 terrible communal
rioting broke out in a mixed 'mahalla' of Ahmedabad because the Mughal
subadar Daud Khan Pani had adjudicated in favour of the Hindus in
celebrating the water festival ('holi') in front of Muslim houses.[83] Social
tension was not confined just to inter-communal groups. Disputes between the
shiᶜa and sunni sects were endemic in medieval Baghdad. In 478 AH sectarian
riots led to the burning of houses in Shiᶜte Karh and Sunnite Bab al-Basra.[84]

A port- or a caravan-city with its heterogeneous population and the large
number of visiting merchants was particularly exposed to the risk of social
tumults. During the popular disturbances of 1186 in Alexandria, the mob
plundered the property of European merchants. The government forces had to
restrain the rioters.[85] The use of separate funduqs and the segregation of ethnic
quarters did not save the minorities from explicit social insults. Centuries later
Carsten Niebuhr bitterly complained that, although Cairo was generally a
law-abiding city, no Christian or Jew was allowed to appear on horses and
could only ride donkeys. When a great Muslim lord rode through the streets,
the infidels were peremptorily ordered by his retainers to dismount. Niebuhr
was mortified to see that on one such occasion, his servants remained seated
on their asses, while he was forced to alight. The previous English consul
always rode horses in Cairo, but his wealth and lavish distribution of gifts to
the rich and the poor had earned him many friends.[86] Incidents which led to
sudden outbreaks of collective social violence were mostly trivial. A Brahman
woman in Surat turned Muslim in 1726 to avoid paying her debts. When the
government ruled in favour of her Hindu creditors, a fanatical Muslim
religious leader Sayyad Ali raised a violent mob in the city. The tense situation
made it dangerous to pass the streets near the Castle green.[87] When European
ships arrived in port at Surat, Madras, or Calcutta after a voyage of eight
months or so, the local inhabitants were warned to be on guard against violent
sailors who got drunk on the fiery local spirits.[88] Sometimes the violence was
quite irrational. A horrified English Council reported from Madras in 1714
that about fifty Europeans from the garrison of Fort St George had gone into
the Black Town and divided themselves into small groups. Then following a
prearranged signal given by a hunting horn they had suddenly fallen on the
local guards, knocked them out with clubs, and attacked everybody who
stood in their way, 'about twenty black people being very much wounded
before the Guards could get up to quell them'. The rioters were paraded in
public and the ringleaders sentenced to whipping, before being sent off-shore

Plate 81 The doorway of Seljuk Madrasa in Konya, Anatolia.

in irons. The Council hoped 'to save the lives of all those that were wounded'.[89]

If the premodern city signified power, artistic aspirations, and the attributes of civilised life, it also pointed to all the negative aspects and structural contradictions inherent in society. Much depended on the attitude, policy, and the political will of the rulers. Sawai Jai Singh (1688–1743) laid out a beautiful capital in 1728 next to the old capital of Amber with the aid of his chief architect Vidhyadhar, who came from Bengal. Jaipur was a planned city based on the grid pattern. A noted astronomer, the Maharaja also composed a mathematical treatise containing astronomical tables made from observations carried out in his own observatories. His immediate ancestors we have already met in Tavernier's account as having studied mathematics with Brahmanic teachers in Varanasi. It is highly likely that they stimulated and encouraged the young prince's interest in the exact sciences. Indian elite interest in town-building was a powerful force towards urbanisation in the subcontinent. Success and continued survival of towns founded by political fiat however depended on the creation of a firm economic base. Very few urban centres of the Indian Ocean could live without the substantial presence of merchants, long-distance trade, and artisan production. Urban planning and the maintenance of physical uniformities in the appearance of streets, the sky-line, and the size of houses might be a function of the political will. More often than not, the social will towards individual or group preferences within the city over-ruled any desire that might have existed on the part of the politically powerful to create visually attractive planned cities.

12

Conclusion

Perpetual memory

The principles of invariance in structural analysis. This study is concerned with two distinct problems inherent in comparative history: the principles identifying the totality of the different civilisations of the Indian Ocean and the reconstruction of the historical patterns of articulation between different forms of social activities such as systems of production, distribution, and consumption which transcend the specific frontiers of each civilisation. Our structural analysis of the economy and civilisation of the Indian Ocean began with a statement of Jakobson's search for the principle of invariance amidst variations.[1] This approach leads to the loss of certain dynamic qualities present in historical processes. By definition the attempt to identify and trace structural continuities and discontinuities most presuppose that these are not continuous functions of time. The clock-work mechanism of a watch, for example, does not undergo any structural changes even though its motions are dynamic. The discontinuity occurs when the mechanical movement is replaced with a quartz movement. A strictly historical description of the economic and social life of the Indian Ocean is possible only after the initial task of establishing the comparative categories is completed. For the time being, our attention must be directed towards answering or at all events investigating some basic questions and problems raised by the analysis so far.

Perpetual memory as a replicative code. It is clear that every society, including those of the Indian Ocean, has a mechanism similar to the genetic DNA code which enables it to copy all the details of a living organism. A 'perpetual memory' seems to replicate not only the demographic foundation of society, the statistical birth and death rates, sex ratios, and the age pyramid, but also a whole range of relationships involving the family, economic practices and institutions, the state, religion, and systems of belief. It may be asked why does the element of imitative behaviour, whether it is collective or individual, not collapse over time so as to make social forms totally unstable? Why is the perception of 'order' in human life valued more than that of 'disorder'? These questions help to highlight the fact that the principle of invariance is more than a convenient theoretical concept for abstract analysis. When measured by an

375

appropriate time-scale, it makes the world what it now is, what it was in the past, and what it will be in future.

It is easily seen that the concept of invariance must always specify the duration of time and that the five basic operators of human thought (equal to, greater than, less than, and, or) assume that the objects of evaluation remain invariant over the relevant unit of time. In his dialogue with Sartre, Lévi-Strauss claimed that 'the characteristic feature of the savage mind is its time-lessness' and that savage thought could be defined as 'analogical' thought because it seeks to grasp the world in a series of discontinuous physical images. Domesticated thought on the other hand not only attached much greater weight to history but attempts to dissolve an original discontinuity by relating objects to one another in an 'analytical' pattern.[2] It can be argued that the difference between the 'savage' and 'domesticated' minds associated here with analogical and analytical thought is less than it first appears. Human mind cannot contemplate certain categories of change without fear and the toler-ance of 'structural' change is limited in most societies, past and present. Did they not show the torture instruments to Galileo when he tried to change the existing *imagines mundi*? There is however no difficulty in accepting the two modes of thought as 'ideal types' and as dialectical principles present in collective social perceptions and norms of behaviour.

A full discussion of 'perpetual memory' and its characteristic operation must await a further study of historical social behaviour. The idea contains two related elements. The biological memory which an individual is born with, of course, does not extend beyond his life. The age-composition of society at any given time admittedly makes it possible to perpetuate social values, traditions, moral systems, and religious faith from one generation to the next. While social traditions and religious rituals might last over a thousand years in a more or less unchanging form, it is not possible for an indi-vidual to identify himself with an ancestor separated by a century. The per-petuation of a collective social tradition is important to the idea of perpetual memory. However, it also transcends a society's conscious awareness of moral systems, collective strategies, and normative actions. The second and by far the most important element of the concept is the ability which each individual has of remembering not only those things which concern himself immediately but also of remembering the same category of things as the rest of the society. In a bread-eating society, an individual will not merely remember that he has eaten bread but is aware that he will go on eating it. There is no question of an alternative choice facing him. The acceptance of bread has no moral force; it is not dictated by habit, though it might become so. A mother who makes bread for her children is not transferring her personal preference for bread to the next generation: that is the consequence of her unconscious action, which she does not question. Her behaviour is governed by the assumption that every one eats bread, has done so in the past, and will go on doing so for all time to come. To take away bread from such a society as staple food is nothing short of removing the basic remembered support of its existence. It is not the collective imitative social behaviour which makes for the perpetuation of collective traditions. On the contrary, it is the possibility and the certainty of imagining the same classes of things, the same processes, and the same safeguards which allows those manifestations of collective action to appear on the containing surface of society. The mental boundary separating perpetual memory from the process of learning, reasoning, conscious strategies, and experience is so uncertain that it is not always possible to make a distinction between them. We are left with a final question. Does the genetic chain also copy and pass on some of the information stored in the individual's memory together with the generative scheme of language, thought, and behaviour?

Population movement as primary form of social replication. The most obvious and fundamental level at which the 'perpetual memory' operated in the history of premodern Asia was the demographic replication. The principle of invariance expressed itself in the perpetuation of the family as a biological unit and as the basic module of social authority. The lineage represented historical continuity and the element of variation is seen in individual responses to social situations and in the different systems of power distribution within the family, in different rules controlling marriage, and different sacramental rituals relating to birth and death. Once the morphism between the family and property had become invariant through laws of inheritance the perpetual memory went on replicating the essential institutional forms. Fernand Braudel began his study of capitalism and material life with a discussion of the 'Weight of Numbers' which he saw primarily as a problem of relating demographic trends with the chronology of economic development, with the relative levels of civilisation, with technological advancement, and exogenous factors such as climatic rhythms.[3] True to his methodology, Braudel addressed himself to the historical demographic manifestations rather than their determinants. If the historian found out what was the rate of world population gorwth, its precise turning-points, and its spatial distribution, over time, then the functional relationship between population, social structures, and historical events subsumed in the discovery of the Atlantic and the Indian Ocean by European people in the fifteenth and sixteenth centuries could be studied and stated accurately. Of course, Braudel also knew that the estimates of total world population between the fifteenth and eighteenth centuries were highly uncertain. 'Statisticians working from conflicting, sparse and uncertain figures offered by historians cannot agree.'[4]

Concepts of over- and under-population. These reservations apply with much greater force when the period of study is as extended as ours. The existing studies which attempt to estimate the population of the Middle East, India, or

China at any given historical time seldom raise the question of why it is important to know the precise extent of absolute figures.[5] In order to place total
demographic magnitudes in proper interpretative context, it is necessary to
relate them to quantifiable economic and social categories. The notions of
over- or under-population are critical for an understanding of the appearance
and disappearance of social tensions, of the formative rules in social practices,
and the use of coercive powers by the state in order to maintain law and order.
The ancient Chinese thinker Han Fei Tzu (*d.* 233 BC) came to a Malthusian
conclusion long before Malthus from his historical observation of population
growth, economic competition, and social harmony. In former times conflict
among people was avoided because the number of people was less than the
means of support. Now the population expansion was so rapid that twenty-
five grandchildren might be born before the death of the grandfather. The
resulting struggle for a livelihood led to social disorder, even when rewards
were doubled and punishments multiplied.[6] While the historical consequences
were directly observable, the notional ratios between population figures,
available economic resources, and attitudes (family size, work ethics, toler-
ation of crime, and acceptable use of force) are impossible to quantify without
accurate census data. If the modern historians display a lively academic
interest and curiosity about the population movements of premodern Asian
societies, it is not justified by the nature of their historical evidence.

Limitation of population data. Comprehensive census records on population
size and its composition were virtually unknown in our period of history. The
centralised bureaucratic empires in the Indian Ocean, the Sasanian, Abbasid,
and the T'ang in the earlier age and the Ming, Ottoman, and the Mughal in the
later, were aware beyond any doubt that the economic success of their
administration required accurate quantitative information on the extent of
agricultural land and its productive yields. The early Islamic historians have
described the detailed and careful Sasanian land management in Iraq before
Arab conquest on which the later Muslim tax practices were modelled.[7] Abu'l
Fazl's *Ain-i-Akbari* and the surviving documentation on agricultural taxation
from the early eighteenth century show the comprehensive and census nature
of the system of data collection on crop production in northern India. However, beyond an elementary enumeration of households and family occupations, few sustained official attempts were ever made in any region of the
Indian Ocean actually to count the total number of people. The government
records betray an acute concern with the level of population densities and the
effects of such densities on agrarian prosperity but it is not matched by a
statistical exercise corresponding to the cadastral land survey and the annual
measurements of the harvests. The notable exceptions to this general state of
affairs were the Ming census of 1391 and Emperor Ch'ien-lung's (1736–95)
decision in 1741 to revise the basis of population enumeration. The Ming

Yellow Registers counted not only the number of households and their size but also specified the composition of families according to age and sex. The purpose of the compilation was to determine the statistical basis of labour services due to the state and the returns show that Ming China in 1393 contained 60,545,812 people.[8] The fact that the demographic exercises of Ming and Ching China were neither comprehensive nor regular over time suggests that there were severe practical and conceptual difficulties in setting up the correct procedures and the forms of enumeration.

The science of demography in the order of knowledge. It seems likely that in the premodern societies of the Indian Ocean the science of demography occupied a position similar to that of economic analysis in the order of knowledge. Neither was seen as a necessary condition of policy-making. Even Ibn Khaldun who had a better grasp than most contemporary thinkers of the articulation between economic factors and social structures could only offer a vague, generalised discourse on the notion of labour and population as a factor of production. Abundant inhabitants in a civilised region, he wrote, added to its prosperity. The amount of the available labour increased total production and

a great surplus of products remain after the necessities of the inhabitants have been satisfied. [This surplus] provides for a population far beyond the size and extent of the [actual one], and comes back to the people as profit . . . This may be exemplified by the eastern regions such as Egypt, Syria, the non-Arab Iraq, India, China, and the whole northern region, beyond the Mediterranean. When their civilisation [population] increased, the property of the inhabitants increased, and their dynasties became great. Their towns and settlements became numerous, and their commerce and conditions improved.[9]

If the productive role of labour appeared as an abstract issue, the shortage of farmland relative to the needs of a growing population was clearly perceived and the social consequence of food production falling behind the rate of demographic growth made itself apparent in numerous urban and rural disturbances. In spite of these recorded instances of demographic imbalances, it is doubtful whether absolute over-population existed in the premodern period in the same form as it manifests itself today in many parts of Egypt, the Indian subcontinent, Java, and China. The evidence for rising rural population is difficult to interpret even when the average size of the holdings appeared to be declining, as a careful study of rural Anatolia during the fifteenth and sixteenth centuries has shown.[10]

Where the problem did occur, the effects of extreme demographic pressure, overcrowding, and chronic malnutrition, were countered by migration, food imports, and by bringing new land under cultivation. The growth and development of wet-rice cultivation in terraced fields could have been a function of population growth. The expansion in rice land which did take place in southern India, Ceylon, Bengal, in the Chao Phraya delta in Thailand, and the lower Yangtze, clearly implied that the labour supply was adequate for the maintenance of the irrigation works and for working the terraces. Internal growth and the migration of people from outside the locality were the only two possible sources for the supply of additional labour.[11] The state was aware of its responsibility in encouraging agricultural productivity if only because a prosperous countryside and contented peasantry implied a greater amount and ease of revenue collections. There was little evidence that population control as opposed to population growth ever troubled the minds of policy-makers. If anything the ruling elites encouraged the people to multiply as a means of strengthening the state in terms of adding to the numerical size of the army and creating new economic resources. Alfred Sauvy, the leading French theoretical demographer, has commented that authoritarian state systems tended to favour the growth of useful subjects and the destruction of dangerous and useless ones. The Malthusian checks, famines, disease, and warfare, were seen as constraints rather than equilibrating factors. Therefore a scarcity of people was feared more than a potential surplus.[12]

Malthus may have turned the historical experience on its head and put forward a generalised population theory which has only proved itself under twentieth-century conditions. This is not to say that disasters in history, whether accidental or systematic, did not have a catastrophic effect on people and communities. What is questionable is the assumption that there is a 'natural' rate of demographic growth which always exceeds the expected rate of economic growth (based on a technology with a constant return to scale).[13] For this statement to be valid, it is not enough to formulate two simple mathematical ratios. Historical evidence is needed on the correlation between statistical birth and death rates and the contribution of population growth to economic expansion. There were certainly recognised practices in Asian societies which prevented successful child-births and hence restricted the family size. Contraceptive techniques, infanticide, limited access to women, marriage rules, all these customs exhibit an acute concern with the social replication of the family.[14] The motivation for selective birth control did not come solely from economic considerations. The preference for male children and the endogamous marriage rules among the higher caste groups in India generated attitudes and cultural values that tolerated, if not actually approved of, female infanticide. Where the custom of bride-price was prevalent, as for example among certain Indian weaving castes, it was difficult for the poorer people to marry until they had collected the dowry. The effect was to raise the age of marriage and perhaps shorten the active period of reproduction. However, it was the rate of birth after marriage which was critical for population growth. The long-run variations in family size hold the real key to an understanding of the historical demography of the Indian Ocean societies and the rationale which determine these changes cannot be recovered by merely pro-jecting the recent experience into the past. The concept of a 'natural' rate of reproduction is a theoretical construct which is contradicted by the history of social practices in most past societies. Even the alleged preference of farming communities for large-sized families is difficult to substantiate in the absence of adequate statistical evidence. The use of family labour in agricultural pro-duction naturally established a correlation between demographic factors and the extent of cultivated land. Without a detailed investigation of different farming techniques, variations in yield relative to soil fertility and crop selec-tion, and the social inclination of different farming groups to use the intensive techniques, it is un-historical to assume that the rate of labour utilisation in agriculture was determined by population growth alone.[15]

Dynamic factors in demographic growth. Were there no dynamic movements at all in Asian population during our period of study? That will be an unwarrantable assumption. Modern census records compiled since the second half of the nineteenth century show that the populations of the Indian sub-continent, Java, and China, to take only three examples, have substantially increased during the past hundred years or so. The rate of expansion, however, was very uneven from decade to decade. The annual average was at around 1 per cent until the turn of the century. From the 1920s the growth rate has accelerated to 2–3 per cent a year. If the rate of expansion historically had been even 1 per cent, the consequences for world population would have been catastrophic. An exercise in astronomical arithmetic suggests that at the rate of 1 per cent annual growth a single couple dating from 10,000 BC would pro-duce enough people to form today 'a sphere of living flesh many thousand light years in diameter, and expanding with a radial velocity that, neglecting rela-tivity, would be many times faster than light'.[16]

The conclusion to be drawn from such theoretical considerations is self-evident. That there was steady demographic growth over time is not in ques-tion. But the historical rate must have been substantially less than one per cent annually. It is not only that the total size of populations even in the densely settled agricultural regions of the Middle East, India, South East Asia, and China expanded very slowly. At times the total numbers declined absolutely. A high infant mortality rate was compounded by sudden disasters. Famines, epidemics, and large-scale warfare, the three horsemen of the Apocalypse, devastated whole communities and left behind survivors barely capable of managing their farm-land. The demographic cycles have been studied in some detail for the Middle East and China. The historians of Egypt in particular have emphasised the effects of Black Death as a pandemic in reducing the absolute level of population in the Nile valley. It has been suggested that the pre-pandemic Egyptian population was about 4 million which was drastically reduced by the abnormal mortality and failed to recover during the next four centuries. When Napoleon's officers took a census, it was still no more than 2.5 million.[17] The general demographic movements for China were well-recorded. From the T'ang period onwards population continued to expand until the twelfth century after which there was a down-turn. Growth was resumed after the Ming dynasty had re-established economic and political stability. The second half of the seventeenth century was another period of demographic and agricultural retrogression. The period from the beginning of the eighteenth to the middle of the nineteenth century on the other hand recorded a spectacular growth. It has been estimated that the population of China expanded from about 60 million in 1393 to 275 million in 1779 and to 430 in 1850.[18] It is evident that in China at least there was a long-term cyclical pattern in demographic growth which may have operated in the case of the Indian subcontinent also. The retrogression in the Middle East is distinctly puzzling. The population of Mughal India in 1600 has been estimated at about 100 million and it is entirely based on conjectural methods.

If the premodern states refrained from counting the number of their members, there may have been sound reason for the failure. In the first place, the omission was at the level of the central government secretariat. The village communities certainly knew the total number of households and the numerical size of each family. The perpetual memory coded this knowledge for the purpose of fixing the theoretical limits of the village as well as for purely practical reasons such as the allocation and utilisation of economic resources within a social consensus. The expected size of Indian or Chinese villages and small district townships display a remarkable constancy over long periods of time. The concept of the state on the other hand excluded a rigid definition of citizenship and even territorial demarcations. Faced with the continuing problem of variable geographical size, internal and external migrations of settled people, the annual movements of nomadic tribes, and the difficulty of maintaining written records in a largely non-literate society, the governments may well have concluded that there were other more urgent tasks on their hands than demographic enumeration. In China and South East Asian states where corvée was an important element of government revenue, it was obviously important to know who and how many people were liable for the labour services. But the exact relationship between historical census records and current service obligations was not easy to interpret.

The dynamic stages in Indian Ocean history

State formation and the world systems of Wallerstein and Braudel. In our analysis of historical time, it was suggested that the period from the rise of Islam to about 1750 constituted a 'life cycle' for the Indian Ocean civilisations. The proposition is validated by the assumption that the average value of certain ratios did not radically change: ratios between population and cultivable land, between the level of technology and the rate of innovation, between expected standards of living and the possibilities of improvement, between the state's capacity to regulate economic life and the autonomy of social groups. While these critical determinants of historical change seemed to obey the rationale of Braudelian *longue durée*, imperial expansion, political conflicts, large-scale migrations of warrior people, and the emergence of strong ruling dynasties introduced the elements of sudden, violent movements. The role of the 'state' in the Indian Ocean history was indeed a dynamic one even though the relevant units cannot always be identified in terms of precise demographic and territorial measurements. The long rhythms of economic activities and the emergence of 'world systems' as defined by Fernand Braudel and Immanuel Wallerstein followed a historical trajectory closely related to state formation and the larger processes of political expansion.

The rise of the capitalist world-economy, Wallerstein has assigned, to the sixteenth century and beyond.[19] The great political and geographical expansion in the territorial limits of Europe began in the early fifteenth century with the Portuguese voyages of discovery in the Atlantic and it culminated in the Spanish conquest of Central and Southern America a hundred years later. The morphism between the economic exploitation of new opportunities and the pattern of spatial identities allows the historian to think in terms of a model with a core area, supported by a semi-periphery and a periphery.[20] For much of the sixteenth century the Habsburg empire in Europe, which included some of the most developed and commercialised regions in the Western world, acted as a metropolitan economy, while the rise of the latifundia in the New World gave an impetus to the capitalist relations of production in the agriculture of the periphery. The description of the historical stages in the emergence of a capitalist world economy is underpinned by a rigorous theory of 'unequal exchange' in which the highest benefits accrue to the core states. The extractive mechanism which transferred economic resources from the semi-periphery and the periphery to the core operated through three antinomies. Firstly, there was an economic structure within which a particular imperial or state system was located. Secondly, world supply was primarily a function of market-oriented and profit-induced production decisions, while world demand remained constrained by socially-determined entitlements and allocation of income. Finally, the accumulation of capital took place as a classic appropriation of labour surplus.[21]

The explanatory power of Immanuel Wallerstein's theoretical construction lies in its capacity to combine a generalised model of dominant relationships with a dynamic sequence of historical developments. Even when historians criticise the model for its lack of inner dynamic quality, the process of transition which leads to the rise of the capitalist world economy, they are not able to dispense with the concept itself. The reason for this apparent paradox is quite simple: Wallerstein's theory is grounded on a fundamental feature of social life: the hierarchical ordering of spatial identities and sources of power. The limitation of the theory, on the other hand, is due to Wallerstein's assumption that dominant relations in the distribution of economic gains are the main motive-force driving the mechanism of a world system. Fernand Braudel accepted the general validity of the world system as a historical concept but gave it a more neutral definition. A world economy was different from the economy of the world. The first was only a fragment of the totality composed of all the different economies but its operational feature was a topological space within which existed a complete system of internal links and exchange.[22] For Braudel the theory of central places propounded by geographers was more important in locating the 'world system' than the idea of unequal economic exchange. Braudel was perfectly aware of the role played by Seville, Antwerp, Amsterdam, and London in the development of capitalism from the sixteenth century to the eighteenth. But capitalism was potentially visible, he believed since the dawn of history and it was a universal phenomenon:

Far in advance, there were signs announcing the coming of capitalism: the rise of towns and of trade, the emergence of a labour market, the increasing density of society, the spread of the use of money, the rise in output, the expansion of long-distance trade or to put it another way the international market. When, in the first century AD, India seized or at any rate penetrated the islands of the East Indies, when Rome held an area even greater than the Mediterranean in her power, when China invented paper money in the ninth century, when the West reconquered the Mediterranean between the eleventh and thirteenth centuries, when a world market began to take shape in the sixteenth century, the 'biography of capital' was starting to be written in one form or another.[23]

Capitalism and the forces of expansion in the Indian Ocean. It is clear that Braudel's capitalism cannot be strictly interpreted as a form of economic domination derived from the monopoly control of one of the factors of production. He is concerned to demonstrate that capitalistic activities are an inseparable part of transcontinental trade which takes its dynamic development from the necessary connection between rural and industrial production, urbanisation, and the use of money as an index of value. The history of maritime trade in the Indian Ocean from the rise of Islam to the end of our period, it can be argued, is neither understood nor explained without explicitly taking into account the role played by capital in production and distribution. For nearly 300 years from the end of the seventh century, the Middle East, southern Mediterranean, and parts of the western Indian Ocean constituted an area of political, economic, and cultural unification which shared some of the core-periphery relationships of a world system. The productive resources of Andalusia, Ifriqiyya, Khurasan, or Sind were not directly transferable to the caliphate's treasury in Damascus or Baghdad. Yet the idea of controlling the periphery of the Balad al-Islam through proconsuls, the settlement of

Muslims, the building of Islamic towns, and the transfer of artistic expressions remained constant. A chain of maritime and caravan trade stretching all the way from the Indian Ocean to the strait of Gibraltar provided the practical means of linking local production with a trans-oceanic system of distribution and consumption.

Maurice Lombard, a contemporary of Braudel, was long aware of the association between the structure of space and the rise of Islam. The centre of the Muslim world he located in the Isthmus region bounded by the Persian Gulf, the Red Sea, the Mediterranean, the Black Sea, and the Caspian Sea:

It was therefore set at the intersection of two major economic units: the Indian Ocean area and the Mediterranean area. These two territories, united in Hellenistic times but later split into two rival worlds, the Roman-Byzantine and the Parthian-Sasanian, were now reunited by the Muslim conquest, so as to form a new, vast territory which was economically one.[24]

The restored unity of the central region rested on large-scale commercial relations along the caravan and maritime routes. It was also fostered by the reintroduction into world trade of the great consuming markets of the western Mediterranean. Urban centres such as Qayrawan, Fez, Seville, Cordoba, and Palermo, added their economic and social strength to the cities at the heartland of Islam to create a complete system of relations, the strong points and the motive force of economic life. According to Lombard, the unity of the early Islamic world rested on three concurrent developments: the adoption of Islam as a universal principle of social and moral integration. Arabisation of the army and the administration through the recruitment of warlike local groups, and finally, the adoption and acceptance of Arabic language for government, education, literary expression, and even mass communication.[25]

There are dynamic elements in this description of the historical expansion during the period of the Umayyad and Abbasid caliphate which share some of the functional attributes of a world system. It is worth recalling, however, that Wallerstein made a careful distinction between a 'world economy' and a 'world empire' and emphasised the structural advantage of the former over the latter as a system.[26] A political empire Wallerstein saw as a sub-set of a larger historical construct, the world system. Nevertheless, it is evident as a general proposition that state formation and its outward projections over space and time create notions of centrality and the hierarchical ordering of spatial units articulated to the structure of the state. The dominant positions of power, however, are not always expressed through economic relationships. These can be political, religious, cultural, and linguistic. Through its assimilation of plural societies, the Islamic world obviously created two fundamental categories of citizens, Muslims who were privileged and non-Muslims who are largely disenfranchised in economic term. But there was no attempt to uphold and encourage the monopoly control of technology leading to an unequal distribution of military power and economic resources. The distinction between Muslim and non-Muslim appeared to be largely theoretical. Capitalistic principles strongly underpinned long-distance trade and economic production for non-local markets. Yet the state and the legal traditions discouraged the accumulation of capital in the hands of merchants and repeated attempts were made to break up the concentration of financial power within selective groups. The historic role of urban centres in the Indian Ocean has all through time accentuated the inter-regional division of labour. Urbanisation was one of the most powerful forces responsible for creating a structural imbalance between different units of space and different groups of people.

The movements towards integration and the contradictory tendencies working in the opposite direction were present not just in the world of the early caliphate but also in all expanding state systems of Asia. It is possible to argue that in the history of the Indian subcontinent and imperial China, the two highly productive regions of the Indian Ocean, the reciprocity of economic interests between the landed classes and the state redistributed both power and wealth. Imperial expansion could never free itself from an ultimate dependence on the elitism of the men of the sword and the men of the pen. The livelihood of both the groups was largely paid for with the economic surplus extracted from agriculture. The primary producers, the peasants and the industrial craftsmen, had to bear the full burden of supporting the state and the intermediaries. The peasants found themselves permanently confined to the margins of social welfare and were vulnerable to an ever-present appropriation of basic rights at the hands of state officials and superior landed classes with armed power at their disposal. A similar position of dependence also bound the artisans to the great merchants and local traders. Control over land rights and control of commercial capital functioned as the two basic instruments of dependent relationships for the farmer and the craftsman. The degree of dependence of course varied in different societies and different periods. Where the state itself was responsible for organising and collecting the agricultural surplus from the peasantry, direct appeal to the central government might save them from the worst excesses of the tax gatherers and the privileged landholders. But if the state delegated some of its administrative functions to local power groups composed of bankers, merchants, and landed magnates in the form of revenue farms, the peasants were faced with severe pressure from competitive maximisation of rents and taxes. In such a situation, rural banditry and mass migrations served as traditional peasant responses to social oppression.

The power of the centralised bureaucratic empires itself could be held in check by a vertical alliance between the different sections of the rural society. The rise of the three great state systems of Asia, the Ming (1368), the Ottoman (*c.* 1453), and the Mughal (1526), was a history of successive attempts to break down the power of local landed magnates through a combination of military and administrative means. The state eventually emerged as the single largest financial enterprise with its income and expenditure forming a significant proportion of total production and consumption. The redistributive function of the centralised state encouraged and fostered a type of commercial capitalism which in strict theory had no institutional basis in law. The great merchants acted as bankers to the state directly. They also converted the agricultural surplus into disposable income for the central treasury and for those officials whose salaries were paid in the form of revenue assignments. The commercial activities of the merchants of course followed an independent logic and the centralised empires could exercise little control over their international economic transactions. The growth of the transcontinental trade of the Indian Ocean operating through a network of commercial emporia benefited from the development of state capitalism and yet it remained firmly linked to an international order of economic specialisation. The mining and the redistribution of large quantities of gold and silver, in the New World and in Japan, accelerated the growth of world liquidity and eased the problem of supporting a metallic currency. The role played by the Europeans in the Indian Ocean as agents of the monetary redistribution was crucial. The emergent forms of new trade patterns and the internal adjustments to the new demand broke down the relative insularity of the Chinese economy and made the economies of the Middle East and India even more open. The origins of the nineteenth century colonialism and Western economic imperialism go back to the 1650s when parts of the Indonesian archipelago lost their economic autonomy to the Dutch East India Company. The final stage in the dynamic movements in the Indian Ocean was reached during the second half of the eighteenth century when British military and naval power fused with European technological revolution to redraw the civilisational map of the Indian Ocean.

Notes

Introduction

1 Braudel, *Une Leçon d'histoire*, 215–17. Fernand Braudel was born in 1902 at Lumeville-en-Ornois (Meuse); he died in Paris on 28 November 1985.
2 *Ibid.*, 202.
3 *Ibid.*, 158.
4 *Ibid.*, 95.
5 *Ibid.*, 157.
6 Braudel, *Civilization and Capitalism*, II, 403–4.
7 *Ibid.*
8 Russell, *My Philosophical Development*, 31, 52.
9 Wittgenstein, *Tractatus Logico-Philosophicus*, 3.
10 For a general description of the methods, see Piaget, *Structuralism*, and Leach, *Lévi-Strauss*.
11 Merleau-Ponty, *Signs*, 69.
12 Braudel, *Civilization and Capitalism*, II, 458–94.
13 Derrida, *Writing and Difference*, 31.
14 Russell, *My Philosophical Development*, 72–6.
15 Descharnes, *The World of Salvador Dali*, 63. See also plate 61.
16 Braudel, *The Mediterranean*, I, 17.
17 'Down narrow streets they come, strange unicorns, from what fields, from what forests of myths?' Lorca, 'Procession', *Obras Completas*, I, 182.

1 The setting: unities of discourse

1 For example, if 0 is taken as the starting point of a series of integers, we can derive 1, 2, 3 . . . N by the inductive process $0+1$, $1+1$, $2+1$. Note that not all numbers have a starting point. Arithmetic fractions have neither a starting number belonging to itself nor a cardinal number. They approach infinities beyond which lie 0 and 1, i.e. two integers. Similarly economic and social history seldom have clear starting dates.
2 See ch. 4, p. 92.
3 See Braudel, 'Histoire et sciences sociales: la longue durée', and *The Mediterranean*, II, 892–903; Lévi-Strauss, *The Savage Mind*, ch. 9, 'History and Dialectic'.
4 The expression 'bricoleur' is defined by Lévi-Strauss as someone 'adept at per-

forming a large number of diverse tasks . . . and the rules of his game are always to make do with "whatever is at hand", that is to say with a set of tools and materials which is always finite and is also heterogeneous'. See *The Savage Mind*, 16–17.

5 For the full text of the paper and explanatory notes on it, see Gödel, *Collected Works*.

6 On the role of 'transformations', see Piaget, *Structuralism*, 10–13.

7 See Wittgenstein, *Tractatus Logico-Philosophicus*, 3.12, 3.13, 4.21, 4.211, 4.25, 4.46, 4.463; Pears, *Wittgenstein*, 69–71.

8 This sequence was pointed out to me by R. Klein.

9 Every word has a time dimension which takes the linguistic form of tense in grammar. But certain words and expressions are generalised through common usage and tense is eliminated, even though they have a hidden history of variable meanings. See also pp. 432–5 and below n. 11.

10 This association of historical facts or events with the 'present' creates the illusion that they are verifiable by experience, hence historical evidence acts as a surrogate for living witnesses.

11 My notes on the theory of historical time and the tensed logic of linguistic expressions were written in the autumn of 1985. In January 1989 I did further work on the subject and read Russell's essay on time published in 1915. It is interesting to compare his theory with that presented here: 'Two pairs of relations have to be considered, namely, (a) sensation and memory, which give time relations between object and subject, (b) simultaneity and succession, which give time relations among objects . . . It will be seen that past, present, and future arise from time relations of subject and object while earlier and later arise from time-relations of object and object. In a world in which there was no experience there would be no past, present or future, but there might well be earlier and later' (Russell, 'On the experience of time', 212).

12 Braudel, *On History*, 76.

13 Braudel, *The Mediterranean*, II, 901.

14 Foucault, *The Archaeology of Knowledge*, 44.

15 *Ibid.*, 3.

16 *Ibid.*, 8.

17 Cantor, *Contributions to the Founding of the Theory of Transfinite Numbers*.

18 Wang, 'The concept of set', 535.

19 Gödel, 'Russell's mathematical logic', 452; Russell, 'Principia mathematica: philosophical aspects', in *My Philosophical Development*, 57–65.

20 Hilbert, 'On the infinite' [address delivered before the congress of the Westphalian Mathematical Society in Munster in honour of Karl Weierstrass], 188, 191.

21 Gödel, 'What is Cantor's continuum problem?', 470.

22 Jakobson, *Verbal Art, Verbal Sign, Verbal Time*, 3.

23 Wittgenstein, *Tractatus Logico-Philosophicus*, 1.13, 2.11, 2.202, 3.42, 4.463.

24 For a discussion of the semiotic theory of Ferdinand de Saussure and its application to urban studies, see Gottdiener and Lagopoulos eds., *The City and the Sign: An Introduction to Urban Semiotics*, 1–21.

2 Comparative civilisations of Asia

1 Ferdinand de Saussure's original work, published after his death (1913) by his pupils, still remains fundamental, see his *Cours de linguistique generale* (1916), English trans. Harris, *Course in General Linguistics* (1983); see also: Barthes, *Élements de sémiologie* (1964), English trans. Lavers and Smith, *Elements of Semiology* (1967), and 'Introduction à l'analyse structurale des récits' (1966), English trans. 'Introduction to the structural analysis of narrative', in Heath, *Image, Music, Text* (1982), 79–124; Derrida, *L'écriture et la différence* (1967), English trans. Bass, *Writing and Difference* (1978); Kripke, *Naming and Necessity* (1972); Davidson, *Inquiries into Truth and Interpretation* (1985); Parsons, *Mathematics in Philosophy. Selected Essays* (1983).

2 For a discussion of this problem, see McGuinness ed., *Wittgenstein and the Vienna Circle*, Appendix A.

3 This point has been extensively discussed by Stover, *The Cultural Ecology of Chinese Civilization*. Stover tried to apply Julian Steward's ecological theories to Chinese history, see Steward, *Theory of Cultural Change: The Methodology of Multilinear Evolution*.

4 On the influence of time rhythm in agricultural calendar, see Bourdieu, *Outline of a Theory of Practice*, 97–109.

5 The logical and philosophical aspects of the problem are discussed in Russell's introduction to Wittgenstein, *Tractatus Logico-Philosophicus*, xix; see also Wittgenstein's theory of 'Totality and system' in McGuinness ed., *Wittgenstein and the Vienna Circle*, 213–17. Foucault has extended the discussion of the problems raised in Wittgenstein's earlier works and examined the interpretation of notions such as 'unities' and 'discontinuities' in historical expositions; see his *The Archaeology of Knowledge*, 21–39.

6 For a general discussion of the problem, see Putnam, *Reason, Truth, and History*, 1–22.

7 The name 'Maha-Chin' or 'Machin' was used mostly in India and the Middle East and was derived from the Sanskrit term Mahacinastana; see Needham, *Science and Civilisation in China*, I, 168–9.

8 Crone and Cook provides a neat description of the civilisational identity of Egypt before 525 BC; see their, *Hagarism*, 50.

9 Beal, *The Life of Hiuen-tsiang by Shaman Hwui Li*, 167–9.

10 Beveridge ed., *The Babur-nama*; Jahangir, *Tuzuk-i-Jahangiri*.

11 For the concept of 'civilisation' in French and English, see Benveniste, 'Civilization: a contribution to the history of the word', in *Problems in General Linguistics*.

12 From the Greek word 'clima', see Ibn Khaldun, *Muqaddimah*, I, 96, n. 18.

13 Al-Jahiz, *Tria Opuscula*, 32, quoted and translated by Watt, *Islam and the Integration of Society*, 1.

14 St Thomas Aquinas, *Summa Theologica*, ix, Ia, 62, 2, pp. 222–3.

15 These two terms were used by Ibn Khaldun to develop his fundamental historical theories of civilisation; see Rosenthal's introduction (1967) to Ibn Khaldun, *Muqaddimah*, I, lxxvi; see also Lacoste, *Ibn Khaldun*, 93–100.

16 For the Qur'anic references to this point, see O'Shaughnessy, *Muhammad's Thoughts on Death: A Thematic Study of the Qur'anic Data* (1969); also Wansbrough, *Qur'anic Studies* (1977).

17 Ibn Khaldun, *Muqaddimah*, I, 80, 289–90; al-Masudi, *Muruj adh-dhahab*, II, 210.

18 The policy of Umar was discussed by the Islamic jurist Abu Yusuf Ya'qub b. Ibrahim (*d.* 798), *Kitab El Kharadj (Le livre de l'impot foncier)*, 43, quoted by Lambton, *Landlord and Peasant in Persia*, 22. See also Baladhuri, *Kitab Futuh al-Buldan* (1866); Løkkegaard, *Islamic Taxation in the Classic Period* (1950); Morony, 'Landholding and social change: lower al-Iraq in the early Islamic period'.

19 al-Tabari, *Ta'rikh*, I, 2664; Ibn Khaldun, *Muqaddimah*, I, 290.

20 Crone and Cook, *Hagarism*, p. 103, quoting Ibn ʿAbd Rabbih, *Kitab al-'iqd al-farid*, III, 404.

21 Lewis, 'The Muslim view of the world', in *The Muslim Discovery of Europe*, 63–4. The question was discussed by the contemporary historian Zia al-din Barani, *Ta'rikh-i Firuz Shahi* (1357), ed. Elliot and Dowson, *History of India*, III, 184.

22 For a discussion of political legitimacy and the senility of dynasties see, Ibn Khaldun, *Muqaddimah*, I, 54, and II, 116–17.

23 al-Masudi, *Muruj adh-dhahab*, VII, 325, English trans. Lunde and Stone, *The Meadows of Gold: The Abbasids*, 282; Ibn Khaldun, *Muqaddimah*, I, 49. The Caliph Musta'in (*r.* AD 862–6) was held a prisoner by two Turkish officers, Bugha and Wasif, and the following verse was composed during his short reign: 'A Caliph in a cage, between Wasif and Bugha. He repeats whatever they say, just like a parrot.' The legitimacy of more than one imam was discussed by various contemporary Islamic thinkers and jurists; see Lambton, *State and Government in Medieval Islam*.

24 Dasgupta, *A History of Indian Philosophy*, III, 165–398.

25 Pellat, *The Life and Works of Jahiz*, 197. For the history of Indian mathematics, see Datta and Singh, *History of Hindu Mathematics*.

26 Sachau, *Alberuni's India*, 23. Albiruni gave an exact translation of the passage in Varahamihira's (*c.* AD 504) *Brhat samhita*; see Bhat ed., *Brhat Samhita*, 20.

27 Sachau, *Alberuni's India*, 100.

28 See Benveniste, 'Tripartition of functions' in *Indo-European Language and Society*, 227–38.

29 Dasgupta, *A History of Indian Philosophy*, IV, 1–50.

30 For a discussion of the points see, Srinivas, 'Sanskritization', in *Social Change in Modern India*, 1–45.

31 For a description of the caste conflicts between the Right-hand and Left-hand trading groups in eighteenth-century Madras and the invasion of economic employment, see Chaudhuri, *The Trading World of Asia and the English East India Company*, 269, 308–9.

32 For a discussion of this point, see Hardy, *Historians of Medieval India*.

33 These interpretative problems are still being debated by historians; see Coedes, *The Indianized States of Southeast Asia*, 14–35, Hall, *Maritime Trade and State*

Development in Early Southeast Asia (1985), 44–54, Aeusrivongse, 'Devaraja cult and Khmer kingship at Angkor', Mabbett, 'The "Indianization" of South-East Asia'.

34 See Chaudhuri, *Trade and Civilisation in the Indian Ocean*, 9–33.

35 See, for example, the descriptions of Chau Ju-kua in his *Chu-fan-chi* (*c.* 1225) and Ma Huan, *Ying-yai Sheng-lan* (*c.* 1433).

36 These points are discussed in Geertz, *The Religion of Java*, Hefner, *Hindu Javanese*, and Tambiah, *Buddhism and the Spirit Cult in North-East Thailand*.

37 On this point see, Hadiwijono, *Man in the Present Javanese Mysticism*.

38 Tambiah, *Buddhism and the Spirit Cult in North-East Thailand*, 253; see also his, *Culture, Thought, and Social Action* (1985).

39 For an analysis of the 'laws' of an earlier Thai Buddhist ruler, King Mangrai (1259–1317), at Chiangmai, see Kirsch, 'Cosmology and ecology as factors in interpreting early Thai social organization', and Wyatt, 'Laws and social order in early Thailand'. These two papers are published, with other contributions in the 'Symposium on social organization in mainland Southeast Asia prior to the eighteenth century', *Journal of Southeast Asian Studies*, XV, 1984.

40 Lucien Hanks in his foreword to the Symposium voices the theoretical difficulty of admitting dual structures in his statement that 'There cannot be both a horizontal and vertical organization of society at the same time.' *Ibid.*, 221. In our theory of 'structures' we dispense with the inadmissability of such 'contradictions' and follow Gödel's proof of the 'incomplete theorem'. See Gödel, *Collected Works*. For a relatively non-technical discussion on the ideas of the theorems, see Nagel and Newman, 'Goedel's proof', and Hahn, 'Infinity'. For a discussion of the apparent contradictions in theoretical physics, see Bohm, *Wholeness and Implicate Order*.

41 *ʿAhbar as-Sin waʾl-Hind* (*c.* 851); Buzurg ibn Shahriyar, *Kitab ʿAjaʾib al-Hind* (*c.* 900–53).

42 al-Masʿudi, *Muruj al-Dhahab* (*c.* 915–16), II, 85–6.

43 Ibn Battuta, *Travels in Asia and Africa 1325–1354*, 235.

44 *Ibid.*, 292.

45 Bary, *Neo-Confucian Orthodoxy*, 9–10. See also Berling, *The Syncretic Religion of Lin Chao-en*, 104–10.

46 See Kahn, *Monarchy in the Emperor's Eyes*.

47 Spence, *Emperor of China: Self-Portrait of K'ang-hsi*, 80. On the concept of Shang-ti as a Supreme Being in ancient China, see Chang, *Early Chinese Civilization*, 156.

48 Spence, *Emperor of China: Self-Portrait of K'ang-hsi*, 69.

49 Mair, 'Language and ideology in the written popularizations of the *Sacred Edict*'.

50 Yang, *Religion in Chinese Society*, 294–340.

51 The Chinese religious practices and the cults were exhaustively examined by de Groot in *The Religious System of China*, 6 vols., Leiden, 1892–1919. See also Osgood, *The Chinese*, III, 1,121–47.

52 Hughes and Hughes, *Religion in China*, 92. See also Granet, *The Religion of the Chinese People*.

53 Lord Macartney was informally received by the Emperor in the garden palace of Jehol; Morse, *Trade and Administration in China*, 23.

54 Spence, *Emperor of China: Self-Portrait of K'ang-hsi*, xii.

55 Bodde, 'Harmony and conflict in Chinese Philosophy' in Wright ed., *Studies in Chinese Thought*, 51; Ping-ti Ho, *The Ladder of Success in Imperial China*. See also Shigeta, 'The origins and structure of gentry rule'.

56 Watson, 'Standardizing the Gods'.

57 Wolf, 'Gods, ghosts, and ancestors'.

58 Needham, *Science and Civilisation in China*, I, 210.

59 *Ibid.*, 219.

60 Pellat, *Life and Works of Jahiz*, 96–7, 197.

61 Cantor, *Contributions to the Founding of the Theory of Transfinite Numbers*.

3 State, society, and economy

1 Brown *Augustine of Hippo*, 322–3.

2 Ibn Khaldun, *Muqaddimah*, I, 423–4.

3 Huang, *1587, A Year of No Significance*, 135; *Taxation and Finance in Sixteenth-century Ming China*, 311–12. See also Handlin, *Action in Late Ming Thought*, ch. 5.

4 See Ziya al-Din Barani, *Ta'rikh-i Firuz Shahi*.

5 (IOR), 1 January 1701–2, Original Correspondence, vol. 59, no. 7, 302.

6 On this point see Lévi-Strauss, *The Savage Mind*.

7 Augustine, *De Civitate Dei*, XXII, 22; translated by Brown, *Augustine of Hippo*, 328.

8 Ghuzuli, *Matali al-budur*, the saying is attributed to Caliph al-Mamun, quoted by von Grunebaum, *Medieval Islam*, 250, n. 67; see also Lewis, 'Islamic political writings', 143.

9 Nizami, 'Some aspects of Khanqah life in medieval India'; the source quoted by Nizami is Amir Khurd, *Siyar al-Auliya*, 135.

10 Huang Liu-hung, *A Complete Book Concerning Happiness and Benevolence*, 515–16.

11 *Ibid.*, 175.

12 Abu'l Fazl, *Akbarnama*, trans. Jarrett, vol. 3, recto 578, p. 875. For the economic development in the Jaipur state see, for example, Rajasthan State Archives, Bikaner, India, *Parwana* from the Durbar to the district *amils*, dated 14 Jesht Vadi Vikram Sambat 1780/1723 AD, in Arhsatta Pargana Hindaun, Bundle no. 9, 1,014–18. The *Parwana* or order instructed the *amils* (revenue officials) to control the level of taxation and collection charges so as not to discourage cultivation.

13 The government, however, was well aware of the need to maintain high grain prices in order to realise a cash income from the sale of state produce collected as taxes; see Inalcik, 'Rice cultivation in the Ottoman Empire', in *Studies in Ottoman Social and Economic History*, VI, 114–15.

14 Lien-sheng Yang, 'Economic justification for spending – an uncommon idea in traditional China'.

15 Al-Muqaddasi, *Ahsan al-Taqqasim*; Al-Tabari, *Ta'rikh al-Tabari*. For the early irrigation system in Mesopotamia, see Adams, *Land Behind Baghdad*, Le Strange, *The Lands of the Eastern Caliphate*, Lapidus, 'Arab settlement and economic development of Iraq and Iran'. It is doubtful if the Mongols were directly responsible for the agricultural decline of Iraq and its nomadisation; rather, it appears to have been a coincidental development. Present explanations are not conclusive.

16 Von Grunebaum, *Classical Islam*, 99.

17 Shiba, 'Urbanization and the development of markets in the lower Yangtze valley'.

18 For a discussion of Marx's Asiatic Mode of Production and its modern critique see, Bailey and Llobera eds., *The Asiatic Mode of Production*, and Hindess and Hirst, *Pre-Capitalist Modes of Production*.

19 Lien-sheng Yang, 'Economic justification for spending – an uncommon idea in traditional China', 47.

20 Li ed., *The Civilization of China*, 201–8, and Williamson, *Wang An Shih*, I, 150–6.

21 Barani, *Ta'rikh-i Firuz Shahi*, 192–6. See also Hardy, *Historians of Medieval India*. Barani's approval of price controls was presented in his treatise on political theory *Fatawa-i-Jahandari* (*c.* 1358–9).

22 Barani, *Ta'rikh-i Firuz Shahi*, 239–40.

23 Huang, *Taxation and Government Finance in Sixteenth-Century Ming China*, 69–74; on the use of rice and silk as money, see Chaudhuri, *Trade and Civilisation in the Indian Ocean*, 223.

24 See Althusser's comment on this point, *Reading Capital*, 178.

25 See the essays in Sabloff and Lamberg-Karlovsky eds., *Ancient Civilization and Trade*.

26 Ibn al-Ukhuwwa, *Maʿalim al-Qurba Fi Ahkam al-Hisba*, ed. and trans. R. Levy (1938), English and Arabic texts, 22, 91.

27 *Ibid.*, 21, 88–90; Barani, *Fatawa-i-Jahandari*, 35. On price regulations in Mamluk Cairo, see Ibn Taghri Birdi, *History of Egypt 1382–1469*, III, 38.

28 For a general treatment of nomadic societies see the essays in *Pastoral Production and Society*.

29 Bray, *Science and Civilisation in China*, 491; for a description of the rice markets in China around 1275, see Balazs, *Chinese Civilization*, 91, and Chaudhuri, *Trade and Civilisation in the Indian Ocean*, 25.

30 Bernier, *Travels in the Mogul Empire*, 248–9.

31 Bray, *Science and Civilisation in China*, 491.

32 Tavernier, *Travels in India*, I, 41.

33 Petrushevsky, 'The socio-economic condition of Iran under the Il-Khans', 501, quoting from the agronomic work *Kitab-i ʿilm-i falahat u Zira't* (1323), ed. ʿAbd al-Ghaffar Najm al-Daulah, Teheran, 1905.

34 See Chaudhuri, *The Trading World of Asia*; Pelsaert, *The Remonstrantie*, 16.

35 Huang Liu-hung, *A Complete Book Concerning Happiness and Benevolence*, 516.

36 Lambton, 'The dilemma of government in Islamic Persia: the *Siyasat-Nama* of Nizam al-Mulk'.

37 Griswold and Prasert na Nagara, 'Epigraphic and historical studies no. 17'.

38 Handlin, *Action in Late Ming Thought*, 23, 151.

39 Lambton, *State and Government in Medieval Islam*, 117, 122.

40 Gardiner, 'Ramesside texts relating to the taxation and transport of corn', 19, 22. Gardiner has warned that the first text is highly ambiguous and corrupt.

4 The structure of time and society

1 For Joseph Needham's exposure of European ignorance of Chinese astronomical clocks and the measurement of time, see *Heavenly Clockwork* (1960), 168. Even in 1956 one author could write: 'The history of Chinese civilisation from its beginnings reflects a timelessness, indeed a lack of preoccupation with time in any form ... It is consequently not altogether surprising to learn that the Chinese never produced any competent clockmakers.' Bedini, 'Chinese mechanical clocks', quoted by Needham.

2 Leibniz, *Selections*, 201–2; van Fraassen, *An Introduction to the Philosophy of Time and Space*, 38.

3 Lévi-Strauss, *The Savage Mind*, 258.

4 The expression 'fire-flies' of history is Braudel's, see *The Mediterranean*, II, 901.

5 Kraus, *Razis Opera philosophica fragmentaque quae supersunt*, I, 304, quoted by Corbin, *Cyclical Time and Ismaili Gnosis*, 30–1.

6 Bernier, *Travels in the Mogul Empire*, 260.

7 Jahangir, *Tuzuk-i-Jahangiri*, II, 49.

8 *Ibid.*, I, 330, and II, 65–6, *Ikbal-Nama-Jahangiri*, in Elliot and Dowson, *The History of India*, VI, 406–7.

9 Quoted by Rosenthal, *A History of Muslim Historiography*, 224–5; Rosenthal explains that the Prophetical tradition does not admit the report of a third person to be equivalent to actual observation.

10 Pomian, 'The secular evolution of the concept of cycles'; Fraser, Lawrence, and Haber eds., *Time, Science, and Society in China and the West*; Sivin, *Cosmos and Computation in Early Chinese Mathematical Astronomy*.

11 For ancient Indian time measurements, see Brennand, *Hindu Astronomy*, and Chakravarty, *Origin and Development of Indian Calendrical Science*.

12 In 751 the T'ang forces commanded by the Korean general Kao Hsien-chih were defeated by the Arabs in the battle of the River Talas, although it was not until much later that Islam made substantial conversions in Central Asia. Similarly, serious conversions in South East Asia did not get under way much before the fifteenth century.

13 Lewis, *The Muslim Discovery of Europe*, 199.

14 *Fort William-India House Correspondence 1757–1759*, 23 March 1759, para 55, 142; Chaudhuri, *The Trading World of Asia*, 56.

15 IOR. Despatches to Bombay, 29 March 1758, vol. 996, para. 21, 587; Chaudhuri, *The Trading World of Asia*, 67.

16 Ibn Khaldun, *The Muqaddimah*, I, 64–5.

17 There is considerable historical evidence that the population of Egypt and Syria did not recover permanently until the nineteenth century. The point will be dis-

cussed later. For a discussion of the historical issues, see Lopez, Miskimin, and Udovitch, 'England to Egypt: long-term trends and long-distance trade'; Dols, *The Black Death in the Middle East*; Lapidus, *Muslim Cities*; Musallam, *Sex and Society in Islam*, ch. 6.

18 See Hartwell, 'A cycle of economic change in imperial China: coal and iron in north-east China, 750–1350'.

19 Needham, *The Grand Titration*, 67; *Gunpowder as the Fourth Power*.

20 Tavernier, *Travels in India*, II, 217.

21 D. Petrovic, 'Fire-arms in the Balkans on the eve of and after the Ottoman Conquests of the fourteenth and fifteenth centuries', 190.

22 Ayalon, *Gunpowder and Firearms in the Mamluk Kingdom*; H. Inalcik, 'The socio-political effects of the diffusion of fire-arms in the Middle East'.

23 Smith, 'The Tahirid sultans of the Yemen', 154.

24 Tavernier, *Travels in India*, I, 48–9.

25 White, *Medieval Technology and Social Change*, 1–38; White, 'The crusades and the technological thrust of the West'; Needham, *The Grand Titration*, 86.

26 Pellat, *The Life and Works of Jahiz*, 92–3 and 'Djahiz et les Kharidjites' in his *Études sur l'histoire socio-culturelle de l'Islam (VIIᵉ–XVᵉ s.)*; Bosworth, 'Recruitment, muster and review in medieval Islamic armies', and 'Barbarian incursions: the coming of the Turks into the Islamic world', in *The Medieval History of Iran, Afghanistan and Central Asia*. The text of al-Jahiz' *Risala fi manaqib al-atrak wa-ᶜammat jund al-khilafa* is edited by G. van Vloten in *Tria Opuscula auctore al-Djahiz* (1903) and for an earlier English translation see Harley-Walker, 'Jahiz of Basra to al-Fath b. Khaqan on the "exploits of the Turks and the army of the Khalifate in general"' (1915). For some curious reason, al-Jahiz contrasts the Turks against the members of the Khawaraj sect, who are presented as fighters. It is possible that he was making a caricature of the Turks.

27 Braudel, *Civilization and Capitalism*, III, 71–88; Braudel, *On History*, 64–80.

28 Ibn Taghri Birdi, *A History of Egypt 1382–1469*, IV, 114.

29 Caetani, *Saggio di un Manuale di Cronologia Musulmana*, 65; Walker, *A Catalogue of the Arab-Byzantine and Post-Reform Umaiyad Coins*, xxv.

30 Grierson, *Numismatics*, 40.

31 The stationary component of time is, of course, the static trend, around which the actual observations will fluctuate in a random distribution with varying amplitudes.

32 On Champa rice, see Bray, *Science and Civilisation in China*, VI, Part II, 492.

33 al-Maqrizi, *A History of the Ayyubid Sultans of Egypt*, trans. Broadhurst (1980), 39, 77, 95, 107, 108, 139, 191, 222. See also Rabie, 'Some technical aspects of agriculture in medieval Egypt', 75–6; Lapidus, 'The grain economy of Mamluk Egypt'.

34 Huang Liu-hung, *A Complete Book concerning Happiness and Benevolence*, 405. On Chinese famines, see also Will, *Bureaucratie et famine en chine au 18ᵉ siècle*.

35 Soothill, *The Hall of Light*, 103.

36 Ibn Khaldun, *The Muqaddimah*, I, 280–1; on Islamic time-keeping for prayers and other regular duties, see King ed., *Islamic Mathematical Astronomy*.

37 Granet, *La Pensée chinoise*, 97. See also Sivin, *Cosmos and Computation in Early Chinese Mathematical Astronomy*.

38 Soothill, *The Hall of Light*, 42–51; Needham, *Time and Eastern Man*, 7, n. 3.

39 For examples in the seventeenth century, see Chaudhuri, *The Trading World of Asia*, chs. 5, 7, 16.

40 E. Zermelo, 'Über Grenzzahlaen und Mengenbereiche', quoted by Rucker, *Infinity and the Mind*, 203; see also, Gödel, 'What is Cantor's continuum problem?'.

5 The structure of space and society

1 For a discussion of the concept of implicated order and enfoldment in quantum physics, see Bohm, *Wholeness and the Implicate Order*, chs. 5 and 6.

2 The irrationality of the 'present' may be compared with the theory of continuity in space proposed by Richard Dedekind in 1872: 'I find the essence of continuity . . . in the following principle. If all points of a straight line fall into two classes, so that every point of the first class lies to the left of every point of the second class, then there exists one and only one point which produces this division of all points into two classes, this severing of the straight line into two portions.' Dedekind, 'Continuity and irrational numbers'.

3 See Ahmad Ibn Majid, *Kitab al-Fawa'id fi usul al-bahr wa'l-qawa'id* [Arab Navigation in the Indian Ocean].

4 For a contemporary description of the overland horse trade, see Ibn Battuta, *Travels of Ibn Battuta AD 1325–1354*, II, 478–9; also, Digby, *War-horse and Elephant*, 34. Horses exported from the Persian Gulf by sea are described in ᶜAbdu-llah Wassaf, *Tazjiyatu-l Amsar* (1300–28), III, 33.

5 al-Muqaddasi, *Ahsan al-Taqasim*, 29.

6 This notion is similar to the mathematical theory of induction. See ch. 1, n. 1.

7 For a critique of the Platonist notion of set theory, as completed entities of infinite classes existing independently of the mind, see Feferman's Introduction in Gödel, *Collected Works*, I, 22, 29; also Introduction in Benacerraf and Putnam eds., *Philosophy of Mathematics*, 30.

8 See Ibn Khaldun, *The Muqaddimah*, I, 266; also, Morony, *Iraq after the Muslim Conquest*, 179.

9 al-Muqaddasi, *Ahsan al-Taqasim*, 48.

10 Ibn Battuta, *Travels in Asia and Africa*, 309.

11 Ibn Khaldun, *The Muqaddimah*, I, 249.

12 Lyall ed., *The Mufaddaliyat*, II, 150.

13 Musil, *The Middle Euphrates*, 113; Musil recorded the event in 1915.

14 On this point, see Lammens, *Le Berceau de l'Islam; le Climat-Les Bedouins*, 146–7.

15 al-Maqrizi, *A History of the Ayyubid Sultans of Egypt*, ed. Broadhurst, 161.

16 Musil, *Arabia Deserta*, 162–3, 279–80; Musil was describing the attack (1909) on the oasis of al-Jawf by the Ruwala prince Nawwaf Ibn Nuri Ibn Shalan, the son of the reigning Amir An-Nuri Ibn Shalan, during the war between the forces of Ibn

Rashid and Ibn Saud. For historical references to similar movements, see also Bailey, 'Dating the arrival of the bedouin tribes in Sinai and the Negev'.

17 Musil, *Arabia Deserta*, 470–1.

18 This conclusion is presented in Adams, *Land Behind Baghdad* and *Heartland of Cities*, on the basis of field survey and taxation records of the late Abbasid period. The conclusion is controversial; for a critique, see Watson, 'A medieval green revolution', 53, n. 29.

19 See Adams, *Heartland of Cities*, 225, figures 52, 53 and Waines, 'The third century internal crisis of the Abbasids'. The question of the exaggeration by the Islamic historians of the effects of the Mongol conquests is discussed in Wu, *The Fall of Baghdad and Mongol Rule in al-Iraq, 1258–1335*.

20 Ma Huan, *Ying-yai sheng-lan*, 69, 179.

21 Ibn Khaldun, *The Muqaddimah*, I, 369–71.

22 Mendes Pinto, *Peregrinacam de Fernam Mendez Pinto*; for a discussion of the fact and fiction in the geography of Mendes Pinto, see Gentil, *Fernao Mendes Pinto*, 36.

23 Lu Yu, *Chajing* [Classic of Tea], quoted by Watson, *Tang and Liao Ceramics*, 35.

24 See Okakura, *The Book of Tea*, 32.

25 Marco Polo, *The Description of the World* [1298], 73.

26 Hamilton, *A New Account of the East Indies*, I, 6.

27 Ibn Khaldun, *The Muqaddimah*, I, 119, 172; the geographical section in the above drew heavily on al-Idrisi, *Nuzhat al-mushtaq*, composed at the court of Roger II of Sicily (1129–1154), French trans. Jaubert, *La Geographie d'Idrisi* (1836–40).

28 For a discussion of these texts see, Needham, 'Geography and cartography', in *Science and Civilisation in China*, III.

29 Ibn Taghri Birdi, *A History of Egypt 1382–1469*, IV, 86.

30 'A letter from Surat in India', 18 January 1671–2, printed in *The Diary of William Hedges*, II, cccv.

31 Fryer, *A New Account of East India and Persia*, II, 159.

32 Orme, *Historical Fragments of the Mogul Empire*, 404, 409.

33 Tavernier, *Travels in India*, I, 205.

34 *The Periplus of the Erythraean Sea*, 52–3; al-Idrisi, *La Geographie d'Idrisi*, I, 87.

35 al-Idrisi, *La Geographie d'Idrisi*, I, 161; Hamilton, *A New Account of the East Indies*, I, 77.

36 See Lamb, *The Changing Climate* and *Climate, History, and the Modern World*, 122, 124, 137; Bryson and Murray, *Climates of Hunger*.

37 al-Baladhuri, *Kitab Futuh al-Buldan*, 292, quoted by Le Strange, *The Lands of the Eastern Caliphate*, 27. See also El-Samarraie, *Agriculture in Iraq during the 3rd Century AH*, 12.

38 For a discussion of the recent climatic theories of the monsoons and the model suggested by George Hadley (1735) and William Ferrel, see Lamb, *Climate, History, and the Modern World* (1982), and *Changing Climate* (1966), 30.

39 For a general discussion of the history of climatic theories, see Chisholm, *Modern World Development: A Geographical Perspective*, ch. 6.

40 Geiger, *Civilization of the Eastern Iranians in Ancient Times*, I, 204–7.

41 Ma Huan, *Ying-yai Sheng-lan* (1433), 152–3.

42 *Ibid.*, 148.

43 Liefrinck, 'Rice cultivation in Northern Bali' (1886–87); van der Meer, *Sawah Cultivation in Ancient Java.*

44 See Goblot, *Les Qanats*; Wilkinson, *Water and Tribal Settlement in South-East Arabia*; English, 'The origins and spread of qanats in the old World'; Lambton, 'Kanat'.

45 Hsu Kuang-ch'i, *Nung-cheng chuan-shu* (1843), 25.15b, translated and quoted by Ping-ti Ho, *Studies on the Population of China*, 179.

46 For a general discussion of some of these points, see Pryor, 'The invention of the plow', and 'Causal theories about the origins of agriculture'; Boserup, *Population and Technology*; Goody, *Technology, Tradition, and the State in Africa.*

47 Ibn Jubayr, *The Travels*, 224.

48 Tavernier, *Travels in India*, I, 47.

49 Fryer, *A New Account of India and Persia*, III, 21.

50 *Ibid.*, 155–65.

51 For a description of the *baoli*, see Jairazbhoy, *An Outline of Islamic Architecture*, 304.

52 The printed version of Fryer's letter contains an error of transcription. The word 'pestilence' written in seventeenth-century handwriting in shortened form was not correctly read; see Fryer, *A New Account of India and Persia*, III, 165. For a discussion of the medieval image of the Ship of Fools, see Foucault, *Histoire de la Folie*. In 1582 one of the English merchants attending William Harbourne, envoy to the Ottoman Court of Murad, described a religious figure in the following language:

> Now, before the great Bassa, and Abraham Bassa, at their returne from the Court (and as we thinke at other times, but at that time for a certaine) there came a man in maner of a foole, who gave a great shout three or foure times, crying very hollowly, the place rebounded with the sound, and this man, say they, is a prophet of Mahomet, his armes and legges naked, on his feet he did weare wooden pattens of two sorts, in his hand, a flagge, or streamer set on short speare painted . . . Hakluyt, *The Principal Navigations*, III, 108.

53 Babar, *Babur-nama*, II, 480, 486–7, 525.

54 Ibn Khaldun, *The Muqaddimah*, II, 269.

55 al-Muqaddasi, *Ahsan al-Taqasim*, 186.

56 Ibn Battuta, *The Travels of Ibn Battuta*, III, 649.

57 See Amir Khusru's description of the treatment of Mongols by the Delhi Sultans in Elliot and Dowson eds., *The History of India*, III, 528–9.

58 Cleaves ed., *The Secret History of the Mongols*, 145–6.

59 Fisher, 'The eastern Maghrib and the central Sudan', 238.

60 On this point, see Chaudhuri, *Trade and Civilisation in the Indian Ocean*, 120.

61 See Ibn Battuta, *The Travels of Ibn Battuta*, I, 160; on the Arab attitude to the desert, see Bell, *The Desert and the Sown*, 60.

62 Ibn Khaldun, *The Muqaddimah*, I, 309.

63 Musil, *Arabia Deserta*, 306, 310.

64 Musil, *The Manners and Customs of the Rwala Bedouins*, 90.

65 For a discussion of the point, see Lammens, *Le Berceau de l'Islam: Le Climat – Les Bedouins*, 144.

66 Musil, *The Middle Euphrates*, 2.

67 Ibn Battuta, *The Travels of Ibn Battuta*, I, 256.

68 Ibn Jubayr, *The Travels of Ibn Jubayr* (1952), 215. On the archaeological sites of the hajj route and the water cisterns see, Al-Rashid, *Darb Zubaydah: the Pilgrim Road from Kufa to Mecca* (1980).

69 Ibn Battuta, *Travels of Ibn Battuta*, ed. Gibb (1958), I, 249, 252. Ibn Battuta was obviously following Ibn Jubayr's account for this part of the journey closely, for the amir of the pilgrims in 1184 also entered the town in combat formation. See Ibn Jubayr, *The Travels of Ibn Jubayr*, 214.

70 Musil, *Arabia Deserta*, 150.

71 *Ibid.*, 292–3.

72 On the problem of teaching the ignorant bedouins the correct Qur'anic prayer forms, see the 'Sira' of al-Hadi ila l-Haqq, the first Zaydi Imam of the Yemen (AD 897–911), discussed by Madelung, 'Land ownership and land tax in Northern Yemen and Najran: 3rd–4th/9th–10th century'.

73 Musil, *Arabia Deserta*, 232, 427.

74 Ibn Jubayr, *The Travels of Ibn Jubayr*, 215. See also Musil, *The Middle Euphrates*, 287–8, *Manners and Customs of the Rwala Bedouins*, 160. The linguistic and historical usage of the term 'qasr' is discussed in Conrad, 'The *qusur* of medieval Islam: some implications for the social history of the Near East', *Al-Abath*, vol. 29, 1981, 7–23.

75 Musil, *Arabia Deserta*, 332; Musil identifies al-Hadita with al-Muhdata mentioned by al-Muqaddasi as a station in the desert.

76 Musil, *Arabia Deserta*, 296; on the removal of tracks in the sand by the Arab guides see, also Ibn Battuta, *The Travels of Ibn Battuta*, I, 72.

77 Bailey, 'Dating the arrival of the bedouin tribes in Sinai and the Negev'; al-Jaziri's work is entitled *Durar al-Fara'id al-Munazzamah fi Akhbar al-Hajji wa Tariq Makkah al-Mu^cazzamah*, Cairo, 1964. See also Stern, 'Petitions from the Ayyubid Period' in his *Coins and Documents from the Medieval Middle East*, VIII, 22–3.

78 Hakluyt, *The Principal Navigations, Voyages, Traffiques and Discoveries*, III, 167–98.

6 Social identities I

1 Braudel, *Civilization and Capitalism*, I, 105.

2 Ying-shih Yu, 'Han', in Chang ed., *Food in Chinese Culture*, 55–6.

3 Devout Muslims generally disliked the presence of dogs. On the miniature, see Stanley Clarke, *Indian Drawings*.

4 See Buzurg ibn Shahriyar, *Kitab ^cAja'ib al-Hind*.

5 Tabari, *Ta'rikh*, II, 863–44. See also Stillman, 'Libas', in *Encyclopaedia of Islam*[2]; Dietrich, 'al-Hadjdjadj', in *Encyclopaedia of Islam*[2]

6 'Dis-moi ce que tu manges, je te dirai ce que tu es', Brillat-Savarin, *Physiologie du Gout*, 1.

7 Ying-shih Yu, 'Han' in Chang ed., *Food in Chinese Culture*, 66, quoting Chia I (*d.* 169 BC).

8 Jahangir, *Tuzuk-i-Jahangiri*, I, 236.

9 Heber, *Narrative of a Journey*, 216–17.

10 *Ibid.*, 221.

11 Ibn Muhammad Ibrahim, *The Ship of Sulaiman*, 34–42.

12 Chardin, *Travels in Persia* (1686), 224.

13 Rodinson, 'Ghidha', in *Encyclopaedia of Islam²*; Broomhall, *Islam in China*, 230–1.

14 Haagen-Smit, 'Smell and taste', in Hoff and Janick (eds.), *Food, Readings from Scientific American*, 8.

15 al-Muqaddasi, *Ahsan al-Taqasim*, 259.

16 Bernier, *Travels in the Mogul Empire*, 233, 248, 252.

17 Della Valle, *The Travels* (1664), I, 95. Della Valle's mental horizon was perhaps no wider than that of Bernier; see Gurney, 'Pietro Della Valle: the limits of perception', 103–16.

18 Hamilton, *A New Account of the East Indies*, I, 168–9.

19 Shway Yoe, *The Burman*, 79.

20 See Lévi-Strauss, *Structural Anthropology*, 86–7.

21 See Needham, *The Grand Titration*, 94; Al-Muqaddasi, *Ahsan al-Taqasim*, 201, 320; the text of the 'waqfiyya' is taken from the second volume of the collected *awqaf* in the Directorate at Damascus and the translated extract printed by Muhammad Adnan al-Bakhit, 'The role of the Hanash family', in Khalidi ed., *Land Tenure and Social Transformation in the Middle East*, 282.

22 For the Islamic regulations on the use of animals in mills see, Ibn al-Ukhuwwa [*d.* 729 AH/AD 1329], *Maᶜalim al-Qurba fi Ahkam al-Hisba*, ed. and trans. R. Levy (1938), 29. On the Chinese pickle making and the tax collected on pickles, see Huang Liu-hung, *A Complete Book Concerning Happiness*, 173.

23 This famous theme of Lévi-Strauss has been re-examined by Goody, *Cooking, Cuisine, and Class.*

24 Shway Yoe, *The Burman*, 280–1.

25 Ying-shih Yu, 'Han', in Chang ed., *Food in Chinese Culture*, 80–1; Hoff and Janick, *Food, Readings from Scientific American*, 8–9, 153–9.

26 Shafer, 'T'ang', and Spence, 'Ch'ing' in Chang ed., *Food in Chinese Culture*, 112–14, 264.

27 See Ibn Ridwan, *Medieval Islamic Medicine: Ibn Ridwan's Treatise*, ed. Dols and Gamal (1984); Hamarneh, *Origins of Pharmacy and Therapy in the Near East*; Meyerhoff, *Studies in Medieval Arabic Medicine.*

28 Macartney, *An Embassy to China*, 83.

29 Chardin, *Travels in Persia*, 232, 237.

30 Tavernier, *Travels in India*, I, 68–9.

31 Chang ed., *Food in Chinese Culture*, 7–8, 46.

32 Chardin, *Travels in Persia*, 222, 225.

33 For a general discussion of the problem, see Ashtor, 'An essay on the diet of the various classes in the medieval Levant' in Forster and Ranum eds., *Biology of Man*

in History; Braudel, *Civilization and Capitalism*, I, 129–30; for the reference to the memorandum of Ssu-ma Kuang see ch. 3, n. 20.

34 Jahangir, *Tuzuk-i-Jahangiri*, 419.

35 Khichri was also a favourite dish of his son Shah Jahan, see Bernier, *Travels in the Mongol Empire*, 152, 381.

36 Al-Mas'udi, *Maruj al-Dhahab*, *Les Prairies d'Or*, VIII, 438; Arberry trans, 'A Baghdad cookery book', 7.

37 Arberry trans., 'A Baghdad cookery book', 37; Ahsan, *Social Life under the Abbasids*, 131; Abu'l Fazl, *Ain i Akbari*, I, 60.

38 Al-Muqaddasi, *Ahsan al-Taqasim*, 207; Goitein, 'The main industries of the Mediterranean areas as reflected in the records of the Cairo Geniza', 195.

39 Ibn al-Ukhuwwa, Diya al-Din Muhammad, *Ma'alim al-Qurba fi Ahkam al-Hisba*, ed. and trans. R. Levy (1938), 35, 142; Bernier, *Travels in the Mogul Empire*, 250.

40 Chardin, *Travels in Persia*, 236. Lane, *An Account of the Manners . . . of the Modern Egyptians*, 318.

41 Freeman, 'Sung', in Chang ed., *Food in Chinese Culture*, 158–60.

42 Ibn Jubayr, *The Travels of Ibn Jubayr*, 117.

43 Jahangir, *Tuzuk-i-Jahangiri*, I, 5, 93, 391, and II, 177.

44 Pigeaud, 'Javanese gold', 192–3.

45 Tavernier, *Travels in India*, II, 177; Abbe Dubois, *Hindu Manners, Customs, and Ceremonies*, 184.

46 Good, 'A symbolic type and its transformation: the case of South Indian Ponkal', 226.

47 Huang Liu-hung, *A Complete Book Concerning Happiness*, 557–64. On the contrast between the rich and the poor, see also Gernet, *Daily Life in China* (1962), 136; Freeman, 'Sung', in Chang ed., *Food in Chinese Culture*, 151. Read ed., *Famine Foods listed in the Chiu Huang Pen Ts'ao*.

48 Nizami, *Studies in Medieval Indian History*.

49 Margoliouth, *The Table-talk of a Mesopotamian Judge*, 14–15, 66. On the Middle Eastern attitude to beef, see the references cited in nn. 13, 33.

50 On the technical aspects of food, see Margaria, 'The sources of muscular energy', Mayer, 'Appetite and obesity', and Kretchmer, 'The physiology of starvation'.

51 For a detailed modern study of food and nutrition in three Javanese villages, see Edmundson, 'Land, food, and work in three Javanese villages'.

52 Al-Mas'udi, *Muruj al-Dhahab*, *Les Prairies d'or*, II, 438–9, and VIII, 336; Ashtor, 'Diet in the medieval Levant', in Forster and Ranum eds., *Biology of Man in History*, 134; Watson, *Agricultural Innovation in the Early Islamic World*, 45.

53 Bray, *Science and Civilisation in China*, VI, Part II, 541, 622, quoting *Chi Min Yao Shu*.

54 Bray, *Science and Civilisation in China*, VI, Part II, 67.

55 Finkel, 'King Mutton, a curious Egyptian Tale from the Mamluk period', quoting al-Shirbini, *Hazz al Kuhuf*; Ashtor, 'Diet in the medieval Levant', in Forster and Ranum eds., *Biology of Man in History*.

56 Chardin, *Travels in Persia*, 222–6.

57 Abu'l Fazl, *Ain i Akbari*, I, 59–60.

58 Pigeaud, *Java in the 14th Century*, IV, X, 250.

59 ath-Thaʿalibi, *The Lataʾif al-maʿarif of Thaʿalibi*, 64–5; Ibn Battuta, *Travels in Asia and Africa*, 86; Ahsan, *Social Life under the Abbasids*, 89–90.

60 Al-Muqaddasi, *Ahsan al-Taqasim*, 326.

61 For a photograph of the Pharaonic loaves, see figure 12.13, reproduced in Darby, Ghalioungui, and Grivetti, *Food: The Gift of Osiris*, II, 521.

62 Pliny, *Natural History*, Libri XVIII.xix.106, 256–7, XVIII.xiii.71, 235, XVIII.xx.85–6, 245.

63 Abu'l Fazl, *Ain i Akbari*, I, 61.

64 Patwardhan and Darby, *The State of Nutrition in the Arab Middle East*, 20–1. Rodinson, 'Recherches sur les documents arabes relatifs à la cuisine', 152, quoting *Kitab al-Wusla*, which calls such bread *iflaqun*.

65 Chardin, *Travels in Persia*, 233. *Lavas* is also called *nan-e hunegi* when it is rolled out thin as a paper. *Sangak* had another name, *nan-e hamiri*, On methods of making Persian bread, see Wulff, *The Traditional Crafts of Persia*, 292.

66 Musil, *The Manners and Customs of the Rwala Bedouins*, 92.

67 Abbé Dubois, *Hindu Manners, Customs, and Ceremonies*, 282–3.

68 The Arab physician al-Razi warned against eating meat other than mutton; see Ashtor, 'Diet in the medieval Levant', in Forster and Ranum eds., *Biology of Man in History*, 130; Rodinson, 'Recherches sur les documents arabes relatifs à la cuisine', 146.

69 Ibn Battuta, *Travels of Ibn Battuta A.D. 1325–1354*, III, 607–8. Bharatchandra, *Bharatchandra-granthavali*.

70 Ibn Muhammad Ibrahim, *The Ship of Sulaiman*, 68–9, 156–7.

71 Lord Macartney, *An Embassy to China*, 121–2.

72 Will, *Embassies and Illusions*, 73, 208–9.

73 Spence, 'Ch'ing', in Chang ed., *Food in Chinese Culture*, 292–3.

74 *New International Larousse Gastronomique.*

75 Al-Muqaddasi, *Ahsan al-Taqasim*, 199.

76 On the cooling properties of earthenware jars, see Niebuhr, *Travels through Arabia*, II, 317; it can also be verified by simply buying one of these vessels in the suqs of Saʿna. On the Iranian and Chinese ice houses, see Chardin, *Travels in Persia*, 239; Fortune, *Three Years' Wanderings in the Northern Provinces of China*; Al-Muqaddasi, *Ahsan al-Taqasim*, 202. Also al-Hassan and Hill, *Islamic Technology; An Illustrated History*, 231.

77 Abu'l Fazl, *Ain i Akbari*, I, 55–6; Bernier, *Travels in the Mogul Empire*, 356.

78 Ahsan, *Social Life Under the Abbasids*, 164; Masʿudi, *The Meadows of Gold: the Abbasids*, 258.

79 Chardin, *Travels in Persia*, 88, 243. Hamilton, *A New Account of the East Indies*, I, 63. Yarshater, 'The theme of wine-drinking and the concepts of the beloved in early Persian poetry'.

80 Tavernier, *Travels in India*, I, 71.

81 For a theoretical discussion of the problem of identity, see Kripke, *Naming and Necessity*, 143–55.

7 Social identities II

1 Ibn Taghri Birdi, for example, describes how in 1434 Sahib Karim ad-Din appeared in the Citadel before Sultan Barsbai of Egypt and was invested with a

tunic from the sultan's own clothing. Next day he was invested a second time with a magnificent robe to retain the position of major-domo. See *A History of Egypt 1382–1469*, IV, 114; Serjeant, *Material for a History of Islamic Textiles*, I, 75, and XVII, 29.

2 Jahangir, *Tuzuk-i-Jahangiri*, I, 384.

3 Ibn Jubayr, *The Travels of Ibn Jubayr*, 75, 91; Ibn Jubayr gives a full description of the *hajj* routine as he found it in AD 1183; on 'ihram' and 'libas' (clothing), see *Encyclopaedia of Islam*², under the above headings.

4 On shawls, see Abu'l Fazl, *Ain-i-Akbari*, I, 91–2.

5 Serjeant, *Material for a History of Islamic Textiles*, 73.

6 Tritton, *The Caliph and their Non-Muslim Subjects*, 115–26.

7 Al-Tabari, *The History of al-Tabari*, XXXII, 61–2.

8 See IOR, Original Correspondence, 24 December 1702, vol. 65, no. 8097.

9 Al-Muqaddasi, *Ahsan al-Taqasim*, 151; see also, Abu'l Fazl, *Ain-i-Akbari*, I, 90–1.

10 Ibn Battuta, *Travels in Asia and Africa*, 230, 244.

11 *Brhat Kalpa Sutra Bhasya*, quoted by Moti Chandra, *Costumes, Cosmetics & Coiffure in . . . India*, 51, 66.

12 Della Valle, *The Travels*, I, 45.

13 For a detailed description and analysis of the symbolism of textiles in Indonesia, see Gittinger, *Splendid Symbols, Textiles and Tradition in Indonesia*.

14 'Je vous avoue que je n'ai aucun attrait pour les modes immobiles des Turcs et des autres peuples de l'Orient. Il semble qu'elles prêtent de la durée à leur stupide despotisme, car les habitudes se tiennent . . . Nos villageois sont un peu Turcs à l'égard des modes.' Say, *Cours complet d'économie politique pratique*, V, 108.

15 Chardin, *Travels in Persia*, 211.

16 Braudel, *Civilization and Capitalism*, I, 312.

17 On the symbolic significance of Chinese robes, see Cammann, *China's Dragon Robes*; Fernald, *Chinese Court Costumes*; Vollmer, *In the Presence of the Dragon Throne*.

18 *Ming shih*, 67.7b.8, quoted by Cammann, *China's Dragon Robes*, 17–18.

19 Vollmer, *In the Presence of the Dragon Throne*, 50.

20 Rifaᶜa, *Al-Rihla*, 119–20, quoted by Lewis, *Muslim Discovery of Europe*, 281–2.

21 Al-Masᶜudi, *Muruj al-Dhahab*, VII, 190, *The Meadows of Gold: The Abbasids*, 239.

22 Kuhnel and Goetz, 'History of costume', in *Indian Book Painting*, 41.

23 Abu'l Fazl, *Ain-i-Akbari*, I, 91–2.

24 Ibn Khaldun, *Muqaddimah* II, 65–6.

25 Kuhnel and Goetz, *Indian Book Painting*, 43.

26 Della Valle, *The Travels*, I, 43–4.

27 Ibn al-Rami, *Kitab al-I'lan bi-Ahkam al-Bunyan* (The Book for Communicating Building Solutions) quoted by Hakim, *Arabic-Islamic Cities*, 25, the citation is from a text handwritten and printed lithographically in Fez, 1332 AH/AD 1913; see also Brunschvig, *Le Berberie Orientale sous Les Hafsides*, II, 183, Ibn Khaldun, *The Muqaddimah*, II, 361, n. 121. The case was recorded by jurist Malik ben Anas al-Asbahi of Medina (711–95).

28 See *New International Larousse Gastronomique*, and Carême, *Le Pâtissier royal Parisien ou Traité élémentaire et pratique de la pâtisserie ancienne et moderne*.

29 For a description of the 'Architecture of power' in Islam, see Grabar's contribution in Grube ed., *Architecture of the Islamic World*, 48–79.

30 Ibn Khaldun, *The Muqaddimah*, 262–3. In spite of what Ibn Khaldun said about the Byzantine origins of the craftsmen employed in building the Dome of the Rock, its architects are still unknown. See Creswell, *Early Muslim Architecture*, I, 100. On the tradition of obtaining builders and building material from the Byzantine emperor, see Ibn Jubayr, *The Travels of Ibn Jubayr*, 272 and Ibn Battuta who repeats Ibn Jubayr, see n. 33 below.

31 For a discussion of the historical works on early Islamic architecture, see Creswell, *Early Muslim Architecture*, I.

32 Al-Muqaddasi, *Ahsan al-Taqasim*, 259–60, 262. On al-Walid's reputation as a builder see also, ath-Thaᶜalibi, *The Lati'f al-ma'arif of Thaᶜalibi*, 97; Wilbur, 'Builders and craftsmen of Islamic Iran'.

33 Ibn Jubayr, *The Travels of Ibn Jubayr*, 288; the place was also described in Ibn Battuta, *The Travels of Ibn Battuta*, I, 148.

34 Abu'l Fazl, *Ain-i-Akbari*, I, 222.

35 Wilbur, *The Architecture of Islamic Iran*, 124; Wilbur, 'Builders and craftsmen of Islamic Iran'.

36 Pelsaert, *The Remonstrantie*, 56.

37 Gil, *Documents of the Jewish Pious Foundations from the Cairo Geniza*, 65, 147; the text of the court records in al-Bab al-ᶜAli, presided over by Qadi al-Qudat is printed in Hanna, *Construction Work in Ottoman Cairo 1517–1798*, 55. See also Goitein, 'A mansion in Fustat: a twelfth-century description of a domestic compound in the ancient capital of Egypt', 163–72, and 'Urban housing in Fatimid and Ayyubid times'.

38 On the Buddhist stupa of Barabodur, see Krom, *Beschrijving van Barabudur*, 5 vols.; Lohuizende Leeuw, 'The Stupa in Indonesia'. On the economic aspects of Buddhist monasteries in China, see Chen, *Buddhism in China*, ch. 10; Gernet, *Les aspects économique du Bouddhisme dans la société chinoise du vᵉ au xᵉ siècle*; Twitchett, 'The monasteries and China's economy in medieval times'; Yang, 'Buddhist monasteries and four money-raising institutions in Chinese history'.

39 Hamilton, *A New Account of the East Indies*, II, 86–7. See also Tavernier, *Travels in India*, II, 229.

40 Tavernier, *Travels in India*, II, 229.

41 Bowrey, *A Geographical Account of the Countries Round the Bay of Bengal*, 293.

42 Ricci, *China in the Sixteenth Century: The Journals of Matthew Ricci*, 19–20. For the plain appearance of ordinary Chinese houses, see Nieuhoff, *An Embassy from the East India Company*, 81.

43 Spence, *The Memory Palace of Matteo Ricci*, 213. The print album apparently never reached the emperor. See also Huang, *1587: A Year of No Significance*, 126–9.

44 Bernier, *Travels in the Mogul Empire*, 281; De Magalhaens, *A New History of China*, quoted by Needham, *Science and Civilisation in China*, IV, Part III, 63.

45 Nieuhof, *An Embassy from the East India Company*, 129.

46 Macartney, *An Embassy to China*, 272.

47 However, in parts of Oman and Lower Iraq reed and thatch houses were quite common; see Abdulak, 'Tradition and continuity in vernacular Omani housing'; Thesiger, *The Marsh Arabs*.

48 Marçais, 'Dar', in the *Encyclopaedia of Islam*[2]; Raymond, *The Great Arab Cities in the 16th–18th Centuries*, 69–70; Hakim, *Arabic-Islamic Cities*, 95.

49 Serjeant and Lewcock eds., *San'a': An Arabian Islamic City*, 461. See also Golvin and Fromont, *Thula, architecture et urbanisme d'une cité de haute montagne . . . du Yemen*.

50 Niebuhr, *Travels through Arabia*, I, 403, 405.

51 *Ibid.*, 255.

52 Goitein, 'A mansion in Fustat: a twelfth-century description of a domestic compound in the ancient capital of Egypt'. See also Revault and Maury, *Palais et Maisons du Caire*.

53 Serjeant and Lewcock eds., *San'a'*, 442b; Aalund, 'The wakalat bazar'a: the rehabilitation of a commercial structure in the old city', 35–6.

54 Gazzard, 'The Arab house: its form and spatial distribution', 20.

55 Bernier, *Travels in the Mogul Empire*, 247; Chardin, *Travels in Persia*, 261.

56 See Serjeant and Lewcock, *San'a'*, plates 2, 50, 53.

57 Ath-Tha'alibi, *The Lata'if al-ma'arif of Tha'alibi*, 48–9. This method of air-conditioning persisted in northern India until the 1930s when thick mats made from thin aromatic roots were used as screens, known as 'khas-khas'.

58 For a detailed description of the construction techniques and building materials see, Serjeant and Lewcock eds., *San'a'*, 468–84.

59 Pelsaert, *The Remonstrantie*, 67.

60 Fryer, *A New Account of East India and Persia*, III, 17.

61 Thevenot, *Indian Travels of Thevenot*, 22.

62 Bernier, *Travels in the Mogul Empire*, 246.

63 *Ibid.*, 246.

64 Pelsaert, *The Remonstrantie*, 61.

65 Bernier, *Travels in the Mogul Empire*, 245.

66 Fryer, *A New Account of East India and Persia*, II, 241.

67 Raymond and Wiet eds., *Les Marches du Caire: Traduction Annotée du Texte de Maqrizi* [Hitat, II, 92–4] 133–45; Hanna, 'Bulaq – an endangered historic area of Cairo', and *An Urban History of Bulaq in the Mamluk and Ottoman Periods* (1983); Aalund, 'The Wakalat Bazar'a' (1987).

68 Niebuhr, *Travels in Arabia*, I, 351.

69 Thevenot, *Indian Travels of Thevenot*, 12–13.

70 Nieuhoff, *An Embassy from the East India Company*, 81.

71 See La Loubere, *A New Historical Relation of the Kingdom of Siam*, 29.

72 See Koentjaraningrat, *Javanese Culture*, 134–5. See also Prijotomo, *Ideas and Forms of Javanese Architecture*.

73 La Loubere, *A New Historical Relation of the Kingdom of Siam*, 31–2.

74 Needham, *Science and Civilisation in China*, IV, Part III, 69.

75 Wu, *Chinese and Indian Architecture*; Boyd, *Chinese Architecture and Town*

Planning, 75–121; Needham, *Science and Civilisation in China*, IV, Part III, 65.
See also Boerschmann, *Picturesque China: Architecture and Landscape*.

76 Mo Tzu, *The Ethical and Political Works of Motse*, 22, 117; Needham, *Science and Civilisation in China*, IV, Part III, 125.

77 Mendoza, *The History of the Kingdom of China*, 26–7.

78 Huang, *1587: A Year of No Significance*, 129.

79 La Loubere, *A New Historical Relation of the Kingdom of Siam*, 28–30.

80 Thevenot, *Indian Travels of Thevenot*, 11.

8 The land and its products

1 The importance of market-gardening for suburban landlords was emphasised in the sixth-century Chinese *Chih Min Yao Shu*; see Bray, *Science and Civilisation in China*, 431–2, 622.

2 Abu'l Fazl, *Ain-i-Akbari*, 52.

3 Helbaek, 'Ecological effects of irrigation in ancient Mesopotamia', 186.

4 For a very fine general account of agriculture and its history in the Far East, see Gourou, *Man and Land in the Far East*.

5 See Gourou, *The Tropical World*, 45, for a different set of calculations.

6 N. I. Vavilov worked at the All-Union Institute of Plant Industry in Leningrad from 1920 to 1940 and organised plant collection and genetic analysis on a world scale. His main conclusions have been translated and published. See Vavilov, 'The origins, variation, immunity, and breeding of cultivated plants'. For a discussion of his work, see Harlan, 'The plants and animals that nourish man'.

7 For a general discussion, see Renfrew, *Palaeoethnobotany: The Prehistory of Food Plants of the Near East and Europe*; Harlan, 'Plant and animal distribution in relation to domestication', and Hutchinson, 'India: local and introduced crops'; Harlan, *Crops and Man* (1975); Allchin, 'Early cultivated plants in India and Pakistan'; Stamp ed., *A History of Land Use in Arid Regions*; Sauer, *Agricultural Origins and Dispersals*.

8 Pliny, *Natural History*, ed. Rackham, Bk. XVIII.x.55, vol. 5, 225.

9 Watson, *Agricultural Innovation in the Early Islamic World*. See also Laufer, *Sino-Iranica: Chinese Contributions to the History of Civilization*.

10 Serjeant and Lewcock eds., *San^ca': An Arabian Islamic City*, 553.

11 al-Abbas, *Bughyat al-Fellahin*, I, 40.

12 See ch. 5, p. 000.

13 Hsu Kuang-ch'i, *Nung-cheng chuan-shu*, 25.15b, translated and quoted by Ping-ti Ho, *Studies on the Population of China*, 179.

14 See Ashtor, 'Diet in the medieval Levant', in Forster and Ranum eds., *Biology of Man in History*.

15 al-Abbas, *Bughyat al-Fellahin*, I, 40–1.

16 On the techniques of cultivation in the Islamic sources, particularly the summary of the text *Kitab al-filaha al-Nabatiyya* [The Book of Nabatean Agriculture] by Ibn Wahshiyya, see El-Samarraie, *Agriculture in Iraq during the 3rd Century, AH*; also Rabie, 'Some technical aspects of agriculture in medieval Egypt'.

17 Bray, *Science and Civilization in China*, 431.
18 Abu'l Fazl, *Ain-i-Akbari*, 63.
19 Rabie, 'Some technical aspects of agriculture in medieval Egypt'.
20 Helbaek, 'Ecological effects of irrigation in ancient Mesopotamia', 195.
21 Loomis, 'Agricultural systems'.
22 Ibn Battuta, *Travels of Ibn Battuta*, I, 63–4. See also Ashtor, 'Levantine sugar industry in the late Middle Ages: a case of technological decline'.
23 See for example, Abu'l Fazl, *Ain-i-Akbari*.
24 Ziya al-Din Barani, *Ta'rikh-i-Firuz Shahi*, III, 242. Muhammad Tughluq was the ruler who had employed Ibn Battuta as an Islamic judge at his court in Delhi.
25 The concept of oasis land as the geographical determinant of cultivable area is discussed in Lombard, *The Golden Age of Islam*, 23.
26 al-Baladhuri, *Kitab Futuh al-Buldan*, 428.
27 The rates levied in Iran for the ninth and tenth centuries have been summarised in Lambton, *Landlord and Peasant in Persia*, 43–5.
28 *Ibid.*, 427.
29 al-Baladhuri, *Kitab Futuh al-Buldan*, 423. For a recent discussion of the problems on early Islamic conquest, settlement, and the taxation of Iraq, see Donner, 'Tribal settlement in Basra during the first century AH', Morony, 'Land holding and social change: lower al-Iraq in the early Islamic period', and North, 'Some remarks on the "nationalization" of conquered lands at the time of the Umayyads', in Khalidi ed., *Land Tenure and Social Transformation in the Middle East*.
30 For Babylonian laws on agricultural production and land, see Driver and Miles eds., *The Babylonian Laws*.
31 See Abu'l Fazl's historical account in *Ain-i-Akbari*, II, 55–8; Lambton, *Landlord and Peasant in Persia*.
32 Ahmed Sousa, *Irrigation and Civilization in the Land of the Twin Rivers*, plates XV–XVII, and notes.
33 For a discussion of the role of the plough and the wheel and their absence in African agriculture, see Goody, *Technology, Tradition, and the State in Africa*, 21–38; the sociological issues in African agrarian production are discussed in Meillassoux, 'From reproduction to production: a Marxist approach to economic anthropology', and Dupré and Rey, 'Reflections on the pertinence of a theory of the history of exchange'.
34 Watabe, *Glutinous Rice in Northern Thailand*, 21, summarises the available information.
35 Hunter, *A Statistical Account of Bengal*, V, 202–3.
36 See Barker *et al.* eds., *The Rice Economy of Asia*, 15–16.
37 See Chang, 'The rice cultures'; Chang, Kwang-chih, 'The beginnings of agriculture in the Far East'; Christiansen, 'Wet rice cultivation: some reasons why'; Geertz, *Agricultural Involution*; Grist, *Rice*.
38 Niebuhr, *Travels through Arabia*, II, 290–1.
39 Braudel, *Civilization and Capitalism*, I, 151; the relative yield figures are also given by Braudel.

40 Bernier, *Travels in the Mogul Empire*, 437; see also the description of Streynsham Master in 1676 in *The Diary of Streynsham Master*, II, 28; Adam Smith, *The Wealth of Nations*, vol. II, bk. IV, ch. IX.

41 See Liefrinck, 'Rice cultivation in Northern Bali [1886–87]', 43; for a critique of Balinese social institutions in colonial mind, see Nordholt, *Bali: Colonial Conceptions and Political Change 1700–1940*, and van der Meer, *Sawah Cultivation in Ancient Java*.

42 Bray, *Science and Civilisation in China*, VI, 491.

43 Chi, Ch'ao-ting, *Key Economic Areas in Chinese History*, 134, quoting T'o, *Sung History*, chuan 173, 'Book on Food and Commodities', 29.

44 Knox, *An Historical Relation of the Island of Ceylon in the East-Indies* (1681), 7–8.

45 al-Hassan and Hill, *Islamic Technology*, 37; Ahmed Sousa, *Irrigation and Civilization in the Land of the Twin Rivers*, plate IX. The beam was also found extensively in India.

46 Hill, *A History of Engineering in Classical and Medieval Times*, 127–52.

47 Quoted in Schiøler, *Roman and Islamic Water-Lifting Wheels*, 59.

48 For Babar's description, see *Babur-nama*, I, 388, and II, 486.

49 See Reade, 'Studies on Assyrian geography'.

50 Davey, 'The Negub tunnel'.

51 Forbes, *Studies in Ancient Technology*, I, 153; Goblot, *Les Qanats: Une Technique d'Acquisition de L'Eau*, 61; English, 'The origin and spread of qanats in the Old World' (1968); Lambton, 'Kanat', in the *Encyclopaedia of Islam*[2].

52 See Krenkow, 'The construction of subterranean water supplies during the Abbasid caliphate'.

53 Wilkinson, *Water and Tribal Settlement in South-East Arabia*, 85; Brohier, *Ancient Irrigation Works in Ceylon*, I, 3; Liefrinck, 'Rice cultivation in Northern Bali'.

54 Polybius, *History*, Bk. X.28.3–4, vol. 4, 169.

55 See article 'Ma' [Water] by Cahen and others in the *Encyclopaedia of Islam*[2], and 'Mizan' by Wiedemann in the *Encyclopaedia of Islam*[1].

56 Forbes, *Studies in Ancient Technology*, I, 154, the reference is to Megasthenes and Strabo, XV. 1.50.c. 707.

57 In this context, see the valuable study by Inalcik, 'Rice cultivation and the Celtukci-Re'aya system in the Ottoman Empire', in *Studies in Ottoman Social and Economic History*, VI, 71–83.

58 See the detailed study of the Omani 'falaj' organisation in Wilkinson, *Water and Tribal Settlement in South-East Arabia*, 100–21; also Lambton, 'Kanat', in *Encyclopaedia of Islam*[2].

59 Morony, 'Lower al-Iraq in the early Islamic period', 217; the reference is to Baladhuri, *Kitab Futuh al-Buldan*, 291. See also el-Sammarraie, *Agriculture in Iraq during the 3rd Century AH*, 151, on Abu Yusuf's recommendation for differential rate of taxation on crops, Abu Yusuf (*d.* AD 798), *Kitab al-Kharaj*.

60 Inalcik, 'Rice cultivation in the Ottoman empire', in *Studies in Ottoman Social and Economic History*, VI, 73–4.

61 Kramers, 'Sokolli Muhammad Pasha', in the *Encyclopaedia of Islam*[1]; Allen, 'The Ottoman and Turkestan: The Don-Volga Canal Project' in *Problems of Turkish Power in the Sixteenth Century*.

62 Shams-i-Siraj Afif, *Tarikh-i-Firuz Shahi*, 299–302.

63 'Inayat Khan, *Shah Jahan-Nama*, VII, 86.

64 Tavernier, *Travels in India*, I, 121–2.

65 See Adiceam, *La Geographie de l'Irrigation dans le Tamilnad*.

66 Ishii ed., *Thailand: A Rice-Growing Society*, 21.

67 Hayami, 'A "Great Transformation": economic and social changes in the late 16th and 17th centuries Japan'; Tomosugi, 'Japan's wet rice agrarian society: a study in genesis, structure, and change'.

68 Quoted by Perdue, *Exhausting the Earth: State and Peasant in Hunan, 1500–1850*, 88.

69 For a discussion of these problems, see Murphey, 'The ruin of Ancient Ceylon'.

70 Brohier, *Ancient Irrigation Works in Ceylon*, 23.

71 The historical details are discussed in Murphey, 'The ruins of ancient Ceylon'; Leach, 'Hydraulic society in Ceylon'; Gunawardana, 'Irrigation and hydraulic society in early and medieval Ceylon' (1971).

72 Gourou, *L'Utilisation du Sol en Indochine française*, 165–70, *Man and Land in the Far East*, 38–46.

73 Braudel, *Civilization and Capitalism*, I, 149; Gourou, *L'Asie*, 30–2.

74 Knox, *An Historical Relation of the Island of Ceylon in the East Indies*, 123–4.

75 *Ibid.*, 4.

76 For the full passage of Ibn Khaldun's text, see ch. 5, p. 101.

77 See Needham, *Science and Civilisation in China*, IV, 236.

78 Lecomte, *Memoirs and Observations, Topographica, Physical . . . Made in a late Journey through the Empire of China*, 111.

79 Schurmann, *Economic Structure of the Yuan Dynasty*, 52. [*Yuan shih*, 93. 4a9–7b9], 52.

80 Weng Cheng, *Nung Shu*, ch. 7, p. 5a, b; the passage is quoted in Chi, Ch'ao-ting, *Key Economic Areas in Chinese History*, 27, and in Needham, *Science and Civilisation in China*, IV, 225.

81 Ching, Ch'ao-ting, *Key Economic Areas in Chinese History*, 113–41; Needham, *Science and Civilisation in China*, IV, 307.

82 Ssu-ma Ch'ien, *Shih Chi*, quoted by Chi, Ch'ao-ting, *Key Economic Areas in Chinese History*, 66.

83 See ch. 5, p. 000.

84 See Orme, *General Idea of the Government and People of Indostan*, printed in *Historical Fragments of the Mogul Empire*; for Marx's theory of the Asiatic Mode of Production see, *Capital*, vol. III, Book III, chapter XX, 'Historical facts about merchants' capital'. For recent discussions, see Godelier, *Rationalité et Irrationalité en Économie*, and *Sur les Sociétés Pre-capitalistes*; Bailey and Llobera eds., *The Asiatic Mode of Production*; Kahn and Llobera eds., *The Anthropology of Pre-Capitalist Societies*; Hindess and Hirst eds., *Pre-Capitalist Modes of Production*.

85 Thomas Robert Malthus, *An Essay on the Principle of Population* (1798). In the later edition of his *Essay*, Malthus introduced in addition to the concept of negative checks, that of positive ones. The conscious attempt to limit the size of families and raising the age of marriage could have significant effects, he thought, on population expansion.

86 For a historical context of the theory of diminishing return, see Schumpeter, *History of Economic Analysis*, 581–8.

87 Bernier, *Travels in the Mogul Empire*, 226–7.

88 Burke, 'Speech on Nabob of Arcot's debts, 28 February 1785', in *The Writings and Speeches of Edmund Burke*, ed. P. J. Marshall, V, 521–2.

89 See Inalcik, 'Rice cultivation in the Ottoman Empire', VI, 73, and 'Military and fiscal transformation in the Ottoman Empire, 1600–1700', V. Cuno, 'Egypt's wealthy peasantry, 1740–1820: a study of the region of al-Mansura'. Huang Liu-hung, *A Complete Book concerning Happiness*, 512–14.

90 For a discussion of the Malthusian problem in the context of European agrarian history, see Aston and Philpin eds., *The Brenner Debate: Agrarian Class Structure and Economic Development in Pre-Industrial Europe*.

91 Løkkegaard, *Islamic Taxation in the Classic Period*; Lambton, *Landlord and Peasant in Persia*, 53–76; Moreland, *The Agrarian System of Moslem India*, 216–23; Inalcik, 'Military and Fiscal Transformation in the Ottoman Empire, 1600–1700'.

92 Tanaka Masatoshi, 'Popular uprisings, rent resistance, and bondservant rebellions in the late Ming'.

93 Perdue, *Exhausting the Earth: State and Peasant in Hunan, 1500–1850*, 21; Ping-ti Ho, *Studies on the Population of China, 1368–1953*, 58–60, 147–8; Adam Smith on the practice of infanticide in China, *The Wealth of Nations*, I, 73. Rice shortages in southern China in the eighteenth century is discussed in Viraphol, *Tribute and Profit: Sino Siamese Trade 1652–1853*, ch. 5. For a graphic analysis of the twentieth-century conditions, see Chen Han-seng, *Landlord and Peasant in China: A Study of the Agrarian Crisis in South China*; Jing Su and Luo Lun, *Landlord and Labor in Late Imperial China*.

94 Khalidi, ed., *Land Tenure and Social Transformation in the Middle East*.

95 For the nineteenth century theory and practice of Indian landholding and its historical interpretation, see Baden-Powell, *The Land Systems of British India*, I; Moreland, *The Agrarian System of Moslem India*; Lambton, *Landlord and Peasant in Persia*; Løkkegaard, *Islamic Taxation in the Classic Period*; Rabie, *The Financial System of Egypt AH 564–741/AD 1169–1341*.

96 On the land usage of South East Asia and social stratification, see Ishii ed., *Thailand: A Rice-Growing Society*; Popkin, *The Rational Peasant: the Political Economy of Rural Society in Vietnam*; Tomosugi, *A Structural analysis of Thai Economic History*; Wales, *Ancient Siamese Government and Administration*; Bremen, *The Village on Java*; Geertz, *Agricultural Involution*; Koentjaraningrat ed., *Villages in Indonesia*; Tjondronegoro, *Social Organization and Planned Development in Rural Java*; Van Setten van der Meer, *Sawah Cultivation in Ancient Java*.

97 See Oyama Masaaki, 'Large landownership in the Jiangnan delta region during the late Ming-early Qing period'; Elvin, *The Pattern of the Chinese Past*, chs. 6 and 15.

98 Rawski, *Agricultural Change and the Peasant Economy of South China*, 10–30.

99 This point was made by Hicks, *A Theory of Economic History*, 102.

100 For a criticism of Hicks' view, see Gerschenkron's review of Hicks, *Mercator Gloriosus*.

9 Animals and their masters

1 See Doerfer, *Turkische und Mongolische Elemente im Neupersischen*, III, 621–5.

2 See Lindner, *Nomads and Ottomans*, 54–5.

3 Bates, 'Differential access to pasture in a nomadic society: the Yörük of South-eastern Turkey'.

4 For a discussion of the term nomadism, see Salzman, 'Is "nomadism" a useful concept?'.

5 Jahangir, *Tuzuk-i-Jahangiri*, II, 233–4.

6 Tavernier, *Travels in India*, I, 32–3.

7 M. Sanudo, *Diarii*, II, column 577, quoted by Braudel, *The Mediterranean*, I, 87.

8 This was the famous finding of Barth from his study of the Basseri nomads; Barth, *Nomads of South Persia*, 101–11. It has been extensively commented upon by other anthropologists and various permutations are now available as case-studies.

9 For the Mediterranean transhumance and the Spanish mesta, see Braudel, *The Mediterranean*, I, 85–94.

10 For a discussion of the historiography of pastoral nomadism, see Khazanov, *Nomads and the Outside World*.

11 Petrushevsky, 'The socio-economic condition of Iran under the Il-Khans', 494; see also Khazanov, *Nomads and the Outside World*, 3, 252.

12 Lambton, *Continuity and Change in Medieval Persia*, 178, n. 97, quoting Rashid al-Din, *Mukatabat-i-Rashidi*.

13 Lindner, *Nomads and Ottomans*, 54.

14 'Henry Bornford's account of his journey from Agra to Tatta', March 1639, IOR, Original Correspondence, vol. 16, no. 1669.

15 Lattimore, 'Herdsmen, farmers, urban culture', in *Pastoral Production and Society*, 481.

16 Stein, *Ruins of Desert Cathay*, 154.

17 One shih was equal to 120 Chinese pounds or the equivalent of 72 kg.

18 Ibn Khaldun, *The Muqaddimah*, I, 304–5.

19 Ibn Khaldun, *The Muqaddimah*, II, 286–91.

20 Khanzanov, *Nomads and the Outside World*, 233.

21 Caetani, *Studi di Storia Orientale*, I, 51–288, and III, 289–400.

22 Musil, *Northern Negd*, 304–15.

23 *Ibid.*, 316.

24 Caskel, 'Bedouinization of Arabia', 41–4.

25 Dostal, 'The evolution of Bedouin life'.

26 Asad, 'The Bedouin as a military force'. See also Lapidus, 'The Arab conquests and the formation of Islamic society'.

27 See Donner, *The Early Islamic Conquests*, 221–6.

28 Cahen, 'Quelques mots sur les Hilaliens et le nomadisme'.

29 Al-Jahiz, *Risala fi manaqib al-atrak wa-ᶜammat jund al-khilafa*, English trans. in C. T. Harley-Walker, 'Jahiz of Basra to al-Fath b. Khaqan on the "Exploits of the Turks and the army of the Khalifate in general" ', *Journal of the Royal Asiatic Society*, 1915, 631–97.

30 Lambton, *Continuity and Change in Medieval Persia*, 8; the source is Zahir al-Din Nishapuri, *Saljuq-nama*, Teheran, AHS 1332/1953.

31 Huntington, *The Pulse of Asia*; *Civilization and Climate*, 316–17, 390–1. The point has also been repeated in Khazanov, *The Nomad and the Outside World*, 235.

32 For a discussion of the military technology of the Delhi Sultanate, see Digby, *War-horse and Elephant in the Delhi Sultanate*; Digby holds the view that the armies of the Delhi sultans did not possess a decisive technological superiority and puts a greater emphasis on the supply of war horses available to the Turks.

33 For a general history of the Mongol expansion, see Morgan, *The Mongols*.

34 Barthold, *Turkestan Down to the Mongol Invasion*, 404.

35 Lambton, *Continuity and Change in Medieval Persia*, 15; Juvaini, *The History of the World-Conqueror*, trans. Boyle (1958), I, 163–4.

36 Juvaini, *The History of the World Conqueror*, I, 96–7.

37 Ibn al-Athar, *Al-Kamil fi'il-ta'rikh*, XII, 358–9, quoted by Spuler, *History of the Mongols*, 30.

38 Amir Khusru, *Kiranu-s Sa'dain*, in Elliot and Dowson, *History of India*, III, 528–9.

39 Musil, *Northern Negd*, 10.

40 Juvaini, *History of the World Conqueror*, I, 30.

41 Juvaini, *History of the World Conqueror*, I, 104. Needless to say, such ascriptions to famous historical figures were based on hearsay in contemporary historiography.

42 For an illuminating discussion of the problem, see Fletcher, 'The Mongols: ecological and social perspectives'.

43 Abu'l Fazl, *Ain-i-Akbari*, I, 134–5.

44 Wassaf, *Tazjiyatu-l Amsar*, in Elliot and Dowson, *History of India*, III, 34. For a summary of Barani's description of the horses imported to India, see Digby, *War-horse and Elephant in the Delhi Sultanate*, 37–8.

45 Zeuner, *A History of Domesticated Animals*, 311–13.

46 Brown, *The Horse of the Desert*, 40–1.

47 Marco Polo, *The Descriptions of the World*, [47], 137.

48 Ibn Battuta, *The Travels of Ibn Battuta*, II, 478.

49 Ferrier, *Caravan Journeys and Wanderings in Persia, Afghanistan, Turkistan, and Beloochistan*, 95.

50 *Ibid.*, 84.

51 Marco Polo, *The Description of the World*, [196], 445.

52 Abu'l Fazl, *Ain-i-Akbari*, I, 133–5.

53 Marco Polo, *The Description of the World*, [195], 445.

54 Wassaf, *Tazjiyatu-l Asmar*, in Elliot and Dowson, *History of India*, III, 32–3.

55 Brown, *The Horse of the Desert*, 148.

56 Brown, *The Horse of the Desert*, 112; for the reverse case, the owners looking for stolen animals, see also Musil, *The Manners and Customs of the Rwala Bedouins*, 379–80.

57 Brown, *The Horse of the Desert*, 96.

58 Lady Anne Blunt, *Bedouin Tribes of the Euphrates*, II, 259.

59 Brown, *The Horse of the Desert*, 98.

60 Lady Anne Blunt, *Bedouin Tribes of the Euphrates*, II, 245; Vire, 'Khayl', in *Encyclopaedia of Islam*².

61 Lady Anne Blunt, *Bedouin Tribes of the Euphrates*, II, 65, 251–2.

62 Salim Bakhit al-Tabuki, 'Tribal structure in south Oman'.

63 Bulliet, *The Camel and the Wheel*, 141–2.

64 Abu'l Fazl, *Ain-i-Akbari*, I, 143.

65 *Ibid.*

66 Pellat, 'Ibil', in *Encyclopaedia of Islam*².

67 Musil, *Northern Negd*, 70.

68 Musil, *The Manners and Customs of the Rwala Bedouins*, 44–5.

69 Cole, *Nomads of the Nomads*, 16.

70 On this point, see Musil, *Northern Negd*, 303.

71 Musil, *The Manners and Customs of the Rwala Bedouins*, 16, 165, 298.

72 Cole, *Nomads of the Nomads*, 28.

73 Musil, *The Manners and Customs of the Rwala Bedouins*, 298.

74 *Ibid.*, 338.

75 Wilkinson, *Water and Tribal Settlement in South-East Arabia* (1977), 60, reporting from Schmidt-Nielson, *Desert Animals: Physiological Problems of Heat and Water*, Oxford, 1964 and Taylor, 'The eland and the oryx, *Scientific American*, no. 220, 1969, 88–95.

76 Musil, *The Manners and Customs of the Rwala Bedouins*, 338–47.

77 Buchanan, *Journey from Madras*, II, 8.

78 Bruen, *Cattle Breeding in the Bombay Presidency*, 1–2.

79 Kristnasamienger and Pease, *Notes on the Cattle of Mysore*, 13, 30.

80 Buchanan, *A Journey from Madras*, II, 10–12.

81 Erskine, *A Gazetteer of the Jodhpur State*, 106–7.

82 Renouf, *Cattle and Dairying in the Punjab*, 4–7.

83 *Ibid.*, 17–18.

84 Baluch, *The Bhagnari Breed of Cattle*.

85 Joslin, *Cattle of the Bombay Presidency*.

10 The human hand and its products

1 The stimulus to technological development given by the Euro-Asian trade was mentioned as early as 1701. The anonymous author of the tract, *Considerations*

on the East Trade, first made a specific reference to the labour-saving effect of using machines, 'A saw-mill with a pair or two of hands will split as many boards as thirty men without this mill; if the use of this mill shall be rejected that thirty may be imployed to do the work', and went on to say: 'The East India Trade, whether by setting forward the invention of Arts and Engines to save the labour of Hands, or by introducing greater Order and Regularity into our English Manufactures, or by whatsoever other means lessens the price of labour. However, Wages are not abated; wherefore, without reducing Wages, this Trade abates the price of Labour, and therefore of Manufactures.' *Considerations on the East India Trade*, 580, 593.

2 Pattullo, *An Essay upon the Cultivation of the Lands and Improvements of the Revenues of Bengal*, 25.

3 Defoe, *The Just Complaint of the Poor Weavers*; *A Brief State of the Question between the Printed and Painted Callicoes and the Woollen and Silk Manufacture*.

4 *Considerations on the East India Trade*, 550.

5 Orme, *Historical Fragments*, 413.

6 Madhavi Bajekal, *Agrarian Production in Eastern Rajasthan in the 18th Century* (forthcoming).

7 Smith, *The Wealth of Nations*, I, Book I, ch. 3.

8 Johansen, B., 'The all-embracing town and its mosques: *Al-Misr Al-Gami*', 141.

9 For example, see Chaudhuri, *The Trading World of Asia and the English East India Company*, 267–8; Chao, *The Development of Cotton Textile Production in China*, 176–7.

10 For a discussion of the highly complex 'caste' structure of the service communities in medieval south India, see Ramaswamy, *Textiles and Weavers in Medieval South India*, 59–62.

11 For a case-study, see Ramaswamy, *Textiles and Weavers in Medieval South India*, 160.

12 Lapidus, *Muslim Cities in the Later Middle Ages*, 82, 102; Keyvani, *Artisans and Guild Life in the later Safavid Period*, 156.

13 Serjeant, *Islamic Textiles*, 102.

14 Buchanan, *Journey from Madras*, I, 212–13.

15 Chaudhuri, *The Trading World of Asia and the English East India Company*, 270.

16 On Islamic associations, see Keyvani, *Artisans and Guild Life in the Later Safavid Period*; Cahen, 'Ya-t-il eu des corporations profesionelles dans le monde musulman classique'.

17 Havart, *Op-en Ondergang van Coromandel*, III, 13–14, quoted by Irwin, *Studies in Indo-European Textile History*, 34–5.

18 Pelsaert, *Remonstrantie*. Thomas Bowrey, however, thought that the South Indian shipbuilders understood the engineering principles involved in their work and adopted European construction techniques; see *A Geographical Account of Countries Round the Bay of Bengal*, 102.

19 For a discussion of theoretical issues in interpreting pottery shapes and designs, see Miller, *Artifacts as Categories: A Study of Ceramic Variability in Central India*.

20 IOR Original Correspondence, 28 January 1664, vol. 28, no. 3019; Chaudhuri, *The Trading World of Asia and the English East India Company*, 247.

21 IOR Despatch Book, 3 March 1731, vol. 105, para. 50, 482.

22 Chao, *The Development of Cotton Textile Production in China*, 20.

23 Marx, *Capital*, III, Book III, Part IV, ch. 20.

24 Goitein, *A Mediterranean Society*; Frantz-Murphy, 'A new interpretation of the economic history of medieval Egypt'.

25 Ibn al-Ukhuwwa, *The Maᶜalim al-Qurba*, 25.

26 Ibn Miskawaihi, *The Eclipse of the ᶜAbbasid Caliphate*, VI, 361; Serjeant, *Islamic Textiles*, 29.

27 Fortune, *A Journey to the Tea Countries of China*, 37.

28 Shih Min-hsiung, *The Silk Industry in Ch'ing China*; E-tu Zen Sun, 'Sericulture and silk textile production in Ch'ing China'; Li, *China's Silk Trade*.

29 Buckingham, *Travels in Assyria, Media, and Persia*, I, 193–4.

30 Chaudhuri, *The Trading World of Asia and the English East India Company*, 251.

31 Elvin, 'The high-level equilibrium trap'.

32 Chao, *The Development of Cotton Textile Production in China*, 57–9.

33 *Ibid.*, 59.

34 Sung Ying-hsing, *T'ien-kung K'ai-wu*, 56.

35 Report of John Taylor, IOR Home Miscellaneous Series, vol. 456F.

36 For a detailed contemporary description, see Sung Ying-hsing, *T'ien-kung K'ai-wu*, 48–50.

37 See the Roque Manuscript of 1678 in the Bibliothèque Nationale in Paris, FR. 14614, printed in Schwartz ed., *Painting on Cotton at Ahmedabad India in 1678*; for processing and dyeing thread, see Buchanan, *Journey through Madras*, I, 213–15. On textile painting and printing, see also Varadarajan, *Traditions of Textile Printing in Kutch*.

38 Chaudhuri, *The Trading World of Asia and the English East India Company*, 275.

39 For a discussion of the textile industry in the Ottoman Empire, see Farooqhi, *Towns and Townsmen of Ottoman Anatolia*, 125–55.

40 Chaudhuri, *The Trading World of Asia*, 254.

41 The organisation of textile weaving in North India during the eighteenth century is discussed in Bayly, *Rulers, Townsmen, and Bazaars*, 144–51.

42 For a discussion of the organisation of Chinese silk weaving, see Shih Min-hsiung, *The Silk Industry in Ch'ing China*, 33–8.

43 *Ibid.*, 37.

44 Hamilton, *The Hedaya or Guide: A Commentary on the Mussulman Laws*, 299, 302, 308.

45 Ibn al-Ukhuwwa, *The Maᶜalim al-Qurba fi Ahkam al-Hisba*, 43. For a general discussion of the early industrial organisation in Europe and India, see Kriedte, Medick, and Schlumbohm, *Industrialization before Industrialization*; Chicherov, *India: Economic Development in the 16th–18th Centuries*; Perlin, 'Proto-Industrialization and Pre-colonial South Asia'.

46 The documents are in IOR, East India Company, Factory Records Surat, vol. 106. See also Chaudhuri, *The Trading World of Asia*, 259.

47 Chaudhuri, *The Trading World of Asia*, 253.
48 Ch'u ta-chun, *Kuangtung Hsin Yu*, quoted by Needham, *The Development of Iron and Steel Technology in China*, 17.
49 Ibn Khaldun, *The Muqaddimah*, III, 271–2.
50 *The Qur'an*, ch. 57, quoted by al-Hassan and Hill, *Islamic Technology, 251.*
51 This was the view of the nineteenth century collector Juan Yuan; see Watson, *Ancient Chinese Bronzes*, 23.
52 Goitein, *Studies in Islamic History and Institutions*, 337, 340.
53 Chardin, *Travels in Persia*, 250.
54 Sung Ying-Hsing, *T'ien-Kung K'ai-Wu*, 162.
55 Abu'l Fazl, *Ain-i-Akbari*, I, 112–13.
56 Wallace, *The Malay Archipelago*, 129–31.
57 Smith, *A History of Metallography*, 14, 16.
58 Egerton, *A Description of Indian and Oriental Armour*, 57; Mas꜀udi, *The Meadows of Gold*, 260; Ath-Tha꜀alibi, *The Lata꜀if al-ma꜀atif of Tha꜀alibi*, 123.
59 On the use of coal in Chinese iron works, see Hartwell, 'A cycle of economic change in imperial China: coal and iron in Northeast China, 750–1350', 108–11.
60 See al-Hassan and Hill, *Islamic Technology*, 252–3, 'Ma꜀din' in the *Encyclopaedia of Islam²*, Needham, *The Development of Iron and Steel Technology in China*, 18–19.
61 Sung Ying-hsing, *T'ien-hsing K'ai-wu*, 249–50.
62 For a detailed account of Indian iron smelting, see Francis Hamilton Buchanan, *Journey from Madras*, I, 171–5, II, 16–23, and III, 361–3. See also Wilkinson, 'On the cause of the external patterns or watering of the Damascus sword-blades', *Journal of the Royal Asiatic Society*, 1837, 187–93; Wilkinson, 'Iron', *Journal of the Royal Asiatic Society*, 1839, 383–9; Heath, 'On Indian iron and steel', *Journal of the Royal Asiatic Society*, 1839, 390–7.
63 Needham, *The Grand Titration*, 96.
64 Hamilton, *A New Account of the East Indies*, I, 217.
65 Buchanan, *Journey from Madras*, II, 16.
66 ath-Th꜀alibi, *The Lata'if al-ma꜀atif of Tha꜀alibi*, 118.
67 al-Hassan and Hill, *Islamic Technology*, 151–4.
68 For a detailed description of Indian glass-making, see Buchanan, *A Journey from Madras*, III, 369–72.
69 Buchanan, *A Journey from Madras*, III, 371–2.
70 For a general survey of fine Islamic ceramics, see Fehervari, *Islamic Pottery*.
71 For a discussion of these points, see Watson, *Tang and Liao Ceramics*, Honey, *The Ceramic Art of China*, and Wirgin, *Sung Ceramic Designs*.
72 Sung Ying-hsing, *T'ien-kung K'ai-wu*, 147, 155.
73 See Maqrizi, *Les Marches du Caire*, 175; Buchanan, *A Journey from Madras*, I, 159–63.
74 Chardin, *Travels in Persia*, 248–9.

11 Historical dimensions of towns and cities

1 These symbols are taken to be a collection or set of concrete objects, such as houses, streets, density of population (crowds), cultivated fields, farm-houses,

ploughs, farm animals, and so on. For powerful theoretical analysis of these mental images and their relationship to towns as physical objects, see Greimas, 'Pour une semiotique topologique'; Ledrut, 'Parole et silence de la ville'; Eco, 'Function and sign: semotics of architecture'; and other essays translated and edited by Gottdiener and Lagopoulos in *The City and the Sign*.

2   Weber, *Economy and Society: An Outline of Interpretative Sociology*, II, ch. 16, 'The city'; Wirth, 'Urban society and civilization'; Redfield, *The Folk Culture of Yucatan*, and his *peasant Society and Culture*; Redfield and Singer, 'The cultural role of cities'; Sjoberg, *The Pre-Industrial City*; Abrams and Wrigley, *Towns in Societies*; Saunders, *Social Theory and the Urban Question*.

3   Braudel, *The Mediterranean*, I, 278.

4   Braudel, *Capitalism and Material Life*, 373. For a criticism of Braudel's views and his reply, see Abrams and Wrigley eds., *Towns in Society*, 23–4, Braudel, *Civilisation and Capitalism*, I, 481.

5   This has been pointed out by Greimas, 'Pour une semiotique topologique'.

6   The theoretical analysis adopted here, which is an application of semiotic studies derived from Saussure's work enables the multiple forms of the city to be studied within a single conceptual category. For an interesting example of the kind of divergence of view which can arise from defining the conceptual category strictly by the physical features of the city, see Wheatley's criticism of Nelson Wu's statement that the ancient Indian and Chinese urban centres were totally different in every respect, Wheatley, *The Pivot of the Four Quarters*, 450, Wu, *Chinese and Indian Architecture*, 114, n. 2.

7   Acharya ed., *Architecture of Manasara*, IV, 62, 93–5.

8   Ibn Khaldun, *The Muqaddimah*, II, 286–7.

9   Social dimensions are meant to include economic activities as well.

10 For a penetrating discussion of this point, see Renfrew, 'Trade as action at a distance: questions of integration and communication', 3–59.

11 Polanyi, 'Marketless trading in Hammurabi's time' and 'The economy as instituted process'.

12 Braudel, *Capitalism and Material Life*, 401, *Civilization and Capitalism*, I, 515.

13 Braudel, *The Mediterranean*, I, 387.

14 For a similar discussion of this, see also Chaudhuri, *Trade and Civilisation in the Indian Ocean*, 176.

15 Braudel himself has done this in his discussion of the divisions of space and time in Europe; see *Civilization and Capitalism*, III, 35–9.

16 For Weber's typology of the 'Consumer', 'Producer', and 'Merchant' city , see his *Economy and Society*, II, 'The City', 1,215–16. For the historical connection between social consumption and urbanisation in the Indian context', see also Bayly, *Rulers, Townsmen and Bazaars*, 201–11.

17 See Pedersen, 'Masdjid', in the *Encyclopaedia of Islam*[1].

18 See Pedersen and Diez, 'Masdjid', in the *Encyclopaedia of Islam*[1].

19 Al-Muqaddasi, *Ahsan al-Taqasim*, 113.

20 Ibn Jubayr, *The Travels of Ibn Jubayr*, 86–7.

21 *Ibid.*, 129.

22 *Ibid.*, 135.

23 Wiet, *Cairo*, 72.

24 The harm done by the early sacrilege of Hindu temples was repaired by the policy of Alp Khan, see Misra, *The Rise of Muslim Power in Gujarat*, 68–71.

25 Pelsaert, *The Remonstrantie*, 19–20.

26 Tavernier, *Travels in India*, I, 56.

27 *Ibid.*, II, 189.

28 Albiruni, *Alberuni's India*, I, 144–7.

29 ʿAbdu-lla, *Tarikh-i-Daudi*, IV, 439–40.

30 Hasan Nizami, *Taju-l Ma-asir*, II, 223.

31 Tavernier, *Travels in India*, I, 97, and II, 180–2.

32 al-Maqrizi, *Khitat*, I, 374, 1.29–34, trans. Casanova, IV, 75–6, quoted by Creswell, *The Origin of the Cruciform Plan of Cairene Madrasas*, 28; Petry, *The Civilian Elite of Cairo in the Later Middle Ages*, 330.

33 For a description of the royal visits to the temples of Auythya, see Tavernier, *Travels in India*, II, 229.

34 Rozman, *Urban Networks in Ch'ing China and Tokugawa Japan* (1973), 35–40, 133; Hall ed., *Japan before Tokugawa*, 194–7.

35 Wright, 'The cosmology of the Chinese city', 56–7, Wu, *Chinese and Indian Architecture*, 35–6.

36 Ibn Jubayr, *The Travels of Ibn Jubayr*, 63–70.

37 *Ibid.*, 70. On the profusion of goods and provisions available in Mecca, see ch. 6, p. 168.

38 Sarkar, *History of Aurangzib*, III, 282.

39 Al-Muqaddasi, *Ahsan al-Taqasim*, 84–5.

40 Weber, 'The city', in *Economy and Society*, ed. Roth and Wittich, II, 1,226–7.

41 Marco Polo, *The Description of the World*, 329.

42 Della Valle, *The Travels*, II, 61, 67. On Broach, see also ch. 5, p. 137.

43 Misra, *The Rise of Muslim Power in Gujarat*, 170–4. On the early history of Ahmedabad, see Gillion, *Ahmedabad: A Study in Indian Urban History*, ch. 1.

44 Pelsaert, *The Remonstrantie*, 19; Tavernier, *Travels in India*, I, 59. della Valle, *The Travels*, II, 96.

45 Jahangir, *Tuzuk-i Jahangiri*, I, 414, 423–5. See also della Valle, *Travels*, II, 94–5.

46 Thevenot, *Indian Travels of Thevenot*, ch. 5.

47 *Ibid.*, 17. See also Pelsaert, *The Remonstrantie*, 19.

48 Thevenot, *Indian Travels of Thevenot*, 60.

49 Grose, *A Voyage to the East Indies*, I, 98.

50 See, for example, the often-quoted passage in Al-Yaʿqubi, *Kitab al-buldan*, VII, 237–8, quoted by Lassner, *The Topography of Baghdad*, 127, and Lewis, *The Arabs in History*, 82.

51 Al-Muqaddasi, *Ahsan al-Taqasim*, 188.

52 Ibn Jubayr, *The Travels of Ibn Jubayr*, 226.

53 Al-Muqaddasi, *Ahsan al-Taqasim*, 196.

54 On the foundation of Fathpur Sikri, see Jahangir, *Tuzuk-i-Jahangiri*, I, 2.

55 For an explanation of the phrase, see ch. 4, n. 4.

56 See Mote, 'The transformation of Nanking, 1350–1400'.

57 El-Ali, 'The foundation of Baghdad', 89.

58 Ibn Jubayr, *The Travels of Ibn Jubayr*, 46.

59 Khafi Khan, *Muntakhabu-l Lubab*, VII, 415.

60 Methwold, *Relations of Golconda*, 2.

61 ʿAbdur Razzak, *Matlaʾu-s Saʾdain*, IV, 105–17.

62 For the urban plan of medieval Herat, see Gaube, *Iranian Cities*, ch. 2.

63 Naqvi, *Urbanization and Urban Centres under the Great Mughals*, 175–7.

64 Ibn Taghri Birdi, *History of Egypt 1382–1469*, IV, 135–6.

65 Pelsaert, *The Remonstrantie*, 58–9.

66 Jahangir, *Tuzuk-i-Jahangiri*, I, 7–8.

67 Surat Factory: Diary and Consultation Book, 2/612, Letter from Cambay, 18 July 1726, quoted by Commissariat, *A History of Gujarat*, II, 419–20. This volume of the Surat Factory Records is missing in the India Office Records.

68 For a discussion of the role of port cities and the relationship between towns and caravan trade, see Chaudhuri, *Trade and Civilisation in the Indian Ocean*, chs. 5 and 8.

69 The reports have been translated by Makdisi in his 'The topography of eleventh century Baghdad: materials and notes (II)', 283–5. For fires in Delhi described by Bernier, see also ch. 7, n. 63.

70 Ibn Ridwan, *Medieval Islamic Medicine*, 104–11.

71 *Ibid.*, 93, 102.

72 *Records of Fort St George: The Diary and Consultation Book 1727*, 27 June 1727, 84.

73 Ibn Ridwan, for example, challenged Ibn al-Jazar's assertion that 'the water of the Nile is noticeably harmful for everyone who inhabits Egypt'. The Nile, Ibn Ridwan said, was the greatest cause for the habitation of this land and 'the bodies of the Egyptians have become accustomed to it. The Nile air is not harmful though it is actually bad . . . the bodies of the Egyptians are not chronically ill, but they are very susceptible to illness.' See *Medieval Islamic Medicine*, 102–3.

74 Maqrizi, *A History of the Ayyubid Sultans of Egypt*, 141.

75 Pelsaert, *The Remonstrantie*, 48, 61.

76 Lane, *An Account of the Manners and Customs of the Modern Egyptian*; Tavernier, *Travels in India*, I, 225, 311; Bernier, *Travels in the Mogul Empire*, 381.

77 *Records of Fort St George: Diary and Consultation Book 1727*, 26 June 1727, 82.

78 *Records of Fort St George: Despatches to England 1727–33*, 22 September 1727, 14; see also Chaudhuri, *The Trading World of Asia*, 52.

79 *Records of Fort St George: Diary and Consultation Book 1736*, 30 April 1736, 77–9. For the sale of children in an earlier famine, see Methwold, *Relations of Golconda*, 3.

80 Thevenot, *Indian Travels*, 21.

81 Pelsaert, *The Remonstrantie*, 1.

82 Della Valle, *The Travels*, I, 30. On the Middle Eastern segregation, see Raymond, *Grandes villes arabes à l'epoque ottomane*, 174–9.

83 Khafi Khan, *Muntakhabu-l Lubab*, VII, 454–6.

84 Makdisi, 'The topography of eleventh century Baghdad: material and notes II', 291.

85 Maqrizi, *A History of the Ayyubid Sultans of Egypt*, 79.

86 Niebuhr, *Travels in Arabia*, I, 81–2.

87 Factory Records Surat, Diary and Consultation Book, 15 October 1726, vol. 12, 12–13.

88 Factory Records Surat, Diary and Consultation Book, 17 October 1670, vol. 3, 96; Despatch Book, 16 September 1675, vol. 88, 196; *Ibid.*, 5 October 1737, vol. 108, 221.

89 *Records of Fort St George: Despatches to England, 1714–18*, 15 July 1714, 7.

12 Conclusion

1 See ch. 1, p. 28.

2 Lévi-Strauss, *The Savage Mind*, 263.

3 Braudel, *Civilisation and Capitalism*, I, ch. 1.

4 *Ibid.*, I, 34.

5 For a discussion of the problem of reconstructing the historical demography of the Middle East and China, see Crecelius, 'Archival sources for demographic studies of the Middle East' and Issawi, 'The area and population of the Arab Empire: an essay in speculation' in Udovitch ed., *The Islamic Middle East, 700–1900*; Cook, *Population Pressure in Rural Anatolia 1450–1600*; Ping-ti Ho, *Studies on the Population of China, 1368–1953*; Lee, 'Food supply and population growth in Southwest China 1250–1850'.

6 Quoted by Bodde in 'Harmony and conflict in Chinese philosophy', *Essays on Chinese Civilization*, 250.

7 For a brief account, see Lambton, *Landlord and Peasant in Persia*, 15, 32.

8 Ping-ti Ho, *Studies on the Population of China, 1368–1953*, 10.

9 Ibn Khaldun, *The Muqaddimah*, II, 280–1.

10 See Cook, *Population Pressure in Rural Anatolia 1450–1600*.

11 For the replication of the village and its social structure over space and time in Ceylon, see Obeysekere, *Land Tenure in Village Ceylon: A Sociological and Historical Study*; for Thailand and China, see Ishii ed., *Thailand: A Rice-Growing Society*; Yoshinobu Shiba, *Crisis and Prosperity in Sung China*, and *Studies in the Economy of the Lower Yangtze in the Sung*.

12 Sauvy, *General Theory of Population*, 101, 110.

13 For a discussion of the population theory of Malthus and the qualifications he himself made, see above ch. 8, p. 251.

14 For a discussion of these factors, see Musallam, *Sex and Society in Islam*.

15 For a discussion of the determinants of population trends, see Chao, *Man Land in Chinese History*; Coale and Watkins eds., *The Decline of Fertility in Europe*; Hanley and Yamamura, *Economic and Demographic Change in Pre-Industrial Japan 1600–1968*; Hanley and Wolf eds., *Family and Population in East Asian History*.

16 Cipolla, *The Economic History of World Population*, 89; Putnam, *The Future of Land Based on Nuclear Fuel*, 18.

17 Issawi, 'The area and population of the Arab Empire', in Udovitch ed., *The Islamic Middle East, 700–1900*; Musallam, *Sex and Society in Islam*, 109–16;

Russell, 'Late ancient and medieval populations'; Russell, 'The population of medieval Egypt'; Hollingsworth, *Historical Demography*.

18 Ping-ti Ho, *Studies on the Population of China, 1368–1953*, 10, 64.

19 Wallerstein, *The Modern World System*, I and II.

20 For an illuminating restatement of the theory and its application to Braudel's concept of historical time, see Wallerstein, 'The inventions of TimeSpace realities: towards an understanding of our historical systems'.

21 Wallerstein, 'An historical perspective on the emergence of the new international order; economic, political, cultural aspects', in *The Capitalist World-Economy*, 272–3.

22 Braudel, *Civilization and Capitalism*, III, 21–2.

23 *Ibid.*, III, 620–1.

24 Lombard, *The Golden Age of Islam*, 9–10. Lombard was born in 1904 and died in 1965. The above book was first published in 1971 under the title *L'Islam dans sa premiere grandeur* and derived from his lectures and notes.

25 Lombard, *The Golden age of Islam*, 5–6.

26 Wallerstein, *The Modern World System*, 179.

Glossary of theoretical terms

Arbitrary By an arbitrary name, phonetic sound, or a sign, it is meant that the truth-possibilities of the expression are not verified by their sense but by associative learning (see also **Proposition**).

Axiom of choice, see **Set theory**

Bricolage Lévi-Strauss defined it as the assembly of heterogenous intellectual methods to create a critical language of discourse (*The Savage Mind*, 16–17). He also thought that bricolage could be a form almost of mytho-poetry. See also Derrida's critique of the concept in 'Structure, sign, and play', *Writing and Différence*, 285.

Bricoleur Following the above definition of bricolage, bricoleur is an intellectual 'handy-man' who borrows a wide variety of methods from different disciplines to construct a structural approach to critical analysis.

Cardinal, number and principle One of the key concepts in mathematical theory, a cardinal number is a *collection* or *set* of objects, identified by an arbitrary phonetic sound or set of phonemes (one, two, three, and so on). The concept does not require direct counting of objects, which follows from the system of ordinal numbers. It only calls for *correspondence* between different collections of objects. Thus the statement 'the lecture-hall is full' needs correspondence between two cardinal numbers, the number of seats in the lecture-hall and the number of people present. The eye and the brain can evaluate the information received from the two physical sets without counting and find out if there are or not any empty seats in the hall (see also **Cognitive process**). In this work, the concept of cardinality is used to identify a group of people with a common religion, culture, or civilisation. Thus the words 'Muslim', 'Hindu', 'Javanese', or 'Chinese' imply the existence of principles by which *all* members of the respective set can be recognised as belonging to the set without exception.

Cognitive process The operation of the senses which establishes correspondence between physical objects and concepts in the mind.

Continuity While the human mind automatically senses continuity and discontinuity, it is not generally aware of the principle which establishes these distinctions. The sense of continuity depends on the perception of the existence of a point or a series of points which divides an entity into two sets. If visual sense is used to validate the existence of the point or points, such sets will appear as a left-hand set and a right-hand set or their mental equivalents. For example, the point 1899 marks the end of the nineteenth century, the twentieth century lies to its right, 1900 marks the beginning of the twentieth century, the nineteenth lies to its left. Thus two points or limits establish the continuity of the nineteenth century, 1800 and 1899. The

423

unconscious existence of such points or the existence of the principles of separation acts as mental signifiers (see **Semiology**).

Continuum (see also **Set theory**)   The concept of a continuum was defined by Georg Cantor as an aggregate which is well-ordered and perfect. That is to say, each number belonging to the set can be recognised by its relative magnitude or the concept of less than / greater than other numbers in the collection, and the limits of the sequence are set by numbers which are members of the same set. The 'continuum problem' in mathematics is the task of actually establishing how many numbers are contained in, for example, a set of integers, a set which is capable of infinite extension and infinite divisibility. The problem is given by a fundamental contradiction present in the human mind which can envisage *possibilities*. Thus it is possible to state that every integer, no matter how large, has a successor and at the same time to think of an infinitely large cardinal number which contains *all* integers. Such uncountable numbers Cantor called the transfinite cardinals. In this work, a continuum is also used in a linguistic sense. A concept, identified by a sound image, will vary over a range of possible states but never transgress its own limits or boundaries. Thus, the limits of the 'urban' concept are set by towns and cities, no matter how large and small, and never by villages and hamlets. Thus, the word town and the symbolic designators such as a collection of houses, streets, people, and abstract qualities constitute a *rigid* set in terms of its own limits. A town does not need the dialectical concept of a village to create its limits, though the principle of exclusion may be applied to perceive the concept itself. It is also important to realise that whereas terms such as 'urban', 'rural', 'Indian Ocean' constitute a continuum, there are other terms which do not have closed boundaries (i.e. infinity, eternity, time, space and so on).

Contradiction see **Proposition**

Differentiation, structural (see also **Inner limit**)   The process of reasoning through which a concept, a word, or a structure is seen as a single entity or an integral can be further partitioned. Thus the expression 'Indian Ocean civilisations' can be divided into religious systems, methods of economic production, nations and states, all grouped together by the name 'Indian Ocean' and the expression 'civilisation', both of which are partially arbitrary (see also **Arbitrary**).

Integration (see also **Symbolic integration**)   The process whereby separate and different entities are made part of a single structure. Thus the problem of discovering the unity and disunity of the 'Indian Ocean civilisations' can be reduced to two separate operations: 1. a structural totality is divided into component parts, 2. a multitude of elements is formed into a structural totality.

Density (see also **Transforms**)   A contradictory notion of an interval between two entities which can take on any values between 0 and infinity. Thus one can go directly from the notion of water to steam but also imagine that the two states of water are separated by an infinitude of physical processes.

Discourse (see also **Reduction** and **Tense**)   In this work, it is used in a specific sense. It is a body of ideas, discussions, opinions, systems of thought, methods of analysis, writings, and principles of action which prevail at any given period of time and which are interlinked by common objective categories. The rules which connect the objective categories and discourse obey certain regularity. Madness, insanity, unreason, as Foucault pointed out (*The Archaeology of Knowledge*, 32–9), are all objective categories which change their meaning and content over time. The discourse associated with the categories also changes consequently. Foucault, however, added the qualification that the relationship between the objects of discourse and discourse itself was a two-way process. Discourse could create new objective categories. If there is a regularity between these categories and the statements or theories, it should be taken as a *discursive formation*. The question whether the Indian Ocean civilisations possess any historical unity can be resolved if there is also a unity of discourse or rules by which such a unity can be perceived.

Disunity see **Continuity**

Enumerable   If a principle exists by which all members of a set can be identified as belonging to that set, it is enumerable. When there is a difference of opinion as to what that principle is or should be, the set is not enumerable. In number theory a set of *all sets of positive integers* is non-enumerable, as it is too large.

Epistemology   Theory of knowledge: a methodology which allows the construction of a theory.

Excluded set see **Set theory**

First order logic   Elementary logic of language based on operators such as *not*, *and*, *or*, *if*, *if then*, and *if and only if*, the universal quantifier *for every value of x* (everyone, everything), and the existential quantifier *for some value of x* (someone, something). Sentences constructed in first order logic are validated by language sense. There is no formal mechanical test or proof which decides their validity. The sentence 'White porcelain cups are best for drinking tea' has no mechanical test (yes and no to a question) which enables one to derive the correct answer. But the statement 'Red is a distinct colour different from all the other colours' does have a mechanical test based on a test of identity (i.e. 'Is this colour red? If the answer is yes, stop further action, if it is no, take the next colour and ask the same question.')

Frequencies, of time see **Time**

Function   A relationship between two entities so that if one changes the other also changes in a specific way.

Implicated order, in space (see also **Symbolic integration**)   This refers to when the original order or shape of an object has been disturbed or transformed subsequently but still remains 'implicated' in space. For example, a square piece of paper when crumpled up into a ball still retains its implicated order; when it is smoothed out into its original shape, the folds will still show how it was transformed into a ball.

Included set see **Set theory**

Incomplete Theorem, of Kurt Gödel   Gödel provided the theoretical basis of the proof that in any system of formal logic or arithmetic operations there is at least one proposition or formula which can be neither proven nor refuted according to the assumptions of that system. Hence, 'The consistency proof for the system S can be carried out only by means of modes of inference that are not formalized in the system S itself', Gödel, 'Some metamathematical results on completeness and consistency' (1930b), in *Collected Works*, 143.

Induction   A principle or a rule by which one entity can be derived from another entity consistently. Thus, the proposition that every number has a successor is valid only if there is a rule by which the successor can be recognised as such a number. It calls for the fundamental operators of the cognitive process, the notion of 'equal to', 'less than', and 'greater than'. This method of reasoning, however, is different from the inductive method in the physical sciences, which draws a general conclusion or creates a theory from an examination of particular cases.

Infinite, infinity   One of the most difficult and controversial topics in the philosophy of mathematics, the idea of the infinite, was regarded before Cantor as an ever-growing process the end of which human reasoning cannot attain, and it was associated with the convergence of sequence, something which again could not actually be reached. Thus the two limits of the set of arithmetic fractions, 0 and 1, can never be reached no matter how infinitely small or large a fraction is. In this sense, the infinite corresponds to the *potential infinity*. Cantor, Dedekind, and Frege however used the idea of *actual infinite* to develop a new set of mathematical concepts. Cantor's theory of transfinite cardinals (see also **Continuum**) suggested that there is actually a set of infinitely large numbers which contain all other numbers. One of the strange results of Cantor's work on the infinite was the conclusion that the part may be equal to the whole. For example, the infinite sets of odd or even numbers equal the set of odd and even numbers taken together, since a one-to-one correspondence (see also **Mapping** and **Isomorphism**) can be established between each term of the two sets. This result is obtained at the expense of order which will of course be different for each set. For historians the concept of infinite sets is useful to show correspondence between different sets of interpretations, as for example, in the statement 'the total number of good men = the total number of good Muslims', i.e. the assumption that only good Muslims are to be regarded as good men. Concepts such as good, bad, true, false, beautiful, are all similar to Cantor's transfinite cardinals, i.e. classificatory terms capable of an infinite extension of meaning. It has also been demonstrated that the number of sentences which a natural language can generate is greater than any transfinite set, see Langendoen and Postal, 'Sets and sentences' in Katz, ed., *The Philosophy of Linguistics*.

Inner limit (see also **Limits**, **Logical space**, and **Outer limit**)   The concept of inner and outer limits is treated as one of the most important elements of the theoretical framework presented in this study. It is one of the two boundaries at which an element of a set ceases to be a member of that set. If a concept or the linguistic sense of a word is taken as a set, there are other associated concepts or words which are its elements. *If the order of these associated elements is arranged from the most general to the most particular*, the inner limit is the point beyond which the process of partition or particularisation cannot go. For example, if the word 'land' represents in agriculture the most generalised expression of space, the elements of the set 'land' are given by expressions such as fertile land, barren land, fields, plots, parcel of land, soil, loam, humus, gravel, sand, nitrogen, phosphates, and so on. It can be easily verified at which point the particular elements cease to be a member of the set 'land' and become members of the set 'chemistry'.

Integration, structural see **Differentiation**

Invariant   An entity or a rule which does not change over time. The concept is essential to structural analysis, because it is important to know whether a structure remains invariant or not over a certain duration of time or whether it is subject to continuous or sudden changes. For example, if social institutions such as marriage rules, laws of inheritance, the ownership of landed property, and so on remain invariant over long periods of time when other elements in society are subject to variations, it has profound historical implications. Jakobson's search for the principle of invariance amidst variation (referred to in ch. 1, p. 28) can be understood from the following simple example. The structure of a sentence 'I am going home' can be kept invariant while the subject, the verb, and the object are all varied, i.e. 'We went to school'.

Isomorphism (see also **Mapping** and **Morphism**)   When the structural characteristics of two or more separate sets appear to be identical, they are treated as isomorphic. The mapping relation between the two sets (or the correspondence between the elements of the two sets) is taken to be in one-to-one or unit ratio. For example, the ritual status of a community of Brahmans (if no other information than that they are all Brahmans is available) must be assumed to be the same as that of any other Brahman community, irrespective of size and location in the Indian subcontinent. It is possible, however, that at a more detailed level of the ritual model, the sets are not isomorphic, though there is a morphism between them. Another physical example of isomorphism is a piece of music played live on instruments by musicians, its recorded version on magnetic tape and on discs. The structural image of the sound is identical in all three cases.

Limits (see also **Inner limit** and **Outer limit**)   In this work, the idea of limits is treated in two ways. Firstly, it is the point or boundary at which a proposition or concept ceases to convey its original sense. Secondly, it is the point in an infinite process beyond which human reasoning cannot go.

Logical necessity   In this work, logical necessity is defined in two ways. [1] The linguistic definition is given to the proposition, 'if there is a fire, there will also be heat'. As Wittgenstein put it, if p follows from q, an inference can be made from q to p or p can be deduced from q (*Tractatus Logico-Philosophicus*, 5.132). Whether the first example is objectively true or not is another matter. 'The freedom of the will consists in the impossibility of knowing actions that still lie in the future. We could know them only if causality were an *inner* necessity like that of logical inference. – The connection between knowledge and what is known is that of logical necessity' (5.1362). [2] It is postulated in this work that such an inner necessity does indeed exist between different causally connected parts of a physical structure. Thus, settled agriculture assumes the existence of a set of logical necessities which must be satisfied, i.e. cleared land, availability of water, seeds of domesticated plants, availability of labour, availability of a stock of food while the plants are growing and so on.

Logical space (see also **Inner limit**)   The expression is used in two separate senses. [1] It is a range of possibilities in the existence of the states of affairs (McGuinness ed., *Wittgenstein and the Vienna Circle*, 260). Every word or expression has a logical space associated with it and its meaning varies within the limits of the logical space. Thus the word 'land' excludes certain possibilities and creates a positive logical space for itself. A simple tautology such as p lacking factual sense excludes nothing from the logical space, while a contradiction *not-p* completely fills it up, i.e. there is only one possibility. [2] Logical space is also defined as the mental or abstract reflection of a **Structural space** (q.v.). It should be noted that the expression 'space' in this context has nothing to do with physical space. It merely refers to a bounded scale of variations.

Longue durée   Fernand Braudel's famous theory of the slow-moving component of time, historical features that change only imperceptibly over time. The shapes of mountains, the level of the sea, climate, pre-modern technology, and even population, are all subject to a slow rate of change.

Mapping pattern, mapping (see also **Isomorphism** and **Morphism**)   Mapping is a process or a function which transfers the structural image of one set to another set either as a static representation or as a causal sequence. Thus a cartographic map of the Indian Ocean is a static image of the physical features of a unit of space. But such structural features of the sea as, for example, its seasonal variations (temporal) and depth and breadth (spatial) can be mapped onto the sailing schedules of premodern ships and the design of ship construction.

Metamorphosis   In this work, the expression is used to describe the transformation of a demarcated unit of space into another recognisably different unit. For example, an area of forested land might be cleared and become cultivated land with dwelling houses. Similarly, drought, floods, and earthquakes can destroy cultivated land and turn it into unusable space.

Metrics   The science of measurement.

Morphism (see also **Isomorphism** and **Mapping**)   The relationship or similarity between two separate structures or sets.

One-to-one ratio see **Isomorphism**

Operators, cognitive   There are five basic logical operations of the mind which enable the human senses to function: (1) equal to, (2) less than, (3) greater than, (4) and, (5) or.

Order   The position of two or more points, entities, and ideas, *relative* to one another. It is essentially a geometric concept fixed in the first instance by the idea of *before* and *after* and subsequently by the idea of *non-identity*. The perception of non-simultaneity creates the notion of before and after and leads to the idea of succession which is a movement from an earlier point to a later one. In the present work, order is also used to analyse the arrangement of demarcated units of space, such as plains, valleys, hills, mountains, and so on, all of which are arranged by their elevation from sea level. The concept of order in a moral system implies the operation of an abstract structure logically necessary for the perpetuation of society.

Partial order is the order of a subset of elements in a set which is different from the order of the rest of the elements.

Ordinal, number (see also **Cardinal**)   A concept in mathematics which is complementary to that of cardinal numbers. It involves arranging objects or mental terms belonging to a collection or set in an *ordered* succession or sequence given by the notion of before and after. The name given to the last term in a finite collection is called its *ordinal number*.

Outer limit (see also **Inner limit**)   The outer limit of a concept or word is fixed by a generalised principle or linguistic sense by which all its elements can be included in the set.

Partial order see **Order**

Perpetual memory   A mechanism which perpetuates the basic behavioural patterns of a society from one time period to another without a conscious awareness on the part of its members. Tradition embodying moral values, religious beliefs, and social structures is one component of the perpetual memory. Its most important component is the capacity of individuals to remember things which are also remembered by other people in exactly the same way. Thus it is a generative scheme which enables society to reproduce collectively its basic strategy of survival.

Perceived time see **Time**

Phoneme Phonetical sounds produced by the human voice. A finite combination of phonemes constitutes a sound-image in the mind.

Power, of time see **Time**

Proposition, linguistic (see also **Logical space**) In the present work, the reasoning suggested by Wittgenstein in *Tractatus Logico-Philosophicus* is followed. Accordingly, a proposition expresses a thought perceived by the senses (3.1).

Classes of propositions Wittgenstein took an elementary proposition to be the most basic module of language and thought, without indicating how it is derived. Subsequently, he defined *two* types of propositions, those which possess *sense* and those which are *true*. Thus, the sentence 'I am going home' possesses a certain sense. Whether it is true or false is not relevant to the comprehension of its meaning. On the other hand, a statement 'There are five people in this room' is immediately verifiable by observation as true or false (McGuinness (ed.), *Wittgenstein and the Vienna Circle*, 213). Of course, the distinction between the two above examples is artificial, because the second sentence also has sense which is conveyed by the syntax of language. Whether there is any correspondence between its sense and an objective property is a secondary question. It might be added that *names* constitute another class of proposition. The correspondence between objects, ideas, concepts and names (arbitrary phonemes) involves a *learning process*. The statement 'Asia is a continent' has neither intrinsic sense nor truth-value, except the fact that it is a grammatical sentence in English (see **Sign**).

Elementary proposition This is the most basic kind of proposition which simply indicates a state of affairs. The test whether a proposition is elementary or not is the fact that it is not contradicted by another elementary proposition (4.21, 4.211).

Tautology If a proposition is true for all truth-possibilities it is called a tautology (4.46); for example, p exists if it is perceived by the senses as p.

Contradiction If a proposition is false for all truth possibilities it is a contradiction (4.46).

Pure sign see **Sign**

Qualitative inequality Inequalities which are evaluated not in terms of physical metrics but by a scale of mental values or preferences, as for example, good, less good, very good, or, good, better, and best.

Real time see **Time**

Reduction (see also **Discourse** and **Tense**)In the present work, the term is used in two senses. (1) It is an abstract process of reasoning which makes a multiplicity of separate objects or concepts appear as a single entity. Thus, it may be surmised there was a very large collection of separate porcelain tea bowls in Chinese history but only one class of proposition called a 'tea bowl'. Again, non-European people, non-European cultures, and units of space beyond Europe may be reduced to a single and finite set called 'Asian'. In this case, a concept or a property called 'non-European' is associated with many different objects and then reduced to a single expression (such as 'non-European food'). (2) It is also a physical process of **Transforms** (q.v.) which changes one category of objects into another.

Reflection principle see **Set theory**

Representative selection see **Set theory, axiom of choice**

Rule of induction see **Induction**

Semiology   Ferdinand de Saussure defined it as the science which studies the life of signs within social life and is a part of its social psychology. He derived it from the Greek word *semeion* (Saussure, *Cours de linguistique générale*, 1949, 33).

Sign   The findamental concept of semiotics. A sign = a signifier (a sound-image or its written equivalent) + a signified (concept). The sign unites a sound-image and a mental thought. A signifier can of course be a physical symbol also.

Pure sign   A sign which contains the *sufficient* condition of a property fixing its limits. Thus, the necessary conditions for an urban space may be taken individually as houses, streets, water supply, rubbish disposal, markets, people, transport, and so on, all of which collected together make up a sufficient condition. Even when an urban area does not have many of the necessary attributes, the pure sign can still evaluate the historical experience of that town or city and designate it as urban.

Semiotic topology   A system of interlinked **signs** (q.v.) associated with a bounded unit of space. Thus, 'towns' and 'cities' are taken to represent units of space which retain their structural features under every transformation. Neither expansion nor contraction, or indeed distortion of any kind, destroys the collection of significations designated by the term 'urban'. See Greimas, 'For a topological semiotics', in Gottdiener and Lagopoulos (eds.), *The City and the Sign*, 28–9. Greimas makes a distinction between two kinds of urban or spatial forms: physical and semiotic, both of which could be topological. Semiotic form, or topological semiotic, he defined as 'the description, the production, and the interpretation of spatial language'. Greimas treats paired oppositions of spatial signs (here/elsewhere, sacred/profane, private/public, external/internal, superior/inferior, masculine/feminine) as a semiotic set which establish the topology of buildings inside a pre-industrial city or which account for the distribution of space inside a spatial complex.

Set of *all* sets see **Set theory, paradox**

Set theory   Set theory provides the philosophical basis of modern mathematics and is a powerful logical tool for identifying and analysing problems of unities and disunities. As such, it is particularly useful for historians working with generalised concepts and with structural relationships over time and space. The properties of the set theory were first systematically investigated by Georg Cantor (1845–1918) and subsequently formalised by A. Fraenkel and E. Zermelo. Cantor defined a set as a collection of objects or abstract entities. According to Cantor, the set theory rests on two separate properties of the mind: (1) individual objects can be collected into a set by some intuitive principle, (2) a given set which is already perceived as an integral entity (such as the human body or a religion) can be further divided into its constituent elements by some consistent principle.

Empty set   A set which contains no elements and is similar to the notion of 0. The iterative method of forming sets follows from the empty set. For example, a set which contains the empty set can be taken as a second set; a set which contains the set which contains the empty set is the third set and so on; (0), ((0)), (((0))).

Axiom of choice   The axiom postulates that if *A* is a disjoint collection of non-empty sets, then there exists a set **B** which has a single member in common with each member of *A*. The formation of such a set involves making a *representative selection* and therefore the axiom assumes the existence of a principle which allows the selection to be made. For example, it is possible to choose a Muslim from the entire set of Muslims at any given time as a representative member of the set. But it is not possible to select a single member who could represent the entire Hindu social order, because a Brahman does not and cannot represent the members of the other *varnas*. To make up a representative element of Hindus at least four members (one from each caste) are needed.

Excluded set   An expression used in this work to indicate a set which is the contradiction of another set and has no common element with it. Thus the principle of being 'non-European' can be used to form sets which are contradictions of 'European'.

Included set   A set which is the starting-point of an iterative process of forming other sets and all elements of the subsets are exclusively members of the included set.

Paradox   In set theory, paradox results from the expression *a set of all sets* (Cantor's paradox). As Bertrand Russell pointed out, if a set is a member of itself it has the following consequence. Suppose a model-maker sets out to make a *perfect* model of London while living in London. Such a model would not be perfect unless it contained a model of London in it. But that does not solve the problem because there are now *two* models of London in London and so the series would continue to infinity like two mirrors reflecting each other. In order to avoid the Russell paradox, it is necessary to assume that no set can contain itself as a member.

Liar's paradox   The ancient Liar's Paradox is of the following form: Epimenides, the Cretan, says that all Cretans are liars. This statement contains two predicates (1) Epimenides is a Cretan, (2) all Cretans are liars. If (1) is true, (2) is false, because as a Cretan Epimenides cannot be speaking the truth. If (2) is true, (1) is false, Epimenides cannot be a Cretan. But the sentence states that both are true. Hence, it can neither be proven nor refuted according to semantic logic.

Reflection principle   The principle was proposed by Zermelo to demonstrate that every model of a set theory can be taken as a member of another model of a higher order. Thus Muslims, Hindus, etc. can be taken as members of the set called the 'Indian Ocean people' who in turn belong to the set human beings, who are members of the set mammals and so on. The principles or the models which allow each set to be formed can be arranged in a hierarchical order.

Set of sets   A set which is the inverse of an *included set*, i.e. which contains other subsets as its elements and the elements of these subsets are only members of the set of sets.

Well-ordered set   A set of numbers or elements one of which has a least value and forms the starting-point of its ordering.

Sign see **Semiology**

Signification see **Semiology**

Signifier see **Semiology**

Steady state   A structure or system which displays only small and insignificant changes over time and which generates outputs which also fluctuate within narrow limits.

Structural contradiction   A contradiction embedded in a structure which is a part of its **logical necessity** (q.v.) and cannot be removed. The most well-known structural contradiction in economic history is the effects of low and high grain prices on cultivators and consumers respectively. Low prices reduced the income of peasants and benefited consumers and vice versa. Since the quantity of grain produced in pre-modern agriculture was imperfectly related to the price variable, it was impossible to establish an equilibrium price which would satisfy both suppliers and consumers.

Structural differentiation/integration see **Differentiation**

Structural space see **Structure**

Structure   In this work, it is used in three different senses. (1) It is a set of relationships between two or more physical entities, such as the functional connection between land, rainfall, and crop-growing. (2) It is also a set of relationships between abstract entities *without a space or time dimension*, as for example, the perception of ties between family members. As such it is called a *Structural relation*. (3) It is also a set of relationships defined in terms of six planes, (i) physical space, (ii) mental concept of space, (iii) real time, (iv) perceived time, (v) physical structure, and (vi) structural relations. This set is defined as *Structural space*. The mental perception of the *structural space with six dimensions or planes of variations* is called *Logical space*. The definition (2) is the most general one in this work and is used throughout as a principle of classification, as defined by Russell (see above, pp. 12, 29–30).

Succession (see also **Order**)   A movement from one point in space to another point which is located next to it. Thus the assumption that every natural number has a successor needs to be defined in terms of both space and time.

Symbolic integration (see also **Implicated order** and **Integration**)   A process in which the unity or coherence possessed by a collection of objects, ideas, and concepts is rearranged to form another integrated structure which has a new symbol to signify it.

Tautology see **Proposition**

Temporal structure see **Time, structure of**

Tense (see also **Discourse** and **Reduction**)   A syntactical device which enables the structure of time to be represented in language as past, present, and future. Tensed logic expresses the temporal sequences correctly in terms of a set of necessary conditions. Every word has an associative conditional tensed logic, whether expressed directly or indirectly. Sunset, sunrise, yesterday, today, tomorrow, all have strong associative tensed logic. But even classificatory terms such as good or bad suggest states of affairs and therefore incorporate the awareness of time or tense. When time is deliberately excluded from the meaning of a word, it is made *tense-less* or *tense is abolished*. Thus the statement X: 'The concept of Asia is only understood as long as there is a concept of Europe' (see ch. 1, p. 23) has a hidden conditional tense attached to the words 'Asia' and 'Europe'. Asia is a valid term *if and only if* Europe is a valid term. Since Europe is a historical concept, it is subject to an indirect tensed logic which is conditionally transferred to Asia. That is to say, the expression 'as long as' can be expanded in the following sequence. Europe is a historical concept. Asia is not-Europe or the opposite of Europe. Therefore not-Europe or Asia is historical. *Once the meaning of the two expressions are mastered by repetitive usage, they become tense-less classificatory terms.* The content of such terms may change over time but the terms themselves remain the same. The necessary connection between names and objects no longer holds strictly. The statement *X* above clearly does possess a temporal structure or tensed logic, even though both Asia and Europe appear semantically *tense-less*. Foucault's main historical inquiry was to trace the ruptures and discontinuities in the contents of the classificatory names and the appearance of new names and concepts. *Tensed experience* is an experience which consciously compares the relevant historical information to form an expectation for the present and the future.

Time   In this work, the definition of time given by Leibniz is taken as a starting-point, that time is the order and succession of non-contemporaneous things, in which the specific measurement of changes is ignored. Thus the sequence of movements from one physical event to another may be taken as *real time* and our perception of the sequence of that movement (first, second, third, and so on) as *perceived time*. When events associated with perceived time are in turn associated with astronomical movements or solar time, the chain becomes *historical time*. It should be noted that historical time is always located in the past and therefore obeys tensed logic (see **Tense**), i.e. every historical event identified by a time-mark expressed in solar, lunar, or regnal system of dating has a past, present, and future.

World line   The axis on which an observer locates his measurement or metrics of time is called a world line. Thus the world line of solar time is given by the relative movements of the earth in relation to the sun and by the intervals of years, months, days, hours, minutes, and seconds. Since the perception of these intervals differs between individuals and communities, their respective world lines also differ. Thus time appears to go slow or fast because the human sense of the duration of the intervals of time or the relationship between two relative motions is imprecise.

Frequency of time   The number of the occurrence of a class of events within a given time interval. Thus according to the metrics of solar time, it can be said that the events associated with an individual's daily life measured over his life-time has a high frequency of time. On the other hand, events such as the birth of a new religion measured over the period of recorded history have a low frequency. The smaller the metrics of measurement (one minute in the case of the human pulse), the higher the frequency.

Power of time   An event which has the capacity to influence future events over a very long period of time is defined as possessing a high power of time. The longer the period and the larger the unit of space over which its influence is felt, the higher the power of the event.

Structure of time   This is made up by four components, (1) *stationary* events which show little or no change in values over time, (2) *random* events which do not occur in a systematic way within the given time intervals, (3) *long-term* events, the average values of which show a steady increase over time, and (4) *cyclical* events, the values of which increase and decrease in a regular and continuous way.

Topology   A branch of mathematics which attempts to measure the area of a bounded unit of space subject to irregular expansion and contraction. In this work, a topological concept or structure is defined as a bounded 'space' which retains its characteristics under every transformation in a one-to-one mapping. Concepts such as Islamic, Sanskritic, or Chinese civilisations are treated as topological. A topological space also indicates the concept of 'inside' and 'outside' by keeping the boundaries always closed. Thus a topological feature subject to any kind of deformation will still continue to indicate points inside and outside its boundaries. The concept is illustrated below. The triangle A is stretched until it becomes circle B. The line which intersects the two sides of A at points C and D still remain in contact with the curve of B. Furthermore, points x, y, z still remain inside and outside B.

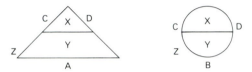

Transform   A process which changes an entity from one form to another. When the two forms are completely dissimilar over the period of transformation, it is defined as one of maximum density. Thus the physiological transformations in the human body from birth to death have different densities in different periods of time sequence. When water becomes steam through the application of heat, the process might be called one of maximum density. It should be noted that the notion of transformation does not need the concept of equilibrium, i.e. the idea that an object is in an ideal state of changelessness does not apply, as everything in the universe can be presented in a state of perpetual transformation.

Transient   A break or rupture in a continuous function.

Unity see **Continuity**, and also **Continuum, Differentiation, Limits**

Variance   The measurement of variation in an entity over a given unit of time.

Well-ordered set see **Set theory**

World line see **Time**

Bibliography

PRINTED SOURCES

Oriental

al-ᶜAbbas al-Malik al-Afdal ibn Ali, *Bughyat al-Fallahin* (*c.* 773AH/AD 1371); 'The cultivation of cereals in mediaeval Yemen', trans. P. B. Serjeant, *Arabian Studies*, I, 1974, 25–74.

ᶜAbdu-lla, *Tarikh-i-Daudi*, in Elliot and Dowson (eds.), *History of India*, vol. 4.

ᶜAbdur Razzak, *Matla'u-s Sa'dain*, in Elliot and Dowson (eds.), *History of India* vol. 4.

Abu Yusuf, Yaᶜqub b. Ibrahim (*d.* 798), *Kitab El Kharadj*, French translation E. Fagnan, Paris, 1921.

Abu'l Fazl, *ᶜAin-i-Akbari* (1595), ed. H. Blochman, 2 vols., Calcutta, 1867–77, in 3 vols.: vol. 1 by H. Blochman, rev. D. C. Phillott; vols. 2 and 3 by H. S. Jarrett, rev. J. Sarkar, Calcutta, 1927–39, 1948–9.

    Akbar-nama, ed. Abdur Rahim, 3 vols., Calcutta, 1877–87; trans. H. Beveridge, 3 vols., Calcutta, 1897–1910.

ᶜAhbar as-Sin wa'l-Hind, Relation de la Chine et de l'Inde redigée en 851 (anonymous), texte établi, traduit et commenté par Jean Sauvaget, Paris, 1948.

Acharya, P. K. (ed.), *Architecture of Manasara: Translated from Original Sanskrit*, London, 1934, reprinted Delhi, 1980, vol. 4.

Babar, Zahir al-Din Muhammad (1483–1530), *The Babur-nama*, ed. A. S. Beveridge, 2 vols., London, 1912–21.

al-Baghdadi, al-Karim al-Katib, *Kitab al-Tabikh*, British Library Or. 5099; trans. A. J. Arberry, 'A Baghdad Cookery Book', *Islamic Culture*, vol. 13, 1939, 20–47, 189–214; reprinted as a separate book, London, 1939.

al-Baghdadi, Katib, *The Topography of Baghdad* (*Ta'rikh Baghdad*), trans. J. Lassner, Detroit, 1970.

al-Baladhuri (*d. c.* 892), *Kitab Futuh al-Buldan*, Arabic text in M. J. de Goeje, Leiden, 1866; *The Origins of the Islamic State*, trans. P. H. Hitti, London, 1916.

Banu Musa bin Shakir, *Kitab al-Hiyal*, English trans. and annotation D. R. Hill, *The Book of Ingenious Devices*, Dordrecht and Boston, 1979.

Barani, Ziya al-Din, *Ta'rikh-i Firuz Shahi*, English trans. in Elliot and Dowson (eds.), *History of India*, vol. 3.

    Fatawa-i-Jahandari (*c.* 1358–9), trans. Afsar Umar Salim Khan, Allahabad, 1969.

Bharatchandra Das, *Bharatchandra-Granthavali*, ed. B. Bandopadhya and S. K. Das, Calcutta, 1944.

al-Biruni, *Alberuni's India*, ed. C. Sachau, London, 1914.

Buzurg Ibn Shahriya (*c*. 900–53), *Kitab ʿAja'ib al-Hind*, English trans. G. S. P. Freeman-Grenville, *The Book of the Wonders of India, Mainland, Sea, and Islands*, London and The Hague, 1981.

Chau, Ju-kua, *Chu-fan-chi* (*c*. AD 1225, 1242–58), trans. F. Hirth and W. W. Rockhill, St Petersburg, 1911.

Cleaves, F. W. (ed. and trans.), *The Secret History of the Mongols*, vol. 1, Cambridge, Mass., 1982.

Driver, G. R. and Miles, J. C., *The Babylonian Laws*, Oxford, 1952.

Elliot, H. M. and Dowson, J. (eds.), *The History of India as told by its own Historians*, 8 vols., London, 1867–77.

Finkel, J., 'King Mutton, a curious Egyptian tale from the Mamluk period', *Zeitschrift für Semitiskik und verwandte Gebiete*, vol. 8, 1932, 122–48, and vol. 9, 1933–4, 1–18.

Gardiner, A. H., 'Ramesside Texts relating to the taxation and transport of corn', *Journal of Egyptian Archaeology*, vol. 27, 1941, 27–74.

Griswold, A. B. and Prasert na Nagara, 'Epigraphic and Historical Studies No. 9: The Inscription of Ramkamhaeng of Sukhothai (AD 1292)', *Journal of the Siam Society*, vol. 59, 1971, 179–228.

'Epigraphic and Historical Studies No. 17: The Judgement of King Mang Ray', *Journal of the Siam Society*, vol. 65, 1977, 137–60.

Hamilton, C., *The Hedaya or Guide: A Commentary on the Mussulman Laws*, London, 1870.

Hanna, N., *Construction Work in Ottoman Cairo 1517–1798*, Le Caire, 1984 (Supplement aux Annales Islamologiques, Cahier N° 4).

al-Hariri, *The Assemblies of Al-Hariri*, ed. and trans. A. Shah, London, 1981.

Hasan, Nizami, *Taju-l Ma-asir* (1205), in Elliot and Dowson (eds.), *History of India*, vol. 2.

Huang Liu-hung, *A Complete Book concerning Happiness and Benevolence* (*Fu-hui Ch'uan-shu*), ed. and trans. Djang Chu, Tucson, Arizona, 1984.

Hudud al-ʿAlam, the Regions of the World: A Persian Geography 372 AH–AD 982, trans. V. Minorsky, London, 1937; 2nd edn ed. C. E. Bosworth, London, 1970.

Hwui Li, Shaman, *The Life of Hiuen Tsiang*, trans. S. Beal, London, 1911.

Ibn al-Ukhuwwa [*d*. 729AH/AD 1329], *The Maʿalim al-Qurba fi Ahkam al-hisba* [British Library Manuscript dated AD 1370], ed. and trans. R. Levy, Cambridge, 1938.

Ibn Battuta (*d*. 1377), *Rihla, The Travels of Ibn Battuta AD 1325–1354*, ed. and trans. H. A. R. Gibb, 3 vols., Cambridge, 1958, 1962, 1971; selected trans. H. A. R. Gibb, *Ibn Battuta: Travels in Asia and Africa 1325–1354*, London, 1929.

Ibn Jubayr, *The Travels of Ibn Jubayr*, trans. R. J. C. Broadhurst, London, 1952.

Ibn Khaldun, Abu Zayd, ʿAbd-ar-Rahman (1332–1406), *The Muqaddimah: An Introduction to History*, trans. F. Rosenthal, 3 vols., Princeton, 1967.

Ibn Majid, Ahmad, *Kitab al-Fawa'id fi usul al-bahr wa'l-qawa'id* (*c*. 1490), Arabic text from MS 2292 Bibliothèque Nationale, Paris, in G. Ferrand (ed.), *Pilote des mers de l'Inde et de la Chine et de l'Indonésie*, 2 vols., Paris, 1921–3; *Arab Navigation in the Indian Ocean*, trans. G. T. Tibbetts, London, 1971.

Ibn Muhammad Ibrahim, *The Ship of Sulaiman*, trans. J. O'Kane, London, 1972.

Ibn Taghri Birdi, *History of Egypt 1382–1469* (*Abul Mahasin Ibn Taghri Birdi*), trans. W. Popper, Berkeley and Los Angeles, 1957–8, vols. 3 and 4.

Ibn Ridwan, Ali (AD 998–1068), *On the Prevention of Bodily Ills in Egypt*, in *Medieval Islamic Medicine: Ibn Ridwan's Treatise*, ed. and trans. with Arabic text, M. W. Dols and A. S. Gamal, Berkeley, Los Angeles and London, 1984.

Ibn Miskawaihi, *The Eclipse of the ᶜAbbasid Caliphate*, ed. and trans. H. F. Amedroz and D. S. Margoliouth, Oxford, 1921.

al-Idrisi [1099/1100–62], *Nuzhat al-mushtaq*; French trans. Pierre-Amedée Jaubert, *La geographie d'Idrisi*, Paris, 1836–40.

'Inayat Khan (*d.* 1666), *Shah Jahan-Nama*, in Elliot and Dowson (eds.), *History of India*, vol. 7.

Jahangir, Nur al-Din (1569–1627), *Tuzuk-i-Jahangiri*, trans. A. Rogers and H. Beveridge, 2 vols., London, 1909–14.

al-Jahiz, *Risala fi manaqib al-atrak wa-ᶜammat jund al-khilafa*, Arabic text ed. G. van Vloten in *Tria Opuscula Auctore al-Djahiz*, Leiden, 1903; translation Harley-Walker, 'Jahiz of Basra to al-Fath b. Khaqan on the "Exploits of the Turks and the army of the Khalifate in general" ', *Journal of the Royal Asiatic Society*, 1915, 631–77; Pellat, C., *Life and Works of Jahiz*, London, 1969.

al-Jazari, Ibn al-Razzaz, *Kitab fi ma 'rifat al-hiyal al-handasiyya*, English trans. and annotation D. R. Hill, *The Book of Knowledge of Ingenious Mechanical Devices*, Dordrecht and Boston, 1974.

Juvaini, ᶜAla al-Din ᶜAta-Malik (1226–83), *Taᶜrikh-i-Jahan-Gusha*, English trans. J. A. Boyle, [*The History of the World Conqueror*], 2 vols., Manchester, 1958.

Khafi Khan, *Muntakhabu-l Lubab*, in Elliot and Dowson (eds.), *History of India*, vol. 7.

Ku-chin t'u-shu chi-chi-ch'eng, 1725.

Li, J. Dun, *The Civilization of China from the Formative Period to the Coming of the West* [English trans. of Chinese texts with an introduction], New York, 1975.

Ma Huan, *Ying-yai Sheng-lan* [The overall Survey of the Ocean's Shores], ed. and English trans. J. V. G. Mills, Cambridge, 1970.

Makdisi, G., 'The topography of eleventh century Baghdad: materials and notes parts I and II', *Arabica: Revue d'Études Arabes*, vol. 6, 1959, 181–97, 280–309.

al-Maqrizi, 'Le traité des famines de Maqrizi', trans. G. Wiet, *Journal of the Economic and Social History of the Orient*, vol. 5, 1962, 14–28.

Les marches du caire: traduction annotée du texts de Maqrizi, trans. A. Raymond, Caire, 1979.

A History of the Ayyubid Sultans of Egypt, trans. R J. C. Broadhurst, Boston, 1980.

al-Masᶜudi (*d.* 956), *Muruj al-Dhahab wa-Maᶜadin an-Jauhar*, Arabic text and French trans. in C. Barbier de Meynard and Pavet de Courteille (eds.), *Les Prairie d'or*, 9 vols., Paris, 1861–77; *The Meadows of Gold: The Abbasids*, trans. P. Lunde and C. Stone, London and New York, 1989.

Mo Tzu, *The Ethical and Political Works of Motse*, trans. Mei Yi-pao, London, 1929.

al-Mufaddal, Ibn Muhammad, *The Mufaddaliyat: An Anthology of Ancient Arabian Odes Compiled by Al-Mufaddal Son of Muhammad*, ed. and trans. C. J. Lyall, 2 vols., Oxford, 1918–21.

Muhammad Ibn al-Hasan al-Hasib, *Anbat al-miya al-khafiyya* (Bringing Hidden Water to the Surface), Hyderabad, 1940, selected English trans. in Krenkow, F., 'The construction of subterranean water supplies during the Abbaside caliphate', *Transactions Glasgow University Oriental Society*, vol. 13, 1947–49 [1951], 23–32.

al-Muhassin, *The Table-talk of a Mesopotamian Judge* (AD 971), trans. D. S. Margoliouth, London, 1922.

al-Muqaddasi, *Ahsanu-t-Taqasim fi Ma'rifati-l-aqalim*, Arabic text ed. Goeje, III; English trans. G. S. A. Ranking and R. F. Azoo, Calcutta, 1901; French trans. A. Miquel, Damascus, 1963.

Nakagawa Chusei, *Shinozoku Kibun*, 1799.

Okakura, K., *The Book of Tea* (*Chajing*), London, 1906.

Shams-i-Siraj Afif, *Tarikh-f-Firuz Shahi*, in Elliot and Dowson (eds.), *History of India*, vol. 3.

Stern, S. M., *Coins and Documents from the Medieval Middle East*, London, 1986.

Sung Ying-hsing, *T'ien-kung K'ai-wu* (1637) [Chinese Technology in the Seventeenth Century, originally published in Chinese in 1637], trans. E-tu Zen Sun and Shiou-chuan Sun, Pennsylvania, 1966.

al-Tabari (*c.* AD 838–923), *Ta'rikh al-Tabari*, Arabic text ed. Th. von Noldeke, Leiden, 1879 and Muhammad Abu al-Fadl Ibrahim, 10 vols., Cairo, 1960–77.

The History of al-Tabari, vol. 32, *The Reunification of the ᶜAbbasid Caliphate*, trans. C. E. Bosworth, New York, 1987.

ath-Thalᶜalibi, ᶜAbd al-Malik Ibn Muhammad, *The Lata'if al-maᶜarif of Thaᶜalibi*, trans. C. E. Bosworth, Edinburgh, 1968.

Varahamihira (*c.* AD 504), *Brhat Samhita*, ed. R. M. Bhat, Delhi, 1981.

Wassaf, ᶜAbdu-llah, *Tazjiyatu-l Amsar wa Tajriyatu-l Asar* (1300–28), trans. in Elliot and Dowson (eds.), *The History of India*, vol. 3.

Weng Chen, *Nung Shu* (1313), Wan-yu wen-ku edition.

Williamson, H. R., *Wang An-shih*, 2 vols., London, 1935–7.

European

Aquinas, St Thomas, *The Summa Theologiciae*, vol. 9, ed. Kenelm Foster, O. P. Blackfriars, Cambridge, 1967.

Augustine, St, *De Civitate Dei*, trans. J. Healey, ed. R. U. G. Tasker, 2 vols., London, 1945.

Bernier, François, *Travels in the Mogul Empire AD 1656–1668*, Irvine Brock, rev. and annotated A. Constable, London, 1891; reprinted Delhi, 1968.

Bowrey, Thomas, *A Geographical Account of Countries Round the Bay of Bengal 1669 to 1679*, ed. Sir Richard Temple, Cambridge, 1905.

Blunt, Lady Anne, *Bedouin Tribes of the Euphrates*, 2 vols., London, 1879.

Brillat-Savarin, Jean Anthelme (1755–1826), *Physiologie du gout ou meditations de gastronomie*, Paris, 1876.

Buchanan, F. (Hamilton), *Journey from Madras through the Countries of Mysore, Canara, and Malabar*, 3 vols., London, 1807.

Buckingham, J. S., *Travels in Assyria, Media and Persia including a Journey from Baghdad by Mount Zargos*, London, 1829.

Burke, E., *The Writings and Speeches of Edmund Burke: Volume V, India: Madras and Bengal 1774–1785*, ed. P. J. Marshall, Oxford, 1981.

Carême, Marie-Antoine, *Le patissier royal parisien ou traité élémentaire et pratique de la pâtisserie ancienne et moderne*, 2 vols., Paris, 1815.

Chardin, Sir John, *Travels in Persia* (1686), ed. Sir Percy Sykes, London, 1927.

Considerations on the East India Trade (1701), in J. R. McCulloch (ed.), *Early English Tracts on Commerce*, London, 1856.

Dapper, O., *Naauwkeurige Beschryvinge Syrie, Palestine*, Amsterdam, 1677.

Defoe, D., *The Just Complaint of the Poor Weavers*, London, 1719.

   A Brief State of the Question between the Printed and Painted Callicoes and the Woollen and Silk Manufacture, London, 1719.

Dubois, A. J. Abbé, *Hindu Manners, Customs and Ceremonies* (c. 1806), ed. H. K. Beauchamp, Oxford, 1906.

Ferrier, J. P., *Caravan Journeys and Wanderings in Persia, Afghanistan, Turkistan, and Beloochistan*, London, 1857.

Forbes, James, *Oriental Memoirs*, 4 vols., London, 1813.

Fortune, R., *A Journey to the Tea Countries of China*, London, 1852.

Fort William–India House Correspondence, vol. II, 1757–59, ed. H. N. Sinha, Delhi, 1957.

Fortune, R., *Three Years' Wanderings in the Northern Provinces of China*, London, 1847.

Fryer, J., *A New Account of East India and Persia being Nine Years' Travels 1672–1681*, ed. W. Crooke, 3 vols., London, 1909, 1912, 1915.

Gonzales de Mendoza, *The History of the Great and Mighty Kingdom of China*, ed. Sir G. T. Staunton, London, 1853–4.

Grose, John Henry, *A Voyage to the East Indies*, London, 1757; 2nd edn, 2 vols., London, 1772.

Hakluyt, R., *The Principal Navigations, Voyages, Traffiques and Discoveries of the English Nation*, 8 vols., London, 1927.

Hamilton, Alexander, *A New Account of the East Indies*, first published Edinburgh, 1727; modern version ed. W. Foster, 2 vols., London, 1930.

Havart, D., *Op-en Ondergang van Coromandel*, Amsterdam, 1693.

Heath, J. M., 'On Indian iron and steel', *Journal of the Royal Asiatic Society*, 1839, 390–7.

Heber, R., *Narrative of a Journey through the Upper Provinces of India . . . 1824–1825*, 2 vols., London; new edn 1861.

Hedges, W., *The Diary of William Hedges (1681–1687)*, ed. H. Yule, 3 vols., London, 1887–89.

Hunter, W. W., *A Statistical Account of Bengal*, London, 1875.

Knox, R., *An Historical Relation of the Island of Ceylon in the East-Indies*, London, 1681.

Lane, E. W., *An Account of the Manners and Customs of the Modern Egyptians . . . 1833, –34, and –35*, London, 1860.

Lecomte, L., *Memoirs and Observations, Topographica, Physical . . . Made in a Late Journey through the Empire of China*, London, 1697.

Leibniz, G. W., *Leibniz: Selections*, ed. P. P. Wiener, New York, 1951.

Loubére, Simon de La, *A New Historical Relation of the Kingdom of Siam by Monsieur De La Loubére*, trans. A. P. Gen, London, 1693.

Macartney, Lord, *An Embassy to China*, ed. J. L. Cranmer-Byng, London, 1962.

Malthus, T. R., *An Essay on the Principle of Population*, London, 1798.

Mandenslo, Albert de, *Les voyages du Sieur Albert de Mandelslo*, Leiden, 1719.

Master, Streynsham, *The Diaries of Streynsham Master 1675–1680*, ed. Sir Richard Temple, 2 vols., London, 1911.

Mendoza *see under* Gonzales de Mendoza.

Methwold, W., *Relations of Golconda in the Early Seventeenth Century* (1626), ed. W. H. Moreland, London, 1931.

Montanus, Arnoldus, *Atlas Chinensis*, London, 1671.

Niebuhr, Carsten, *Travels through Arabia and Other Countries in the East*, trans. R. Heron, Edinburgh, 1792.

Nieuhoff, J., *An Embassy from the East India Company of the United Provinces to the Grand Tartar Chan Emperor of China*, London, 1669.

Norden, F. L., *Voyage d'Egypte et de Nubie*, vol. I, Copenhagen, 1755.

Orme, R., *General Idea of the Government and People of Indostan* (1753), printed in his *Historical Fragments of the Mogul Empire*, London, 1805.

Pattullo, H., *A Essay upon the Cultivation of the Lands and Improvements of the Revenues of Bengal*, London, 1772.

Pelsaert, Francisco, *Jahangir's India: The Remonstrantie of Francisco Pelsaert*, ed. and trans. W. H. Moreland and P. Geyl, Cambridge, 1925.

Periplus Maris Erythraei, ed. and trans. G. W. B. Huntingford [*The Periplus of the Erythaean Sea*], London, 1980.

Pinto, Fernao Mendes, *Peregrinacam de Fernam Mendez Pinto*, Lisboa, 1614.

Pires, Tomé, *The Suma Oriental of Tome Pires: An Account of the East, from the Red Sea to Japan, Written in Malacca and India in 1512–1515*, ed. and trans. Armando Cortesao, 2 vols., London, 1944; reprinted Wiesbaden, 1967.

Pliny, *Natural History*, trans. H. Rackham, vol. 5 [Libri XVII–XIX], London, 1950.

Polo, Marco, *The Descriptions of the World* [1298], ed. and trans. A. C. Moule and P. Pelliot, London, 1938.

Polybius [the historian], *History*, trans. W. R. Paton, vol. 4, London, 1925.

Prisse D'Avennes, *L'art arabe d'après les monuments du Kaire depuis le VIIe siècle jusqa'à la fin du XVIIIe*, 2 vols., 1877.

Ricci, Matteo, *China in the Sixteenth Century: The Journals of Matthew Ricci 1583–1610*, trans. L. J. Gallagher, New York, 1953.

Say, Jean-Baptiste, *Cours complet d'economie politique pratique*, vol. 5, Paris, 1829.

Schwartz, P. (ed.), *Painting on Cotton at Ahmedabad India in 1678*, Ahmedabad, 1969.

Smith, Adam, *An Enquiry into the Nature and Causes of the Wealth of Nations* (1776), reprinted from the 6th edn, London, 1905.

Solvyns, B., *A Collection of Two Hundred and Fifty Coloured Etchings: Descriptive of the Manners, Customs, and Dresses of the Hindoos*, Calcutta, 1799.

Tavernier, Jean-Baptiste, *Travels in India* (1640–67), trans. John Phillips, London, 1677; new edn trans. V. Ball, 2 vols., London, 1889; Ball's translation rev. and ed. W. Crook, London, 1925.

Texier, Charles Felix Marie, *Description de l'Asie Mineure, faite par ordre du Governement Français, de 1835 à 1837*, 3 vols., Paris, 1839–49.

Thevenot, J. de, *Indian Travels of Thevenot and Careri*, ed. S. Sen, New Delhi, 1949.

Valle, Pietro della, *The Travels of Pietro della Valle in India* (1664), ed. E. Gray, 2 vols., London, 1892.

Wallace, A. R., *The Malay Archipelago*, London, 1890.

Wilkinson, H., 'On the cause of the external pattern or watering of the Damascus sword-blades', *Journal of the Royal Asiatic Society*, 1837, 187–93.

'On Iron', *Journal of the Royal Asiatic Society*, 1839, 383–97.

MODERN WORKS

Aalund, F., 'The wakalat bazar^c a: the rehabilitation of a commercial structure in the old city', in Meinecke (ed.), *Islamic Cairo: Architectural Conservation and Urban Development of the Historic Centre, Art and Archaeology Research Papers*, 35–41.

Abdulak, S., 'Tradition and community in vernacular Omani housing', *Art and Archaeology Research Papers*, 1977, 18–41.

Abdulfattah, K., *Mountain Farmer and Fellah in 'Asir Southwest Saudi Arabia: The Conditions of Agriculture in a Traditional Society*, Erlangen, 1981.

Abrams, P. and Wrigley, E. A. (eds.), *Towns in Societies: Essays in Economic History and Historical Sociology*, Cambridge, 1978.

Adams, R. M., *Heartland of Cities: Surveys of Ancient Settlements and Land Use on the Central Floodplains of the Euphrates*, Chicago and London, 1981.

Land behind Baghdad: A History of Settlement on the Diyala Plains, Chicago and London, 1965.

The Evolution of Urban Society, London, 1966.

Adiceam, E., *La géographie de l'irrigation dans le Tamilnad*, Paris, 1966.

Auesrivongse, N., 'Devaraja cult and Khmer kingship at Angkor', in K. R. Hall and J. K. Whitmore (eds.), *Explorations in Early Southeast Asian History: The Origins of Southeast Asian Statecraft*, Ann Arbor, 1976.

Ahsan, M. M., *Social Life under the Abbasids, 170–289AH/AD 786–902*, London, 1979.

Alam Khan, I., 'Early use of cannon and musket in India: AD 1442–1526', *Journal of the Economic and Social History of the Orient*, vol. 24, 1981, 146–64.

Allan, J. W., *Persian Metal Technology AD 700–1300*, London, 1979.

Allchin, F. R., 'Early cultivated plants in India and Pakistan', in Ucko and Dimbleby (eds.), *The Domestication and Exploitation of Plants and Animals*.

Allen, W. E. D., 'The Ottomans and Turkestan: The Don-Volga Canal Project', in *Problems of Turkish Power in the Sixteenth Century*, London, 1963.

Arnold, T. W., *The Caliphate*, Oxford, 1924.

Asad, T., 'The bedouin as a military force: notes on some aspects of power relations between nomads and sedentaries in historical perspectives', in Nelson (ed.), *The Desert and the Sown*.

Ashtor, E., 'L'administration urbaine en Syrie médiévale', in *The Medieval Near East: Social and Economic History*, London, 1978.

'L'évolution des prix dans le Proche-Orient à la basse époque', *Journal of the Economic and Social History of the Orient*, vol. 4, 1961, 15–46.

'Republiques urbaines dans le Proche-Orient à l'époque des croisades', in *The Medieval Near East*.

'The Levantine sugar industry in the late Middle Ages: a case of technological decline', in Udovitch (ed.), *The Islamic Middle East*.

'The diet of salaried classes in the medieval Near East', *Journal of Asian History*, vol. 3, 1969, 1–24; reprinted in Forster and Ranum (eds.), *Biology of Man in History*.

Aston, T. H. and Philpin, C. H. E. (eds.), *The Brenner Debate: Agrarian Class Structure and Economic Development in Pre-Industrial Europe*, Cambridge, 1985.

Athar Ali, M., *The Mughal Nobility under Aurangzeb*, Delhi, 1968.

Ayalon, D., *Gunpowder and Firearms in the Mamluk Kingdom: A Challenge to a Medieval Society*, London, 1955.

Baal, J. van *et al.* (eds.), *Bali, Further Studies in Life, Thought, and Ritual*, The Hague, 1969.

Bachelard, G., *La poetique de l'espace*, Paris, 1958.

Baden-Powell, B. H., *The Land Systems of British India*, Oxford, 1892.

'Badw' (Bedouin), in *Encyclopaedia of Islam*^{2}.

Bacon, E. E., 'Types of pastoral nomadism in central and southwest Asia', *Southwestern Journal of Anthropology*, vol. 10, 1954, 44–68.

Bailey, A. M. and Llobera, J. R. (eds.), *The Asiatic Mode of Production*, London, 1981.

Bailey, C., 'Dating the arrival of the bedouin tribes in Sinai and the Negev', *Journal of the Economic and Social History of the Orient*, vol. 28, 1985, 20–49.

Bakhit, M. A., *The Ottoman Province of Damascus in the Sixteenth Century*, Beirut, 1982.

'The role of the Hanash family', in Khalidi (ed.), *Land Tenure and Social Transformation in the Middle East*.

Balazs, E., *Chinese Civilization and Bureaucracy: Variations on a Theme*, ed. and trans. H. M. Wright and A. F. Wright, New Haven, 1964.

Baluch, P., *The Bhagnari Breed of Cattle*, Delhi, 1926.

Barbir, K. K., *Ottoman Rule in Damascus, 1708–1758*, Princeton, 1980.

Barker, R., Herdt, R. W., and Rose, B., *The Rice Economy of Asia*, Washington, 1985.

Barth, F., 'A general perspective on nomad–sedentary relations in the Middle East', in Nelson (ed.), *The Desert and the Sown*.

Nomads of South Persia: the Basseri Tribe of the Khamseh Confederacy, Oslo and London, 1964.

Barthes, R., *Image, Music, Text*, trans. S. Heath, London, 1977.

Barthold, W., *Turkestan Down to the Mongol Invasion*, London, 1928.

Bary, W. T. de, *Neo-Confucian Orthodoxy and the Learning of the Mind-and-Heart*, New York, 1981.

Basham, A. L. (ed.), *Kingship in Asia and Early America*, Mexico, 1981.

Bates, D. G., 'Differential access to pasture in a nomadic society: the Yoruk of South-eastern Turkey', in Irons and Dyson-Hudson, *Perspectives on Nomadism*.

Bayly, C. A., *Rulers, Townsmen and Bazaars: North Indian Society in the Age of British Expansion, 1770–1870*, Cambridge, 1983.

Beck, L., *The Qashqa'i of Iran*, New Haven and London, 1986.

Bedini, S., 'Chinese Mechanical Clocks', *Bulletin of the National Association of Watch and Clock Collectors*, vol. 7, no. 4, 1956.

Bell, G. M. L., *The Desert and the Sown*, London, 1907.

Benacerraf, P. and Putnam, H. (eds.), *Philosophy of Mathematics: Selected Readings*, Cambridge, 1985.

Benveniste, E., *Problems in General Linguistics*, trans. M. E. Meek, Coral Gables, 1971.

Indo-European Language and Society, trans. E. Palmer, London, 1973.

Berling, J. A., *The Syncretic Religion of Lin Chao-en*, New York, 1980.

Birks, J. S., 'Development or decline of pastoralists, the Bani Qitab of the Sultanate of Oman', *Arabian Studies*, vol. 4, 1978, 7–19.

Bodde, D., *Essays on Chinese Civilization*, Princeton, 1981.

'Harmony and conflict in Chinese philosophy', in Wright (ed.), *Studies in Chinese Thought*.

Boerschmann, E., *Picturesque China: Architecture and Landscape*, n.p., n.d.

Bohm, D., *Wholeness and the Implicate Order*, London, 1980.

Boserup, E., *Population and Technology*, Oxford, 1981.

Bosworth, C. E., 'Recruitment, muster, and review in medieval Islamic armies', in Parry and Yapp (eds.), *War, Technology, and Society in the Middle East*.

The Medieval History of Iran, Afghanistan and Central Asia, London, 1977.

Bourdieu, P., *Distinction: A Social Critique of the Judgement of Taste*, trans. S. Heath, London, 1984.

Outline of a Theory of Practice, trans. R. Nice, Cambridge, 1977; reprinted 1985.

Boyd, A., *Chinese Architecture and Town Planning*, London, 1962.

Boyle, J. A. (ed.), *The Cambridge History of Iran*, vol. 5, Cambridge, 1968.

Braudel, F., *Afterthoughts on Material Civilization and Capitalism*, P. M. Ranum, Baltimore, 1977.

Civilisation materielle: économie et capitalisme, XVe–XVIIIe siècle, I, *Les structures du quotidien: le possible et l'impossible*, II, *Les jeux de l'échange*, III, *Le temps du monde*, Paris, 1979; English trans. S. Reynolds, London, vols. 1–2, 1981–2, vol. 3, 1984.

Ecrits sur l'histoire, Paris, 1969; trans. S. Matthews, London, 1980.

'Histoire et sciences sociales: la longue durée', *Annales: Economie, Sociétés, Civilisations*, vol. 13, 1958, 725–53; trans. in Burke (ed.), *Economy and Society in Early Modern Europe*.

La mediterranée et le monde mediterranéen à l'époque de Philippe II, 2nd edn, Paris, 1966; trans. S. Reynolds, 2 vols., London, 1972–3.

L'identité de la France, Paris, 1986; trans. S. Reynolds, London, 1988.

Une leçon d'histoire de Fernand Braudel: Chateauvallon/octobre 1985, ed. M. Paquet, Paris, 1986.

Bray, F., *Science and Civilisation in China, vol. 6, Biological Technology, Part II: Agriculture*, Cambridge, 1984.

Bremen, J., *The Village on Java*, Rotterdam, 1980.

Brennand, W., *Hindu Astronomy*, London, 1896.

Brett, M., 'Ibn Khaldun, and the arabisation of North Africa', *Maghreb Review*, vol. 4, 1979, 9–16.

'The city-state in medieval Ifriqya: the case of Tripoli', *Cahiers de Tunisie*, vol. 34, 1986, 69–94.

'The way of the peasant', *Bulletin of the School of Oriental and African Studies*, vol. 47, 1984, 44–56.

Brohier, R. L., *Ancient Irrigation Works in Ceylon*, 2 vols., Colombo, 1934–5.

Broomhall, M., *Islam in China*, London, 1910.

Brown, P., *Augustine of Hippo*, London, 1969.

Brown, T. B., 'Early bread wheat', *Antiquity*, vol. 24, 1950, 40.

Brown, W. R., *The Horse of the Desert*, New York, 1929, reprinted 1977.

Bruen, E. J., *Cattle Breeding in the Bombay Presidency: Principles and Progress*, Poona, 1927.

Brunschvig, R., *La berberie orientale sous les Hafsides: des origines à la fin du XV siècle*, 2 vols., Paris, 1940–7.

Bryson, R. A. and Murray, T. J., *Climates of Hunger*, Madison, 1977.

Bulliet, R. W., *The Camel and the Wheel*, Cambridge, Mass., 1975.

Conversion to Islam in the Medieval Period: An Essay in Quantitative History, Cambridge, Mass., 1979.

The Patricians of Nishapur: A Study in Medieval Islamic Social History, Cambridge, Mass., 1972.

Bunting, E. J. W., *Sindhi Tombs and Textiles, the Persistence of Pattern*, Albuquerque, New Mexico, 1980.

Burke, P. (ed.), *Economy and Society in Early Modern Europe: Essays from Annales*, London, 1972.

Caetani, L., *Saggio di un manuale di cronologie musulmana estratto dalla chronolgraphia islamic*, Roma, 1923.

Studi di Storia Orientale, vols. 1 and 3, Milano, 1911, 1914.

Cahen, C., 'L'évolution de l'Iqta du IXe siècle: contribution à une histoire comparée des sociétés médiévales', *Annales: Économie, Sociétés, Civilisations*, vol. 8, 1953, 25–52.

Makhzumiyyat: Études sur l'histoire économique et financière de l'Egypte médiévale, Leiden, 1977.

'Movements populaires et autonomismes urbains dans l'Asie musulmane au Moyen Age', *Arabica*, vol. 5, 1958, 225–50, and vol. 5, 1959, 25–6, 223–65.

'Quelques mots sur les Hilaliens et le nomadisme', *Journal of the Economic and Social History of the Orient*, vol. 11, 1968, 130–3.

'Y-at-il eu des corporations professionelles dans le monde musulman classique', in Hourani and Stern (eds.), *The Islamic City*.

Cammann, S., *China's Dragon Robes*, New York, 1952.

Cantor, G., *Contributions to the Founding of the Theory of Transfinite Numbers* (1897), trans. P. E. B. Jourdain, New York, 1915; reprinted 1955.

Caskel, W., 'The bedouinization of Arabia', in Grunebaum (ed.), *Studies in Islamic Culture*.

Cassirer, E., *Determinism and Indeterminism in Modern Physics*, trans. O. T. Benfey, New Haven, 1956.

Chakravarty, A. K., *Origin and Development of Indian Calendrical Science*, Calcutta, 1975.

Chang, K. C. (ed.), *Food in Chinese Culture: Anthropological and Historical Perspectives*, New Haven and London, 1977.

Chang, Kwang-chih, 'The beginning of agriculture in the Far East', *Antiquity*, vol. 44, 1970, 175–85.

Chang, Te-tzu, 'The rice culture', in Hutchinson (ed.), *The Early History of Agriculture*.

Chao, K., *Man Land in Chinese History: An Economic Analysis*, Stanford, 1986.
  The Development of Cotton Textile Production in China, Harvard, 1977.

Chaudhuri, K. N., 'Capitalisme commercial et production industrielle en Asie avant 1800', in Braudel (ed.), *Une leçon d'histoire de Fernand Braudel*.
  'Some reflections on the town and country in Mughal India', *Modern Asian Studies*, vol. 12, 1978, 77–95.
  The Trading World of Asia and the English East India Company 1660–1760, Cambridge, 1978.
  Trade and Civilisation in the Indian Ocean: An Economic History from the Rise of Islam to 1750, Cambridge, 1985.
  'World silver flows and monetary factors as a force of international integration 1660–1760 (America, Europe, and Asia)', in Fischer, McInnes, and Schneider (eds.), *The Emergence of a World Economy 1500–1914*.

Chen, K., *Buddhism in China: A Historical Survey*, Princeton, 1972.

Chen Han-sheng, *Landlord and Peasant in China: A Study of the Agrarian Crisis in South China*, Shanghai, 1936.

Chi, Ch'ao-ting, *Key Economic Areas in Chinese History as Revealed in the Development of Public Works for Water-control*, New York, 1963.

Chicherov, A. I., *India: Economic Development in the 16th–18th Centuries: Outline of Crafts and Trade*, Moscow, 1971.

Chisholm, M., *Modern World Development: A Geographical Perspective*, London, 1982.

Christiansen, S., 'Wet rice cultivation: some reasons why', in Norlund, Cederroth, and Gerdin (eds.), *Rice Societies*.

Chuang, Han-sheng and Krauss, R. A., *Mid-Ch'ing Rice Markets and Trade: An Essay in Price History*, Cambridge, Mass., 1975.

Cipolla, C. M., *Clocks and Culture 1300–1700*, London, 1967.
  The Economic History of World Population, London, 1978.
  Guns and Sails in the Early Phase of European Expansion 1400–1700, London, 1966.

Clark, S., *Indian Drawings*, London, 1921.

Clerget, M., *Le Caire*, 2 vols., Cairo, 1934.

Coale, A. J. and Watkins, S. C. (eds.), *The Decline of Fertility in Europe*, Princeton, 1986.

Coedes, G., *The Indianized States of Southeast Asia*, ed. and trans. W. R. Vella and S. B. Cowing, Honolulu, 1968.

Cole, D. P., *Nomads of the Nomads: The al-Murrah Bedouin of the Empty Quarter*, Chicago, 1975.

Commissiariat, M. S., *A History of Gujarat 1573–1758*, Bombay, 1957.

Conrad, L. I., 'The *qusur* of medieval Islam: some implications for the social history of the Near East', *Al-Abath*, vol. 29, 1981, 7–23.

Cook, M. A., *Population Pressure in Rural Anatolia 1450–1600*, London, 1972.
   (ed.), *Studies in the Economic History of the Middle East*, Oxford, 1970.

Corbin, H., *Cyclical Time and Ismaili Gnosis*, London, 1983.

Crecelius, D., 'Archival sources for demographic studies of the Middle East', in Udovitch (ed.), *The Islamic Middle East*.

Creswell, K. A. C., *A Short Account of Early Muslim Architecture*, revised and supplemented by J. W. Allan, London, 1989.
   Early Muslim Architecture, 2 vols., Oxford, 1969.
   The Origin of the Cruciform Plan of Cairene Madrasas, Cairo, 1922.

Crone, P. and Cook, M., *Hagarism: The Making of the Islamic World*, Cambridge, 1977.

Crook, N., 'On the comparative historical perspective: India, Europe, the Far-East', in Dyson, T. (ed.), *India's Historical Demography*, London, 1989.

Cuno, K. M., 'Egypt's wealthy peasantry, 1740–1820: a study of the region of al-Mansura', in Khalidi (ed.), *Land Tenure and Social Transformation in the Middle East*.

'Dar' (Dwelling place), in *Encyclopaedia of Islam*².

Darby, W., Ghalioungui, P., and Grivetti, L., *Food: The Gift of Osiris*, 2 vols., London, New York, and San Francisco, 1976–7.

Dasgupta, S. N., *A History of Indian Philosophy*, 5 vols., Cambridge, 1922–55.

Datta, B. and Singh, A. N., *History of Hindu Mathematics*, Lahore, 1935.

Davey, C. J., 'The Negub Tunnel', *Iraq*, vol. 47, 1985, 49–55.

Davidson, D., *Inquiries into Truth and Interpretation*, Oxford, 1967.

Dedekind, R., 'Continuity and Irrational Numbers', in *Essays on the Theory of Numbers*, Chicago, 1901; reprinted, New York, 1963.

Derrida, J., *L'écriture et la différence*, Paris, 1967; *Writing and Difference*, trans. A. Bass, London, 1978.

Desharnes, R., *The World of Salvador Dali*, London, 1979.

Digby, S., *War-horse and Elephant in the Delhi Sultanate: A Study of Military Supplies*, Oxford, 1971.

Doerfer, C., *Turkische und Mongolische Elemente im Neupersischen*, 4 vols., Wiesbaden, 1963–75.

Dols, M., *The Black Death in the Middle East*, Princeton, 1977.

Donner, F. M., 'Tribal settlement in Basra during the first century AH', in Khalidi (ed.), *Land Tenure and Social Transformation in the Middle East* (1984).
   The Early Islamic Conquests, Princeton, 1981.

Dostal, W., 'The evolution of Bedouin life', in Gabrieli (ed.), *L'Antica Societa Beduina*.

Dummett, M., *Frege: Philosophy of Language*, 2nd edn, London, 1981.

Dumont, L., *Homo Hierarchicus: The Caste System and its Implications*, London, revised edn 1980.

Dunn, R. E., *The Adventures of Ibn Battuta: A Muslim Traveller of the 14th Century*, London, 1986.

Dupre, G. and Rey, Pierre-Philippe, 'Reflections on the pertinence of a theory of the history of exchange', *Economy and Society*, vol. 2, 1973, 131–63.

al-Duri, Khidr Jasmin, *Society and Economy of Iraq under the Seljuqs (1055–1160) with Special Reference to Baghdad*, Ph.D. thesis, University of Pennsylvania, 1970.

Ebrey, P. B., *The Aristocratic Families of Early Imperial China*, Cambridge, 1978.

Eco, U., 'Function and sign: semiotics of architecture', in Gottdiener and Lagopoulos (eds.), *The City and the Sign: An Introduction to Urban Semiotics*.
Semiotic and the Philosophy of Language, London, 1984.

Edmundson, W. C., *Land, Food, and Work in Three Javanese Villages*, Ph.D. thesis, University of Hawaii, 1972.

Egerton, Lord, *A Description of Indian and Oriental Armour*, London, 1896.

El-Ali, S., 'The foundation of Baghdad', in Hourani and Stern (eds.), *The Islamic City*.

Elvin, M., 'The high-level equilibrium trap: the causes of the decline of invention in the traditional Chinese textile industries', in Willmott, W. E. (ed.), *Economic Organization in Chinese Society*, Stanford, 1972.
The Pattern of the Chinese Past, Stanford, 1973.

English, P. W., 'The origins and spread of qanats in the Old World', *Proceedings of the American Philosophical Society*, vol. 112, 1968, 170–81.
City and Village in Iran: Settlement and Economy in the Kirman Basin, Madison, 1966.

Erskine, K. D., *A Gazetteer of the Jodhpur State and Some Statistical Tables*, Ajmer, 1909.

Farooqhi, S., *Towns and Townsmen of Ottoman Anatolia: Trade, Crafts and Food Production in an Urban Setting, 1520–1650*, Cambridge, 1984.

Febvre, L., *A Geographical Introduction to History*, London, 1925.

Fehervari, G., *Islamic Pottery*, London, 1973.

Fernald, H. S., *Chinese Court Costume*, Toronto, 1946.

Fischer, W., McInnes, R. M., and Schneider, J. (eds.), *The Emergence of a World Economy 1500–1914*, Wiesbaden, 1986.

Fisher, H. J., 'The eastern Maghrib and the central Sudan', in Oliver (ed.), *Cambridge History of Africa*, III.

Fleet, J. F., 'The ancient Indian water-clock', *Journal of the Royal Asiatic Society*, 1915, 213–30.

Fletcher, J., 'The Mongols: ecological and social perspectives', *Harvard Journal of Asiatic Studies*, vol. 46, 1986, 11–50.

Forbes, E. J., *Studies in Ancient Technology*, 9 vols., Leiden, 1955–64.

Forster, R. and Ranum, O. (eds.), *Biology of Man in History, Selections from the Annales: Economies, Societes, Civilisations*, Baltimore, 1975.

Foucault, M., *Histoire de la folie à l'age classique*, Paris, 1964; *Madness and Civilization*, trans. R. Howard, London, 1971.

    L'archeologie du savoir, Paris, 1969; *The Archaeology of Knowledge*, trans. A. M. Sheridan Smith, London, 1972; reprinted 1982.

    Les mots et les choses, Paris, 1966; *The Order of Things: An Archaeology of the Human Sciences*, trans. London, 1970, reprinted 1982.

Fraassen, B. C. van, *An Introduction to the Philosophy of Time and Space*, New York, 1985.

Frantz-Murphy, G., 'A new interpretation of the economic history of medieval Egypt', *Journal of the Economic and Social History of the Orient*, 1981, vol. 24, 19.

    'Land tenure and social transformation in early Islamic Egypt', in Khalidi (ed.), *Land Tenure and Social Transformation in the Middle East*.

Fraser, J. T., Lawrence, N. and Haber, F. C. (eds.), *Time, Science, and Society in China and the West*, Amherst, 1986.

Freedman, M., *Lineage Organization in Southeastern China*, London, 1958.

    Chinese Lineage and Society: Fukien and Kwangtung, London, 1966.

    (ed.), *Family and Kinship in Chinese Society*, Stanford, 1960.

Fritz, J. M., 'Vijayanagara: authority and meaning of a South Indian Imperial Capital', *American Anthropologist*, vol. 88, 1986, 44–55.

Fritz, J. M., Michell, G., and Nagaraja Rão, M. S., *The Royal Centre at Vijayanagara*, Melbourne, 1984.

Gabrieli, F. (ed.), *L'Antica Societa Beduina*, Roma, 1959.

Gardiner, A. H., 'Ramesside Texts relating to the taxation and transport of corn', *Journal of Egyptian Archaeology*, vol. 27, 1941, 19–73.

Garthwaite, G. R., *Khans and Shahs: A Documentary Analysis of the Bakhtiyari in Iran*, Cambridge, 1983.

Gaube, H., *Iranian Cities*, New York, 1979.

Gazzard, R., 'The Arab house: its form and spatial distribution', in Hyland and Ahmed Al-Shahi (eds.), *The Arab House*.

Geertz, C., *Agricultural Involution: The Process of Ecological Change in Indonesia*, Berkeley and Los Angeles, 1963.

    The Religion of Java, Glencoe, Illinois, 1960.

Geiger, W., *Civilization of the Eastern Iranians in Ancient Times*, vol. 1, London, 1885.

Gellner, E., *Muslim Society*, Cambridge, 1981.

Gentil, G. Le, *Fernao Mendes Pinto: un précurseur de l'exotisme au XVIe siècle*, Paris, 1947.

Gernet, J., *Daily Life in China on the Eve of the Mongol Invasion 1250–1276*, trans. H. M. Wright, London, 1962.

    Les aspects économiques du Bouddhisme dans la société chinoise du Ve au Xe siècle, Saigon, 1956.

Gerschenkron, A., '*Mercator Gloriosus*' [Review of Hicks, *A Theory of Economic History*], *Economic History Review*, vol. 24, 1971, 653–66.

'Ghida' (Food), in *Encyclopaedia of Islam*[2].

Ghurye, G. S., *Indian Costume*, Bombay, 1951.

Gibson, M. and Biggs, R. D. (eds.), *The Organization of Power in Aspects of Bureaucracy in the Ancient Near East*, Chicago, 1987.

Digard, J. P., *Techniques des nomades baxtyari d'Iran*, Cambridge and Paris, 1981.

Gil, M., *Documents of the Jewish Pious Foundations from the Cairo Geniza*, Leiden, 1976.

Gillion, K. L., *Ahmedabad: A Study in Indian Urban History*, Berkeley and Los Angeles, 1968.

Gittinger, M., *Splendid Symbols, Textiles and Tradition in Indonesia*, Oxford, 1985.

Goblot, H., *Les qanats: une technique d'acquisition de l'eau*, Paris, 1979.

Gödel, K., *Kurt Gödel: Collected Works, Volume I, Publications 1929–1936*, ed. S. Feferman *et al.*, Oxford, 1986.

 'Russell's mathematical logic', in Benacerraf and Putnam (eds.), *Philosophy of Mathematics: Selected Readings*.

 'What is Cantor's continuum problem', in Benacerraf and Putnam (eds.), *Philosophy of Mathematics: Selected Readings*.

Godelier, M., *Rationalité et irrationalité en économie*, Paris, 1966.

Goitein, S. D., 'A mansion in Fustat: a twelfth-century description of a domestic compound in the ancient capital of Egypt', in Miskimin, H. A., Herlihy, D., and Udovitch, A. L. (eds.), *The Medieval City*, New Haven and London, 1977.

 'The main industries of the Mediterranean area as reflected in the records of the Cairo Geniza', *Journal of the Economic and Social History of the Orient*, vol. 4, 1961, 168–97.

 'Urban housing in Fatimid and Ayyubid times', *Studia Islamica*, vol. 24, 1978, 5–23.

Golvin, L. and Fromont, Marie-Christine, *Thula, architecture et urbanisme d'une cité de haute montagne en république arabe du Yemen*, Paris, 1984.

Good, A., 'A symbolic type and its transformation: the case of South Indian Ponkal', *Contributions to Indian Sociology*, vol. 17, 1983, 223–44.

Goody, J., *Cooking, Cuisine and Class: A Study in Comparative Sociology*, Cambridge, 1982.

 Technology, Tradition, and the State in Africa, London, 1971.

Gottdiener, M. and Lagopoulos, A. Ph. (eds.), *The City and the Sign: An Introduction to Urban Semiotics*, New York, 1986.

Gourou, P., *Man and Land in the Far East*, trans. S. H. Beaver, London, 1975.

 L'utilisation du sol en Indochine française, Paris, 1940.

 L'Asie, Paris, 1953.

 The Tropical World: Its Social and Economic Conditions and its Future Status, trans. S. H. Beaver and E. D. Labourde, London, 1978.

Graaf, H. J. de and Pigeaud, G. Th., *Chinese Muslims in Java in the 15th and 16th centuries: The Malay Annals of Semarang and Cerbon*, ed. M. C. Ricklefs, Melbourne, 1984.

Grabar, O., *The Formation of Islamic Art*, New Haven and London, 1973.

Gramsci, A., *Selections from Prison Notebooks*, ed. and trans. Q. Hoare and G. N. Smith, London, 1971; reprinted 1984.

Granet, M., *The Religion of the Chinese People*, trans, M. Freedman, Oxford, 1975.

 La pensée chinoise, Paris, 1934.

Greimas, A. J., 'Pour une semiotique topologique', in Gottdiener and Lagopoulos (eds.), *The City and the Sign: An Introduction to Urban Semiotics* (1986).

Grewal, J. S. and Banga, I. (eds.), *Studies in Urban History*, Amritsar, 1981.

Grierson, P., *Numismatics*, London, 1975.

Grist, D. H. *Rice*, London, 1965.

Groot, J. J. M. de, *The Religion of the Chinese*, 6 vols., Leiden, 1910.

Grove, L. and Daniels, C. (eds.), *State and Society in China: Japanese Perspectives on Ming-Qing Social and Economic History*, Tokyo, 1984.

Grube, E. J. (ed.), *Architecture of the Islamic World*, London, 1978.

Grunebaum, G. E. von, *Classical Islam: A History 600–1258*, London, 1970.

   Islam: Essays in the Nature and Growth of a Cultural Tradition, Menasha, Wisconsin, 1955.

   Islam and Medieval Hellenism: Social and Cultural Perspectives, ed. D. S. Wilson, preface by S. Vryonis, London, 1976.

   Medieval Islam, Chicago, 1953.

   Studies in Islamic Culture, Menasha, Wisconsin, 1954.

Gunawardana, R. A. L. H., 'Irrigation and hydraulic society in early and medieval Ceylon', *Past and Present*, no. 53, 1971, 3–25.

Gurney, J. D., 'Pietro della Valle: the limits of perception', *Bulletin of the School of Oriental and African Studies*, vol. 49, 1986, 103–16.

Habib, I., *Agrarian System of Mughal India*, Bombay, 1963.

   An Atlas of the Mughal Empire, Delhi, 1982.

Hadiwijono, H., *Man in the Present Javanese Mysticism*, Amsterdam, 1967.

'Hadjadjadj', in *Encyclopaedia of Islam*[2].

Haeger, J. W. (ed.), *Crisis and Prosperity in Sung China*, Tucson, Arizona, 1975.

Hahn, H., 'Infinity', in Newman (ed.), *The World of Mathematics*, III.

Hakim, B. S., *Arabic-Islamic Cities: Building and Planning Principles*, London, 1986.

Hall, J. W., Keiji, N. and Yamamura, K. (eds.), *Japan before Tokugawa: Political Consolidation and Economic Growth*, Princeton, 1981.

Hamarneh, S. K., *Origins of Pharmacy and Therapy in the Near East*, Tokyo, 1973.

Handlin, J. F., *Action in late Ming Thought*, Berkeley and Los Angeles, 1983.

Hanks, L. M., 'Forward', 'Symposium on social organization in mainland Southeast Asia prior to the eighteenth century', *Journal of Southeast Asian Studies*, vol. 15, 1984, 219–23.

Hanley, S. B. and Yamamura, K., *Economic and Demographic Change in Pre-Industrial Japan 1600–1968*, Princeton, 1977.

Hanna, N., *An Urban History of Bulaq in the Mamluk and Ottoman Periods*, Le Caire, 1983 (Supplément aux annales islamologiques, cahier N° 3).

   'Bulaq – an endangered historic area of Cairo', in Meinecke (ed.), *Islamic Cairo*.

   Construction Work in Ottoman Cairo 1517–1798, Le Caire, 1984 (Supplément aux annales islamologiques, cahier N° 4).

Hardy, P., 'Force and violence in Indo-Persian writing on history', in Israel and Wagle (eds.), *Islamic Society and Culture*.

   Historians of Medieval India, London, 1966.

   'The oratio recta of Barani's *Ta͑rikh-i-Firuz Shahi* – fact or fiction?', *Bulletin of the School of Oriental and African Studies*, vol. 20, 1957, 315–22.

Harlan, J R., *Crops and Man*, Madison, 1975.

   'Plant and animal distribution in relation to domestication' in Hutchinson (ed.), *The Early History of Agriculture* (1977).

'The plants and animals that nourish man', *Scientific American: Food and Agriculture*, San Francisco, 1976.

Hartwell, R. M., 'A cycle of economic change in imperial China: coal and iron in northeast China 75–1350', *Journal of the Economic and Social History of the Orient*, vol. 10, 1967, 102–59.

'Demographic, political, and social transformation of China, 750–1550', *Harvard Journal of Asiatic Studies*, vol. 42, 1982, 365–442.

Hassan, A. Y. and Hill, D. R., *Islamic Technology: An Illustrated History*, Cambridge and Paris, 1986.

Hayami, A., 'A "Great Transformation": economic and social changes in the late 16th and 17th centuries Japan', Paper presented to the third international studies conference on Japan, The Hague, 20–3 September 1982.

Hefner, R. W., *Hindu Java: Tengger Tradition and Islam*, Princeton, 1985.

Helbaek, H., 'Ecological effects of irrigation in ancient Mesopotamia', *Iraq*, vol. 22, 1960, 186–96.

Hicks, J., *A Theory of Economic History*, Oxford, 1969.

Hilbert, D., 'On the infinite', in Benacerraf and Putnam (eds.), *Philosophy of Mathematics: Selected Readings*.

Hill, D., *A History of Engineering in Classical and Medieval Times*, London, 1984.

Hills, E. S. (ed.), *Arid Lands: A Geographical Appraisal*, London, 1966.

Hindess, B. and Hirst, P. Q., *Pre-Capitalist Modes of Production*, London, 1975.

Ho, Ping-ti, *Studies on the Population of China, 1368–1953*, Cambridge, Mass., 1959.

The Ladder of Success in Imperial China, New York, 1967.

Hoff, J. E. and Janick, J. (eds.), *Food: Readings from Scientific American*, San Francisco, 1973.

Hollingsworth, T. H., *Historical Demography*, Ithaca, 1969.

Honey, W. B., *The Ceramic Art of China and Other Countries of the Far East*, London, 1955.

Hourani, A. H. and Stern, S. M. (eds.), *The Islamic City*, Oxford, 1970.

Huang, P. C. C., *The Peasant Economy and Social Change in North China*, Stanford, 1985.

Huang, R., *1587, A Year of No Significance*, New Haven and London, 1981.

Taxation and Finance in Sixteenth-century Ming China, Cambridge, 1974.

Hughes, E. R. and Hughes, K., *Religion in China*, London, 1950.

Huntington, E., *The Pulse of Asia*, Boston, 1907.

Civilization and Climate, 3rd edn, New Haven and London, 1924.

Hutchinson, J. B. (ed.), *The Early History of Agriculture*, Oxford, 1977.

Essays on Crop Plant Evolution, Cambridge, 1965.

'India: local and introduced crops', in *The Early History of Agriculture*.

Hyland, A. D. C. and Ahmed Al-Shahi (eds.), *The Arab House*, Newcastle, 1986.

'Ibil' (camel), in *Encyclopaedia of Islam²*.

'Ihram' (Ritual clothing in Islam), in *Encyclopaedia of Islam²*.

Inalcik, H., 'The socio-political effects of the diffusion of fire-arms in the Middle East', in Parry and Yapp (eds.), *War, Technology, and Society in the Middle East*.

Studies in Ottoman Social and Economic History, London, 1985.

Irons, W. and Dyson-Hudson, N. (eds.), *Perspectives on Nomadism*, Leiden, 1972.

Ishii, Y. (ed.), *Thailand: A Rice-Growing Society*, Honolulu, 1978.

Islamoglu-Inan, H., 'Les paysans, le marché et l'état en Anatolie au XVIᵉ siècle', *Annales: Economie, Sociétés, Civilisations*, vol. 43, 1988, 1025–43.

(ed.), *The Ottoman Empire and the World Economy*, Cambridge, 1987.

Ismail, O. S. L., 'The founding of a new capital Samarra', *Bulletin of the School of Oriental and African Studies*, vol. 31, 1968, 1–13.

Israel, M. and Wagle, N. K. (eds.), *Islamic Society and Culture*, Delhi, 1983.

Issawi, C., 'The area and population of the Arab empire: an essay in speculation', in Udovitch (ed.), *The Islamic Middle East*.

Jahn, K., 'Paper currency in Iran', *Journal of Asian History*, vol. 3, 1970, 101–35.

Jairazbhoy, R. A., *An Outline of Islamic Architecture*, Bombay, 1972.

Jakobson, R., *Verbal Art, Verbal Sign, Verbal Time*, Oxford, 1985.

Jing Su and Luo Lun, *Landlord and Labor in Late Imperial China: Case Studies from Shandong*, trans. E. Wilkinson, Cambridge, Mass., 1978.

Johansen, B., 'The All-Embracing Town and its mosques: *Al-Misr Al-Gami*', *Revue de l'Occident Musulman et de la Mediterranée*, No. 32, 1981, 139–61.

Joslin, F., *Cattle of the Bombay Presidency*, Bombay, 1905.

Juynboll, G. H. A. (ed.), *Studies on the First Century of Islamic Society*, Carbondale and Edwardsville, Illinois, 1982.

Kahn, H. L., *Monarchy in the Emperor's Eyes: Images and Reality in the Ch'ien-lung Reign*, Cambridge, Mass., 1971.

Kahn, J. S. and Llobera, J. R. (ed.), *The Anthropology of Pre-Capitalist Societies*, London, 1984.

'Kanat' (Underground canal), in *Encyclopaedia of Islam²*.

Karashima, Noburu, *South Indian History and Society: Studies from Inscriptions AD 850–1800*, Delhi, 1984.

Katz, J. J. (ed.), *The Philosophy of Linguistics*, Oxford, 1985.

Keyvani, M., *Artisans and Guild Life in the Later Safavid Period: Contributions to the Socio-Economic History of Persia*, Berlin, 1982.

'Khayl' (horse), in *Encyclopaedia of Islam²*.

King, D. A. (ed.), *Islamic Mathematical Astronomy*, London, 1986.

King, G., 'Some examples of the secular architecture in Najd, *Arabian Studies*, vol. 4, 1978, 113–42.

Kirsch, A. T., 'Cosmology and ecology as factors in interpreting early Thai social organization'. 'Symposium on social organization in mainland Southeast Asia prior to the eighteenth century', *Journal of Southeast Asian Studies*, vol. 15, 1984, 253–265.

Khalidi, T. (ed.), *Land Tenure and Social Transformation in the Middle East*, Beirut, 1984.

Khare, R. S., *Culture and Reality: Essays on the Hindu System of Managing Food*, Simla, 1976.

The Hindu Hearth and Home, Delhi, 1976.

Khazanov, *Nomads and the Outside World*, trans. J. Crookenden, Cambridge, 1984.

'Khubz' (Bread), in *Encyclopaedia of Islam²*.

Koentjaraningrat, R. M., *Javanese Culture*, Singapore, 1985.

(ed.), *Villages in Indonesia*, Ithaca, New York, 1967.

Kraeling, C. H. and Adams, R. M. (eds.), *City Invincible: A Symposium on Urbanization and Cultural Development in the Ancient Near East*, Chicago, 1960.

Kramers, J. H., 'Sokolli Muhammad Pasha', in *Encyclopaedia of Islam*[1].

Krenkow, F., 'The construction of subterranean water supplies during the Abbaside caliphate', *Transactions Glasgow University Oriental Society*, vol. 13, 1947–49 [1951], 23–32. See also under Muhammad Ibn al-Hasan in the Oriental section of the bibliography.

Kriedte, P., Medick, H., and Schlumbohm, J., *Industrialization before Industrialization: Rural Industry in the Genesis of Capitalism*, trans. B. Schempp, Cambridge, 1981.

Kristnasamienger, A. and Pease, H. T., *Notes on the Cattle of Mysore*, Calcutta, 1912.

Kripke, S., *Naming and Necessity*, Cambridge, Mass., 1972.

Krom, N. J. and Erp, van T., *Beschrijving van Barabudur*, 5 vols., The Hague, 1920–31.

Kuhnel, E. and Goetz, H., *Indian Book Paintings from Jahangir's Album in the State Library in Berlin*, London, 1926.

Kulke, H., 'Fragmentation and segmentation versus integration? Reflections on the concept of Indian feudalism', *Studies in History*, vol. 4, 1982, 237–63.

Kunt, I. M., *The Sultan's Servants: The Transformation of Ottoman Provincial Government, 1550–1650*, New York, 1983.

Lacoste, Y., *Ibn Khaldun: The Birth of History and the Past of the Third World*, London, 1984.

Lamb, H. H., *Climate, History, and the Modern World*, London, 1982.
  The Changing Climate, London, 1968.

Lambton, A. K. S., *Continuity and Change in Medieval Persia: Aspects of Administrative, Economic and Social History, 11th–14th Century*, London, 1988.
  'The dilemma of government in Islamic Persia: *Siyasat-nama* of Nizam al-Mulk', *Iran*, vol. 22, 1984.
  'The evolution of the Iqta in mediaeval Iran', *Iran*, vol. 5, 1967, 41–50.
  'Kanat' in *Encyclopaedia of Islam*[2].
  Landlord and Peasant in Iran, London, 1953
  'Reflections on the role of agriculture in medieval Persia', in Udovitch (ed.), *The Islamic Middle East 700–1900: Studies in Economic and Social History*.
  State and Government in Medieval Islam, London, 1981.

Lamm, C. J., *Cotton in Medieval Textiles of the Near East*, Paris, 1937.

Lammens, Henri S. I., *La cité arabe de Taif: à la veille de l'Hegire*, Beyrouth, 1922.
  Le Berceau de l'Islam: l'Arabie occidentale à la veille de l'Hegire, 1er volume, Le Climat – Les Bedouins, Rome, 1914.

Lancaster, W., *The Rwala Bedouin Today*, Cambridge, 1981.

Lancaster, W. and Lancaster, F., 'Thoughts on the bedouinisation of Arabia', *Proceedings of the Seminar for Arabian Studies*, vol. 18, 1988, 51–62.

Langweis, L. and Wagner, F. A., *Decorative Art in Indonesian Textiles*, Amsterdam, 1964.

Lapidus, I. M., 'Arab settlement and economic development of Iraq and Iran in the age of the Umayyad and early Abbasid caliphs', in Udovitch (ed.), *The Islamic Middle East 700–1900: Studies in Economic and Social History*.

Muslim Cities in the Later Middle Ages, Cambridge, Mass., 1967; new edn, Cambridge, 1984.

'The Arab conquests and the formation of Islamic society', in Juynboll (ed.), *Studies on the First Century of Islamic Society*.

'The grain economy of Mamluk Egypt', *Journal of the Economic and Social History of the Orient*, vol. 12, 1969, 1–15.

Larousse Gastronomique, New International, London, 1977.

Lassner, J., 'Municipal entities and mosques: an additional note on the imperial center', *Journal of the Economic and Social History of the Orient*, vol. 10, 1967, 53–63.

The Shaping of Abbasid Rule, Princeton, 1980.

The Topography of Baghdad in the Early Middle Ages: Texts and Studies, Detroit, 1970.

Lattimore, O., 'Herdsmen, farmers, urban culture', in *Pastoral Production and Society*.

Inner Asian Frontiers of China, Boston, 1962.

Laufer, B., *Sino-Iranica: Chinese Contributions to the History of Civilization in Ancient Iran*, Chicago, 1919.

Leach, E. R., 'Hydraulic society in Ceylon', *Past and Present*, no. 15, 1959, 2–26.

Lévi-Strauss, London, 1970; revised edn, 1985.

Le Strange, G., *The Lands of the Eastern Caliphate*, Cambridge, 1905.

Ledrut, R., 'Parole et silence de la ville', in Gottdiener and Lagopoulos (eds.), *The City and the Sign: An Introduction to Urban Semiotics*.

Lee, J., 'Food supply and population growth in southwest China 1250–1850', *Journal of Asian Studies*, vol. 41, 1982, 711–46.

Lévi-Strauss, C., *Anthropologie structurale*, Paris, 1958; *Structural Anthropology*, trans. C. Jacobson and B. G. Schoepf, London, 1968; reprinted 1969.

La pensée sauvage, Paris, 1962; *The Savage Mind*, trans. London, 1966; reprinted 1981.

Mythologie I: Le cru et le cuit, Paris, 1964; trans. London, 1970.

Lewis, B., 'On the quietist and activist traditions in Islamic political writings', *Bulletin of the School of Oriental and African Studies*, vol. 49, 1986, 141–7.

The Arabs in History, London, reprinted 1984.

The Muslim Discovery of Europe, London, 1982.

Li, L. M., *China's Silk Trade: Traditional Industry in the Modern World 1842–1937*, Cambridge, Mass., 1981.

'Libas' (Clothing), in *Encyclopaedia of Islam*[2].

Liefrinck, F. A., 'Rice cultivation in northern Bali' (1886–7), in van Ball *et al.* (eds.), *Bali, Further Studies in Life, Thought, and Ritual* (1969).

Lindner, R. P., *Nomads and Ottomans in Medieval Anatolia*, Bloomington, 1983.

Lohuizen-de Leeuw, J. E., 'The Stupa in Indonesia', in Dallapiccola and Lallemant (eds.), *The Stupa: Its Religious and Architectural Significance* (1980).

Loizou, A., *The Reality of Time*, Aldershot, 1986.

Løkkegaard, F., *Islamic Taxation in the Classic Period*, Copenhagen, 1950.

Lombard, M., *The Golden Age of Islam*, trans. J. Spencer, Amsterdam, 1975.

Loomis, R. S., 'Agricultural systems', in *Scientific American: Food and Agriculture*, San Francisco, 1976.

Lopez, R., Miskimin, H., and Udovitch, A. L., 'England to Egypt, 1350–1500: long-term trends and long-distance trade', in Cook (ed.), *Studies in the Economic History of the Middle East.*

'Ma' (Water), in *Encyclopaedia of Islam*².

Mabbett, I. W., 'The "Indianization" of Southeast Asia: reflections on the prehistoric sources', *Journal of Southeast Asian Studies*, vol. 8, 1977, 1–14, 143–61.

'Maᶜdin' (Mining and metallurgy), in *Encyclopaedia of Islam*².

Madelung, W., 'Land ownership and land tax in Northern Yemen and Najran: 3rd–4th/9th–10th century', in Khalidi (ed.), *Land Tenure and Social Transformation in the Middle East.*

Mann, M., *A History of Power from the Beginning to AD 1760*, vol. 1, Cambridge, 1986.

Mair, V. H., 'Language and ideology in the written popularization of the Sacred Edict', in Johnson, Nathan, and Rawski (eds.), *Popular Culture in Late Imperial China* (1985).

Makdisi, G., 'Autograph Diary of an eleventh-century historian of Baghdad', parts 1–5, *Bulletin of the School of Oriental and African Studies*, vol. 18, 1956, vol. 19, 1957.

   The Rise of Colleges, Institutions of Learning in Islam and the West, Edinburgh, 1981.

Marçais, G., 'Dar' (house), *Encyclopaedia of Islam*².

Masaaki, O., 'Large landownership in the Jiangnan delta region during the late Ming-early Qing period', in Grove and Daniels (eds.), *State and Society in China.*

Masatoshi, T., 'Popular uprisings, rent resistance, and bondservant rebellions in the late Ming', in Grove and Daniels (eds.), *State and Society in China.*

Massignon, L., *Mission en Mesopotamie*, 2 vols., Cairo, 1910–12.

'Masdjid' (Mosque), in *Encyclopaedia of Islam*².

Masters, B., *The Origins of Western Economic Dominance in the Middle East: Mercantilism and the Islamic Economy in Aleppo, 1600–1750*, New York, 1988.

Mayer, L. A., *Mamluk Costume*, Geneva, 1952.

Meer van der, van Setten, *Sawah Cultivation in Ancient Java*, Canberra, 1979.

Meillassoux, C., 'From reproduction to production', *Economy and Society*, vol. 1, 1972, 92–105.

Meinecke, M., *Islamic Cairo: Architectural Conservation and Urban Development of the Historic Centre, Art and Archaeology Research Papers*, London, 1978.

Melville, C. P., 'Earthquakes in the history of Nishapur', *Iran*, vol. 18, 1980, 103–20.

Merleau-Ponty, M., *Signes*, Paris, 1960; trans. R. C. McCleary, Northwestern University Press, 1964.

Meyerhof, M., *Studies in Medieval Arabic Medicine*, ed. P. Johnstone, London, 1984.

Miller, D., *Artefacts as Categories: A Study of Ceramic Variability in Central India*, Cambridge, 1985.

Miskimin, H. A., Herlihy, D. and Udovitch, A. L. (eds.), *The Medieval City*, New Haven and London, 1977.

Misra, S. C., *The Rise of Muslim Power in Gujarat: A History of Gujarat from 1298 to 1442*, London, 1964.

'Mizan' (Balance), in *Encyclopaedia of Islam*².

Moreland, W. H., *From Akbar to Aurangzeb: A Study in Indian Economic History*, London, 1923.

India at the Death of Akbar: An Economic Study, London, 1920.

The Agrarian System of Moslem India: A Historical Essay with Appendices, London, 1929.

Morgan, D. O., 'The "Great Yasa of Chingiz Khan" and Mongol law in the Ilkhanate', *Bulletin of the School of Oriental and African Studies*, vol. 49, 1986, 163–76.

'The Mongol Armies in Persia', *Der Islam*, vol. 56, 1979, 81–95.

The Mongols, Oxford, 1986.

Morony, M. G., *Iraq after the Muslim Conquest*, Princeton, New Jersey, 1984.

'Land holding and social change: Lower al-ʿIraq in the early Islamic period', in Khalidi (ed.), *Land Tenure and Social Transformation in the Middle East* (1984).

Morse, H. B., *Trade and Administration in China*, Shanghai, 1921.

Mote, F. W., 'The transformation of Nanking, 1350–1400', in Skinner (ed.), *The City in Late Imperial China*.

Moti Chandra, *Costumes, Textiles, Cosmetics and Coiffure in Ancient and Medieval India*, Delhi, 1973.

Mukhia, H., 'Was there feudalism in Indian history?', *Proceedings of the Fortieth Session of the Indian History Congress*, Waltair, 1979, 229–59.

Murphey, R., 'The ruin of Ancient Ceylon, *Journal of Asian Studies*, vol. 16, 1957, 181–200.

Musallam, B. F., *Sex and Society in Islam: Birth Control before the Nineteenth Century*, Cambridge, 1983.

Musil, A., *The Manners and Customs of the Rwala Bedouins*, New York, 1928.

Arabia Deserta: A Topographical Itinerary, New York, 1927.

The Middle Euphrates, New York, 1927.

The Northern Negd, New York, 1928.

Nagel, E. and Newman, J. R., 'Goedel's proof', in Newman (ed.), *The World of Mathematics* (1960), III.

Naji, A. J. and Ali, Y. N., 'The suqs of Basrah: commercial organization and activity in a medieval Islamic city', *Journal of the Economic and Social History of the Orient*, vol. 24, 1981, 298–309.

Naqvi, H. K., *Urbanization and Urban Centres under the Great Mughals 1556–1707*, Simla, 1972.

Needham, J., *Science and Civilisation in China, vol. 1, Introductory Orientations*, Cambridge, 1954.

Science and Civilisation in China, vol. 4, Part 3, Civil Engineering and Nautics, Cambridge, 1971.

Science and Civilisation in China, vol. 5, Chemistry and Chemical Technology Part 7: Military Technology: The Gunpowder Epic, Cambridge, 1986.

Grand Titration: Science and Society in East and West, London, 1969.

Gunpowder as the Fourth Power, Hong Kong, 1985.

The Development of Iron and Steel Technology in China, London, 1958.

'Time and Eastern Man', Henry Myers Lecture, 1964; reprinted in *Grand Titration* (1969).

Needham, J., Wang, L. and Price, D. J. de S., *Heavenly Clockwork*, Cambridge, 1960.

Nelson, C., *The Desert and the Sown: Nomads in the Wider Society*, Berkeley and Los Angeles, 1973.

Newman, J. R. (ed.), *The World of Mathematics*, vol. 3, New York, 1960.

Nizami, K. A., 'Some aspects of Khanqah life in medieval India', *Studia Islamica*, vol. 8, 1957, reprinted in *Studies in Medieval Indian History*, Aligarh, 1966.

Nordholt, H. S., *Bali: Colonial Conceptions and Political Change 1700–1940*, Rotterdam, 1986.

Norlund, I., Cederroth, S., and Gerdin, I. (eds.), *Rice Societies: Asian Problems and Prospects*, Copenhagen, 1986.

North, A., 'Some remarks on the "nationalization" of conquered lands at the time of the Umayyads', in Khalidi (ed.), *Land Tenure and Social Transformation in the Middle East*.

Obeysekere, G., *Land Tenure in Village Ceylon: A Sociological and Historical Study*, Cambridge, 1967.

Oliver, R. (ed.), *Cambridge History of Africa Volume 3: from c. 1050 to c. 1600*, Cambridge, 1977.

Osgood, C., *The Chinese: A Study of a Hong Kong Community*, 3 vols., Arizona, 1975.

O'Shaughnessy, T., *Muhammad's Thoughts on Death: a Thematic Study of the Qur'anic Data*, Leiden, 1969.

Pargiter, F. E., 'The telling of time in ancient India', *Journal of the Royal Asiatic Society*, 1915, 699–715.

Parry, V. and Yapp, M. E. (eds.), *War, Technology, and Society in the Middle East*, Oxford, 1975.

Parsons, C., *Mathematics in Philosophy: Selected Essays*, New York, 1983.

Pastoral Production and Society: Proceedings of the International Meeting on Nomadic Pastoralism, Paris, 1–3 Dec. 1976, L'équipe écologie et anthropologie des sociétés pastorales, Cambridge, 1979.

Patwardhan, V. N. and Darby, W. J., *The State of Nutrition in the Arab Middle East*, Nashville, 1972.

Pears, D., *Wittgenstein*, London, 1971.

Pellat, C., *Études sur l'histoire socio-culturelle de l'Islam (VIIe–XVe s.)*, London, 1976.

'India and Indians as seen by an Arab writer of the 3rd/9th century – al-Djahiz', in *Studies in Asian History: Proceedings of the Asian History Congress 1961*, New Delhi, 1969.

'Khubz' (bread), in *Encyclopaedia of Islam²*.

Life and Works of Jahiz, London, 1969.

Pellet, P. L. and Shadarevian, S., *Food Composition: Tables for Use in the Middle East*, Beirut, 1970.

Perdue, P. C., *Exhausting the Earth: State and Peasant in Hunan, 1500–1850*, Cambridge, Mass., 1987.

Perlin, F., 'Proto-Industrialization and pre-colonial South Asia', *Past and Present*, no. 98, 1983, 30–95.

Petrovic, D., 'Fire-arms in the Balkans on the eve of and after the Ottoman conquests of the fourteenth and fifteenth centuries', in Parry and Yapp (eds.), *War, Technology, and Society in the Middle East* (1975).

Petrucci, R., *Encyclopédie de la peinture chinoise,*

Petrushevsky, I. P., 'The socio-economic conditions of Iran under the Il-Khans', in Boyle (ed.), *The Cambridge History of Iran*, V.

Petry, C. F., *The Civilian Elite of Cairo in the Later Middle Ages*, Princeton, 1981.

Piaget, J., *Structuralism*, London, 1973.

Pieper, J., An outline of architectural anthropology in relation to the general history and theory of architecture', *Art and Archaeology Research Papers*, 1980, 4–10.

Pigeaud, Th., 'Javanese gold', *Bijdragen tot de Taal-Land-en Vokenkunde*, vol. 114, 1958, 192–6.

   Java in the 14th Century, vol. 4, The Hague, 1962.

Pijper, G. F., *Studien over de Geschiedenis van de Islam in Indonesia 1900–1950*, Leiden, 1977.

Planhol, X. de, *Les fondements géographiques de l'histoire de l'Islam*, Paris, 1968.

Polanyi, K., *The Great Transformation*, Boston, 1957.

Polanyi, K., Arensberg, C. M., and Pearson, H. W. (eds.), *Trade and Markets in the Early Empires*, New York, 1957.

Pomian, K., 'The secular evolution of the concept of cycles', in *Enciclopedia Einnaudi*, vol. 3, Torino, 1977; reprinted *Review: Fernand Braudel Center*, vol. 2, 1979, 563–646.

Poncet, J., 'Le myth de la catastrophe hilalienne', *Annales: Économie, Sociétés, Civilisations* vol. 22, 1967, 1999–1120.

Popkin, S. L., *The Rational Peasant: The Political Economy of Rural Society in Vietnam*, Berkeley, Los Angeles, London, 1979.

Prior, A. N., *Time and Modality*, Oxford, 1957.

   Papers on Time and Tense, Oxford, 1968.

Prijotomo, J., *Ideas and Forms of Javanese Architecture*, Yogyakarta, 1984.

Pryor, F. L., 'The invention of the plow', *Comparative Studies in Society and History*, vol. 27, 1985, 727–43.

   'Causal theories about the origins of agriculture', *Research in Economic History*, vol. 8, 1982–3, 93–125.

Putnam, H., *Reason, Truth, and History*, Cambridge, 1981.

Rabie, H., 'Some technical aspects of agriculture in medieval Egypt', in Udovitch (ed.), *The Islamic Middle East*.

   The Financial System of Egypt 564–741 AH/AD 1169–1341, London, 1972.

Ramaswamy, V., *Textiles and Weavers in Medieval South India*, Delhi, 1985.

Rao, A. and Casimir, M. J., 'Mobile pastoralists of Jammu and Kashmir: a preliminary report', *Nomadic People*, no. 10, 40–50.

al-Rashid, Saad A., *Darb Zubaydah: the Pilgrim Road from Kufa to Mecca*, Riyad, 1980.

Raymond, A., *Artisans et commercants au Caire au XVIIIe siècle*, 2 vols., Damascus, 1974.

   The Great Arab Cities in the 16th–18th Centuries: An Introduction, New York, 1984.

'Les grands waqfs et l'organisation de l'espace urbain à Alep et au Caire à l'époque ottomane (XVIᵉ–XVIIᵉ siècles)', *Bulletin d'Études Orientales*, vol. 31, 1979.

Grandes villes arabes à l'époque ottomane, Paris, 1985.

Read, B. E., *Famine Food Listed in the Chiu Huang Pen Ts'ao: Giving their Identity, Nutritional Values and Notes on their Preparation*, Shanghai, 1946.

Reade, J., 'Studies in Assyrian geography', *Revue d'Assyriologie*, vol. 72, 1978, 42–72, 157–80.

Redfield, R., *Peasant Society and Culture*, Chicago, reprinted 1969.

The Folk Culture of Yucatan, Chicago, 1941, reprinted 1970.

Redfield, R. and Singer, M., 'The cultural role of cities', *Economic Development and Cultural Change*, vol. 3, 1954, 53–73.

Reid, A., *Southeast Asia in the Age of Commerce 1450–1680*, vol. 1, New Haven and London, 1988.

Renfrew, C., 'Trade as action at a distance: questions of integration and communication', in Sabloff and Lamberg-Karlovsky (eds.), *Ancient Civilization and Trade* (1975).

Renfrew, J. M., *Palaeoethnobotany: the Prehistory of Food Plants of the Near East and Europe*, London, 1973.

Renouf, W. C., *Cattle and Dairying in the Punjab*, Lahore, 1910.

Revault, J. and Maury, B., *Palais et Maisons du Caire du XIVᵉ au XVIIIᵉ siècles*, Paris, 1975.

Rodinson, M., *Islam and Capitalism*, London, 1980.

'Recherches sur les documents arabes relatifs à la cuisine', *Revue des Études Islamiques*, 1949, 95–165.

Rosenthal, F., *A History of Muslim Historiography*, Leiden, 1952.

Rotberg, R. I. and Rabb, T. K., *Hunger and History: The Impact of Changing Food Production and Consumption on Society*, Cambridge, 1985.

Rozman, G., *Urban Networks in Ch'ing China and Tokugawa Japan*, Princeton, 1973.

Population and Marketing Settlements in Ch'ing China, Cambridge, 1982.

Rucker, R., *Infinity and the Mind: The Science and Philosophy of the Infinite*, Brighton, 1982.

Russell, B., *My Philosophical Development*, London, 1959.

'On the experience of time', *Monist*, vol. 25, 1915, 212–33.

Russell, J. C., 'Late ancient and medieval populations', *Transactions of the American Philosophical Society*, new series, vol. 48, 1958.

'The population of medieval Egypt', *Journal of the American Research Center in Egypt*, vol. 5, 1966, 69–82.

Sabloff, J. and Lamberg-Karlovsky, C. C. (eds.), *Ancient Civilization and Trade*, Albuquerque, New Mexico, 1975.

Salim Bakhit al-Tabuki, 'Tribal structure in south Oman', *Arabian Studies*, vol. 4, 1978, 51–6.

Salzman, C., 'Is "nomadism" a useful concept?', *Nomadic People*, vol. 6, 1980, 1–7.

El-Samarraie, H. A., *Agriculture in Iraq during the 3rd Century AH*, Beirut, 1972.

Sarkar, J., *History of Aurangzib*, vol. 3, Calcutta, 1921.

Sauer, C. O., *Agricultural Origins and Dispersals*, New York, 1952.

Saussure, F. de, *Cours de linguistique générale*, ed. C. Bally and A. Sechehaye, Paris, 1916; revised edn 1922, 1971; *Course in General Linguistics*, trans. A. Harris, London, 1983.

Sauvaget, J., *Alep: essai sur le development d'une grande ville syrienne, des origines au milieu du XIX siècle*, 2 vols., Paris, 1941.

   'Esquisse d'une histoire de la ville de Damas', *Revue des Études Islamiques*, vol. 4, 1934, 421–80.

   La Mosquee Omeyyade de Medine, Paris, 1947.

Sauvy, A., *General Theory of Population*, London, 1969.

Schiøler, T., *Roman and Islamic Water-lifting Wheels*, Copenhagen, 1973.

Schumpeter, J., *History of Economic Analysis*, London, 1967.

Schurmann, H. F., *Economic Structure of the Yuan Dynasty*, Cambridge, Mass., 1956.

Schwartz, P. R., *Printing on Cotton at Ahmedabad, India in 1678*, Ahmedabad, 1969.

Scientific American: Food and Agriculture, San Francisco, 1976.

Scott, J. C., *The Moral Economy of the Peasant*, New Haven, 1976.

   Weapons of the Weak: Everyday Forms of Peasant Resistance, New Haven and London, 1985.

Serjeant, R. B., 'The cultivation of cereals in mediaeval Yemen', *Arabian Studies*, I, 1974, 25–74. See also under al-Abbas in the Oriental section of the bibliography.

   'Some irrigation systems in Hadramawt', *Bulletin of the School of Oriental and African Studies*, vol. 27, 1964, 33–76.

   Islamic Textiles, Beirut, 1972.

   Material for a History of Islamic Textiles, London, 1942.

Serjeant, R. B. and Lewcock, R. (eds.), *Saʿnaʾ: An Arabian Islamic City*, London, 1983.

Shih Min-hsiung, *The Silk Industry of Ch'ing China*, Ann Arbor, 1976.

Shiba, Yoshinobu, *Studies in the Economy of the Lower Yangtze in the Sung*, Tokyo, 1988 [Japanese text and English summary].

   'Urbanization and the development of markets in the lower Yangtze valley', in Haeger (ed.), *Crisis and Prosperity in Sung China*.

Shigeta, Atsushi, 'The origins and structure of Gentry rule', in Grove and Daniels (eds.), *State and Society in China: Japanese Perspectives*.

Shway Yoe, *The Burman: His Life and Notions*, London, 1910.

Sivin, N., *Cosmos and Computation in Early Chinese Mathematical Astronomy*, Leiden, 1969.

   'On the limits of empirical knowledge in the traditional Chinese sciences', in Fraser, Lawrence, Haber (eds.), *Time, Science, and Society in China and the West*.

Sjoberg, G., *The Pre-Industrial City*, Glencoe, Illinois, 1960.

Skelton, R., 'Europe and India', *Europa und die Kunst des Islam 5. bis 18. Jahrhundert*, 5, 33–42.

Skinner, G. W. (ed.), *The City in Late Imperial China*, Stanford, 1977.

Smith, C., 'Kawkaban: some of its history', *Arabian Studies*, vol. 6, 1982, 35–49.

Smith, C. S., *A History of Metallography: the Development of Ideas on the Structure of Metals before 1890*, Chicago and London, 1960.

Smith, J. M., 'Turanian Nomadism and Iranian politics', *Iranian Studies*, vol. 9, 57–81.

Smith, R., *Medieval Muslim Horsemanship: A Fourteenth-century Arabic Cavalry Manual*, London, 1979.

'The Tahirid Sultans of the Yemen (858–923/1454–1517) and their historian Ibn al-Dayba', *Journal of Semitic Studies*, vol. 29, 1984, 141–54.

'Sokolli Muhammad Pasha', in *Encyclopaedia of Islam*[2].

Soothill, W. E., *The Hall of Light: A Study of Early Chinese Kingship*, London, 1951.

Sourdel, J., 'Mosquée et madrasa', *Cahiers de Civilisation Médiévale*, vol. 13, 1970, 97–115.

Sousa, Ahmad, *Irrigation and Civilization in the Land of the Twin Rivers*, Baghdad, 1969 [English and Arabic text].

Spence, J. D., *Emperor of China: Self-Portrait of K'ang-hsi*, New York, 1974.

The Memory Palace of Matteo Ricci, New York, 1984.

Spuler, B., *History of the Mongols*, London, 1970.

Srinivas, M. N., *Social Change in Modern India*, Berkeley and Los Angeles, 1967.

Stamp, L. D. (ed.), *A History of Land Use in Arid Regions*, Paris, 1961.

Stein, Sir Aurel M., *Ruins of Desert Cathay*, 2 vols., London, 1912.

Stein, B., *Peasant State and Society in Medieval South India*, Delhi, 1980.

Stern, S. M., *Coins and Documents from the Medieval Middle East*, London, 1986.

'The constitution of the Islamic city', in Hourani and Stern (ed.), *The Islamic City* (1970).

Steward, J. H., *Theory of Cultural Change: the Methodology of Multilinear Evolution*, Urbana and Chicago, 1955.

Stover, L. E., *The Cultural Ecology of Chinese Civilisation: Peasants and Elites in the Last of the Agrarian States*, New York, 1974.

Sun, Ching-chih *et al.* (eds.), *Hua-tung Ti-ch'u Ching-chi Ti-li*, Peking, 1959; *Economic Geography of the East China Region*, trans. Washington, 1961.

Sun, E-tu Zen, 'Sericulture and silk production in Ch'ing China', in Willmott (ed.), *Economic Organization in Chinese Society*, 1972.

Takaya, Y., 'An ecological interpretation of Thai history', *Journal of South East Asian History*, vol. 6, 1975, 190–5.

Tambiah, S. J., *Buddhism and the Spirit Cult in North-East Thailand*, Cambridge, 1970.

Culture, Thought, and Social Action: An Anthropological Perspective, Cambridge, Mass., 1985.

World Conqueror and World Renouncer: A Study of Buddhism and Polity in Thailand against a Historical Background, Cambridge, 1976.

Tannahill, R., *Food in History*, London, 1988.

Thesiger, W., *The Marsh Arabs*, London, 1964.

Tomosugi, T., 'Japan's wet rice agrarian society', paper presented at School of Oriental and African Studies, South Asia Area Studies Centre, University of London, 1985.

A Structural Analysis of Thai Economic History, Tokyo, 1980.

Tritton, A. S., *The Caliph and their Non-Muslim Subjects*, London, 1930.

Twitchett, D., *Financial Administration under the T'and Dynasty*, Cambridge, 1963.

'The monasteries and China's economy in medieval times', *Bulletin of the School of Oriental and African Studies*, vol. 19, 1956–7, 526–49.

'Lands under state cultivation during the T'ang dynasty', *Journal of the Economic and Social History of the Orient*, vol. 2, 1959, 162–203, 335–6.

Ucko, P. J. and Dimbleby, G. W. (ed.), *The Domestication and Exploitation of Plants and Animals*, London, 1969.

Udovitch, A. L. (ed.), *The Islamic Middle East, 700–1900: Studies in Economic and Social History*, Princeton, 1981.

Varadarajan, L., *Traditions of Textile Printing in Kutch: Ajrakh and Related Techniques*, Ahmedabad, 1983.

Varisco, D. M., 'The production of Sorghum (*Dhurrah*) in highland Yemen', *Arabian Studies*, VII, 1985, 53–88.

Vavilov, N. I., *The Origin, Variation, Immunity, and Breeding of Cultivated Plants: Selected Writings of N. I. Vavilov*, trans. K. S. Chester, *Cronica Botanica*, vol. 13, 1949 [Issued 1951], 1–366.

Viraphol, S., *Tribute and Profit: Sino Siamese Trade 1652–1853*, Cambridge, Mass., 1977.

Vollmer, J. E., *In the Presence of the Dragon Throne*, Toronto, 1977.

Waldman, M. R., *Towards a Theory of Historical Narrative*, Columbus, Ohio, 1980.

Wales, H. G. Q., *Ancient Siamese Government and Administration*, London, 1934.

Walker, J., *A Catalogue of the Arab-Byzantine and PostReform Umaiyad Coins*, London, 1956.

Wang, H., 'The concept of set', in Benacerraf and Putnam (eds.), *Philosophy of Mathematics: Selected Readings* (1985).

Wansbrough, J., *Quranic Studies: Sources and Methods of Scriptural Interpretation*, London, 1977.

The Sectarian Milieu: Content and Composition of Islamic Salvation History, Oxford, 1978.

Watabe, T., *Glutinous Rice in Northern Thailand*, Kyoto, 1967.

Watson, A. M., 'A medieval Green Revolution', in Udovitch (ed.), *The Islamic Middle East*.

Agricultural Innovation in the Early Islamic World, Cambridge. 1983.

Watson, J. L. and Rawski, E. S. (eds.), *Death Ritual in Late Imperial and Modern China*, Berkeley, Los Angeles, and London, 1988.

Watson, J. L., 'Standardizing the Gods', in Johnson, Nathan, and Rawski (eds.), *Popular Culture in Late Imperial China*.

Watson, W., *Ancient Chinese Bronzes*, London, 1977.

Tang and Liao Ceramics, London, 1984.

Watt, J. R., *The District Magistrate in Late Imperial China*, New York, 1972.

Watt, M., *Islam and the Integration of Society*, London, 1961.

Weber, M., *Economy and Society: An Outline of Interpretative Sociology*, ed. G. Roth and C. Wittich, 2 vols., Berkeley, Los Angeles, London, 1978.

Wheatley, P., *The Pivot of the Four Quarters: A Preliminary Enquiry into the Origins and Character of the Ancient Chinese City*, Edinburgh, 1971.

White, L., *Medieval Technology and Social Change*, New York, 1964.

'The Crusades and the technological thrust of the West', in Parry and Yapp (eds.), *War, Technology, and Society in the Middle East.*

Studies in Ottoman Social and Economic History, London, 1985.

Wiet, G., *Cairo: City of Art and Commerce*, trans. S Feiler, Oklahoma, 1964.

Wilber, D. N., 'Builders and craftsmen of Islamic Iran: the earlier periods', *Art and Archaeology Research Papers*, 1976, 31–9.

The Architecture of Islamic Iran: The Ilkhanid Period, Princeton, 1955.

Wilkinson, J. C., *Water and Tribal Settlement in South-East Arabia: A Study of the Aflaj of Oman*, Oxford, 1977.

Will, P. E., *Bureaucratie et famine au Chine au 18e siècle*, Paris, 1980.

Williamson, H. R., *Wang An-shih: A Chinese Statesman and Educationalist of the Sung Dynasty*, 2 vols., London, 1935–7.

Willmott, W. E. (ed.), *Economic Organization in Chinese Society*, Stanford, 1972.

Wills, J. E., *Embassies and Illusions: Dutch and Portuguese Envoys to K'ang-hsi, 1666–1687*, Cambridge, Mass., 1984.

Wirth, L., 'Urban society and civilization', *American Journal of Sociology*, vol. 45, 1940, 743–55.

Wirgin, J., *Sung Ceramic Designs*, London, 1979.

Wittgenstein, L., *Philosophical Investigations*, London, 1953.

Tractatus Logico-Philosophicus, trans. D. F. Pears and B. F. McGuinness, with an introduction by Bertrand Russell, London, 1961; reprinted 1981.

Wittgenstein and the Vienna Circle: Conversations Recorded by Friedrich Waismann, ed. and trans. B. McGuinness and J. Schulte, London, 1979.

Wolf, A. F., 'Gods, ghosts, and ancestors', in A. F. Wolf (ed.), *Studies in Chinese Society*, Stanford, 1978.

Wong, R. Bin and Perdue, P. C., 'Famine's foes in Ching China' [Review article on Will, *Bureaucratie et famine en Chine*], *Harvard Journal of Asiatic Studies*, vol. 43, 1980.

Wright, A. F., 'The cosmology of the Chinese city', in Skinner (ed,), *The City in Late Imperial China* (1977).

(ed.), *Studies in Chinese Thought*, Chicago, 1953.

Wu, N. L., *Chinese and Indian Architecture*, London, 1963.

Wu, Pai-nan Rashid, *The Fall of Baghdad and Mongol Rule in al-Iraq, 1258–1335*, Ph.D. thesis University of Utah, 1974, University of Michigan microfilm, 1979.

Wulff, H. E., *The Traditional Crafts of Persia: Their Development, Technology, and Influence on Eastern and Western Civilizations*, Cambridge, Mass., 1966.

Wyatt, D., 'Laws and social order in early Thailand: an introduction to the *Mangraisat*', 'Symposium on social organization in mainland Southeast Asia prior to the eighteenth century', *Journal of Southeast Asian Studies*, vol. 15, 1984, 245–52.

Yang, C. K., *Religion in Chinese Society*, New York, 1967.

Yang, Lien-sheng, 'Buddhist monasteries and four money-raising institutions in Chinese history', *Harvard Journal of Asiatic Studies*, vol. 13, 1950, 174–91.

'Economic justification for spending – an uncommon idea in traditional China', *Harvard Journal of Asiatic Studies*, vol. 20, 1957, 36–52.

'Numbers and units in Chinese economic history', *Harvard Journal of Asiatic Studies*, vol. 12, 1949, 216–25.

Yarshater, E., 'The theme of wine-drinking and the concept of the beloved in early Persian poetry', *Studia Islamica*, vol. 13, 1960, 43–54.

Yao, shan-yu, 'The chronological and seasonal distribution of floods and droughts in Chinese history 206 BC–AD 1911', *Harvard Journal of Asiatic Studies*, vol. 6, 1941, 273–312.

Zeuner, A. F. E., *A History of Domesticated Animals*, London, 1963.

Zermelo, E., 'Über-Grenzzahlen und Mengenbereiche: Neue Untersuchungen über die Grundlagen der Mengenlehre', *Fundamenta Mathematicae*, vol. 16, 1930, 29–47.

Index